The Institute of Chartered Accountants in England and Wales

BUSINESS STRATEGY

For exams in 2014

Question Bank

 ICAEW

www.icaew.com

Business Strategy
The Institute of Chartered Accountants in England and Wales

ISBN: 978-0-85760-726-3
Previous ISBN: 978-0-85760-461-3

First edition 2008
Seventh edition 2014

British Library Cataloguing-in-Publication Data
A catalogue record for this book is available from the British Library

Printed in the United Kingdom by Polestar Wheatons

Polestar Wheatons
Hennock Road
Marsh Barton
Exeter
EX2 8RP

Your learning materials are printed on paper obtained from traceable,
sustainable sources.

Contents

Title	Marks	Time allocation Mins	Page Question	Page Answer
Business strategy questions				
1 Security Parking Ltd	30	45	3	138
2 Pasta2Go Ltd	37	55	4	143
3 Monteverdi Master Appliances plc	26	39	6	149
4 The Complete Furniture Group plc	40	60	7	152
5 Holiday Cottage Company Ltd	33	49	9	160
6 The Slate Snooker Table Company Ltd	32	48	11	164
7 Furbiton & Frobisher plc	40	60	12	168
8 Cabot Tours Ltd	28	42	14	176
9 Jenny and Bob	21	31	15	180
10 Chibb plc	30	45	16	182
11 TE plc	30	45	17	187
12 DA plc (03,2008)	40	60	19	190
13 Kraftvagen Gmbh (KV) (03,2008)	28	42	21	198
14 Campaign for Trading Equitably (03,2008)	32	48	23	207
15 Embury Ltd (09,2008)	42	63	25	214
16 DT Ltd (09,2008)	32	48	27	223
17 Taylor-Thorne plc (TT) (12,2008)	27	40	29	229
18 CWI International Ltd (note 1) (03,2009)	20	30	30	232
19 Kemmex Ice Cream plc (KIC) (06,2009)	43	64	32	239
20 Evara Electrical Engineers Ltd (EEE) (06,2009)	32	48	35	247
21 Rugeley Tableware plc (09,2009)	40	60	37	253
22 Pitstop Ltd (09,2009)	27	40	39	260
23 Somborne Zoological Park Ltd (09,2009)	33	49	41	268
24 Green Cards Ltd (GC) (12,2009)	43	64	43	276
25 Efficiency Systems Ltd (ES) (12,2009)	32	48	45	284
26 Total Equipment Hire Ltd (TEH) (12,2009)	25	37	48	288
27 Blazing Bicycles Ltd (BB) (03,2010)	42	63	49	292
28 Deeshire Council (DC) (03,2010)	36	54	52	300
29 NP Ltd (NP) (03,2010)	22	33	54	309
30 Executive Travel Ltd (ET) (06,2010)	42	63	55	315
31 Hutton Haulage plc (HH) (06,2010)	31	47	58	320
32 Cutting Edge Ltd (CE) (06,2010)	27	40	59	324
33 Supaspeed Ltd (Supa) (09,2010)	43	64	60	329
34 e-Parts Ltd (EP) (09,2010)	21	32	63	336
35 Marcham plc (09,2010)	36	54	64	341

Note 1: The original exam question was 25 marks but has been amended to remove a 5 mark requirement on project management which is no longer examinable.

Question Bank

Your exam will consist of three questions   100 marks

Time available   2½ hours

1 Security Parking Ltd

Note: Assume that the current date in the question is January 20X7.

Security Parking Ltd (SP) is a large, private company that operates ten city centre car parks in the UK. Members of one family own 75% of the ordinary shares of SP.

Company history

SP was set up 20 years ago. It acquired rough land near the city centre of Birmingham and turned it into a car park by installing, at minimal cost, an exit barrier and a cabin. Employees were hired working shifts to staff the site and take customers' money. By 20X5, SP had acquired another nine sites of rough land near the centres of different cities in the UK and developed them into car parks.

By 20X7, land was becoming increasingly expensive near city centres and it was becoming difficult to make a reasonable return on investment. Some rival car parking companies have been selling land to be redeveloped as offices or apartments. Also, due to environmental concerns, it has become increasingly difficult to obtain local government planning permission to develop land into car parks near city centres.

Strategic plan

A meeting of the board of directors of SP was called to discuss the problems:

The **marketing director** put forward a proposal: 'I believe that we have maintained a steady operating performance for our existing business but further expansion of city centre car parks is difficult and costly. I suggest that we try a different type of car park by acquiring out-of-town land cheaply and providing a regular bus service to take people to the city centre by operating a 'park-and-ride' scheme. The bus fares could be charged to customers separately.'

The **finance director** has reservations: 'The buses can be leased, but the land will need to be purchased. However, we have reached our borrowing capacity and we cannot raise more share capital. As a result, the only way we could fund the new car parks would be to sell one or more of the existing car parks. However, we need to be sure that the car parks we are buying will perform better than the car parks we are selling. I would suggest we sell the current car park, or car parks, with the lowest residual income or the lowest return on investment.'

The **chief executive** has some issues: 'We cannot assess the potential performance of the new car parks unless we know the likely volume of business and the prices we are to charge for parking and for the bus service. We need to do some market research to determine these, but it is clear that people will not pay as much for out-of-town parking as they will for in-town parking. Indeed, the price to park out-of town could be only half of the in-town price. I also have a problem with which car parks we should sell to finance the new venture. I think we should sell the oldest car parks, as the land was cheap then, and we will make a large profit on disposal.'

The **chief accountant** has put together some illustrative data (see **Exhibit**). As an example, he has reported actual performance achieved for two current in-town car parks (Birmingham and Liverpool), which could be divested to fund the new out-of-town car park strategy. The illustrative data also shows estimates of a possible new out-of-town site, although there are a number of similar sites that could also be acquired in addition to this one.

SP uses a required annual interest rate of 10% to determine residual income and as the required return on investment. Customers are currently charged per day or any part thereof. All car parks are open 360 days per year.

Exhibit – Illustrative data

	Birmingham	Liverpool	Proposed site out-of-town (estimates)
Purchase date	20 years ago	20X6	20X7
Original cost	£750,000	£3 million	£1 million
Current value	£2 million	£3 million	£1 million
Capacity	100 cars	160 cars	400 cars
% Utilisation	80%	70%	unknown
Revenue (p.a.)	£288,000	£403,200	unknown
Operating costs (p.a.)	£38,000	£43,200	£400,000*

* Including lease payments and other costs of operating the buses.

Requirements

(a) Using the data and other information provided in the question,

    (i) Determine the return on investment (ie return on capital employed) and the residual income of the Birmingham and Liverpool car parks using both original costs and current values to value the capital invested.

    (ii) Explain how SP should determine which of the current car parks, if any, should be divested in order to finance the new out-of-town car parks. Where appropriate, refer to your answers in (i) and make any additional relevant calculations. **(15 marks)**

(b) As an external consultant, you have been asked to consider the proposal for acquiring new out-of-town car parks. Write a memorandum to the board of SP which explains, and critically appraises, the following:

    (i) The benefits and disadvantages that may arise from the strategy of switching from in-town to out-of-town car parks.

    (ii) The market research that SP should undertake in order to determine the likely volume of customers and the most appropriate prices, specifying data sources where appropriate. **(15 marks)**

(30 marks)

2 Pasta2Go Ltd

Pasta2Go Ltd (hereafter Pasta2Go) operates a chain of 25 outlets, located throughout the North of England, providing take-away food and a home-delivery service of hot pasta and pizza meals.

All meals are cooked to order. For take-away food, customers call in person to collect their meals, although some customers may telephone their order in advance to save waiting. For home-delivery meals, orders are normally telephoned to outlets by customers and deliveries are made to them (within five miles) at no extra charge if the order exceeds £10. Any greater distance is considered individually.

Company history

The business was set up by Carlos Alberto and Roberto Riva 20 years ago. Six years later it became incorporated with the entire shareholding held equally by the two founders, who were also the only directors. Expansion has been rapid in recent years with the opening of two new outlets in each of the past five years. There is also a central depot located in Northern England from which outlets are supplied with ingredients. All property is leased.

The target market for the company is busy, young professionals, working long hours, who do not wish to cook when getting home from work. The menu is constantly revised to accommodate their changing tastes and market conditions.

Competitive positioning

The directors believe that their success, compared with competitors, is due, firstly, to their closely guarded recipe using fresh ingredients; and secondly, they have a rapid and reliable motorbike delivery service which guarantees that, within five miles, hot meals will be with the customers in less than 30 minutes of their telephone order. The motorbikes also include an insulated box to retain heat.

The food is competitively priced and, although this means a low margin on each sale, it generates a high revenue.

Competition comes in a number of forms.

- Other types of take-away and home-delivery food are available in most areas operated by Pasta2Go.

- This includes Chinese, Indian and British food as well as other providers of Italian meals
    - From restaurants
    - From home-cooked food

Board meeting

A recent board meeting identified two significant problems.

(1) Measuring the performance of individual outlets and that of the company as a whole.
(2) The most appropriate method of future expansion.

(1) Measuring performance

While revenue has increased rapidly, profitability has grown much more slowly. In particular, the directors are concerned about the costs involved in setting up new outlets and the fact that it takes at least two years for each new outlet to become established and achieve profitability.

The directors do not believe that financial measures alone would be a reasonable reflection of the strategic success of the company or of individual outlets. Moreover, in assessing the performance of managers it is considered unreasonable to use only profit, particularly in new outlets.

(2) Future expansion

Proposal 1

Carlos Alberto believes that expansion should be more rapid and is in favour of considering offering franchising arrangements to expand the network of outlets in all areas of Britain.

Proposal 2

Roberto Riva agrees that the rate of expansion should be increased but has been negotiating with BurgerGrill plc (hereafter BurgerGrill), a large company with an international chain of 20,000 hamburger restaurants. He has negotiated a potential arrangement whereby:

- BurgerGrill would take up a one-third shareholding in Pasta2Go by subscribing for new share capital. There would be an option to extend this to a 50% holding after five years.

- BurgerGrill would also provide significant loans to Pasta2Go which are likely to be much greater than its new share capital investment. These loans would be at commercial interest rates.

- Expansion in the number of Pasta2Go outlets would take place mainly in the South of England. There would also be expansion into the restaurant market, setting up a new division which would use the new brand name, Pasta2Stay. These restaurants would be mid-market and would be located throughout Britain, with some adjacent to BurgerGrill restaurants. Identical meals to those currently served would be offered.

- There would be a shared distribution network between Pasta2Go and BurgerGrill for inward deliveries.

- Pasta2Go would help to develop the recipe for a new 'pasta-burger' to be sold in BurgerGrill restaurants.

Requirements

(a) Identify and explain **two** key critical success factors (CSFs) relevant to companies operating in the market for home-delivery meals. Explain how such companies may implement the use of these two CSFs to promote competitive advantage. **(7 marks)**

(b) Prepare a balanced scorecard for Pasta2Go using **each** of the following headings.

    (i) Financial perspective
    (ii) Customer perspective
    (iii) Internal business perspective
    (iv) Innovation and learning perspective

Note: Ignore potential expansion plans. **(12 marks)**

(c) As a strategic consultant, write a memorandum to the directors of Pasta2Go which describes and evaluates the key factors with respect to the two proposals for expansion put forward by the directors. Use the following headings.

    (i)   Economies of scale
    (ii) Operating, financial and strategic risks
    (iii) Competitive positioning   **(18 marks)**

                                                                       (37 marks)

3 Monteverdi Master Appliances plc

Monteverdi Master Appliances plc (hereafter MMA) is a company listed on an international stock exchange. It manufactures electrical kitchen appliances and sells in the low to medium price sector of the market.

Company profile

MMA manufactures three different types of electrical appliances: cookers, washing machines and fridges.

The company currently has four manufacturing sites located in Malaysia, Russia, England and the United States. Each of the factories currently manufactures all three products and, in general, sells them in the region of the world in which that factory is located.

While sales are internationally diversified, market research has shown that different geographical regions require different designs and features. As a result, each factory has developed each of the products separately with different features and capabilities which are appropriate to the market in its own geographical region.

Cost competitiveness and cost reduction

Each of the factories is a separate profit centre. Profitability has declined in all four of the factories in recent years and thus profitability for the company as a whole has fallen steeply.

The central board has attempted to improve matters by reviewing costs, engaging in internal benchmarking exercises and applying a series of cost reduction programmes. Each of these cost reduction programmes tended to focus on one factory at a time and extended over periods of up to a year. At a board meeting to discuss the results of the latest cost review exercise the finance director summarised the results.

'It is clear that some of our factories can produce at a lower cost than others, but the results are not consistent. Take, for example, the Malaysian factory. It produces fridges and cookers cheaper than any of our other factories, but it is the highest cost producer of washing machines. What is more, when there is a major change in the exchange rate, the whole cost comparison exercise changes.

Another concern is that we have repeatedly engaged in cost reduction programmes by: selective redundancies, shifting production, changing reporting structures, reducing capacity and outsourcing functions, to name but a few. Despite all this, there has been no permanent cost reduction of any significance.

Also, there has recently been an unexpected major new entrant into the industry from South East Asia, which has low costs and low prices. If we are to compete we will have to reduce costs much more significantly than we have able to do in the past.'

Global production

In response to the concerns of the finance director a proposal was put forward to globalise production. The key features of the proposal are as follows:

- Each of the three products would be made in only one basic design, and all of the world production of each product would be made at a single factory.

- As a result only three factories would be needed in future; one factory would therefore close.

- Each factory would be a cost centre and marketing would be centralised functionally worldwide. It would therefore be outside the responsibility of the factory managers in future.

- The change would be pushed through urgently with the aim of completion of the change programme within six months.

- It is intended that larger scale specialist production would significantly reduce production costs, but the situation would be reviewed in two years' time given the uncertainties involved in such a major change.

Requirements

(a) Compare the type of change programme engaged in by MMA in the previous cost reduction exercises with the current proposal to globalise production. **(10 marks)**

(b) Examine how the globalisation change programme is likely to impact upon key stakeholders. Assess the implications for MMA in communicating the nature of the changes in each case. **(8 marks)**

(c) Give examples of barriers to change that may arise and which may cause resistance to the implementation of the globalisation change programme in MMA. **(8 marks)**

(26 marks)

4 The Complete Furniture Group plc

Note: Assume that the current date in the question is March 20X7.

The Complete Furniture Group plc (CFG) is the UK's largest furniture manufacturer. Listed on the London Stock Exchange, it manufactures and sells a wide range of furniture to businesses in the building trade (trade sales) and to individual retail customers (retail sales).

Company profile

CFG has always positioned itself as a low cost provider, but has recently experienced a continued decline in performance resulting in an overall published loss, and as a result the share price is depressed. In the year ended 31 December 20X6 CFG made an operating loss of £0.45 million (20X5: £48.2m profit) on revenues of £1,054 million (20X5: £1,038m). CFG's average share price was £0.81 in 20X6 and £1.08 in 20X5. No final dividend was declared by CFG for 20X6.

The business is currently organised into three divisions: retail sales, trade sales and manufacturing.

Retail sales

The loss-making retail division operates nationwide, from 120 out-of-town furniture showrooms and 15 high street stores.

The out-of-town showrooms are located on dedicated retail shopping parks, situated away from the town centre, with good road links and ample parking. The high street stores are significantly smaller and located in the centre of major towns and cities, with good public transport links and favouring access by pedestrians.

Information for each type of store for 20X6 is set out below:

	Typical out-of-town store	Typical high street store
Revenue	£4,677,563	£1,969,500
Space occupied	2,500 m^2	1,000 m^2
Rental per square metre	£150	£250
Number of transactions pa	11,700	7,800

The stores range in size between 1,000 and 3,000 square metres. Each offers a complete range of furniture for the kitchen, living room, bedroom, bathroom and home office, on direct sale to the general public.

The product margins vary considerably and some products are not price-competitive after allocation of store and delivery costs in the pricing calculation.

Kitchens and bedroom furniture account for over 80% of revenue and gross margin, but a significantly lower proportion of selling space.

Trade sales

The trade sales division supplies kitchens, doors, window frames and other wood products to the building trade. Customers are mainly local builders, small developers and specialist kitchen installers. This division has seen rapid growth and rising profits and is currently the star of the group. It has around 300 sales centres across the UK, 15 of which were opened in 20X6. The board expects a similar number of new sales centres to be opened in 20X7.

Manufacturing division

The manufacturing division consists of four factories and eight distribution centres. It has historically manufactured and supplied the majority of components and finished goods for the retail and trade sales divisions. It only supplies products internally and the goods are priced at cost.

The board meeting

CFG's board is under pressure to improve performance and so it urgently needs to improve margins, control costs and generate cash. As a result the directors are currently assessing the store portfolio and the supply chain and need help implementing the strategic review.

The directors have expressed some views:

Director of manufacturing division:

'Our high street stores are simply not big enough to carry a sufficient range of stock and the rent is very high. Sales from the high street have fallen as internet sales have become more popular. Besides, anyone with transport tends to go to one of our out-of-town locations. The high street shops are an obvious candidate for closure.'

Director of retail sales division:

'We have always had a reputation as a low cost supplier but the problem is we can no longer compete with our rivals who have increasingly outsourced production to low cost countries. I believe it is time to close our in-house manufacturing division which is inflexible and inefficient. This will give us more flexibility and allow us once again to compete on price. It would also allow us to save costs by halving the number of distribution centres.'

Director of trade sales division:

'Whatever we decide, we need to ensure the changes are handled carefully and communicated properly to our staff and our shareholders. In trade sales we have a successful business model and I am concerned that our reputation might be damaged by all the bad publicity surrounding job losses. We don't want anything to get in the way of our growth plans.'

Appendix 1: Financial performance

	20X6 £m	20X5 £m
Retail sales		
Revenue	591	618.82
Operating loss	(78.15)	(23.47)
Trade sales		
Revenue	463.35	419.32
Operating profit	77.7	71.7

Requirements

(a) Using the information available, identify and calculate appropriate Key Performance Indicators (KPIs) for a typical out-of-town and a typical high street store. Suggest further financial and non-financial measures that could be used to provide management with more information as to the performance of the various stores. **(9 marks)**

(b) Referring to your calculations in (a) where appropriate, and addressing the comments made at the board meeting where relevant, set out and evaluate:

(i) Potential strategies for the retail sales division.

(ii) The proposal to close the manufacturing operation and outsource production. **(16 marks)**

(c) Assume it is decided that the closures suggested by the directors take place. As an external consultant, prepare a memo for the board of CFG addressing the following aspects of the change management programme:

(i)   Planning the change
(ii) Explaining barriers to change and how staff can be motivated in the period
(iii) Communicating the change plan to stakeholders   **(15 marks)**

(40 marks)

5   Holiday Cottage Company Ltd

Note: Assume that the current date is mid-December 20X5.

Norman Hogg had been a director of a large holiday company for 25 years, but he was made redundant in 20X4. Using his redundancy money, he set up the Holiday Cottage Company Ltd (hereafter HCC) in December 20X4. His initial business model was to provide a link between: owners of holiday cottages who wished to rent them out and families looking to rent this type of accommodation for their holidays. Revenues are generated for HCC by charging the owners of properties a percentage of the rentals generated.

Industry background

The UK holiday property rental market consists of a range of different properties including cottages, flats, caravans and lodges. Many are individual privately owned properties, but there are also large sites with many properties, owned by major holiday companies and which provide a range of additional recreational facilities including swimming pools, bars, and organised activities.

Within the private rental market many individuals have purchased second homes in holiday areas in recent years in order to take advantage of increases in property prices, to earn rental income, and to enjoy holidays themselves. Some property owners attempt to rent out their properties themselves, through advertising and personal contacts, while others offer a block of perhaps 30 weeks a year to intermediaries such as HCC to market and administer rentals on their behalf.

Commissions charged by holiday property intermediaries, such as HCC, range from 10% of rentals for a basic service, to about 30% charged by some large companies. The larger companies tend to sell their services on the basis of significant advertising and exposure to a large population, rather than by providing a comprehensive and individual service to property owners.

HCC's current business model

Norman's vision is that, although the holiday rentals industry is competitive, profits can be made at the upper end of the market with good quality properties being let out to high income holiday-makers, where both parties would appreciate a premium service.

The HCC business focuses on the South West of England, where Norman lives and where HCC is based. This geographical concentration enables a knowledgeable, manageable and high quality service to be provided on behalf of property owners. His mission statement, which captures this idea, is: 'We worry about your property, so you don't have to.' The premium service provided includes administration, insurance, advertising, cleaning and a hand-over service between rentals.

The company employs cleaning and administration staff on a casual basis due to the uncertainty over the volumes of lettings and the seasonality of the business.

HCC advertises in quality newspapers and magazines offering holiday accommodation. Also, Norman writes articles in magazines and newspapers about the benefits and pitfalls of holiday letting, and uses this platform to advertise his own company and its services to potential property owners. HCC also has a website giving details of the properties and the services that the company offers.

At the current date of mid-December 20X5, HCC is expected to achieve the following results for 20X5:

- A total of 400 holiday lettings at an average gross rental fee to the holiday-maker of £800 per property

- Fixed costs for the year will be £80,000

- Average commissions charged by HCC will be 25% of the rental fee generated (ie £200 for the average rental)

- Variable costs will be 5% of each rental fee generated (ie £40 for the average rental)

Customer feedback has been good for the 20X5 season with a number of repeat bookings from property owners and holiday-makers for 20X6. Despite this, Norman is conscious of the fact that he has done little more than break into the market and that he needs to expand the business significantly if he is to make adequate profits.

Norman is also aware that this is a very competitive market with large companies at one end of the spectrum and many individual owners selling directly to the public at the other end.

Future growth

If HCC is to continue with the current business model then the expected growth in rental incomes generated from the 20X5 base is expected to be 10% per annum in terms of the volume of rentals, and 5% per annum in the fees per rental. Fixed costs are expected to grow at 5% per annum. HCC's commissions are expected to remain at 25% of rental incomes generated. Variable costs are expected to remain at 5% of rental incomes generated.

Norman is, however, considering departing from the current business model by expanding the HCC product range and he has identified the following two strategies for expansion.

Strategies for expansion

Strategy 1

Many UK residents have purchased properties in Northern France in recent years. This is a popular holiday destination for UK tourists. Norman therefore believes that he could rent out properties in Northern France with UK owners to UK tourists. This strategy would use the existing website and hence few additional fixed overhead costs would be incurred, but the variable costs of service and support would be higher per property than in the UK.

Strategy 2

In addition to offering a premium service, Norman believes he can offer a 'no frills, introduction only' service via the Internet. This would involve property owners buying a HCC website subscription. HCC would heavily advertise the website and charge the property owners for each successful rental, but no further service would be offered. The charge in this case could be as low as 10% of rental income generated. This strategy would require a significant new investment in the website and new advertising, but there would be almost no additional variable costs per rental.

Requirements

(a) Ignoring the strategies for expansion, determine each of the following:

    (i) Calculate what would have been the break even revenue for HCC in 20X5 using the data provided for that year.

    (ii) Using the projected growth figures, determine the first calendar year in which HCC will make a profit. (Show all workings clearly.) **(8 marks)**

(b) Prepare a memorandum for Norman which:

    (i) Explains the critical success factors for HCC and the key performance indicators that may be used to measure these.

    (ii) Develops HCC's marketing strategy for:

       – Property owners
       – Holiday-makers **(14 marks)**

    For this purpose ignore the strategies for expansion.

(c) Identify and explain the following for each of the two new strategic proposals.

    (i) Core competences necessary to deliver each strategy successfully
    (ii) Risks **(11 marks)**

(33 marks)

6 The Slate Snooker Table Company Ltd

Note: Assume that the current date is June 20X5.

The Slate Snooker Table Company Ltd (hereafter SSTC) is a large private company which manufactures snooker tables.

Industry background

Snooker is a traditional game, which enjoyed a major revival in the late 1970s when it was first televised on a widespread basis. Since that time, snooker's popularity has varied but it still maintains enthusiastic support.

Slate snooker tables vary in price, with new slate tables in the UK selling from about £2,000 to over £20,000. There is also an active second hand slate snooker table market, which competes with the new market. Increasingly, both new and used snooker tables are sold by individuals and by companies over the Internet. Few tables are exported, or imported, as the transportation costs would be high given their weight and the risk of damage.

Many low cost wooden and toy snooker tables exist, but these are of a significantly poorer quality than slate tables making them unsuitable for serious players. In general, wooden tables are regarded as a separate market from slate tables.

The company background

SSTC was established in 1879. It has specialised in making slate snooker tables and, unlike many competitors, it does not sell any other products. Indeed, it makes only one type of table, 'The Standard', which sells for £3,000.

SSTC has two types of customers: snooker clubs and private homes. Tables are supplied to the customers' premises and assembled on site by SSTC employees. The company takes pride in its reputation of providing customers with a good service and it has a good reputation for quality in the industry.

SSTC is organised functionally with production, marketing and administration being the three sections. SSTC's main factory and showroom is in central England, but it also has showrooms in Scotland and in London.

Estimated financial information for the year to 30 June 20X5

	£'000	£'000
Sales		
Private homes	9,000	
Clubs	6,000	
		15,000
Variable costs	2,500	
Fixed costs		
Direct labour (fitters)	500	
Other fixed costs	13,000	
		(16,000)
Loss		(1,000)

At a board meeting a number of strategic proposals were put forward to improve the poor results.

The board meeting

Proposal 1

The **marketing director** suggested: 'Our basic problem is that we are a quality company but we are not charging enough for our product. A great opportunity has arisen for us to sponsor the national snooker championship in July 20X5 as the original sponsor has withdrawn. They will use our tables, which will be seen on national television. The sponsorship cost would be £2 million but the exposure would mean that we will be able to increase our prices immediately, or alternatively sell a lot more tables.'

Proposal 2

The **finance director** disagreed: 'The problem is that we only sell one product. We should sell a range of tables and accessories, but more immediately an opportunity has arisen for us to acquire the entire share capital of National Snooker Clubs Ltd (NSC). This company runs a chain of about 100 snooker clubs around the UK and, at the moment, they are not one of our customers. They have only been breaking even so we should not need to pay any more than the value of the assets to acquire the company. NSC could then be run as a separate division from the existing SSTC business, with each division having its own divisional manager.

I estimate that the SSTC division would provide the NSC division with 500 tables a year. This alone would be enough to turn our existing SSTC business into profit and it would mean lower cost tables for NSC. It could also provide 100 new sales outlets if we expanded into snooker accessories.'

Proposal 3

The **human resources director** saw the problem from a different perspective: 'Our fitters who install the tables on site are paid a fixed weekly wage and a two-man team is expected to install one table per day. The problem is that our direct labour is in effect a fixed cost. When there is no work they still get paid. I also understand that they sometimes finish the day around mid-afternoon and go home. They are capable of doing more, but they do not have the incentives. If we start paying overtime they will just stretch the job out to earn more money. Also, when there has been a big snooker tournament on television the demand is high, but they just cannot cope with the volume of work. What we need is more flexibility by turning direct labour into a variable cost by introducing payment by results, rather than by time worked. We also need to measure the performance of our fitters in order to improve efficiency and maintain quality.'

Requirements

(a)   Using the marketing director's information under Proposal 1, calculate:

    (i)   The amount by which selling price; and
    (ii)   The amount by which the volume of sales

    would need to increase in order to achieve break-even profit for the year ending 30 June 20X6.

    Assume that, other than any changes arising from the marketing director's suggestion, variable costs per unit and fixed costs remain as they were in the year ending 30 June 20X5.

    Ignore Proposals 2 and 3. Consider (a)(i) and (a)(ii) separately.   **(6 marks)**

(b)   Appraise the marketing director's suggestion under the following headings:

    (i)   The scale of the changes required to break-even
    (ii)   Strategic and operating risks
    (iii)   Competitive position   **(9 marks)**

(c)   Evaluate the merits and demerits of the finance director's suggestions in Proposal 2.   **(9 marks)**

(d)   Adopting the human resource director's suggestion, calculate the impact on the break even output if all direct labour costs (ie the cost of the fitters) became variable costs. Ignore Proposals 1 and 2. Assume, for the purpose of these calculations that there is no change in the fitting time per table.
    (4 marks)

(e)   Briefly identify non-financial indictors that might be used to measure labour performance by fitters.
    (4 marks)

    (32 marks)

7   Furbiton & Frobisher plc

Note: Assume that the current date is December 20X5.

Furbiton & Frobisher plc (hereafter FF) is a listed company which operates a small chain of up-market department stores throughout the UK.

Company history and background

FF was established in 1948 with a single store in London selling only top quality clothing. The business grew rapidly in the following years and, according to the chairman, the factors leading to this success were:

- Strong brand name and reputation

- Access to internationally known suppliers with up-market brands

- Inelastic demand for sales, based upon a high income customer base, resulting in high profit margins

- Recruitment of good quality staff with high salaries for the industry

By 20X5, the FF chain had grown to ten stores spread throughout the UK. Each store has 2,000 to 3,000 square metres, with two or three floors. This is smaller than many large rival store companies, but FF sells only four types of product in each store through separate departments: clothing, furnishings, cosmetics and electrical.

All the stores have prime, city centre locations and are leased. The lease rentals vary considerably, depending on the location, size, lease terms and condition of the building.

The four departments within each store are profit centres. The rental costs of each store are charged to the four departments in that store on the basis of floor area occupied. Other fixed costs, including head office costs, are divided equally between the departments.

Staff are recruited with the help of the human resources section at head office, but the departmental manager has the final decision. Staff are not usually transferred between departments as the departmental managers have autonomy to retain their own staff. Also, there is specialist knowledge in selling each of the different types of products which makes staff transfers difficult.

The departments

Clothing

The clothing departments are normally considered to be the core of the business. Only well-known, quality brands are sold. A few of the very best international brand companies supply a restricted number of outlets in the UK, so competition for FF is constrained in respect of these designer labels. Unfortunately, one of the very best Italian designers informed FF that it will no longer supply it after the end of 20X5. Part of the reputation of FF depends on selling these international quality labels.

Furniture

The furniture departments were introduced into FF stores in 20X2, but revenues have grown rapidly, with an emphasis on modern styles from quality manufacturers. The departmental managers of five of the furniture departments were recently recruited by a rival company and left FF in November 20X5. These were five of FF's best departmental managers.

Cosmetics

FF commenced selling luxury cosmetics in 1980. FF places itself at the top end of the cosmetics market by its products and by the level of service it offers, including make-overs and special evenings for loyal customers. Profit margins are high but revenue generated is smaller than the other three departments and it has not grown in recent years. A high proportion of sales are in November and December prior to Christmas.

Electricals

This department has performed poorly in recent years due to increased price competition from rival department stores, specialist suppliers and Internet suppliers.

Performance

The estimated financial performance for the year to 31 December 20X5 is:

	Clothing £m	Furniture £m	Cosmetics £m	Electrical £m	Total £m
Revenue	80	30	20	70	200
Direct costs	(55)	(20)	(8)	(65)	(148)
Rental costs	(8)	(4)	(4)	(8)	(24)
Other fixed overheads	(6)	(6)	(6)	(6)	(24)
Profit/(loss)	11	0	2	(9)	4

A board meeting

At a recent board meeting the possibility of closing all the electrical departments was considered. A dilemma that arose was what to do with the vacated floor space if the closures took place. Two strategies were put forward:

Strategy 1

Lease the space vacated to an external specialist retailer, Thinebury Brothers, which sells up-market glassware and tableware. It has previously expressed an interest in taking space in FF stores. The lease agreement would need to be for at least five years.

Strategy 2

Expand the remaining three departments to take up the vacated floor space. To make this strategy credible it would be necessary to expand the product range for each department. The board has suggested that a 'Furbitons' own-label brand should be used. These products would be good quality but not as up-market as existing goods. The brand name of the new suppliers would not be shown, as these goods would be sold under the 'Furbitons' label, utilising the company's own reputation, rather than that of the suppliers. Selling prices for 'own-label' goods would be lower than for existing products.

Requirements

(a) Explain how each FF store should measure:

(i) Departmental performance
(ii) The performance of departmental managers

In so doing, evaluate the factors that should be considered in deciding whether to close the electrical departments. Provide supporting calculations where appropriate.

For this purpose ignore the proposed future strategies. **(15 marks)**

(b) Assume that the electrical departments are to close. As a consultant, prepare a memorandum for the board of FF addressing each of the following aspects of the change management programme:

(i) Planning the change programme
(ii) Explaining the barriers to change and how staff can be motivated during the change period
(iii) Communicating the change plan to stakeholders **(13 marks)**

(c) Evaluate the likely financial and strategic effects for FF of the two proposed strategies. **(12 marks)**

(40 marks)

8 Cabot Tours Ltd

Note: Assume that the current date in the question is March 20X7.

Cabot Tours Ltd (CT) is an established tour and travel operator which provides UK clients with a full range of package holidays through high street shops and also an online travel agency. In an attempt to capitalise on the growing market for medical tourism, CT is considering offering 'Sun & Surgery' holidays to India. Customers would be offered a complete package which would include arrangements for surgery, travel, accommodation in a private hospital and a post-operative holiday with recuperation time.

Market information

There are two types of market for surgery:

(1) Elective surgery – this includes cosmetic surgery, fertility treatment, cosmetic dentistry and weight reduction.

(2) More urgent medical treatment – this includes heart surgery, joint replacement and kidney transplants.

A study by the Confederation of Indian Industry suggests that the medical tourism market could be worth 100 billion rupees (approx £1.2 billion) by 20Y2. It is estimated that around 150,000 medical tourists visited India in 20X6, with the numbers currently rising by 15% p.a. The Indian government is planning to introduce medical visas to facilitate the process which would allow patients to return up to four times in a year for check-ups and post-operative care.

The growth in demand has arisen because of:

- The rising cost of healthcare and the ageing population in Western Europe

- The ease and affordability of international travel

- Favourable exchange rates – the rupee has continued to decline in value against both sterling and the euro

- Improving technology and infrastructure in India

- Certain patients being rejected for treatment in their own countries eg due to obesity or age

- The availability in India of a large pool of highly skilled doctors

Packages range in price from £1,500 to £8,000 depending on the treatment required. A knee operation costing £10,000 in the UK would cost around £4,900 in India, including travel and accommodation.

The directors of CT have some concerns about the risks of the 'Sun & Surgery' venture and want help putting together a business plan and deciding on a suitable structure. In particular they are concerned about the necessary medical provision and are considering a possible arrangement with a private medical group who have hospitals in three cities in India.

Requirements

As an external consultant, brought in to help with the business plan,

(a) Prepare, for initial discussion by the board of Cabot Tours Ltd, a PESTEL analysis for entry into the medical tourism industry in India. **(9 marks)**

(b) Identify and explain the potential business risks associated with the proposed venture. **(8 marks)**

(c) Identify alternative business structures that could be used for the venture and advise the directors of the advantages and disadvantages of each arrangement. **(11 marks)**

(28 marks)

9 Jenny and Bob

Jenny and Bob Lindsay are directors of Lindsay Leisure Ltd (3L), a small entertainments and leisure company which they formed in 1988. 3L currently owns a DVD and computer game rental business with three small outlets in neighbouring towns in the West Midlands. The business has traded profitably since its formation, but has recently suffered reduced margins due to competition from large national rental companies, and from the increased access to cable and satellite television in the area.

For some time Jenny has been suggesting to Bob that they consider expanding their business into related areas, and they have now been offered the opportunity to buy a cinema in the town of Bridge Stanton. 'The Bijou' is a fully operational 200-seat cinema, with a lounge bar and refreshments kiosk, situated on the main market square of the town. It was built in 1924 and traded profitably as a cinema until the late 1960s when, due to falling audiences, it was converted into a bingo hall.

The Bijou is owned by Stan Collymore, an 81-year-old businessman, who wishes to retire and is asking £180,000 for the freehold premises and a further £20,000 for goodwill and inventory. Jenny estimates that an additional £200,000 would be required to refurbish the cinema and install new projection equipment. 3L has £100,000 available to invest, but the remainder would need to be raised from external sources.

Jenny has an article from a recent issue of *Leisure World* magazine which reports a five per cent annual growth in cinema audiences over the last three years, and this has led her to believe that it will be possible to run the Bijou profitably. Bob is less confident, but agrees that the modern 'multiplex' cinema ten miles away in Broadley is always very busy when he drives past on Friday or Saturday evenings.

In order to proceed 3L needs to approach its bank with a view to raising the additional finance required. The bank has requested a business plan for the proposed venture, and Jenny has approached your firm to assist with the preparation of the plan.

Requirements

As a member of staff with the 3L accountants, prepare an initial memorandum to 3L which covers the following:

(a) The likely contents of a business plan which will be suitable for submission to the bank in connection with raising the required finance.

(b) An indication, under each of the general plan headings, of factors relevant to the proposed venture.

(21 marks)

10 Chibb plc

Chibb plc is a company listed on the London Stock Exchange, with a year-end of 31 December. Chibb manufactures and retails fine china tableware at the upper end of the market, operating through two divisions, the manufacturing division and the retail division.

The manufacturing division sells exclusively to the retail division with no external sales. The manufacturing site is at one factory in South Wales which has several processes for making and painting its range of china tableware.

Similarly, the retail division purchases only from the manufacturing division. It operates from shops located throughout the UK, normally sited in large towns and cities. The transfer price between the two divisions is set at the retail selling price minus 30%.

The fine china industry has suffered a decline in sales in the past few years. However, the performance of Chibb has been particularly poor, with a sharp decline in its sales, profits and share price over the last year. As a result, a meeting of the directors was called.

The board meeting

Chairman: 'This situation cannot go on. The company is under-performing in terms of profitability and share price. What we need are some key measures of performance and a means to improve performance.'

Finance director: 'I agree, but what we do not know is which division is under-performing, as the transfer price between them is arbitrary. What we need is to set transfer prices based upon market values – then we will see which division is the problem. I have provided some projections for the year to 31 December 20X4.' **(Exhibit 1)**.

Managing director of retail division: 'How can we set a transfer price based upon market prices? We only buy and sell from each other, which is the whole point of our strategy of protecting the brand by keeping it in-house throughout the supply chain. While competitors' products may be similar, they are not identical, and thus there is no readily observable market price. I vote that we stay with the current system but also look at non-financial measures of performance.'

Managing director of manufacturing division: 'We need a fair transfer price that ensures both divisions make a profit. If the company makes a profit, we both contribute to it and we should therefore both share it.'

Chief executive: 'I think the problem is that we do not know whether we are a manufacturer or a retailer. Perhaps we should just concentrate on one or the other. I think we should use benchmarking to determine which division is performing well relative to standards set outside the company. We can then use the knowledge we get from benchmarking to improve performance or, if not, divest ourselves of that part of the business.'

Exhibit 1 – Projections for the year to 31 December 20X4

	Manufacturing division £m	Retail division £m
Estimated retail sales	–	24
Variable costs	8	3
Fixed costs	10	2

The above figures exclude the cost of goods transferred between the two divisions.

Requirements

(a) Using the figures provided in Exhibit 1 determine:

    (i) The expected profit or loss to be made by each division in the year to 31 December 20X4, assuming transfer prices are set on the existing basis of retail price minus 30%.

    (ii) The transfer pricing formula (ie the retail price minus a specific profit percentage), which would enable the manufacturing division to break even in the year to 31 December 20X4.

    (6 marks)

(b) Examine the benefits and problems of Chibb using transfer prices based on retail price minus a profit margin. Refer to your calculations above where appropriate. **(6 marks)**

(c) As an external consultant, write a memorandum to the board of Chibb which evaluates the comments made at the board meeting with respect to divisional performance measurement and the potential divestment decision. Use each of the following headings:

    (i) Profit based divisional performance measurement
    (ii) Non-financial divisional performance measurement
    (iii) Benchmarking
    (iv) Closure of a division – relevant criteria   **(18 marks)**

    (30 marks)

11 TE plc

TE plc (TE) is an unquoted company which runs bus and train franchises. The franchises are awarded by the government, and last for a maximum of ten years. Most of TE plc's franchises have another eight years to run. When the transport sector was privatised, the government took some trouble to ensure that competition was introduced and the company has to compete with other suppliers on many of its routes.

The information technology and information systems used by TE are mainly legacy systems, inherited a few years ago from the old nationalised industry which had previously run all public transportation.

The systems at TE are focused mainly at the transaction processing and office automation levels – wages, salaries, maintenance records and non-current asset recording. When public transportation was in the public sector and was effectively a monopoly, this level of information provision was enough to allow the organisation to function. Whether a good service was provided was another matter and, as with many public sector monopolies, the public had no choice in the services that were provided.

The system is poor at reporting passenger numbers on each train, poor at reporting seasonal (often daily) fluctuations in demand and poor at identifying route profitability. That information can be obtained, but it requires considerable manual manipulation of data to yield useful results. Inevitably, manual intervention can introduce errors and delays into the system.

The board of the company has largely been recruited from outside the state sector, and there has been astonishment at the lack of investment in the company, not only in trains and buses but also in the information infrastructure and staff training. A team of consultants called in to evaluate the information systems at TE recently prepared the following as part of their report:

'Information can be described as data with meaning. Ways in which meaning can be generated include:

- **Processing the data**: For example, identifying credit balances on a receivable data, or working out statistical results.

- **Presentation of data**: Descriptions attached to data or numerical data presented graphically.

Knowledge can be defined as 'information in someone's head'. It is only when information is accessed by someone and used for decision-making that it becomes actively useful. A filing cabinet or computer disc full of files which no-one has ever accessed is of little use.

Knowledge can be divided into two categories:

- **Explicit knowledge**: Usually written down or recorded on some way, but its existence is known and it can be accessed. An example of explicit knowledge is when a report, showing revenue generated by TE's major routes, is read and discussed by management.

- **Tacit knowledge**: This information is normally not formally written down or recorded in some other way. An organisation or indeed individuals might not even be aware of its existence, yet it could be used regularly and could be very important to organisational success. An example of tacit knowledge is when a member of TE management knows of plans to set up a new bus route, but does not record this anywhere.

At TE formal reports could appear to present information inadequately. This will interfere with the assimilation of explicit knowledge by employees. However, the real challenge facing organisations such as TE is dealing with tacit knowledge – knowledge which they might not even know exists. They need to develop ways of:

- Uncovering tacit knowledge
- Recording tacit knowledge (often it is qualitative)
- Distributing tacit knowledge
- Ensuring that it is kept up-to-date.'

Although many people are involved in processing the data at TE, they are not always capable of identifying significant information, or showing initiative in analysing and presenting data in different ways. For example, the company feels that additional marginal revenue could be earned if fares were varied, for example, between peak and off peak travelling times. However, no information is available which might support or refute this belief.

Almost no information about competitors is available.

The company's mission can be summarised as:

'We aim to be the most responsive and safe transport operation in the UK.'

In the two years after privatisation, about 50% of employees left as they were unwilling to adapt to operating in a market economy. While TE management understands that resistance to change can arise for a variety of reasons (such as fear of redundancy or a fear of reduced status, coupled with the stress of a new job), many of the employees who left voluntarily were the ones that the company would have preferred to keep. Many had very deep knowledge of operating a complex transport operation, especially a railway where timetabling and line utilisation is very skilled and specialised. Running a railway operation has become more complex since privatisation because rolling stock from different companies now share train lines and stations.

Requirements

(a) The board of TE urgently wants to review the provision of information within the company. As a first step, the quality of the information provided by the current IS/IT system is to be evaluated. Suggest headings under which this evaluation could be carried out and, so far as the scenario allows, comment on the current system. **(8 marks)**

(b) Most organisations require different information to be available at different functional levels. Describe these functional levels, and the nature of the information they provided in TE plc. **(8 marks)**

(c) Explain why developing a good knowledge management system is likely to be both challenging and important for TE plc. **(6 marks)**

(d) The privatisation of the company meant that employees were faced with major changes, and around 50% left. The employees at TE might have resisted change. Suggest what steps management could take to minimise resistance. **(8 marks)**

(30 marks)

12 DA plc

DA plc (DA) is an information solutions company, listed on the London Stock Exchange.

Company background

DA began trading in 1980, providing credit reference services for business customers. Although this remains its primary activity, it has grown organically and now provides financial and statistical information to a variety of UK businesses to help them manage the risk of commercial and financial decisions.

The company is split into three divisions:

- Credit reference services – provides factual information to clients, via credit searches of an individual's financial history, to assist them to lend profitably or offer trade credit.

- Decision software – assists clients in improving the consistency and quality of business decisions in areas such as credit risk, fraud prevention and customer account management.

- Vehicle history – provides financial and statistical information to the automotive industry to help clients understand the risks associated with the purchase or sale of a particular second-hand vehicle.

A breakdown of key data, by division, for 2007 is as follows:

	Credit reference services	Decision software	Vehicle history	Total
Sales (£m)	166	115	64	345
Operating profit (£m)	41	34	13	88
Growth in sales from 2006	3%	15%	0%	6%
Number of employees	686	490	300	1,476

Credit reference services

Clients for credit reference services can be split into two groups:

(1) Banks, credit card companies and other financial services organisations which need help assessing the risk associated with lending decisions; and

(2) Commercial companies seeking credit references before supplying goods on credit to other businesses and private customers.

When an individual or business makes an application for credit, the lender or supplier usually asks a credit reference agency (CRA) for a credit search to check the applicant's identity and credit worthiness. The database system operated by a CRA enables different lenders, such as banks, to share information about their customers' credit accounts and repayment histories. Applicants have to give permission for their credit report information to be shared when they apply for credit.

Although a number of companies are currently licensed as CRAs in the UK, DA is the largest, with a 58% market share. DA has built its market position by compiling and managing the most comprehensive credit database in the UK. Communication and information technology are a core part of DA's business. Online systems allow lenders to update data directly, resulting in more accurate information and efficiency gains for DA.

DA's main competitor, CC Inc (CC) is an American-based business with an acknowledged expertise in credit scoring (a statistical technique that combines several financial characteristics to form a single score to represent a customer's creditworthiness). CC has recently announced that, as part of its global expansion strategy, it plans to increase its share of the UK credit market, which is currently 32%. CC intends to use low cost web-based systems to deliver online consumer credit scores directly to lenders and companies extending trade credit. In this way, it hopes to reduce DA's market dominance in the UK.

DA's strategic development

Decision software

Having created a reputation for holding the most comprehensive credit database in the UK, DA went on to develop analytical software to enable clients to process credit applications and manage customer credit accounts more efficiently.

The software takes data from DA's credit management database and other sources, such as the client's own customer account information, and uses analytical tools and scoring systems to provide decision support. Typical users of this product are banks, credit card companies, mortgage providers and other organisations that grant personal or trade credit. DA's software enables them to assess quickly and accurately whether to accept a new customer or extend credit arrangements for existing customers. It can also define the processes the businesses should adopt in managing an account that has fallen into arrears.

Vehicle history

Recognising that it had a core skill in the management of large databases for the financial services industry, DA also decided to provide similar services to the automotive industry. It compiles and manages data on the histories of 30 million vehicles and 25 million car insurance policies in the UK.

This data is used to provide vehicle history information to car dealers, finance providers and insurers. Fraudulent representation of used vehicles is a significant risk for private consumers and a potential financial liability for the businesses involved in the sale or purchase. The vehicle history can assist in establishing the market value of a vehicle; and whether a vehicle is registered as stolen or has outstanding finance.

Proposed diversification

Recently, DA has decided to target a new market, the individual consumer market, with a new online service: 'Checksta'.

Under current UK legislation, individuals have a legal right to see the information about them held by a CRA. In return for a statutory fee of £2, the CRA is legally obliged to provide a written copy of the information held on the individual's credit report. Instead of making a written application for a statutory credit report, individual consumers will be able to pay to subscribe to Checksta.

The Checksta service will allow individuals to check online that their credit report is accurate and up-to-date, as many times as they want. Checksta will send a text or e-mail alert every time there is a significant change to the information held on an individual's credit report. This alert service assists in identifying identity fraud (where somebody applies for credit in another person's name). Individuals will also be able to order a credit score, based on their DA credit report, which will give them an idea of how a lender would view the information, if they were to apply for credit.

The introduction of Checksta is partly in response to the aggressive marketing stance currently being adopted by CC and also as a reaction to the following changes in the external environment:

- Changing attitudes to money and credit

  An increase in spending has led to an increase in demand for credit and it is very easy to apply now, both by telephone and online. This means that individuals are more likely to shop around for credit and lenders have to carry out more credit checks.

- Changes in legislation

  DA has to conform to the UK laws that govern the way it does business. Government concerns that debt levels are too high have caused a tightening of the legislation to give consumers better access to information held on them, more rights regarding disputes with lenders and more protection from rogue lenders. As a result, CRAs have had to implement a consumer education programme, working closely with consumer organisations to help consumers understand how credit referencing works.

- The growth of e-commerce (products bought online)

  This has necessitated more frequent and rapid credit checks and a subsequent upgrading of DA's information technology systems.

- An increase in identity fraud

  Identity criminals steal people's personal information and use these details to commit crimes, usually obtaining credit illegally.

Marketing

To date, DA has worked mainly with business clients, attracting business customers through personal selling and retaining them by developing strong client relationships. The sales director is aware that to succeed in the consumer market, DA will need to use a different marketing strategy for Checksta.

DA intends to use its knowledge of consumers who have applied for their statutory credit reports in the past, to build up a profile of the consumers it wants to target with its online service. Preliminary market research suggests that those most likely to be interested are people who are Internet users, credit users and those keen to manage their financial affairs effectively. Such people are likely to read the financial pages in newspapers or visit personal finance websites.

Requirements

(a) Explain the factors that may have contributed to DA's competitive advantage. **(6 marks)**

(b) Using relevant strategic models, analyse the ways in which DA has chosen to expand its business since it began trading, including its plans for Checksta. **(10 marks)**

(c) Prepare a PESTEL analysis on the credit reference industry, clearly explaining the implications for DA's plans to implement the Checksta product. **(8 marks)**

(d) Advise DA on an appropriate marketing strategy for Checksta. **(8 marks)**

(e) Identify the strategic and operational risks arising from DA's use of Information Technology and Information Systems and outline the measures that can be implemented to deal with such risks.

(8 marks)

(40 marks)

13 Kraftvagen Gmbh (KV)

Kraftvagen GmbH (KV) is a car manufacturer, based in Germany. It produces a range of luxury cars.

KV has production facilities in a number of continents, normally located where labour is cheap and it can take advantage of economies of scale, enabling costs of production and assembly to be minimised. KV cars are sold worldwide although its core markets are in the USA, Europe and Japan (see **Exhibit 1**).

Market development

KV has been attempting to identify a new sales market and has recently identified a potential opportunity in India. There is an increasing trend for organisations to outsource service provision to India because of the availability of a low cost but skilled workforce. In addition, rapid economic growth (9% per annum) is attracting investment from an increasing number of entrepreneurs and professionals such as investment bankers, accountants and software engineers, drawn by the prospect of significant returns. This has started to create demand for luxury cars, which currently represent less than one per cent of new car sales in India. The luxury sector in India is widely forecast by the automotive industry to grow significantly in the next ten years (see **Exhibit 2**).

The Indian government has allocated significant funding to improving the infrastructure of the country and in particular the national highways. It has a ten-year plan to improve and widen 25,000 kilometres of highway and to build a new motorway linking India's four largest cities. There is some concern however about the speed with which this may be achieved.

Last year KV decided to test the market by exporting a number of luxury cars to India. The trial was successful, resulting in the sale of 300 cars. KV's Chief Executive, Walter Bergen has decided that KV should actively pursue this business opportunity.

Walter Bergen commented: 'I am keen to pursue this venture as I believe there are significant growth opportunities for those who are first in the market place. This would give us the chance to establish our brand reputation, build market share, develop economies of scale and create barriers to entry. However, I am mindful that our experience in other emerging markets suggests that initial sales may be low and that it may take some time to recover the costs of our investment. Whatever we do, I am keen to minimise the downside risk.'

Plans for implementation

Options available for KV's planned sales expansion into the Indian market are as follows:

(1) Continue to export luxury cars to India, using KV's existing production operations.

(2) Set up an assembly-only plant in India. This plant will import the parts for the luxury cars in kit form from KV's existing production operations and then assemble the final car locally. The plant would occupy 7,500 square metres and could make 1,700 cars per year, on a single shift operation. The number of shifts, and therefore output, could be doubled if demand increased.

(3) Invest in a full scale production operation, which would build the cars in India. This would have an annual production capacity of 8,000 cars. Initially any spare capacity could be used to produce cars for export to KV's other markets.

The Indian government does not currently place restrictions on the level of imports. It has, however, recently announced that it is 'looking at this area, because it is keen to promote jobs for the local population and ensure spending contributes to the growth of the domestic economy'. One possibility being considered is the introduction of quotas restricting the volume of imports; another is an import tax, which would be levied on the value of any finished goods entering the country. There are currently no plans to impose similar restrictions or taxes on exports.

Expected competition

Two other car manufacturers, which both compete in KV's core luxury car market (see **Exhibit 3**), are also considering entering the Indian market:

• Lima plc (Lima) a UK company which produces a wide range of cars, has recently announced plans to create an assembly-only plant for its luxury car model.

• Durant Inc (Durant), an American company, primarily seen as a maker of mid-range cars in USA and Europe, but considered a luxury brand in India, is considering opening up a full production operation, with a complete range of cars.

Conrad SA (Conrad), a French manufacturer of luxury cars and the European market leader, currently has no plans to enter the Indian market.

Exhibit 1: Analysis of KV's 2007 sales by location of market and also by location of production, (expressed in Euros)

Market	Sales revenue	Production (valued at selling price)
	(€m)	(€m)
USA	22.4	18.3
Europe	53.6	45.3
Japan	43.7	25.2
Other	9.5	40.4
Total	129.2	129.2

Exhibit 2: Indian domestic car sales volumes, 2002 – 2017

Sales volumes '000 cars	2002 actual	2007 actual	2012 forecast	2017 forecast
Luxury cars	3	12	28	56
Total passenger cars	600	1,300	1,900	2,800

Exhibit 3: Extract of market information for volume of luxury car sales, 2007

Number of cars sold	USA '000	Europe '000	Japan '000
KV	280	670	546
Lima	750	308	150
Durant	120	295	434
Conrad	405	714	240
Other manufacturers	765	233	190
Total luxury car sales	2,320	2,220	1,560

Average annual market growth

2002-2007 actual	0%	-4.6%	+5.5%
2007-2012 forecast	-2.5%	-6.2%	+3.2%

As an external consultant, Walter Bergen has asked for your help in assessing the proposed development in India.

Requirements

(a) Using the data provided, evaluate the relative product and market positioning of KV. Identify, with reasons, any other information that would be necessary to make a more complete assessment of KV's competitive position and performance. **(10 marks)**

(b) Explain the possible reasons for targeting the emerging markets for sales expansion and the issues, including risk, that KV needs to take into account with this strategy. **(7 marks)**

(c) Assuming that the decision is taken to develop the Indian market, prepare a report advising KV as to:

(i) The factors to consider in selecting the most appropriate of the three options for implementation; and

(ii) Ways in which it could minimise the downside risks associated with each of the three options. **(11 marks)**

(28 marks)

14 Campaign for Trading Equitably

The Campaign for Trading Equitably (CTE) is a charity, registered in the UK.

Mission and founders

CTE's mission statement is 'to promote the relief of poverty and suffering arising in connection with the conduct of trade in any part of the world. This will be achieved by providing assistance to disadvantaged producers and workers in order to help improve their social and economic position.'

CTE was founded in 2003 by a number of charitable bodies with an interest in the developing world. All the founder members have a strong interest in helping promote CTE and they contribute significant funds to the organisation.

Activities

CTE promotes fair trade by providing independent certification of the ethical nature of a product, via the 'CTE logo'. This acts as a consumer guarantee as to the adherence of standards by producers and traders. As such, consumers can be confident that in purchasing a product bearing the CTE logo, they are contributing to fairer trading terms for developing nation producers and their workers.

Currently the CTE logo applies to a range of products including food, wine, clothing, cosmetics and flowers. CTE receives a licence fee from companies whose products carry the CTE logo. In addition to the payment of the licence fee, those businesses adopting the CTE logo are required to offer overseas producers and farmers a guaranteed income, as well as a social premium to support local community projects.

In its Constitution, the charity's primary activities are listed as:

- Establishing and maintaining the CTE licence agreements, including the monitoring of adherence to standards and terms

- Assisting new producers and products to enter the supply chain for CTE certified products

- Activities to promote the knowledge and awareness of the CTE logo and the need for more equitable trade

- Fundraising, including the sale of promotional items to CTE supporters

Funding

In addition to the annual contributions of the founder members, the charity's major sources of funds are:

- Licence fees for the use of the CTE logo
- European Union grants and other grant funding
- Corporate sponsorship
- Donations and other miscellaneous income
- Sale of CTE merchandise

Medium-term priorities

As consumers become more supportive of ethical goods, the number of retailers keen to stock CTE certified products is increasing. Although retailers have to accept a lower margin on CTE goods, the volume of sales makes them more profitable overall. As a result of this trend, the work of the charity is increasing and it has recently appointed a new director, Ellen Bates. Ellen has a commercial background and has no previous experience of working in the charitable sector. Ellen has identified the charity's medium-term priorities as:

- To widen the range of products currently operating under the CTE logo;

- To ensure that the UK market for CTE certified goods delivers benefits to an increased number of producers and farmers; and

- To enhance the impact of CTE as an organisation.

This involves creating strategies for:

- Raising awareness so consumers can make more informed choices
- Influencing UK companies to develop better trading relations with overseas suppliers
- Persuading more companies to adopt the CTE logo and take up CTE licences

Governance issues

Ellen is concerned that, as CTE's activities become more prominent, the Board of Trustees should not do anything to create exposure to risk. In particular, she is aware that there has been much discussion among the founder members about:

- Spending money on promoting the CTE logo and CTE as an organisation, which might be seen as a waste of resources

- Offending the ethics of current and potential stakeholders, by accepting donations and corporate sponsorship from large multinationals that might be seen as having previously operated unfair trade practices

Requirements

(a) Discuss the extent to which the objectives of the charity will differ from those of a typical profit focused organisation. **(4 marks)**

(b) Critically evaluate the content of CTE's mission statement, making recommendations for any improvements. **(5 marks)**

(c) Identify the key stakeholders of CTE, explain their interests and analyse the influence they are likely to have in their relationship with the charity. **(6 marks)**

(d) With reference to the concerns of the founder members, advise Ellen on the specific governance issues facing the charity. **(5 marks)**

(e) Explain how Ellen could measure the performance of CTE, suggesting appropriate key performance indicators. Describe the nature and sources of data or information that would assist Ellen in measuring CTE's performance. **(12 marks)**

(32 marks)

15 Embury Ltd

Extract taken from *The Digby Herald* newspaper, 5 September 2008:

Local firm Embury Ltd (Embury), which manufactures garden equipment, plans to close its two factories in this area, and move all of its UK manufacturing operations to an extended factory at its main site in Birmingham. The Digby Herald discovered this shocking news when a copy of some recent board minutes was e-mailed to our news desk just hours before we went to press. Up to 400 jobs could be lost. The decision is being blamed on poor product sales which resulted from recent water shortages and the subsequent local government restrictions placed on the use of garden watering equipment such as hosepipes.

When asked to comment on the plans, the managing director of Embury said:

'This proposal is part of an attempt to move to a flexible manufacturing strategy. This will allow the company to counter high UK production costs and the impact that these have had on our margins.

'The rationalisation of our UK production under one roof will save overheads, reduce transportation and communication costs and improve cost effectiveness in our supply chain. In line with our European competitors, we also intend to outsource the manufacturing of selected product ranges to China, in the face of escalating raw material costs.

'It is extremely regrettable that these measures will result in a reduction of up to 35% of the company's UK workforce. However we need to take this opportunity to consolidate so we can meet the challenges in our market.'

Company information

Embury is the UK's leading manufacturer of watering equipment such as hosepipes, water sprinklers and irrigation systems for use in domestic gardens. Embury's products are sold to consumers via retailers, such as supermarkets, home improvement superstores and garden centres and are also available through independent mail order catalogues and internet retail sites.

The major challenges currently facing Embury's business are three-fold:

(1) The availability of low cost products produced in China and other countries where labour costs are low;

(2) The difficulty of predicting demand; and

(3) Pressures as a result of environmental issues and the impact of changing weather patterns.

Industry information

The garden equipment industry is divided into four market segments:

- Hand-held garden tools;
- Powered garden equipment;
- Irrigation and watering equipment; and
- Garden pond and ornamental water features.

There are a number of large, multinational manufacturers which produce a complete range of garden equipment across all four segments and sell to a variety of geographic markets. Most of these companies have large manufacturing facilities to take advantage of economies of scale, typically sited in areas where labour costs and other operating costs are low.

The European market leader, GartenZwerg Gmbh (GZ) is a German company which began as a manufacturer of small hand-held garden tools. By developing new products and extending existing product ranges, GZ has evolved from a small, family-run business to a multinational public company with a strong reputation for innovative garden products across all four market segments. In an attempt to expand into the UK market, GZ has recently signed a long-term contract with a major chain of UK garden centres, to stock its products on an exclusive basis, rather than those of other manufacturers, including Embury.

In addition to the large multinationals, there are a number of other smaller manufacturers, such as Embury, which have chosen to focus on individual segments of the market and/or domestic markets only. Embury's products also face competition from retailers' own brand products which are always competitively priced.

Factors affecting industry demand

Although there has been an increase in the number of households in the UK and hence the number of garden owners, sales of gardening equipment have remained static in value terms since 2000, because of a trend towards smaller gardens.

A recent report from the UK Gardening Trade Association suggests that future prospects for the garden equipment industry depend on:

- The general level of economic wealth
- Personal disposable incomes
- The number of households and hence gardens
- The age distribution of the population
- Consumer attitudes to leisure and gardening

Historically, gardening has been seen as the preserve of the older generation but the industry has identified the need to appeal to new and younger target groups.

Recent market research now predicts an increasing interest in gardening across all age groups. This is a result of a desire for a better quality of life, a home environment that includes natural surroundings, an increased focus on leisure time, and the availability of a better climate to enjoy the outdoors. Thus gardening is widely expected to gain importance in the future, causing the market for gardening equipment products to expand at higher rates over the next few years.

Environmental issues

The garden equipment industry requires consumers to have access to adequate, reliable and secure water supplies.

Governments around the world are paying increasing attention to issues of water quality and quantity, as climate and lifestyle changes mean that water demand increasingly exceeds supply. Shortages of water have led to greater focus on the need for the sustainable use of resources in order to secure the water supply for current and future generations. As a result, in many countries, the national government sets water conservation regulations and standards and environmental groups promote the efficient use of water.

In recent years, environmental pressures have given rise to demands by the UK government and the water companies for households to reduce the pressure on limited water supplies by cutting their domestic water consumption. This has led to restrictions on the non-essential use of water during periods of extreme shortage.

Thus, for example, in dry summers, bans have been imposed on the use of hosepipes and water sprinklers in some areas of the UK. In other areas households have been encouraged to avoid washing their cars and to adopt other water conservation measures, such as the collection of rainwater for use on the garden and the installation of special irrigation systems that deliver only limited amounts of water directly to plants.

In addition to the scarcity of water supply, charges for water services across the UK (using water meters to determine charges according to the amount used) have increased significantly in the last decade and as a result more households are making attempts to conserve water to reduce their monthly running costs.

Changing weather patterns and the increased focus on water conservation have caused significant issues for Embury. Periods of warm spring weather cause a surge in demand for watering equipment, which puts enormous pressure on the business and creates problems in the supply chain for raw materials and components. Conversely restrictions on the use of water imposed in times of water shortage prevent consumers from using Embury's products. These factors, which give rise to varying seasonality of demand, have resulted in periods of both stock-outs and over-stocking.

Plans for product development

In response to the fluctuations in demand caused by the weather, the increasing pressure from the government and environmental groups, and the threat posed by GZ's expansion into the UK, Embury has decided to increase spending on research and development. It plans to develop a new water-efficient product range that will help conserve water usage.

New products currently under development include:

- An underground tank and pump which allows rainwater to be stored and used for various outdoor purposes thus avoiding the use of expensive drinking water;

- A garden irrigation system that waters plants directly from the underground water tank; and

- A watering device which allows household waste water to be pumped onto the garden.

Requirements

(a) Prepare a PESTEL analysis on the garden equipment industry. **(8 marks)**

(b) (i) Describe the issues facing Embury in respect of production capacity planning and procurement; and

    (ii) Explain how outsourcing elements of production might benefit Embury and describe the possible problems and risks associated with outsourcing. **(12 marks)**

(c) Embury is considering introducing an ethical procurement policy. Explain the impact this could have on any outsourcing agreement. **(5 marks)**

(d) Explain the change management problems that are likely to occur as a result of the newspaper article and the planned factory closures. Discuss how these problems might be addressed.

(11 marks)

(e) Discuss the advantages and disadvantages of Embury's plans for product development. **(6 marks)**

(42 marks)

16 DT Ltd

DT Ltd (DT) was established in 2005 by David Thomas, a software specialist with a keen interest in driving cars. David owns 100% of the share capital and is the sole director. DT operates in the vehicle driver education industry, providing training for learner drivers, via a virtual reality driving simulator, similar to those used in airline pilot training. The simulator is used in addition to traditional road-based instruction and learning.

DT's mission is 'to provide high quality, convenient and comprehensive driver education courses at the lowest cost'.

Industry information

In the UK, all learner drivers are required to pass a driving test before they can obtain a full driving licence to drive a car. Most choose to prepare for the test by taking driving lessons provided by a self-employed driving instructor or driving school.

The driver education industry is fragmented into two different types of businesses. 55% of the market consists of self-employed driving instructors. There is significant variation in the cost of the driving education provided, the quality of instruction and the overall success rate of the learner.

The remaining 45% consists of a few national or international companies, known as driving schools. The driving schools are well funded, have excellent facilities and services and provide high quality tuition. However as a result they also adopt a premium pricing policy.

The industry is highly seasonal. Most learner drivers undertake lessons during spring or autumn, with numbers of learner drivers declining in the summer months due to holidays and falling even more substantially in winter when the daylight hours are short and road conditions are poor.

Barriers to entry are low. Anybody can set up as a driving instructor provided that they have a driving licence, access to a vehicle, and the necessary insurance. Most driver training providers obtain their clients through some form of referral and as a result of the large number of competitors, the industry is very price competitive.

DT's competitive position

Using his software expertise and driving knowledge, David spotted a gap in the market and developed a driving simulator to help new drivers prepare for the test to obtain a full driving licence. It is also used to help existing drivers prepare for high risk driving conditions including driving on busy roads and national highways, extreme weather such as ice and snow, and brake failure.

David identified the potential for DT to create a new low cost position, using modern training techniques, while still being able to compete with the larger companies on quality.

The use of a simulator reduces the total hours that a learner driver takes to become competent. If a learner driver uses a simulator, the total time spent altogether on the simulator and the road is less than 50% of the normal learning time required under the traditional model on a road only. Training in a safe environment reduces accidents and driver stress and it has also been shown to improve the success rate in passing the test to obtain a full driving licence.

In addition there are significant benefits for DT. As less time is spent on the road, there are reduced costs of fuel, vehicle acquisition and repair and since one driving instructor can control up to four simulators at a time, this training can be offered for a lower price than competitor driving schools which offer only on-road experience.

An added benefit is the positive effect on the environment as a result of reduced fuel consumption.

Although DT's core market is learner drivers wishing to acquire a full driving licence, there is also a market in existing drivers, who want to refresh or enhance their driving skills, and commercial drivers, who are required to undertake regular and rigorous training to maintain their licences.

Expansion

After early tests of the simulator concept had proved successful, David successfully applied for a software patent. The business grew much faster than David had originally anticipated and by mid-2008 DT had developed a good reputation locally and expanded to five outlets based in and around the London area. To finance the growth David had reinvested the profits generated and personally borrowed considerable sums of money.

David now wants to increase the rate of growth but is unsure about the best way to do this:

'We are a small business and our financial and physical resources are limited. I believe the product has the potential to be successful on a national and international basis but I am not really sure what is the best way to go about expanding outside London. Also I think I will need help to sell the idea to prospective investors.'

David is currently considering two mutually exclusive proposals for expansion:

- DT could expand the network of outlets across the UK by offering franchise arrangements to individuals seeking to become driving instructors. This would give the franchisee the right to use the DT name and software. DT would receive an upfront capital payment and ongoing commission based on sales revenue generated.

- The International Motoring School (IMS) has approached DT. IMS currently operates a network of driving schools across Europe but has no UK presence. IMS would take up a one third share in DT by subscribing for new share capital. There would be an option for IMS to extend this to a 50% holding after five years. IMS would also provide significant loan finance at a commercial rate of interest and support with marketing activities and instructor training. In return, IMS would gain access to the simulator software for use in its existing driving schools.

Requirements

(a) Prepare a SWOT analysis of the current strategic position of DT and clearly identify what you consider to be the major issues. **(8 marks)**

(b) Evaluate the key factors to be considered with respect to the two proposals for expansion. Use the following headings:

    (i)   Governance and control
    (ii) Risks
    (iii) Resource requirements **(12 marks)**

(c) David has asked for your help in producing a business plan to attract potential franchisees.

Write the sections of the plan which cover:

(i) DT's business model
(ii) The basis of DT's competitive advantage
(iii) The benefits for a franchisee

(12 marks)

(32 marks)

17 Taylor-Thorne plc (TT)

Taylor-Thorn plc (TT) is a small listed company which manufactures ladies handbags under the brand name 'Timy'. The handbags are sold to upmarket fashion retailers.

Company background

The company operates at the luxury end of the market with its handbags retailing for an average price to the end consumer of £3,000 per item. The Timy brand name is famous throughout the world and its handbags are used by celebrities.

The TT directors take an active interest in day to day operations, with the head office and factory being located in the same building. The board is small, including three members of the Taylor-Thorn family. There are also two other directors including the chief executive.

Only the very best leather from Italy is used and it is sourced from one quality supplier which delivers in its own vans on a regular basis. Delivery instructions are provided by the purchasing director.

The production process is labour intensive with highly skilled, well paid staff taking a significant amount of time to cut and stitch the leather by hand for each handbag. Despite this expensive process, the cost of manufacture is a small proportion of selling price. The major non-manufacturing cost is marketing expenditure to support the brand name. TT uses an advertising agency, but a range of other product placement and upmarket promotions also take place using celebrities. However, retailers have a profit margin of around 25% of retail price.

Distribution of the product is tightly controlled and retailers are subject to a strict appraisal before TT will supply Timy handbags to them. Only retailers of bags and other fashion items at the very top end of the market are supplied by TT. Orders are taken from approved retailers over the Internet and TT delivers to them in its own vans, using its own staff.

Inventory, receivables and payables systems are all manual as there are relatively few suppliers, customers and product lines.

The company's advertising slogan is: 'A handbag for life'. TT offers a 'repair and care' service which will guarantee the handbags for 10 years and thereafter, for a charge, TT will repair and periodically maintain the handbag (by treating the leather) for life.

The company makes a substantial profit per item, but a key barrier to expansion is sales volume, as only a small number of people can afford Timy handbags. Sales volumes have been constant at around 15,000 items per year for some time. As a consequence, despite worldwide recognition of the brand, the company has struggled to grow and in October 2008 the chief executive and finance director were replaced. The new board set up a strategic review to develop options for expansion.

Strategic proposals

The new chief executive summarised the situation. 'Our major asset is our brand, but if we continue only making very expensive handbags, then we will never be able to exploit the Timy brand by selling to a large customer base. In short, we will carry on earning good profit margins in percentage terms, but we will never make large profits overall because we will never be big enough when we only sell to the rich and famous.

I have set out three proposed strategies for expansion which will leverage the brand over a wider customer base. We need to implement one of these options by the end of the year. We simply do not have the resources to implement more than one of these strategies.'

Strategy 1 – Licensing

A fashion house, Lume plc, sells a wide range of ladies' clothing. Lume's clothing is very good quality, but the company was established in 1995 and it does not have a large advertising budget. As a consequence, the Lume brand name is not well recognised by consumers as a leading fashion brand.

Lume has approached the management of TT asking if they could sell their best quality clothing through upmarket retailers using the Timy brand name, under licence.

Strategy 2 – Brand diffusion

Brand diffusion includes the use of a variant of an existing brand to access a wider market. The proposal in this case is to manufacture ladies' handbags under the brand name 'Miss Timy' (MT). These handbags would sell at an average retail price of £400 per item which, while still expensive, is within the price range of a much larger group of potential consumers. Retailers would continue to take a 25% profit margin. The MT handbags would use a lower quality of leather than Timy handbags, they would have a modified version of the distinctive Timy logo and they would not be sold through the same retailers as the premium price Timy handbags. The MT handbags would also be made largely by machine, rather than by hand as are the Timy handbags. There is therefore a significant capital investment required to commence production of MT handbags.

Strategy 3 – Acquisition of a retailer

An opportunity has arisen to acquire Skin-Deep Ltd (Skin-Deep) which owns a chain of 20 retail outlets selling fashion items including handbags, clothing and jewellery. All of these stores are upmarket and are in prime city centre locations. Skin-Deep is an existing customer of TT. Timy handbags currently make up about 3% of Skin-Deep's revenue.

Requirements

(a) Ignoring the strategic proposals:

    (i)   Prepare a value chain diagram for TT. It should include brief notes for each of TT's relevant activities within the diagram

    (ii)   Briefly explain the TT value chain and describe how TT creates value   **(13 marks)**

(b) With respect to the three proposed strategies:

    (i)   Explain the benefits and problems of each strategy in developing and expanding TT; and

    (ii)   So far as the information permits, recommend, with reasons, which strategy should be implemented and explain any amendments to the strategy that you would recommend.

        (14 marks)

        (27 marks)

18 CWI International Ltd

CWI International Ltd (CWI), whose head office is in the UK, operates a chain of English language schools in a range of African, European and Asian countries.

Background information

CWI schools offer two types of English language course for students wanting to learn English. The majority of CWI students are aged 16-18 years and want qualifications to improve their employment prospects or to fulfill the English language entry requirements for higher education in the USA and the UK. In common with most language schools, CWI operates a selective entrance system where prospective students are required to attend an interview and undertake a skills assessment, based on their academic ability.

All CWI schools, irrespective of size, offer courses for the following two qualifications:

- **International Baccalaureate Diploma (IBD)**

  The IBD programme offered by CWI is a 12-month course of study that leads to an examination set by an external board, once a year. IBD holders are eligible for admission to premium universities throughout the world. The total course fee for the one year programme is £7,200. The course consists of nine weeks' tuition, comprising a three-week introductory course at the start of the programme, a five week interim course and a one week revision course before the IBD exam. Throughout the year students undertake home study in between the tuition phases, with tutorial support as required.

- **Test of English as a Foreign Language (TOEFL)**

   The TOEFL is a five week course of study leading to a test, which is set by an external board, eight times a year. The test measures the ability of non-native speakers of English to use and understand English as it is read, spoken, written and heard in college and university settings. The course fee is £1,250.

All CWI schools are approved exam centres so the IBD exams and TOEFL tests are sat in school.

Each CWI school offers at least one course per exam/test sitting. The larger schools have the facility to offer up to five courses per sitting for each qualification. CWI primarily generates income by charging tuition fees but also receives some educational grants.

CWI has an outstanding academic record and achieves excellent results. Many CWI students progress to Higher Education, normally to their 'first choice' universities or colleges. To maintain the highest teaching standards CWI only employs tutors with specialist qualifications in English language teaching. It encourages tutors to improve their qualifications by providing them with financial support for further study and training, and all CWI schools offer regular training for tutorial staff.

Performance measurement

CWI has recently decided to apply for accreditation by the English Language Board (ELB). A wide range of schools offer English language courses and accreditation by the ELB is the main internationally recognised guarantee of quality. To be accredited CWI must demonstrate that it meets the ELB performance criteria in all of its schools. Every aspect of each school's English language provision will be scrutinised, based on stringent criteria covering tutors, results, class sizes, materials, management, student welfare and premises.

Currently the internal evaluation of performance at CWI schools derives mainly from annual results in the external examinations, IBD and TOEFL. These are monitored closely by reference to the average world-wide pass rate for the particular examination.

In order to receive accreditation from ELB, CWI's chief executive believes that it will need to introduce a more rigorous and wide-ranging system of performance measurement and has written to your firm asking for help. An extract from the letter is as follows:

> 'We need reliable information that will assist us in evaluating the profitability and performance of our schools. This should include financial analysis as well as providing us with other non-financial information in preparation for ELB accreditation and the subsequent two-yearly inspection that is a condition of retaining it. In addition, the market for English language courses is becoming more competitive due to the global economic downturn and I believe better performance information will help us to differentiate CWI when talking to prospective students. Finally, I believe that there is significant variation of performance between each CWI school and the different qualifications. I hope to use the measures from the new performance measurement system to increase consistency and to identify underperforming tutors and schools, and I would like some suggestions as to how to go about this.
>
> I need to select a member of my staff to manage the implementation of this performance measurement project, but I need some advice on the project management skills they will need and the barriers to change that they are likely to face.
>
> Exhibits 1 and 2 contain some data that I have collated for the last two years, which will help you.'

Requirements

As a consultant, prepare a report which:

(a) Using the data provided, evaluates the financial and non-financial performance of CWI, providing supporting explanations of your data analysis. Identify and justify any additional information that you would require in order to assess the performance of the individual CWI schools. **(14 marks)**

(b) Explains the barriers that may be encountered in implementing a new performance measurement system and indicates how these might be overcome. **(6 marks)**

(20 marks)

Note: Exhibits 1 and 2 are below.

Exhibit 1: Financial performance data

Reporting period ending 31 December

	2008 £'000	2007 £'000
Income		
Tuition fees:		
IBD	3,600	2,304
TOEFL	3,840	3,360
Total tuition fees	7,440	5,664
Grants	600	560
Total income	8,040	6,224
Expenditure		
Tutor costs	3,250	2,240
Premises	1,525	1,260
Course and study materials	446	336
Marketing	745	392
Administration including support staff	1,050	840
Total expenditure by schools	7,016	5,068
Contribution	1,024	1,156
Head office costs	(450)	(420)
Profit before interest and tax	574	736

Exhibit 2: Other relevant data

		2008	2007
Number of schools		10	8
Number of tutors		145	104
Number of courses:	IBD	30	16
	TOEFL	240	224
Course fee per student:	IBD	£7,200	£7,200
	TOEFL	£1,250	£1,250

Pass rates	IBD		TOEFL	
	2008 %	2007 %	2008 %	2007 %
CWI pass rate	85	89	90	89
Worldwide pass rate	81	79	75	74

19 Kemmex Ice Cream plc (KIC)

Ralph Reines is the recently appointed chief executive of Kemmex Ice Cream plc (KIC), which is a listed company manufacturing ice cream.

Company background

KIC was established in 1959. Its only factory is located within a reasonable distance of both London and the major seaports which serve France and other North European countries. The company produces low cost ice creams in the 'economy' sector of the industry. All its ice creams are for the 'take home' market, being sold in large containers of one litre or two litres in a range of flavours.

Manufacturing costs have been kept low due to the low cost of ingredients, the narrow product range and a basic production process. Distribution costs have been kept low by maintaining a customer base of ice cream retailers including small shops, cafés and low cost independent supermarkets, all located within 100 miles of the factory – an area that includes London. This has also enabled KIC to compete with larger ice cream manufacturers by offering a good level of service. In particular, the company's willingness to deliver small quantities at short notice appeals to many retailers.

Ralph Reines took over as chief executive from his father, David Reines, on 30 November 2008. David had run the company for many years and, while there had been little expansion during this period, it had generated reasonably stable profits in its local market.

Falling profits at KIC

The management accounts for the quarter ended 30 May 2009 (**Exhibit 1 on page 5**) did not make pleasant reading when Ralph first saw them. He immediately called the finance director, Charlie Milton, and the marketing director, Jane Chang, into his office. Ralph was first to speak:

'Just look at the latest management accounts. They are a disaster. We have increased sales, but we are not making any profits.'

Charlie was quick to interrupt: 'Well, I told you so when we devised the strategy to cut prices, grow sales volumes and build market share. The board took too much notice of Jane and her marketing team. We took our eye off the bottom-line profit.'

Jane was not pleased with Charlie's remarks: 'That's just typical of accountants. You can't see beyond the next quarter's profit figures. We cannot stay where we are. We need to grow, or the company will stagnate.'

Ralph had indeed wanted to expand the company rapidly and had initially supported Jane Chang's plan to lower prices by 10% from 1 March 2009 to encourage growth. The poor results for the quarter to 30 May 2009, however, caused him real concern so he called a board meeting in early June 2009 to review future strategy.

The ice cream industry and the UK market

The global ice cream manufacturing industry is dominated by two major international food and drinks companies which manufacture about 25% of the world's output of ice cream by value. There are a few other large manufacturers, but the remainder of the industry is highly segmented with many smaller manufacturers. In the UK alone, there are in total around 200 ice cream manufacturing companies.

Ice cream, in economy form, can be manufactured using a simple low-cost process, but large scale production or higher quality ice creams require significant capital investment.

The European ice cream market generates sales of about £13,000 million at retail selling prices, with the UK market making up about £1,000 million of that total. The ice cream consumer market can be divided into two separate sectors. First, there is the 'impulse' sector, which are ice creams bought for one person for immediate consumption, typically wrapped in bars, or being held on a stick or cone.

Second, there is the 'take-home' sector, which are purchases made in large units, typically at supermarkets or grocers, for consumption normally by a number of people some days or weeks after purchase. The 'take-home' market consists of large containers of ice cream (eg one or two litres) or multipacks (several individual wrapped bars, normally of the same type as sold individually as 'impulse' purchases). In the UK, the take-home sector makes up about 72% of the total market, but in many other European countries there are different tastes and there is a more equal split between the impulse and take-home sectors.

The global ice cream industry is segmented by price and quality as follows:

- **Economy**. At the lower end of the market is economy ice cream, produced using low cost ingredients, mainly by smaller manufacturers using basic processes. This is a large market, but is low value added and is price competitive. There is little branding other than supermarket 'own labels'. Distribution is to local markets to reduce transport costs. Retailers are small outlets or low cost supermarkets.

- **Regular**. Regular ice cream incorporates standard quality ingredients with some limited branding, normally being the manufacturer's name. It is a large market with moderate value added. It is mainly produced by larger manufacturers using capital intensive, large-scale production and it is distributed nationally and internationally to a wide range of retailers.

- **Premium branded**. Good quality ingredients with some branding of individual products and advertising to support the brand are found in the premium branded segment, which is a moderate, but growing, market with high value added. It is almost entirely produced by larger manufacturers using capital intensive, advanced technology processes and it is distributed nationally and internationally to a range of large and specialist retailers.

- **Superpremium branded**. Very high quality ingredients with significant dedicated branding of individual products and high spending on advertising to promote the brand are found in the superpremium branded segment. This is a small, but rapidly growing, market with high prices and very high value added. It is produced solely by larger manufacturers, using capital intensive processes and is distributed nationally and internationally to selected retailers. New product developments are constantly taking place.

There is some seasonality in the industry but this is less pronounced for the take-home market and for premium and superpremium products.

A key factor in the industry is distribution. This needs to be in chilled conditions for transport, but also the freezer space of retailers is a constraining factor on sales and storage.

The UK is a net importer of ice cream from the EU. There is limited trade outside the EU for UK manufactured ice creams due to transport costs.

Retailers impact on the industry significantly. Supermarket chains are significant buyers and they force down the prices that they pay to suppliers in all sectors of the market, but particularly at the lower end. Last summer, for instance, a large supermarket chain reduced ice cream prices in the 'regular' sector so significantly that they were below prices in much of the 'economy' sector. This price reduction was, however, only on a temporary basis.

Future strategy – board meeting

At the board meeting two mutually exclusive strategies were put forward.

Strategy 1 – Continue with the low price strategy. This strategy was suggested by Jane who argued that: 'The strategy adopted from 1 March 2009 of reducing all our prices – to both existing and new customers – by 10% needs to be given time. Sales volumes will continue to increase as our pricing policy becomes better known. The number of existing customers and the quantity of ice cream sold to them has remained unchanged since the quarter to 28 February 2009 despite the price reduction. This means that our sales volume growth has been entirely due to new customers.

In particular, we are now appealing to retailers well beyond the 100 mile limit in the UK that we used to have and this is where our new customers have arisen. We are beginning to have national UK coverage. I expect that revenues will improve, with sales volumes eventually growing 25% from that achieved in the quarter to 31 May 2009, mainly from customers in the north of England up to 350 miles away.'

Strategy 2 – Enter the premium branded sector. The research department has developed a new high quality ice cream. The board has discussed a possible contract with a large, international confectionery manufacturer, Yocolate plc, which does not produce ice cream products. The agreement would be that the new ice cream could be branded to look like one of Yocolate plc's well-known chocolate bars, the 'Chocnut', and KIC would use the same name. Yocolate plc would require a fixed annual royalty of £1 million, plus 5p per item sold. The annual fixed costs of making 'Chocnut' ice creams would be £3 million and the variable production and distribution costs would be 20p per item. Typically, ice creams of this type produced by other manufacturers sell to retailers for around 50p per item. Sales of the 'Chocnut' ice cream would be through existing retailers to the 'take-home' market in multipacks and KIC would also attempt to enter the 'impulse' market, selling individual bars through the same retailers. It would also be necessary to sell the 'Chocnut' throughout the whole of the UK and in some other European countries in order to achieve an adequate sales volume. This strategy would require reversal of the 10% price reduction made on 1 March 2009 for existing economy ice creams.

Requirements

(a) Explain the barriers to entry that exist in the ice cream industry, identifying particular issues that affect the four separate industry segments. **(8 marks)**

(b) Briefly evaluate KIC's current market share. Describe how KIC's '*market*' should be defined most appropriately for the purpose of determining its market share. **(6 marks)**

(c) Using the data in Exhibit 1 and the other information provided:

  (i) Assess and explain the performance of KIC during the quarter ended 31 May 2009. Provide appropriate data analysis to support your arguments.

(ii) So far as the information permits, evaluate *Strategy 1* and establish whether this continued price reduction policy is the appropriate strategy for the future, even though it has produced a short-term financial loss. **(17 marks)**

(d) Assess the proposed *Strategy 2* under each of the following headings.

    (i)   Risks

    (ii) Marketing strategy   **(12 marks)**

                                                                     (43 marks)

Exhibit 1 – Quarterly, summary management accounts

	3 months to	
	28 Feb 2009	31 May 2009
	£'000	£'000
Sales	10,000	10,350
Production costs		
Variable	5,000	5,750
Fixed	2,500	2,500
Distribution costs		
Variable	500	750
Fixed	250	250
Administration and other fixed operating costs	1,250	1,250
Operating profit/(loss)	500	(150)
Number of customers (ie retailers)	2,500	3,000

20 Evara Electrical Engineers Ltd (EEE)

Evara Electrical Engineers Ltd (EEE) is a medium-sized private company which carries out electrical contract work, including wiring, electrical repairs, safety inspections and supplying and fitting electrical devices.

Company background

EEE was established in 1988 in Manchester by Eric Evara, the managing director and sole shareholder. Initially, Eric ran the business from his home, carrying out electrical work alongside the three other electricians whom the company employed. Eric did all the administration tasks himself in the evenings, including invoicing, estimates and quotes, preparing wages, collecting of cash and writing up the accounts.

From mid 1993, Eric's sole role was to manage the business, no longer doing any electrical work himself. In 1994 he opened small business premises in Manchester for administration, and for storing materials. By the end of 2008 EEE employed 25 electricians and two support staff.

Despite the growth, in early 2009 EEE still had a basic organisational structure with Eric, as sole manager, taking all the key decisions, including negotiating prices with customers, allocating work to staff, overseeing work in progress, ordering materials and managing the office. Eric has external professional support from his accountants, legal advisers and occasionally from electrical engineering consultants where the jobs are particularly difficult technically.

Electricians are split into teams and there are five team leaders who are paid more than other employees. There are normally between two and seven electricians allocated to each job, depending on the size of the task. A team leader is in charge of each job on site, but their authority is informal, as employees tend to socialise together and regard each other as equals.

Eric exercises control informally. Team leaders telephone Eric about every two days to report the progress of work in general terms. Eric also visits each site personally, once a week, to review progress.

Eric keeps basic records of how much he spends on materials and labour for the business overall. He does not have any formal system of recording the material and labour costs incurred by each job. Through his day to day contact with operations Eric is, however, generally aware of whether costs differ significantly from his calculations made for the initial price estimate for each job.

Customers and pricing

EEE generates about £1 million in annual sales revenue. EEE's largest customer by far is Briggs Builders plc (BB), a UK listed company, which has factories in and around the Manchester area. BB has historically made up about half of EEE's annual sales revenue. Prices on the BB contract are set on a strict cost plus formula basis.

Other than BB, EEE's customers are smaller businesses (such as builders and property developers), almost entirely located within 35 miles of Manchester. Some of these customers offer regular work to EEE, whilst others are one-off jobs, frequently acquired through local reputation. Eric once described his pricing policy for these smaller customers as follows:

'I price jobs for smaller customers according to what I think they are willing to pay. I always negotiate directly with the budget holder who will effectively be the decision maker. Also, the price quote initially agreed is subject to 'variations', which means I can charge extra if there are unforeseen problems in the building structure, or additional faults are discovered when hidden wiring is exposed or the customers change their minds. I always find some of these variations so I can add on 10% to the price even if the problem is fairly trivial. The customers normally don't understand electrics so it is hard for them to dispute any variation. Also, if there is a problem in price variation negotiations, I give the budget holder tickets to sports events or concerts. That normally makes them more co-operative.'

A major expansion

In May 2009 BB was acquired by Sharrow & Sline plc (SS), a major listed company with sites located throughout Europe. Eric was concerned at this time that EEE would lose the BB contract following the acquisition and began to make tentative plans to downsize his business. To Eric's surprise, however, he was offered a one-year contract to be the preferred supplier of electrical contracting services to the entire SS group, including BB, commencing on 1 January 2010. Under this contract, about 10% of EEE's jobs for SS would be in continental Europe, with the remainder spread throughout the UK.

The conditions offered to EEE on the SS group contract for 2010 were as follows:

- The pricing formula is the same as that used previously on the BB contract

- The contract is estimated to be worth £4 million for the first year, but it may be more or less than that depending on requirements

- Assurances are needed by SS that EEE can cope with the volume of work required

- If EEE refuses the contract it will be offered elsewhere, including the work for BB

- Renewal of the contract for 2011, and beyond, will depend on performance in the first year. To judge this, SS requires detailed data reports for each job including labour hours analysis, materials used and technical updates of the work completed

- Details of EEE's project management procedures are to be presented to SS prior to commencement of the contract

- EEE must act in accordance with SS's strict ethical code. This will also impact on EEE's behaviour towards its other customers

New equipment and procedures would be required to fulfil the contract. As a consequence, EEE would be unlikely to make a significant profit in the first year. In addition, some of the operational work would be complex and outside the experience of Eric and his current employees.

Eric is keen to take on the new contract, but he has two major concerns about it.

(1) The only way he can see to staff the new contract is either to recruit 100 new electricians by January 2010 or to outsource the new work by sub-contracting it to other electrical firms.

(2) Irrespective of whether outsourcing is used or not, Eric knows that EEE would need a new organisational structure and new information systems to enable him to manage the individual jobs and the business overall. Eric also realises he would no longer be able to carry out all management functions and all quality control procedures himself. He appreciates that he would need better information systems to generate the data reports required by SS to judge performance and to decide whether the contract should be renewed.

Requirements

(a) Ignoring the potential new contract with SS, explain how far EEE's organisational structure and information systems are suitable for managing its current strategy and operations. **(10 marks)**

(b) Discuss the ethical issues that arise from EEE's current pricing policy for its smaller customers.

(6 marks)

(c) As a business adviser, prepare a draft report for Eric giving advice relating to the proposed SS contract as follows:

   (i) Describe, and justify, potential new organisational structures for EEE which would be suitable if the SS contract is undertaken. From these alternatives, make a recommendation of the most suitable structure for EEE.

   (ii) Explain the factors that Eric should consider in deciding between outsourcing and recruitment of more staff, in order to meet the needs of the SS contract.

   (iii) Briefly advise Eric, with reasons, whether he should accept the SS contract. **(16 marks)**

(32 marks)

21 Rugeley Tableware plc

Rugeley Tableware plc (Rugeley) is a niche manufacturer of quality ceramic tableware, based in the UK.

Company history

Rugeley was founded in 1779 by William Rugeley, a local businessman and entrepreneur. It specialises in the design and manufacture of exclusive ceramic tableware (sets of plates, bowls etc), which is sold direct to the hotel and restaurant industry and also to individual consumers. Rugeley's products are stocked by major retailers and can be purchased online via its website.

From the beginning, Rugeley created a reputation for manufacturing tableware of the highest quality which it originally sold to wealthy individuals. For more than two centuries, Rugeley tableware was used at dinner tables in sophisticated private houses and hotels and the brand name became associated with an elegant lifestyle. As a result of its innovative patterns and designs, Rugeley was recognised as a prestigious brand throughout Europe and the US and was sought after because of its quality and English heritage.

Rugeley enjoyed many years of profitability and was converted into a public limited company in 1989 at the peak of its success, when it became listed on the London Stock Exchange. 40% of the equity share capital remains in the hands of the Rugeley family, 45% is held by institutional investors and the remainder is owned by individual investors.

Declining fortunes

Several years after it was listed, Rugeley's results began to deteriorate. In 2000, Rugeley decided to outsource some of its manufacturing operations to Asia, in an attempt to reduce costs and to address competition from the following sources:

- Cheaper imports, which were almost entirely being produced in low labour cost countries.

- Large global retailers that had begun to introduce mass produced, own-label product ranges, designed to resemble high quality tableware.

- More diversified competitors in the tableware market that also offered glassware and table linen.

- Major international companies that were able to benefit from economies of scale by manufacturing a wider range of ceramics for use in the home (including bathroom sanitary ware, kitchen sinks, tiles and tableware).

These sources of competition have become more powerful since 2000 and sales and profits have continued to decline, despite the outsourcing decision. The most recent results (for the year ended 30 June 2009) show a fall in revenue of 15%, a fall in profit of 25% and negative operational cash flow. The business urgently needs to make changes if it is to avoid becoming loss making.

For nearly a year, institutional shareholders have been openly critical of the chairman and chief executive, Belinda Rugeley (a direct descendant of William). Belinda runs the company in an authoritarian manner. She has refused to appoint non-executive directors, on the basis that they would not be as committed to the company as its executive directors, whose remuneration is based on the financial performance of the business. Some institutional investors have suggested the company should consider seeking a buyer from among the major international manufacturers.

Future options

At a recent board meeting to discuss Rugeley's future strategic options, the following views were expressed:

Marketing director (Malcolm Enderby): 'For years we have set worldwide standards in tableware design and manufacturing, but people's attitudes to dining have changed. As formal dining has given way to more relaxed eating habits, so our traditional products have become unfashionable. As a result, our sales to individual customers are now concentrated on a very narrow market, consisting largely of customers over 40 years of age. What's more the recession is unlikely to help matters as it will inevitably depress sales of what is seen as a luxury item.

I think we have taken too narrow a view of Asia as the solution to our manufacturing. I believe we should also focus on Asia as a new sales market. There is an opportunity here to build a brand image of exclusive tableware, based on our English style and heritage.

We also need to target the new, younger generation who are unfamiliar with our products. The recession may work in our favour here, as more people choose to dine at home instead of eating out. We can exploit this by introducing a new range of everyday designer tableware. Melinda James, the famous chef, owns a well-respected design and marketing business and she has agreed to cooperate with us in a joint venture to launch such a product.'

Production director (Alex Rodin): 'I think the lack of sales is more about supply chain issues than anything else and these have impacted on our customer service capabilities. At the moment there is a mis-match between the high quality of our product and the level of service we are providing to customers. Although we carry very high levels of inventory, these are not always of the right product lines. Because of the lead times associated with overseas manufacturing, production and delivery times have increased and our level of overdue orders is unacceptably high.

The problem is exacerbated by the fact that all our key strategic and operational decision making is carried out by the board, so production is based on centrally produced sales forecasts and not driven by real customer demand. Our centralised management structure has given rise to inflexibility and slow response times. It has also stifled local sales initiatives and design innovations. I believe we need to address our supply chain issues and at the same time change our decision making structure so that more authority is delegated, and sales planning is undertaken by the local manager within each sales market.

A former colleague of mine now works at PCE plc, a company which manufactures portable consumer electronics such as digital radios, MP3 and DVD players. They have just completed a review of their own supply chain with amazing results, and they've published some of their data on this. I think we could learn something from what they have achieved.'

Chairman/chief executive (Belinda Rugeley): 'I really don't see how we can learn anything from PCE plc – they are in a completely different industry from us. Surely they don't know anything about the manufacture of ceramic tableware and any targets they set for their supply chain will not be a relevant benchmark for ours?'

Requirements

Acting as a consultant to the board of directors:

(a) Prepare a SWOT analysis of Rugeley's current strategic position, and highlight the key issues facing the company. **(8 marks)**

(b) Using Ansoff, analyse the proposals made by the marketing director. **(8 marks)**

(c) Evaluate the production director's proposals to decentralise decision making. Explain the change management issues that Rugeley would need to address if it were to go ahead with the proposed new decision making structure. **(10 marks)**

(d) Discuss the comments made by the production director and the chairman/chief executive in respect of PCE plc. **(7 marks)**

(e) Explain the principles of good corporate governance which would be relevant and the ways in which non-executive directors would be of benefit to the running of Rugeley. **(7 marks)**

(40 marks)

22 Pitstop Ltd

Pitstop Ltd (Pitstop) operates a well-known chain of roadside restaurants in the UK.

Company information

Pitstop's target market is road users, in particular business travellers and families with children, who want to break up a long journey and stop for refreshments. Pitstop has 65 restaurants, which occupy prime sites along major roads.

The restaurants all have the same internal design, décor, menu and prices. They are open 07:00 to 19:00 for 360 days in each year, and each has the capacity to seat 50 customers.

All procurement is done centrally and Pitstop sets strict guidelines regarding staff levels and the purchasing and preparation of food. Each restaurant is set a target for cost of sales of 68% of revenue so that waste is kept to a minimum and food and labour costs are carefully controlled.

All other costs incurred by Pitstop are fixed. These include the salaries of the restaurant managers, rent, marketing, procurement administration and other central costs. For reporting purposes, these are totalled and then divided equally across the 65 restaurants in the chain.

Key factors that influence performance for an individual restaurant are customer numbers and average amount spent by each customer. Pitstop's restaurants are all leased. Results have suffered recently as rents have increased considerably, whilst at the same time customer numbers have fallen.

The market is highly competitive and there is a variety of other outlets which cater for a similar need to Pitstop: petrol station forecourt shops, roadside facilities operated by regional and national chains, fast food outlets, coffee chains and local family friendly bar/restaurants. In addition, the volume of customers is highly affected by roadworks, the weather and the time of year.

The current focus on healthy eating has given rise to criticism that Pitstop's traditional menu places too much emphasis on fried food with a high fat content. In addition there have been changes in driving habits. The advent of in-car entertainment systems has made it easier for families to occupy children on a long journey. Many drivers prefer to purchase a snack that can be eaten quickly rather than stop for the time required to order and consume a meal.

Strategic proposals

Pitstop's board of directors has been discussing two possible strategies to improve profitability:

Strategy 1: Widen the appeal of the restaurant

Pitstop would attempt to increase customer volumes by a third in all its restaurants by:

- Targeting local families who could be encouraged to make regular visits to Pitstop as a neighbourhood restaurant

- Encouraging business executives to view the restaurant as a meeting point, by creating a special office area within each restaurant, with facilities for laptop computers and free internet access

- Attracting more road users with the introduction of a new snack menu. This would provide an alternative for customers who are short of time and wish to resume their journeys as soon as possible

The finance director is on long-term sick leave. In her absence, the sales director has produced a forecast of the likely impact of this strategy on an **average** Pitstop restaurant, which is set out in **Exhibit 1** along with actual results for an **average** restaurant in the year ended 31 July 2009. On the basis of these figures he is keen to implement the strategy across all Pitstop restaurants.

Exhibit 1: Strategy 1 projections for an average Pitstop restaurant

Year ended 31 July	Actual Results 2009 £	Forecast Strategy 1 2010 £
Revenue	486,000	648,000
Food costs	170,100	226,800
Labour costs	160,380	213,840
Cost of sales	330,480	440,640
Gross profit	155,520	207,360
Marketing	20,000	20,000
Rent	75,000	75,000
Other overheads	60,000	60,000
Profit before interest and tax	520	52,360
Average amount spent by each customer	£9.00	£9.00

Strategy 2: Reduce prices

This strategy would involve reducing prices by 15% to make Pitstop more competitive. Although gross profit margins would fall as a result, the sales director is confident that the increase in customers would more than compensate for this.

The operations director is concerned about the downside risk associated with this strategy. In particular he has pointed out that if the lower prices do not attract more customers, then the majority of Pitstop's restaurants will fail to break-even.

Risk assessment

To assist in assessing the risk of the two strategies, the operations director has provided some information about the variability of customer numbers, average spend and margins during the year ended 31 July 2009. This is set out in **Exhibit 2**, together with his estimate of the impact that Strategy 2 would have on gross profit margins.

Exhibit 2: Variability of Pitstop customer numbers, average spend and margins

	Worst performing restaurant	Average restaurant	Best performing Restaurant
Year ended 31 July 2009 (actual)			
No of customers per day	95	150	245
Average amount spent by each customer	£7.50	£9.00	£10.50
Actual gross profit margin	30%	32%	34%
Year ended 31 July 2010 (estimate)			
Estimated gross profit margin with Strategy 2	18%	20%	22%

Requirements

(a) Using both exhibits and the other information provided:

    (i) Analyse Strategy 1 and evaluate its impact on an average restaurant.

    (ii) Assess the reasonableness of the sales director's forecast and assumptions as a basis for projecting the results for all Pitstop's restaurants.

    Show any additional calculations that are relevant. **(12 marks)**

(b) For Strategy 2:

    (i) Prepare calculations which demonstrate the increase in customers per day that would be required to maintain existing gross profits for an average restaurant.

    (ii) Discuss the likely impact of the proposed price reduction on the profitability of the company as a whole, showing any additional calculations. **(10 marks)**

(c) Explain any other factors that Pitstop should consider when making a decision about how to improve the company's profitability. **(5 marks)**

(27 marks)

23 Somborne Zoological Park Ltd

Somborne Zoological Park Ltd (Somborne) is a charitable, not-for-profit company. It is engaged in animal conservation and research and operates a well-known zoo in the UK. (Note: conservation is the securing of long-term populations of species in natural ecosystems and habitats wherever possible.) Somborne is home to more than 2,600 animals and attracts around two million visitors a year. In addition to income from visitors, the zoo receives financial support from corporate sponsors, grants for research, donations from benefactors and subscription income from its membership programme.

Governance and regulation

Somborne is managed by a board of trustees which has overall responsibility for the zoo's operations. Somborne is a member of The International Zoo Federation (IZF), a global industry body, which requires each member to achieve certain standards in conservation, education and animal care and to meet certain inspection criteria annually in order to maintain its licence to operate.

Staffing

Somborne has a staff of about 200 paid employees, and more than 1,500 volunteers. The zoo is led by a manager who is responsible for the maintenance and growth of the animal collection and who has overall responsibility for the staff. The day-to-day care of the animals is undertaken by zookeepers, supported by qualified vets. In addition Somborne employs a number of staff in catering and retail roles at the zoo's café and shop.

Aims and objectives

Somborne's mission is 'To focus the zoo's resources on animal conservation and to support this through sustainable commercial activities, including managing the zoo as a first class visitor attraction.'

Somborne's strategic goals are stated as follows:

- To maximise the impact of our conservation activities and to undertake research activities which make contributions to conservation programmes both in captivity and the wild

- To promote and support the zoo through marketing and the provision of learning opportunities for the public

- To identify and develop alternative income streams to reduce dependency on visitor income

In addition, as part of a desire to gain accreditation for sustainability and environmental management from the IZF, the board has recently identified a fourth goal:

> To follow ethical principles to guarantee the well-being of our animal collection and to manage the operations and development of the zoo to ensure long term sustainability

A new chairman has recently been appointed to assist the board in implementing this sustainability initiative and has approached you, as a member of the zoo's finance department, for help:

'I think I am clear about the vision for the zoo but there appears to be a lack of detail on how the zoo intends to implement that vision. Please could you explain to me the relevance of strategic planning for a not-for-profit organisation such as ours, and give me some specific examples of detailed operational objectives that would allow us to meet our first three strategic goals.

As you are well aware we only have a finite budget and so the other thing I am concerned about is how to allocate the resources that we do have, between the various goals and projects that we could undertake.

In order to gain accreditation from the IZF we need to carry out an environmental audit to establish some baseline performance measures in four areas: financial, environmental, human resources and social. These measures will be used for monitoring during the first year of implementation of the sustainability initiative and subsequently. I have attached an extract of the guidance issued by the IZF on sustainability and environmental management in the **Exhibit** below which should explain more.'

'The board of trustees has spent some time defining what sustainability means for the zoo in the four areas identified by the IZF:

- **Financial** – Somborne's income needs to match the zoo's growing expenditure. We want to ensure the application of environmental and ethical standards to our purchasing, sponsorship and investment.

- **Environmental** – Somborne must conduct activities in a way which minimises any negative impact on the environment (water, waste, energy, transport). Many zoo animals spend considerable periods of time in water and all rely on a plentiful daily supply for health and survival. The zoo intends to implement measures to reduce, reuse and recycle water. Our special exhibits, such as the reptile house, use lots of energy, and in addition to the volume of waste generated by visitors, care of the animals generates considerable natural waste. We need to reduce the amount of energy used and increase efficiency. We want to encourage staff to adhere to environmentally friendly principles and promote environmentally friendly methods of transport for staff and visitors.

- **Human resources** – We are committed to the management and development of talent and the application of ethical employment practices.

- **Social** – We are committed to extending the concept of corporate social responsibility to the wider community. Somborne will only use suppliers and contractors that follow ethical principles. In addition we are keen to increase our participation in the local community, in particular with local schools, to help educate the future generation about the need for sustainable living.'

Requirements

Prepare a report, in response to the chairman's request for help, which covers the following:

(a) (i) Explain the benefits of strategic planning for the zoo.

    (ii) Give two examples of specific objectives for each of the first three strategic goals identified in the scenario. **(8 marks)**

(b) Identify the issues that Somborne is likely to face in deciding how to allocate limited resources. **(6 marks)**

(c) (i) Explain the likely costs and benefits for the zoo of implementing a sustainability initiative.
    (ii) Assess the likely impact of such an initiative on the zoo's staff and one other key stakeholder. **(9 marks)**

(d) Explain how the zoo could use an information system to assess the success of its sustainability initiative and suggest some appropriate performance measures that could be used for each of the four areas identified by the IZF. **(10 marks)**

(33 marks)

24 Green Cards Ltd (GC)

Green Cards Ltd (GC) is a specialist retailer of good quality greeting cards, operating through a chain of shops.

Industry background

Greeting cards are traditionally purchased by consumers and sent by post to celebrate special occasions such as birthdays, religious festivals, weddings, births, and other important personal events.

The greeting card market in the UK is substantial, with estimated retail sales of £1,500 million in 2009. It is a mature market which has experienced slow, but steady, growth (**Exhibit 1 on page 5**).

There are several different types of retailer of greeting cards. Specialist retailers, such as GC, are those companies which sell greeting cards as their only, or major, product. These retailers are dominated by the 'big five' companies with large chains of shops spread throughout the UK. Non-specialist retailers include department stores, supermarkets, stationery shops, charity shops and small general shops.

There is significant competition in the industry at all levels, with smaller retailers constantly leaving and joining the industry. The larger retailers tend to be mid-market, selling for an average of about £2.50 per card and paying suppliers about £1.50 per card. The smaller retailers try to compete on the quality of the cards and customer service. The highest quality hand-made cards with special design features are sold through small specialist shops. A recent entrant to the retail market, Cardworld Ltd, sells very low price cards, all at £1.00 each, while paying suppliers about £0.90 per card.

A recent alternative to a traditional greeting card is electronic cards (e-cards) sent via the internet. While there has been rapid growth in the use of e-cards, they have not, to date, significantly affected the traditional greeting card market.

Suppliers of cards

Greeting cards are supplied to retailers by card manufacturers, as even the largest retailers do not design and print their own greeting cards. The card manufacturing industry is concentrated, with 88% of the UK market being controlled by the 19 largest companies. In developing the market, card manufacturers have shown innovation in designs and features and have invested heavily in highly specialised greeting card printing machines.

The card manufacturers sell their cards to retailers, but also sell directly to UK and international consumers through mail-order and the internet.

Company history

GC currently has over 40 shops located in large towns and cities in the UK. It sells good quality cards with up-market designs. GC has retail prices averaging about £4.00 per card and it pays suppliers an average of £3.00 per card. GC's sales have grown slowly, but steadily (**Exhibit 2 on page 5**). The company chairman, Louise Green, explained the company's strategy:

'We cannot compete with the larger retailers on price or range as we do not have their scale. By far the largest retailer in the industry is Mood Cards plc (Mood Cards), (**Exhibit 3 on page 5**). We therefore sell in a market niche of higher quality cards, although this niche is only around 10% of the total market, as most people do not want to pay any more than necessary. We do not, however, sell the most expensive hand-made cards, which retail at two or three times the price of our cards, as the market is very small. Also, we pride ourselves on customer service.

We import most of our cards from a large card manufacturer in the Netherlands, Haad Cards. We have formed a good relationship with Haad Cards and they don't sell to many other retailers in the UK, so our cards tend to be different from those of other retailers. However, prices from Haad Cards have risen over the past year or two.

We are constantly looking to expand. When we see an opportunity to open a new shop in a new town or city, we will take advantage, but it can take some time for it to become known in a new local market. We try not to have more than one of our shops in the same town or city.'

Environmentally friendly cards

'Last year we launched a range of cards to take advantage of consumer support for environmental issues. These 'environmentally friendly' cards are displayed on separate shelving units in each shop, occupying about 5% of floorspace. The cards are purchased from new suppliers at an average cost of £3.00, and they retail at an average price of £5.00. They are printed on a mixture of 10% recycled paper and 90% ordinary paper, and we have made sure they contain the label '*Made from Recycled Paper*'. For each card sold, we donate £0.01 to environmental charities supporting the sustainable planting of trees.

After a recent review it was decided we are not making enough profit on these cards, so we will withdraw from this market as soon as possible.'

Proposals for a new strategy

Louise and the board have become impatient with slow growth, despite the fact that profits are being made. Two alternative strategies have therefore been put forward.

Strategy 1

GC has been approached by a high quality cake and confectionery company, Cakes4Occasions Ltd (C4O), with a business proposal. C4O makes cakes and other decorated confectionery for particular occasions such as birthdays, weddings and birth celebrations. It makes the decoration specific to the customer (i.e. with the individual's name or a special message written onto the cake).

C4O has proposed that it takes 20% of the floorspace in all GC shops, in order to make its own sales. C4O's marketing director explained the proposal at a recent meeting between the two companies:

'Our proposal would give us space in key locations, and it would link our product to GC's cards which are also up-market and are bought for special occasions. This cross-branding would benefit both companies. We would be prepared either to pay GC a rental of £100 per square metre per annum, or to pay a fee of 10% of the revenue that we generate in GC shops. Initially a one year agreement would be appropriate.'

Strategy 2

GC's finance director has proposed an alternative strategy. He argued: 'If we can't increase sales, then we need to improve profit by cutting costs. Staffing is the largest cost, so I propose we reduce staff by the equivalent of one full-time employee in each GC shop. I think we will see the benefits in profits quickly.'

It is not possible to undertake both *Strategy 1* and *Strategy 2*.

Exhibit 1 – UK greeting cards retail sales data

	2009 estimated	2008	2007
Sales revenue (£m)	1,500.0	1,435.0	1,396.0

Exhibit 2 – Data for GC

	2009 estimated	2008	2007
Sales revenue (£m)	10.58	10.08	9.50
Operating profits (£m)	0.846	0.806	0.760
Number of shops	46	42	38
Total floorspace (000s sq metres)	6.9	6.3	5.7
Number of employees	460	420	380

Exhibit 3 – Data for market leader – Mood Cards plc

	2009 estimated	2008	2007
Sales revenue (£m)	460.0	418.0	380.0
Operating profits (£m)	46.0	37.6	30.4
Number of shops	920	930	940
Total floorspace (000s sq metres)	184	186	188
Number of employees	9,200	9,300	9,400

Requirements

(a) Prepare analyses for the following sections of the Porter's Five Forces model for the greeting cards retail industry in the UK.

   (i) Power of suppliers
   (ii) Threats from substitutes   **(7 marks)**

(b) Using the Exhibits and other information provided for the years 2007, 2008 and 2009:

   (i) Prepare an analysis of GC's competitive position in the greeting cards market, and explain any threats to GC's competitive position

   (ii) Evaluate the performance of GC and draw comparisons with Mood Cards plc's performance
        (18 marks)

(c) Discuss the ethical and business implications of GC's participation in, and withdrawal from, the environmentally friendly cards market.   **(6 marks)**

(d) As an assistant to the finance director of GC, prepare briefing notes which:

   (i) Evaluate each of the two proposed new strategies; and
   (ii) Give clear and reasoned advice as to which of the strategies GC should choose.

   Use relevant data and calculations to support your arguments where appropriate.   **(12 marks)**

        (43 marks)

25 Efficiency Systems Ltd (ES)

Jon Toman and Mike Landowne resigned their lecturing posts in Computer Science at the University of Northern England in 2007 in order to set up Efficiency Systems Ltd (ES), which develops and markets software for operational processes in businesses and public sector organisations.

Expanding the business

After an initial two year period establishing ES, it became apparent that more finance would be needed to expand. Great Western Bank (GWB) offered to consider making a loan, provided that ES produced an appropriate business plan.

Jon and Mike, the two directors, have drafted some sections of the business plan, but have approached their firm of business advisers for assistance in completing the plan in a form that can be presented to GWB. The directors also require advice on the likely risks arising from their strategy and operations that may concern GWB.

Exhibit

Efficiency Systems Ltd

Contents

1. Introduction and management
2. Products and services
3. Fees
4. Marketing
5. Competition
6. Financing requirements
7. Revenue and cash flow
8. Mission statement **(to be completed)**
9. Critical success factors **(to be completed)**

1. Introduction and management

ES was established in 2007 by ourselves (Jon Toman aged 45 and Mike Landowne aged 62) in order to develop software to promote efficiency in clients' operational processes. We are the sole shareholders and directors and we do not currently have any employees.

2. Products and services

ES's key product is a process scheduling software programme, Comax. This measures and monitors the efficiency of operational processes in a wide range of industries by recording and monitoring the time and resources spent on individual tasks. This data can be applied to optimise how labour and other resources are used in operational processes. Comax works as a standard programme, but it can also be adapted and customised to suit the needs of each client.

ES owns the intellectual property rights to its products and has recently rejected an offer of £500,000 from a large company for the rights to all its programmes currently in operation and under development.

Example – Case study

One existing client provides gas maintenance, repairs and fitting services to individuals and businesses. The use of our Comax software enabled:

- Visits to be scheduled more efficiently, thereby improving labour usage
- Inventories of parts held on vans to be managed more effectively to prevent return visits
- The client to monitor the output of its service engineers more effectively

We intend to develop ES by writing new programmes which will link to mobile phone technology. We call this 'Z-Info'. This will enable real-time monitoring of clients' operations and the immediate capture of information. Z-Info has not yet been fully completed, but initial testing is promising.

3. Fees

Fees are generated from a number of sources:

(a) Initial sale and installation of our software

(b) Initial training of client's staff to use the software

(c) Continuing advisory work on systems and operations to enhance cost reduction by using the software

As most of the fees are earned from initial installation and training undertaken in the first year with a new client, it is essential that more new clients are attracted in future. New finance for the development of the Z-Info system is therefore essential for the expansion of ES.

4. Marketing

Our existing client base comprises small companies. In order to obtain larger clients we need to win competitive tenders. Public sector organisations, service companies, and industrial maintenance and repair businesses are our key target markets. To win tenders we need to operate on a larger scale.

With the additional funds Mike will complete the development of Z-Info. A pilot version has been well received in a trial run at one client. However, it needs further refinement before it can be sold commercially. We will also employ two support staff.

5. **Competition**

The key competition comes from eight medium-sized firms (with over 10 employees) offering similar services to ours.

We expect between three and five credible tenders to be made for each contract we try to win. These will mainly be from among the medium-sized firms, but one or two will come from smaller companies such as ourselves.

We believe ES's competitive advantage comes from a product that is superior to that of most of our immediate competitors.

6. **Financing requirements**

We each initially invested £100,000 in the business through personal borrowing. ES currently has no debt as it previously had no historic record of trading.

ES needs to borrow £250,000 and we are prepared to use our homes, in which there is equity of £400,000, as security for the company loan.

7. **Revenue and cash flow**

	Revenue	Net operating cash flows	
2007	£200,000	£50,000	
2008	£320,000	£60,000	
2009	£350,000	£60,000	(estimated)
2010	£550,000	£100,000	(forecast)
2011	£750,000	£200,000	(forecast)

Assumptions

- Directors' remuneration will continue at £40,000 per year each

- Sales of Comax and Z-Info for 2010 and 2011 are stated on the assumption that new finance will be available to finish the development of Z-Info and that one tender in three is won (which has been the average achieved to date)

Requirements

As a senior in the firm of business advisers acting for ES:

(a) Prepare the following sections for inclusion in the business plan:

   (i) Critical success factors
   (ii) Mission statement   **(8 marks)**

(b) Critically assess each section of the directors' draft business plan (see **Exhibit**) to be presented to GWB to raise the required finance. Identify additional information that should be included.

                                                                             (15 marks)

(c) Explain the key risks facing ES, assuming that the required finance is provided by the bank.

                                                                             (9 marks)

                                                                             (32 marks)

26   Total Equipment Hire Ltd (TEH)

Total Equipment Hire Ltd (TEH) hires out plant and equipment to construction companies and small building firms. The company has a high level of debt.

Company background

TEH has three product lines:

Product line	Examples	Customer type and period of hire	% of TEH's revenue
Heavy equipment	Bulldozers, cranes, diggers, excavators and concrete pumping vehicles (includes trained operator)	Large construction companies for periods of over a month	70%
Small tools and equipment	Hand tools and small items of plant, such as generators and pumps	Small building firms for periods of less than two weeks	20%
Scaffolding	Scaffolding	Existing customers who will also hire large or small equipment at the same time as scaffolding	10%

Each product line is run as a separate division, although all equipment is stored and maintained at one site, so many of the costs are incurred jointly.

TEH's equipment is of good quality, reasonably new and well maintained. The company's support service is also good, with prompt and efficient delivery to the customer's site for all items. As a result, the business is perceived as being above average quality and hire charges therefore include a price premium over many rivals.

Total revenue was £240 million in the year ended 31 December 2008, but is estimated to fall to around £180 million in the year ending 31 December 2009. The reduction is reasonably evenly spread, in proportionate terms, across the three divisions and is due to both volume reductions and price discounts.

Impact of the recession

he building and construction industry has suffered in the recession. As a consequence, demand for equipment hire has reduced very significantly in 2009 compared to 2008. There has been a significant reduction in the number of days hiring, but also there is fierce competition in the industry resulting in downward pressure on hire charges.

The key industry benchmark is a utilisation rate of 90% (ie equipment is being hired out nine working days in every ten) but, up to the end of 2008, TEH operated with a utilisation rate of around 80%. This lower utilisation rate was due to TEH holding a wide variety of equipment to satisfy customers' occasional needs for infrequently used equipment. Customers were therefore attracted to TEH for all their equipment needs as a comprehensive service was provided. In 2009 TEH's utilisation rate has fallen to 70%, compared to an industry average of 78%.

TEH estimates that it will make a loss for the year ending 31 December 2009. Operating cash flows have been negative and the company is unable to borrow further. As a result, there is doubt over whether the company will be able to make the half yearly interest payment of £15 million that is due on 1 January 2010. A board meeting has recently taken place.

The board meeting

Helen Chen, the *finance director*, opened the meeting: 'We need to generate cash quickly by selling some of our equipment. I know we will make a loss on sale, but I think we need to sell off about 20% of our equipment in order to generate cash of around £60 million. Where we have more than one item of the same type of equipment we could sell off one, so we maintain our product range. We also need to cut costs. We spend far too much on customer service and delivering equipment promptly. We need to reduce our labour and transport costs, even if the service to customers deteriorates.'

Paula Penny, a *non-executive* director, interrupted: 'I agree that cash needs to be generated from selling equipment, but we should be more focused on closing down one division: either small tools or scaffolding. The performance of these divisions needs to be measured to decide which one to close.'

Frank Fitt, the *operations director,* was furious with these suggestions: 'If we sell off that amount of equipment we will destroy our whole strategy, as we will lose customers who want a complete product range from one hirer. During the recession, we know we will also only raise cash for about half what the equipment is worth.'

The *managing director,* Jeff Jones, joined in: 'I prefer not to sell equipment. Instead, I have entered into some tentative negotiations with a multinational shipping and transport company, International Transport and Trading plc (ITT). A central African country is having a major dam constructed and it has an urgent, but temporary, need for heavy plant and machinery. ITT has suggested a joint venture whereby, under a three year contract, we would make available up to 40% of our heavy plant and machinery.

According to the proposed contract, this equipment needs to be available for immediate transport to Africa on request. ITT would transport the equipment to Africa and deal with the customers in return for 50% of the rental fee. ITT would collect the fees directly from the client and then pay TEH its share. It is estimated that the gross rental fees would be about 75% of the equivalent hires in the UK, but utilisation will be near 100% for requested items during their time in use on the project in Africa. ITT has offered, on signing the agreement, to make an upfront payment of £10 million to TEH in respect of our share of future hirings on the project, to help us with our short-term liquidity problem.'

Requirements

(a) Explain the potential impact on TEH's strategy and operations which could arise from Helen Chen's proposals for divestment of equipment and cost reduction. **(8 marks)**

(b) Discuss the issues to be considered in measuring the financial and non-financial performance of the small tools and scaffolding divisions in order to determine which division should be considered for closure, in accordance with Paula Penny's suggestion. **(8 marks)**

(c) Evaluate the benefits and problems of Jeff Jones' proposed joint venture arrangement with ITT. Identify any matters that need to be clarified between TEH and ITT before a decision on whether to proceed with it can be made. **(9 marks)**

(25 marks)

27 Blazing Bicycles Ltd (BB)

Blazing Bicycles Ltd (BB) is an independent bicycle retailer which operates a chain of ten stores across the UK, selling high quality bicycles and bicycle accessories.

UK bicycle industry information

The number of bicycles sold in the UK since 1930 and key dates in the history of the UK bicycle industry are set out in the graph and table in **Exhibit 1**.

Exhibit 1

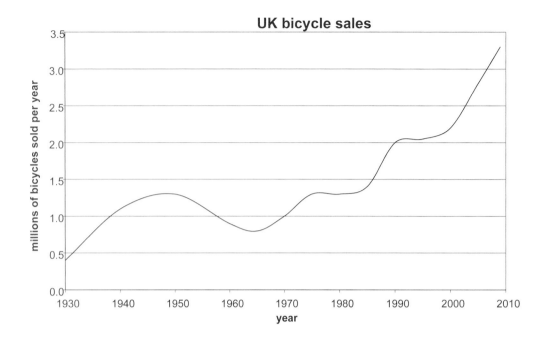

UK bicycle sales

Key dates

1930s	Bicycles become popular as a form of transport
1950s	Motor cars become more affordable
Mid 1960s	Development of small-wheeled bicycles gives rise to the concept of leisure cycling
Early 1970s	Range of popular children's bicycles developed based on the small-wheeled design
	Popularity of motorcycle cross-country rallying leads to the creation of the bicycle motor cross (BMX) market – a range of small-wheeled 'off-road' bicycles specifically for children
Mid 1980s	The concept of off-road cycling is extended to adults with the development of small-wheeled mountain bikes for recreational cycling
Late 1990s	Technological advances including suspension bicycles and carbon fibre frames lead to radical changes in competitive cycling
Early 21st century	Concerns about health and the environment increase the popularity of cycling as a lifestyle activity and mode of transport for short journeys

History of the UK bicycle manufacturing industry

After the bicycle in its modern form was developed in the UK in the late 1800s, the UK became a major manufacturer of bicycles, using the metalwork and engineering expertise of its armaments and sewing machine industries to facilitate production. For the first half of the 20th century, the UK was the world leader in bicycle manufacturing, exporting bicycles to the USA and mainland Europe, and it remained a net exporter until the early 1980s.

By 1999 all the major bicycle manufacturers had ceased production in the UK. Although a number of UK-based small-scale bicycle manufacturers remain, UK-manufactured bicycles now only account for around 5% of UK bicycle sales. The majority of bicycles and parts are imported from China and Taiwan, where wages (which account for approximately 25% of production costs) are less than a third of those paid in the UK.

The UK bicycle retailing industry today

Bicycle retailing is a fragmented industry. There are over 2,000 independent bicycle retailers with a collective market share of approximately 45%. Some, like BB, are regional chains, but many are local owner-managed businesses operating from a single shop. Some cater for a wide range of cycling interests, while others specialise in a particular market segment eg top of the range bicycles for the competitive racing cyclist.

The UK's leading mass-market bicycle retailer, 'Benhonda', has approximately a 30% market share. The remainder of the industry consists of large sports retailers, supermarkets, toy shops, mail-order catalogues and online retailers which often offer a wide range of sporting and outdoor equipment.

Total UK bicycle retailing industry revenues amounted to approximately £510 million in 2009 and are forecast to reach £550 million in 2010. The breakdown of the average independent bicycle retailer's revenue is 47% bicycles, 36% parts and accessories and 17% bicycle repair services. The average retail price in 2009 of a bicycle was just over £150. Prices typically range from £45 for a basic child's bicycle to £2,000 for a high specification racing bicycle. Gross margins on bicycles average 37% of revenue, whereas margins on parts and servicing are generally higher at 48% of revenue. As a result of the recession, people are keeping their current bicycles for longer periods and so revenues from specialist workshop and repair services are increasing.

Market environment

The industry relies on discretionary spending and sales are affected by economic conditions and unusual weather.

Technological innovation has played a key part in the industry. In the 1950s most bicycles were made of low cost metals, had thick rubber tyres and a single gear. Since the mid 1980s new materials such as titanium and carbon fibre have become more common in bicycles and multiple-gear systems have become standard. There has also been increasing focus on aerodynamically efficient designs for racing and competition bicycles.

Concerns about environmental sustainability, escalating fuel prices and increased traffic congestion have led to the return of the bicycle as a mode of transport for short journeys, including use by commuters. Folding bicycles, which can be taken on public transport, and e-bicycles (a pedal bicycle with a small electric motor to aid with hills and speed) are becoming increasingly popular. E-bicycles are already in widespread use in countries such as China where there is a strong cycling culture. In addition to offering consumers a fast, environmentally-friendly mode of urban transport, they also have commercial applications (eg for postal deliveries).

The UK Government has introduced a number of cycling initiatives to address health problems related to inactivity and to tackle climate change. These include funding for cycle training in schools, and tax incentives for employees and employers under 'cycle to work' schemes. The UK bicycle industry has also benefited from public enthusiasm for cycling as a competitive sport, generated by the success of the British cycling team in the Beijing Olympics and the prospect of the 2012 Games in London.

Company information

In addition to selling high quality bicycles and accessories, BB provides limited repairs and servicing for customers who have purchased a bicycle from BB. Its ten out-of-town stores are held under operating leases. BB only employs staff with a keen interest in cycling and appropriate technical knowledge and expertise.

At a recent Board meeting the managing director expressed some concern about the external issues and risks facing the company:

'We have recently analysed the external environment and the nature of our industry, based on PESTEL and Porter's Five Forces. Using the results from this I have undertaken a risk analysis and identified the following four principal commercial risks that might prevent BB achieving its long term strategic objectives:

1   Economic and industry conditions
2   Competition
3   Responsiveness to changing consumer preferences
4   Reliance on foreign manufacturers

We have always operated in a difficult market but competition has intensified as a result of the recession. Although we have opened several new stores since 2007 our profits have fallen.'

Exhibit 2: BB financial performance in 2007 and 2009

Year ended 31 December	2007	2009
Number of stores	6	10
Total number of bicycles sold	9,200	11,000
	£000s	**£000s**
Sales:		
Bicycles	3,245	4,380
Accessories and servicing	2,198	2,798
Total sales	5,443	7,178
Gross profit:		
Bicycles	1,091	1,314
Accessories and servicing	938	1,268
Total gross profit	2,029	2,582
Administration and Distribution overheads	(928)	(1,493)
Profit before tax	1,101	1,089

Future direction of the business

In response to the managing director's concerns, the sales director outlined two possible strategies:

Strategy 1

'We could consider expanding the product range to offer sporting and outdoor equipment (for activities such as camping, hiking and surfing). This is consistent with what the larger retailers are doing and will reduce our reliance on the uncertain bicycle market.'

Strategy 2

'A significant proportion of our customers come to us to buy high specification bicycles, because of the knowledge and expertise of our staff. We could capitalise on this by setting up specialist bicycle workshops within each store. These will offer a range of services to new and existing customers, such as expert assembly, repairs and annual service plans. Our Manchester store has recently started doing this with excellent results.'

Requirements

(a) Using the data in Exhibit 1 and the other information provided, discuss the extent to which the concept of the industry and product life cycle can be applied to the UK bicycle retailing industry and to sales of different types of bicycle. **(7 marks)**

(b) Identify the factors that may have resulted in the UK's competitive advantage in bicycle manufacture for a significant period in the industry's history. Explain why this advantage now appears to have passed to countries such as China and Taiwan. Where appropriate, refer to relevant models of international trade. **(7 marks)**

(c) Using the data in Exhibit 2 and the other information provided, analyse the performance of BB and its competitive position within the UK bicycle retailing industry. **(12 marks)**

(d) Explain the relevant external factors that have led the managing director to identify the four commercial risks listed. **(8 marks)**

(e) Discuss the merits of Strategy 1 and Strategy 2 as possible future directions for the business.
(8 marks)

(42 marks)

28 Deeshire Council (DC)

For the purposes of local government, the UK is divided into different administrative regions. Deeshire is one such region, covering an area of 2500km^2 with a population of one million people. It is run by Deeshire Council (DC), an administrative body made up of elected, paid councillors who represent the views of the people within the region. DC receives funds from the UK central government, together with local taxes paid by the residents and businesses within Deeshire. This income is used to provide services for the community, and DC has to decide which services to provide and how much money to spend on them in areas such as education, health, housing, policing, transport, leisure and waste management.

Waste management

DC provides domestic waste collection and disposal services to its residents. The services are currently operated 'in-house' by DC's own employees. Each household is required to leave its waste at the boundary of the property for collection on the appointed collection day. There are two types of household waste: general refuse and recycling.

- General refuse is collected once per week and then disposed of by being buried in the ground ('landfill').

- Recycling is waste such as aluminium, glass, plastic and paper which can be re-used or re-processed into other materials. This is collected once every two weeks and taken to a disposal site for sorting, before being sold for re-use/re-processing.

Two million tonnes of household waste are collected annually by DC, of which up to 50% is suitable for recycling. The waste management costs that will be incurred by DC in the financial year ended 31 March 2010 are estimated to be £17.65 million and are detailed in **Exhibit 1**.

**Exhibit 1: Estimate of waste management costs incurred by Deeshire Council
Year ending 31 March 2010**

		£ million	£ million
General refuse			
Direct costs	1.5m tonnes @ £3 per tonne		4.50
Overhead costs			6.50
			11.00
Recycling			
Direct costs	0.5m tonnes @ £4 per tonne	2.00	
Overhead costs		3.20	
		5.20	
less Revenue generated from sale of recycling	0.5m tonnes @ £2.50 per tonne	(1.25)	
			3.95
Other central overheads			2.70
Total waste management costs			17.65

The UK central government has set DC a target for reducing waste, and for recycling as much as possible, so as to minimise the amount of general refuse going to landfill. Failure to meet the targets would involve DC incurring financial penalties in the form of a 'landfill tax'. DC is therefore considering two options to reduce costs and increase recycling rates (the options could be undertaken at the same time).

Option 1

Save £2.5 million annual overhead costs by reducing the collection of general refuse to once every two weeks and running a recycling campaign which will result in households converting a further 20% of their existing general refuse into recycling.

Option 2

Outsource the recycling element of DC's waste collection. The collection and disposal of general refuse would continue to be operated in-house. To comply with legislation, the contract has to be awarded by tender to an external contractor on the basis of the following three factors:

- The tender price submitted
- The contractor's capability to provide the recycling services required
- The financial strength of the contractor.

DC will need to improve its existing information systems in order to manage the outsourcing contract and measure the performance and delivery standards of the external contractor. DC would therefore incur costs related to the management of the contract which have been estimated at £100,000 pa. As a result of the outsourcing decision, all the current costs specifically attributable to recycling would however be saved.

Tenders have been received from two applicants: Contractor A has submitted a tender price of £5 per tonne for the duration of the contract. Contractor B has quoted an overall total fixed tender price of £4 million pa. The successful contractor will be awarded a contract for the next four years.

The chief executive of Contractor A, who is also chairman of a prestigious golf club in the region, has approached a group of councillors, who are all members at the club. He has offered to fund life membership of the golf club for these councillors, if they ensure that his company obtains the contract.

You are employed by DC's strategic planning and policy group. The chairman of DC has asked you to prepare a briefing note which will be circulated to all councillors in advance of the next DC meeting, where the waste management strategy is to be discussed.

Requirements

Prepare the briefing note on waste management requested by the chairman of DC:

(a) Using the data in Exhibit 1 and the other information provided, evaluate the financial impact of both options to be considered by DC and comment on the implications of your figures for DC's waste management strategy. **(13 marks)**

(b) Explain the change management issues that need to be considered by DC under each option. In your answer you should refer to change management models where appropriate. **(10 marks)**

(c) With respect to Option 2 only:

    (i) Explain the principles of public sector governance that the councillors must apply when choosing between Contractor A and Contractor B. Recommend any appropriate action the councillors should take. **(6 marks)**

    (ii) Describe how DC could use an information system to monitor performance if an outsourced contractor is appointed. **(7 marks)**

(36 marks)

29 NP Ltd (NP)

NP Ltd (NP) is a small company which manufactures and sells steam cleaning machines in the UK only. These are used to clean surfaces and equipment in the healthcare and leisure industries. The use of steam reduces water and chemical usage and results in surfaces that are instantly clean and dry. NP is owned and managed by Nilesh Patel, a former research scientist with a keen interest in sustainability and the environment.

Applying the knowledge gained from operating the steam cleaning business, Nilesh has developed a new energy-efficient washing machine technology for laundering clothes and fabrics. This involves the use of special nylon beads to dissolve and absorb dirt and stains during the washing process. The beads reduce the amount of detergent required, and also reduce water consumption by 90% compared with conventional washing machines. As a result the clothes are almost dry at the end of the washing process and therefore considerable savings are made in terms of energy.

The technology has been fully tested in laboratory conditions and initial research suggests it would be appropriate for use in both the domestic and industrial laundry markets.

The domestic laundry market consists of consumers who purchase small washing machines for use in their own homes.

The industrial laundry market consists of commercial businesses which use large-scale industrial washing machines to provide washing services to:

- Companies – cleaning corporate clothing such as protective garments and uniforms, and linen for the hotel and leisure industry.

- Consumers – cleaning of specialist items of clothing, and household textiles such as duvets and curtains.

The majority of washing machines are manufactured by a few large international companies. Each company manufactures machines under a variety of different brand names for both the domestic and industrial laundry markets.

Nilesh has been granted worldwide patents for the new technology but recognises that, as a small company, NP may need additional help and expertise to exploit its full potential. He is currently considering three development strategies:

Option 1

CDT plc (CDT) is a company that specialises in helping organisations successfully develop new technological products. CDT would contribute finance and commercial support in exchange for a 50% equity stake in NP, with a view to growing the company as a manufacturer in order to obtain a listing on a stock exchange within five years. The commercial support would include creating a supply chain, developing a distribution network and identifying appropriate commercial partners.

Option 2

Eco Laundry (Eco) is a well-known, environmentally-friendly industrial laundry company that does not use chemical solvents. Eco owns a chain of industrial laundry businesses across the US, with an established customer base of both companies and consumers. Eco wants to create a strategic alliance with NP to promote the use of the new technology in its own business and also to sell it to other companies operating in the industrial laundry market in North America.

Option 3

NP would remain independent and set up a licensing arrangement whereby NP grants the right to use the technology to manufacturers of domestic and industrial washing machines.

Requirements

Prepare a report for Nilesh which:

(a) Advises him on the issues to address when selecting the best market for the new technology, using the following headings:

   (i)   Market research
   (ii) Segmentation and targeting

   For this part only, ignore the three proposed development strategies.   **(10 marks)**

(b) Discusses the desirability of pursuing a development strategy with a third party and advises him as to the relative merits of the three options being considered.   **(12 marks)**

(22 marks)

30 Executive Travel Ltd (ET)

Executive Travel Ltd (ET) operates a chain of 21 upmarket travel agent outlets which are located in major cities throughout the UK.

The travel industry

Tour operators traditionally sell trips (ie holidays and business trips) that include flights, accommodation and other services to consumers through travel agents which act as intermediaries. After offering a consumer advice and information from tour operators' databases, the travel agent makes a booking of a trip with the tour operator for the consumer using a sophisticated IT-based booking system. In return for these services, the travel agent receives a commission from the tour operator for each booking, based on a percentage of the value of the booking. For example, if a consumer pays £1,000 to a travel agent for a holiday, the commission earned by the travel agent may be £100 and then the net price paid over by the travel agent to the tour operator would be £900.

Since about 1995 travel agents have faced competition from internet bookings made on-line directly by consumers with the tour operators. Until 2005, the tour operators' on-line price to consumers was the same as the consumer would have paid when booking via a travel agent, so in saving the travel agent's commission the tour operators made a higher profit. Since 2005, however, tour operators have lowered on-line prices to consumers to around the net price paid by travel agents to the tour operators. As a consequence, there has been intense competition in the industry with many small travel agents ceasing to trade.

There are approximately 6,800 travel agent outlets in the UK. The 'big three' chains of travel agent outlets are part of vertically integrated companies which also comprise tour operators, airlines and hotels. They have about 1,750 travel agent outlets between them. The remainder are mainly small, independent chains.

Executive Travel Ltd

ET's business model is to sell upmarket leisure and business trips to long distance locations. These normally include business class or first class air tickets and luxury hotel accommodation. The trips are frequently designed by ET to meet the individual requirements of a consumer, rather than being a standardised package.

ET also attempts to make high margins from selling 'extras' such as car hire, travel insurance and limousine airport transfers.

ET has maintained a network of 21 travel agent outlets since 2001. Of these, 20 are shops in city centres, but a key part of the ET business is called Outlet21. This is located in an office within a large investment bank, Garrett Inc (Garrett), in London. Outlet21 deals with all the business travel arrangements for Garrett's London-based staff. Garrett employees needing to make a business trip provide details to ET staff, who make all the arrangements and the booking. ET staff are authorised to make payments to tour operators from the bank's funds and then to record the costs against the appropriate cost codes in the bank's management accounting system. ET is paid fees by Garrett at the end of each month based on a percentage of the value of the trips arranged. Garrett's finance staff make very few checks on the costs incurred through ET and considerable discretion is given to ET employees over the cost and quality of the trips booked.

A crisis board meeting

The global economic downturn has caused a decline in ET's sales. As a consequence, a crisis board meeting was called. Jo Walker, the chief executive, explained the problem: 'In the recession, higher-priced upmarket travel has suffered even more than other sectors of this market. In order to compete and make sales therefore, since January 2009 the managers of each ET outlet have been given the authority to reduce the price that the consumer pays. This is done by reducing our commission percentage by up to a half. Unfortunately, many managers seem to be discounting too often and our margins have suffered.'

The finance director, Carol Gull, who is a chartered accountant, added: 'I don't believe that discounting is the right pricing strategy for an upmarket travel agent. It sends out the wrong message to consumers. On the positive side, however, we have tried to keep sales volumes high by giving managers an incentive to increase the number of bookings being made: the number of bookings is now a key performance indicator, and part of the managers' remuneration is based on this figure.'

The marketing director, Henry Hall, was looking ahead. 'I think the way forward for increasing volumes is in entering into a contractual arrangement with an upmarket provider of travel or accommodation. I have had tentative negotiations with the Snooty Hotel Company (SHC). This company operates 25 luxury hotels, situated in high quality resorts around the world. Normally SHC would charge consumers £300 per room per night, but they are suffering low utilisation in the recession. To improve utilisation, SHC is willing to reduce its price to consumers. SHC has therefore offered to sell to our clients for £200 per room per night. We would need to guarantee to SHC that we would book a minimum of 1,600 room nights over the next year. Any shortfall would be payable by ET itself. Consumer bookings for SHC through ET were about 1,000 room nights last year, all at the full price of £300 per room per night. The commission rate for ET from SHC would remain at 10% of the room night price charged by SHC.'

At the board meeting the finance director provided data on the UK travel industry and on ET (**Exhibit**). It was agreed at the end of the meeting to conduct a thorough review of ET's business.

Exhibit

UK industry data

Years to 31 December	2007	2008	2009
Revenue of tour operators (£m)	36,500	35,800	35,300
Commissions of travel agents from making bookings (£m)*	4,380	3,938	3,530
Number of bookings through travel agents (000's)	68,600	65,200	64,100

* Includes transfer prices of vertically integrated companies

Company data – ET

Years to 31 December	2007	2008	2009
20 city centre outlets			
Revenue of tour operators (£m)	90	84	78
Commissions from making bookings (£m)	9	7.56	6.24
Number of bookings (000's)	30	27	24
Sundry commissions (car rental, travel insurance etc) (£m)	1	1.1	1.1
Outlet21			
Fees from Garrett (£m)	3	3	3

Ethical issue

One of the ET employees working at Outlet21 recently resigned and sent the following letter to Carol Gull, the finance director.

> I want to draw your attention to a couple of matters that have concerned me whilst working in Outlet21. ET employees have considerable discretion over the quality of the hotels and flight tickets being booked. As a result, relatively junior Garrett employees are being given the best accommodation and travel by some ET employees who are then 'rewarded' with gifts from these bank employees – sometimes amounting to over £100 per gift.
>
> Also, Garrett has a charitable trust for education in Africa to which the bank's clients, employees and suppliers voluntarily contribute. Senior bank employees sometimes book with ET to go to Africa to open new schools that have been purchased from the trust's funds, and so gain publicity for the bank. When they do so, they stay in the best hotels and travel first class. I think that if this had been bank business then it would be fine, but it is becoming a major cost for the charitable trust and it seems unnecessary and inappropriate. Sometimes the travel costs of the trips are even charged in full to the charitable trust, even though some commercial banking business also takes place.

Requirements

(a) Using the Exhibit and other information provided, evaluate the performance of ET over the period 2007 to 2009. Make comparisons with the performance of the industry as a whole where appropriate. Indicate any additional key information that would be needed to make a fuller assessment of ET's performance in the period. **(16 marks)**

(b) As part of ET's review of its business:

    (i) Discuss the likely effects of the pricing policy of discounting by reducing commission percentages; and

    (ii) Assess the likely impact of the incentives for outlet managers being based on the key performance indicator of the number of bookings.

    Ignore the contract with SHC. **(11 marks)**

(c) Regarding the proposed contract with SHC:

    (i) Assess the benefits and risks that need to be taken into account before deciding whether to enter into the contract; and

    (ii) Explain how risk can be managed if the contract is entered into. **(8 marks)**

(d) Discuss the key ethical issues that arise from the letter sent to Carol Gull and explain what actions she should take. **(7 marks)**

(42 marks)

31 Hutton Haulage plc (HH)

Hutton Haulage plc (HH) is a listed company which currently specialises in road haulage operations. It is one of the largest companies in the UK haulage industry.

Industry details

The road haulage industry offers a transport service by road for the goods of its customers and it accounts for 65% of all goods moved within the UK. The UK road haulage industry is in competition with transport by rail, water and air, while competition also arises from road haulage operators based in other EU countries, where diesel fuel for commercial vehicles is cheaper than in the UK. A relaxing of transport regulations by 2012 will allow EU haulage companies even greater access to UK markets in the coming years.

Barriers to entry in the industry are low but, during the recession, many haulage companies merged or ceased trading due to cash flow problems caused by narrow profit margins.

Company background

HH has a fleet of 1,500 trucks, most of which are less than five years old and are reasonably fuel-efficient. Twenty of the most recent trucks purchased have been fitted with 'green technology' engines and are significantly larger than the other trucks. This reduces the number of journeys, cuts total emissions and saves HH money over time, although the initial outlays are significant for this type of vehicle.

HH's major area of expansion in recent years has been to specialise in the road haulage of chilled and frozen food and drinks, which requires specialised containers. HH is one of the market leading road haulage companies for food and drinks manufacturers and for small to medium-sized retailers of these products but, to date, it has managed to secure only one specialist contract with a major supermarket. This is a five-year contract with Goonhill plc signed in November 2006.

About 75% of HH's journeys are within the UK but, in the last two years, HH has successfully expanded its trade to, and from, EU countries. A key location is Spain, from where fresh fruit and vegetables are imported for HH's UK customers in chilled conditions. About 50% of this trade with Spain is for Goonhill plc.

Part of HH's competitive advantage has been in controlling its costs. Its utilisation level is 85% (i.e. only 15% of the annual distance covered is with an empty load). This is achieved through detailed scheduling of journeys using IT systems which link resources with HH's wide network of customers. The utilisation rate is also facilitated by high annual volumes, which enable the goods of several customers to be transported in a truck at the same time (a shared load). In addition, HH's trucks enable drivers to sleep in their vehicles during rest breaks and at night. The truck and driver can therefore undertake journeys over several days serving a network of different locations for several customers, before returning to the home depot.

Current plans: Contract with Freshco

HH has been trying to finalise an outsourcing arrangement to supply transport services to Freshco, a large supermarket. Freshco has a good reputation for selling fresh food and it sources about 15% of this from Spain, with another 15% from other EU countries. The outsourcing arrangement would have no fixed term or any minimum guarantee of volume or value of services required. It would therefore be on a 'pay-as-you-go' basis. Freshco would however declare its intention to use HH as its preferred road haulage company for its distribution of fresh, chilled and frozen food and drinks from its suppliers to its central warehouses and to its 209 supermarkets located throughout the UK.

Freshco currently uses its own trucks to transport its fresh, chilled and frozen food and drinks, but it has been concerned that its supply chain operations have not been efficient with low utilisation rates and an aging fleet of vehicles. It is looking for service improvement and cost reduction. Freshco is therefore asking HH to show how it can improve Freshco's supply chain management compared to their existing, internally-resourced transportation policy.

In the negotiations with HH, Freshco has, in the last month, introduced new conditions. All Freshco's suppliers, including HH, are now required to present a plan showing how they will reduce their carbon emissions and enhance environmental sustainability in their activities to supply Freshco.

Current plans: Acquisition of RailTrans plc

RailTrans plc (RailTrans) operates rail transport facilities across Europe including the chilled transport of food and drink products. HH is considering whether to acquire RailTrans, as this would enable HH to offer more flexible transport methods to customers. Its trucks could collect or deliver goods at a rail terminus close to a major ferry port in the south of England, enabling efficient connections to many EU countries.

The fixed initial investment in RailTrans would be significant, but the variable cost of transporting goods on long journeys by rail across Europe would be up to 50% cheaper than by road, although this depends on a large volume of goods being transported on a regular basis. Food would be chilled more efficiently and trains are quicker than road transport. In addition the carbon emissions from trains are substantially lower than from trucks.

Requirements

(a) Prepare a SWOT analysis for HH, explaining each of the points made. Highlight the key issues in a summary. **(10 marks)**

(b) Prepare a memorandum for discussion by the HH board that explains:

   (i) How the outsourcing arrangement with HH can improve the efficiency of Freshco's supply chain; and

   (ii) The actions that HH can take in order to enhance environmental sustainability in its activities for Freshco. **(12 marks)**

(c) Explain the factors which should be considered in deciding whether to acquire RailTrans. **(9 marks)**

(31 marks)

32 Cutting Edge (CE)

Cutting Edge Ltd (CE) is a private company that owns 50 hairdressing salons (ie outlets), located in six cities in the north of England. CE is owned by an upmarket hairdressing company, Cupitt Inc (Cupitt), which is based in New York.

Company history

CE was established by Stella Edge in 1976 with a single salon. Stella was both entrepreneurial and a good hairdresser, expanding her business and winning national awards. Prices charged were about 30% higher than the average for hairdressing salons in similar locations. In 2005, when CE had 75 salons, Stella retired and her son, Peter, took control of the business.

Peter was a good hairdresser, but he had poor management skills and the business therefore suffered. Peter sold 25 salons in the period 2005-2009 as they became unviable due to falling revenues.

New ownership

In March 2010, Peter sold CE to Cupitt. Within the UK, Cupitt had salons only in London at that time and it believed the acquisition of CE was a good entry into the non-London, UK market. Marketing surveys show that the Cupitt brand name is well-known and valued in the London area, mainly among higher socio-economic groups, but it is not well-known outside London. Cupitt's prices are about 20% higher than those of CE.

On acquisition, the Cupitt board set up a separate division (the new 'CE division') to manage and monitor the performance of the CE salons. Jane Jackson, a young manager in Cupitt's Paris office, was transferred to take charge of the CE division. The Cupitt board made it clear to her that they expected the performance of the CE division to improve substantially within three years. During the initial three years to March 2013, however, Jane would have no central funds to open new salons; any new openings would therefore need to be financed from the operating cash flows of the CE division.

After an initial review, Jane prepared a document summarising what she considered to be the key issues facing the business. These were as follows:

• The good reputation of the Cutting Edge brand had been damaged in the period 2005-2009 but, in the cities where CE had salons, it was still a well-recognised and valued brand.

- Staff turnover is high. Newly-appointed employees possess only basic hairdressing skills and are poorly paid.

- Salon managers are generally of low quality and are poorly paid. Prices are standardised, so managers have no control over the price list. They also have no discretion to make purchases of equipment. They can however recruit new employees within the overall salon budget.

Jane's two main strategic concerns are: first, to decide on the most appropriate divisional structure for developing the CE division; and second, how to monitor the performance of each salon in both financial and non-financial terms.

Jane is considering the following mutually exclusive options on how to structure the CE division:

Option 1

All salons to provide detailed weekly reports directly to Jane covering staffing, inventory requirements, sales and other operational matters. All detailed operational decisions for each salon would in future be taken by Jane, including staffing, services offered, purchasing and setting prices.

Option 2

Franchise the salons, whereby franchisees would control the prices and services offered in each salon.

Option 3

Give salon managers authority and control over all key operational decisions for their salon, including staffing, purchasing, pricing and the opportunity of widening the services offered to include beauty treatments. Jane would monitor each salon's performance using a balanced scorecard.

Requirements

(a) Prepare notes for Jane which set out the advantages and the disadvantages of Option 1 and Option 2.

(15 marks)

(b) Assuming that Jane decides to follow Option 3:

(i) Prepare a balanced scorecard for the CE division describing goals and key performance indicators for each salon; and

(ii) Discuss whether a balanced scorecard is likely to be the best method of monitoring the performance of each salon. (12 marks)

(27 marks)

33 Supaspeed Ltd (Supa)

Supaspeed Ltd (Supa) is a parcel delivery company which specialises in the home delivery of parcels to consumers on behalf of business clients in the Business-to-Consumer (B2C) market. Supa's main clients are mail order companies, traditional store-based retailers fulfilling consumer orders, internet retailers and businesses selling via online auction sites.

Parcel home delivery industry

The parcel home delivery market is highly competitive. There is a wide variety of choices open to clients, both in terms of the number of companies operating in the industry and the range of different services that each delivery company offers.

Within the UK, the parcel home delivery market is fragmented:

Parcels delivered to UK households (B2C market)	*Market share*
UK national postal service operator (overall market leader)	30%
Four international courier groups (the Big Four)	45%
Eight national companies (including Supa) and over 1,000 smaller businesses	25%

Outside the UK, in view of their global coverage, the Big Four dominate the market for parcels delivered from UK businesses to international consumers, with a combined market share of 70%.

Most parcel delivery companies offer a choice between speed and price, ranging from speed-sensitive urgent delivery (same-day or next-day), to price-sensitive non-urgent delivery within 2-3 working days. In the B2C market, the required speed of delivery is usually chosen by the end consumer when placing an order.

Some companies, like Supa, concentrate only on the B2C market. Others, including the Big Four, also operate in the Business-to-Business (B2B) and Consumer-to-Consumer (C2C) markets.

Industry developments

The demand for parcel home delivery services predominantly comes from retail businesses which need to distribute goods to a variety of consumers. Free trade and increasing globalisation have led to these businesses expanding into new international markets and this has increased demand for the worldwide transportation of goods. Economic growth in the Asian market has created a need for new distribution networks, and the trend towards outsourcing has led many businesses to turn to parcel delivery companies as part of their supply chain.

Before the internet changed the way that businesses operate, clients for the UK parcel home delivery market mainly consisted of UK mail order businesses which needed to send goods to consumers, with delivery taking up to two weeks. The home delivery sector has benefited from the continued growth in online shopping. However, this has also led to increased consumer expectations regarding the speed, security and tracking of delivery, and to reduced tolerance of delays.

Margins within the industry have come under pressure as a result of the recession and high fuel prices. Measures to tackle pollution and congestion have increased costs for road-based delivery services, and heightened security measures have increased the costs of air freight operations. This has led to the failure of a number of smaller operators and some consolidation, as other small operators have been acquired by the Big Four.

Supa's operations

Supa's distinctive purple delivery vans are based at 20 depots across the UK. The vans deliver parcels to consumers in their area in the morning and then make collections from business clients in the afternoon, although a minority of clients take parcels directly to the depot for onward delivery.
Once a parcel arrives at the depot it is sorted according to its address and area code and then transported to its final destination via land, air or sea depending on the speed of delivery requested by Supa's client or the consumer. To meet client requirements, Supa has developed a chain of overseas partners, giving it cost-effective access to a global network of distribution centres. These strategic alliances also provide Supa with links to international businesses wanting to deliver to consumers in the UK.

Parcel delivery is a cyclical business so Supa has a core of full-time employees, who all belong to a trade union, supplemented by part-time staff at peak periods. Employees are treated as a valuable resource and Supa invests heavily in training, so employees are familiar with the range of services Supa offers, understand how to use the technology and are able to communicate with clients and consumers. To promote Supa's corporate identity, all employees wear a purple uniform.

The condition of the contents of a parcel is affected by the quality of its packaging. To reduce the risk of damage, Supa encourages clients to make use of its own-brand, environmentally-friendly packaging materials (bags, boxes, tubes, tape etc). Supa was the first UK company to introduce a carbon-neutral delivery service, which is available at a premium price.

Change of strategy

Supa found it hard to compete effectively in the non-urgent market, dominated by the major international and national companies. In July 2008 therefore it withdrew its non-urgent delivery service and focused entirely on urgent deliveries by offering a time-guaranteed next-day delivery service. Clients and consumers have a choice of specified 2-hour time slots at different prices, the most expensive slot being the first delivery of the day (between 07:00 and 09:00). The latest delivery slot ends at 19:00.

In order to achieve this, Supa has invested heavily in information and communications technology to increase the efficiency of distribution. All parcels are labelled with a Supa delivery notice, and bar-coded with a unique parcel identification code (PIC). This facilitates the sorting and tracking process. All delivery vehicles are fitted with global positioning systems (GPS). Drivers have a notebook computer, with handheld scanner linked to a centralised database, which captures electronic information about each parcel, including the time of collection and delivery and the consumer's signature. Supa's ability to track electronically both drivers and parcels throughout the delivery process facilitates more efficient scheduling of collections and deliveries, and provides clients and consumers with accurate information about expected delivery times, reducing the need for costly redeliveries. Using the unique PIC, both clients and consumers can access information via Supa's website so they can trace a parcel, ascertain expected arrival time or verify proof of delivery. Supa also sends a text message or e-mail reminding the consumer of the impending delivery and reconfirming the time.

Supa is now carrying out a post-investment audit in order to decide whether the strategy it has implemented in the two years since July 2008 has been successful. Summary financial results for Supa and for the next-day delivery market leader in the year ended 30 June 2010, together with a budget, historical data and a Balanced Scorecard of performance measures, are set out in **Exhibits 1 and 2**.

Supa's operational director has suggested that further service improvements could be made by rationalising its depots and restructuring its distribution system. This would involve halving the number of depots and creating a new centralised sorting facility. The remaining depots would no longer undertake any sorting but would simply act as a local base for Supa's vehicles.

Exhibit 1:   Summary financial results

Years to 30 June	Supa Old strategy Actual 2008	Supa New strategy Budget 2010	Supa New strategy Actual 2010	Market leader Actual 2010
Revenue	£35m	£42.3m	£46m	£380m
Operating profit	£1.05m	£2.1m	£1.61m	£17m
Number of parcels handled	4.7m	4.7m	4.6m	42m
Number of UK depots	20	20	20	50

Exhibit 2:   Balanced Scorecard for the time-guaranteed next-day B2C delivery market

Year ending 30 June 2010

Key performance indicator	Supa Budget 2010	Supa Actual 2010
Financial		
Revenue growth percentage } to be calculated from	?	?
Operating margin percentage } Exhibit 1	?	?
Customer		
% of deliveries made within allocated time slot	99%	97.5%
% packages lost or unable to be delivered	2.5%	3.5%
Internal business		
% of successful first attempt deliveries	70%	65%
Average number of trips per vehicle per day	4	4.5
Innovation and learning		
% staff achieving certification for training on new technology	80%	95%
Information systems availability – % downtime	2%	5%

Requirements

(a) Explain how the parcel home delivery industry has evolved in the face of changing consumer demand and other key external factors.   **(8 marks)**

(b) Analyse Supa's value chain and describe clearly its key value drivers. A value chain diagram is not required.   **(10 marks)**

(c) Using both exhibits and the other information provided, assess whether implementation of the strategy to focus on time-guaranteed next-day B2C deliveries since July 2008 has been a success.

You should:

(i) Prepare calculations for each financial indicator (budget and actual) that is indicated as being missing from Exhibit 2, together with other relevant financial performance measures;

(8 marks)

(ii) Use your calculations in (i), and the Balanced Scorecard in Exhibit 2, to evaluate the impact of the new strategy, justifying any further information that you would require in order to reach a conclusion. **(10 marks)**

(d) In relation to the operational director's proposal, explain how the depot sorting staff, as key stakeholders, would be affected by and have the power to resist rationalisation of the depots.

(7 marks)

(43 marks)

34 e-Parts Ltd (EP)

e-Parts Ltd (EP) is an online retailer which sells spare parts and accessories for a variety of domestic appliances. EP was established two years ago by Kamal Sheikh, who identified a gap in the market after he struggled to find a reasonably priced replacement part for his oven. EP has two types of customer:

- Small specialists who repair and service domestic appliances for individuals and need to access parts quickly at low cost; and

- Individuals who need either parts such as door hinges and seals to carry out their own simple, non-electrical repairs, or accessories such as fridge shelves or dishwasher cutlery baskets.

EP has grown as people try to save money in the recession and seek to extend the life of their existing domestic appliances by servicing them rather than replacing them. It now has a database of over two million customers. 90% of orders are placed and paid for online, with the remaining 10% handled by a call centre, which also offers after-sales service and support for online customers. In its warehouse, EP stocks 100,000 different products covering the appliances of 250 different manufacturers. EP's inventory control system allows it to despatch most items on the day that the order is placed.

Competition

Domestic appliance manufacturers charge premium prices for spare parts and accessories, primarily to encourage customers to buy new appliances, but also because they do not find it cost-effective to supply parts and accessories directly to customers. Domestic appliance retailers only stock items for the most popular appliances. EP prices are significantly lower than those charged by the appliance manufacturers. As a result, its only real competition is from other similar online businesses.

Brand and marketing

Kamal has positioned EP as 'a service business which helps customers to repair and enhance appliances'. Via the EP website's advice page, customers can access articles and videos to guide them through the most common repair processes. EP also takes advertising revenue from repair businesses in exchange for listing their services on the website. EP relies heavily on customer feedback. As well as a 'product and service review' facility on the website, Kamal has recently created a social networking page where customers can take advantage of special promotions, exchange information and access free advice from experts.

Risk management and business continuity

At a recent management meeting, Kamal made the following comments:

'Keeping our website operational is key for our business. If the site is down we don't make any money. If new customers visit our site and the online shop is not functioning effectively, they don't come back again. The other key issue for us is our inventory control system which allows us to identify quickly whether an item is in stock and where it is located. So far we have handled everything ourselves, but as a result of our rapid growth I am thinking of outsourcing all our operational systems to a specialist information technology (IT) provider. I have also been told that we should have a formal risk management policy, including a business continuity plan, for the business as a whole, so that if a major incident occurs we can continue to function.'

Requirements

(a) Explain the relevance of risk management to the business as a whole and identify the main factors that would be covered in EP's business continuity plan. **(6 marks)**

(b) Identify the key risks arising for EP as a result of its reliance on IT (other than those relating to business continuity) and recommend how they can be managed. **(8 marks)**

(c) Explain the factors to be considered by EP in deciding whether to use outsourcing as a method of implementing its IT strategy. **(7 marks)**

(21 marks)

35 Marcham plc

Marcham plc (Marcham) is a major supermarket chain with a loyal customer base and a 30% share of the UK supermarket sector.

MarchamBank

Marcham is proposing to take advantage of recent turmoil in the banking sector and public mistrust of some retail banks by launching its own banking services, under the name of MarchamBank. This will reduce the pressure felt by Marcham's traditional mature retail business as a result of lower consumer spending during the recession, and will take advantage of rising margins for financial products. MarchamBank will operate from 30 branches within the largest existing Marcham stores and will also provide online banking facilities. The strategy is to offer Marcham customers simplified financial products and the marketing literature will emphasise 'face-to-face, relationship-driven banking from a name that our customers can trust'. Initially MarchamBank will offer simple savings products, short term loans, and a credit card. Once these have all been launched successfully, it will offer current accounts and a mortgage broker service to source mortgages for customers. It does not intend to offer mortgages itself.

Unlike other competitors which have moved into selected personal finance products via joint ventures with major UK banks, Marcham is planning to control its own banking operations. It will hire its own financial services specialists to run its branches and staff its customer service call centre. In view of the collapse of several banks during the financial crisis, the UK government is keen to increase competition in the banking sector and Marcham has already been granted a banking licence. Establishment of the customer service call centre in Scotland (rather than Asia where most competitors base their support services) will allow Marcham to receive a £5 million grant from the UK government.

Customer loyalty card scheme and integrated information system

Marcham has over 20 million customers in the UK and manages its relationship with them via a customer loyalty card. The loyalty card allows customers to earn points in return for cash spent in Marcham stores. Points can be converted into vouchers that can be used to reduce the cost of future purchases. The loyalty card forms part of an integrated information and knowledge management system which allows Marcham to track the shopping habits of its customers.

The other key element of the integrated system is a sophisticated Electronic Point of Sale (EPOS) and inventory control system. As soon as a sales transaction is recorded, this system updates inventory records, provides valuable sales information regarding product demand and profitability, and facilitates automated purchasing from suppliers. This has enabled Marcham to reduce costs by increasing the frequency and accuracy of ordering, leading to lower levels of inventory and wastage.

The data collected from the various elements of the integrated system are logged in a centralised database with an advanced search engine. Marcham uses the resulting customer profiling information for a variety of purposes including pricing, decisions as to which product ranges to stock, research, marketing and customer service. One of the key benefits is improved customer segmentation, enabling Marcham to promote low price or high quality items as appropriate. The information is also sold to a number of the company's suppliers which use it to refine and develop their products.

Whilst most other supermarkets operate similar customer loyalty schemes, none is as far-reaching as Marcham's, which was the first of its kind. Marcham's research suggests that one in four UK adults belongs to its customer loyalty scheme. A key advantage for Marcham is that the scheme enables it to extend its share of customer spend by identifying other products that the customer is likely to be interested in, based on their profile and spending patterns.

Marcham plans for the loyalty card scheme to be a key driver of competitive advantage for its expansion into banking services, especially as none of the existing retail banks operates a loyalty card scheme. It will provide an immediate customer list for direct marketing purposes and the data may help to assess a customer's credit-worthiness.

Marcham intends to offer its customers a MarchamBank credit card to stand alongside the standard loyalty card scheme. This will further enhance its database by giving it access to information about non-Marcham purchases made by its customers.

Marcham criticised

The following is an extract from an article that appeared recently in a national newspaper:

'Supermarket giant Marcham has been criticised recently. Its customer loyalty card scheme has been labelled as a sophisticated spy system by some critics, allowing it to exploit customers by capturing information that they are not in a position to withhold and then using it to sell them things they don't need. As well, there is a risk that this private shopping information could fall into the wrong hands and might one day be used against people.

Marcham has also been accused of further tightening supplier payment terms to improve its own cashflow, despite continuing to make huge profits – indeed this may be where the money for its proposed expansion into banking services is coming from. Suppliers are, of course, prevented from complaining about low margins and onerous terms and conditions because of fears that they will lose Marcham's business.'

Requirements

(a)   In preparation for a meeting of Marcham's senior executives, the operations director has asked you to prepare a report which:

    (i)   Explains the potential benefits of an effective information system for a supermarket and discuss how Marcham has used its information systems to create competitive advantage in the supermarket industry **(8 marks)**

    (ii)   Assesses the suitability, feasibility and acceptability of Marcham's proposed expansion into the banking sector **(12 marks)**

    (iii)   Discusses the relative merits of Marcham's intention to expand into banking via organic growth rather than having an established bank as a business partner **(8 marks)**

(b)   Discuss the ethical issues raised by the newspaper article in respect of Marcham's customer loyalty card and its treatment of suppliers. **(8 marks)**

(36 marks)

36   Quantum Agencies Ltd

Quantum Agencies Ltd (QA) is a medium-sized estate agent, with branches located in a prosperous area of the south of England. The business focuses entirely on residential properties (ie individuals' homes). It has no dealings with commercial properties.

The UK industry

Estate agents can provide a number of services relating to properties for individuals. The most important for estate agents, in terms of revenue generation, arises from assisting private individual vendors (ie sellers) with the sale of their residential properties. The services provided in this context include agreeing an asking price with the vendor, advertising the property, taking potential purchasers to view the property and assisting with price negotiations between the vendor and purchaser. A commission charge is made for these services averaging between 1.0% and 1.5% of the final agreed selling price of the property. This is paid by the vendor to the estate agent on completion of the sale. There is no charge if a sale is not made. Estate agents also normally offer other property services such as property management, valuations, surveys, auctions and financial services.

Branches of estate agents, which are usually located on busy town or city centre streets, are effectively offices with large front windows used as advertising spaces for vendors' property details (eg photographs of the property). Staff in the offices aim to persuade vendors to sign contracts which commit the vendors to the agency for the sale of their properties. Staff then encourage potential purchasers to inspect and then buy the vendors' properties.

In the 13 years from 1994, the estate agent industry experienced strong growth with increasing selling prices and high volumes of sales.

From 2008, the economic downturn caused a reversal of fortunes in the UK industry, causing many estate agent branches to close in the period 2008-2010. Key features of this decline were: falling selling prices (from a UK average of about £203,000 in 2007 to about £162,000 in 2010); declining sales volumes; reduced availability of loans for property purchases; and increased competition among estate agents. The decline in volumes arose mainly from potential vendors being reluctant to sell at historically low prices, while potential purchasers were waiting for market prices to fall further.

Late 2010 has seen some tentative signs of recovery, but property sales volumes continue to be well below their 2007 level. Both vendors and purchasers remain cautious about undertaking a major financial transaction in the current economic climate.

Estate agents are facing increasing competition from individuals who advertise and sell their own properties directly through the internet. There is also low-price competition from internet-based estate agents. A further issue in the industry is recent legislation stating that vendors must provide a certificate showing the energy efficiency of their properties.

Predictions for population growth show that, over the next 20 years, there will be a significant increase in demand for residential properties and therefore a worsening of the UK's historical long-term shortage of housing. To address this issue the government has required some local authorities, particularly in areas where there is high demand such as the south of England, to construct many new homes, including ecology-friendly towns and low-cost social housing.

Company background

QA was formed in 1987 by Neil Smith and Steven Richards, its only directors. It deals with residential property sales, but it also offers a range of other property services.

QA started with only one branch but grew over the years and now has 20 branches. The branches are all held under operating leases and hence there are few owned assets. Each branch is located in a town where there are normally two or three branches belonging to other estate agents. QA branches are all of similar size and are normally at least 15 miles from each other.

In 2007 each QA branch had seven staff with a further 20 staff at head office. Following the reduction in sales volumes, there are now only six staff at each branch and 15 at head office. Significant cost savings have also been made in branch rents since 2007, as a number of operating leases have been renewed at lower cost.

QA operates in the comparatively upmarket sector of the industry, offering high quality customer service. Up to 2007 it maintained a normal commission charge to the vendor of 1.5% of the selling price for each property sold but, in order to compete during the economic downturn, a policy of offering extensive discounts on commission to vendors was introduced in 2008. By 2010, QA's profits had reduced significantly.

Steven and Neil decided to call a meeting in early December 2010 to plan a new strategy for 2011 and beyond.

The meeting

Each director proposed a different strategy. They agreed it would not be possible to implement both proposals.

Proposal 1

Neil opened the meeting: 'The recession has been longer and more severe than expected. We can no longer sustain our present network of branches and staff. I've been thinking we need to close at least five of our 20 branches.

However, recently, a friend of mine who owns a firm of solicitors, GTA, suggested to me that QA and GTA link up. In the five towns where GTA has branches, GTA's large front windows would be used to advertise our clients' properties. When a potential purchaser or vendor makes an enquiry at that branch, GTA's staff would take their details and communicate these to us. GTA would therefore be our first point of contact with vendors and purchasers. We would deal with the customer as previously, but by visiting their homes rather than having our own premises.

In return, where a QA property is sold following an introduction by one of GTA's branches, GTA would receive a half of one percent of the selling price as commission. QA would keep the remainder of the commission (eg 1.0%, if a full 1.5% is charged to the vendor). GTA may also benefit from selling legal services to the vendor or the purchaser. We could adopt this arrangement in the five towns where GTA operates. This would save about 75% of our branch costs in those towns, as there would be no need to rent premises, and staff costs would be significantly reduced.'

Proposal 2

Steven disagreed: 'I believe that the recession is ending and we need to start growing again.
Jim Terra, the owner of a rival firm of estate agents, Terra Ltd (Terra), told me recently that Terra has suffered in the recession as much as QA. He indicated that he would consider a merger of our two companies to form a new company, Terra & Quantum (TQ), with Jim having 50% of its ordinary share capital and each of us having 25%.

This seems like a generous offer to me, as Terra has 30 branches. There would be 10 towns where TQ would initially own two branches, but one branch could be closed in each of these towns to save costs. Jim has provided the following background details about Terra to help us evaluate a potential merger:

- Terra commenced trading in 1994 and operates a chain of 30 branches. It only operates in the residential property market.

- Terra's business model is to attract as many vendors' properties as possible by offering a lower commission charge than most rivals. Terra normally charges 1.0%, but discounts may be given.

- Terra expanded rapidly with high volumes from 1994 to 2007 but it has made losses every year since then. Branches are all held under operating leases, of varying duration, so there are few owned assets.'

Performance data

The following data shows estimated figures for the year ending 31 December 2010 for both QA and Terra, plus QA's figures for the year ended 31 December 2007 (which was the peak of the housing market in terms of house prices and sales volumes).

	Quantum Agencies (QA)		Terra
	2007	2010 Estimated	2010 Estimated
	£000	£000	£000
Total value of properties sold	600,000	375,000	625,000
Commission from properties sold	9,000	4,500	6,000
Fees from other services	3,000	2,000	2,700
Branch costs	(8,500)	(5,000)	(7,200)
Head office costs	(1,500)	(1,400)	(2,000)
Pre tax profit/(loss)	2,000	100	(500)
	Units	Units	Units
Number of residential properties sold in the year	2,000	1,500	2,500
Average number of properties, advertised at any one time as available for sale	600	700	1,200
Number of branch employees	140	120	150
Number of branches	20	20	30

Requirements

(a) Prepare a PESTEL analysis for the UK estate agent industry. **(11 marks)**

(b) Using the data and other information available, analyse the performance of QA in 2010 compared with 2007, explaining the key factors that have caused profit to decline. **(12 marks)**

(c) Discuss the merits and problems of the strategic alliance with GTA in Proposal 1. **(7 marks)**

(d) With reference to the merger in Proposal 2 and the analysis in requirement (b):

   (i) Compare the performance of QA and Terra in 2010; and

(ii) Explain the benefits and problems of the merger. Give advice on whether the merger should be undertaken by QA on the terms suggested by Jim. **(14 marks)**

(44 marks)

37 SkinDeepe plc

SkinDeepe plc (SD) manufactures and markets a range of skin creams and lotions.

Company background

SD's product range includes 33 different types of face creams, sun creams and body lotions.

About 75% of SD's products by volume are sold under SD's own brand, the 'Le Beauty' label. These are upmarket products selling at about double the average retail price for the industry. 'Le Beauty' products are sold through selected retailers across Europe in order to enhance the reputation of the brand. The other 25% of its products are sold to Tatton plc (Tatton) which owns a chain of exclusive department stores across Europe. These products are identical in substance to 'Le Beauty' products, but are packaged under the Tatton brand. The price paid by Tatton is about 20% lower than that paid by other customers due to the high volume purchased.

SD has two factories which produce and package its products. These are both located near Southampton, a major seaport in the UK. They are situated about ten miles from each other. Factory A employs 150 staff and produces the creams and lotions in bulk form. They are then transported by road to Factory B where they are packaged by inserting the bulk products into a variety of attractive containers, suitable for retailing. These include sprays, tubes and tubs. Factory B employs 100 staff. SD's own fleet of trucks then distributes the packaged products to customers throughout Europe. Orders for Tatton go directly to its central storage facility.

A reduction in sales volumes and an increase in costs have caused pressure on profits and forced SD to reconsider its business model. The company recognises that a key asset is its brand and that its strength is in marketing and selling, rather than in production.

A cost reduction plan

Given the new challenges, in early December 2010 the board decided to implement the following plan in order to reduce costs:

(1) *Phase 1* – Immediately outsource production of the bulk cream and lotion products to a manufacturer in China, Huang Inc (Huang), to be delivered by ship to Factory B. Within one month, therefore, close Factory A.

(2) *Phase 2* – If phase 1 is successful, in one year's time SD will close Factory B and Huang will then also package the products before transporting them to the UK by ship. On arrival in the UK, a distribution company, Fell plc (Fell), will collect the products from the ship, hold the inventory in a large warehouse, then deliver products directly to customers when requested to do so by SD.

SD will continue to be responsible for sales and marketing from its head office which is adjacent to Factory B, but in a separate building. About 30 of the Factory A and Factory B employees will be offered transfers, some to head office and some to China in quality assurance roles. These roles arise as quality assurance procedures are being put in place at Huang and in SD as part of SD's supply chain management procedures. All other employees will be made redundant.

SD's board is particularly concerned about how to implement and monitor the new strategy. The workforce at Factory B has tended to be loyal and most staff have been in employment with SD for many years. Factory A's workforce is mainly unskilled labour, on short-term contracts. Levels of job satisfaction in Factory A are low and there have been several strikes in the recent past.

Huang does not currently have the equipment to package the products during Phase 1, so this is purely a production phase. Also, even though operational due diligence procedures have been carried out to demonstrate that Huang can deliver on the contract, SD wants to implement the plan in two phases in order to obtain evidence about the level of service that Huang actually provides. A draft service level agreement with Huang is in place which emphasises quality management and quality assurance. This contains clearly defined measures for product quality and delivery times.

The plan is currently confidential but, as part of its implementation, the board has recently informed its biggest customer, Tatton, about it. A reply has just been received from Tatton as follows:

Thank you for your confidential email. We understand the need to cut costs, but the proposed plan to outsource production when both phases are fully implemented causes us some concern. We would therefore seek assurances on the following matters as a condition of Tatton continuing to do business with SkinDeepe:

(i)   How do you intend to continue to assure the quality of your products when you no longer have direct control of production?

(ii) How do you intend to guarantee the reliability of delivery dates, particularly at short notice, when your supply chain stretches across the globe and therefore lead times are likely to be long?

Helen Wong

Purchasing Director

Requirements

(a)   With respect to the plan to source products from China, identify and justify the position of the following key stakeholder groups in Mendelow's power-interest matrix:

- Factory A employees
- Factory B employees
- Tatton   **(9 marks)**

(b)   Explain how barriers to change for Phase 1 may differ from those for Phase 2.   **(8 marks)**

(c)   Identify and explain the key performance indicators that SD could use to monitor the performance of Huang in Phase 1 of the plan, in order to decide whether to continue with Phase 2.   **(6 marks)**

(d)   As a senior, working for SD on its cost reduction project, draft a response to the two matters raised by Tatton.   **(10 marks)**

(33 marks)

38   Heaton Home

Heaton Home (HH) is a not-for-profit charity established in 1976 by Lady Alice Heaton when she gifted a large house to the charity. HH has a board of trustees responsible for its governance and strategy.

HH's history

The gift from Lady Heaton is a building of historical and architectural significance. The conditions attaching to the gift require the charity's board of trustees to use the house 'to provide reduced cost residential care home places for elderly people who have lived in the local town of Northport for ten years or more'. The trustees have always interpreted 'elderly' as meaning 'over 65 years old' when determining whether an individual is eligible for a place. The conditions of the gift by Lady Heaton also stated that the house itself should be 'maintained in good order'.

Lady Heaton also gave HH just enough money to establish the house as a residential care home, but not enough to cover annual running costs. There are no funds remaining from the original gift. Lady Heaton died in 1990.

Managers were appointed by the trustees and established three sources of funding to finance the running of the home:

- Fees from residents. These are currently £10,000 per year, per resident, which is much lower than the fees charged by other care homes in the region. However, fees were increased from £8,500 two years ago in order to meet the care home's rising costs.

- Contributions from local government have been agreed as a lump sum of £300,000 per year and an additional £5,000 per resident, per year. Local government has been willing to make a contribution since the alternative is for them to accommodate the elderly people in other care homes, which would cost local government substantially more. A condition of the contribution is the appointment of a trustee on the board who specifically represents local government.

- Charitable donations and bequests from the local community. These have been constant at around £250,000 per annum in recent years.

Experienced managers and care assistants are employed at a total cost of £800,000 per year. A quarter of the total labour hours required to run the home are provided by unpaid volunteers from the local community, where the home is well known and supported.

Some recent issues

The trustees have recently appointed a new manager to run the home. He identified a few problems in his initial review:

- The home has 50 places and historically these have been full, with a waiting list. Over the past two years, however, the number of occupied places has fallen to only 45 and there is no waiting list. Under the terms of HH's agreement with local government, £100,000 of the lump sum payment will be withdrawn if average occupancy in a year falls to 40 or below.

- There has been some deterioration in the state of the house which affects its appearance, but not the way it functions. The estimated cost of restoring the house is £300,000.

- The number of volunteer hours is falling by about 5% per year.

- Some residents will struggle to pay the full amount of their fees next year. Demand for places in the home has been sensitive to the increased price charged to the residents.

- The estimated full cost of running the home in 2010 is £1.25 million, which is almost entirely fixed costs and includes salaries. HH currently has cash accumulated from surpluses of previous years of only £100,000.

Meeting of the Board of Trustees

At a recent meeting, the trustees agreed that the current situation was financially unsustainable. There was also concern that the charity was failing to meet the needs of its residents, as evidenced both by the fall in demand, and by its failure to meet its obligation under the conditions attaching to Lady Heaton's gift, which required the house to be maintained. Legal advice suggests that the trustees are required to continue to comply with this building maintenance aspect of Lady Heaton's gift.

Hannah Khan, the local government trustee, put forward a series of proposals:

- To increase fees to residents by 20%

- In order to increase demand, to offer places to people living in a slightly wider geographical area around Northport, and to extend the eligible age range down to people who are at least 60 years old

- To reduce the staffing levels in order to save costs

Hannah argued that the conditions attaching to Lady Heaton's gift were not relevant to running the home in today's environment, but that any additional surplus arising from Hannah's proposals should be accumulated to restore the house.

Requirements

(a) Prepare a mission statement for HH and briefly explain why a mission statement may be useful for HH. **(6 marks)**

(b) Based on the new manager's review, identify the key risks facing HH and briefly describe how these can be managed. Show any relevant supporting calculations. **(10 marks)**

(c) Evaluate the ethical implications of the proposals made by the local government trustee. **(7 marks)**

(23 marks)

39 Family Entertainment Company

The Family Entertainment Company plc (FEC) is a UK-based company which operates a chain of 20 family-oriented theme parks throughout Western Europe. Its mission is to provide 'a great all-round family entertainment experience'. Each FEC theme park consists of roller coasters and other thrill rides, live entertainment and themed exhibits (attractions linked to a specific concept such as outer space or sea-life). Each park also offers a variety of food outlets plus retail outlets that sell FEC branded merchandise. FEC's target market in each country is domestic customers and foreign tourists.

The theme park industry in Western Europe

In Western Europe the leisure and entertainment industry is mature. As well as an increasing number of theme parks, there is a wide range of alternative forms of entertainment available to tourists and domestic customers eg films, sports, zoos, and tourist and cultural attractions. Theme parks range from major complexes, operated worldwide by large multinational entertainment corporations, to regional chains such as FEC, to much smaller, simpler local parks. The multinational entertainment corporations gain marketing benefits from linking rides with film and television characters, and are also able to access the significant capital and technology required to develop the latest rides. Most multinational and regional chains add at least one new ride per year per park to attract visitors, and they spend on average 20% of annual revenue on building new rides and attractions.

Costs and revenues

Theme parks have relatively low variable costs and high fixed costs. They have low, mid and high seasons in terms of volumes of visitors. Seasonal attendance means that the effective cost per visitor is much lower in the high season. In addition, demand for rides fluctuates during the day, which can cause problems such as congestion and queuing at peak times.

Typically theme parks operate one of two pricing schemes:

Pay as you go – visitors pay a nominal price for entry to the park. Once inside the park, a separate price is payable for each ride or attraction, based on its popularity, with the most popular ones costing up to four times the price of the least popular.

Single admission price – visitors pay a single substantial admission price for which they receive unlimited use of nearly all attractions and rides. A small number of highly popular rides/attractions may not be included in the price or may incur a premium.

Competition is fierce. To improve profits in each period, parks need to attract more visitors, keep them in the park longer and increase the amount they spend. The key factors for a successful theme park are:

(i)   Convenience of location;
(ii)   Uniqueness/popularity of rides (performance and excitement);
(iii)   Price;
(iv)   Availability and quality of wider amenities (food, merchandise etc); and
(v)   Health and safety.

The impact of the difficult economic climate on consumer spending has led to many theme parks suffering declining attendance and a fall in profitability. In view of increasing competition in the traditional markets of the USA and Western Europe, and the fact that land for expansion is expensive and restricted, a number of operators have started to look at other markets in Asia and South America. FEC has come under pressure recently from its shareholders, who are unhappy about falling earnings per share. To address this, FEC is now considering expanding into India.

Expansion into India

FEC's board believes that the Indian market is attractive for the following reasons:

* Strong economic growth

* Availability of large areas of dormant/unused land

* Government promotion of tourism and incentives for investment in the leisure industry

* Rising average household incomes and an increased willingness by the local population to spend resources on recreation and entertainment

There are over 100 theme parks in India, operated mostly by domestically-owned regional or local businesses, which tend to have a cultural or historical theme. These parks tend to be small, with fairly simple rides, partly because the owners lack the financial resources and technology to establish large parks with advanced, state-of-the art attractions.

FEC's theme park in India would be built on the outskirts of a major city (population of 14 million) that is recognised as one of the wealthiest in India; the residents are typically viewed as trendsetters in fashion and lifestyle. The city attracts many visitors and its tourist industry is very large.

FEC believes that the emphasis on families that is prevalent in Indian culture is a good fit with FEC's own values, and that there is an opportunity for an initial market entrant to establish a high degree of brand loyalty.

Financial projections for the Indian venture are to be produced on the basis of the assumptions set out in Exhibit 1.

Exhibit 1: Assumptions to be used for financial projections in respect of the Indian theme park

1. All costs and revenues will be incurred locally and will be denominated in US$

2. Figures are for revenues and expenses once the park is fully established

3. Total average revenue per visitor is made up of 50% admission price and 50% food and merchandise

4. The average admission price is $10 per visitor

5. Variable costs per visitor (excluding food and merchandise) are 20% of admission price. There is a 100% mark up on all food and merchandise

6. Estimated attendance figures:

	Attendance per month
High season (3 months)	90,000
Mid season (5 months)	75,000
Low season (4 months)	50,000

7. Annual fixed costs are $9,000,000

Health and safety

The theme park industry is in its development stage in India. Each theme park must undergo an annual inspection in order to retain a licence from local government in accordance with local certification standards. A national regulatory body for theme park health and safety has not yet been established so standards vary across the country.

FEC's operations director commented:

'Obviously the initial costs of creating and opening the new theme park will be huge, but once the park is open the annual overheads, including labour, will be much lower than in our European parks. This is important as the admission prices will need to be affordable to local customers. The industry is still at an early stage of development and regulation, and we can take advantage of this by reducing what we are normally forced to spend on park safety and ride maintenance. That should mean higher profits to keep the shareholders happy.'

Requirements

(a) Prepare the following sections of the Porter's Five Forces model for the theme park industry in **Western Europe**:

   Threat of new entrants

   Competitive rivalry

   Substitutes   **(8 marks)**

(b) Discuss the benefits and risks of FEC's proposed strategy to expand into India.   **(7 marks)**

(c) Using the data in Exhibit 1 and the other information provided about the Indian park:

   (i)   Estimate the park's annual net profit, once it is established;

   (ii) Calculate the park's break-even attendance figure at the estimated average revenue per visitor;

   (iii) Calculate the sensitivity of the park's profits to both the estimate of fixed costs and the estimate of average admission price;

(iv) Comment on the significance of your calculations in (i) to (iii) above and set out any additional information that would be useful to verify the accuracy of the assumptions provided and improve the quality of the financial projections. **(15 marks)**

(d) Explain how the market might be segmented by FEC as part of its approach to marketing for the Indian park and discuss appropriate pricing strategies. **(8 marks)**

(e) Discuss the ethical issues raised by the operations director's comments on health and safety and the potential for stakeholder conflict that might be present. **(7 marks)**

(45 marks)

40 MPW Ltd

MPW Ltd (MPW) is a mobile phone wholesaler. It purchases mobile phone handsets from all of the major manufacturers and then sells them to independent mobile phone retailers in the UK.

Strategy for growth

Mobile phone wholesaling is a very competitive business with narrow margins. At the end of 2009, in order to increase sales volumes, MPW embarked upon an ambitious growth strategy. The board decided that to attract more retailers it was necessary to improve service levels by widening the range of handsets on offer and guaranteeing a next-day delivery service for all orders placed. To meet these service levels and to accommodate the increased inventory requirements, MPW acquired a large, conveniently-located warehouse.

Incentives and performance measurement

In an effort to keep costs down and revenue high, at the same time MPW implemented an incentive scheme under which bonuses are payable as follows:

- **Purchasing manager** – based on the amount of discount negotiated on purchases from phone manufacturers

- **Sales team** – each salesperson receives a bonus based on the average gross profit they achieve across all their orders (measured as the actual selling price to the retailer less the actual purchase price paid to the manufacturer)

The board's new performance measurement scheme used the following Key Performance Indicators (KPIs) to track the success of the strategy:

- Revenue growth
- Percentage gross margin
- Percentage of deliveries made on time (next-day)

During 2010 MPW's sales volumes increased by over 20% and the number of retail outlets served grew significantly. Large bonuses were paid to the purchasing manager and the sales team. However when the draft financial statements were prepared for 2010 it became apparent that the strategy had not been successful in profit terms.

Board meeting to assess the success of the growth strategy

The managing director called a board meeting to discuss the draft financial statements, at which the following comments were made by the directors:

Managing director

'I thought we agreed that growth was imperative to our future success. Why, when we have met our KPI targets for revenue growth and percentage gross margin and 99% of our deliveries are made on time, has our net profit fallen? Are we losing money on some customers or product lines and not others?'

Sales director

'The handsets my team are actually selling are all making a positive gross margin; otherwise we wouldn't be selling them. However I can't help feeling the problem is with our purchasing strategy. Having lots of inventory is not necessarily a good thing - we are often out-of-stock of the new, highly popular handsets that our retailers want, yet 40% of our inventory consists of earlier models which have been in our warehouse for over two months. Once the inventory is this old, we are going to struggle to do much more than recover what it cost us.'

Purchasing director

'It's our sales strategy that's the issue. Our emphasis on customer service might have attracted some new retailers but it has been a disaster as far as our original customers are concerned. Before they tended to order in large quantities, a month or so in advance, based on their expected demand. Now we are offering next-day delivery they have reduced their own inventories and are placing orders with us for smaller quantities, much more frequently. In total our original customers are buying the same quantity from us, so our revenues are the same, but our costs of order processing and distribution, which are a significant element of selling and administration costs, have increased significantly.'

Finance director (recently appointed)

'I agree that the level of inventory and the volume of orders may be costing us money, but I think that the problem also lies with our incentive schemes and with the fact that our KPIs have a very narrow focus.'

Requirements

As a business strategy consultant brought in by the managing director, prepare a report for the board of directors which:

(a) Evaluates the comments made by the sales, purchasing and finance directors, in order to explain the reasons for the unexpected decline in net profit highlighted by the managing director;

(13 marks)

(b) Advises on the steps that MPW can take to improve the efficiency of its entire supply chain and hence the performance of MPW; and **(10 marks)**

(c) Identifies MPW's critical success factors and discusses how it can improve its performance measurement in order to focus on them. You should identify four specific performance measures.

(8 marks)

(31 marks)

41 SPV plc

SPV plc (SPV) is a world market leader in the manufacture of thin-film solar panels for installing on the rooftops of commercial and domestic buildings. SPV was formed in 1999 and in 2002 it began commercial production of panels, which it sells to companies and individuals in North America, Europe and Asia Pacific. SPV's revenue has grown from £15 million in 2006, when it obtained a full listing on the London Stock Exchange, to just under £200 million in 2010. Since listing, the company has had a profitable track record, a strong financial position and positive cash flows.

How solar panels work

Solar panels work by converting light into electricity. The amount of power generated is determined by the amount of light falling on the panels, which is in turn determined by the weather and time of day. 40-60% of the annual electricity requirement of an average building can be generated in this way, replacing some or all of the highest-cost electricity that the building uses at peak times.

Solar panels are expensive to purchase and install but, once installed, they have low maintenance costs and can produce free energy for the building for many years. The panels are connected to the local electricity network or grid. This means the owner of the panels can buy electricity from the network when solar power is insufficient (eg at night and during winter months), and any surplus solar power generated can be sold to the network under a scheme known as the solar Feed-In-Tariff (FIT).

The payback period for the investment in each panel depends on the savings in network electricity bills and the revenue earned from FIT, but is typically in excess of 10 years. To be successful, therefore, solar panel manufacturers need proven technology and an established track record, because customers want confidence that the manufacturer will be in business for the duration of the panel warranty period.

Demand for solar energy

As the price of solar panels falls and that of traditional power sources increases, the global market for solar energy, which has grown rapidly since 2005, is predicted to double again by 2014. However, demand for solar energy is unpredictable and varies considerably from country to country. Demand is driven by:

(i)   Climate (the panels operate in daylight hours whatever the weather, however solar energy is most successful in areas of high sunshine);

(ii) The price of electricity from traditional power sources;

(iii) Public awareness of and attitudes towards sustainability;

(iv) The state of the national economy; and

(v)   Government policy/incentives for renewable energy.

The political and economic framework

Government incentives offered to households and businesses to install solar energy systems vary from country to country but typically come in one of two forms:

• Investment incentives, where grants or loans are available to subsidise the initial cost of purchase and installation.

• Varying levels of FITs, where the owner of the panels receives payment for all solar generated electricity that they feed back into the local network

In view of the long payback period for panels and to ensure stability of demand, government support schemes need to be available in the long term. As a result of its proven FIT scheme, finance opportunities, availability of skilled solar energy companies, and good public awareness, Germany has the highest proportion of solar power installations, followed by Italy, Japan and the USA. However each country's relative position is very dependent on its political and economic framework. For instance Spain, which had until recently been ahead of Germany, was forced to reduce solar energy subsidies in the face of its critical short-term budgeting and funding problems, resulting in an immediate and marked decline in demand.

SPV's competitive advantage

SPV uses special patented thin-film technology which is much lighter and cheaper to produce than the silicon used by other solar panel manufacturers, and which has a higher energy yield in the absence of sunshine. SPV owns factories around the world, including the USA, Germany and Malaysia, and derives economies of scale from its vertically-integrated manufacturing process which facilitates high-volume, low-cost production of efficient panels.

The uncertain industry environment and an increase in the number of Asian manufacturers offering quality products at low prices mean that, to maintain its competitive advantage, SPV needs a structure and culture which allows it to be forward-looking, innovative and quick to respond to changes in demand in different markets.

Recently, a number of environmentally-aware governments have set targets for their domestic utility companies requiring them to obtain up to 33% of energy from renewable sources by 2020. In view of this, SPV has approached UTILCO, a major utility company operating throughout the USA, to set up a joint venture where SPV's solar panels are attached to UTILCO's telephone and electricity poles. The solar energy will be captured and fed directly into the national electricity network.

Requirements

(a) (i)   Recommend and justify an organisational structure that is suitable for SPV given the nature of its environment. Refer to relevant models.   **(5 marks)**

     (ii) Suggest operational strategies which SPV could adopt to encourage the culture necessary to maintain its competitive advantage.   **(5 marks)**

(b) Explain how the need for sustainability influences SPV's strategy, and assess the extent to which, as a result, SPV's success is driven by factors outside its control.   **(8 marks)**

(c) Discuss the relative merits of the proposed joint venture from the point of view of both UTILCO and SPV.   **(6 marks)**

                                            (24 marks)

42   Cauldron Cereals plc

Cauldron Cereals plc (CC) manufactures boxed breakfast cereals. It purchases grains such as wheat, corn and barley, processes them into breakfast cereals, packages the cereals in a range of box sizes and sells them to retailers which, in turn, sell to consumers.

Industry background

The boxed breakfast cereals industry in the UK is large and long established, with retail sales that make up about 2.3% of the UK grocery market. Despite being a mature industry, there was steady, long-term annual volume growth in UK retail sales of over 3% until the end of 2008, since when retail sales revenues have been constant at around £1,200 million. The price to retailers and the final price to consumers of the average box of cereals have both been stable since 2005 due to competitive factors in the industry and the economic recession.

One of the main drivers of growth in consumer demand up to and including 2008 was a general trend among consumers towards healthy eating, in relation to which breakfast cereals have a positive image. This was exploited by manufacturers and retailers through new product development and marketing of innovative breakfast cereals designed to target healthy-eating consumers. More recently, however, the healthy-eating reputation of the industry has been tarnished by reports that, during the manufacturing process, high levels of sugar and salt are added to enhance taste. Manufacturers have been concerned about this publicity, but have had problems producing breakfast cereals of an equivalent taste with reduced sugar and salt content.

Competition in the industry is intense. Manufacturing output is dominated by the 'big three' (Astra Inc, Benn Inc and Ceel plc) which are all large international companies with manufacturing sites both in the UK and abroad. Jointly, they have dominated the UK industry for many years, defending their competitive positions with high marketing expenditure and regular launches of new products. The wide product range of the 'big three' includes the full spectrum of size, price and quality choices, including market niches such as healthy-eating and children's cereals. Many companies outside the 'big three' tend to focus on these market niches. Overall there is a wide diversity of companies in the industry (**Exhibit 1 on page 5**). There are insignificant exports and imports of boxed breakfast cereals due to their bulk nature.

90% of sales by manufacturers of boxed breakfast cereals are made directly to supermarkets and other multi-outlet retailers, with the remainder to independent shops. The largest supermarket chains therefore have significant market power and use this to put pressure on all manufacturers to lower their prices. Many manufacturers, including some of the 'big three', supply 'own brand' products to supermarkets. These are products which are sold under the supermarket's brand label, so the consumer is unaware of which manufacturer made the product.

Company background

CC is a long-established manufacturer of boxed breakfast cereals focusing on the niche market of healthy eating. Within this niche it makes a range of products in terms of quality, price and size. It markets them to both adults and children. CC is small by comparison to the 'big three' but there are other companies in the industry of similar size, some of which have products in the same market niche (**Exhibit 1 on page 5**).

CC sells directly to a wide range of retailers including the largest supermarket chains. CC products are currently only sold under the CC brand label.

CC historically used high quality grains in its breakfast cereals and the sugar and salt content was low at only 3% and 1% respectively, compared with 6% and 3% for many lower quality breakfast cereals. These figures have always been prominently disclosed on every box of CC cereal and are a key feature of advertising. Grains are bought on international commodities markets and represent nearly all of the variable cost of production. Current commodity prices are set daily by open market trading and tend to fluctuate significantly. Other variable costs of breakfast cereal manufacture, including sugar and salt ingredients, are negligible.

2009 – A change in strategy

Despite the growth in sales in the UK breakfast cereal market as a whole up to 2008, CC sales have not grown for some years and, at the beginning of 2009, CC's chief executive was replaced.

The new chief executive, Eric Land, reviewed the company's strategy and decided that there was little CC could do to improve sales in the short term due to market competition and the economic recession. He therefore decided on the immediate tactic of cost cutting by reducing the quality of the grain purchased. Eric's instruction to production staff was: 'produce the same taste, at lower cost'. The cheaper grain was imported from Eastern Europe under a fixed-price, two-year contract signed in January 2009. This fixed price contract proved surprisingly beneficial in saving further costs, as CC gained from lower grain prices in both 2009 and 2010 when world grain commodity prices unexpectedly increased by 10% each year. Further increases in grain prices are now expected from 2011 onwards.

As a consequence of the cost-cutting policy, CC's profits increased in 2009, despite there being some evidence that consumers were not as happy with the taste as they had been previously, resulting in a fall in sales volumes (**Exhibit 2 on page 5**).

2010 – An ethical issue

Alarmed by the fall in sales volume, at the end of 2009 Eric held an informal meeting with a small number of directors closest to him. They decided to increase the sugar and salt content of CC's products in order to improve taste and to compensate for the reduction in grain quality. The sugar and salt content was increased to 3.49% and 1.49% respectively from 1 January 2010. Eric explained at the meeting: 'We can legitimately continue to show sugar and salt content at 3% and 1% on our boxes, as these are now figures rounded to the nearest whole percentage point. I do not intend to disclose the fact that we have increased sugar and salt content, even to the other directors, as it may cause unnecessary problems.'

The change in sugar and salt content helped to improve the taste a little and, as a consequence, demand recovered slightly in 2010.

In March 2011 the finance director Jenny Jones, a chartered accountant, discovered the undisclosed increases in the sugar and salt content. She resigned immediately and then informed a number of newspapers. As a consequence of the bad publicity, weekly sales of CC products immediately fell to about 80% of their previous level. Eric was forced to resign. At the board meeting prior to his resignation he declared: 'How can you run a business when you can't trust your fellow directors to keep confidentiality as a basic principle of professional and ethical conduct? I improved the business and what she did was unprofessional and unethical. She has ruined this company.'

June 2011 – A new start

A new board was appointed and in May 2011, after reviewing the situation, they restored both the original grain quality and the previous sugar and salt content. Nevertheless, the reputation of CC had been damaged and sales were expected to remain at around 80% of their previous level for some time.

An offer has recently been received from a low-cost supermarket, FoodSave plc, to buy CC products at an average price of £2 per box. The cereals would be 'own branded' under the FoodSave name. Volumes would be a minimum of 400,000 boxes per year for two years.

Requirements

(a) Using the data in Exhibit 1 and other information available, evaluate CC's long term competitive position in the UK boxed breakfast cereals manufacturing industry. For this purpose ignore the decisions made from 1 January 2009. State any additional information that would be needed to make a more complete assessment of CC's competitive position. **(12 marks)**

(b) Using the data in Exhibit 2 and other information provided:

    (i) Describe and evaluate the financial and strategic performance of CC in the period 2008-2010. In so doing, assess the impact on performance of the decisions to reduce costs and to change the quality of the grain content from 2009; and

    (ii) Explain the risks facing CC in 2011 and beyond. **(16 marks)**

(c) Explain the ethical issues arising from:

    (i) The decision to increase the sugar and salt content; and

    (ii) Jenny's public disclosure of this decision. **(8 marks)**

(d) Prepare a brief report which provides reasoned advice to the CC board on whether the new contract with FoodSave plc should be accepted. Include supporting calculations. **(8 marks)**

(44 marks)

Exhibit 1 – UK boxed breakfast cereal industry – average annual revenue 2008–10

Company	Average annual revenue from retailers in each year £m	Comment
Astra Inc	295	The 'big three' have international operations and sell a wide range of boxed breakfast cereals.
Benn Inc	127	
Ceel plc	112	
Rival 1	65	Focuses on market niche of healthy cereals. Average wholesale selling price per box is £2.25.
Rival 2	40	Niche market of healthy cereals specifically for children. Average wholesale selling price per box is £3.
Rival 3	38	High quality producer using best grains. Sells a range of products but no particular emphasis on healthy cereals. Average wholesale selling price per box is £3.50.
CC	35	
Other smaller companies	268	There are about 125 other smaller companies in the UK manufacturing boxed breakfast cereals
Industry total	980	

Exhibit 2 – Additional data

Financial data for CC

	2008 £m	2009 £m	2010 £m
Revenue	36	34	35
Fixed operating costs	(16)	(16)	(16)
Variable operating cost (grains)	(16)	(13)	(13.4)
Operating profit	4	5	5.6

Other data

	2008	2009	2010
Boxes sold by CC (millions)	12	11.33	11.67
Boxes sold by UK industry (millions)	490	490	490

43 Henford plc

Henford plc (Henford) is a conglomerate company with a diversified range of products.

Company history

Henford commenced trading in 1955 as a manufacturer of traditional toys and games (eg, board games, models, wooden toys and soft toys). The Henford brand is well respected and sells at a premium price, but operating cash flows are modest. Sales volumes have been falling for some years as the company has struggled for market share. There is severe competition from other toy companies, and particularly from companies which manufacture technology-based toys.

In 2001, Henford appointed a new chief executive, Ian Palmer, who attempted to diversify while retaining the original toy business. His diversification policy was to make acquisitions, irrespective of the type of company or the industry in which the opportunity arose, using two criteria:

(i) The target company could be acquired at a price which represented good value; and
(ii) Henford management could add value.

Since 2001 Henford has acquired two other companies: Premium Paper Products Ltd (PPP) in 2006 and Medicarex Ltd (Medicarex) in 2009.

PPP was established in 2001 and manufactures paper for all types of computer printer and copier. The paper is high quality and high price. The paper has been designed using significant research and development and has been shown to be one of the most efficient in the market in reducing blockages and solving other quality problems when printing. PPP has a very small market share compared to the market leader, but it has experienced rapid growth. Due to rapid expansion and new investment it has moderate profits, but a large negative cash flow.

Medicarex is a manufacturer of specialist containers for pharmaceuticals. In this niche sector Medicarex is a market leader, but growth rates for the company and the industry are low. Profit margins are reasonably high and, as the production technology is stable and long established, limited new investment is needed, so significant cash flows are being generated.

Each manufacturing site for toys, paper and pharmaceuticals is located in a different region of the UK. Henford's head office is located at the same site as toy production. Data is provided for each product (**Exhibit on page 8**).

Organisational structure

Until 2001, Henford was managed by the Henford family with a fairly rigid, functional structure and a bureaucratic management style. Since 2001, despite the two acquisitions expanding the size of Henford, the organisational structure had not been changed. However, Ian Palmer decided to modify the organisational structure with effect from 1 January 2011. As a consequence, the old and new structures were as follows.

Director	Old Structure (Pre 2011)	New Structure (2011 onwards)
Ian Palmer	Chief executive	Chief executive
Holly Huang	Finance director	Finance director
Simon Smart	Procurement director	Toys division director
Lisa Langford	Production director	Paper division director
Ali Akbar	Marketing director	Pharmaceuticals division director
Claire Cullen	Human resources director	Human resources director

All directors report to the chief executive under the old and new systems.

Under the old system each director had a small group of senior managers reporting to him or her.

Within the new structure, each of the three products forms a separate operating division under the leadership of a director who, as divisional head, is responsible for that division's profit. Each division carries out its own procurement, production and marketing, but finance and human resources remain as group-wide functions, each headed by a director as under the old structure.

The various senior managers in the old procurement, production and marketing functions have been allocated to the new divisions and each reports to the relevant divisional head.

Reaction to the change

Ian Palmer believes that the senior marketing managers have been very reluctant to accept the changes. He summarised the situation as he saw it at a board meeting:

'I made a decision to make changes in our organisational structure and I expect staff to implement that decision fully. It is clear that the senior marketing managers have been against these changes from the beginning, with a series of excuses as to why we should not carry out any proposed change every time we ask for consultation. Sales performance has fallen and this is not acceptable.'

Ali, the marketing director under the old structure, was much more sympathetic than Ian: 'The senior marketing managers and other marketing staff all used to be based at head office, but they are now spread across all three locations. We are all still in communication with each other, as we feel strongly that marketing should have remained as a centralised functional activity, like finance and human resources. Procurement and production staff were already spread across the three locations so they have not been affected much by the changes. Moreover, it has been reported to me that the other two new divisional heads do not understand the complexities of marketing and so can neither appreciate, nor control, the marketing staff's work. This is causing demotivation and a reluctance to perform to the best of their ability.'

Requirements

(a) Using the data in the exhibit and the other information provided, for each of Henford's three products (ie, toys, paper, pharmaceuticals):

    (i) Explain and justify its positioning within the Boston Consulting Group (BCG) matrix; and

    (ii) Based on your BCG analysis, explain where it is located within its product life cycle.

(13 marks)

(b) In respect of Henford's organisational structure:

    (i) Draw organisational charts for both Henford's old structure (ie prior to 2011) and its new structure; and

    (ii) Evaluate whether the change from the old functional structure to the new structure is likely to be beneficial for Henford.

(13 marks)

(c) As far as the information permits, explain the barriers to change that the senior marketing managers could potentially create.

(8 marks)

(34 marks)

Exhibit – Product data

	Annual market growth rate	Sales	Largest competitor sales
		£m	£m
Toys	zero	25	50
Paper	20%	5	50
Pharmaceuticals	3%	110	100

44   Felan Fashions plc

Felan Fashions plc (FF) is a designer, producer and retailer of ladies' fashion clothing. It has 27 retail outlets located in major cities throughout the UK, plus a central production site.

Current business model

FF has been very successful since being established by Tanya Felan in 1980. Tanya had been a fashion designer working for a major fashion house when she decided to set up her own business.

Her business model was to base her latest designs on current trends set by the major international fashion houses, but to tailor FF products to UK market tastes and sell at prices well below those of the leading international fashion brands. These prices are still much higher than those of most good quality UK clothing retailers. FF's target market is young female professionals with high disposable incomes.

All the outlets are owned by FF and sell only FF products. FF clothes are made in a range of standard sizes at the central production site, but are fitted and adjusted to individual customer needs by FF's skilled staff at each retail outlet. The retail outlet staff also provide general advice and assistance for individual customers in making their fashion choices.

The business model has been successful and the FF brand has become well known in the UK, with 80% of young professional women recognising the FF brand name in market surveys. Specifically, the FF brand is perceived as desirable with an exclusive image, which is nevertheless affordable by young consumers on high incomes.

Future development

By 2011 Tanya believed that the UK market was saturated and therefore decided to expand by opening retail outlets in other parts of Europe. Only FF branded clothes would be sold.

An initial market survey showed that brand recognition among the target market in key European countries was only 20%, although it was 25% in France. As a result, Tanya recognised that marketing would be a key issue.

Tanya has identified two mutually exclusive strategies for European expansion as follows:

Strategy 1 – to open independent stores across four European countries (Germany, France, Italy and Spain) as opportunities arise for suitable prime locations in major cities in these countries.

Strategy 2 – to use floorspace within a chain of large, mid-market to upper-market French department stores, UneShop. This strategy would limit the expansion to France, but FF outlets could be opened immediately in all ten UneShop stores located in French cities. The available floorspace of each 'shop within a store' would be equivalent to one of FF's independent retail outlets.

Requirements

(a) Explain the factors to be considered in developing a suitable marketing plan for FF's Strategy 1 using the marketing mix. **(12 marks)**

(b) Compare and evaluate the two strategies for expansion and provide a reasoned recommendation as to which, if either, of the strategies should be adopted. **(10 marks)**

(22 marks)

45 Brownroll plc

Brownroll plc (Brownroll), a company listed on the London Stock Exchange, operates in the UK leisure industry. Brownroll has two separate divisions, each trading under a different brand name – a chain of budget hotels called 'Value Lodge' (VL), and a chain of up-market coffee bars called 'Café Premium' (CP). Extracts from the company's management accounts for the year ended 31 August are provided in the Exhibit below.

Exhibit: Extracts from management accounts for year ended 31 August

	2010 £ million	2011 £ million
Revenue		
VL	243	290
CP	109	116
	352	406
Divisional contribution (revenue less all directly traceable costs)		
VL	29.3	32.4
CP	18.3	22.7
	47.6	55.1
Reported operating profit (after central costs)		
VL	20.6	23.3
CP	9.6	13.6
	30.2	36.9
Net assets		
VL	148.4	160.2
CP	52.5	57.2
	200.9	217.4

Value Lodge (VL)

VL currently has 350 budget hotels across the UK which provide basic value-for-money accommodation to business and leisure customers. In order to create brand identity, the individual rooms and communal areas conform to the same design and layout for each hotel. Unlike many businesses, VL has continued to perform well since 2008 despite the recession. It has attracted an increasing number of business travellers who have switched to VL from more up-market accommodation, in order to control their costs. VL's competitively priced room rates have also helped to attract a weekend tourist market which ensures overall occupancy rates are high. 90% of VL's bookings are made online.

VL's major competitor is Budgetbeds (BB), the only other national budget hotel chain which, with recently reported annual revenue of £208 million, holds 31% of the UK budget hotel market. Apart from VL and BB the budget hotel market is fragmented, with a variety of small independent hotels, but the standards of accommodation and service vary widely.

Café Premium (CP)

CP's financial performance continues to be strong although revenue growth has slowed over the course of the recession. CP currently has 370 stand-alone branded coffee bars located throughout the UK. CP markets itself as 'providing a unique blend of high quality espresso-based coffee in a local community setting'. There is no standard design – CP coffee bars are customised to incorporate local features and reflect the neighbourhood in which they are located. CP invests heavily in customer service training for all staff.

The UK branded coffee bar market is increasingly competitive and is seen as approaching saturation by many in the industry, with a total of 3,500 outlets and annual revenue of £1.2bn. There are three branded coffee bar chains which all have a UK-wide presence and are all larger than CP. These three chains currently have 2,015 outlets and a 72.5% market share (by revenue). The branded coffee bar market also faces competition from independent coffee shops and other restaurants and cafés that are not exclusively coffee specialists.

Future strategy

At a recent board meeting to discuss the provisional results for 2011, there was some dispute about the future direction of Brownroll.

The VL director stated that: 'We have established a reputation for consistently offering the best value-for-money business accommodation and our week-day occupancy rate is over 80%. We need to capitalise on this by buying some more hotels to ensure that we have complete UK-wide coverage and to consolidate our position in the market place. There is little, if any, synergy between our two divisions. Continued revenue growth is one of our shareholders' key requirements. As the future growth prospects for the UK coffee bar market are disappointing, I suggest we sell off the CP business and use the cash to expand VL. The company's financial results would look much better without CP.'

The CP director disagreed: 'It is fair to say that the UK coffee bar market is becoming saturated, but we have continued to demonstrate year-on-year growth by opening new outlets. Also, our margins are excellent, especially when benchmarked against our competitors. There is a lot of growth potential in other European markets so I think we should consider expanding our outlets outside the UK by franchising our brand name.'

Brownroll's finance director held that: 'What we need to do is consider what's best for our shareholders. Our two divisions operate in very different markets with different strategies. An international food and beverage company has approached us because it is interested in entering the UK coffee bar market, so we might be able to get a good price if we sell CP now. Alternatively we could demerge the two divisions and create two separate listed companies, then let the shareholders decide for themselves.'

Requirements

(a) Explain why Brownroll operates its business under two separate brand names. **(6 marks)**

(b) Using the data provided in the **Exhibit** and the other information available:

    (i) Compare the current market share and financial performance of Brownroll's two divisions
        (8 marks)

    (ii) Explain the usefulness of benchmarking for Brownroll and recommend two specific KPIs for each division that would help benchmark performance in relation to the wider industry
        (6 marks)

    (iii) Ignoring strategic considerations, evaluate the VL director's comment that 'the company's financial results would look much better without CP'. Justify any assumptions made and suggest any further internal information that would be useful. **(8 marks)**

(c) Evaluate the comments made at the Board meeting with respect to the future direction of the company. Use the following headings:

    • Sale of CP to fund expansion of VL

    • Demerger

    • Expansion of CP outside the UK by franchising **(12 marks)**

        (40 marks)

46   Dearman Cranes plc

Dearman Cranes Ltd (Dearman) is a family-owned business, based in Scotland, in the North of the UK. Dearman manufactures mobile cranes (i.e. heavy duty lifting equipment which is capable of being transported to and used at different locations) for use in a variety of construction-related industries. The company's managing director is Rob Price, the son of the original founder. Rob's sister, Jane Price, is research and development director.

Background of Scotland's industry

During the 19th and early 20th century Scotland was a world leader in heavy engineering and was most famous for its shipbuilding, undertaking around 50% of the world's production. A concentration of industry specialising in heavy engineering (including shipbuilding, marine engineering and aerospace engineering) developed in Scotland as a result of port facilities, a ready supply of raw materials from the local steel industry and access to a pool of skilled labour. This clustering was also driven by demand for ships and aero-engines from the defence industry.

By the 1960s however, lack of investment and innovation led to growing competition from countries like Japan and Germany, leading to a period of relative economic decline for Scotland and rapid de-industrialisation, as many shipbuilding sites in particular closed. Fortunately, in the late 1960s oil was discovered in the North Sea off Scotland, and by the early 1980s Scotland had become the centre of the UK's North Sea offshore oil/gas production and petrochemical industries. The petrochemical industry remains a major source of employment and income in Scotland today.

Company history

Dearman was established by Rob's and Jane's father, in the late 1940s, at a time when the construction industry in Scotland was booming and there was significant demand for mobile cranes for shipbuilding work. National and regional government support was also available in the form of grants and cheap loans.

The growth of the oil, gas and petrochemical industries meant that, during the late 20th century, demand for Dearman's mobile cranes continued to exceed supply, since most major operations in these industries require the use of heavy-lift cranes and associated equipment. Today Dearman supplies the most technologically advanced cranes to all the major petrochemical companies.

One issue for Dearman, however, is that the end of Scotland's traditional shipbuilding industry has led to many people working in service industries rather than manufacturing. There is now a shortage of relevant skilled manufacturing labour locally and as a result Dearman has recently brought in labour from Eastern European countries.

Mobile crane manufacturing industry

Historically the mobile crane manufacturing industry was dominated by large American and Japanese manufacturers. The rapid development of the Chinese economy has led to increased competition, as domestic manufacturers in China expand production capacity to cope with increased domestic demand and also seek to export. The Chinese market for mobile cranes now accounts for over 70% of global sales.

Dearman specialises in mobile cranes capable of lifting very heavy loads. It is a small player in the context of the overall industry but, within its market niche, it has developed a worldwide reputation for technological innovation, product quality and safe operation, and it has a loyal international customer base.

Product development

Dearman sells both new and refurbished mobile cranes. The product life of a typical crane is 20 years, although new product development can create technical obsolescence. Customers wishing to have the most advanced technology often trade in their existing cranes to obtain new models. The old cranes are then refurbished and sold in less technologically demanding markets or for lower specification work.

Product development and protection of the consequent intellectual property are key to success. The major international crane manufacturers spend at least 5% of annual revenue on research and development. Road regulations are a primary driver of product innovation. As regulation enforcement measures have strengthened, mobile crane designers have had to respond with lighter and more manoeuvrable machines. Regulations vary considerably between countries however; Japan, for example, has continued to accommodate cranes of heavier road weights than those allowable in Europe and North America.

Strategic options

Jane Price has suggested that the company considers a joint venture with a major Scottish university to establish an engineering research centre. This would allow Dearman to access world-class researchers and improve research outcomes. In exchange Dearman would provide industry placements for student engineers and the university would share in the commercial benefits of any resulting intellectual property.

At the same time Rob Price is considering an Alternative Investment Market (AIM) listing to raise more funds for research, but he has some concerns: 'Our accountant says that if we offer some shares to the public there are governance implications for the way we run the company, and for our responsibility to society and the environment. I thought we'd been running the company properly – I've always made sure we had processes in place that add value to the business, and attitudes that help build our reputation and ensure long-term success. If having a wider group of stakeholders means we aren't allowed to take the same risks, then I'm worried our results will suffer, even if we do have better access to finance for research.'

A customer dilemma

Dearman has recently received an e-mail from a customer, YXL Ltd, which is a major construction company. Dearman's board is concerned that this e-mail raises both legal and ethical issues for the company.

To: Rob Price
From: Jo Blunt, YXL Ltd
Date: 1 September 2011
Re: Crane modifications

As you know, YXL Ltd does a lot of work in the city of Abbeyville. As a result of two recent accidents, Abbeyville's local government has introduced new regulations which only permit mobile cranes to be used on the city's construction sites if they are fitted with an alarm and a shut-down device. The alarm is required to sound automatically if the crane load exceeds a specified safe capacity set by the local government. The alarm must also initiate an automatic shut-down of the crane's mechanism, in order to prevent dangerous movement or further overload.

Can you help us out? I'd like Dearman to upgrade all our cranes by fitting alarms and shut-down devices in order to comply with the new regulations. However at the same time I would like you to install a bypass switch. If the alarm sounds, the crane operator will be able to use the bypass switch to prevent the shut-down device automatically shutting the crane down. This will allow the crane to continue to operate with loads in excess of the new limits.

We've never had an accident so I don't see the need for these stricter rules and limits. They will simply slow the work down and reduce our margins. Fitting the alarms and devices should be enough to keep Abbeyville's local government happy, but the bypass switch will allow us to continue operating as we always have.

If you can do this for us at short notice, I will commit YXL Ltd to a contract to buy five new Dearman cranes in 2012.

Regards

Jo

Requirements

(a) Using Porter's diamond, explain the reasons for the clustering of the shipbuilding industry in Scotland. **(6 marks)**

(b) Identify the major risks arising from Dearman's current strategic position. **(6 marks)**

(c) Identify the benefits, for both Dearman and the university, of pursuing the joint engineering research venture, and any issues that might arise. **(8 marks)**

(d) Explain to Rob Price the impact that an AIM listing is likely to have on stakeholders' expectations of the company's governance and risk management. **(8 marks)**

(e) Discuss the issues which arise for Dearman from YXL Ltd's email request. **(5 marks)**

(33 marks)

47 Happy Valley Yoga Centre

Sam Bikram previously worked as the manager of a gym in a local hotel, but after being made redundant, she decided to train as a yoga instructor (yoga is a form of exercise intended to improve physical and mental well-being). Since then Sam has been running yoga classes on a self-employed basis, at a local health and recreation centre. These have proved very popular and Sam has developed a loyal client base. In view of the demand for her classes, Sam has now decided to set up her own yoga centre and has approached the firm of accountants where you work. Set out below is an extract of the e-mail your firm has received from Sam:

> I have found a great location for my Happy Valley Yoga Centre (HVYC), on the town's local business park, within easy walking distance of most of the office buildings, but with plenty of free parking for those who drive. Having talked to a number of my existing yoga clients who are employed in the business park, I intend to offer a programme of 45-minute classes which will allow them to attend in their breaks and lunch hours. Yoga will provide my clients with relief from the pressure of work and increase their sense of well-being. I am planning to run some free introductory sessions, and once people have tried yoga I am sure word-of-mouth will bring in more clients. I have also been talking to the human resources manager of one of the local businesses. He is keen to sponsor corporate membership for its employees, as part of a flexible benefits package.
>
> Whilst I was pretty good at my job, which involved managing people and being responsible for a budget, I know very little about setting up a business. Obviously I know it will take a while for HVYC to be successful but from an earnings point of view, I don't want to be any worse off than I am at the moment.
>
> In addition to annual rental of £15,000, which includes all costs of using the premises, I estimate that the set-up costs for the HVYC will be about £30,000. This will include the cost of fitting out the yoga studios and changing rooms, yoga equipment and inventory. Initially there will be myself and one other self-employed instructor, who will be paid on a per hour basis.
>
> I have about £20,000 of redundancy money and savings, so I have approached my local manager at Bourne Bank (BB) for a £10,000 loan. He tells me that all such finance has to be approved by BB's regional small business team. As a result I need to submit a business plan, using BB's standard template, with content structured under the following headings:
>
> • Executive summary
>
> • Detailed description of the business
>
> • Financial data
>
> • Supporting documents
>
> One thing I am not sure about is pricing – at the moment the leisure centre pays me £30 per hour for every class I run. This is irrespective of the number of attendees, who each pay the leisure centre £6 per one-hour class. Should I charge everyone the same price or is it worth offering a discount to encourage people to come back again?

Requirements

Produce a report for Sam which:

(a) (i) Explains the benefits for Sam of preparing a business plan **(4 marks)**

    (ii) Provides a brief overview of what Bourne Bank is likely to expect to see under each of the four headings of HVYC's business plan and why such content would be important to the bank. You are NOT required to draft the specific sections of the plan. **(8 marks)**

(b) Identifies and explains the key weaknesses and threats for HVYC that are likely to be of concern to Bourne Bank, setting out any factors that could mitigate these. **(7 marks)**

(c) Advises Sam on the factors to consider when deciding on a pricing policy (include any relevant supporting calculations). **(8 marks)**

(27 marks)

48 KoganAir

KoganAir plc (KoganAir) is a listed, low-cost airline based in the UK. It flies only on 'short-haul' routes within Europe.

Industry background

The passenger airline industry consists of two sectors, scheduled and non-scheduled. The scheduled sector operates to a published timetable. It includes long-established airlines (eg, British Airways, Emirates, Lufthansa) operating flights on both short-haul and intercontinental, 'long-haul' routes. It also includes low-cost airlines (eg, easyJet, Ryanair) which operate flights almost exclusively in the short-haul sector. The non-scheduled sector comprises all other air transport which, in respect of passenger transport, consists mainly of charter flights operated exclusively by holiday companies to take their customers to a particular holiday destination.

Competition is particularly intense in the European airline industry as many low-cost airlines operate in this geographical region, competing with the established airlines of each country. Historically, the established airlines dominated the industry due to their size, enabling economies of scale. They were also often government-subsidised, national carriers with monopolies over certain routes (ie. rights to operate flights between specified airports) and landing slots (ie. rights for a given period, allocated to an airline by an *airport*, to schedule *landings* or *departures*).

However, international deregulation of airlines (sometimes referred to as the 'open skies' policy) has meant lower barriers to entry, which has led to many new entrants to the industry in the past two decades. Reduced government regulation over permitted routes has allowed market forces to increase access to landing slots and to determine mergers between airlines and pricing.

Despite deregulation, there is not yet full open access to routes and landing slots, as established airlines have retained some of their historical dominance at key airports. However, newer airlines entering the industry have cost advantages over traditional airlines, for example by setting up lower cost wage agreements.

Many of the new entrants have been low-cost airlines which have penetrated the scheduled market by attracting individual customers with low fares, popular routes, frequent flights and ease of booking on-line directly with the airline. In the past 15 years, many of these entrants have become market leaders in terms of short-haul passenger numbers.

The airline market has experienced long-term growth but has, more recently, suffered a decline in revenues and passenger numbers as a result of the global economic downturn. In addition, airline profits have been affected by high and volatile fuel prices, which comprise a high proportion of total costs. Other concerns facing the industry are: security issues, regulatory intervention, specific taxes on airlines, industrial action and ecological issues.

Company history

KoganAir was established in 1996 and immediately acquired aircraft, along with the rights to landing slots and routes, from the liquidator of an insolvent airline. The fleet has since been expanded by both purchasing and leasing aircraft in approximately equal numbers.

As a low-cost airline, KoganAir quickly penetrated the scheduled market and has significantly increased its total number of passengers each year.

In order to offer low fares, KoganAir aims to operate at the lowest possible cost in its sector of the industry. It operates a 'no frills' service to passengers (eg, no free food, drinks or films during flights) and it also constantly seeks to minimise the turnaround time spent by its aircraft at airports in order to maximise utilisation.

KoganAir has continued to expand but the November 2011 management accounts, released internally last week, make clear that profits for the year ending 31 December 2011 will be significantly lower than last year. This decrease has been expected and profit warnings were given to financial markets in October 2011. However, since then, analysts have made increasing demands for more details, including information about how much of the fall in profit is due to industry-wide factors, and how much due to company-specific factors. A meeting of executive management was called to evaluate the issue in more detail and to determine an appropriate strategy for moving forward.

Executive management meeting

The *chief executive* summarised the situation: 'In many ways we have been successful but, despite increasing revenues in 2011, we have suffered a significant decrease in profits and I do not believe we have adequately analysed the underlying reasons for this. Fuel costs increased, on average, by 17% per tonne in 2011 compared with 2010, driven by the world price of oil, but fuel costs are only one factor. I need an analysis of our basic financial and operating data (**Exhibit 1**) to explain in more detail why profits have fallen. I am also worried about the impact of further increases in global oil prices next year, as I fear these could cause our fuel costs to rise by as much as 30% per tonne. I have provided some key working assumptions for 2012 (**Exhibit 2**) to enable some scenario planning to be carried out. The aim is to better evaluate our risks and improve our forecasts for 2012.'

The *marketing director* had a different issue: 'I know costs are important, but we need to consider our long-term positioning in the market. We entered the market in 1996 as a low-cost airline and, until recently, this approach has served us well, enabling us to penetrate the market and expand market share. Now, I think we need to reconsider our market positioning and pricing policies. Our margins are just too low to cover even modest cost increases. My proposal is to move to a mid-market position, sitting between the low-cost airlines and the higher priced, long-established airlines. My view is that we should increase passenger seat prices by, on average, 10% next year.'

Requirements

(a) As an external adviser, prepare a report to the board which:

   (i) Analyses the data in Exhibit 1 and the other information provided to explain, with supporting calculations, why the operating profit in 2010 is expected to turn into an operating loss in 2011, despite an increase in revenue generated; and **(15 marks)**

   (ii) Calculates the forecast operating profit for 2012 using the working assumptions in Exhibit 2. In addition, comment on the working assumptions and on the sensitivity of operating profit to fuel cost changes during 2012. (For this purpose ignore the suggestions of the marketing director.) **(9 marks)**

(b) Explain the key risks for KoganAir that arise from factors within the economic, ecological and legal sections of the PESTEL framework. For each risk identified, explain how it might be managed by KoganAir. (For this purpose ignore the suggestions of the marketing director.) **(10 marks)**

(c) Evaluate the suggestion of the marketing director, referring to Porter's generic strategies and any other appropriate strategic models. **(9 marks)**

(43 marks)

Exhibit 1 – Financial and operating data

	Note	2010 Actual	2011* Estimated	2012** Forecast	% change 2010 to 2011
Total revenue (£m)	(1)	313	337		+7.7%
Fuel costs (£m)		(76)	(96)		+26.3%
Operating costs of aircraft fleet (£m)	(2)	(25)	(26)		+4.0%
Other costs (£m)		(211)	(227)		+7.6%
Operating profit/(loss) (£m)		1	(12)		
Available passenger seats (millions)	(3)	6.4	7.0	7.7	
Actual passenger seats sold (millions)	(4)	5.4	6.0	6.7	
Load factor %	(5)	84.4%	85.7%	87.0%	
Number of aircraft		49	50	53	
Routes operated		62	64	66	
Available seat kilometres (ASK) (millions)	(6)	7,271	7,868	8,500	

* The estimates for 2011 have a high degree of certainty as there are only a few weeks remaining in the financial year.

** Forecasts for 2012 use the working assumptions in Exhibit 2.

Notes:

(1) Seat prices increased on average by 2% in 2011 compared with 2010.

(2) Comprises: (i) leasing costs and (ii) depreciation of owned aircraft.

(3) Available passenger seats are the total number of seats available for passengers to occupy on all flights in the year (across all routes and based on the total number of aircraft in operation).

(4) Actual passenger seats sold are the total number of passenger journeys (ie seats occupied) actually flown in the year.

(5) Number of actual passenger seats sold as a percentage of available passenger seats (ie (4) as a % of (3)).

(6) Available seat kilometres (ASK) is the number of available passenger seats, multiplied by the average kilometres per flight.

Exhibit 2 – Key working assumptions for 2012

In 2012, compared with 2011, the following are assumed:

- The cost of fuel per tonne will increase by 30%
- The average price per passenger seat will remain constant
- The amount of fuel used and revenue will vary approximately according to ASK
- The operating costs of the aircraft fleet will remain constant
- Other costs will increase by 3%

49 Universal Office Supplies

Universal Office Supplies plc (UOS) manufactures office equipment for businesses and the public sector.

Products

UOS manufactures two product lines: communication systems hardware (including videoconferencing, audio conferencing and data sharing equipment) and office furniture (including desks, chairs and storage cabinets).

UOS began manufacturing office furniture in 1990 as Office Supplies Ltd and added the communications systems hardware operation in 1995 on acquiring Universal Systems Ltd. After merging, the company became UOS and obtained a listing in 1997, setting up a single factory where each product line is manufactured in a separate section and operated independently. The product lines use very different methods of manufacturing. UOS has many clients who are customers for both product lines.

The communications systems hardware section aims to offer its customers the latest technology. Its products are differentiated from those of rivals by the nature and quality of the features provided. Jim Snape, head of communications systems manufacturing, is constantly changing the design and range of the products being offered in order to compete effectively in the market. New clients are frequently attracted to UOS by this product line, although existing clients are also lost to rivals on a regular basis. Prices are above the average for the sector.

The head of office furniture manufacturing is Pauline Parks. Office furniture is a mature industry so Pauline has tended to make few changes to manufacturing methods or to the nature of the final products. UOS produces mid-market office furniture and competes on price and service.

Current structure

UOS has three main operating divisions which are currently vertically integrated, being Procurement, Manufacturing and Marketing. There are also three support divisions: Research and Development (R&D), Finance and Human Resources.

By far the largest division is the Manufacturing Division, and the divisional head is Chen Li. This division has responsibility for manufacturing both product lines.

UOS attempts to maintain the autonomy of the operating divisions in its use of transfer pricing and by treating each operating division as a profit centre.

Inter-divisional transfer prices

The Procurement Division sources materials and parts according to the specifications provided by the Manufacturing Division. These materials and parts are sold by the Procurement Division to the Manufacturing Division at budgeted prices agreed between divisional heads at the beginning of the year. These prices include the budgeted direct cost of purchase, plus an allocation (based upon the value of the order) of the budgeted overheads of the Procurement Division. Any purchase discounts achieved by the Procurement Division therefore add to its divisional profit.

About 95% of the Manufacturing Division's output is sold to the Marketing Division at negotiated transfer prices which approximate to wholesale market prices. The remaining 5% of the output of the Manufacturing Division, consisting of both product lines, is sold directly to central government under a long-term contract. These items are not dealt with by the Marketing Division at all, but the prices in the government contract are used as a guide for the negotiated prices of all other transfers between the Manufacturing and Marketing Divisions.

The Marketing Division sells products to customers at the highest price it can obtain and also aims to sell, for both product lines, additional services such as installation and extended warranties. In recent years, however, the Marketing Division has struggled to break even.

The objectives of the R&D Division are product innovation and also cost reduction through improved efficiency. It is autonomous, initiating research projects that it believes will improve processes and products for communications systems hardware. Once a successful R&D project is completed, Jim Snape and Chen Li are informed and implementation of the development work is discussed. No charge is made by the R&D Division to the Manufacturing Division. No work is undertaken by the R&D Division in respect of the office furniture product line.

Proposed restructuring

The chief executive of UOS, Anna Tudor, wants to restructure the company after Chen Li retires next month. She proposes that, in future, divisionalisation should be on a product line basis, with two operational divisions – Communications and Furniture. Each division would have its own manufacturing, procurement and marketing sections.

For operational reasons the R&D Division would remain a separate cost centre and recharge its full costs, including overheads, to the Communications Division, which would initiate all R&D projects. The details, including costings, would be agreed between the two divisions before each R&D project commences.

The Human Resources and Finance Divisions would continue to operate as previously.

As part of the restructuring, Anna Tudor proposes changes in key positions which include the following:

	Current structure	Proposed structure
Chen Li	Head of Manufacturing Division	Retired
Andy Worrell	Head of Marketing Division	Head of Communications Division
Pauline Parks	Head of office furniture manufacturing	Head of Furniture Division
Jim Snape	Head of communications systems hardware manufacturing	Deputy head of Communications Division

Anna explained these changes to a fellow director. 'The communications systems hardware section has been underperforming and I largely blame Jim. He is a good engineer, but not a good manager. The focus has been too much on the technological features of the products and not enough on the needs of customers. I want to appoint Andy as head of the new Communications Division to address this problem. We need more of a market focus.'

Requirements

(a) In respect of the R&D function:

    (i)   Explain how it can contribute to the business strategy of UOS; and   **(6 marks)**

(ii) Compare and evaluate the current and the proposed structuring and recharging arrangements. **(7 marks)**

(b) Comment on the merits and problems of the company's current divisional structure in respect of the three operating divisions. Include an evaluation of performance measurement and transfer pricing arrangements. **(12 marks)**

(c) Evaluate the proposed restructuring of the three operating divisions. In so doing, suggest and justify the most appropriate method of divisional performance measurement under the proposed new structure. **(8 marks)**

(33 marks)

50 Conchester Theatre

The Conchester Theatre (CT) is a regional theatre, located 250 miles from London. It has a good artistic reputation and is operated on a not-for-profit basis.

History and background

CT was established in 1948 with a mission: 'To promote, in the local community around Conchester, traditional plays and musicals with high artistic merit. CT aims to break even financially'.

Plays are often the work of local playwrights, both current and those who lived in the region in previous centuries. Musicals are traditional and classical, as the theatre has avoided populist musicals in order to remain close to CT's mission. Each production of an individual play or musical normally has between one and seven performances.

Membership and demand

The theatre building is owned by the local government and leased to CT at a favourable rent of about half the full commercial rental. The theatre holds 800 people and is available for productions five days a week, 50 weeks a year, but it is not normally filled to capacity. It tries to stage many small productions (eg, with local drama groups, colleges and schools) in order to keep the theatre in use even when utilisation is well below capacity.

The local population, living within 20 miles of the theatre, is approximately 200,000 people.

CT has 1,500 Members who each make an annual donation of £30. The membership is restricted to 1,500 and there is a long waiting list. The Members elect the board of Trustees which runs CT. If CT has any debts it cannot pay, the individual Trustees are potentially personally liable.

CT also has a mailing list of Friends of the Conchester Theatre ('Friends') who receive information on the latest productions, but they do not need to make any donations. CT maintains a database of Friends with their details (address, age, profession, productions attended) so it can target mailings to those most likely to be interested in certain productions. There are about 4,000 people (including all Members) on this database.

Financing

The main source of revenue has always been sales of tickets, but ticket sales alone have never been sufficient to cover costs. Tickets all sell for £15 and there are currently no discounts available. Seats are sold to the public on a 'first come, first served' basis. However, Members are offered the opportunity to purchase up to four tickets for each production, one week before the general public. As a result, for popular performances, the Members sometimes take up the entire 800 seats available.

The other main source of revenue has been a government grant from the Arts Council. Following reductions in public spending by central government, in 2012 the grant will only be half its previous level, and will disappear altogether in 2013. A basic revenue summary is provided (**Exhibit**).

A dispute

The board of Trustees has met to discuss ways in which more revenue can be raised to compensate for the loss of the government grant.

The *chairman* started the meeting: 'We have had an offer of £125,000 in 2012 and £250,000 a year thereafter from a local businessman, Henry Strong. This would replace the government funding that we are losing. There are, however, some conditions attached, including that he sits on the board as a new Trustee. He would also have the right to choose ten productions each year and, as Mr Strong is a keen supporter of populist productions, we do not expect these to be the type of production we would normally put on. I do not like these conditions, but without this money we would start making large losses and we, as Trustees, could be personally liable. I think we should therefore accept Mr Strong's offer.'

The *treasurer* of CT objected strongly: 'Taking up the offer would be contrary to the historic culture of CT and the wishes of Members and other stakeholders. I do, however, recognise that we need to raise more revenue so I suggest we have more flexible pricing. We should stop charging £15 for every ticket and attempt to charge different prices, to different people, for different productions.'

Requirements

(a) Discuss the ethical issues for CT's board of Trustees arising from the offer from Henry Strong.

(8 marks)

(b) Explain each of the following:

    (i)   The purposes of market segmentation for CT;

    (ii)   How the CT database may be used to segment the market; and

    (iii) How different prices may be set by CT in order to increase revenue.   **(16 marks)**

(24 marks)

Exhibit – Revenue summary

Year	Ticket sales £000	Government grant £000	Membership donations £000
2009	1,380	250	45
2010	1,440	250	45
2011*	1,500	250	45

* 2011 data has been reliably estimated given that the year is nearly complete.

It is estimated CT will break even in 2011, but it incurred small operating losses in 2010 and 2009.

51 Debt Crisis Aid

Debt Crisis Aid (DCA) is a UK not-for-profit organisation working in the personal debt advice sector. It provides free support and assistance to individuals ('clients') with financial problems. DCA is **run by a Board of trustees, some of whom are chartered accountants.**

Background

A large number of commercial debt management companies exist which charge for the services they provide. However, for these companies there is often a conflict of interest: the debt management services which generate the greatest profit for the company are often not the best course of action for the client who is in debt. As a result, some commercial debt management companies have been criticised for not treating clients ethically and for charging high initial fees for services.

DCA was set up in 2005, with backing from the UK central government, to increase the availability and effectiveness of free, independent debt advice, with a focus on the best interests of the individual client. DCA's **core activities** include:

- Providing access to free, independent information and financial/legal advice for clients with debt problems (face-to-face, telephone and online)

- Helping clients to negotiate with lenders to reschedule loan repayments

- Providing education and training to clients to develop financial awareness and financial management skills

- Researching issues related to personal debt, the availability and cost of credit, and financial advice

DCA's main source of income is a fixed annual budget provided by the government. This is awarded in two separate elements: an amount to cover DCA's overheads (employment and administration costs) and a separate budget to pay for the cost of financial/legal advice which is provided to clients by approved external experts. DCA supplements government funding by raising donations from organisations which benefit from offering credit to consumers, including a number of large retailers, banks and building societies.

As a publicly-funded organisation, DCA must deliver services efficiently within budget. The government sets annual targets which include: the number of clients DCA helps each year; how quickly and successfully those clients are helped; and how efficiently the budget has been managed. Success is measured using a 'balanced scorecard' approach, reporting against key performance indicators.

Operations

DCA has a small number of its own employees, who are located at 12 regional offices, each operating independently. When a prospective client approaches a DCA regional office, an employee undertakes an initial interview to assess the client's situation. The employee then refers the client to an approved external expert (an accountant and/or solicitor) who provides the relevant financial/legal advice. The expert then invoices the DCA regional office for the services provided.

Accountants and solicitors who wish to undertake work as approved external experts on behalf of a DCA regional office are required to complete and submit an Approved Expert Questionnaire, together with supporting evidence, which is assessed by local DCA employees. To be approved, experts must demonstrate that they meet quality standards, are capable of delivering results that benefit clients and will make effective use of public money. Once accepted there is no on-going review process, so an expert can remain on the Approved Expert List indefinitely.

DCA's policy states that advice which is likely to cost under £2,000 should be allocated to the most appropriate approved expert at the discretion of the DCA employee. In all other cases at least two competitive quotes from persons on the Approved Expert List must be obtained. A sole practitioner expert, or firm of experts, cannot carry out more than 10% of the total advice work (by value) provided by a DCA regional office in any financial year.

UK industry environment

DCA has to work within a changing environment and it can be difficult to predict demand for debt advice services. The number of clients seeking advice fluctuates with the performance of the economy, interest rates and the cost of credit.

In the last decade, there has been a significant increase in consumer spending on communications and technology, and on leisure and recreation. Changes in technology have also led to increasing use of the internet for financial transactions and the purchase of goods and services. There has been a general trend of decreasing savings and increased spending, with households using credit cards and other forms of credit to increase their expenditure. The government is keen to encourage sustainable lending and borrowing and has introduced regulations to ensure that consumer credit markets operate in a way which is fair.

Future plans

DCA's core budget is under pressure due to government funding cuts. In addition, from 2012 DCA is subject to an annual cost and quality compliance audit. To demonstrate that they can increase efficiency and reduce costs, DCA's trustees have decided to create a central shared service centre (SSC). The SSC will undertake the screening of all professionals wishing to become approved experts and will handle all payments to experts - activities which are currently conducted on a regional office basis. It will also introduce procedures for monitoring levels of service quality from experts.

DCA will retain a small number of employees at each regional office and the remaining employees will be asked to apply for roles at the new SSC. It is envisaged that approximately 50% of the current workforce will be made redundant.

To assist with the proposed changes DCA plans to introduce a new information system including a central database. This will allow Approved Expert Questionnaires to be submitted and assessed online; it will also allow experts to submit invoices for payment electronically. Finally it will gather the information required for the government's balanced scorecard performance measurement reporting system and the cost and quality compliance audit.

The trustees of DCA have recently been approached by Mary Bourne, the managing partner of a national chain of solicitors, Longparish LLP. Not all Longparish offices are on DCA's current Approved Expert List. Mary has suggested to the trustees that they would be able to save time and money if, in future, all DCA offices allocated legal advice work under £2,000 directly to her firm. In return, Longparish would produce a single consolidated monthly invoice for all work undertaken.

Requirements

(a) Explain the political, economic and social factors that DCA's trustees need to take into account when developing strategy.   **(8 marks)**

(b) Using Mendelow's power-interest matrix, identify and justify the position of the following stakeholder groups for DCA:

  - UK government
  - External experts
  - Clients   **(8 marks)**

(c) (i)   Discuss the advantages and disadvantages of the trustees' plans to centralise shared services.
                                                                                         (7 marks)

  (ii) Assuming that the shared service centre (SSC) goes ahead, explain how the trustees should manage the change. In your answer you should refer to change management models where appropriate.   **(8 marks)**

(d) Explain what outputs will be required from the information system to enable DCA to measure performance.   **(7 marks)**

(e) Discuss the ethical and public sector governance issues arising from Mary Bourne's proposal to the trustees.   **(6 marks)**

                                                                                         (44 marks)

52 Bootwear

Bootwear plc (Bootwear), a company listed on the London Stock Exchange, specialises in the production and sale of high quality, waterproof protective footwear (boots and shoes), originally designed for use by outdoor workers.

Company information

Bootwear products are sold through its own stores and also via specialist outdoor retailers which sell clothing and equipment for a range of outdoor sports and activities. Over 90% of people who buy Bootwear footwear are male, the majority of whom are aged 25-35.

Bootwear places great emphasis on corporate social responsibility and sustainable business practices. The company is publicly committed to reducing its environmental impact.

Future strategic options

Bootwear markets its products as 'Footwear for life', reflecting the fact that its boots and shoes are functional and long-lasting and do not need to be replaced frequently. Consequently, although the business is profitable, Bootwear needs to expand its customer base if the business is to grow. It is currently considering two mutually-exclusive acquisition targets, BHC Ltd (BHC) and MK Ltd (MK):

- BHC is an online retailer of premium-priced sports-style fashion clothing for males and females. Since its launch in 2005, BHC has created a perception of a luxury lifestyle brand, based on its classic British heritage. The clothes are targeted at affluent young people, aged 18-25, interested in traditional sporting and country pursuits such as polo, hunting, rugby and rowing. BHC specialises in a fast turnover of items. Each season a new range of products is launched, based on existing designs, but using different colours and fabrics. Marketing is undertaken via its monthly lifestyle magazine 'BHC Life' and the use of social network sites which promote the latest 'must-have' items to BHC's global customers. BHC has grown rapidly because its wealthy target market does not appear to have been significantly affected by the economic downturn. However it has been criticised in the newspapers for being 'an over-priced disposable-fashion brand'. BHC's majority shareholder is rumoured to be considering benefiting from the company's success by selling some, or all, of her investment.

- MK is an established family company which produces a wide range of climbing equipment, including a small range of clothing for mountaineering. MK products are sold in the UK to specialist climbing shops. It also has a long-term contract to supply MK branded goods to a well-known outdoor retailer, Whiteout plc (Whiteout), which operates a chain of stores throughout the UK. MK invests heavily in marketing by sponsoring famous climbers. Its brand is recognised in the climbing world for its technical attributes and safety and, as a result, it has a loyal customer base. MK's products are designed in-house but manufacturing has been outsourced to various suppliers in Asia. MK has an ethical procurement policy and insists on contracts that ensure fair terms and appropriate working conditions for suppliers and their employees. This means that its cost base is higher than that of competitors which creates pressure on margins, especially when there are adverse movements in exchange rates. MK's senior management team are all family members, some of whom are hoping to retire soon, although there is no succession plan in place.

Bootwear is currently conducting a preliminary appraisal of the potential targets. It has not yet entered discussions with either company regarding the price or the form of consideration, should it decide to go ahead with an acquisition.

Exhibit

Financial information for all companies for the year ended 31 December 2011 is set out below:

	Bootwear £'000	BHC £'000	MK £'000
Revenue	23,509	7,028	12,109
Cost of sales	15,385	3,722	9,410
Gross profit	8,124	3,306	2,699
Operating expenses	5,227	1,548	2,256
Operating profit	2,897	1,758	443
Interest	235	54	88
Profit before tax	2,662	1,704	355
Net assets	9,915	2,943	3,903
Debt/Equity	46%	21%	25%
Revenue growth 2010-2011	6%	18%	4%

Requirements

You are a consultant assisting Bootwear with the preliminary appraisal of the acquisition targets.

Using the data in the Exhibit and the other information provided, prepare a report for the board which compares the two potential target companies, clearly identifying any further information required.

Use the following headings in your report:

(a) Strategic fit   **(10 marks)**

(b) Financial performance and other relevant financial issues   **(14 marks)**

(c) Future risks   **(6 marks)**

(d) Preliminary conclusions and recommendations   **(4 marks)**

                                                                                                              (34 marks)

53 Vicaro Ltd

Vicaro Ltd (Vicaro) is a small research and development company which was set up in India by a group of local entrepreneurs. Vicaro develops new business ideas which it normally commercialises by granting licences to other companies to use its intellectual property within India and the rest of Asia. Vicaro's latest development is aimed at making a low-cost personal computer (PC) accessible for the first time to the domestic Indian population.

PC industry background

The PC industry emerged from the market for mainframe computers - large, costly systems owned and used by big corporations. The invention of the microprocessor in 1971 led to the creation of much smaller computers targeted at individuals.

Early PC owners were computer technicians and enthusiasts, who purchased their PC as a kit of electrical components from which they built their own desktop machine.

The development of colour graphics in the 1980s made it easier for non-technical users to work with PCs. This created a market for ready-assembled desktop PCs with associated devices such as a keyboard, monitor, disk drive and printer. Product standardisation gave rise to economies of scale for the manufacturers and lowered the cost so PCs were an affordable consumer good, popular for domestic as well as business use.

In the late 1980s the laptop PC was developed, integrating all the components of a desktop PC into a single portable unit. The advent of the internet in the 1990s made PCs in their various forms a household item, providing instant access to information. In 1977 48,000 PCs were sold worldwide, increasing to over 100 million by 2001. This growth continues: in 2010, the number of PCs in use worldwide was 1.4 billion, forecast to reach 2 billion by 2015.

Laptops have become increasingly popular for both business and personal use and since 2008 the sale of laptops has exceeded that of desktops. Within the last decade, the popularity of email, social networking, e-commerce and e-reading has given rise to the development of even smaller PCs and recently the introduction of 'tablet' PCs. A tablet is a hand-held, touch-screen PC, larger than a mobile phone but smaller than a laptop. There has also been increased competition for PCs from the smartphone – a sophisticated mobile phone with advanced computing capability and internet connectivity, which can also operate as a camera and portable media player.

The tablet market is currently dominated by one multi-national company, which sold 14.8 million units in 2010 when it launched its tablet (over 75% in volume of worldwide tablet sales). Industry predictions suggest that over 25 million people will buy tablets instead of laptops during 2012. Despite a number of other competitors entering the market in the last year, the tablet remains a premium-priced product.

The Sibal

Aware that the price of PCs is prohibitive for a large proportion of the domestic Indian population, Vicaro has recently developed a prototype of a low-cost touch-screen tablet ('the Sibal'). The Sibal has an on-screen keyboard, word processor, and internet browser. It runs on solar power. There is no need to download and install applications on the Sibal, as all processing and storage is maintained remotely on a server accessed via the internet.

Due to its limited specification and lack of internal memory, the Sibal will cost less than 15% of the price of other tablets currently on the market. Initial market research in India suggests that high demand for the Sibal is likely for family and educational use due to its cheap purchase price, low running costs and ease of operation.

In order to make production viable, economies of scale are required to reduce costs. Vicaro is currently considering choosing one of the following options for the financing and commercial development of the Sibal:

(1) Approach a global PC manufacturer which does not currently have its own tablet with a view to a joint venture. Vicaro would provide the intellectual property in exchange for access to the partner's manufacturing and distribution facilities.

(2) Exploit the intellectual property rights by granting a licence to use the technology to those wishing to manufacture and sell the tablet in India and the rest of Asia.

(3) Create a new company. Finance would be sought from private investors. The Indian government would also be approached for sponsorship on the basis that the Sibal could contribute to education and to the growth of the Indian economy.

Requirements

(a) With reference to the industry and product life-cycle models, explain how the personal computer (PC) industry has evolved. **(8 marks)**

(b) Explain the issues that Vicaro needs to consider when choosing the appropriate method of commercial development for the Sibal.

Use the following headings:

- Resources
- Control
- Risks and returns **(14 marks)**

(22 marks)

54 Palladium Printing

Palladium Printing Ltd (PP) is a printing company which produces high quality printed products for business customers.

The UK printing industry

Scope and structure

The UK printing industry generates about £10,100 million in annual revenues. It is highly fragmented comprising almost 14,000 companies, with approximately 61% of these having annual revenues of less than £250,000. At the other extreme, a few very large companies generate annual revenues in the range of £100 million to £500 million.

Products and markets

Printed products take many different forms, including advertising literature, tickets, business stationery, labels, brochures, newspapers, magazines and books. Customers are also diverse, encompassing private sector businesses, public sector organisations, charities and individuals. Contracts with customers vary significantly in nature and size. These range from large annual contracts to one-off jobs. Some printing companies provide related services, such as binding (of books and magazines) and graphic design.

Imports and exports

UK printing companies are major exporters to the rest of Europe. However, the UK market is also served by low-cost imports for some types of printed product, particularly from large-scale, efficient, low-cost printing companies located in developing economies.

Technology and processes

There are two main types of printing process in use in the industry – digital printing and lithographic ('litho') printing. Smaller printing companies use only digital printing. Larger printing companies use both processes.

With digital printing, digitally recorded data and images are stored, reorganised and adapted on computer, then transferred to a printing machine and printed onto paper, plastics, metal and various other materials. Digital printing has a relatively high average cost per page, but set-up costs of the printing machines are low for each print run, and turnaround times from order to delivery are quick, so printing short or medium-sized print runs at short notice ('on-demand printing') is cost-effective. The initial capital cost of the computers and printing machines is relatively low. With some digital printing systems, printed products can be customised for each item printed.

Litho printing is suitable for long, standardised print runs and for printing of items with complex or very high quality features such as metallic ink on greetings cards. It requires significant capital investment in complex printing presses. Litho printing can have a low cost per page for long print runs, however there is significant time and cost in setting up a printing press for each print run. Labour costs for litho printing are also high because of its highly skilled nature. With litho printing, each item produced within a print run is identical.

Suppliers

The major raw material input for print companies is paper. Paper prices rose by an average of 15% at the beginning of 2011. This was because paper mills suffered an increase in energy and transportation costs which were passed on, in full, to printing companies. There are over 50 major paper manufacturers operating in Europe and they tend to be large, highly mechanised companies.

Industry profitability

The profitability of the UK printing industry has fallen significantly in recent years and, as a consequence, approximately 16% of UK printing companies ceased to trade in 2011. Most of these were small companies. One cause has been the recession, whereby customers have put pressure on prices and reduced the volumes demanded (ie, the number of print runs, the length of print runs and also the number of pages of each printed product). The other major cause has been the growth of electronic communication, including the internet, e-books, email and other on-line forms of media. Conversely, however, technology has also been a means of lowering costs within the printing industry (eg, digital printing) and of improving the quality and flexibility of printed products.

There has been a short-term boost in volumes as a result of the 2012 London Olympics but, conversely, there has been a trend towards reducing paper communication for environmental and sustainability reasons.

Company background

PP uses only digital printing. For a minority of jobs, PP also provides the add-on service of graphic design, whereby PP's graphic designers help customers produce the required images for printing.

PP aims to produce at the upper end of digital printing quality, to offer on-demand printing and to give a customised service that meets individual customer needs. PP cannot compete on a cost basis with litho printing companies for long-term contracts with long print runs, so currently it focuses on medium-sized, one-off jobs in the business market.

PP has performed poorly in recent years, although demand improved in 2012. The chief executive, John Johnson, summarised the situation at a recent board meeting. 'Quite frankly, we are struggling to compete. We are being squeezed between the very small local printing companies for short print runs, and the major litho printing companies for long print runs. Price competition is severe and margins have fallen.'

Strategic review

A board meeting was called to assess PP's current position and initiate a strategic review.

The finance director commenced the meeting: 'I have provided some financial and operating data (**Exhibit 1** on pages 4 and 5) and it is clear to me that our graphic design activities should be closed. We need to be ruthless if we are to survive.'

The technology director offered an alternative view: 'We need to offer a service that better meets the needs of customers. There is new software and supporting technology available, variable data printing (VDP). This would let us use client databases to provide a customised service for them by personalising every item printed, even on longer print runs.

'For example, one of our customers is a department store which currently sends out a 200-page brochure to its customers. The VDP software would enable us to print only the pages which are relevant to each customer's interests, and we can print each customer's name on each brochure.'

The marketing director, Haraj Harris, was enthusiastic about combining VDP with PP's printing machines. 'This is just what we need. I am negotiating a possible three-year contract with Southern University (SU) which would be a large contract for us.

'SU currently sends 20,000 full prospectuses out each year to students who are considering applying to study at the university. The full prospectus describes every academic course SU offers. However, most potential applicants are interested in only two or three of those courses. Also, they complete a prospectus request form with personal details (eg courses considered, home address, interests, gender) which are then held by SU on a database.

'SU usually places the annual print run with a large litho printing company, so we cannot compete on cost under the current arrangements. However, using VDP, combined with our ability to print on demand, may help as we could print personalised mini-prospectuses which contain only material that is relevant to each potential applicant. I have provided some data on the potential SU deal (**Exhibit 2** on page 5).'

Requirements

(a) Evaluate the competitive forces in the UK printing industry using Porter's Five Forces model.

(10 marks)

(b) Using the data in Exhibit 1 and the other information provided, analyse and explain the performance of PP in each of the accounting periods from 1 January 2010 to 30 June 2012.

(15 marks)

(c) Draft a letter to SU for Haraj Harris which explains the benefits to the university of changing to PP for the printing of mini-prospectuses, instead of using a litho printing company for the printing of full prospectuses. You may assume that PP will make use of VDP and that SU has a database available of details from potential applicants. **(8 marks)**

(d) With respect to PP's strategic review:

    (i) Determine the break-even price per mini-prospectus for PP for the SU contract. (Ignore the time value of money.)

    (ii) Explain the factors that PP should consider in determining whether it should close the graphic design section. **(12 marks)**

(45 marks)

Exhibit 1 – Financial and operating data

	Notes	Year to 31 December 2010	Year to 31 December 2011	Estimate for six months to 30 June 2012
Financial data:		£	£	£
Revenue:				
Printing	1	2,400,000	2,500,000	1,330,000
Graphic design	2	60,000	60,000	30,000
Total revenue		2,460,000	2,560,000	1,360,000
Fixed operating costs	3	(800,000)	(800,000)	(400,000)
Variable operating costs:				
Employee costs		(600,000)	(600,000)	(300,000)
Paper		(790,000)	(845,000)	(460,000)
Other		(190,000)	(245,000)	(160,000)
Operating profit		80,000	70,000	40,000

	Notes	Year to 31 December 2010	Year to 31 December 2011	Estimate for six months to 30 June 2012
Other operating data:				
Employees	4	30	30	30
Print runs completed		1,200	1,300	800
Pages printed (in millions)		65	68	42

Note 1 – *Printing revenue*
The London Olympic Games added significantly to revenue in the year ended 31 December 2011 and in the six months to 30 June 2012, but no reliable estimates can be made to measure this effect as many jobs were only indirectly related to the Olympic Games. No further revenues are likely to arise from the Olympic Games after 30 June 2012.

Note 2 – *Graphic design revenue*
Graphic design work is performed for a minority of customers and always as part of a particular print run. In these cases, a general formula is applied that graphic design revenue is 10% of the total amount charged for the print run.

Note 3 – *Fixed operating costs*
Fixed operating costs include premises and machine costs and are incurred on a time basis. They have been reasonably consistent per month over recent years.

Note 4 – *Employees*

Three employees work in the graphic design department.

Exhibit 2 – Data on the potential SU contract

The contract with SU would be for three years.

In the past, full prospectuses of over 200 pages were all identical and were printed in August each year in one long print run of 20,000 units. If the contract were to be awarded to PP it would use VDP and would produce only personalised mini-prospectuses of a fairly standard length (around 40 pages). Printing would take place once a month over the period August to December. Each month, SU would provide a database of potential applicants' personal and academic details one week prior to printing to enable the latest data to be incorporated.

SU estimates that 20,000 mini-prospectuses will be required in 2012. Due to SU's expansion and improving reputation it will require 32,000 mini-prospectuses in 2013 and 35,000 in 2014.

Total variable operating costs will be £1.60 per mini-prospectus. Incremental fixed operating costs for this contract will be £11,600 per year.

SU requires the price it pays per mini-prospectus to be the same over the whole of the three-year contract.

55 Flambard Foods

Flambard Foods plc (FF) is a manufacturer and retailer of frozen ready-made meals.

Company history and operations

FF was established by Brendan Bantam in 1988. He is still the main shareholder and chief executive.

Ingredients used to make the meals, including vegetables, dairy products, fish and meat, are bulk purchased by FF from the lowest cost source within Europe. This is normally from large, low-cost farms in Eastern Europe, which deliver directly to the FF factory in the UK. The quality of ingredients is the minimum acceptable to consumers. The range of ingredients is small to keep logistical processes simple and distribution costs low.

Ingredients are prepared and cooked by FF to create ready-made meals (for example, chicken with rice). These are then packaged and frozen. Each is a complete meal and the consumer has no need to carry out any food preparation beyond heating the meal.

FF employs mainly unskilled workers at the legal minimum wage. Factory operating rules are strictly applied to employees in order to maximise labour efficiency and comply with health and safety laws. Staff turnover is high, but there is significant local unemployment. This means that FF can always employ new staff at the legal minimum wage.

Brendan personally maintains tight operational and financial controls over the business to minimise all costs.

The production process is automated, but simple. A small range of meals is manufactured so production runs are long and operating efficiency is high. Manufacturing scheduling is in regular weekly production cycles, so ordering of ingredients is predictable and can be planned weeks in advance. The limited product range facilitates a simple, but efficient, inventory control system. With only a few suppliers, control of accounts payable is a very basic operation.

Once frozen, the meals are stored in a large freezer warehouse next to the factory. FF has its own fleet of 10 lorries, which have freezer facilities and are in use 24 hours a day, five days each week. This fleet collects the frozen meals in cartons from the warehouse and distributes them to FF's chain of 200 shops located throughout the UK.

FF shops currently only sell FF frozen ready-made meals. Prices undercut almost all rivals in the sector. There are no credit sales.

The industry background

The ready-made meals industry has two sectors: frozen meals and chilled meals. The chilled meals sector comprises about 65% of the UK ready-made meals market and is growing. The frozen meals sector makes up the remainder and is declining.

Chilled meals are stored at temperatures just above zero, whereas frozen meals are stored at around minus 20 degrees Celsius. As a result, chilled meals are higher quality than frozen meals, but have a higher price. Chilled meals can be displayed in shop fridges for only a few days before being discarded if unsold, whereas frozen meals can be displayed in shop freezers for months.

Profit margins are much higher for ready-made meals than they are for produce sold in shops as raw ingredients. Margins are higher for chilled meals than for frozen meals.

In recent months, supermarkets have reduced the prices of their chilled meals and increased marketing expenditure to boost volumes. This has put pressure on the frozen meals sector.

A new venture

While FF remains profitable, sales have fallen across the frozen ready-made meals sector.

Brendan has therefore put a proposal to the FF board that the company should enter the chilled ready-made meals sector. He summarised his proposal:

'The chilled meals market is growing, while the frozen meals market is declining. We can no longer be excluded from the chilled meals market. There are some problems though. FF's existing operations are suitable for frozen meals, not chilled ones, so we will need capital investment in chilled storage and transport alongside our existing frozen facilities. However, most production processes, prior to freezing or chilling, will be common to both types of product.

'Also, if we try to copy our competitors we will merely be seen as a late entrant. I think we should focus on a theme of food by geographical origin. The market is already well served by meals in Italian, Chinese and Indian cooking styles, including some of our own frozen meals.

'My idea is therefore to produce chilled meals in cooking styles where existing supply is currently limited. I favour Polish, Lebanese and Vietnamese cooking styles. These have a growing reputation in restaurants, but they do not have much presence on the chilled meals shelves of supermarkets. I would like to sell them in our existing shops alongside our frozen meals.

'My problem is that whilst I believe they will sell, I cannot be sure how many and at what price.'

Requirements

(a) Based on the existing frozen meals operation and ignoring the proposed new venture:

    (i) Prepare a value chain diagram for FF. Include brief notes describing each section of the diagram; and

    (ii) Briefly explain the FF value chain and describe how FF creates value.   **(14 marks)**

(b) Explain the factors that the FF board should consider before deciding whether to enter the chilled ready-made meals market. For this purpose, ignore the specific types of cooking style that Brendan has suggested.   **(10 marks)**

(c) Assuming that FF decides to enter the chilled meals market, describe the market research that should be undertaken to determine whether FF should produce the meals in the three types of cooking style suggested by Brendan.   **(8 marks)**

                                                 (32 marks)

56   Keeler Kinetics

Keeler Kinetics plc (KK) is an AIM listed company which manufactures small electrical appliances for use by consumers.

Company history

KK was listed on AIM in 2011 when it was spun off from a large multinational electronic company, Vaart Inc (Vaart). Until then, KK had been a separate division within Vaart, manufacturing small electrical appliances. All the appliances had the Keeler brand and KK has retained this brand name.

KK's product range has 12 lines including vacuum cleaners, blenders, toasters and irons.

Introducing the new business model

In a presentation to financial analysts shortly after the establishment of KK in early 2011, the new chief executive, Michael George, had summarised the changes necessary at that time as follows:

'It is not possible to continue to operate leading edge technology as we did when we were part of Vaart. The new business model is therefore to aim only to achieve basic consumer acceptability in terms of technical features. Typically, KK will introduce new technology about two years after the market leaders, when it is cheaper, well-established and has become a consumer expectation.

'Instead of offering the latest technology to consumers, KK will produce attractive designs in terms of shapes, materials and colours for all products, helped by engaging a world-leading firm of designers from Milan.

'This change in business strategy will require changes in our employees' skills. We need some voluntary redundancies to reduce the size of the workforce and reduce costs. However, lower costs and the absence of the latest technology should not mean a poor quality product. I want KK to be a producer of well-designed, good quality products.

'This new business strategy is likely to take some time to be recognised in the market and therefore operating losses may occur up to 2012 and for some time afterwards. Nevertheless, the board believes this is the right strategy which will eventually produce the right results.'

Monitoring the strategy

Since early 2012, when a loss was announced for 2011, there has been some adverse comment by analysts about the operating losses and scepticism about the time it will take before generating a profit. Analysts want to know how KK is measuring success in the meantime.

Michael responded at a board meeting in May 2012: 'We need to make sure that we have the right strategy even though we are not making any profit. I need relevant financial and non-financial measures to evaluate and manage KK's performance.'

An ethical issue

A new employee, Jack Eccles, joined KK having worked as an independent business adviser to the electrical appliances industry. On his computer at home, Jack has detailed files containing the KPIs (key performance indicators) used by several companies he advised which are rivals of KK. He also has data on the actual performance achieved in respect of these measures. Jack has offered to copy these files for KK management to help them set appropriate benchmarks. Alternatively, he has offered to join the KK team in setting KPIs, using his experience of rivals' businesses.

Requirements

(a) Prepare a Balanced Scorecard for KK which can be used to monitor its new business strategy. Explain why each of the four perspectives within this scorecard is important to KK and why the KPIs for each perspective are important for monitoring performance. **(16 marks)**

(b) Assess the ethical implications for KK of accepting either of the offers from Jack. **(7 marks)**

(23 marks)

57 Bigville Council

Bigville Council (the Council) is the local government body responsible for providing community services to residents of Bigville, a large city in the UK. The Council is financed by central government, together with local taxes paid by residents and businesses in the area. Bigville is relatively strong economically. It has a respected university and is well-known as both a business and tourist destination. Around 500,000 people live and/or work in Bigville.

Demand for a community stadium

Bigville's professional rugby club leases its current sports stadium from the Council. As a result of recent success, the club is attracting large crowds to matches played at its stadium (home matches) and this stadium is at full capacity. Aware that Bigville's professional football club is also in need of a new stadium, the rugby club has asked the Council to consider the creation of a council-owned community stadium on a new site, with a shared pitch suitable for both rugby and football. It would also incorporate additional sports facilities which would be available for use by schools, colleges, clubs and other community groups throughout the year. On days when there are no home matches for either rugby or football teams the stadium could be used for a range of other commercial and social events (concerts, weddings, etc).

In the UK, football clubs compete in a series of hierarchical leagues, with the top clubs being promoted to the league above at the end of the playing season and the bottom clubs being relegated to the league below. The same system applies to rugby.

The attendance (number of people attending home matches at the club's stadium) and financial performance of any club is heavily dependent on its team's performance in the league. Bigville's two clubs currently play home matches on different days (football on Saturdays and rugby on Sundays) and their seasons overlap. The football season runs from August through to April, and the rugby season runs from February to September. Both clubs have a strong support base but have lower attendance than their respective league competitors due to restricted capacity. Neither stadium has the scope to be extended.

A new stadium would benefit the two clubs by allowing for increased attendance, which generates revenue from ticket sales, refreshments and merchandising. The improvement in facilities would increase the scope to raise some ticket prices by offering premium seating. For this reason, if the shared stadium goes ahead, the rugby and football clubs have pledged to make initial contributions of £1 million and £2 million respectively towards the capital cost.

Council's strategic priorities

The Council has recently stated publicly that its strategic priorities are as follows:

- To maintain and develop Bigville's successful economy and provide suitable employment opportunities for residents

- To ensure accessible opportunities for all to engage in culture, leisure and recreational activity

- To promote and provide support for local people to make healthy lifestyle choices

- To create, enhance and maintain cleaner, safer and more sustainable environments

The Council believes that a new community stadium would potentially assist in meeting some of these aims. It is therefore making a preliminary assessment of the business case for the community stadium. If this indicates viability, a more detailed feasibility study and financial analysis will be undertaken. The vision is to create a stadium with 6,000 seats, which both the football and rugby clubs will use for home matches and training.

The new stadium will incorporate a community sports centre with an athletics track and all-weather sports pitches. There is an option to enhance the stadium by adding a second level, which could be used commercially as a conference and events centre.

The Council has identified three criteria which it will use to assess the business case:

(a) Ability to raise finance for the initial capital investment

(b) Whether it is a commercially sustainable venture

(c) Alignment with the Council's overall strategic priorities

Council-owned land has already been identified as a suitable site for the stadium. This land is expected to meet the necessary planning criteria. The stadium would be partly sunk into the ground to limit noise problems, reduce the impact on the landscape and maximise environmental efficiency.

Capital costs and financial projections

The new stadium would be partly funded by the sale of the council-owned land on which the rugby club's current stadium stands. If sold to a developer for the construction of a retail site, this land would be expected to realise in the region of £6 million. Initial research suggests that some additional public sector funding would be available in the form of central government grants, provided certain criteria are fulfilled by the new stadium. These criteria include whether it can be demonstrated that the stadium actively increases community participation in sports, creates additional employment or contributes to the sustainability of the local environment. A sponsorship deal would be sought with a large credit card company, Finanex plc, whose headquarters are in Bigville and which is Bigville's largest private sector employer. The company has indicated that it would be prepared to pay an initial £1 million for the stadium to be named 'The Finanex Stadium', and then it would also contribute an amount annually for the right to display its company logos on the exterior and interior of the stadium.

The stadium is likely to cost a total of £10 million to construct. This comprises £6.75 million for the basic stadium and £3.25 million for the community sports facilities. An enhanced stadium, with an additional second level for conference and events facilities, would cost a further £1.1 million. Any shortfall in funding would need to come from the Council's cash reserves and /or debt finance. The Council's strategy department has researched similar community stadia funded by other councils and has produced some initial forecasts for the potential costs and revenue streams associated with the new stadium. These are set out in **Exhibits 1 and 2**.

Management and operation

If the new stadium goes ahead as planned, it will be owned by the Council and operated by a stadium management company (SMC) created as a joint venture between the Council and the two sports clubs. The Council will lease the stadium to SMC, which will then retain any profits or losses made from its operation. The Council, the football club and the rugby club will each have two directors on the board of SMC, although the Council will have a casting vote on certain specified issues. The Council is keen to ensure that it minimises its level of risk and, in particular, the financial liability to which it is exposed. It also wants to retain the ability to control the governance of SMC and the pricing, events scheduling and promotion of the stadium.

Exhibit 1: Forecast annual match revenues and costs for new stadium

	Number of home matches	Expected attendance per match	Total annual attendance	Total annual revenue	Total annual contribution	Traceable annual fixed operating costs	Forecast annual profit/ (loss)
	Note (i)	Notes (ii) & (iii)		Note (iv)			
Football	25	3,200	80,000	£800,000	£640,000	(£644,000)	(£4,000)
Rugby	15	3,000	45,000	£450,000	£270,000	(£214,000)	£56,000

Notes to Exhibit 1:

(i) Based on the average number of home matches played last season in each club's existing stadium. This can increase if a club is successful in various additional competitions which are run during the season.

(ii) Initial estimate of expected future attendance provided to the Council by each club, on the basis that it increases its capacity by moving to the new stadium and remains playing within its existing competitive league.

(iii) The average home match attendance at each club's current stadium is: football: 2,863; rugby: 2,234. Comparable data for similar clubs are as follows:

	Average attendance per match for typical club in:		
	League below	Existing league	League above
Football	1,800	3,050	5,000
Rugby	1,900	2,840	4,000

(iv) Based on expected average total spend per visitor on tickets, refreshments and merchandising.

Exhibit 2: Forecast annual non-match revenues and costs for new stadium

	Basic stadium	Enhanced stadium with conference facilities
	£	£
Revenues		
Net income from community use of facilities	50,000	50,000
Stadium advertising/sponsorship from Finanex plc	200,000	250,000
Revenue from non-match day activities	187,000	537,000
Costs		
Stadium running costs, not directly traceable to rugby or football matches	(375,000)	(525,000)

Requirements

(a) Discuss how the objectives of the key stakeholders (the Council, the rugby club and the football club) may conflict in relation to the shared stadium. You should ignore SMC as a separate entity for the purposes of this requirement. **(7 marks)**

(b) (i) Using the data in Exhibit 1 relating to the new stadium, estimate the break-even attendance figures for each rugby and football match. **(4 marks)**

    (ii) Explain the implications of your calculations in (i) for the forecast match profits and discuss the potential variability in the annual attendance for each club, including the impact this is likely to have on the forecast in Exhibit 1. Show any supporting calculations. **(9 marks)**

(c) Using the data in Exhibits 1 and 2 and the other information provided, prepare a report for the Council which evaluates the business case for the new stadium against the Council's three stated criteria, clearly identifying any further information required. **(14 marks)**

(d) Assess the key risks for the Council in relation to the construction of the stadium and its operation by SMC. **(8 marks)**

(42 marks)

58 Beauty Soap

Beauty Soap Ltd (BS) is a large UK-based company which manufactures and sells personal care products (eg. hand soap, deodorant, shampoo, face cream, toothpaste and other personal hygiene products) throughout Europe.

Company history

BS was established in 1904 as a producer of soap. BS quickly established itself as a major player in the market because of the range of different product sizes and fragrances offered. Initially BS grew organically by investing in research and development to create a wider range of personal care products including shampoo and face cream. As the UK market became increasingly competitive, consolidation took place and the number of competitors reduced. BS however continued to expand through the acquisition of a UK company specialising in dental care products. It also acquired several manufacturers of personal care products in mainland Europe.

Strategic options

BS wants to reduce its dependence on the European market, as the market is mature and market prices are under pressure (see **Exhibit**).

Exhibit: European market for personal care products

	Revenue	
	2010 €m	2011 €m
Total European market	11,690	10,989
Market leader	1,489	1,297
BS	444	417

A number of competitors have targeted other international markets. BS is keen to expand into Latin America, as forecasts suggest there is considerable growth potential in some areas of the personal care products market, particularly in Brazil. The population of Brazil is culturally diverse. There are a number of affluent cities, but approximately one third of people live in rural areas, and there is significant poverty. BS is currently considering two alternative methods of development for expansion into Brazil:

(1) Acquire Gomera, a personal care products business based in Brazil. Gomera has an existing product range tailored to the needs of the local market and established supply chain and distribution networks. BS could either rebrand Gomera's products under the existing BS brand or keep Gomera's local brands and gradually introduce other brands from the BS range.

(2) Expand organically. Preliminary research has suggested that the market in Brazil would prefer smaller product sizes and lower prices than BS's traditional European product model, which the market perceives to be priced at a premium compared to local companies. BS plans to introduce new versions of products such as soap, shampoo and toothpaste in small packets containing enough product for a single use. BS already produces a range of similar single-use products for a major European hotel chain but does not currently sell these to individual consumers. The Brazilian government wants foreign-owned companies to demonstrate that they are creating value for the Brazilian economy. BS would therefore use a direct selling model with a workforce of local people, working from home and paid on a commission basis.

Competition

In Brazil the main competition in the personal care product market consists of:

- Two large multinational companies which have entered the market with their own global personal care brands

- Three domestic companies, one of which is Gomera, which produce a range of personal care products

The three domestic companies have established a strong presence in a variety of product segments and have the following advantages:

- An existing wide distribution network which extends to remote rural regions
- Low cost local manufacturing
- An established local supply chain network

They produce good quality products at competitive prices and make reasonable margins, although they lack the advertising budget and product innovation capacity of the multinational firms.

Educational marketing campaign

BS has recently announced plans to launch an education campaign, in conjunction with the governments in the countries in which it operates, to promote the regular washing of hands with BS soap to reduce infection and disease. The campaign will involve posters within schools and hospitals. If undertaken in Brazil there will be an advertising campaign featuring a well-known Brazilian footballer. BS's education campaign has been criticised by some as unethical marketing.

Requirements

(a) (i) Using relevant strategic models, explain both the ways in which BS has previously chosen to expand its business and its future plans for Brazil. **(7 marks)**

   (ii) Using the data in the Exhibit and the other information provided, evaluate the appropriateness of BS's plans to target markets outside Europe, given its current position. For the purposes of this requirement you should ignore the specific methods of expansion being considered. **(8 marks)**

(b) Explain the choice that companies such as BS face between standardisation and adaptation of products in the context of the global market for personal care products. **(5 marks)**

(c) Advise BS on the relative merits of the two options being considered for expansion into Brazil. **(8 marks)**

(d) Discuss the ethical marketing issues raised by BS's proposed education campaign. **(5 marks)**

(33 marks)

59 Maureen's Motors

Maureen's Motors (MM), named after its female founder Maureen Docherty, sells motor insurance policies to car owners.

In the UK it is a legal requirement for drivers to have a minimum level of motor insurance cover. This provides compensation in respect of injury or damage to other people or their property resulting from an accident caused by the driver. The main driver of the car is usually the policy-holder, but the policy may also cover additional named drivers. Policy-holders can reduce their premium (the annual price of the policy) by agreeing to an excess (a fixed amount which, in the event of a claim under the policy, will not be paid out by the insurer).

Company background

A gap in the motor insurance market was identified by MM when industry research revealed that although there are many women drivers, a significant number were just covered as a named driver on their partner's car insurance policy rather than being the policy-holder.

MM therefore focuses on motor insurance for female policy-holders, by offering product and service benefits specifically tailored to women, which are not offered by standard car insurers.

MM provides additional cover for handbags and contents, pushchairs and child car seats; 24-hour accident and breakdown recovery (including a guarantee to be there within an hour of any call); a network of female-friendly car repairers; a helpline giving policy-holders advice on all vehicle-related matters; and, if a car is involved in an accident, MM provides a replacement child car seat even if the existing seat has not been damaged.

MM wanted to remove the image of 'insurance as a necessary evil' and to create a reassuring brand for 'real women with real lives'. Three famous actresses from a well-known TV comedy played the role of the

'3 Maureens' in a long-running TV advertising campaign. Following this, MM was featured heavily in women's magazines. MM then ran a competition for existing and potential customers to star in a TV and poster advertising campaign. This campaign has significantly increased brand recognition, and using customers rather than celebrities has had the additional benefit of reducing marketing costs.

Pricing

The pricing of motor insurance premiums involves a risk assessment by the insurer of the likely risk of a claim being made and the amount that the insurer may have to pay out. The final price incorporates a number of factors, including:

- The insurance benefits offered
- The policy excess
- The type of vehicle, the expected annual mileage, and the location where the vehicle is normally kept
- The age and claims history of the policy-holder and any named drivers.

The larger the pool of insured drivers, the more the risk is spread out for the insurer and the lower the premiums can be. MM offers discounts for customer loyalty and for referring a friend, to help retain customers and market share.

An EU Directive prohibits motor insurers from price discrimination between equivalent men and women. MM therefore offers its car insurance policies to male drivers at the same price as an equivalent female driver and men can also be named as drivers on a female partner's policy. However because of its brand image and the nature of its product offering, MM's current customer base of policy-holders is 90% female.

Insurance industry statistics show that women typically drive fewer miles than men, are responsible for fewer driving convictions and make significantly fewer claims. Where women do make claims, these are usually for less serious accidents and therefore smaller amounts. Statistically women are also less likely to switch insurer and this, coupled with their reduced risk profile, allows MM to make higher margins.

MM has recently attracted some adverse publicity in the national newspapers. It has been criticised for focussing too much attention on marketing to attract new customers rather than on delivering efficient claims handling and customer service to its existing ones.

Requirements

(a) With reference to relevant models, discuss MM's generic strategy and market positioning.

(7 marks)

(b) Explain the key elements of the service marketing mix adopted by MM. (12 marks)

(c) In light of the criticism received by MM, recommend with reasons three KPIs that MM can implement to help improve its claims handling and customer service. (6 marks)

(25 marks)

60 Grassgrind Garden Mowers

'I really do not believe that accepting this bid is in the best interests of our shareholders. The board needs to convince shareholders that they should reject the bid and support our strategy for growth.' The chief executive of Grassgrind Garden Mowers plc (GGM), Sundeep Shiller, was speaking at a board meeting last week.

GGM is a UK company that manufactures two types of upmarket, petrol-powered mower for use by UK households in cutting grass in their gardens. The meeting was held to discuss a take-over bid for GGM by Boston Batteries Inc (BB), a large US company.

You are a senior working for a firm of chartered accountants and business advisers, Puller and Platt LLP (PP). Following the board meeting, Sundeep asked a partner in your firm, Jeff Nelson, to come to see him. You accompany Jeff.

The meeting

It was Sundeep who opened the meeting:

'In making the offer to GGM shareholders, BB has been critical of our strategy and our performance. The GGM board however believes that it has produced a reasonable performance recently and has a better strategy for future growth than BB.

'The board needs PP to provide a report to shareholders which evaluates GGM's performance and compares the board's proposed strategy for growth with that of BB.

'PP has not carried out any business advisory work for GGM in the past, so I have provided you with:

- Some background notes about GGM (**Exhibit 1**);
- A trade newspaper cutting about the mower industry (**Exhibit 2**);
- Details of the growth strategies proposed by both GGM and BB (**Exhibit 3**);
- Some financial, operating and market data about GGM (**Exhibit 4**).

'In looking at the data in Exhibit 4, I am concerned that we allocate fixed operating costs between our two types of mower on the basis of volumes sold. Is this distorting our assessment of profitability? I am wondering whether we should, instead, allocate such costs on the basis of the sales revenues generated by each type of mower, as this would provide a better measure of performance of each product line.'

An ethical issue

GGM recently received an email from Hetty Inc (Hetty), a company located in Eurasia, which is a developing nation. The following is an extract from that email:

'We would like to become your first export customer by placing a major order with GGM. However, in order to keep the price low, we would require a modification to your mowers, which is the removal of the safety guard. Unlike the UK, it is not a legal requirement in Eurasia, so it is not necessary for us to have this feature.'

Requirements

(a) Using the data and other information provided, draft the report requested by Sundeep. In the report you should:

    (i) Analyse the performance of GGM, and of each of its two products, in the financial years 2011 and 2012. **(15 marks)**

    (ii) Determine the current UK market share of GGM, highlighting any problems that arise in defining market share in order to produce a useful figure. **(5 marks)**

    (iii) Explain the competitive positioning of GGM in the UK mower market, and assess how this has changed between 2011 and 2012. **(7 marks)**

(iv) Compare the growth strategy of the GGM board with that of BB. Make relevant calculations and refer to appropriate strategic models. **(12 marks)**

(b) Explain the ethical issues that arise for GGM from Hetty's request to modify its mowers, and outline how GGM should respond. **(6 marks)**

(45 marks)

Exhibit 1 – GGM company background

GGM was established in 1956 and has always produced upmarket, petrol-powered mowers. Two types of mower are produced by GGM: (i) large mowers with a seat and a steering wheel for the user ('tractor mowers'); and (ii) conventional mowers which the user steers by hand while walking. Tractor mowers are sold to high income households as they are only suitable for very large gardens. All tractor mowers are powered by petrol engines, while conventional mowers are powered in a variety of ways.

A feature of both types of GGM product is their high-quality steel cutting blades, which outperform most rivals. All of GGM's sales are in the UK.

GGM's customers are large do-it-yourself (DIY) stores, garden centres and other large retailers. As is normal in the industry, these retailers sell on to households at the price charged by GGM plus 25%.

While most companies in the mower industry also manufacture other types of powered garden tools and equipment, GGM has, to date, only produced mowers.

Exhibit 2 – Extract from article in Mower Chronicle, 4th December 2012

> **Mowers – Battery power is cutting into the market**
>
> Sales of mowers to consumers in the UK amounted to £396 million in 2011 at retail prices, making up 45% of the overall gardening tools and equipment market.
>
> The mower industry can be divided into sub-sectors in a variety of ways. These include by style of blade, by type (tractor or conventional) or according to how they are powered (petrol, electric, battery or hand-propelled).
>
> Petrol-powered mowers have the largest market share by value as they are more expensive than electric mowers but, in terms of volumes, electric and hand-propelled mowers have a larger market share.
>
> Conventional petrol-powered mowers have maintained approximately the same market share by value at about 35% of the UK mower market in the last five years, while tractor mowers make up about 9% of the UK mower market.
>
> A recent development in the mower industry has been cordless mowers powered by batteries. Their market share by value reached 10% in 2011, from 5% in 2007.

Exhibit 3 – Proposed strategies for growth

GGM strategic plan

The GGM board proposes a new strategy, to diversify into a range of petrol-powered garden tools and equipment, including hedge trimmers, strimmers and chainsaws. The new range would use a smaller version of the petrol engine developed for the GGM mower. Customers (ie retailers) for the new products would be the same as for the mowers and the same GGM brand name would be used.

Budgets have been produced for the new range of petrol-powered garden tools and equipment, based on market research. The most realistic estimate indicates that 25,000 units will be sold each year, at an average price of £150 and with a 40% contribution margin on selling price. Additional annual fixed operating costs are expected to be £1.4 million. The market researchers have indicated that their estimate of sales volume could be up to 20% higher or 20% lower than their most realistic estimate, depending on market conditions.

BB strategic plan

BB is a US manufacturer of high performance lithium-ion batteries and has diversified in recent years by acquiring companies in industries producing industrial and domestic equipment which uses its batteries.

BB does not manufacture mowers, nor do any of its subsidiaries. As a result, its strategic plan is to acquire GGM and allow it to continue to produce petrol-powered mowers, and to commence producing mowers powered by lithium-ion batteries, using the same cutting blades as currently used by GGM. BB plans to encourage GGM to export battery-powered mowers to the US in future. BB has no plans for GGM to diversify away from mowers into other garden tools and equipment.

In the UK, battery-powered mowers would be sold to the same customers (ie retailers) as the existing products. The petrol-powered mowers would continue to be branded as GGM, but the battery-powered mowers would be branded under the BB name.

Budgets have been produced by BB that indicate 20,000 battery-powered mowers would be sold worldwide each year at an average price of £500 and with a 30% contribution margin on selling price. Additional annual fixed operating costs are expected to be £2 million, but could be as high as £3 million, or as low as £1 million.

Exhibit 4 – GGM financial, operating and market data for years to 31 December

Profit per unit data	2011		Estimated 2012	
	Conventional mowers	Tractor mowers	Conventional mowers	Tractor mowers
	£	£	£	£
Price	400.0	2,000.0	400.0	1,800.0
Variable operating costs	240.0	1,000.0	240.0	1,000.0
Fixed operating costs*	112.5	112.5	120.0	120.0
Operating profit per unit sold	47.5	887.5	40.0	680.0

*   Fixed operating costs are currently allocated to each mower based on GGM's total sales volume (see Sundeep's comments).

Operating and market data	2011		Estimated 2012	
	Conventional mowers	Tractor mowers	Conventional mowers	Tractor mowers
Volume sold by GGM (units)	8,100	2,700	7,380	2,820
UK market - volume sold (units)	1.5m	30,000	1.5m	30,600
UK market - sales value (at retail prices)	£360m	£36m	£368m	£36m

61   Care 4U Ltd

Care 4U Ltd (C4U) is a large private company which owns a chain of retail pharmacy outlets in the UK. These outlets supply consumers with prescription items (drugs and other products prescribed by health professionals for individual patients), general medicines and a range of other health and personal care products.

Industry background

Products and services

Retail pharmacies have two main sources of revenue:

(i)   About 80% from the provision of prescription items to patients by an appropriately qualified pharmacist

(ii)   About 20% from retail sales by non-qualified staff of over-the-counter (OTC) general medicines and other products

In the UK, the key role of pharmacies is to provide patients with drugs and other items under prescriptions from their doctor or other health professional. Many prescriptions are wholly government-funded and provided free-of-charge to patients. Where the patient is required to pay a charge for a prescription item, this is a fixed amount which is the same irrespective of the purchase cost of the item. Most of a pharmacy's revenue therefore comes directly from the government which pays an amount for each prescription item supplied and makes an additional payment for the service the pharmacy provides to patients.

Many drugs can be obtained only on prescription from qualified pharmacists. However, many types of OTC general medicines, plus other health and personal care products, can be bought at their market price from non-qualified staff at pharmacies and other general retailers.

The retail pharmacy market

Total revenue for pharmacies has the potential to grow, as the volume of demand for prescription items is expected to increase. This is due to an ageing population and constant improvements in healthcare. However, reductions in government expenditure create doubt over the amount of future government funding that will be available for prescription items.

Despite increases in industry revenues, the number of retail pharmacy outlets has declined in recent years. This has been partly due to increased competition in the industry created by deregulation which has permitted price competition on OTC general medicines since 2001. Since that time, supermarkets have introduced low-price, in-store pharmacies that are open, in some cases, 24 hours a day.

C4U company background

C4U was established in 1970. Since that time, commercial success through good centralised management has enabled expansion of the number of pharmacy outlets to 150 and significant growth in revenue per pharmacy.

All purchases are undertaken centrally at head office where key decisions are made. C4U's information technology system helps monitor and manage the performance of individual pharmacies. Typically, an average size C4U pharmacy, once established, would generate annual revenues of about £600,000 and an operating profit of 20% of sales revenue (this is before any central management charges, but after product purchases, salaries and overheads).

C4U has a reputation as a community pharmacy that offers services which are free to customers, including basic health tests (eg blood tests and health screening) and medical advice. The C4U brand has high and favourable consumer recognition throughout the UK.

At each C4U pharmacy there is a senior qualified pharmacist who, in addition to preparing prescription items, also runs the pharmacy's business activities, including being responsible for: ordering prescription drugs, OTC medicines and other products from head office; administration; hiring staff; and financial arrangements. Depending on the size of the pharmacy, there may be one or more other qualified pharmacists in addition to a senior qualified pharmacist.

A problem has arisen of high staff turnover among qualified pharmacists. Generous salaries are paid which have been successful in recruiting qualified pharmacists to C4U, but there have been problems in motivating and retaining them. In particular, many of C4U's pharmacists carry out the technical functions required of them, but have failed to manage professionally the business activities of the pharmacy by winning new customers, expanding sales and controlling costs. Other C4U pharmacists, having accumulated enough savings, have resigned from C4U to set up their own pharmacies on a self-employed basis.

C4U has borrowing facilities to obtain funding for its desired objective of further expansion, but the C4U board wants to ensure that available funds are used to best effect by opening as many new pharmacy outlets as possible.

C4U proposed expansion

The board has proposed two alternative strategies for expansion. Both strategies are designed to attract independent-minded, qualified pharmacists who wish to operate their own pharmacy, but who do not have enough funds to be self-employed by buying one outright. The two strategies are franchising and shared ownership:

Strategy 1 - Franchising

Under this proposal the number of C4U pharmacy outlets would be increased across the UK by offering qualified pharmacists franchise arrangements with the right to use the C4U brand name. Franchisees (ie the qualified pharmacists) could choose to benefit from some limited support and advice with respect to purchasing and administration, but could choose to reject this help.

C4U would purchase the property and basic fittings for each pharmacy outlet at an average cost of £200,000. The property would be acquired specifically for the purpose of opening a new pharmacy outlet. No existing pharmacy outlets would be franchised.

Each franchise agreement would last for five years and then would either be terminated (ie C4U would take full ownership of the property and control of the business) or, if both parties agreed, renegotiated on new terms. C4U would charge the franchisee an initial fixed fee of £25,000 and also an annual franchise fee of 5% of total annual revenue. Each franchisee would manage their own performance and would be entitled to all residual profit after franchise fees had been paid.

Franchisees would have strict responsibilities to abide by the terms of the franchise arrangement so C4U can protect its reputation. There would be no constraints on prices charged for non-prescription items, which can be determined by the franchisee.

Strategy 2 – shared ownership
Under this proposal each new pharmacy outlet would be owned by a limited company, with ownership of the company shared equally between C4U and a qualified pharmacist. C4U would lend money to each new company to finance the remaining initial cash requirement of the pharmacy outlet. Typical funding for an average-sized pharmacy outlet would be as follows:

Share capital contributed by C4U	20%
Share capital contributed by pharmacist	20%
Loan from C4U to the company	60%

The average cost of opening a pharmacy outlet would be £200,000, so each qualified pharmacist would need to contribute £40,000 on average to acquire their share capital.

Each pharmacist would be paid a market salary by their company. C4U would receive a management fee from each company for providing intensive support, advice, administration and IT facilities at a market rate averaging £20,000 per annum. This support and monitoring would be a compulsory part of the agreement, so C4U can manage the performance of its investment. If the pharmacist wanted to sell his/her shares to C4U (or conversely to buy C4U's shares) at any stage in the future, this would be possible at a fair value, to be independently determined.

Requirements

(a) Prepare a SWOT analysis for C4U. Each point should be clearly explained. Conclude by identifying the key issues and justify why they are significant. Ignore the strategies for expansion.   **(12 marks)**

(b) Explain and compare the two strategies for C4U's expansion under each of the following headings:

- Operating profit **for C4U** in respect of one outlet for one year (you should provide supporting calculations)

- Control and management

- Incentives for franchisees compared to shared owners.

(19 marks)

(31 marks)

62 The Mealfest Corporation

The Mealfest Corporation (MC) owns a chain of over 100 mid-market restaurants, located in four countries across Europe: France, Germany, Switzerland and the UK. France and Germany have the euro as their currency.

Company structure and pricing

Until January 2012, each restaurant manager was responsible for performance and reported directly to the company's head office in Germany. Menu prices were fixed centrally in euro at 1 January each year and were uniform across all restaurants. The prices in euro were translated into Swiss Francs (CHF) and sterling (£) using exchange rates prevailing at that date.

Head office specialists took responsibility for recruiting permanent staff for each restaurant. The same wage, which was reset and retranslated annually, was paid to all staff within each staff grade throughout the company.

On 1 January 2012 the company was restructured by having a separate division for each country. Each division has a divisional head. Restaurant managers now report their performance to their divisional heads, who then report total divisional performance to the company's head office. As with the previous structure, performance is evaluated by three measures: revenue, profit and return on assets.

From 1 January 2012 a new pricing policy was implemented. Menu prices are now set by divisional heads for their division each year, and can therefore vary between countries, but prices are required to be consistent within each country. Similarly, staff recruitment and remuneration are now decided at divisional level.

In both the pre- and post- 2012 structures, all meal ingredients are purchased centrally by MC from a French wholesaler. They are recharged to restaurants in euro at cost. Similarly, decisions on investment in new restaurants have always been centralised.

Monitoring the new structure and strategy

The MC board is having problems monitoring the success of the new structure and the new pricing strategy. It wishes to evaluate whether the method of assessing performance has improved following the restructuring.

The finance director summarised just one of the issues: 'It is very difficult to compare performance between countries due to exchange rate movements. Under the old pricing policy this meant that we set menu prices centrally in euro, then for the UK and Swiss operations we translated these to sterling and Swiss Francs each year. Fluctuations over the year in exchange rates meant restaurant prices in the UK and Switzerland sometimes changed significantly when they were reset the following year. Under the new pricing system there is more pricing flexibility at national level, but we still need to make performance comparisons in euro as a common currency.

'I am not interested in hedging or in financial reporting issues, but I am concerned about the commercial impact of exchange rates on restaurants and customers, and their effect on measuring divisional financial performance.'

The chief executive responded: 'That is all very well in terms of financial performance, but I am interested in measuring all aspects of performance and in whether we now have the right structure and pricing strategy.'

Requirements

(a) Compare MC's pre- 2012 and post–2012:

- Organisational structure and performance measurement; and
- Pricing strategies. **(14 marks)**

(b) Explain how benchmarking may be used by MC to evaluate the performance of divisions and individual restaurants. **(10 marks)**

(24 marks)

63 Mayhews Ltd

Mayhews Ltd (Mayhews) is a family-owned business which runs three garages from freehold sites in prime locations in central England. Each garage operates a filling station, which sells fuel (petrol and diesel), and has a facility offering maintenance and repairs for motor vehicles.

Fuel retailing in the UK

Fuel retailing in the UK is a high volume, low margin business, characterised by strong competition. In the industry there are three types of filling station:

- Branded filling stations are either owned and managed by one of the major fuel wholesalers or operated on their behalf by licensees.

- Independent retailers, like Mayhews, are free to obtain fuel supplies from any wholesaler. Over 50% of all filling stations in the UK are independently owned.

- The big supermarket chains operate filling stations alongside their major stores. In recent years, whilst the number of branded filling stations and independent retailers has declined, the number of supermarket-owned sites has increased. This has coincided with the expansion of large out-of-town supermarkets with more people driving to do their shopping and buying fuel at the same time. As a result of their supply chain efficiencies and the large volumes of fuel that they sell, the supermarkets incur lower overheads per litre of fuel sold and are able to charge lower prices. In addition, many offer discounts on fuel based on the amount customers spend on goods in the main store. The average retail price charged by supermarkets in 2012 was 130.9 pence per litre compared to an overall UK average of 133.8 pence per litre.

Supply of fuel and pricing in the UK industry

The wholesale supply of fuel to retailers is dominated by a few large companies which produce and refine crude oil into a range of products including fuel. These wholesalers supply fuel to their own branded filling stations and to the supermarkets and independent retailers. 60% of the UK retail fuel price per litre consists of fuel tax and sales tax. On average 35% is paid to the wholesaler and the retailer earns 5% towards overheads and profit. Wholesale fuel prices in the last three years have been very volatile as the price of crude oil has varied significantly. Price volatility is a major problem for independent retailers. When market prices fall, independent retailers are often left with fuel supplies previously bought from the wholesaler at a high price. If they reduce the retail price then they may make a loss. If they keep retail prices high this is likely to have a negative effect on sales volumes. Conversely, when wholesale prices rise, the independent retailer may struggle to afford the increased cost of replenishing fuel supplies.

Demand for fuel in the UK market

Despite increased numbers of cars on the road, sales volumes of fuel are under pressure because of the improved efficiency of vehicle engines, increased fuel prices and the difficult economic climate. Government figures suggest congestion on motorways and major roads has been falling, indicating that people are undertaking fewer journeys by car.

Fierce competition between fuel retailers has led to a significant decline in the number of filling stations. There are now fewer than half the 18,000 filling stations that existed twenty years ago (Exhibit 1).

A fuel station's viability depends on two key factors: the gross margin per litre and the volume of fuel sold. Independent filling stations and those in less well-populated rural areas are at the greatest risk of losses due to declining sales volumes and below average margins. They also struggle to justify the additional capital expenditure required to comply with increasingly strict environmental and safety regulations. Many have tried to reduce their reliance on fuel revenue by creating alternative revenue streams such as on-site shops selling snacks, groceries and vehicle accessories. Mayhews does not currently operate a shop at any of its garages.

420 filling stations closed in the UK in 2012, of which two-thirds were independent. Some of these filling stations have been bought by property developers, although because of environmental regulations, sites have to be closed and the fuel tanks filled with concrete before being capable of alternative use.

Mayhews' business

The first Mayhews garage was set up in 1950 by John Mayhew. The 1950s boom in vehicle ownership and the later development of the UK motorway network led to a significant increase in demand for fuel and maintenance/repairs and Mayhews soon opened a further two garages. The business is now owned and managed by John's son Barry (aged 60), who is a well-known businessman in the region. After many successful years, Mayhews has been finding the filling stations market increasingly difficult and this is reflected in the company's recent results (**Exhibit 2**).

Although Mayhews has been experiencing a decline in fuel sales, the revenue and profit from maintenance and repairs have been increasing. This part of the business undertakes MOT testing (a compulsory annual test of safety for vehicles over three years old); replacement of parts due to wear and tear (brakes, tyres, wiper blades, lights etc); annual maintenance; and repairs.

Due to the economic climate, people have been slow to replace their old vehicles with new ones. Time pressure, lack of skills and the complexity of vehicles mean people no longer maintain their own vehicles, but they are reluctant to pay the high prices charged by the vehicle retailers for maintenance. Because of its longstanding presence in the region, and also as a result of Barry's contacts, each Mayhews garage has a loyal base of local customers. Mayhews also has contracts with a number of local companies for the maintenance of their corporate vehicles.

There are 32 million vehicles on the UK's roads and the maintenance and repairs market is fragmented. There are around 24,000 garage outlets in the UK offering motor vehicle repairs and maintenance. They are operated by retailers of vehicles, national and regional repairs and maintenance chains, fast-fit centres (specialising in tyres, exhausts and brakes) and many independents.

Strategic dilemma

Your firm acts as business advisers to Mayhews. At a recent meeting, Barry commented:

'We seem to be selling so little fuel these days I can't believe we are making much money from this side of the business. What do you think about us closing one or more of the filling stations and focussing on maintenance and repairs? This is a service-based market with many different providers where trust is really important to the customer. We already have a reputation for being honest and reliable and our brand is well-known locally.

'We also have much lower overheads and labour costs than the main vehicle retailers. We can use this to differentiate ourselves by offering vehicle retailer quality service at affordable local garage prices.

'Unfortunately, we simply don't have the appropriate technology to deal with the engine management systems in the more modern vehicles so currently we have to refer them to the vehicle retailer. We would need to invest in information technology by purchasing the relevant engine diagnostic equipment and a new computer system.

'The new computer system would improve parts management and have marketing benefits. By maintaining their vehicles in good working condition our customers can improve fuel efficiency and drive safely. A key way we can help customers is to anticipate their needs for MOTs and maintenance and contact them in advance based on the age and mileage of their vehicle. The new system would provide us with an advanced data management system to do this, as well as allowing us to offer customers online booking for repairs and maintenance.'

Requirements

(a) Prepare a Porter's Five Forces analysis of the UK fuel retailing industry which might be used to inform further discussions regarding the viability of Mayhews' filling station operations. **(9 marks)**

(b) Using the data in the Exhibits, your answer to requirement (a), and the other information provided, evaluate the performance of Mayhews' overall business and compare the performance of the individual garages. Make and justify a preliminary conclusion as to whether Mayhews should consider closing one or more of its filling stations to focus on maintenance and repairs. **(17 marks)**

(c) Discuss the advantages and disadvantages of making the investment in information technology referred to by Barry. **(6 marks)**

(d) Explain how the use of critical success factors (CSFs) may assist Mayhews in establishing a strategic control system. Justify three CSFs for Mayhews' maintenance and repairs business and suggest one appropriate key performance indicator for each CSF identified. **(9 marks)**

(41 marks)

Exhibit 1: UK filling stations – market data 2012

	Branded filling stations	Independents	Supermarkets	Total
Number of sites	2,605	4,425	1,470	8,500
Millions of litres sold	10,520	7,425	14,950	32,895

Exhibit 2: Mayhews Ltd recent financial performance

	Breakdown of 2012			Total company	
	Garage A 2012 £'000	Garage B 2012 £'000	Garage C 2012 £'000	Mayhews Ltd 2012 £'000	Mayhews Ltd 2011 £'000
Sales:					
Fuel (note 1)	878	738	776	2,392	2,686
Maintenance & repairs	688	454	755	1,897	1,604
Total sales	1,566	1,192	1,531	4,289	4,290
Gross profit:					
Fuel	103	76	91	270	304
Maintenance & repairs (note 2)	355	218	415	988	836
Total gross profit	458	294	506	1,258	1,140
Operating costs (note 3)	269	184	219	672	679
Profit	189	110	287	586	461
Litres of fuel sold (millions)	1.63	1.34	1.43	4.40	5.21

Notes:

1. Fuel revenue is stated net of tax, ie, at 40% of the retail fuel price.

2. The gross profit on maintenance & repairs is based on the sales value of work done less the cost of parts and materials.

3. Operating costs include the wages and salaries of all garage staff. The operating costs for garage A also include £45,000 for Barry's salary.

64 Cabezada Ltd

Cabezada Ltd (Cabezada) is a relatively new company which uses steel shipping containers to create short-term living accommodation. The standard-sized containers can be transported anywhere by road, rail or sea, modified and then stacked to create the desired number of rooms.

The business is owned and managed by two directors: Sam Lowe, previously chief executive of a hotel group, and Anka Bien, formerly operations director of a large construction company.

Cabezada has two markets:

(1) Events clients, which require short-term accommodation for employees, media representatives, visitors and participants at a variety of sporting and leisure events.

(2) Contract clients, including the construction industry, the military and government, which typically require longer-term accommodation. Recent projects include key-worker accommodation and a temporary hospital.

Since starting the company, a number of projects have been completed very successfully for both markets. Cabezada's directors believe the business has significant global appeal and have started to draft a business plan which will be used to attract appropriate local partners to develop a worldwide business. The directors have already written some of the plan, which is included in the **Exhibit**, and have asked your firm of business advisers for help in developing it further.

Requirements

(a) As a senior in the firm of business advisers, write the sections of the draft business plan indicated in the Exhibit, to cover:

    (i)   Strengths and realistic market opportunities (section 2.2.1);

    (ii)   Weaknesses and threats (section 2.2.2);

    (iii) Benefits of partnership for both Cabezada and its local partners (section 3).

    You should present your answer in an appropriate style and format, written in such a way as to help Cabezada to attract potential partners. **(16 marks)**

(b) Recommend any further information that you believe should be included in the plan to enable potential partners to adequately assess Cabezada's partnership proposition. **(8 marks)**

(c) Cabezada currently segments its market between events and contract clients. Explain the purpose and benefits of market segmentation and discuss other approaches to segmentation which Cabezada could adopt. **(8 marks)**

(32 marks)

Exhibit: Draft Business Plan provided by Cabezada's directors

---

DRAFT: Cabezada Local Partnership Programme 2013

1.   Cabezada Local Partnership model

Cabezada uses steel shipping containers to create temporary living accommodation. Cabezada is regarded as a pioneer in the container accommodation industry and our brand name is well-recognised and trusted. The demand for cheap, flexible, temporary accommodation provided under a sustainable model is a global one. However we believe global business is best done using a local model and we are seeking the right local partners to help us target a wide range of potential markets.

Each local partner will set up a new company in their country or region called 'Cabezada (country/region name)'. Cabezada will have partial ownership of the company with a stake of 20%. The new company will pay a one-off franchise fee for exclusive rights to operate under the Cabezada brand in its defined area. There will be a monthly management charge for the use of all Cabezada information and infrastructure and a royalty fee on all container accommodation sold in the local market.

2.   The Business

2.1. Our product concept

Shipping containers are highly durable and provide an ideal building module suitable for all climates and locations. Most new shipping containers are manufactured in China to international-standard sizes at a cost of approximately £4,000 each. Many countries import manufactured goods from Asia in shipping containers. Rather than pay to have these containers shipped back empty, it is often cheaper for Asian suppliers to buy new containers in Asia. As a result there is a plentiful supply of used shipping containers available globally, costing on average £1,000 per container.

Since the containers are designed to be easily transported by ship, road or rail, distribution costs are low, so accommodation can be provided in whatever location the client requires. Once adapted to make them suitable for living accommodation, the shipping containers can be quickly and easily combined in several storeys without requiring additional structural support.

The modular system offers flexibility of design and the standard of accommodation can range from very basic to luxurious. Depending on the client and location there is scope to create a building façade of brick, timber or marble. Cabezada's design system includes any necessary foundations, communal access arrangements, ventilation and connections to utilities.

For buildings up to five storeys high, container accommodation is significantly cheaper than the cost of erecting a brick-built structure, which takes much longer and requires larger, expensive foundations. Cabezada's whole product concept is more environmentally friendly, ideal for temporary use and consistent with the need for sustainability. Once a project is over, the containers can be refurbished and re-used. There is also a ready market for the sale of containers after use if Cabezada no longer requires them.

2.2. **Cabezada position analysis**

2.2.1 Strengths and realistic market opportunities (to be completed)
2.2.2 Weaknesses and threats (to be completed)

3. Benefits of partnership for both Cabezada and its local partners (to be completed)

65 Chiba

Chiba is a Japanese company which manufactures a range of liquid foods including rice vinegar and soy sauce.

Different countries make vinegars from their indigenous crops, for example rice vinegar in Japan, oat vinegar in Korea, cider vinegar in the US, wine vinegar in Europe and malt vinegar in the UK. Rice vinegar has no fat or cholesterol and is very low in calories. It is also known for its anti-bacterial properties.

UK expansion strategy

Malegar, a division of a large UK listed food business, makes the UK's leading brand of malt vinegar. The division is currently for sale because Malegar's parent company (VM plc) has incurred significant borrowings and is now moving to a strategy of focusing on a few key profitable food brands.

Chiba wants to increase its market share in the UK and is considering setting up a subsidiary company, Chiba UK, to acquire Malegar, because of Malegar's strong UK heritage and identity. As well as targeting Malegar's traditional food market, Chiba is also keen to promote vinegar as a health product and as a cleaning product. However, Chiba's marketing director is concerned that VM plc would not be selling Malegar if it were a profitable business.

Contamination issue

The directors of Malegar are aware of a recent complaint from a major wholesaler concerning a contaminated batch of malt vinegar. The cause has not yet been confirmed and they are unsure whether the contamination arose in the glass bottles, which are purchased from an external supplier, or within the Malegar factory. Malegar takes health and safety and quality control very seriously, so the directors believe the fault is most likely to lie with the supplier. As Malegar was probably not responsible for the incident, the directors are planning to keep this issue confidential from all parties, including Chiba.

Human resource management

If Chiba's acquisition of Malegar goes ahead, all Malegar employees will transfer their contracts to Chiba UK following an appropriate consultation process. This may take up to twelve months.

Chiba's approach to human resource management is very different from Malegar's. Malegar has a hierarchical structure with a focus on short-term results, and with individual functional managers held accountable for the performance of their function. Employees within Malegar's factory have little involvement in the decision-making process and there is high staff turnover. In contrast, Chiba's approach emphasises job security for core employees, co-operation and mutual trust between employees and managers, collective responsibility and shared decision making. Chiba's directors are concerned about the change management issues that will arise from the integration of the Malegar employees into the Chiba culture.

Requirements

(a) Explain the ethical issues that arise for Malegar's directors in relation to concealing the possible contamination. **(5 marks)**

(b) In light of the comments by Chiba's marketing director, discuss the possible reasons for the divestment of Malegar by VM plc and the benefits to Chiba of growing by acquisition in the UK.

(8 marks)

(c) (i) Contrast Chiba's and Malegar's differing approaches to human resource management.

(5 marks)

(ii) Explain the change management issues that Chiba is likely to face when integrating the Malegar employees. Refer to relevant models where appropriate. **(9 marks)**

(27 marks)

66   Hire Value Ltd

Hire Value Ltd (HV) operates in the car hire industry throughout the UK.

The UK car hire industry has two sectors: renting cars to users for the short term, typically between one day and two weeks (the car rental sector); and leasing cars to users for the longer term (the leasing sector). These sectors are of approximately equal size in terms of revenue.

The UK car rental sector

There are about 100 companies operating in the car rental sector in the UK. In 2012, these companies generated total revenue of £5,000 million. A few large companies dominate the sector. These larger companies tend to be international, with some companies being subsidiaries of car manufacturers. The car rental sector is also characterised by many medium-sized companies. Some of these have a regional focus, but most operate throughout the UK from airports, where there are clusters of car rental companies providing wide consumer choice.

The larger companies tend to maintain a modern fleet of cars, usually owning each vehicle for an average of only 13 months.

The car rental sector can be segmented in two main ways: by customer (business or leisure) or by location of outlets (airport or non-airport). A high proportion of rentals are dependent on the airline industry. Business customers tend to be companies which negotiate flexible contracts for renting many vehicles for short periods so that, for instance, visiting overseas executives can drive to meetings straight from the airport. An account is set up for each business customer and preferential prices are offered, compared with those for individual customers hiring cars for leisure purposes.

The car rental business tends to be seasonal, with spring and summer (the peak periods for leisure customers) each generating about 30% of annual revenues.

Strategic partnerships are common in the sector. The main examples are partnerships between car rental companies and airlines, which allow the customer to book car rentals on-line with a partner company at the same time as booking flights.

UK car rental market leader

Kerr Karrs plc (KK) is the UK market leader in the car rental sector, which is the only sector in which it operates. KK offers a high level of standard service by renting out modern, relatively good quality cars, charging a price premium compared with the industry average. In addition to its standard range of vehicles, it has a premium range of luxury cars for affluent individuals and senior business executives.

KK operates throughout the UK. It has many large, listed companies as its business customers and has partnerships with many airlines including special arrangements for their first class and business class customers. It tends not to have partnerships with budget airlines.

Hire Value Ltd - company history

HV was established in 1991 by the current members of its board. HV's business model is to operate in the car rental sector throughout the UK. Its particular focus is to locate its outlets at airports in order to attract business and leisure travellers. The airport outlets also serve customers living or working in the cities closest to these airports. Each outlet consists of a customer service desk in the airport terminal, plus a vehicle collection site in the parking area. Both are distinctively branded to attract travellers and promote brand image. Staff are well trained in customer service.

HV's accounting information system provides an analysis of revenues from business customers and leisure customers separately. However, there is no separate analysis of costs or profit for each of these customer groups, as individual cars are used interchangeably between them.

HV aims to operate mid-market in terms of the service it provides. However, in order to control costs, HV buys cars which are about two years old and then operates them for a further three years. HV has adopted this policy as it believes that customers are more sensitive to price and the type of car they hire than its age.

All customer bookings are made on-line. Car rental charges are payable by credit card or debit card at the time of booking by leisure customers. Business accounts are on credit terms.

Expansion and the business plan

In March 2012, the HV directors obtained new equity finance from a venture capital company, TopFin, to expand the business. The business plan included the acquisition of more vehicles and the development of more locations to provide greater economies of scale and more efficient operations. A forecast of rapid growth was therefore a key element in obtaining the new finance from TopFin. The original board members continue to hold 60% of the ordinary share capital of HV; the remaining 40% is owned by TopFin.

A formal agreement was made between the director-shareholders and TopFin that there would be an independent review after a year to monitor the success of HV's growth strategy. In April 2013 accountants and business advisers, Gatter LLP, therefore reviewed how the business plan was being implemented and monitored. They reported that, for the year ended 31 March 2013, revenues had grown, but the projections in the business plan had not been achieved (see **Exhibit** on page 5). TopFin has now asked for a detailed analysis of the data to explain why actual performance has varied from the business plan.

Ethical issues

The review by Gatter LLP also reported that executive directors used some HV assets for personal use, raising a number of ethical issues:

(1) HV cars are sometimes loaned overnight to various executive directors when not rented out to customers. This is done on a casual basis without records. It appears to be accepted by employees as part of HV's corporate culture but, as no records are kept, TopFin has, to date, been unaware of this practice.

(2) One director, Mike Knight, provided an HV car to his friend for a few hours without charge. He told one of the other directors about this, prior to lending the car.

(3) Another director, Sandra Bevan, rented out an HV car for cash under a private arrangement. Initially, she held the cash received in her personal bank account but, after a month, paid it over to HV. This was just prior to the start of the Gatter investigation.

Requirements

(a) For the year ended 31 March 2013 compare the actual performance and competitive position of HV with that of the market leader, KK. Use the data in the Exhibit and the other information provided. **(10 marks)**

(b) Using the data in the Exhibit and the other information provided, analyse and explain the shortfall between HV's actual performance for the year ended 31 March 2013 and its forecast performance in the business plan for the same period. In addition, you should indicate **three** significant matters which require further investigation in order to provide a more complete analysis. **(16 marks)**

(c) Prepare a risk register for what you consider to be the **four** most significant risks of HV. Use a table with three columns which, for each risk, explains:

    (i)   The nature of the risk;
    (ii) The possible impact of the risk and likelihood of it occurring;
    (iii) Possible risk management procedures. **(9 marks)**

(d) Prepare notes for a presentation to the HV board which explain the ethical issues, and the implications that arise from these, for the HV directors (both individually and collectively) as a result of the review by Gatter LLP of HV asset use. **(10 marks)**

(45 marks)

Exhibit – Financial and operating data for HV and KK

Year ended 31 March 2013	HV forecast in Business Plan	HV actual	KK actual
Revenue:			
Business customers (£'m)	13.00	7.00	620.00
Leisure customers (£'m)	17.00	20.00	580.00
Operating profit (£'m)	1.20	1.00	56.00
Number of cars owned (average in year)	3,000	2,800	68,000
Total days of hiring ('000 days)	870	820	21,100
Market values of assets:			
Cars (£'m)	20.25	16.80	816.00
Other assets (£'m)	10.00	10.00	664.00

67 Up 'n' Over Plc

Up 'n' Over plc (UnO) manufactures garage doors for domestic properties. It sells entirely to retailers on a business-to-business basis.

Company history

UnO was established in 1994 and obtained a listing in 2005. The directors own 20% of the ordinary share capital, with the other 80% being held by financial institutions.

From incorporation, UnO produced reasonable quality, basic garage doors at relatively low cost. It did not aim to be the cheapest, but it did aim to offer best value to customers, selling garage doors at prices towards the lower end of the market. UnO established a good reputation with end-consumers, who demand a reliable product at reasonable prices.

UnO sells to retailers located throughout the UK. They range from small shops, which buy from UnO only when they receive an order from a customer, up to very large retail chains, which have three-year purchase contracts with UnO. Large chains carry high inventories of UnO doors for immediate delivery to consumers.

A cost reduction policy

In December 2011 a new chief executive, Helen Earth, was appointed by UnO to increase profitability. After briefly reviewing the operations of the business, she decided on a cost reduction exercise, commencing in January 2012. This involved: reducing the quality of the materials used to make the garage doors; reducing staffing levels; replacing some staff at a lower skill level; freezing any unnecessary capital investment in machinery; and reducing maintenance. Strict performance management procedures were introduced to ensure that output volume was maintained, despite the changes.

The changes had a favourable effect on reported profit in the year ended 31 December 2012 (see **Exhibit** on page 7) but by June 2013 some problems were being reported. A board meeting was arranged.

Board meeting

Helen, the *chief executive,* explained the reasoning for her cost reduction plan. 'We have not yet developed a long-term strategy, but the cost reductions were immediately necessary just to make a profit.

'We've had some quality problems lately, but the cost of correcting these faults is small in comparison with the cost savings we have made. I realise that the durability of the current products is questionable. Problems will increase after about 18 months of usage of the garage doors, and there may be serious problems after three years of usage. I have made sure, however, that this is not going to be too costly to UnO, by reducing the guarantee period to customers from five years to two years. This means that by the time most doors start to develop serious faults after usage, they are out of guarantee and we have no obligation to repair them.

'As a result, I have prepared a schedule (see **Exhibit** on page 7) which shows that we expect to make a profit in the year to 31 December 2013, whereas we made a loss in 2011, and the share price is higher now than then. This demonstrates that the strategy is working. This is a competitive market and we need to compete on low prices, so we must keep our costs low.'

The *marketing director* disagreed: 'This business model is not sustainable. The number of complaints from our customers is growing and our reputation is declining. One of the large retailers has given us a final warning about quality standards and is threatening to stop buying our products when its long-term agreement period with UnO is completed. This cost reduction policy is just to improve short-term profits and share price. We should try to keep our customers happy in the longer term, so we must return to our previous policy of best value.'

The *chairman* joined the discussion: 'We need to balance the cost of rectifying faults with operating cost savings, but it's an increasingly competitive market. Personally, I doubt we can sustain our position as a manufacturer. One possibility is to close down our manufacturing facility and import garage doors from Thailand at a cost (including transport) that is just below our expected operating cost per door for 2013. In effect, we would become an importer and wholesaler of garage doors. To do this cost-effectively, we would need to order in large batches so we can fill a whole shipping container with each order, as there is a high fixed cost for transporting each container. I would like your views on whether we should consider this possibility further.'

Exhibit

Years to 31 December	2011	2012	2013 (expected)
Revenue	£32m	£32m	£30m
Selling price to retailer per door	£400	£400	£400
Fixed operating costs	£15m	£14m	£14m
Operating profit/(loss)	£(1m)	£3m	£2m
Number of doors repaired under guarantee	8	24	96
Price per share	£2.10 at 31 Dec 2011	£4.50 at 31 Dec 2012	£3.20 at 31 May 2013

Requirements

(a) On the basis of the information in the Exhibit, determine:

   (i)   The expected variable cost per garage door for 2013; and

   (ii) The break-even level of sales by volume for UnO in each of the years ended 31 December 2011 and 31 December 2012.

   Briefly comment on the implications for operating risk of these calculations.

   (9 marks)

(b) As a business adviser, prepare a report that evaluates the benefits and problems of each of the three strategies for UnO that were discussed at the board meeting:

   (i)   Return to the original strategy of producing in the UK at low cost and selling at best value, as suggested by the marketing director;

   (ii) Continue with the cost reduction programme introduced by the chief executive; or

   (iii) Cease manufacturing and import garage doors from Thailand, as suggested by the chairman.

   In each case, include a brief assessment of the sustainability of each strategy. Provide a reasoned recommendation, justifying your preferred strategy. **(21 marks)**

   (30 marks)

68 Moogle plc

You have recently joined Moogle plc (Moogle), one of the largest supermarket chains in the UK. You are the senior executive manager responsible for all Moogle's pet product sales in all its UK stores.

Initial briefing – chief operating officer

At an initial briefing, Moogle's chief operating officer, Fred Trueblood, outlined what he expected from you in your role:

'Moogle's pet products have underperformed compared with those of our rivals in recent years. I want you to make a difference. You will be responsible for procurement, pricing and profits in respect of all our pet product sales in the UK. This includes pet food and other pet-related accessories (eg, toys, bowls, bedding).

'I need you to think strategically and get ahead of market trends. Don't just copy what our competitors have already done, as your predecessor did. He also got too involved in what was happening at individual stores and did not see the bigger picture.

'I have outlined a few details for you about the UK pet products retail industry (see Exhibit 1 on page 9) and about Moogle (see Exhibit 2 on page 9), as initial guidance.

'I have also arranged for you to meet our head of IT, Walter Weasil. I want you to agree an information strategy, so you have the information that is necessary to guide the strategic and operational decisions you will need to take.'

Meeting with the head of IT

Walter Weasil opened the conversation:

'I need to know what key pieces of information you will need to guide your decision making and to help you monitor and control your area of responsibility. Your predecessor wanted every possible piece of information and just could not cope with it all. Try to be more selective and ask only for information that is appropriate to your function and level of management. Include any information you need to monitor any new strategies you may wish to adopt.

'We can review matters later but, as a start, set out your regular monthly information needs by identifying three internal and three external pieces of information. In accordance with company policy, you must justify why you need each piece of information.'

Requirements

(a) Prepare a PESTEL analysis for the UK pet products retail industry. **(11 marks)**

(b) Respond to the head of IT's request by identifying **three** pieces of internal information and **three** pieces of external information that you will require each month in your role. Explain why you will need each piece of information. **(14 marks)**

(25 marks)

Exhibit 1 – An overview of the UK pet products retail industry

The UK pet products retail industry grew steadily by around 3% per year until 2008 when it reached total retail sales of £2,500 million. Since 2008, UK pet products sales have grown more slowly at 1% per year due to the recession.

Pet food makes up about 75% of pet products sales. The remainder comprises: pet accessories (eg, toys, bedding); veterinary services; and pet insurance. Pet insurance sales are growing rapidly, but insurance is highly regulated. Expenditure on products for dogs and cats makes up 93% of UK pet products sales. The highest growth in the pet food sector has been premium quality moist food, which has the highest price, largest margins and lowest consumer price resistance.

Animal welfare has become a key issue with new laws being passed requiring minimum standards of pet living accommodation, diet and medical care.

Pet owners now use social media network sites to share experiences and ideas and to recommend pet products to each other.

There has been a growing trend to tag dogs and cats electronically with microchips, so they can be recovered if they are lost.

On-line sales of pet products are increasingly common. There is also significant competition from pet superstores.

Exhibit 2 – Moogle company background

Moogle is one of the largest supermarket chains in the UK, with stores throughout the world. Overall, Moogle positions itself as mid-market, but it has many low cost ranges and many premium product ranges.

Stores vary from large out-of-town superstores, to small in-town stores. All Moogle stores carry pet products. However, the proportion of total sales made up by pet product sales at each store varies significantly.

Moogle has a narrow product range for pets, focussing mainly on dogs and cats with a wide range of foods, plus a moderate range of accessories.

69   Funzie Ltd

Funzie Ltd (Funzie) is a small, UK-based, independent TV production company that produces factual television programmes featuring computer graphics. These programmes are sold to a variety of broadcasters which pay for the right to transmit Funzie's programmes on their TV channels.

Funzie was set up by Vivian Campbell and Sanaya Dhami, both experienced programme makers. Its mission is to produce high quality programmes that are educational and informative. Vivian and Sanaya each own 20% of the company's ordinary share capital. The remaining shareholders are private investors, who each own less than 10%.

Industry information

Although some large organisations exist, most TV production companies are small businesses, owned and managed by highly skilled, artistic people with years of industry experience.

TV programmes are commissioned by broadcasters for a fixed price which depends on the type and length of the programme and its expected audience (see **Exhibit 1** on page 5). Prices for factual TV programmes vary from £100,000 to £300,000 per hour for the most popular programmes. The price entitles the broadcaster to transmit the original programme and any repeat showings on specified channels in the UK. If the original programme is successful the broadcaster may commission the production company to make additional programmes (re-commissioning). Prices for re-commissioned programmes are typically 20% lower than the original commission.

Intellectual property (IP) rights to UK broadcasting of a programme usually belong to the broadcaster. However, the production company normally retains the intellectual property (IP) for international sale of the programme or the programme format (the right to make the same style of programme for broadcast in another country). International sales generate high margins for the production company because the incremental costs are low.

Company information

Funzie's reputation relies on its people and ideas. It is recognised as a specialist in current affairs, natural history and documentaries.

Funzie employs 40 staff. There is a small administration and finance department. The other employees are creative people who work on ideas, programme directors who manage programme production and computer graphics specialists. The company does not own production studios or production equipment, so relies on outsourcing. Programme presenters and technicians such as sound recordists are engaged as independent sub-contractors.

Funzie's operating profit margin for UK broadcast programmes depends on the difference between the commissioned price and the actual costs of making each programme. Programme directors are responsible for ensuring costs stay within the programme budget, but there is often conflict between cost control and quality of output.

Accurate budgeting of detailed costs is critical, since cost over-runs cannot be passed on to broadcasters once the fixed-price commission has been agreed. Most of the budgeted variable costs relate to outsourced activities and sub-contractors. Studio time is the most expensive cost at £30,000 per day, and Funzie has to pay a premium if facilities are required at short notice. If a programme director is not satisfied with the programme output, additional studio time and technicians may be required over and above the original budget.
In addition, some programme presenters arrive late at the studio, wasting time that has already been booked and necessitating additional studio hours.

Future profitability

Broadcasters are under pressure due to falling revenues. They want to reduce their costs and have told Funzie that they will only pay premium prices for its factual programmes if they are entertaining as well as informative and educational.

To ensure the company's future profitability, Funzie needs to manage its costs more effectively and/or review the range of programme types it makes. At a recent shareholder meeting to assess the company's financial performance (see Exhibit 2 on page 5), the other shareholders suggested to Vivian and Sanaya that Funzie could make more money if it expanded its programmes to include drama documentaries. A competitor has recently enjoyed success with one such programme based on a real-life survival story, consisting of re-enacted scenes and narrative from the survivor and his family.

One shareholder argued that: 'This type of real-life programme has wide audience appeal and, more to the point, is quite low budget to produce, since we won't have to pay expensive fees for scriptwriters and actors, and little actual studio time is required. Also, there would be lots of scope to re-commission further programmes and to sell the format internationally.'

Vivian disagreed: 'I think we should stick to our original mission or we will damage our reputation for high quality educational and informative programmes. It isn't the revenue that is the problem, but our approach to budgeting and cost control. If we had a better understanding and control of costs then we would definitely make more profit.'

Computer graphics (CG)

In early 2012 Funzie's reputation was enhanced when its new series of documentary programmes 'The March of Time' won an industry award for innovative use of computer graphics (CG). CG software is used to create scenery, simulate crowds and generate special effects. It allows small companies to produce high-quality programmes without the same scale of resources as the larger production companies. Funzie's programmes increasingly rely on CG. In 2012 it used 500 days of CG time, outsourcing approximately 50% of these at a cost of £2,250 per day. Funzie is considering the acquisition of new CG software, costing

£1.2 million, which would remove its requirement for outsourcing. Since technology changes rapidly, the software is likely to need replacing or upgrading in two to three years.

Ethical issue

A programme director, Conrad Jack, has recently joined Funzie from a rival UK production company (Dayze). At Dayze, Conrad had been developing an idea for a documentary about some of the UK's landmark structures, and the engineering that went into them, making considerable use of CG. Shortly before Conrad left, Dayze began discussions with its lawyers about protecting the IP for this new programme format, however Dayze has not yet discussed the idea for the new programme with any UK broadcasters. Conrad has connections with some Australian broadcasters and has suggested that he approaches them on Funzie's behalf, with a view to selling them a similar programme idea based on famous Australian landmark structures.

Requirements

(a) Using the data in the Exhibits on page 5 and the other information provided, evaluate Funzie's actual financial performance for 2012 in relation to both the 2012 budget and 2011 actual performance. Explain any further information required. **(14 marks)**

(b) Discuss Funzie's options for improving future profitability and the implications for its key stakeholders.

Use the following headings:

- Budgeting and cost control
- Options for increasing sales revenue

For this purpose ignore the specific proposal for the purchase of computer graphics software. **(13 marks)**

(c) Discuss the financial implications and strategic considerations of the proposal to bring all computer graphics in-house. Show any supporting calculations. **(10 marks)**

(d) Explain the ethical issues presented by Conrad Jack's suggestion and advise Funzie on appropriate next steps.

(6 marks)

(43 marks)

Exhibit 1: TV production industry average statistics year ended 31 December 2012

Programme type	Average commissioned price/programme hour £'000	Producer's average operating profit margin
Factual	200	10%
Period drama	425	8%
General entertainment	150	13%
Comedy	225	11%
Drama documentary	250	12%

Exhibit 2: Summary of Funzie Ltd's financial performance year ended 31 December

	Budget 2012 £'000	Actual 2012 £'000	Actual 2011 £'000
UK programme revenue	19,550	20,436	16,330
International programme revenue	1,000	1,200	860
Total revenue	20,550	21,636	17,190
UK operating profit (Note 1)	2,150	1,541	1,796
International operating profit	550	720	473
Total operating profit	2,700	2,261	2,269

Note 1: Analysis of UK operating profit

	Budget 2012	Actual 2012	Actual 2011
Number of UK programme hours completed and sold	85	91	71
	£'000	£'000	£'000
UK programme revenue	19,550	20,436	16,330
In-house variable programme costs	(3,870)	(3,660)	(3,236)
Outsourced variable programme costs	(12,836)	(14,550)	(10,648)
Fixed costs	(694)	(685)	(650)
UK operating profit	2,150	1,541	1,796

70 RESQ Ltd

RESQ Ltd (RESQ) is a London-based key-holding company, founded by entrepreneur Gemma Devereux. It provides a 24-hour emergency service for customers in London who have mislaid their house or car keys and need a spare set urgently so they can access their home or car.

Business model

Customers pay RESQ a monthly subscription to hold spare keys on their behalf. Subscriptions cost £3 per month (house keys) or £4 per month (house and car keys). This compares favourably to the call-out fees charged by local locksmiths if they are called out to access a house or car in an emergency.

If a customer urgently needs a spare set of keys, they call RESQ's 24-hour phone helpline. A courier collects the keys from the relevant RESQ depot and hands them to the customer at a pre-arranged meeting point, in exchange for a unique password. Delivery of the keys, in the London area, is guaranteed within a one-hour time slot. There is no call-out fee provided the customer makes fewer than four RESQ requests in a rolling 12-month period. After a request, the customer is responsible for returning the spare set of keys to RESQ.

RESQ is very security conscious. All RESQ employees and courier staff undergo a criminal records check and a financial credit check. Each customer's keys are kept at a secure depot, and labelled with a unique barcode so they can be identified but not linked to the customer's name and address. When requesting a spare set of keys, customers go through a rigorous security process.

RESQ currently has 15,000 customers and annual revenue of £700,000. There is a basic organisational structure. Gemma, the managing director and sole shareholder, makes all the decisions and manages a small team of employees who staff the 24-hour phone helpline, sign up customers, organise couriers, and conduct security checks and other administration. Gemma arranges external professional support from accountants, legal advisers and security experts when needed. RESQ leases space at three secure depots across London and sub-contracts all courier work to a London-based courier company.

New contract

Gemma believes RESQ will grow much faster if she targets corporate clients, such as banks or insurance companies, with an existing customer base. However she is aware that if this happens, she would no longer be able to carry out all the management herself. RESQ has been approached by a large insurance company, Genysis plc (Genysis). Genysis wants to enter into a contract with RESQ, whereby it will pay RESQ a fixed price annually to provide the key-holding service to 100,000 of its customers as part of its premium home insurance package. As Genysis's customers are located UK-wide, RESQ would need to develop the ability to cope with a national scale operation in the UK, rather than just London-based customers.

Genysis has asked for a large discount on RESQ's standard prices. All Genysis customers will be offered storage of both house and car keys and will be entitled to unlimited RESQ requests. Storing keys has a direct cost of £8 per customer per annum regardless of the number or type of keys held, or the location.

The chances of a request for keys being made by a Genysis customer in any one year are estimated as follows:

Number of requests per annum	0	1	2	3	4
Probability	40%	30%	20%	5%	5%

The average courier cost to RESQ for key collection and delivery is £15 per request and the secure depot charges £2 to RESQ each time a set of keys is accessed. RESQ estimates its existing fixed costs are £75,000 per annum, and that these would increase by £150,000 per annum as a result of accepting the contract with Genysis.

Requirements

As a senior in a firm of business advisers, write a report to Gemma Devereux which includes:

(a) An explanation of RESQ's current organisational structure and advice on how this may need to adapt if the new contract with Genysis is undertaken. Refer to relevant models.   **(9 marks)**

(b) A summary of the advantages and disadvantages of developing the business by working with a large corporate customer such as Genysis.   **(7 marks)**

(c) A discussion of the factors that would affect the profitability of the Genysis contract. Show supporting calculations including a break-even price, and state any assumptions.   **(8 marks)**

(24 marks)

71 Inkpen Ltd

Inkpen Ltd (Inkpen) is a family-owned chain of bookstores which specialises in the sale of textbooks to customers including school children, students, and teachers. Inkpen has 40 bookstores across the UK, many in university towns or on university campuses. Inkpen has a reputation for superior service and its staff are known for their advice, expertise and love of books. Stores hold regular discussion groups, technical talks and book readings and have a coffee area where customers can relax and/or study.

UK retail book industry information

The UK retail book industry is dominated by a small number of national and regional chains but there are also many independent bookstores. Some, like Inkpen, specialise in a particular market niche; others target a wide market. The industry changed radically after the internet led to the arrival of large online retailers which, because of their economies of scale, are able to undercut bookstore prices. Such competition at a time of economic pressure has led to the closure of many bookstores.

Recent technological developments have led to many people reading e-books rather than printed ones. E-books are digital versions of printed books which are downloaded and read on a PC, tablet, smart-phone or e-reader device (a portable reading device specifically designed to display written material in digital form). E-books are priced at a discount of 10 – 20% on the printed book. In 2012 e-books accounted for 13.5% of UK book sales by volume and 6.5% by value. One of the major online retailers

(Sahara plc) is also the main supplier of e-reader devices. In the UK, Sahara plc has 80% of the e-reader device market and 60% of the e-book download market.

There is fundamental uncertainty about the future of the industry and experts disagree on potential scenarios. Some believe that, as technology evolves, and e-books overwhelm printed books, traditional bookstores will disappear almost completely. Others believe that both types of reading media will continue to co-exist, as each has its own advantages. A small number believe e-books will prove to be a passing fashion that will only appeal to a very small niche market.

Impact of technology in relation to textbooks

Printed textbooks are mostly bought in-store rather than online, as customers like to browse before purchase, but price is a key factor. Many specialist bookstores lose sales because customers get advice on book selection from the bookstore, then buy the chosen textbook cheaper from an online retailer. Bookstores also face competition from local libraries and from a thriving student market in the sale of second-hand printed textbooks.

Although digital technology has had some impact, the majority of textbooks are still bought as printed books. New textbooks are often published in both digital and printed versions, but existing textbooks tend to be available in printed form only. Some publishers have been slow to produce e-textbooks, preferring to offer supplementary e-learning packages to enhance their printed textbooks, as this maximises their revenue. Research shows that printed textbooks support a wider range of reading and learning styles than e-textbooks. In a recent study commissioned by Inkpen, two-thirds of students said it was important to them to have access to printed copies of textbooks even when digital versions were available.

Future strategy

Inkpen was the first UK bookstore to provide an online shop in 1998. This allowed it to offer customers a wider range of books than it could carry in-store. Inkpen has worked hard to integrate its online business and physical stores: customers can now reserve books online and collect in-store. Customers can also place online orders in-store for printed books that are not in stock, the majority of which can be delivered next day from a central warehouse. Approximately 70% of all books sold by Inkpen are textbooks and 11% of Inkpen's total sales are made online.

Inkpen is considering a strategic alliance with a well-known American retailer of textbooks, Livro Inc (Livro). Livro has developed its own low-cost e-reader device, the Cartilla, designed to provide significant advantages over downloading e-textbooks to a PC, tablet or smart-phone. The Cartilla is very successful in the US because it has special text annotation facilities, is easy to read in all lighting conditions and consumes little battery power. Inkpen will have exclusive rights to sell the Cartilla in the UK. Inkpen's in-store coffee areas will be fitted with wi-fi technology to allow customers to test the Cartilla before purchase and to download e-books. Inkpen will earn commission on every Cartilla sold and generate revenue from every e-book downloaded onto a Cartilla by customers in its store. Customers who purchase a Cartilla will receive recommended reading lists and in-store promotional offers from Inkpen.

'This move will help us to guarantee our future in the digital age, without forsaking our roots,' said Inkpen's chief executive. 'The Cartilla will attract more people into our stores who will then buy printed books as well as e-books, so we can recapture some market share from the online retailers. We are aiming at readers who want to access both printed texts and e-books and who buy in-store as well as online. We can also increase our share of customers' spending on books other than textbooks.'

To increase e-book sales, Inkpen intends to offer special pricing deals for customers who purchase textbooks in both the printed and digital version. For example, it might be attractive for a student to acquire the printed textbook, but also be able to download it onto their Cartilla.

Requirements

(a) Explain how Inkpen might benefit from scenario planning when developing strategic responses to the uncertainty facing its industry. **(6 marks)**

(b) Analyse Inkpen's current strategic position, identifying the **key** internal and external issues and explaining why they are significant. For this purpose, ignore the proposed strategy to link up with Livro. **(8 marks)**

(c) From Inkpen's point of view, evaluate the proposed alliance with Livro.

Use the following headings:

- Strategic fit
- Resources and competences required
- Risks   **(12 marks)**

(d) Discuss the factors that Inkpen needs to consider in developing suitable pricing strategies for both printed books and e-books.   **(7 marks)**

(33 marks)

Exhibit 1 – An overview of the UK pet products retail industry

The UK pet products retail industry grew steadily by around 3% per year until 2008 when it reached total retail sales of £2,500 million. Since 2008, UK pet products sales have grown more slowly at 1% per year due to the recession.

Pet food makes up about 75% of pet products sales. The remainder comprises: pet accessories (eg, toys, bedding); veterinary services; and pet insurance. Pet insurance sales are growing rapidly, but insurance is highly regulated. Expenditure on products for dogs and cats makes up 93% of UK pet products sales. The highest growth in the pet food sector has been premium quality moist food, which has the highest price, largest margins and lowest consumer price resistance.

Animal welfare has become a key issue with new laws being passed requiring minimum standards of pet living accommodation, diet and medical care.

Pet owners now use social media network sites to share experiences and ideas and to recommend pet products to each other.

There has been a growing trend to tag dogs and cats electronically with microchips, so they can be recovered if they are lost.

On-line sales of pet products are increasingly common. There is also significant competition from pet superstores.

Exhibit 2 – Moogle company background

Moogle is one of the largest supermarket chains in the UK, with stores throughout the world. Overall, Moogle positions itself as mid-market, but it has many low cost ranges and many premium product ranges.

Stores vary from large out-of-town superstores, to small in-town stores. All Moogle stores carry pet products. However, the proportion of total sales made up by pet product sales at each store varies significantly.

Moogle has a narrow product range for pets, focussing mainly on dogs and cats with a wide range of foods, plus a moderate range of accessories.

Answer Bank

Guidance on mark plans

Introduction

This guidance has been put together by the examining team. It is possible, over time, as a result of candidates' performance in the real exams, that there may be further developments in the way in which mark plans are constructed. This approach builds on that applied in the old syllabus Business Management exam.

A document such as this can only ever provide broad guidance. The examining team set mark plans for each question on an individual basis, taking account of the overall structure of the question, the scenario, and the complexity of the analysis and argument required.

Allocation of marks

Typically it is not possible to allocate a half/one mark per point as it is in the more numerical papers. This type of approach would encourage a scatter-gun approach and reward answers making a long list on minor point, even where they fail to identify and explain the key issues.

Marks are therefore awarded in small pools which attempt to give an assessment of a candidate's performance for each sub-set of a requirement.

In fact it is often the case that the more succinct answers are better, since it is the quality rather than the number of points which attracts marks in Business Strategy.

As a general rule, the mark plan is constructed according to the following principles:

- **Numerical elements**

  Where the requirement includes a specific calculation, the total marks available will be broken down into a series of computation for the components of the calculation. Marks will be awarded for workings and not just for the correct final figure. Additional marks will be available for stating assumptions.

- **Data interpretation/analysis**

  One of the features of the new Business Strategy paper is that at least one of the questions will include data analysis.

  Specific marks for any necessary calculations/numerical analysis will be awarded as for numerical elements above. Also, however, appropriate calculations will need to be identified by the candidate and marks will be awarded for addressing the key issues.

  A greater proportion of the total marks available will be awarded for the following skills:

  - Interpretation of data
  - Considering cause and effect relationships
  - Identifying implications of the analysis
  - And for linking the data analysis to the wider strategy or issue in the scenario

  In these respects 'making the numbers talk' will be a key feature.

  Additional marks will be awarded for highlighting additional information required and/or the limitations of the analysis undertaken, even if not specifically asked for (although this may form part of the requirement).

- **Use of specific theories/models**

  Requirements will generally be open ended and candidates may be expected to identify the appropriate model to use in a particular situation. For example, a requirement to analyse the ways in which the business has grown might be answered by considering Ansoff and Lynch.

  Where a requirement calls for the application of a particular theory or model, there will be a limited number of marks for identifying the correct model and explaining its use. A greater proportion of the total marks will be awarded for applying the model to the scenario and discussing its limitations in the particular context.

- **Written elements**

  Each component of the requirement will be assigned a 'pool' of marks. An element of the marks in the pool will be available for demonstrating the correct knowledge but the majority will then be awarded to a candidate based on the degree of application, analysis and judgement demonstrated by the answer. Thus it is possible to identify the characteristics of various possible answers, together with their mark scoring potential:

  (a) Generic comments from the learning materials, which are not expressed in the context of the scenario. Answer includes lists of unprioritised, undeveloped and/or irrelevant points. Points listed but not explained.

  This constitutes a poor answer, scoring less than half the marks available in the pool and hence a 'fail' on the particular section of the requirement.

  (b) A number of generic comments but with some attempt to apply knowledge to the scenario in the question and to link points together in the form of key issues.

  An adequate attempt, scoring a little over half the marks available in the pool normally generating sufficient marks to attain a marginal pass.

  (c) Succinct points, made in the context of the question with little irrelevant comment. Some insights demonstrated. Logical argument backed up by analysis of the data/scenario. Demonstrates judgement by providing clear recommendations or advice where required by the question.

  A high scoring answer which would be awarded the majority of marks available in the pool (in some cases the maximum) and achieve a clear pass.

Presentation marks and workings

Generally, where specifically requested in the requirement, one mark would be awarded for presentation of a report/memo/briefing notes in an appropriate format.

Headroom

As can be seen from the sample paper and previous real exam papers, all written questions contain a degree of 'headroom', (ie potentially there are more marks available than the maximum for the requirement) as a range of different answers are possible. For example, the requirement totals, say, 20 marks, but the mark plan contains a total of, say, 25 marks. This means that a candidate could, in fact, score 100% without producing an ideal answer.

The published answers are mark *plans* and are designed to encompass many possible valid comments that a marker may see. As a result they are often more detailed than even a strong candidate would give in his or her answer.

Mark plans in the learning materials

The summary mark plans in the learning materials have been reviewed by the examining team. However, tutors should bear in mind that the mark plans in the learning materials have not undergone the full development process as those for the real exams where mark plans are tested over a large sample of candidates' answers.

Nonetheless, the above guidance can be illustrated by looking at the past real exam papers included in the question bank.

The mark scheme provided with each solution indicates relative emphasis of the sub-areas of the question.

Note that the marks awarded in the real paper may exceed these where the candidate's answers merit this.

1 Security Parking Ltd

				Marks	
(a)	(i)	Original costs	2		
		Current values	2		
				4	
	(ii)	Factors identified	5		
		Judgement skills	3		
		Use of data	3		
				11	
(b)	(i)	Switching strategy – Benefits	4		
		– Problems	4		
	(ii)	Market research – Nature and argument	5		
		– Data sources	2		
				15	
				30	

(a) (i) **Original cost**

Birmingham (ROI)

$$\frac{£250,000}{£750,000} = 33\%$$

Liverpool (ROI)

$$\frac{£360,000}{£3m} = 12\%$$

Birmingham (RI)

£250,000 – (£750,000 × 10%) = £175,000

Liverpool (RI)

£360,000 – (£3m × 10%) = £60,000

Current value

Birmingham (ROI)

$$\frac{£250,000}{£2m} = 12.5\%$$

Liverpool (ROI)

As above for cost (12%)

Birmingham (RI)

£250,000 – (£2m × 10%) = £50,000

Liverpool (RI)

As above for cost (£60,000)

(ii) Given that there is insufficient cash available, then the adoption of the new out-of-town strategy is dependent upon divestment of one, or more, of the existing car parks. This raises two issues:

- The performance (however measured) of the new car park(s) should be better than the old divested car park(s) being replaced.

- There is a change in strategic direction from an in-town strategy towards an out-of-town strategy that needs to be considered in the wider context of the capabilities and performance of the company as a whole.

In terms of operating performance, the illustrative data provided by the FD is actual historic data. However, in making any decision it is only the future that matters. Thus, for instance, the Liverpool site is relatively new and the data may reflect a 'bedding-in' period, whereby sales need to be established and customers won over by changing their parking and travel habits. This may take some time and thus the current performance would not reflect future performance.

In terms of the capital invested the RI and ROI should both meaningfully be based on current values rather than on the original cost (although given the recent purchase of the Liverpool site these values are the same).

If, however, the company has 'maintained a steady operating performance', as the marketing director indicates, then the change in RI and ROI for the Birmingham site indicates that performance relative to capital invested has decreased significantly (eg from a 33% ROI to 12.5%) mainly because of the increase in land values.

If, in future, land values continue to rise in city centres, then ROI and RI will continue to fall and may fall below the 10% threshold. However, operating performance is only one aspect of total performance. If land values rise in city centres, due to scarcity and planning regulations, then a gain would be made by SP from holding the asset, which would be independent from any operating profit achieved from car parking fees.

The capacity to make such capital gains in future must therefore be considered for in-town versus out-of-town sites alongside their relative operating performance. It is recognised, however, that predicting future property prices is a difficult task.

In terms of ROI and RI operating performance then, under normal circumstances, RI is the preferred measure as it gives an absolute gain after recognising a capital charge. In these circumstances of constrained capital, however, RI is not such a good measure as it fails to reflect the scarcity of capital. In these circumstances, the 10% is an inadequate measure of the cost of capital and the ROI % return would have more credibility than is usually the case.

What is really required is the RI per £1 invested or a credible marginal opportunity cost of capital. Thus, for instance, although the Liverpool site has a larger RI than the Birmingham site, this is largely because of the larger scale of the Liverpool site, rather than reflecting the efficiency with which it is using its capital. Therefore, if the Liverpool site were to be sold, it would finance three new out-of-town sites. Compare this to the Birmingham site, which would only finance two out-of-town sites. The opportunity cost of retaining the Liverpool site is thus larger.

Another way of examining the issue, to compare like-with-like, is that if we had three sites like Birmingham or alternatively two like the Liverpool site (so we had an equivalent £6 million invested in each) the three Birmingham type sites would yield an RI of £150,000 and the two Liverpool type sites would yield an RI of £120,000 using current values.

Leaving aside the relative operating performance of the two existing sites, it is clear that in absolute terms, they are only marginally profitable (ignoring capital gains). If land prices rise further, and operating performance fails to improve, then it may be that the return will fall below the threshold of 10% and should thus be divested, irrespective of whether the funds are reinvested in out-of-town sites. In these circumstances the investment and divestment decisions would be independent.

(b) **Memorandum**

To: Directors of Security Parking Ltd
From: External consultant
Subject: Out-of-town parking strategy
Date: XX/XX/XXXX

(i) **Strategic benefits and problems**

Strategic benefits

The new strategy is different in terms of location to the existing business but, other than the operation of the buses, it is a similar operational activity with similar core competences to the existing in-town business.

The major advantage of the new strategy is the lower cost of land. The illustrative data shows that 400 parking spaces are available for a land cost of £1 million (ie the capital cost of providing one parking space is £2,500). This can be compared to town centre capital costs per parking space of £20,000 for Birmingham and £18,750 for Liverpool at current values. Thus, in these cases the in-town cost per space is 7.5 or 8 times greater than out-of-town spaces.

The lower land prices may yield benefits which may be viewed in a number of ways:

- Lower fixed costs and thus lower operating gearing

- Potential from capital gains in future if land prices rise from their current low level (although this is dependent on market conditions)

- Lower capital cost for market entry when capital is constrained

- Potentially, a better return on investment with a lower investment cost

Of course, to generate value the available parking spaces need to be occupied by customers, but the indicative capital cost base is favourable.

A further benefit of the out-of-town strategy is that it is appropriate to environmental policies being put forward by national and local governments, which are likely to encourage out-of-town parking and discourage in-town parking. These policies may reduce in-town parking capacity and therefore increase demand for out-of-town facilities. Similarly, there is a growing culture, among some individuals at least, to behave in an environmentally friendly manner.

There may be greater ease of access to out-of town car parks where cities are congested. Bus lanes and other facilities may then ease access to city centres by using the park-and-ride system.

The bus service may attract additional customers and generate additional revenue. If priced separately from parking it may attract new revenue streams. Also, however, people living close to the out-of-town car parks may use the buses, but not the car park, if it is preferable to the local bus services.

Problems

While the land cost is lower for out-of-town parking, the annual operating costs are higher after the bus service costs are taken into account. Thus, for out-of-town car parks the illustrative data shows that 400 parking spaces are available for an annual operating cost of £400,000 (ie the operating cost of servicing one parking space per annum £1,000). This can be compared to town centre costs of £380 for Birmingham and £270 for Liverpool. Thus, in these cases the annual in-town cost is significantly lower than the out-of-town.

More significantly, these figures are based upon maximum capacity. To the extent that operating costs are fixed (eg lease rentals for buses) then operating gearing may be higher in the out-of-town sites. Thus, if only 50% utilisation is achieved then the operating cost per annum for each space actually used will rise to £2,000.

In terms of cost structure therefore the balance between capital costs (which favour out-of-town) need to be balanced against operating costs (which favour in-town).

The revenue side is considered in more detail below (under (ii) *Market research*) but it should be noted that the new strategy is likely to be subject to more risk as revenue streams at the existing sites are likely to be reasonably predictable on the basis of past experience. On the other hand, the revenues from the new out-of-town venture are more uncertain, even with the benefit of market research.

It may therefore be appropriate to increase the required return above 10% to compensate for the additional risk – at least in assessing performance in the early years.

Alternative aspects of risk are:

- **Exit route**: If the out-of-town venture fails then the exit costs from the venture would appear to be low. Land normally has a ready market value, particularly if there are limited additional development costs incurred, as is the case here where rough land has been used with little modification. The lease contracts on the buses may have some problems in being terminated but initial short-term contracts would limit this.

- **Barriers to entry**: If land is readily available out-of-town and the venture is successful then there are few barriers to entry for competitors. As a result there is likely to be a contestable market in the out-of-town sector, that was not the case in the in-town sector, where land is scarce and regulations prevent new entrants.

- **Barriers to re-entry**: If the out-of-town strategy fails it may be difficult to re-enter the in-town sector as sites are scarce. This out-of-town strategy therefore has the risk of being difficult to reverse if it fails.

(ii) **Market research**

Introduction

Market research is the systematic gathering, recording and analysing of information about problems relating to marketing of goods and services. Market research therefore involves gathering information about the 4Ps of marketing. The particular focus in this case is price but the other 3Ps will affect the price that can be charged and will be relevant to the volume of business achievable at that price.

In particular, the key objective for market research in this case is to determine the likely volume of customers and the most appropriate prices. Relevant to this objective are the following:

Place: The location of the car park is likely to be critical to the price and level of demand. This means that any market research is only likely to be valid with respect to a particular car park location. The idea of assessing the out-of-town strategy in the abstract without specific locations is therefore likely to be largely invalid.

Price: The price that potential customers are willing to pay is clearly a specific objective of the exercise although the current policy of charging 'per day or any part thereof' may be reviewed, and possibly changed, as a result of the research.

Product/service: In this case, the service needs to be considered in terms of the attributes that are likely to generate demand: (eg convenience; security; availability; frequency of buses).

Promotion: As a new venture, the initial impact of advertising and other promotion on price and demand should be considered.

A further factor to consider in market research is that essentially two separate services are being provided, and these may need to be priced, and researched, separately – ie car parking and the bus service.

In this case the subject matter being provided by SP is a service. Compared to market research on a product, this can limit the type and method of market testing that is possible or that is likely to be valid. The two broad areas of market research are however:

- Desk research

- Field research

Desk research

Desk research is the gathering and analysis of existing or secondary data.

In particular, this might relate to the total size of the potential car parking market for a particular city and the likely market share a new out-of-town car park may achieve.

Data sources for the total market size may include:

- Local government surveys of traffic volumes or car ownership
- Other transport economics research (eg universities)
- Environmental studies
- Any information made available by government authorities (eg the DVLA)
- Programmes of regular or special events (football and other sports matches)

In reviewing the information above, particular reference may be made to:

- Any 'day of the week' effects (eg weekend v commuters on weekdays)
- Any planned developments of out of-town shopping centres (which would reduce demand) or in-town facilities (which may increase demand)

Data sources for likely market share include:

- Locations of existing car parks
- Utilisation levels of existing car parks (are any full on a regular basis?)
- Total capacity of existing parking facilities
- Any planned changes in parking facilities in future (eg new car parks being built; closure or redevelopment of existing car parks)
- Consider the sub-market of a city where any car park might be located. Thus, if an out-of-town car park is located to the north of a city, the target market is likely in most cases to be only those people travelling to that city from the north. Any data sources should then specifically relate to this sub-area

Data sources for price include:

- Prices being charged by existing in-town car parks
- Prices being charged by existing out-of-town car parks
- Prices being charged by local trains that include station parking
- Prices being charged by local buses and the density and frequency of service

Field data

Data sources for the market size may include:

- Surveying existing car parks to count vehicles on a sample basis at different times of the day and the week.
- Interviewing local government personnel responsible for traffic
- Interviewing other local researchers
- Review planning applications for new developments
- New housing developments or population changes in the sub area which SP is targeting with a specific out-of-town car park

Data sources for likely market share and price include:

- Questionnaires of potential customer using other car parks/trains/buses
- Internet survey of local potential customers
- In depth interviews
- Surveying existing car parks to count vehicles on a sample basis at different times of the day and the week
- Target closest competitor car park to do in-depth analysis of prices and traffic movements

Examiner's comments:

Requirement (a) (i) asked candidates to determine the residual income and the return on investment for two of the original sites based on their original costs and on their current values.

In general, candidates performed well on this requirement, with many obtaining the correct solution and thus achieved full marks. Nearly all candidates appreciated that the cost calculations and the current value calculations were identical for the Liverpool site.

(a) (ii) requested candidates to explain how the company should select which of the current car parks should be divested in order to finance the new out-of-town car parks. Candidates were also asked to make additional calculations and to refer to previous calculations in requirement (a)(i).

There were some good arguments put forward by stronger candidates, supported by commercially realistic calculations that backed up the conclusions on the divestment.

Weaker candidates tended to provide purely descriptive answers, or only referred to their calculations in (a) (i). Many candidates uncritically favoured residual income as the sole criterion for a decision, without regard for the constrained nature of the company's financing position in this scenario.

(b) asked candidates, as an external consultant, to write a memorandum to the board to assess the merits of the expansion strategy and how market research should be undertaken to determine the pricing strategy and the volume of trade under the new strategy.

Candidates' answers were reasonable, but only the better candidates identified commercially realistic benefits and disadvantages of the proposed strategy changes relative to the existing strategy.

In relation to market research, answers were reasonable, but there was too much emphasis on defining the different types of research, rather than how the information should be collected and applied. There was generally not enough detail identifying appropriate data sources.

2   Pasta2Go Ltd

Marking guide

				Marks
(a)		Identify 2 key CSF	1	
		Explain 2 key CSF	2	
		Implementation	4	
				7
(b)	(i)	Financial perspective	3	
	(ii)	Customer perspective	3	
	(iii)	Internal business perspective	3	
	(iv)	Innovation and learning perspective	3	
				12
(c)		Ansoff matrix	2	
	(i)	Economics of scale	6	
	(ii)	Risk – Operating	2	
		– Financial	2	
		– Strategic	2	
	(iii)	Competitive position	4	
				18
				37

(a) **Critical success factors**

Critical success factors (CSFs) can be defined as 'those components of strategy where the organisation must excel to outperform competition. These are underpinned by competences which promote this success.'

Two CSFs may be

(i)   **Meal quality**: The nature and quality of the meals, which distinguishes the product from other similar suppliers of take-away and home-delivery meals.

(ii) **Delivery**: The speed and quality of delivery from order to customer receipt. This includes transport and cooking times, but also maintaining the food's temperature in transit. Most obviously this applies to home-deliveries, but waiting times for take-away food may also be a source of competitive advantage. Such times need not only to satisfy the customer but also to outperform rivals to give a competitive advantage.

Having identified appropriate CSFs, such as those above, the following stages might be appropriate in their implementation to establish a competitive advantage.

(1)   Identify the underpinning core competences for each CSF which generate a competitive advantage. These might include:

(a)   Meal quality

(i)   Ability of cooks relative to competitors
(ii)   Access to non-standard ingredients
(iii) Superior cooking equipment
(iv)   Quality and variety of recipes

(b)   Delivery

(i)   Delivery vehicles compared to competitors (eg insulation facility, or motorbikes to avoid queues)

(ii)   Local knowledge and reliability of the driver

(iii) Delivery charges

(iv)   Geographical areas of operation (proximity to areas of dense population compared to rivals)

(2)   Ensure that core competences continue to give competitive advantage by constant comparison with rivals.

(3)   Identify the Key Performance Indicators (KPIs) necessary to outperform rivals. These might include measures to assess the following.

(a)   Meal quality

(i)   Number of customer complaints or expressions of satisfaction
(ii)   Sample test results
(iii) Number of new customers (particularly recommendations)
(iv)   Amount of repeat business (number of regular customers)
(v)   Results of surveys of customers

(b)   Delivery

(i)   Average time from order to completion of cooking
(ii)   Average time from completion of cooking to receipt by customer (for home delivery)
(iii) Variances between promised delivery times and actual times
(iv)   Number of complaints about slow delivery
(v)   Number of complaints about cold food

(4) Ensure that competitors cannot imitate core competences.

    (a) Use of secret recipe(s)

    (b) Constant improvement in meals and service

    (c) Lower cost base enabling lower prices

    (d) Geographical dominance acts as barrier to entry (eg loyal customer base, insufficient local market to sustain more similar take-away outlets)

(5) Respond appropriately to new moves by competitors concerning their product, delivery or price that may affect competitive advantage.

(b) Balanced scorecard

(i) Financial perspective

Goals	Measures
Survive	Cash flow
Succeed	Total profit Profit per outlet Return on capital employed Total revenue Revenue per outlet
Prosper	Increase in revenue Increase in revenue per outlet Local market share

(ii) Customer perspective

Goals	Measures
Meal quality	Number of customer complaints Results of sample testing Number of new customers Amount of repeat business
Delivery on-time	Promised delivery times vs actual times Average time from order to cooking Average time from cooking to receipt Number of complaints about slow delivery Number of complaints about cold food
Competitive price	Comparison with competitors Price-based complaints Response of customers to price changes
Improve perception	Advertising Promotions Special offers

(iii) Internal business perspective

Goals	Measures
Quality of supply	Wastage of meals/ingredients New sources of supply of ingredients Orders received on time from suppliers
Quality of output (ie meals)	Staff training Quality of equipment (new cooking equipment) Quality of delivery and service Staff training Speed of cooking (new/more equipment) Speed of delivery (new/more motorbikes) Geographical span

(iv) Innovation and learning perspective

Goals	Measures
New products	Number of new menu items Proportion of sales from new items
New cooking techniques	Use of new recipes Use of new ingredients
New peripherals	Response to new packaging Response to new outlet refurbishment Response to new service
New ordering	Email (number of email orders) Regular customer priority (increased sales)

(c) Memorandum

To: Directors of Pasta2Go
From: A strategic consultant
Subject: Proposals for expansion
Date: Today

Introduction

This memorandum considers two proposals for expansion:

(i)   Franchising
(ii) The arrangement with BurgerGrill

While this memorandum will consider the relative merits of the two proposals, they may not entirely be mutually exclusive and expansion may be able to take place using both methods.

Expansion can be viewed within the Ansoff matrix.

	Products	
	Existing	New
Existing	Core business	New menu items
New	Franchising (in South of England) Pasta2Stay	Pasta-Burger

(Markets)

Economies of scale

Economies of scale are likely to take different forms and may provide different benefits in different circumstances.

The different types of expansion, which may give rise to economies of scale, include the following.

(i)   Growth of the number of outlets in the existing region (increased concentration)
(ii) Geographical expansion (into the South of England)
(iii) Product expansion (restaurant market)

Franchising

Under a franchise a firm grants other firms or individuals the right to use its brand, its product or its know-how. There is likely to be a degree of central control and support. In return, the franchisee will provide a lump sum, share of earnings and specific payments.

The benefits of franchising the Pasta2Go brand in the context of economies of scale are likely to include:

(i)   Quicker business expansion than using Pasta2Go's own financial resources alone, as there are new sources of capital from franchisees

(ii)   Retains incentives with franchisees keeping residual rewards and using local knowledge, thus profitability per outlet may be greater than by employing managers

(iii)   More franchised outlets may increase both concentration in the existing regions and geographical expansion. Given the lack of experience in the restaurant industry, this type of expansion may, however, be more difficult when using franchising

The consequential benefits include:

(i)   Reduced distribution costs (if concentration increases)
(ii)   Little increase in central fixed costs
(iii)   More effective advertising
(iv)   More income-generating units without an equivalent increase in capital invested by Pasta2Go

The drawbacks of franchising in respect of economies of scale include:

(i)   The need to share profits means less profits are being reinvested to expand the business

(ii)   Franchisees are likely to be small and thus may help with retail expansion but, unlike BurgerGrill, they are unlikely to provide any help with large-scale distribution into the South of England

BurgerGrill

BurgerGrill is providing economies of scale in two respects – increased financial capital and access to BurgerGrill's operations.

(i)   Increased financial capital is provided by BurgerGrill in the form of both share capital and loans. This enables increases in the number and the type of outlets.

        The benefits of this include those already cited above, except that franchisees are residual claimants whereas, in respect of their equity holding at least, BurgerGrill is a proportionate claimant.

(ii)   Access to BurgerGrill's operations involves significant synergistic benefits to Pasta2Go. These include:

        • Access to BurgerGrill's distribution network
        • Access to BurgerGrill's expertise in the restaurant market
        • Access to a new market outlet in the form of the 'pasta-burger' through BurgerGrill's restaurants
        • Common benefits where restaurants are adjacent (eg car park, reduced building costs)
        • Common advertising, promotions and offers

Risk

Franchising

Franchising can affect risk in a number of ways.

(i)   **Strategic risk**

        • Poor franchisees may generate the risk of harming the brand name beyond their individual outlet.
        • It may be more difficult to change the strategic direction of the business in future if franchisees have a degree of autonomy over the operation of their outlets.

(ii)   **Financial risk**

        • Reduced risk by having franchisees' own capital, thus the cost of failure is shared by the franchisee. This reduces the maximum potential loss from the failure of an outlet, but also provides an increased incentive for franchisees to succeed.

- Given that it takes two years for an outlet to achieve profitability, there may be early financial failures by franchisees due to lack of liquidity.

(iii) **Operating risk**

- There is a need to monitor franchisees as, while franchising maintains some central control, there is a risk that franchisees will have different objectives, methods and abilities compared to Pasta2Go.
- There is a reduced risk in that if franchising is to be taken up by many small operators, then Pasta2Go is not dominated by its business partner.

BurgerGrill

The following risks may arise from the arrangement with BurgerGrill.

(i) **Financial risk**

- Increased financial gearing arising from the new loans (which are greater than the increase in equity provided by BurgerGrill).
- Given that the company is not listed, a market value needs to be determined for Pasta2Go in order for BurgerGrill to buy-in at an appropriate value. Similarly, if an increase in BurgerGrill's shareholding to 50% is to be achieved, then a valuation method needs to be agreed on a pre-determined basis. An inappropriate valuation method risks losing value for existing shareholders.
- The new division, Pasta2Stay, may be set up as a subsidiary to reduce risk using limited liability. In reality, however, lenders are likely to require security against the assets of the parent company, or else charge a significant risk premium.
- Rapid expansion carries the risk of overtrading.

(ii) **Operating risk**

- Pasta2Go's existing shareholders risk losing control of the company if BurgerGrill takes up the option to increase its equity holding to 50%. This may result in a stalemate situation regarding important decisions.
- There may be confusion in the market-place over the two separate brands.

(iii) **Strategic risk**

- Expansion into the restaurant market is new, with a new brand name, and risks failure, as it is different from BurgerGrill's existing product and Pasta2Go's existing method of delivery. As a result, customers and competition may respond in an unexpected manner.
- The South of England is a different geographical market, which may have different types of consumer and competitor.

Competitive positioning

Franchising

Increased size arising from franchising should give Pasta2Go a stronger competitive position due to:

(i) Stronger market presence in existing markets
(ii) Stronger market presence in new geographical markets
(iii) Lower cost base from economies of scale to enable improved price competition

Overall, however, if franchising is to affect only the size of the current operations, and not its nature, then there should not be a significant effect on the market positioning of Pasta2Go.

BurgerGrill

There appears to be some scope for market confusion on the competitive positioning of Pasta2Go.

(i) The new Pasta2Stay restaurants are mid-market, but take-away food tends to operate in the down-market sector of the hot food industry. Yet they are presumably selling the same, or very similar, food.
(ii) The partnership with BurgerGrill is therefore one between a down-market provider (burgers) and a mid-market provider (Pasta2Stay).

(iii) The original market segmentation strategy of targeting young professionals returning from work may not be appropriate to Pasta2Stay customers, who might also be different from BurgerGrill's target market.

The prices to be charged are likely to reflect this confusion over market position, with perhaps very different prices for eat-in and take-away pasta/pizza. This can be compared with very similar prices normally charged for eat-in and take-away burgers.

This is particularly likely to be the case where the different products are being offered in the same geographical market.

Examiner's comments:

This was the largest question carrying 37 marks. It was also the written test question in which candidates performed best.

The scenario was that of a company with a chain of outlets selling hot take-away and home-delivery food. It is concerned about the most appropriate method of measuring performance. It is also intending to expand in the UK market, but it is undecided whether to use (i) franchising or (ii) a joint venture with an international hamburger chain.

Most candidates tended to answer the first part of part (a) very well, in identifying appropriate critical success factors. Unfortunately, it was a common weakness in the second part of this requirement that candidates failed to spell out how the company could implement these critical success factors to generate a competitive advantage.

The balance scorecard in part (b) produced variable answers. Most candidates identified the usual four perspectives of a scorecard, but too many failed to appreciate that the scorecard identifies specific goals and measures and, instead, tended to discuss general issues under each of the four headings.

Part (c) was in general reasonably well answered, although there was some variability in performance.

The economies of scale arguments tended to be too thin and merely suggested that bigger meant better, without thinking through what this actually meant in terms of the operating activities of this particular business.

There was also a failure by many candidates to distinguish adequately the different risks and market positioning strategies of the two proposals.

3 Monteverdi Master Appliances plc

Marking guide

			Marks
(a)	Levels of change	4	
	Types of change	6	
			10
(b)	Shareholders	2	
	Employees	2	
	Management	2	
	Customers	1	
	Suppliers	1	
			8
(c)	Cultural	3	
	Groups	2	
	Personal	3	
			8
			26

(a) **Comparison of types of change programmes**

(i) **Levels of change**

Change can take place at different levels within an organisation.

- Strategic level
- Structural level
- Process level

The current proposal for the change to globalisation is at the strategic level. This is a change that affects the long-term direction of the entire organisation both in terms of its production capability and in terms of its market competitiveness.

Previous cost reduction exercises appear to have been at a lower level in the company, being restricted to individual factories. This has included changes at the structural level. This is change in organisational structure which appears to have arisen from changes in reporting structures according to the FD, but may also have arisen from outsourcing if this was significant.

Previous cost reduction exercises have also included changes at the business process level. These are the changes necessary in processes, activities and the management of people in order to implement the chosen strategy. These are likely to have occurred as a result of selective redundancies, shifting production, and reducing capacity reported by the FD.

It should be noted, however, that while the new proposal is primarily at the strategic level the implementation of this strategy will also include changes at the structural and process levels.

(ii) **Types of change**

The current proposal also differs from the previous cost reduction exercises in terms of the type of change. There are four main types of change identified by the scale of change involved for the organisation. Two measures of scale can be used – impact and predictability.

- Impact

    - Adaptive – limited change which does not disrupt existing working methods

    - Fracturing – which disrupts current structure and working practices and requires a major change in culture

- Predictability

    How much is known about the effect of change on technology, finances, human resources.

By combining the two measures it is possible to see not only the four main types of change but also obtain guidelines for the best approach to change management. Regarding impact, the current proposal for globalisation appears to be fracturing change, as it would appear to be necessary to disrupt production worldwide. There are also changes in the current structure (profit centres to cost centres) and working practices, and requires a major change in culture.

By contrast the previous cost reduction exercises appear to be more localised and largely adaptive, taking place within a longer timescale and of more limited impact.

Regarding predictability, the entry of a new competitor appears to be unexpected. Moreover, the change is so fundamental that the consequences are likely to be uncertain. This is also implied by the need for a post implementation review after two years. By contrast the previous cost reduction exercises appear to be more repetitive, limited and thus predictable.

In summary the globalisation proposal involves high impact and low predictability. This is sometimes called transformational change (or revolution).

By contrast the previous cost reduction exercises involve low impact and high predictability. This may be regarded as small scale project planning (sometimes called evolution).

If the cost reduction exercises were major, they could be regarded as large scale project planning (sometimes called reconstruction).

(b) **Impact of globalisation change programme**

Shareholders

Shareholders require reassurance that the strategy will be implemented successfully and will result in a successful overall strategy that will enable MMA to compete and add value despite the new competition.

Regular and effective communication with shareholders about the nature and impact of the changes is important (having regard to insider trading regulations which require that information must be communicated openly and equally).

Employees

Production employees in one factory are to be made redundant – unless relocated internationally which seems unlikely in most cases.

Other production employees may have greater security arising from the changes. In particular if the new entrant in South East Asia is to focus on its local market the Malaysian factory may be most at threat under the existing structure but may be more secure under the new structure in serving a global market.

Marketing employees at each site may be made redundant or subject to a new reporting structure, given that marketing is to be global rather than at factory level.

Management

Local management may be made redundant in the factory which closes but may be more likely to be relocated than production staff. Other management will need to work under a new cost centre structure with less autonomy. Management may also be key figures in implementing change and acting as change agents. Management support is thus vital to the implementation of the change programme. They therefore need to be consulted and informed of the changes.

Customers

Customers may be affected by:

(i)   Short-term disruption of supply
(ii) No longer obtaining a product which is adapted to different geographical markets
(iii) Cheaper prices if costs are reduced
(iv) Longer lead times if supply is from a greater distance (depending on inventory holding policies)

Customers may be reassured by advertising. Stockpiling may also be necessary prior to the change to ensure continuity of the quantity of supply and the type of supply during the factional change period.

Suppliers

Given the geographical shift in production there may need to be major changes in suppliers. These changes could be favourable to some suppliers where new production is located to their local factory.

To other suppliers the change may result in the termination of the relationship with MMA.

Suppliers need to be informed of the changes if increased quantities or changes in the types of supply are to be satisfied under the new arrangement.

Where long-term contracts exist that are to be breached, then negotiation of contract termination needs to commence with possible legal advice.

(c) **Barriers to change**

There may be a number of barriers to change arising from:

(i)   The organisational culture
(ii) Groups of stakeholders with common interests
(iii) Individuals

(i) Cultural barriers

Structural inertia is the cumulative effect of all the systems and procedures the organisation has installed over the years to ensure consistency and quality. These act as barriers to change.

The new proposal for MMA puts forward fundamental changes that will affect the culture of the organisation. In order to change this, Lewin argues that the old culture of profit centres and geographical responsibility will need to be unfrozen; the changes made; and then a refreezing of the new culture should take place.

Power structures may be threatened by the redistribution of decision-making authority or resources, or the changing of lines of communication. In particular the change from profit centres to cost centres is indicative of a reduction of decision making authority in each division and increased centralisation of decision making, including for example the marketing function.

This will in particular affect management and thus management may be reluctant to implement changes which will be against their own interests.

(ii) Groups

Group inertia may block change where the changes are inconsistent with the norms of teams and departments, or where they threaten their interests. The factory most likely to close is most probable in forming a group. Also however the marketing employees in all four factories may form a group to resist change knowing that their jobs are most at risk.

(iii) Personnel barriers

There are also barriers which affect individuals and result in them seeing the change as a threat. This may affect not only the factory that is closed, but also the employees in the other factories where there are likely to be substantial changes in work practices and also redundancies of old skills in favour of new skills.

Habit, because habitual ways of work are hard to change, and the new and unknown is often uncomfortable. For example, the cost reduction programmes may involve greater mechanisation which will affect work patterns.

Security is almost inevitably threatened – job security and the security of familiarity. This may vary according to which site is seen as most under threat of closure.

Effect on earnings – continuing cost reductions and changes in work practices may affect the earnings of individuals.

Fear of the unknown reduces people's willingness and interest in learning new skills; they may lack the confidence to take on a new challenge where work practices change. While there is uncertainty over which factory will close, this may affect all employees.

4 The Complete Furniture Group plc

Marking guide

				Marks
(a)		KPI calculation	3	
		Financial measures	3	
		Non-financial measures	3	
				9
(b)	(i)	Strategy for retail division	9	
	(ii)	Outsourcing proposal	7	
				16
(c)	(i)	Planning the change	5	
	(ii)	Barriers to change	5	
	(iii)	Communication plan	5	
				15
				40

(a) Performance indicators

KPI calculations

	Out-of-town		High street	
Revenue per square metre	£1,871	$\dfrac{4,677,563}{2,500}$	£1,970	$\dfrac{1,969,500}{1,000}$
Revenue per £ rental	£12.47	$\dfrac{(4,677,563}{2,500 \times 150}$	£7.88	$\dfrac{1,969,500}{1,00 \times 250}$
Average transaction value	£ 400	$\dfrac{4,677,563}{11,700}$	£253	$\dfrac{1,969,500}{7,800}$

Other KPIs for stores

Financial measures

(i) Year on year sales growth
(ii) Store gross margin
(iii) Operating income as % revenue
(iv) Contribution per square metre
(v) Contribution per £ rental
(vi) Product sales as % total sales, by store and also for retail division
(vii) Product contribution as % total contribution, by store and also for retail division
(viii) Sales per £ spent on wages
(ix) Inventory turnover
(x) Store ROI

Non-financial measures

(i) Sales per hour
(ii) Orders per week
(iii) Conversion rate (number of walk-ins that convert into customers)
(iv) Number of items sold per transaction
(v) Level of returns per store
(vi) Number of product lines carried
(vii) Inventory obsolescence
(viii) Staff turnover

(b) Strategy for retail division

Options for retail division include some or all of the following:

(i) Sale of whole division to allow management and resources to be focused on more profitable trade sales division

Currently the retail division is making a sizeable loss (£78m) which in 20X6 has entirely negated the operating profit made by the trade sales division. Sales have fallen 4.5% from 20X5 to 20X6.

By contrast the trade sales division has seen a growth in sales of 10.5% and maintained operating profit at around 17% turnover.

If CFG cannot compete on cost then they may need to assess the viability of the whole division retail sales division.

Do CFG need to retain any stores? Closing stores and promoting an online home delivery business would considerably reduce wages and rental costs. It would also free up management time to focus on expanding the profitable trade sales business.

(ii) Closure of high street stores as suggested by the manufacturing director

The manufacturing director has suggested closing all high street stores. These account for 11% of the store portfolio by number, 5% of total sales and 8% of total rental costs.

Potentially they are taking a disproportionate amount of management time. However if CFG want cost reductions on a large scale, simply closing the high street stores is unlikely to be sufficient.

Calculations in (a) imply that high street stores are typically making better utilisation of selling space (higher revenue per square metre) but due to rental costs, the revenue per £ rental is significantly lower.

A typical high street store is 40% of the size of the out-of-town store but makes two-thirds the number of transactions. As a result a high street store is making more sales per day than the out-of-town store. This could mean that the high street staff are better able to convert walk-ins to sales but out-of-town staff are better at trading up the sale. Alternatively the higher average transaction value for out of town could be due to the fact that they have the space to carry higher value items. CFG should promote a home delivery function for the higher value items in their high street stores.

CFG may be less likely to lose sales/customers to competitors if there is another CFG store nearby. Most customers are likely to be mobile. In the event of closure, CFG should promote their nearest out-of-town store to try and prevent loss of customers to competitors. Alternatively lost sales could be minimised by setting up an online business.

(iii) **Possible closure of out-of-town stores**

KPI's suggested in (a) could be used to identify weak performers and therefore additional candidates for closure.

Different stores may be at different stages in their life cycle, eg a newly opened store may be in the growth phase, a more mature store may be seen as a cash cow. As a result their performance may not be comparable.

Poor store performance may be down to store location/ market conditions/central decisions rather than the manager – CFG should identify and retain their most able store managers ie decision re closure of store and termination of manager contracts should be made separately.

In deciding which stores to close, CFG should assess the relevant exit costs and likely savings:

- Penalties may apply to terminating the lease on certain stores

- Costs of redundancy may vary from one store to the next depending on profile of staff

- Need to consider savings likely to be made on closure eg some rents will be higher than others. If objective is to improve cashflow and profits, may target most expensive locations

- Other central costs/allocated overheads may not be eliminated by closure

(iv) **Remodel/downsize/relocate stores**

If CFG believe they have a competitive product (or will have after relocating manufacturing) they could try to remodel weak stores, rather than close them:

- Relocate stores to locations where rental is cheaper

- Consider changing the nature of the high street stores to offer a design and ordering service for later delivery. This would minimise the stockholding, reduce the space required and hence rental cost but keep the name on the high street

- The fact that kitchens and bedrooms are contributing 80% of turnover/gross margin but occupying significantly less than this proportion of space implies that CFG could reduce rental costs by reducing the size of their stores without significantly affecting profitability

Other initiatives to improve performance of stores could include:

- Improve operating efficiency
- Train sales staff
- Increase cross selling/trading up of sales eg sell kitchens as 'fitted'
- Implement a customer loyalty programme
- Improve delivery options

(v) **Change product mix**

- Streamline product range to exit unprofitable products and focus on ranges with the highest sales and profit potential, as demonstrated by KPIs suggested in (a), eg kitchens and bedrooms.

Issues to consider if decide to focus on certain product lines include:

- Interdependence of product lines – do customers expect a one-stop shop?

- Some locations within store will be better than others eg opposite front entrance v corner of top floor. This needs to be taken into account when comparing product performance

- Who controls costs of floor space and allocation of space to products – sales could be influenced by changing the allocation of floor space

(vi) **Set up Internet sales business**

- Develop online shopping with home delivery as an alternative distribution method

- Provides sales opportunity without need for high rental costs

- This could be done from the existing distribution centres if the manufacturing facility is retained

- May minimise the impact that store closures have on sales

- Could be used for the product lines that take up considerable store space but make lower margins

- Online market likely to be very competitive and need to consider whether management have the necessary expertise

Closing manufacturing and outsourcing production

Issues to consider

(i) **Closing manufacturing**

- Currently all production is sold internally – is this a strategic decision/a capacity issue or because there is no external demand for goods manufactured by CFG as they are too costly? Lack of external market pressures may have led to complacency and inefficiency.

- The division may not be manufacturing sufficient volumes to generate economies of scale.

- In-house manufacturing requires significant capital investment and WC.

- CFG have a fixed source of supply so are therefore less flexible in responding to changes in market/technology/buyer preferences.

- Manufacturing requires different management skills from management of retailing. Closure would free directors up to concentrate on sales side of business.

- There is an argument for manufacturing in house if it contributes to competitive advantage but the retail division director's comments imply this is not the case here.

- According to the retail director there will be knock on effects in terms of savings in distribution costs.

(ii) **Outsourcing**

- May give access to cheaper products eg through low cost labour and/or exchange rate advantages.

- May improve competitive advantage. Closing the manufacturing division and outsourcing the production overseas as suggested by the retail director may reduce the costs and improve sales and performance of the retail division. The director's comments imply that competitors have benefited from this.

- Reduces fixed costs and hence operating gearing.

- Reduces risk exposure.

(iii) **However CFG may encounter potential problems if closure occurs**

- May be problems in controlling supply chain: there will be admin costs and time spent in co-ordination.

- May be harder to guarantee supply.

- Delays in delivery may arise if products are being imported from overseas locations.

- May be harder to control quality, particularly with a variety of suppliers.

- There may be hidden costs eg impact of 'kick backs' required to do business in certain countries.

- Managing this change will require considerable time and effort on the part of management.

- Closure costs may be prohibitive: redundancies, exit penalties etc.

(iv) **In order to make the decision, CFG need to consider the impact on the other divisions**

- Is weak performance of retail division down to poor selling/store location or poor buying/uncompetitive cost of manufacture?

- What is anticipated impact on sales and operating income of both sales divisions of reducing costs of manufacture through outsourcing?

- Problems with supply, quality, timing of delivery etc may have adverse impact on growth of trade sales division.

- It may be better to consider whether costs can be reduced by rationalising existing set up and improving efficiency – reducing number of factories and distribution centres, moving to Just In Time manufacturing etc.

(c) **Memorandum**

To: Directors of CFG plc
From: A N Consultant
Date: XX/XX/XXXX
Re: Change management programme

As requested this memo sets out the issues that the Board need to consider in planning and implementing the various strategic changes under consideration.

(i) **Planning the change**

In order to plan there is a need to understand the context for change:

- Timescale: To what extent is CFG in immediate crisis or do they have the time available to plan carefully? For example, gradual closure of high street stores.

- Scope of change: The closure of the UK factory could be considered a transformational change, requiring a major shift in culture. The closure of some retail outlets and the remodelling of others is more likely to be brought about within the current paradigm and could therefore be seen as realignment.

- Capability: Do CFG management have the capacity and capability to implement the change.

- Power: Does the change leader have the power to bring about the changes?

- Readiness: Are staff aware of the need to change and willing to do so? What management approach is needed to ensure success?

- Resources: Are there adequate resources (people, finance, equipment) for the change?

- Culture: Does the existing culture represent a barrier to change? Does there need to be an interim internal programme to develop the structures, competences and commitment to tackle the major changes ahead of the adoption of the strategic change?

- Stakeholders: Level of power and interest of the various groups that are likely to be affected. Has CFG communicated the need for change to all stakeholders? How will CFG handle resistance from unions and employees? Is the change cosmetic eg to placate shareholders or will it deliver real results?

Effective change planning involves considering:

- What are the aims and intended outcomes for the change programme?
- How will the change be resourced?
- How much support/resistance is there to the change?
- What are the practical methods to be used?

A blueprint should be prepared which needs to record for each desired outcome:

- What action is to be taken, when the action will start, how long it will take and when it will finish
- Who will do what
- How will the actions be carried out
- Why – the purpose of the actions
- How, when and by whom evaluation will be carried out
- Must include launch: how to position the changes to gain most support

Monitoring and co-ordination is required to ensure everything keeps moving forward according to the blueprint:

- A senior and influential group of CFG executives must take responsibility for overall leadership and co-ordination.
- There must be a clear blueprint even if some of the precise timings are provisional.
- The blueprint must cover the whole range of activities planned.
- Carrying out the actual work of investigating what is needed and implementing new systems and policies should involve key people in the change target group.
- Change leaders should be carefully chosen for their skill and support.
- Methods of making changes following evaluation should be included.

(ii) **Barriers to change**

There may be a number of barriers to change in CFG arising from:

(1) The organisational culture
(2) Groups of stakeholders with common interests
(3) Individuals

(1) **Cultural barriers**

- Structural inertia is the cumulative effect of all the systems and procedures that CFG has installed over the years to ensure consistency and quality. These act as barriers to change.
- The new proposal puts forward changes that will affect the culture of the organisation. In order to change this, Lewin argues that the forces which maintain behaviour in its current form need to be unfrozen; the changes made; and then a refreezing of the new culture should take place.
- Redistribution of decision-making authority or resources, or the changing of lines of communication may threaten the existing power structures within CFG.
- This will in particular affect management who may be reluctant to implement changes if they perceive them to be against their own interests eg director of manufacturing division.
- CFG employees will be suspicious of changes to the comfort zone in which they are used to working. There may be conflicts due to changes in roles and responsibilities eg relocation of high street staff to out of town stores.

(2) **Stakeholder groups**

Group inertia may block change where the changes are inconsistent with the norms of teams and departments, or where they threaten their interests.

Examples include:

- Strikes and other forms of resistance to change implementation by CFG staff to be made redundant.

- Shareholders selling shares as a result of the changes.

(3) **Individuals**

- There are also barriers which affect individuals and result in them seeing the change as a threat. This may affect not only the UK factory that is to be closed but also the employees in the other divisions, particularly if there are some store closures.

- Habitual ways of working are hard to change, and the new and unknown is often uncomfortable.

- Job security and earnings will inevitably be threatened and changes to the usual environment cause uncertainty.

- Focus on continuing cost reductions and changes in work practices may bring concerns about the impact on earnings.

- Fear of the unknown reduces people's willingness and interest in learning new skills; they may lack the confidence to take on a new challenge where work practices change.

- Selective information processing results in employees ignoring management argument for change.

Motivating staff during the change period

- Communication about the reasons for change, the implications for jobs etc

- Participation in the process may improve motivation

- Emphasise training and development opportunities

- Prospects of retention or transfer within CFG may limit resistance to change

- Offer assistance for staff who are to be made redundant

- If staff are to be made redundant, they may be motivated by making negotiation of redundancy terms, references and assistance with alternative employment contingent on smooth transition

(iii) **Communication plan**

Stakeholders	Interests	Needs	Communication method
Shareholders	Interested in impact on share price and profitability/dividends. Have seen share price fall 25% in 20X6. Institutional investors may have different view to smaller shareholders	Reassurance re state of their investment and how strategy will benefit them/improve results	Press Website AGM Financial statements

Stakeholders	Interests	Needs	Communication method
Staff	Will be concerned re earnings and job security. Possibility of redundancy will increase their resistance to change. Could employ tactics to delay closures	Help to adapt to changes Training and support Information about impact on earnings and job security Counselling/help finding new employment	Briefings/team meetings One-to-one interviews with HR/line manager
Management	Will want to know how they are going to be involved in the process. Likely to be supportive of change, unless like manufacturing director or certain store managers they believe their jobs are under threat	Acknowledgement and involvement in the process Reassurance re position/ power Up-to-date information	One-to-one meetings Senior group meetings
Customers	Availability of supply Impact on quality and price Reliability of delivery	Motivation to stay loyal	Adverts Website Press releases/coverage
Financial press/ analysts	How and why has decision been made and how will it be implemented. What will future impact be on the business?	Knowledge of what is happening A good story	Briefings
Potential suppliers	CFG will represent a new source of business. What supplies will they want in future and on what terms?	Information	Trade press/magazines Website Meetings/letters/e-mail depending on size of prospective supplier

CFG should ensure groups are informed in a logical sequence to minimise unrest and rumours. Timing of communication will be critical to success.

5   Holiday Cottage Company Ltd

				Marks
(a)	(i)	Break even calculation	4	
	(ii)	Year of first profit	4	
				8
(b)	(i)	CSFs	3	
		KPIs	3	
	(ii)	Marketing strategy – owners	4	
		– Holiday makers	4	
				14
(c)	(i)	Core competences	6	
	(ii)	Risks	5	
				11
				33

(a)   (i)   Contribution per rental = £200 – £40 = £160

$$\text{Break even} = \frac{£80,000}{£160} = 500 \text{ rentals}$$

Break even for commissions = 500 × £200 = £100,000

Break even for gross rentals = 500 × £800 = £400,000

(ii)   Revenue is growing at (1.1)(1.05) = 15.5% per annum

Current revenue is £800 × 400 = £320,000

	20X6	20X7	20X8
Revenue (15.5% growth)	369,600	426,888	493,056
Contribution (20% × Revenue)	73,920	85,378	98,611
Fixed costs (5% growth)	84,000	88,200	92,610
Profit/(loss)	(10,080)	(2,822)	6,001

Thus HCC will make a profit in 20X8 for the first time in the absence of any expansion strategies.

(b)   **Memorandum**

To: Norman Hogg
From: An Accountant
Date: Mid-December 20X5
Subject: Holiday Cottage Company – CSFs and marketing strategy

(i)   **CSFs**

Critical success factors (CSFs) can be defined as:

Those components of strategy where the organisation must excel to outperform competition. These are underpinned by competences that ensure this success.

An alternative definition of CSFs is: 'A small number of key goals vital to the success of an organisation' ie 'things that must go right'.

As a relatively small player in the industry and still a new entrant it seems unreasonable to compete with the major companies across a wide spectrum of the market or attempt to copy the level of facilities they can provide. In competing in a niche market it may however be possible to outperform rivals. In this context the key issues for competitive advantage from the above appear to be:

- Maintaining and developing the relationship with customers

- Maintaining a good reputation with existing customers for repeat business

- Offering a level of support service that is difficult to copy

- Offering knowledge and specialisms and local presence in the geographically constrained SW England market

Key performance indicators can be used to measure CSFs including the following.

- Rebooking rate by property owners
- Rebooking rate by holiday makers
- Growth in lettings
- Lettings made divided by lettings available
- Market satisfaction surveys
- Exposure rate
- Number of enquiries

(ii) Marketing strategy

There are two markets that need to be considered for marketing:

- Property owners
- Holiday-makers

Promotion

Both need to be attracted simultaneously in order to bring the two aspects together. Property owners need to be encouraged to use HCC by perceiving there to be a supply of holiday-makers visiting the website. However, holiday-makers will only visit the website if there are available properties.

There are three aspects to HCC's advertising:

(1) The website – to encourage people to enter the website there needs to be advertising elsewhere including on the Internet, in books and magazines etc to encourage holiday-makers to visit HCC's website rather than rival websites and other rival advertising media for holiday cottages.

(2) The properties on the website – once potential holiday-makers enter into the website each home needs to be advertised to its maximum potential in order to encourage further enquiries and bookings.

(3) Other advertising in magazines and newspapers causing customers to book holidays or offer properties directly without using the website.

General promotion strategies

- Writing more articles – perhaps in specialist or travel press.
- Obtaining customer lists from clubs/associations of holiday home owners

Segmentation strategy

Property owners

A geographical segmentation strategy is suitable for property owners given the focus on the SW of England. This might include:

- Databases of self catering holidays in SW England
- Estate agents selling new buy-to-let properties
- Advertising by other local holiday letting companies

A key problem is that while all the properties are located in the SW, the owners are likely to live elsewhere.

Given the concentration in the SW other segmentation strategies (eg socio-economic groups) may be too wide-ranging and thus ineffective. To the extent that socio-economic segmentation is valid then higher income groups may be targeted.

Holiday makers

The segmentation strategy is likely to include higher income groups given the premium nature of the properties and the service provided. This might include professionals and high income groups.

The nature of the target market also includes families so advertising in upmarket family magazines may be appropriately for targeted advertising.

Pricing strategy

One aspect of the marketing strategy is the pricing strategy.

There are two aspects to pricing:

(1) The price charged for a week's rental to holiday-makers.

(2) The percentage commission fee charged by HCC to the property owners (based on the rental).

(1) **Rental charge**

The rental charge to holiday-makers needs to be agreed between the owner and HCC. If it is too high there is no point in HCC taking the client as it is unlikely to be rented out.

The target market is the quality end of the properties and customer base, thus the price should be in accordance with this as:

- Where the customer cannot fully observe the product or service prior to purchase then perceived value pricing indicates that the price is a signal of quality.

- If the properties are of good quality then a high price consistent with this can be attained and repeat business based on full information is still possible.

Constraints on the price may however include:

- Prices charged by direct competitors for similar accommodation.
- Prices charged by comparable accommodation (eg hotels, holiday sites) in the SW of England.

(2) **Commission**

The success of HCC in renting out property is based upon the actual and perceived service delivered to the clients. This consists of:

- The comprehensiveness of the service for any one letting (administration, advertising, cleaning, a hand-over service between rentals and insurance).

- The volume of lettings achieved by HCC and thus the utilisation achieved by the property owners.

Prices charged by direct competitors for similar services will be a key constraint, but as a newcomer to the industry HCC might need to consider charging a lower fee to break into the market, despite its high level of service.

(c) (i) **Core competences**

Core competences are linked with the critical success factors noted above for the existing business. The two new strategies however operate in different sectors of the market from the existing business. The key question is therefore whether the existing core competences can be transferred into these new market sectors for the proposed strategies.

Strategy 1 – France

- Local knowledge no longer applies as it does in SW England so this core competence of local knowledge is lost.

- SW Cornwall is similar in some respects to NW France, therefore there may be a similar customer base of property owners with which HCC is familiar (ie the same customer base may generate a similar segmentation strategy).

- The target market for holiday makers is also similar, except for the geographical difference.

- Core skills in website design and marketing enables cross selling between the two markets.
- There is a language advantage for UK holiday-makers and UK property owners over French competitors although this becomes a disadvantage in managing local services, employment etc.
- No experience in the French market (locations, pricing, competition).

Note the key question is not whether HCC has the above skills but whether they are superior to those of competitors and potential competitors, based in the UK and in France, and that they can be sustained to generate a competitive advantage.

Strategy 2 – No frills

- Existing high service, high price, culture and expertise is lost.
- Specialist knowledge of the SW is not relevant so it is not clear where there is any competitive advantage over similar websites and holiday property agents.
- The target market for holiday-makers is different from the existing market, being broader. So there is little market knowledge transfer from the existing business as the client base is wider.
- There appears to be little to suggest that HCC has an industry cost advantage other than the fact that it has an established web site.

It would seem therefore that HCC has few core competences to support this strategy.

(ii) **Risks**

Strategy 1 – France

- Currency risk as some costs are in euros but rentals and commissions are in sterling.
- Low operating gearing as there are few additional fixed costs. This lowers risk.
- Unknown market with limited experience of service provision.
- Diversion of management attention from core market.
- The market may be saturated already with French providers of holiday homes. These may have advantages of language, communication and local contacts over UK providers, even for UK holiday makers.

Strategy 2 – No frills

- High initial fixed costs mean these costs are sunk and irrecoverable if the venture fails.
- High risk from high operating gearing.
- Could lose some existing business as there may be a substitution effect between the existing and the new business.
- Brand confusion (down market vs up market). The two products may confuse customers as to whether the company offers a premium service or a no frills service.

Break even

The break even calculations in (a) show that the company has existing rentals of 400, whilst 500 are needed to break even. The new strategies thus need to be seen in the light of a loss making business. Strategy 1 incurs few additional fixed costs and thus the break-even point would be similar. Additional sales in France combined with more sales in the core market may enable break even to be achieved.

Strategy 2 however will incur more fixed costs and raise the break-even position.

Examiner's comments:

This scenario considers a start-up business which acts as an intermediary between individuals who own holiday properties and individuals wishing to rent such properties for their holidays. A key issue for the business is the need to generate sufficient commission revenue to cover fixed costs while it is attempting to establish itself in the market during the start–up period. A key aspect of this problem is for the business to market itself both to owners and to users of properties, but also to provide a distinct service from other intermediaries which are already established in the industry. Two new strategies for expansion are being considered for the second year of operation.

Requirement (a) asked candidates to make two calculations. Firstly, they were required to determine what would have been the break-even revenue for the current year; and secondly, using the projected growth figures, what is expected to be the first year in which the company breaks even.

Candidates' performance in the calculations was, in the main, disappointing. The break-even required a little thought, given that the company was an intermediary rather than a retailer or a manufacturer, but should nevertheless have presented few problems.

More candidates were able to identify the first year in which profits were achieved, although a variety of methods were used. Some candidates stopped at 20X7 thereby assuming, but not demonstrating, that a profit would be made in 20X8.

Requirement (b) requested candidates to identify the critical success factors for the company and to develop marketing strategies for both property owners and for holiday-makers.

The identification of critical success factors was well answered, although links with KPIs were not always noted. Weaker candidates failed to develop the particular CSFs that would be appropriate to this type of business.

In relation to the marketing strategy, better candidates clearly thought out their approach and separately identified different marketing strategies for each of the two customer groups. Some were able to put forward reasonable commercial ideas as a consequence.

Unfortunately, however, too many candidates merely listed out the 'Four Ps' model in a very standardised form and then squeezed the circumstances of the question around this model, thereby producing relatively unimaginative ideas. Indeed, in recent sittings where a question has included the topic of marketing, there has been a tendency by candidates to use this model as the standard approach to all marketing problems of any kind.

Requirement (c) asked candidates to address the two new proposed strategies of international expansion and a low cost, 'no-frills' service. For each strategy candidates were required to identify and explain the core competences and risks.

In general, candidates performed reasonably well on this section. The better candidates were able to link the core competences to the critical success factors in requirement (b). Similarly, the better candidates linked part of their analysis of risk to the calculations of break-even in part (a).

6 The Slate Snooker Table Company Ltd

Marking guide

				Marks
(a)	(i)	Selling price change	3	
	(ii)	Volume change	3	
				6
(b)	(i)	Scale of changes	3	
	(ii)	Risks	3	
	(iii)	Competitive position	3	
				9
(c)		Profit	3	
		Performance measurement	3	
		Other issues	3	
				9
(d)		Calculations		4
(e)		Non-financial performance measures		4
				32

(a)   Snooker tables sold $= \dfrac{£15m}{£3,000}$

$= 5,000$ tables

Variable cost per table $= \dfrac{£2.5m}{5,000}$

$= £500$

Contribution per table $= £3,000 - £500$

$= £2,500$

(i)   Existing loss $= £1,000,000$

Additional cost $= £2,000,000$

Additional revenue required $= £3,000,000$

Additional revenue per table $= \dfrac{£3m}{5,000}$

$= £600$

(ii)   Number of additional tables to break even $= \dfrac{£3m}{£2,500}$

$= 1,200$ tables

(b)   **Scale**

(i)   **Price change**

An increase in price of 20% would be needed to break even. A price increase of 13.3% would be needed just to cover the sponsorship costs. This however assumes that the reputation effect of the sponsorship only lasts for one year.

Volume change

An increase in volume of 24% would be needed to break even.

A volume increase of 800 tables (ie 16%) would be needed just to cover the sponsorship costs.

Thus break even is 6,200 tables with the marketing director's suggestion.

Existing break even is $= \dfrac{£13.5m}{£2,500}$

$= 5,400$ tables

Beyond 20X6 this would also approximate to the break even position as sponsorship costs are only incurred in one year (under current proposals). If reputation, and thus demand, are improved in the long term then a break-even position may be more readily attained beyond 20X6.

(ii)   **Strategic and operating risks**

The higher level of fixed costs with sponsorship will increase operating gearing very significantly in 20X6. This will lead to significantly increased operating risk if the estimates of increases in selling prices and sales volume are not achieved.

Volatile demand in the industry will cause uncertainty in the sales prices and sales volumes achieved by SSTC.

There is a risk of losing customers by increasing the price. While there might be a short term reputation effect from sponsorship there is a risk that the increased price is unsustainable in the longer term. This may cause confusion in the market about the positioning of SSTC's product.

There is a risk of competitor reactions to a price or volume change in terms of their own marketing/advertising in order to change their own reputation and competitiveness. They may also change price to respond to SSTC's price change.

(iii) **Competitive position**

The price increase from £3,000 to £3,600 will lead to a different strategic positioning in the market for SSTC. This may alter SSTC's market position bringing it into more direct competition with higher quality producers than previously. While sponsorship may improve the perceived quality of the product it will not improve actual quality.

The sponsorship, however, is a short-term effect and whether this reputation improvement is sustainable on the basis of one year's sponsorship is questionable. Alternatively, a long term sponsorship commitment may be required to sustain the improved reputation, but this will increase fixed costs in the long term.

SSTC also operates in two distinct markets – snooker clubs and the home market. It is possible that snooker clubs will be less concerned than the home market about reputation.

The snooker clubs market may also be more concerned about price than the home market and thus demand may be more elastic.

One possibility would be to price discriminate by considering market positioning separately in each of the two markets.

(c) **Impact on profitability**

This suggestion is one of downstream vertical integration. It is, however, unusual in that the vertical integration is not with an existing customer. There may therefore be some increase in profitability to the group entity, as snooker tables are in effect being acquired at their variable cost of manufacture rather than the price previously paid by NSC to their previous supplier.

Strategically however SSTC has no core competences in snooker club management and thus there are questions over management's strategic ability to control and improve the profitability of NSC from its current break-even position.

The expansion into snooker accessories may also enhance group profit although this is a new business where there appear to be few existing core competences in either division and the business would need to compete with other established suppliers of accessories.

Divisional performance measurement

The transfer price will partly determine the relative performance of the two divisions. Unless this is set at an arm's length market price this will distort divisional performance.

Even where the transfer price is at arm's length, it is suggested by the finance director that NSC will purchase its tables from SSTC in future while it does not do so at present. This implies some form of compulsion on the divisional head of NSC in changing the supplier of tables from the existing supplier. If this is the case, it becomes difficult to measure the performance of that division, and that of its manager, as there are restrictions on their decision making.

If the finance director's other suggestion of selling accessories is implemented then it is unclear whether they will be sold by one, or by both, divisions. In the latter case there may be some inter-divisional conflict in making sales.

New reporting structures and management information systems will be required.

Risk

Risk adjusted performance will need to be considered. A significant fixed cost investment has taken place in NSC which will increase operating gearing.

Conversely, however, there is some diversification into other products. Unfortunately, these are still all systematically linked to the popularity of the sport of snooker so a common and systematic industry risk exists from fluctuations in the sport's popularity.

New organisational structure

The new organisational structure is a mixture of divisions and functions if the existing functional lines of reporting are maintained. This may then look like a matrix structure.

Alternatively the functions could be kept within the divisions.

The separation of management of the divisional structure may be appropriate as:

(i)   This would maintain autonomy with transfer prices and assist divisional performance measurement.

(ii)   The core competences of each business could be developed separately to maintain existing management skills.

Other issues of vertical integration

Other issues include:

(i)   There is reduced flexibility for NSC to change the suppliers of its tables. This may be restrictive as SSTC only makes one type of snooker table.

(ii)   Liquid resources will be consumed in the acquisition of NSC.

(d) Snooker tables sold   = $\dfrac{£15m}{£3,000}$

                            =   5,000 tables

Variable cost per table   =   £3m/5,000

                            =   £600

Contribution per table   =   £3,000 – £600

                            =   £2,400

Number of tables for B/E   =   £13m/£2,400

                            =   5,417 tables

Thus the break-even position has increased from 5,400 to 5,417 by changing labour into a variable cost.

(e) Measures might include:

(i)   Quality measures – faults, complaints, customer call outs.

(ii)   Balanced scorecard – financial, innovation, customer, internal business.

(iii)   Benchmarking – internal (against other fitters), competitive (other companies), activity (other similar self-assembly activities), generic (fitters in other industries eg kitchens).

(iv)   Budget targets – targets per month for number of jobs without additional call outs, low rectification costs.

Examiner's comments:

The scenario was that of a manufacturer of snooker tables, which is currently suffering losses. The directors are considering three new strategies to improve profitability: sponsorship; vertical integration with diversification; and changes in the method of remuneration for some employees.

Candidates performed reasonably on this question but the major discriminating factor between good and weak candidates was the ability to do the calculations correctly. The weakest candidates failed to make a serious attempt at the calculations.

Requirement (a) was well attempted, with most candidates correctly determining the required answers in each case. Surprisingly, however, a number of candidates obtained the correct break-even price but were unable to determine the correct break-even quantity.

A number of answers with the correct calculations showed the required new break-even price and volume, rather than the required increases in price and volume, but this was a reasonable approach.

Some weaker candidates failed to score any marks on this requirement. Many of these candidates made only a nominal attempt at the calculations.

Requirement (b) requested candidates to appraise the marketing director's strategy proposal, including: the scale of the changes required to break-even; strategic and operating risks; and the competitive position.

Regarding the break-even section, candidates' attempts were reasonable. Few candidates, however, considered the longer-term effects on break-even. For example, few made the point that the existing break-even would also be similar to the break-even beyond 20X6, as the sponsorship cost is only incurred in one year.

Where candidates made incorrect attempts to calculate break-even in requirement (a) full credit could be given in this section for a correct analysis of their (incorrect) figures. Candidates making no attempt at the calculations in (a) were more restricted, although some made an assumption of the break even amount and based their analysis on this assumed figure, which was an acceptable approach.

The section on strategic and operating risks was fairly well answered. The key weakness for many candidates was to focus on one risk, or one type of risk, thus restricting their analysis.

Regarding competitive position, few candidates observed that the firm operates in two separate markets.

Requirement (c) asked candidates to assess the merits of the finance director's suggestion regarding vertical integration and diversification. This was fairly well answered, although only a minority managed to do full justice to some key points including the impact on profitability, divisional performance, transfer pricing and risk.

Many weaker candidates tended to provide a list of merits, then a list of demerits, without any overall analysis or any particular logic to the order of presentation.

Requirement (d) requested candidates to determine the impact on break-even of the HRM director's suggestion to make some employee costs variable with production. Those candidates answering requirement (a) correctly, generally managed to answer this part correctly as well, but this was not always the case.

As with requirement (a) some weaker candidates failed to make a serious attempt at the calculations in this requirement.

Requirement (e) examined the impact of the HRM director's suggestions on non-financial measures. This was reasonably well answered, on the whole.

7 Furbiton & Frobisher plc

Marking guide

				Marks
(a)	(i)	Departmental performance	6	
	(ii)	Departmental managers	6	
		Closure of electricals	3	
				15
(b)	(i)	Planning the change	4	
	(ii)	Barriers to change	3	
		Motivating staff	2	
	(iii)	Communicating the change	4	
				13
(c)	Strategy 1	– Financial	3	
		– Strategic	3	
	Strategy 2	– Financial	3	
		– Strategic	3	
				12
				40

(a) (i) **Departmental performance**

Financial measures

The measure of performance used should be consistent with the company's overall objectives in order to assess the contribution that each department makes towards achieving the goals of the organisation.

As a listed company, the objective would normally be to maximise the wealth of the shareholders, which would be equivalent to the discounted future income stream of each department. In measuring current performance therefore it is difficult to identify one indicator of future earnings generation.

Current performance therefore does not need to be measured by only one criterion but rather by a range of measures that may capture aspects of both current performance and potential future performance.

Comparative measures

The existing measure of performance used by FF appears to be profit, as each of the departments is a profit centre. On its own, however, profit is not enough, as some benchmark is needed against which to judge profit in order to judge performance. This might be:

- Budgeted profit
- Profit per unit of a constrained resource, such as floor space
- Return on investment (ROI)
- Residual income (RI)

The particular method used will also depend upon the purpose to which the performance measure is to be used. Two possible uses are as a comparative measure (i) between different departments within one store and/or (ii) between similar departments in different stores.

In this case, any basis of comparison needs to be valid. For instance if ROI or RI is to be used then the capital base on which the measure is determined needs to be constant. Thus for instance, the historic cost of a store built in the 1950s would not be comparable with a new store which was recently purchased. The depreciation figure and the capital base would both be distorted.

Even measures such as floor space may not be comparable. Within any store a square metre of floor space in the corner of the third floor would not be as valuable as a square metre by the ground floor main entrance to the store.

Allocating costs

A related issue is that of charging departments with overheads. Allocations of fixed costs are arbitrary (eg head office costs) and this is likely to distort performance in any circumstances. The equal allocation of such costs irrespective of size as in the case of FF appears to be particularly distortionary.

Allocations of floor rental costs is also arbitrary. This is partly due to the fact that there is no direct cause and effect relationship between the amount of floor space and the profit generated. This is partly because, as already noted, floor space is not homogeneous as certain areas of floor space are more valuable than others depending on the location within the store.

Also, however, what is really important with respect to the allocation of store space between the departments is to maximise overall performance. This is achieved not by how much profit is generated on average per square metre, but which department can use space, at the margin, to generate the greatest marginal profit.

One method of reducing profit measurement problems is to examine the contribution per department rather than the profit. However, while this reduces cost allocation problems, many of the other issues cited above remain.

The contributions generated by each department are as follows:

	Clothing £m	Furniture £m	Cosmetics £m	Electrical £m	Total £m
Revenue	80	30	20	70	200
Direct costs	(55)	(20)	(8)	(65)	(148)
Contribution	25	10	12	5	52

This table shows that all departments make a positive contribution but it leaves unresolved the issue of rental costs which are avoidable at the individual store level of performance and are a constrained resource.

Contribution per £1 of rent (which reflects floor space) are:

	£
Clothing	3.13
Furniture	2.50
Cosmetics	3.00
Electricals	0.63

This shows that, on average, Clothing departments use floor space most effectively and Electricals least effectively. The difficulties of assessing contribution from marginal usage of floor space and future contribution also remain. For instance, will Clothing be as profitable next year having lost the Italian supplier?

Non-financial measures

In addition to measuring the financial performance of departments a series of non financial measures can be used to widen the basis on which performance is measured and capture, to a greater extent, the objectives of the organisation.

Non financial measures can include:

- Benchmarking – internal benchmarking can look at the performance of the best FF store and measure the others against this. Competitive (ie external) benchmarking could look at the best performing stores in the industry.

- Balanced scorecard – looks at CSFs and measures these with KPIs appropriate in each case. The four perspectives include: financial, customer; innovation and learning; and internal business.

- Customer satisfaction measures – surveys of customers, field research.

- Stakeholder relationship surveys – employees, suppliers (eg for clothing the reasons for losing the Italian supplier).

Other issues

The performance measures should fit in with the wider strategy. Thus, for instance if reputation is a key CSF for long term profit then this should be a major issue in selecting the non-financial performance measures.

There may be conflict between objectives. For instance short term profits could be made by raising prices significantly, or by cutting costs by reducing sales staff, but in the longer term this may damage reputation and thus may be value reducing.

Different strategies may be appropriate for different departments. As a result, different performance measures may be appropriate for different departments. For instance, the furniture department is recently established and may be in the growth phase of its life cycle (a question mark in the BCG matrix). Growth objectives and breaking into the market may be thus more important for furniture than for other departments. For instance, clothing is a mature department and may be seen as a cash cow in the BCG matrix, and thus different objectives such as cash generation may be appropriate.

(ii) Department managers' performance

Many of the same issues arise for measuring the performance of managers as for measuring divisions' performance. In addition, however, there is an emphasis on controllability of costs and revenues and on autonomy.

The key issue here is that it is unreasonable to hold managers responsible for factors over which they have little or no control. Unfortunately, this leaves a large 'grey area' for the many issues that managers can influence, but which are also affected by internal and external factors which they do not control. Such areas are a matter for qualitative judgement rather than precise quantitative measurement.

The idea of control is manifest in responsibility centres and the responsibility centre used by FF is that of a profit centre. This requires that managers have control over revenues and any costs included within the profit centre calculation.

The costs that should be included are controllable costs, but this raises some questions in the context of FF.

In terms of revenues, the managers of the electrical departments may be very able but adverse market and competitive conditions, beyond their control, seem to have meant that the market is very weak.

In terms of costs of acquiring inventories, it is not clear whether the managers are responsible for sourcing the products sold in their departments. If not, then any weak performance may be as a result of poor buying, rather than poor selling, which would be beyond the control of the departmental manager. One way to bring such costs within the control of managers would be to give them responsibility for purchasing policy but they may have no competence in performing this function.

Control over floor space costs may similarly be beyond the managers' control. However allocations of floor space costs need not relate to actual rental costs. One way to give managers more control would be for managers to bid for floor space so there is an internal market pricing mechanism like a transfer price. This would make floor space costs a more relevant opportunity cost, and bring them within the control of mangers for performance measurement purposes.

Other overhead cost allocations appear to be entirely beyond managers' control. It would appear unreasonable to include these within controllable costs for the purpose of assessing the performance of managers.

One particular point of note is that the furniture managers in five departments have left to join a rival company. This may suggest:

- They were performing well as a rival company has 'poached' them from FF.

- In a competitive labour market that they were not being remunerated sufficiently to retain them or that the measure of performance used to determine remuneration was not capturing their 'true' performance as discerned by the external labour market for this type of manager. In the furniture departments' case there was no profit earned on which to pay a bonus but, as a new and growing department, this may not have captured their managers' achievements.

Closure of electrical departments

The electrical departments currently make a positive contribution of £5 million per annum. However, this is not enough, on its own, to keep them open as:

- Future forecasts may be for continued decline given the difficult market conditions and it is only the future that matters in the closure decision.

- Alternative strategies may generate a contribution of more than £5 million using the vacated floor space.

- The wider strategy of product mix needs to be considered not just short-term contribution.

It may be that an intermediate solution of closing only the worst performing electrical departments is possible as it is unlikely they are all performing the same. This however leaves open the question of whether a critical mass remains (eg to obtain quantity discounts in purchasing).

(b) **Memorandum**

To:	The Board of Furbiton and Frobisher plc
From:	A Consultant
Date:	Today
Subject:	Change management programme

Planning the change programme

Initially it is necessary to consider the aims of the change programme to close Electricals and replace them with the decided alternative strategy.

Blueprint

The blueprint needs to record for each desired outcome:

(i)   What action is to be taken

(ii) When the action will start, how long it will take and when it will finish

(iii) Who will do what

(iv) How the actions will be carried out

(v)   Why – the purpose of the actions

(vi) How, when and by whom evaluation will be carried out

(vii) Must include launch: how to position the changes to gain most support

Monitoring and co-ordination

There is a wide variety of ways to monitor and co-ordinate the change programme to ensure everything keeps moving forward according to the blueprint. The key principles are:

(i)   There must be a senior and influential group of executives to take responsibility for overall leadership and co-ordination. Perhaps a senior executive of FF overall and store managers have control at a lower level.

(ii) There must be a clear blueprint, even if some of the precise timescales are provisional. This might be limited however by the timing of any contract with Thinebury Brothers.

(iii) The blueprint must cover the whole range of activities planned to deal with the three elements of financing, competition and resourcing.

(iv) Carrying out the actual work of investigating what's needed and implementing new systems and policies should involve key people in the change target group.

(v)   Change leaders should be chosen carefully for their skill and support.

(vi) Methods of making changes following evaluation should be included.

Barriers to change

Specific points

Electrical department – there are limited employee transfers despite replacement of floor space with other strategy options. There is therefore a high probability of redundancy for any given employee. This will increase the self-interest of employees in electrical departments to resist change, but reduce their ability for resistance given the transformational nature of the change and that they will not be involved in the new regime.

Some employees if they cannot stop closure may press for Strategy 2, replacing electrical departments as there may be more jobs generated within FF, thereby facilitating at least some employee transfers within the company. Given the different skills this may, however, be limited.

A further means of resistance would be to delay the closure as long as possible in order to extend the employment period.

Other non-electrical department employees may favour the change, particularly under Strategy 2 as there may be more opportunities for promotion in larger departments.

General change issues

Cultural barriers

(i) Group inertia – the closure may disrupt group norms eg if other departments have to expand and adopt different procedures. These will need to be overcome.

(ii) Structural inertia – the new strategies may involve new structures and therefore there may be resistance to abandoning existing structures.

(iii) Power structures – the existing hierarchy within stores may change and resistance by those groups affected may be incurred.

Personal barriers

(i) Effect on earnings – those made redundant will lose significant earnings and will probably be most resistant to change, perhaps moderated by the size of any redundancy payout.

(ii) Security – the potential for change of work, pay, position, status etc may cause loss of security and thus potential resistance.

(iii) Habit – existing habits of work may need to be changed.

(iv) Fear of the unknown – if the new regime is not explained and believed then fear of the unknown may cause individuals to attempt to maintain the *status quo*.

(v) Selective information processing – people may hear what they want to hear and thus not believe management reassurances about change processes and consequences.

Motivating staff during the change period

If it is certain that staff are to be made redundant then they may be motivated by:

(i) Negotiation of redundancy terms (above statutory minimum) being dependent on smooth transition.

(ii) References for another job, and help with alternative employment, being dependent on smooth transition.

If it is less certain about redundancy, then the prospects of retention (subject to legal redundancy requirements) may limit resistance in the hope of replacement jobs elsewhere in the company.

A policy of communication to employees and participation by employees in the change process may also help motivation.

Communicating the change plan to stakeholders

There should be a detailed communication plan for stakeholder groups for the closure of the Electricals departments and the implementation of the new strategy once it is decided. This should specify who the key stakeholders are, and what their information needs are, for each part of the change process. The timing of the release of information will also need to be considered.

The following table summarises the key elements of such a plan for FF:

Stakeholder	Their needs	What they want to know	How to communicate
Shareholders	Reassurance	That there is well thought through strategy. How the strategy will benefit them	The press Financial statements AGM Website
The press	A good story	What's happening, the rationale, and that the changes are under control	Briefings
Suppliers	Information	How the changes will affect their working relationship (if any, for electrical suppliers)	Meetings face-to-face with major suppliers. Letters or e mail to small suppliers
Customers	Motivation	That service in the stores will continue uninterrupted	The press Advertisements
Departmental managers	Acknowledgement and involvement	How they will be involved and any role in the new structure. Reassurance, or at least clarity, over employment position	One-to-one meetings
Staff	Help to adapt or to facilitate redundancy	Retraining and support Redundancy terms for Electrical Departments	Briefings One-to-one with line manager/HR

(c) **Strategy 1**

Financial

Electrical departments generate a positive contribution of £5 million. This could therefore set a floor price for the contract with Thinebury. However, this does not compare like-with-like as the Thinebury contract is for five years.

An assessment therefore needs to be made in terms of the present value of the likely contributions that Electricals would have generated over the next five years. This then needs to be compared to the rental charges that could be made to Thinebury.

Also, while the electrical departments as a whole are generating a modest contribution, it needs to be considered whether electrical departments in all of the stores should be closed or whether some are profitable and should be retained with Thinebury taking up space only in selected stores. As already noted, the availability of quantity discounts from suppliers might determine the feasibility of a partial closure strategy.

Within the five-year period the rentals are reasonably certain so there is a reduction of financial risk in this period.

Strategic

A key consideration is whether the alternative strategies are consistent with the longer-term strategic plan of FF (ie 'strategic fit'). This might be in terms of the product mix, the ethos of the stores and the customer requirements.

Given that the Thinebury contract is for a five-year fixed term this locks FF into the contract and reduces future strategic flexibility if markets change. This increases strategic risk.

Reputation is important to FF thus there is a reputation risk to the contract with Thinebury as there may be limited control over its procedures, unless controls are built into the contract. In particular, customers are unlikely to distinguish FF from Thinebury in their perception of quality and service.

Conversely, Thinebury may walk away after five years so this can only be a medium-term strategy unless renewal is reasonably certain.

Strategy 2

Financial

There may be loss of contribution on existing sales if customers buy the new brands instead of the old brands (substitution effect).

There is likely to be substantial up-front cost from reorganisation and establishing new supply chains, whereas the additional initial cost may be small with Thinebury. The up-front cost includes additional investment in working capital for new inventories.

Despite the higher initial fixed costs with Strategy 2 there is likely to be more upside potential if sales are high and contributions similarly increase.

It is necessary to compare any additional expected contribution over a five-year period with the rental that can be negotiated with Thinebury. The estimated probability of renewal will also need to be considered.

Compare the risk of Strategy 2 with the Thinebury contract which may be largely risk free income. Thus a risk adjusted premium may be required from Strategy 2 compared to Strategy 1.

The new product mix may not actually increase total sales.

Strategic

There may be an impact on reputation of going 'downmarket' by using less well know brands that are perceived to be lower quality.

Own labels may have limited brand value if unknown to customers as a product brand. While the FF name is currently known to customers, it is as a retailer brand rather than a product brand.

There may be a better 'strategic fit' as there is more control over service and products than with Strategy 1.

There is more strategic flexibility to change Strategy 2, (compared to Strategy 1) if it does not work out, as it is within the control of FF. There is thus a more immediate 'exit route' with Strategy 2 than Strategy 1.

Examiner's comments:

The scenario was a small chain of up-market department stores. Candidates were provided with information about the nature and performance of the company segments, including data about the financial performance of each of the four types of department. The electrical departments are performing poorly and the directors are considering closing them. The board is also discussing two alternative strategies for the utilisation of the floor space that would be made available by the closure of electrical departments.

Requirement (a) asked candidates to explain how each store should measure (i) departmental performance and (ii) the performance of departmental managers. Candidates were also required to evaluate the factors that should be considered in determining whether the electrical departments should be closed. This part of the question was well answered. Most candidates divided their answer into its constituent elements, separating departmental performance from manager performance. However, only a minority of candidates supported their arguments by providing supporting calculations (as requested in the question) or by making reference to the financial data provided in the question. Some candidates argued that electrical departments should be kept open solely because they are making a positive contribution.

Requirement (b) requested candidates to address the change management aspects of the closure of the electrical departments, including planning, barriers to change, motivation and communication. The majority of candidates correctly dealt with the key issues of change management. A small minority tried to deal with the requirement by providing an Ansoff's matrix approach. The weakest aspect of candidates' answers was to take materials entirely from the learning materials with little added value in terms of application to the circumstances of the scenario. The major strength in most candidates' answers was the detailed coverage of barriers to change.

Requirement (c) asked candidates to assess the financial and strategic effects of the two proposed strategies. In general, this was reasonably well answered with most candidates separately identifying the key financial and strategic issues for each of the change strategies. A weakness with some candidates was a failure to draw any comparisons between the two alternative strategies. Weaker candidates failed to mention more than a few basic points on this section.

8 Cabot Tours Ltd

Marking guide

			Marks
(a)	Political	2	
	Economic	2	
	Social	2	
	Technological	2	
	Environmental	½	
	Legal	½	
			9
(b)	Identifying/classifying risks	1.5	
	Explaining risks	6.5	
			8
(c)	Organic growth	3	
	Joint venture	3	
	Strategic alliance	3	
	Other	2	
			11
			28

(a) **PESTEL analysis**

Political

(i) Introduction of medical visas by the Indian government will encourage travel

(ii) NHS budget constraints and limited resources mean certain patients are rejected for UK treatment

(iii) Waiting lists are increasing and people are less prepared to wait/may not have the luxury of time

(iv) Private treatment in the UK can be very expensive so cheaper options will be attractive

(v) NHS has begun sending patients to Europe to address backlog so idea of overseas treatment is not new

(vi) Need to consider political stability of Indian government and region. Future governments may not support medical tourism

(vii) Continuing barriers to medical tourism expansion, including a lack of governmental agreements on payment for treatment abroad and insurance coverage

(viii) UK Government may place constraints on patients getting post-operative follow up care back in UK

Economic

(i) Rising cost of healthcare in the UK

(ii) Favourable exchange rates – a strong pound reduces the effective cost of treatment. However, future changes in exchange rates may increase cost

(iii) Affordability and availability of travel

(iv) CII study suggests favourable market growth

(v) Increasing supply of medical tourism products, leading to greater competition

(vi) An increasing role for tourism suppliers in the packaging and marketing of medical tourism

(vii) Growing international private sector investment and joint ventures

Social/demographic

(i) People live longer and have a more active retirement so want to be comfortable/well enough to enjoy it

(ii) The population is much more willing and accustomed to travel

(iii) Increasing media publicity re hospital league tables, care for the elderly and MRSA may encourage some people to look overseas

(iv) People may have a preference for Europe rather than India due to shorter and cheaper flights

(v) Growing ethical concerns about medical tourism, which may limit growth or damage reputation

(vi) Geographical distance may be an issue for relatives of the patient

(vii) Potential clients may be concerned re risks of surgical failure or hygiene overseas (MRSA etc).

Technological

(i) Medical staff highly trained so have the requisite skills

(ii) Internet facilitates shopping around for information and provides lots of choice

(iii) Improving technology and infrastructure in India to support the venture

(iv) Equipment in private hospitals likely to be as sophisticated as that of UK

(v) May be additional logistical requirements for transporting sick patients

(vi) Indian software sector have already been successful in providing outsourcing facilities for UK, USA etc which may pave the way for other sectors

Environmental

Growing environmental concerns may have an impact on affordability/ease of travel in future.

Legal

Potential litigation costs if things go wrong/need to consider insurance.

(b) **Business risks**

Exchange risk

(i) If sterling weakens the cost of packages increases and demand may fall

(ii) CT need to consider whether they can pass on costs of unexpected exchange rate changes

Political risk

(i) Subject to vagaries of Indian economy and Indian government, eg should they decide to withdraw medical visas or increase costs or create legislation to prevent influx of overseas nationals requiring treatment

(ii) Changes in NHS or UK private medical care may reduce demand

(iii) Potential for UK government reaction, eg may act to create barriers to overseas treatment or refuse to accept patients for follow up in UK

(iv) Increased bureaucracy eg need to arrange visas will increase costs and potentially create barriers to travel

New venture/market inexperience

(i) As with any new venture, risks are higher due to uncertainty

(ii) No experience of medical sector – need to choose partner carefully

(iii) Will need funds to establish operation and likely volume of transactions is uncertain – impact on existing cashflow?

(iv) Language issues/differing tax and legal systems

(v) Diversion of management attention from core business

(vi) Possible change in operating gearing eg high initial FC to establish venture

(vii) Will be easy for competition to set up similar ventures

Reputation and other ethical issues

(i) Medical treatment is not without risk

(ii) Increased risk of ill health/fatality whilst patient in ML's care eg risks of flying post surgery may lead to emergencies in the air

(iii) If complications arise there will be a need to extend accommodation/change or delay flights etc – disruption costs

(iv) Potential litigation claims may be costly

(v) Spotlight may fall on CT even if poor treatment is down to the hospital

(vi) Bad publicity may damage CT's reputation

(vii) Public disapproval of the venture may lead to boycott of CT's existing core business

(viii) Even if no medical complications, travellers likely to be older and in a higher risk category – more costly in terms of time/staff input/increased reliance on holiday reps etc

(ix) Quality of partner may affect/damage CT reputation

(c) Business structures

Options for structuring the venture include the following:

(i) Organic growth, ie ownership of new venture
(ii) Joint venture
(iii) Alliance

Organic growth

Set up new venture themselves with full ownership

Advantages:

(i) Direct involvement may give a better understanding of the market
(ii) Does not require sharing of expertise/knowledge/information
(iii) CT retains control and gets all rewards
(iv) No problems of conflicting culture/expectations
(v) Would not be tied to one group of hospitals

Disadvantages:

(i) CT lack expertise in medical market
(ii) May be language and cultural barriers
(iii) Higher risk
(iv) Increased costs
(v) May be looked on less favourably by Indian government as no local involvement

Joint venture

Form a separate company, both businesses take an equity stake and management decisions are shared. Most JVs are separate legal entities with own board, appointed by the shareholders.

Advantages:

(i) Reduces risk as this is shared

(ii) Access to skills of each party: can use the specialist skills of both CT and the medical group to maximise the effectiveness of the new business

(iii) Cost savings for CT as these new skill sets need not be learnt or bought in eg experience and understanding of Indian market

(iv) Cost savings as CT only contributing half of the capital needed for the new venture

(v) Because the joint venture is a separate entity, CT can sell its stake in the company at a later date if it so desires relatively easily

Disadvantages:

(i) Potential conflicts with the medical group over strategic and cultural issues of the new business could be difficult to resolve

(ii) Could be possible disputes over how business should be run/costs incurred/management charges etc

(iii) CT may have to move key staff to the operation of the JV which may affect profitability and effectiveness in the running of the core business

(iv) CT may not like the fact that they do not have complete control over the business

(v) Rewards of the new business will have to be shared

(vi) The objectives of the business may not be totally clear or communicated to the staff involved

(vii) There may be an imbalance in the amount of expertise, investment or assets brought into the joint ventures by the respective parties

Strategic alliance

Similar to a joint venture in some respects but a strategic alliance is some form of contractual relationship designed to secure an international venture without involving a shareholding. CT would have a looser arrangement with the medical group such that they work together but do not go as far as forming a separate company.

Advantages:

(i) Like JV, uses joint expertise and commitment, allowing each party to focus on what they do best
(ii) CT keeps its independence and does not lose key staff
(iii) Less commitment required as the nature of the agreement is looser

Disadvantages:

(i) Arrangement may fail if both parties are not committed to it
(ii) Needs constant work to keep the relationship on a sound footing
(iii) Nature of linkage is essentially weak so less likely to survive in long term

May also mention the following:

Supplier arrangement

MT simply contracts with the Indian hospitals to provide the medical element of the service.

Agency agreement

Indian medical group acts as the agent for MT and bears the operating risk.

Conclusion

Risks associated with the venture are high, so CT would be advised to structure the venture separately to avoid damaging their existing brand/reputation. They could set up the new division as a separate company to limit risk but as they do not have the necessary medical expertise would be best entering into some form of partnership. Careful consideration must be given to the choice of partner and the nature of the agreement to ensure CT minimise risk and enjoy maximum possible returns.

9 Jenny and Bob

Marking guide

	Marks
Structure of the business plan	3
Details of business background and operations	4
Industry information	4
Financial data	3
Additional information	3
Other factors and conclusions	4
	21

Memorandum

To: Lindsay Leisure Ltd
From: Accountant
Date: Today
Subject: Preparation of a business plan for the 'Bijou Cinema' project

General issues

- The business plan will cover a time period appropriate to the business and industry. Commonly this is three to five years, but in this case the period of the plan will be the period of the loan, with less detail for later years.

- The plan document should make use of graphs and charts to aid understanding, and should not be too detailed. Any large tables such as financial forecasts should be presented in detail in the appendices and summarised, or referred to, in the text.

- If the plan document is very long an 'executive summary' should be included, which should highlight key issues and summarise the main conclusions of the document.

The major sections of the plan document will include the following.

Statement of purpose

This will include the circumstances behind the 'Bijou cinema' project and the need for finance.

The business

This section will summarise:

- A description of the business
- The general history of 3L (in so far as it is not already known to the bank)
- Marketing information on the new and existing businesses (eg 5% growth)
- Competition (eg the multiplex ten miles away)
- Operations details (eg size, staffing, sourcing films)
- Personnel
- Insurance

Financial data

(a)   Loan applications (existing and proposed)

(b)   Capital equipment and supply list (cost of property, goodwill and inventory of £200,000 and the further refurbishment cost of £200,000)

(c)   Balance sheet

(d)   Breakeven analysis

(e) Pro-forma income projections (forecast income statements)

  (i)   Three-year summary
  (ii)   Detail by month, first year
  (iii) Detail by quarters, second and third years
  (iv)   Assumptions upon which projections were based

(f) Pro-forma cash flow

  Follow the headings as above for income statement projections

(g) Supporting documents

  (i)   Tax returns of the existing business and owners for last three years
  (ii)   Personal financial statement (all banks have these forms)
  (iii) Copy of proposed purchase agreement for the cinema
  (iv)   Copy of licences and other legal documents (eg copyrights)
  (v)   Copy of CVs of Bob and Jenny and managers
  (vi)   Copies of letters of intent (or contracts) with suppliers of films etc

Industry factors relevant to the proposed venture

Specific industry issues relevant to the project may include:

- Political issues relevant to the cinema industry might include industry-specific legislation on copyright or restrictive practices, health and safety on licensing. 3L should also consider any government assistance available to the West Midlands or the cinema industry.

- Economic factors will include an assessment and forecast of consumer spending on leisure, and any relevant macroeconomic variables such as inflation and unemployment.

- Social factors relevant to the project will include the demographics of the population within the area of the cinema, together with any forecasts of changing attitudes to leisure pursuits which might significantly affect demand levels.

- Any recent or predicted developments in entertainment technology must be considered, such as video, cable, satellite or Internet developments. These may all have an impact on the success of the cinema.

- The industry structure should be analysed in terms of rivalry from other cinemas such as the nearby multiplex, but also to predict the impact of substitutes such as video, television and sports. Any likely new entrants should also be identified, and barriers to entry discussed. It is likely that the film companies may have a very strong bargaining position in the industry.

Environment/industry analysis

In this section the plan will summarise the context within which the business will operate, using 'PESTEL' analysis and the cinema industry structure. In addition to the current environment, the plan should highlight any trends and attempt to predict any major changes.

Objectives

The objectives of the business, both financial and non-financial, should be stated in a form which will make it possible for the organisation's performance to be assessed. As the plan is for discussion with the bank it is likely to focus on financial performance, and an appendix will contain detailed forecasts of balance sheet, profit and loss and cash flow. Appropriate key ratios may also be forecast, such as ROCE and ROI, interest cover and liquidity.

Position analysis

As this is a new venture there will be no analysis of the current position in terms of trading performance. However, the plan may describe the current business in terms of the premises, facilities and any staff.

Strategy

This section should evaluate the alternative strategies available to the cinema, and select those most appropriate in the light of the previous sections. The issues considered will include the following:

- The general positioning and marketing of the cinema. Will it be specialising in less well-known films or competing head-to-head with the multiplex?

- Any additional products to be offered, such as restaurant, bingo or conference facilities.

- Assumptions used in forecasting prices, customer numbers and spending in order to derive the profit and loss and cash flow forecasts included in the appendix.

Financing

As this is primarily a plan for raising finance, this section will be comprehensive. The £300,000 required will be analysed to show exactly what it will be its use, and this section will propose repayment terms and security offered. Some discussion will be necessary of the impact of changing interest rates and risk assessed in view of the PEST analysis.

Conclusions and recommendations

In addition to being necessary for raising the required finance, the business plan will also achieve other objectives.

- It will allow Jenny and Bob to assess the viability of the project, particularly as Bob seems to be less confident in the project.

- It will increase their understanding of the business and industry.

- It will form a basis for the management and control of the cinema business.

3L should therefore prepare a detailed business plan for the project, based on the advice contained in this report. My assistance is offered, if required, to ensure that the application for finance is successful.

Note: There is some flexibility as to the precise headings and structure used in the business plan. The key issue is that it is appropriate for the purpose for which it is to be used.

10 Chibb plc

Marking guide

			Marks
(a)	(i)	Profit/loss calculation	3
	(ii)	Transfer pricing formula	3
			6
(b)		Benefits	2
		Problems	4
			6
(c)	(i)	Profit divisional performance measurement	5
	(ii)	Non-financial divisional performance measurement	4
	(iii)	Benchmarking	5
	(iv)	Closure of a division – relevant criteria	4
			18
			30

(a) **Profits and losses**

   (i) **TP set on existing basis**

	Manufacturing division £m	Retail division £m
Estimated retail sales	–	24.0
Estimated internal sales/purchases	16.8	(16.8)
Variable costs	(8.0)	(3.0)
Fixed costs	(10.0)	(2.0)
(Loss)/profit	(1.2)	2.2

   (ii) **TP set on break-even basis**

     Sales needed to break even = £18m

     $18 \div 24 = 0.75$

     Thus transfer price to enable manufacturing to break even is retail price minus 25%.

(b) **Problems and benefits**

Problems

The use of retail price less a profit percentage as a method to set selling prices has a number of problems.

(i) It is not clear how the profit margin is determined.

(ii) No apparent attempt is made to determine a market price for the goods at the point in the supply chain relating to internal transfers.

(iii) The price appears to be imposed by head office, rather than negotiated by the parties; thus autonomy is damaged as is any attempt to measure the performance of the divisions, or their managers, using a profit based performance measure (eg absolute profit, residual income, ROI).

(iv) The transfer price does not affect overall profit in the short term as the total company profit is the same. It may, however, affect motivation and thus influence overall profit in the longer term.

(v) There is no effective measurement of divisional performance, given that the arbitrary nature of the profit margin means an artificial selling price for the manufacturing division and an artificial purchase cost for the retail division.

(vi) The retail division controls the ultimate retail selling price and thus can, to a large extent, determine the transfer price. Thus, if it lowers its selling price to increase sales, the manufacturing division would suffer 80% of the price cut without any control.

(vii) Moreover, if retail prices are volatile then the transfer price may be difficult to determine at the time of transfer.

Benefits

(i) There is an incentive to cut costs for each division – unlike cost plus.

(ii) The transfer price is derived from an externally determined market price.

(iii) If the profit margin has been based upon that applying in the outside market (after adjusting for difference in product, service and delivery) then it may be a reasonable measure of performance. The margin would, however, need to be kept under constant review to ensure it is in line with market conditions, rather than being fixed in the long term.

(c) **Memorandum**

> **To:** The Board of Chibb
> **From:** External Consultant
> **Date:** 11 June 20X3
> **Subject:** Divisional performance measurement and management

Profit based divisional performance measurement

As noted in Appendix A (ie part (a)) the arbitrariness of the transfer pricing formula makes the profit of each division artificial, and thus weak as a measure of performance. However, any other basis for setting transfer prices would suffer similar problems unless a market price can be determined.

Even so, using profit to measure the divisional performance of Chibb would have problems. If the market price could be determined, it would still need to be imposed by head office as a transfer price as there is no actual trading with the outside market in terms of transfers (ie the manufacturing division does not sell outside the company and the retail division does not purchase inventory from outside the company).

While the price may be set in terms of market rates, the volume of business is determined by retail division and yet affects the performance of the manufacturing division as well. Thus if retail division determines an inappropriate selling price, or fails to market the product properly, then sales volumes would fall and the manufacturing division would also suffer as fixed costs per unit would rise – indeed, due to higher operating gearing, it would suffer more than the retail division.

Profit measures (including those measures derived from profit such as residual income and ROI) only measure short-term performance, and historic performance at that. While this may be appropriate for some purposes, it is more important that long-term wealth is created. In this case, however, the fall in the share price would indicate that the stockmarket's assessment of long-term wealth is falling just as profit is falling – though not necessarily to the same extent.

Measuring performance involves not only measuring divisional performance but also managerial performance. In this case the key element is controllability. It is clear that an imposed transfer price does as little to meet this criterion of measuring the performance of managers as it does to measure the performance of the divisions that they operate.

The suggestion of the MD that the transfer price should be set on the grounds of fairness is inappropriate in assessing the performance of the two divisions. It is not appropriate to set a transfer price, on the grounds of fairness, that creates an artificial profit for an under performing division that is damaging the performance of the company as a whole.

Given the problems of setting transfer prices, the use of profit centres to measure divisional performance may be inappropriate. The manufacturing division could become a cost centre and its performance could be based upon cost targets.

Non-financial divisional performance measurement

In order to obtain the broadest possible measure of performance the company should use as wide a range of measures as possible, both financial and non-financial. Non-financial measures can include the following:

Manufacturing division

(i) Number of new products developed
(ii) Employee turnover
(iii) Returns inwards from retailing division
(iv) External recognition of achievements
(v) Speed of supply to retail division

This is an approach for linking performance measurement systems to broader strategic goals by first identifying the crucial elements of the firm's business strategy. These are critical success factors (CSFs) which are 'those components of strategy where the organisation must excel to outperform competition. These are underpinned by competences which ensure this success. A critical success factor analysis can be used as a basis for preparing resource plans.'

The attraction of the approach lies in the fact that it provides a methodology for identifying strategic goals (or CSFs) by basing them on the strengths, or core competences, of the firm. These are implemented though the development of KPIs which give milestones in the processes for delivering the CSFs.

One tool by which this can be achieved is the balanced scorecard. This includes multiple performance measures based on financial and non-financial criteria. They employ the methodology of CSFs and KPIs to measure objectives and targets. The four perspectives used by the balanced scorecard are:

(i)   Financial
(ii) Customer
(iii) Innovation and learning
(iv) Internal business

Benchmarking

Benchmarking can be defined as 'the establishment, through data gathering, of targets and comparators, through whose use relative levels of performance (and particularly areas of underperformance) can be identified. By the adoption of identified best practices it is hoped that performance will improve.'

The problem with accounting indicators such as profit, is that they are of limited use in steering a company, eg they may indicate to what extent a fall in revenue is due to a fall in sales volume and how much to a fall in price. They do not indicate why people are less inclined to buy Chibb's product or are now only prepared to buy it at a lower price.

The purpose of benchmarking is to help management understand how well the firm is carrying out its key activities, and how its performance compares with competitors and with other organisations who carry out similar operations.

(i)   **Internal benchmarking**: These are other branches within the same organisation. The basis of this approach is to identify which branch conducts each measured activity the best, to enable best practice to be identified and transferred to other branches. For retailing division this may be the best performing shop. For manufacturing division it could be the most efficient process.

(ii) **Competitive benchmarking**: This involves comparing performance with rival companies. This presents problems with data access and hence is usually carried out through a benchmarking centre. This will be 'a central authority' – such as an industry association. It will collect data from each participant then supply an analysis to each firm showing its relative performance against the 'best in class' under each activity as well as its overall relative position in the industry. This requires identification of a similar company but would indicate best practice as to what could be achieved under difficult industry conditions.

(iii) **Activity (or process) benchmarking**: The firm may share operations in common with non-competitor external organisations which might be 'best in the class' for a particular function. This might include inventory management, manufacturing processes or customer service.

(iv) **Generic benchmarking**: This is benchmarking against a conceptually similar process. It is unlikely that this will result in comparison of detailed measures, eg with respect to glazing pottery it could be that high temperature paint technology could be used from the chemical industry. For the retail division it could be that employee training could draw upon the practices of accounting firms!

The point is that benchmarking is not solely a means of measuring performance relative to a best performing unit – although it fulfils this function. It is also a means of identifying why the best performing units have achieved this and thereby attempting to implement this in the other areas of the business.

Closure of division

To some extent division closure would represent an extension of performance measurement, as it would be based upon an assessment of inadequate performance. There are, however, some further considerations depending upon which of the two divisions was being considered for closure.

A key problem would be the interdependencies between the two divisions. For example, if the manufacturing division were closed, then the key core competence of the retail division could also be lost in terms of access to the unique resource of Chibb products.

Similarly, if the retail division were closed if would be necessary for the manufacturing division to establish retail outlets willing to stock its goods and pay appropriate prices for them.

Other considerations include the following:

(i) Strategic implications of closure in terms of protecting the brand throughout the supply chain

(ii) Sunk costs locked into the divisions, ie how much would be earned by a sale of assets or as a going concern

(iii) Ability of external replacement to add as much value as internal function closed

(iv) Whether the decision is irreversible

(v) Whether the decision can be delayed until a more informed judgement can be made

(vi) Whether the resources generated by divestment can be usefully redeployed by the remaining division

Examiner's comments:

The scenario is that of a company that manufactures and retails fine china tableware at the upper end of the market, operating through two divisions, a manufacturing division and a retail division. The company is concerned with its overall performance but, due to problems in setting an appropriate transfer price, it is unaware of whether either division is under-performing. On the basis of improved performance measures, closure of one of the divisions is being considered. The question aims to make candidates consider three areas of the syllabus. Firstly, the inter-relationship between performance measurement and transfer pricing, secondly, benchmarking and, finally, strategic choice in relation to a possible divestment strategy.

In general part (a) was well answered, with many candidates scoring full marks. Common errors included the omission of the cost of transfers in the calculation of the retail division profit.

Part (b) was not well answered by most candidates. Only a minority of candidates clearly stated that there is no effective measurement of divisional performance given the arbitrary nature of the setting of the transfer price. On the positive side, many candidates did point out the incentive to cut costs, however, only a few compared this to other approaches such as cost plus pricing.

Part (c) was well answered on the whole. Many candidates raised the issue of controllability in assessing managerial performance. With regard to non-financial measures, many gave examples of CSFs and KPIs in the context of the balanced scorecard framework. Benchmarking was also generally well understood. The issue of divisional closure was, however, less well addressed, with many answers not explicitly considering key issues such as: the interdependence between the two divisions, the use of resources generated from disposal and implications for the brand. Many candidates simply discussed the individual costs and benefits of closing each division.

11   TE plc

			Marks
(a)	1 mark per quality factor (ACCURATE) including explanation and an example from the scenario, where available		8
(b)	Description of functional levels	3	
	Description of nature of information	5	
			8
(c)	Importance of good knowledge management system (1 mark per valid point)		6
(d)	Steps to minimise resistance (up to 2 marks per valid point)		8
			30

(a)   The quality of information can be assessed with reference to the 'ACCURATE' mnemonic.

	Explanation	Example from the scenario, where available
Accurate	Arithmetic and classifications should be accurate; no typing errors	The scenario states that manual intervention in producing reports introduces errors.
Complete	Everything relevant should be included	It is suspected that not all relevant information is included as staff are 'not always capable of identifying significant information'.
Cost-beneficial	Information should not cost more to produce than the benefit derived from having it	The employment of many clerks to produce manually information from data suggests that the system is not likely to be cost-beneficial.
User-targeted	Information should meet the needs of the user	Again, 'staff are not always capable of identifying significant information or showing initiative in analysing and presenting data in different ways'. Users appear to have little control over the information they are given.
Relevant	Irrelevant information should be omitted from reports	No information available.
Authoritative	The source of information should be reliable; assumptions should be stated	Presumably, as all of the information is from internal sources, provided initial recording is reliable, the information will be authoritative (though as stated above, errors may be introduced before the information is used).
Timely	Information should be available quickly enough to contribute to the decision-making process	The manual preparation of reports will introduce delays. Almost certainly some of these will interfere with the efficient running of the operation.
Easy to use	Clearly presented, not over-whelming, suitable medium	No information available.

(b) The functional levels in a business are typically illustrated using the following diagram:

As one goes up through the hierarchy, the nature of the information needed changes:

Strategic information	Operational information
Highly summarised	Very detailed
Often forward-looking and involving estimates	Usually historical recording of transactions
Often from outside sources	Usually from inside sources
Concerned with the whole organisation	Deals with small aspects of an organisation
Often *ad hoc*	Routine
Quantitative and qualitative	Mostly quantitative

The qualities of management level information lie between these two levels.

Using examples from the scenario at TE, many people at a low level in the accounting department will be concerned that cash is accounted for correctly. Many ticket sales will be for cash, collected by drivers and ticket inspectors during journeys and there it is an important aspect of internal control to ensure that cash collected and banked can be reconciled to ticket sales. The information needed for that task is: very detailed, historical, from inside sources, dealing with a specialist area, routine and quantitative.

At the strategic level, directors will be dealing with new route planning and with designing fare structures. They will require information which allows them to see demand historical patterns and to project those into the future. The information will be non-routine and will often be needed in response to competitor action or environmental events. Much of the information will be from external sources, such as competitors' timetables and fare structures.

A good IS/IT system should be capable of serving the different levels.

(c) Making full efficient use of all the information in an organisation by turning it into knowledge is very important because:

(i) For most organisations information/knowledge is now the route to gaining competitive advantage.

(ii) Knowledge is perishable, and increasingly so in a fast moving environment.

(iii) Higher staff turnover means that there can be continual leakage of tacit knowledge.

With respect to TE plc, now operating in a high-profile and competitive environment, good knowledge management will be important in the following areas:

(i) The company wants to be responsive, presumably to market demands and preferences. The company will not know what the market wants without market knowledge.

(ii) The company wants to generate marginal revenue by changing fares – demand management. How passenger demand changes from hour to hour and day to day will be important knowledge to discover.

(iii) It is not clear if high staff turnover is still a problem. Staff who leave often take valuable tacit knowledge with them.

(iv) Running a railway over a shared infrastructure will probably make use of a high proportion of tacit knowledge. The official timetable for all trains will be known explicitly, but knowing how best to make use of rolling stock if there are delays or cancellations is likely to be knowledge acquired through practice and experience and will probably be tacit.

(d) Management at TE can try to reduce resistance to change by using the following approaches:

(i) Participation in deciding what changes are necessary. In the case of TE plc, management could say to employees something along the lines of 'Like it or not, we are now a private business, dependent on profit, and in a competitive environment. All our jobs depend on delivering a good service, better than our competitors deliver, to the public. We would be grateful for any suggestions as to how the company can succeed'. Once someone has suggested a change, it becomes difficult for them to subsequently resist it.

(ii) Communication. Much unease can be caused by rumours about changes that might never be planned. If members of staff worry about loss of benefits, and the company has no plans to change those, then make this clear at an early stage.

(iii) Financial incentives. For example, if management wants flexible working practices to be introduced, there might be scope for pay rises.

(iv) Lewin's three-step approach to change:

1   Unfreeze
2   Effect the change
3   Refreeze

The unfreeze step is often accompanied by participation and communication: making employees realise why change is necessary and preparing them for it. The refreeze step is a period of consolidation to make sure the new practices are working well and that there is no regression to previous methods.

(v) Lewin's force field model

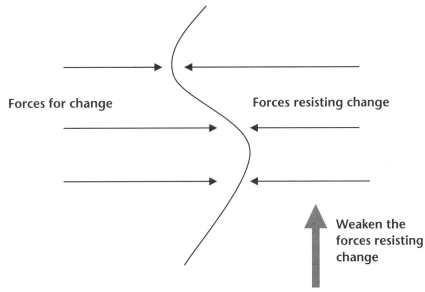

Examiner's comments:
Lewin suggests that forces for change generate opposing, resisting forces. Rather than both sides 'pushing harder' and the *impasse* escalating, Lewin suggests that change will be effected more easily if the resisting forces are weakened. This could be done by participation, communication, financial incentives and envisioning a better future after the change.

12 DA plc

		Marks	
(a)	Total possible marks	7	
	Maximum full marks		6
(b)	Total possible marks	12	
	Maximum full marks		10
(c)	Total possible marks	10	
	Maximum full marks		8
(d)	Total possible marks	10	
	Maximum full marks		8
(e)	Total possible marks	10	
	Maximum full marks		8
			40

(a) **Factors creating competitive advantage**

Competitive advantage is anything that gives one organisation an edge over its rivals. Critical success factors (CSFs) are the areas where an organisation must excel if it is to achieve sustainable competitive advantage. DA's critical success factors concern not only the resources of the business but how these can be used to advantage in the competitive environment in which it operates.

Here a key strategic resource is the possession of a licence to operate as a CRA. Complying with the terms of this licence is fundamental to DA's ability to continue in operation. Possession of the licence acts as a barrier to entry and while it does not give DA an advantage over CC Inc, it does protect its market share from new entrants.

DA may gain competitive advantage over CC Inc by virtue of being the only UK-based CRA.

According to the resource-based view of strategy, firms develop competencies and then exploit them. Sustainable competitive advantage is obtained by the exploitation of unique resources. Thus a firm should focus only on products where it has a sustainable competitive advantage and focus on core competences which competitors do not possess or would find it difficult to copy.

A threshold competence for CRAs is compliance with the relevant UK legislation, eg consumers have specific rights in relation to the information CRAs hold about them. Complying with this and other relevant legislation is crucial to DA's business, as it is to the business of competitors. Going beyond mere compliance, eg by extending its free advisory and education services may give DA a competitive advantage over CC Inc.

The key factors that appear to have given rise to DA's competitive advantage would include:

(i) First to market – DA began business in the 1980s and as one of the first to market, and a primary player, it has created a strong reputation and market dominance as a result of this.

(ii) Scale – With 58% of the market there are scale economies in search costs and IT costs which would give DA an advantage over its main competitor and any potential entrants.

(iii) Information and knowledge systems – DA's core competences are its ability to compile and manage vast quantities of information, giving it 'the most comprehensive credit database in the UK'. It also maintains a large database for the automotive industry.

For competitive advantage DA must have superior skills in Database management:

- Continuous access to a wide variety of information sources to ensure that the consumer profile or vehicle history is complete and accurate

- The ability to integrate vast quantities of information and organise it in a user friendly form

- Maintenance of up-to-date information

(iv) Product development skills/Innovation – DA have a core competence in helping businesses reduce risk. Processes for new product development have enabled DA to expand the products and services it offers and the markets it serves, eg the development of the analytical decision business. By making this proprietary software, DA is able to protect their competitive position and prevent copying.

(v) Relationship management skills – DA's experience in personal selling has attracted business customers in the first instance. These customers have been retained through relationship management and by developing additional products to meet their risk management needs. As a result there is significant brand loyalty.

(vi) Technical resources – DA's IT systems will be important in delivering an efficient service to customers, where customers will particularly value:

- Speed of processing
- Flexibility of delivery (online, phone etc)
- Confidentiality

(vii) Organisation structure – DA has divisionalised by product or brand. This should facilitate communication and decision-making, at the level of the brand and allow a fast response to a rapidly changing market.

(viii) As a listed company DA will also have good access to finance.

(b) **Analysis of strategic development**

The Ansoff model is a two-by-two matrix of Products (new and existing) and Markets (new and existing).

By relating product opportunities to markets, this mix identifies four broad alternative strategies open to DA.

Market penetration

This involves selling more of existing products to existing markets. This increases the organisation's market share. DA is the largest credit reference agency in the UK market and in this field the company has only one major competitor, CC Inc. As a result each company can only increase market share at the expense of the other, unless they can each persuade businesses to carry out searches with both organisations. To some extent DA's position is protected by the fact that organisations wishing to compile credit information need a licence. As DA is clearly the market leader it could be argued that they have been very successful in achieving market penetration. This has been based on their ability to create and retain successful client relationships and their core skills of database compilation and management.

Product development

This means developing new products for existing markets. As a credit reference business, DA initially focused on financial services businesses as its potential customers. It was then able to expand by developing the technology around its existing product. Knowledge of the specific needs of this market in terms of speed of decision making, reduction of risk etc enabled DA to build and develop a wider range of products relevant to its customers, eg the decision analysis software that E introduced was based on the premise that businesses would value analytical rather than just factual information.

Market development

This strategy takes existing products and finds new markets for them. Having recognised a core competence in database management, DA used this strategy to offer information products to the automotive industry. This market is similar to the financial services market, in that customers value information that assists in reducing the risk associated with decisions.

Diversification

This involves moving away from core activities and developing new products for new markets. Diversification stands apart from the other strategies. It involves the greatest risk of all strategies. It requires new skills, new techniques and different ways of operating.

Having focused on the business-to-business market, DA plans to diversify into the business-to-consumer market with its new product Checksta. While the broad product area is still credit information there are overtones of diversification because it is for individual consumers. This decision recognises that many consumers want to be more in control of their credit status, to be able to monitor their credit report at any time and to protect themselves against identity fraud.

Note: Although the company perception is that Checksta represents a new market, It could be argued that this is product development rather than diversification, since DA already offers the statutory credit report to the consumer market.

Lynch Expansion method matrix

The Lynch model is another two-by-two matrix of company growth (organic growth and external development) and geographical location (home (domestic) and international). Under this model, all of DA's growth appears to have been carried out organically and products/markets have been developed domestically rather than internationally.

DA has been able to grow organically as a result of having been an initial player in the market, allowing it to develop critical mass.

Overseas expansion

It is likely that a large number of existing customers, who value the DA brand, are global businesses. In the same way that CC Inc has expanded into the UK, DA could exploit this brand loyalty and apply its information management skills to Europe or the USA. If it wishes to target overseas markets in the future, then growth by acquisition might be considered as a faster way of getting access to the necessary licences and databases.

(c) **PESTEL analysis**

Political

(i) Only companies that are licensed CRAs can provide credit reference services and access to consumer credit files. DA and CC Inc are the two largest CRAs. Lending organisations and retailers offering trade credit have a choice of organisation with which to do a credit search, and consumers may not know which business their prospective lender will use, thus consumers are likely to want to access their file with each organisation.

(ii) Changes in regulation may restrict DA's freedom of operations, eg regarding pricing or ability to advertise.

(iii) Government may choose to discourage credit, reducing the need for credit checks and hence DA's product.

Economic

(i) A consumer's willingness to take on credit depends on his or her confidence in their ability to repay the money. This confidence comes in part from job stability and faith in the economy. The relatively low and stable interest rates and stable employment have made consumers more willing to take on credit. While currently favourable, future changes, eg in interest rates, may reverse this trend.

(ii) Consumer spending is often used as an indicator of how well the economy is doing. Credit is a key factor in fuelling an economic boom. Any boom in consumer spending will mean that there is an increase in the number of credit checks lenders make through DA.

(iii) The rejection of credit applications, especially if it is unexpected, may be an opportunity for DA as it is likely to cause individuals to want to access their credit report.

Social

(i)   Changing attitudes to money and credit have meant it is no longer traditional to save up for things. More and more people use credit as a way of buying things they do not have the money for.

(ii) People can apply for credit from almost anywhere: over the Internet, by telephone, in a shop or supermarket, or in response to direct marketing campaigns.

(iii) Consumers are much less loyal to one bank or finance provider and are more likely to shop around and approach several lenders to find the best deal. The above factors mean that individuals are more likely to shop around for credit and lenders have to carry out more credit checks. A desire to obtain credit on the best terms is likely to increase consumers' awareness of their credit history and increase demand for the credit scoring service provided in conjunction with Checksta.

Technological

(i)   The credit industry has made huge technological advances. Financial products and services can now be bought online and e-commerce is now an important part of the global economy.

(ii) The boom in e-commerce will continue to necessitate more frequent and rapid credit checks by businesses and increase the number of consumers who are likely to want real time online access to their credit history.

(iii) DA has already upgraded its IT systems in response to changing technology but will need to ensure that these are kept up to date and that the necessary security systems are in place.

(iv) The increase in identity crime represents a major opportunity for Checksta as individuals become increasingly aware of the possibilities of fraudulent access to their information and identities and will be keen to protect themselves against this.

Environmental

(i)   Not really of major significance, though there could be a reduction in credit if society moves towards consuming less and conserving energy and resources.

(ii) Environmental concerns, such as the desire to go 'paperless' may boost demand for an online product.

Legal

(i)   UK legislation exists which governs how organisations can collect, use and share personal information and giving consumers specific rights in relation to the information CRAs hold about them. Continuing to comply with this and other relevant legislation is crucial to DA's business. DA needs to ensure that its plans for Checksta do not contravene this legislation or the terms of its licence.

(ii) The consumer education programme that DA had to implement as a result of the tightening legislation has given it an opportunity to increase the awareness of its brand name among consumers and also consumer organisations.

In conclusion the environmental analysis would suggest that there is considerable scope for a product such as Checksta and that its planned introduction is well timed.

(d) **Marketing strategy**

In the first instance DA should ensure that it has undertaken the appropriate market research. Market research is the systematic gathering, recording and analysing of information about problems relating to marketing of goods and services. Market research will therefore involve gathering information about the 7Ps of marketing (see below).

Target market

To the extent that it has identified customer needs and developed a product accordingly, DA would appear to have undertaken some preliminary market research and used this to identify the segments containing those potential customers that it wants to target.

In DA's case it wants to target a specific type of customer: personal rather than business, with certain behaviour preferences: users of credit and also of the Internet. As a result it will need to take account of people's ages, their gender and socioeconomic grouping in deciding on an appropriate marketing mix.

Checksta is a new UK brand. It is important to develop an image that would be appropriate for the product that is being offered. Having a profile of the most likely customer will help DA to develop a promotional campaign that positions the product in the minds of its potential customers.

Marketing mix

Next, DA needs to develop its marketing strategy using the marketing mix, which is traditionally done using the 4Ps.

Product

Checksta is based on a product that existed already – the consumer credit report. The product has been developed by allowing real time online access and augmented via support for ID fraud.

In this case, the service needs to be considered in terms of the attributes that are likely to generate demand (eg 24-hour availability; convenience of online access; security of information; ability to predict lender's scoring).

Checksta's unique selling points (USPs) are that it allows consumers to see their credit reports online and automatically alerts them to important changes to the information held about them. This helps consumers understand what makes them creditworthy and can help them to manage their credit commitments. If there is a problem, consumers get free phone advice from credit reference specialists.

Price

The price that potential customers are willing to pay could clearly be a specific objective of any market research exercise.

DA needs to consider whether there are any regulations governing the pricing of their service. Presumably the starting point for price is the price of the statutory report = £2.

It then needs to assess the value of real time access to the customer and the value of the other services on offer.

One possibility is to price elements of the package separately eg a basic price for online access, and then extra charges for the additional service elements such as the alert service, credit score and so on.

Some form of monthly membership scheme, with an initial free trial period would encourage new users to consider take up of the service. If they do not think the service is for them, members would then have to remember to cancel their membership, say at the end of the 30-day free trial.

DA could consider price skimming for early adopters or alternatively discounts for those who are quick to sign up, so as to build market share quickly.

Place

Checksta developed because of the growth in e-commerce communications technology. Its 'place' or channel by which it reaches its users is the electronic medium of the Internet – Checksta is an e-commerce product, available online for consumers.

Some of the support services are offered online but also via different channels – the alert service is offered via e-mail or text (mobile phone) and the free phone help-line can presumably be accessed via landline or mobile. Thus in addition to Internet users, DA is also targeting those with mobile phones.

Promotion

As a new venture, the initial impact of advertising and other promotion on price and demand should be considered.

Until recently, DA has worked mainly in the business-to-business (b2b) market. Its expertise is based on personal selling and relationship building. To succeed in the business to consumer (b2c) market, DA will have to use a different promotional mix and needs to develop a range of different promotional strategies.

As a result of the tightening of credit legislation DA has already implemented a consumer education programme and been working with consumer groups. When DA launches its Checksta product in the UK, it should build on this existing awareness of its brand by ensuring that all free advice guides, consumer education programmes and conferences it attends also promote Checksta.

It could produce literature both online and as a paper product informing people of the dangers of identity fraud and explain how a monitoring service like Checksta could help protect them from the effects of this crime.

DA should consider using a public relations agency to help advertise the new online credit report with press releases and a television advertising campaign.

Advertising could be placed in the money/financial review sections of the press and appropriate financial/credit/consumer advice magazines.

DA could sponsor exhibitions such as the Ideal Home Show and events such as Credit Awareness Week 2007, which its target customers may attend.

As the product is an online one and DA are targeting internet users, web-based advertising would also be appropriate. DA need to ensure there are links to its website from the various money supermarket and personal finance websites. Research should be done to ensure that DA and the Checksta brand appear when a potential customer uses a search engine.

DA could exploit links with other areas of its business, eg advertise the Checksta service to those customers seeking finance for vehicle purchases. Direct mail those people who have previously applied for a statutory credit report and include a leaflet about Checksta with each statutory report.

Note: As DA is a service company, the marketing mix could be extended to consideration of 7 Ps.

People

This refers to anyone that is to have regular interaction with the customer. In this case a lot of the service will be provided automatically and a substantial amount of any interaction will be electronic by text or email. Customers may make personal contact if they use the free advice phone line.

DA needs to ensure that the nature of any communication gives a good impression of the company, that staff have appropriate training on the new product and the flexibility to provide a good service and that staff manning the helpline are informative and suitably concerned and reassuring.

Processes

Accuracy of information, secure access and confidentiality will be key to determining how effective the service is. DA needs to implement standard operational procedures and ensure that staff apply these consistently.

The ease of application for membership and navigation through the website will be important.

There will need to be security systems in place to verify the identity of members both online and by phone.

DA needs to ensure that the IT systems operate efficiently and that there are no significant delays in the provision of the real time information or periods when the website is down.

Physical evidence

This is the evidence that the service has been performed. It may include electronic confirmation of membership, the online report, any alerts. DA could issue a credit card sized Checksta membership card, with membership number and key contact numbers/website addresses.

(e) IT/IS risks

Strategic Risks	Risk Management
DA will lose competitive advantage if it fails to utilise IT/IS as effectively as CC Inc, particularly given its renewed focus on the UK market.	DA needs to keep up to date with new technology, continuously upgrade systems and ensure continuous advancements in the products/services offered. It should undertake regular benchmarking against competitors such as CC Inc.
Since all of DA's information management and in particular the Checksta product depends on IT/IS, a breakdown in its operations threatens the business. This could arise from systems failure or natural threats such as fire, flood, electrical storms.	DA should ensure that if major failures or disasters occur, the business will not be completely unable to function. It should implement protection measures to ensure continuity of operations and to minimise the risk of systems failures, eg back-up servers in alternative locations and regular back-ups of data.
The cost of updating and maintaining IT/IS and implementing the necessary security controls and risk management systems may reduce the operating margins that DA has enjoyed to date (currently around 25% on average). This is particularly true if, as a result of CC Inc offering a low cost web-based solution, DA has to reduce the price of its services.	The costs of the necessary systems controls and security measures need to be considered in the light of the benefits that these will bring.
Market dominance may result in DA being criticised for anti-competitive practices or investigated by the Competition Commission.	Care should be taken to ensure DA does not abuse its position and actively lay itself open to criticism.

Operational Risks	Risk Management
Loss of information as a result of corruption of the system by viruses or human error.	Particularly important is protection from viruses and the need for regular back-ups. DA needs to protect data and systems from unauthorised modification, eg via passwords and levels of access/modification authority.
Theft of information or deliberate misuse of data by hackers/employees.	DA must recruit trustworthy employees, and ensure detection and reporting of security-related incidents, eg unauthorised activity. Training is particularly important, with the aim that users are aware of information security threats and concerns and are equipped to comply with the security policy.
Penalties or intervention as a result of non compliance with regulations such as the *Data Protection Act* which could be imposed by courts if data is wrongly used or control procedures are not in place.	DA must put controls in place to ensure it monitors compliance with any relevant legal requirements such as the *Data Protection Act*.

General comments:

The scenario in this question considers a credit reference agency, DA, which is the UK market leader. DA provides information to financial services organisations and commercial businesses which want to check the credit rating of potential customers. It has developed its business by extending its database management skills to apply to other industries (eg vehicle history for automotive industry) and also by developing analytical software to help clients making lending decisions. DA is now considering a new online credit report service, Checksta, for individuals who are concerned about their credit ratings and also about the possibility of identity fraud.

At 40 marks, this was the longest question on the paper, although the requirements were broken down to help candidates in developing answer headings and assessing mark allocation. This seems to have been of benefit, as question 1 was well attempted, with the highest average score, although some candidates wrote too much, which was then reflected in their scores for questions 2 and 3.

Requirement (a) asked candidates to explain the factors that may have contributed to DA's competitive advantage. This was reasonably well answered by most candidates, who were able to extract key information from the scenario to evidence their comments (first to market, scale economies, core competences in database management, information technology and customer relationship management). Only the stronger candidates made reference to the need to outperform the competition, in this case CC Inc. Better candidates also discussed the possession of a licence to operate as a CRA as a barrier to entry for new competitors.

Requirement (b) requested an analysis of the ways in which DA had chosen to expand its business, using relevant strategic models. Answers to this part of the question were variable. A number of candidates simply repeated the information in the question about the development of DA's different divisions without examining it in the context of a strategic model. Those candidates who did apply a model, usually chose to use Ansoff's product market matrix, which was the obvious choice given the structuring of the information in the scenario. Weaker candidates simply described where each of the divisions would fall in the matrix, eg identifying the move into vehicle history as a new market for an existing product. Better candidates provided some analysis of the reasons for the choice of strategy and questioned whether the new product, Checksta, was indeed diversification as identified by DA. Although there was also scope to look at the method of growth adopted, only a few candidates identified that DA has chosen to grow organically, and only one candidate mentioned Lynch's expansion matrix in this context.

Requirement (c) asked candidates to prepare a PESTEL analysis on the credit reference industry. These points were largely contained in the narrative and as a result most answers were reasonable, however the weaker candidates simply repeated the facts from the scenario without considering the implications for DA's new product, which had been specifically requested.

Requirement (d) asked candidates to advise on an appropriate marketing strategy for the new product. This part of the question was the least well attempted, with candidates often restricting their comments to possible promotional strategies. Better marks were obtained by those who used the traditional 4Ps of the marketing mix to structure their answers. Since this was a service organisation there was scope to apply 7Ps although none of the candidates did so.

Requirement (e) required candidates to identify the strategic and operational risks associated with DA's use of information technology and to outline measures to deal with such risks. This requirement was well answered with candidates demonstrating a good awareness of the issues. Those who adopted a tabular approach, linking the risk management measures to each specific risk identified, tended to score very well.

13 Kraftvagen Gmbh (KV)

			Marks
(a)	Total possible marks	12	
	Maximum full marks		10
(b)	Total possible marks	9	
	Maximum full marks		7
(c)	Total possible marks	13	
	Maximum full marks		11
			28

(a) Sales and market analysis

Note: The answer that follows covers the range of points that might have been made by candidates and is significantly longer than would be expected for the marks available.

Analysis of KV sales by market/production location

Market	Sales	Production	Sourcing by KV
	%	%	%
USA	17.3	14.2	82 local
Europe	41.5	35.1	85 local
Japan	33.8	19.5	58 local
Other	7.4	31.2	76 sold outside
Total	100.0	100.0	

Analysis of market share in core markets

	USA	Europe	Japan
Total luxury vehicle sales	2,320	2,220	1,560
Market share			
KV	12%	30%	35% (ML)
Lima	32% (ML)	14%	10%
Durant	5%	14%	28%
Conrad	17%	32% (ML)	15%
Relative share of KV compared to mkt leader	0.37	0.94	1.0
Average annual market growth			
2002-2007 actual	0%	–4.6%	+5.5%
2007-2012 forecast	–2.5%	–6.2%	+3.2%
BCG analysis	Dog	Cash cow	Possible Star

Analysis of sales and market position

The market analysis highlights the dependence of KV sales on the European and Japanese markets. Over 75% of its sales come from these two markets, although it is not clear whether these contribute in the same ratio to the operating profit.

KV is the market leader in the Japanese market and very close to the market leader in Europe. It would be useful to know how long it has held this position and whether, in the case of Europe it was previously the market leader.

Europe – KV is one of two key players in the market but as with the USA the market is in decline, indeed the annual decline is forecast at 6.2% for each of the next five years. The decline is very significant and may give rise to damaging overcapacity. Protecting and gaining market share should be the strategy.

Japan – KV is the market leader with 35% of market and its nearest rival is Durant. Durant is maybe not a true luxury carmaker but has gained that perception in the Japanese market; this could be the result of clever promotional activities and may be giving them a high margin. KV could counter-attack by emphasising its true quality. Market research needs to be undertaken to find out why Durant is succeeding in this way.

USA – KV is well behind the market leader in volume of sales, in a market that is forecast to decline. There may be potential to take market share to achieve growth. The market share of the top three is less than half the total market indicating the presence of section of smaller players who could be attacked but some are possible niche players which may give them competitive advantages. Lima, the market leader, has greater diversity in its product range that may give it advantages over KV.

KV's current share of 12% of the US market, while low in relation to its share in Europe and Japan, may represent an increase on previous years.

Other markets – In India last year KV sold 300 cars, which is a market share of 2.5% (300/12000). The growth projections show that opportunities are available here despite decline in other markets. Were KV to set up the new factory, producing and selling 8,000 cars then they would have a market share of 28.6% in 2012 (8,000/28,000) or 14.3% in 2017 (8,000/56,000).

We do not know why the US and European markets are in decline, this may indicate switching from luxury vehicles to sports or smaller vehicles or maybe due to customers attempting to reduce their carbon footprints. Economic factors including taxation could also be causing a downsizing. It is unlikely to be due to population changes or socio-cultural reasons.

It would be interesting to undertake comparative analysis of the three main markets to explain why Japan is bucking the trend in luxury vehicles.

Location of production

The spread of production would tend to imply that KV continue to manufacture significant volumes from its original base in Europe (35.1%) and have then located production facilities in other markets outside Europe, USA and Japan (31.2%) – perhaps in order to take advantage of lower labour costs and scale economies.

To assess the benefits of this strategy it would be useful to have information about relative production costs and capacity for each location. The forecast decline in USA and Europe is likely to bring increased competition and pressure on margins and there may be scope for KV to reduce costs by closing factories and consolidating operations in areas where production costs are cheapest (subject to the increasing distribution costs that this may give rise to).

Stage of industry/product life cycle.

The available information suggests that the market for luxury cars could be assessed as follows in terms of the product/industry life cycle:

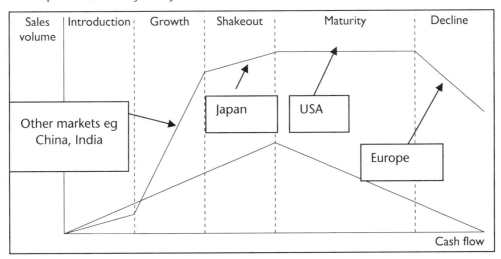

KV would appear to have markets at each stage of the life cycle, which should help smooth cashflows and create a balanced portfolio.

The major reliance on Europe may be of concern because industry information suggests a shrinking market for luxury cars. KV may be able to identify certain elements of this market that will continue to grow however and target these, eg the super luxury market where demand is probably relatively inelastic, alternatively it may be true that within Europe, demand varies by country and some countries are still exhibiting market growth.

The declines in sales of luxury cars are dramatic given that replacement cycles normally keep sales buoyant when taken across several years.

BCG analysis

Although traditionally used to assess product portfolios, A BCG analysis could also be undertaken of KV markets. Again on this basis there seems to be a reasonable spread:

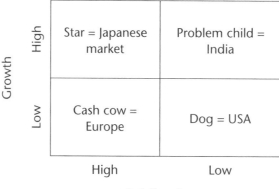

Other information that would be helpful:

External information

(i)   A thorough analysis of the whole market and by vehicle type is required.

(ii)   The data we have may also need to be checked to ensure that the definition of luxury is being consistently applied.

(iii) Details of the size of the passenger car vehicle market in total and the projected growth or otherwise, to ascertain whether the trend in luxury car sales is different from the underlying trend. This would help KV assess whether they should consider additional models/ranges of cars if the future for luxury cars is declining.

(iv)   Details of any individual trends within the luxury car market eg it may be that demand for cars at the lower end of the premium market is reducing as consumers are hit by higher taxes, environmental penalties etc but that at the highest level demand remains consistent.

(v)   Information regarding the market leader in Europe, their range of vehicles and position in other markets. Also any plans they have to enter the Indian market (or whether they are there already).

(vi)   More detailed historic data on market size, growth and share to better identify the stage in the product life cycle.

(vii) More competitive information for benchmarking costs and profitability, also to better understand KV's source of competitive advantage.

(viii) We do not know the pricing, promotion and placing strategies of the key players nor do we know how their sales have been changing in recent years. It would be very useful to have information about the product life cycles of key models including refreshment and re-launching information. While it is likely that manufacturers use single global designs with local variants, an analysis of models with data on extent of design and component sharing would be useful. It would also be important to receive future model plans and examine trends in prototypes.

(ix)   Customer survey data is regularly collected for the motor industry and may help to explain competitive positions.

Internal information:

(i) A breakdown of the 'other market' sales for KV and industry information on market shares, growth and so on.

(ii) An analysis of production across the 'other markets' – in particular number and location of factories, and capacity.

(iii) Information regarding the range of luxury vehicles and a sales analysis by brand to assess stars and underperformers.

(iv) Sales prices and margins by car model and market to assess performance.

(v) Historic analysis, by market, of sales, production and market share to better assess KV's business unit portfolio and understand the trends in its performance.

(vi) Information as to when KV entered each market to assess the degree to which it has benefited from first mover advantage and the time taken to build its market share.

(vii) Sales prices and margins by car model and market to assess performance.

(viii) More internal information is needed to assess financial performance (gross margins, operating costs, operating profit, marketing spend, capacity utilisation).

(ix) Information on production costs per vehicle at each geographical location in order to determine profitability.

(x) Exchange rates used for translation.

(b) **Reasons to target emerging markets:**

(i) Reduces dependence on other core markets and therefore spreads risk, particularly given forecast decline in demand in USA and Europe.

(ii) KV will face increased competition in its mature markets eg US/UK – it may face less rivalry in developing markets such as India initially and therefore enjoy better margins.

(iii) Increased restrictions on carbon emissions/ fuel etc are changing tastes in mature markets like Europe. The governments of developing countries are probably not yet imposing environmental restrictions.

(iv) UK and US tax systems now penalising luxury cars, so targeting other markets extends the possible life of this product.

(v) Stage of product life cycle is likely to be different in India and similar markets, eg China where the market for luxury cars is only just emerging. This offers the opportunity for increased profits and cashflow over a significant period.

(vi) Western products and brands becoming very attractive in Indian market so this represents a good opportunity to increase sales volumes.

(vii) Government spending on infrastructure will facilitate more luxury vehicles.

(viii) Economic growth is likely to boost demand for vehicles in general and industry forecast suggests promising growth in luxury market.

(ix) Production arguments for locating production in low cost countries and ensuring volumes are sufficient for economies of scale. May also reduce transportation costs to other countries outside core markets.

(x) Lack of export restrictions may mean cheaper to service KV's other markets from India.

(xi) May be financial arguments for setting up:

- Grants and incentives from Indian government
- Lucrative emerging market
- Possible tax benefits
- Lowering of trade barriers

(xii) Widen brand and enhance reputation/image as a truly global company.

(xiii) Level out possible seasonal fluctuations in turnover and cashflow.

(xiv) May be an opportunity to dispose of excess production and ensure factories in other countries are operating at capacity.

(xv) Competitors are also doing this and KV needs to be either lead the way or follow.

Risks and issues to consider:

(i) **Risk profile**

On the one hand, expansion into a developing market represents an opportunity to reduce reliance on other markets and spread risk. On the other it involves considerable extra risk, particularly as the market is an emerging one and is likely to change rapidly in ways that may be difficult to forecast.

(ii) As with any overseas venture, KV will face political risk, dealing with a new country and an unknown government. Any political instability could adversely affect KV, as could changes in government attitudes to foreign ownership/investment, changes in legislation etc designed to discourage international trade or protect home producers.

(iii) Economic and transaction risk will affect the exchange rate, the underlying cost of materials and labour, the value of profits extracted and so on.

Exchange control regulations could be applied which might affect the remittance of funds.

(iv) Government spending on infrastructure may not happen/may be delayed and as a result demand for luxury vehicles may not grow as expected.

(v) Economic growth may not continue as expected reducing the number of entrepreneurs and professionals attracted to India and hence the demand for luxury cars.

(vi) The move to impose quotas/taxes on imports could affect KV's flexibility and prevent it continuing to export to India (see above on economic and transaction risks).

(vii) Competition: As the market is predicted to grow there is a high threat of other potential entrants who may establish a reputation faster. Competitors, such as Durant, whose mid-range car is considered to be a luxury vehicle in India, may be able to make better returns from a cost-leadership perspective. KV may also face competition from local manufacturers.

(viii) Is the financial return acceptable? Need to produce forecast profits and cashflow, and to consider the opportunity cost of investment, ie what else could have been done with the funds?

(ix) Does KV have the necessary resources and management skills to exploit the opportunity – cash for investment, ability to recruit local workforce, people with experience of doing business in the Indian market? Again, experiences in other markets would suggest that it is able to manage this.

(x) KV will need to invest time and money understanding customer needs and preferences in the new market. It also needs to consider the extent to which production and marketing needs to be adapted for success in the Indian market.

(xi) Are there any specific regulations that must be complied with or any hidden costs, eg restrictions on the acceptable mix of workforce, hours or days of operation?

KV may run the risk of legal penalties of it fails to comply with the law or bad publicity if it is seen to apply less strict standards than it does in other countries.

(c) **To:**   Walter Bergen
From: A N Consultant
Date: XX March 2008
Subject: Developing the Indian market

This report sets out:

(i) Factors to consider in selecting the most appropriate option for implementation
(ii) Ways to minimise the downside risks associated with each option

(i) **Options for implementation in India**

In choosing a method of development, there are two considerations for KV:

(1) To what extent the product, in this case the luxury car model, can be standardised across national boundaries or whether it needs to be adapted to local market conditions. It would appear that the basic manufacture of vehicles is likely to be quite standardised but that tailoring to the local market may be required in terms of branding, marketing and possibly additional features eg superior suspension.

(2) The extent to which the organisation's activities can be centralised or concentrated in a few limited locations as opposed to being widely distributed internationally. Concentration of production in countries with low cost labour would allow KV to take advantage of economies of scale but might increase the costs of distribution and potentially affect the quality of the vehicles produced.

Option 1

*   Lower risk as no additional capital investment is required.

*   It may be more cost effective to utilise spare capacity available at existing production plants – economies of scale are likely to be greater if KV concentrates production in a few core plants, rather then fragmenting it across all the different countries to which it is selling.

*   India's reputation for restrictive labour laws may deter KV from setting up production locally.

*   The trial run means KV may already have tried and tested distribution channels available for export.

*   People are attracted by the Western brand name and brand image, so there may be no need to have a local brand image as a selling proposition.

*   Would guarantee the existing quality – this is important given the luxury nature of the cars.

*   Avoids any restrictions on KV's ability to extract profits from its Indian investment.

However:

*   Possible supply chain delays if the product is not manufactured locally, although people are more likely to be prepared to wait for luxury car models, so any minor delays in the supply chain would not be a problem.

*   Trade agreements may affect the freedom of movement and costs of imports/exports.

*   Tariffs/quotas likely to be imposed by the Indian government on the import of finished goods, making the option to export finished vehicles to India more costly.

*   Exchange rate movements may affect the costs and hence profitability/competitiveness if the product is not made locally.

*   Lima and Durant are investing in plants in India. Their greater commitment to local expansion could enable them to establish a reputation and build market share faster than KV. In addition KV may face competition from local based auto manufacturers.

Option 2

*   Will avoid any issues with restrictions on finished goods imports, although not on raw materials/components.

*   Local government incentives/grants on offer may reduce costs of capital investment.

*   Retains the quality of the existing components and yet gives a degree of local image. KV is seen to be promoting wealth for the local economy.

*   May give KV the chance to test the market potential if it can build an assembly plant with the flexibility to expand production capacity or switch to assembly of a smaller luxury vehicle for example if Indian tastes prove to be different.   ·

*   A local presence may deter competition setting up facilities and help gain KV market share.

*   This strategy is in line with the actions of Lima (KV's key competitor in the USA).

However:

- Would require significant capital investment and lead to an increase in operating gearing, although less than Option 3.

- Does not maximise access to low cost labour as a significant amount of costs will be incurred elsewhere in manufacturing the kits.

- Capacity is limited to 3,400 cars (two shifts at 1,700), whereas demand in five years is forecast to be 28,000. Unless there is scope to increase capacity beyond the doubling of shifts, this significantly limits KV's ability to fulfil an increase in demand and would require it to export production to India from other countries.

- Suitable premises will need to be located and staff recruited and trained.

Option 3

- Gives more scope to meet growing demand, although production is still limited to 8,000 cars, so if demand increase significantly then some top up of capacity by exporting to India will still be required.

- Full production in India may give KV access to low cost labour, raw materials, property, equipment and even capital.

- Any spare capacity in initial years could be exported to other markets but this will depend on trade agreements, tariffs/quotas and distribution costs.

- Speed of response to changes in demand is likely to be faster if production is based locally.

- KV may experience better hedging of foreign exchange risk through the matching of all revenues and costs in the same currency.

- Being seen to support local economy and the rapidly developing countries, may enhance/promote KV's image globally and avoids any import restrictions.

- Allows tailoring of the vehicle to the local market needs eg enhanced suspension to deal with lower quality roads.

- This is the strategy being pursued by Durant, KV's closest competitor in Japan.

However:

- Will benefit from lower labour and other costs but production numbers may still be too small to generate economies of scale.

- It will take time to establish a full production operation – premises will need to be located, machinery sourced, staff and management will need to be recruited and trained.

- There may not be a local supply chain eg available component manufacturers to support manufacture in India.

- If demand does not materialise then this strategy leads to highest exit costs: redundancies, penalty clauses on leases, reputational damage.

- Higher risk due to increased operating gearing from the additional capital investment.

- There may be quality implications of manufacturing the vehicles in India. KV's brand image and reputation would easily be damaged.

(ii) **Ways to minimise downside risk**

Risk reduction can be achieved through the following:

- KV has already reduced some of the risk they face by conducting trial sales. It could also undertake more market research to obtain a more accurate forecast of the likely levels of demand.

- Risk would be reduced by adopting a 'wait and see' strategy and letting others such as Durant and Lima be first in the market. This will reduce the potential downside risk but also lose the returns associated with first mover advantage.

- Production strategies: The issues concerning production options have been discussed above. KV's management must strike a balance between contracting out production to local sources (thus losing control) and producing directly (which increases the investment and hence increases the potential loss). Alternatively to minimise losses, it may be better to locate key parts of the production process or the distribution channels abroad.

- Insurance: If KV decides to export, trading risks may be reduced with the help of banks, insurance companies, credit reference agencies and government agencies, which provide protection against various threats including nationalisation, currency conversion problems, war and revolution.

- KV may transfer risks contractually, eg obliging distributors to pay for any losses.

- Political risk may also be addressed by negotiations with Indian government to obtain a concession agreement. This would cover matters such as the transfer of capital, remittances and products, access to local finance, government intervention and taxation, and transfer pricing.

- Risk can also be reduced by cultivating relationships with legislators and influential individuals.

- Any foreign exchange risk could be addressed through hedging.

- If KV decides to produce in India, it should create a cost structure where costs are mainly variable, thus reducing operating gearing eg via use of outsourcing. It should also consider the use of Flexible Manufacturing systems to facilitate ability to switch production to other vehicles in response to demand changes.

- Risk of poor quality assembly or production can be minimised by implementing rigorous recruitment and training processes and maybe employing expatriate managers.

- KV may consider the use of strategic partners to share risk and give it the benefit of knowledge of local legislation, practice and cultural tastes.

- Possible methods include joint ventures or ceding control to local investors and obtaining profits by a management contract.

- If KV are producing and selling in India then this moderates exchange risk as revenues and costs are both incurred in Rupees.

- Internal control procedures may be designed to minimise the risks from legal action, for example human resource policies, health and safety polices.

- Also KV can reduce risk to reputation through social and commercial good citizenship, complying with best practice and being responsive to ethical concerns.

The range of options facing KV is typical of an organisation looking to expand overseas.

Often risk of such expansion is reduced by achieved it in stages ie:

(1) Initially the market is targeted as an export market, possibly through an intermediary such as a sales agent.

(2) Some sort of base is established in the target market eg a distribution outlet or sales office.

(3) Full scale production is undertaken in the overseas market once demand is established.

This is typically the pattern that has been followed by the Japanese and European motor manufacturers.

General comments:

This scenario considers a German-based car manufacturer, KV, with a strong market position for luxury vehicles in USA, Europe and Japan. The chief executive has identified that the core markets are experiencing a decline and is looking to expand sales to India, to take advantage of growth opportunities there. Possible methods of expansion being considered range from export to setting up a full production plant.

Despite disappointing attempts at the data analysis element in part (a), candidates generally scored well on the rest of the requirements and as a result overall performance on this question was reasonable.

Requirement (a) asked candidates to evaluate the relative product and market positioning of KV and identify further information that might help assess its competitive position and performance. Most candidates produced calculations showing the sales mix across the various markets and KV's market share in each. Fewer candidates considered the sourcing of production and some misinterpreted this data, ignoring the fact that the question clearly states the production is valued at selling price and using it, incorrectly, to calculate a profit margin for each market. Having done some numerical analysis, many candidates then simply went on to describe their figures, producing little by way of interpretation or explanation. More analysis and reasoning, for example, might have elicited comments as to why the majority of KV's production is sourced from Europe (due to KV's origins in Germany) and other developing markets (perhaps to take advantage of cheaper labour). Better candidates used the market growth and share information to position KV's markets using the BCG analysis and to discuss the future implications for KV of having almost 60% of its sales in declining markets. Only one or two candidates discussed the likely position of each market within the industry life cycle.

A small number of candidates failed to do any numerical analysis and instead chose to apply a Porter's Five Forces analysis, scoring limited marks as a result.

The 'further information' element of the requirement was answered reasonably well and candidates appeared to be well prepared for this part of the requirement.

Requirement (b) requested candidates to explain the possible reasons for targeting emerging markets and the risks and issues to be taken into account.

This requirement was well answered, with candidates making good use of the information in the scenario to explain the reasons why India, in particular, might be attractive and the possible risks involved. Stronger candidates used their analysis from (a) to point out that emerging markets are likely to be at a different point in the industry life cycle and as such represent an opportunity for KV to reduce reliance on the more mature markets like Europe and USA which are forecast to decline.

Requirement (c) asked candidates to prepare a report advising on the factors to consider in the choice of expansion method and the ways that downside risks could be minimised. Again this was well attempted by the majority of candidates, who made sensible comments about the need to consider relative costs of production and distribution, possible barriers to imports, the need for a local image, balancing capacity and future demand, and the actions of competitors.

Candidates seemed well prepared to comment on risk management, with most making the obvious points about hedging foreign exchange risk and sharing risk though some form of JV arrangement.

14 Campaign for Trading Equitably

Marking guide

			Marks
(a)	Total possible marks	5	
	Maximum full marks		4
(b)	Total possible marks	6	
	Maximum full marks		5
(c)	Total possible marks	7	
	Maximum full marks		6
(d)	Total possible marks	6	
	Maximum full marks		5
(e)	Total possible marks	15	
	Maximum full marks		12
			32

(a) **NFP vs profit-focused organisation**

As a charity, CTE can be considered a not-for-profit organisation (NFP).

The primary goal of a typical profit-focused trading organisation will be the wealth maximisation of its stakeholders.

The goals/objectives of CTE will not be based on profit achievement but rather on achieving a particular response from a much wider range of stakeholders, including:

> Founder members and others with an interest in equitable trade, donors and volunteers, beneficiaries such as targeted producers and workers, consumers, licensee companies and corporate sponsors. (See (c))

When CTE sets objectives it must balance the interests and concerns of these audiences, which will often conflict. This may result in a range of objectives, rather than a single over-riding one.

In order to allow for this balance to be achieved, NFPs will typically feature much wider participation in the objective setting process. Indeed, it may be a legal condition in their constitution and essential to maintaining their legal status.

CTE's objectives are likely to be more intangible and less financially measurable than those of a trading organisation. Thus primary goals may include meeting the founder members' needs, contributing to the well-being of workers and producers, generating the support of consumers and pressing for political and social change.

Secondary goals will include the economic goal of remaining solvent and, ideally perhaps generating a financial surplus to invest in promotional activities or to give to specific projects to benefit those disadvantaged by trade.

To the extent that CTE, will seek to maximise the benefit derived from limited resources eg funds, they might be similar to a profit-focused trading organisation.

However CTE's objectives are likely to involve a much greater degree of corporate social responsibility than a profit-orientated organisation.

CTE's objectives are also likely to be more heavily influenced by external stakeholders such as the government than in a typical trading organisation.

(b) CTE's mission statement

CTE's mission statement might be expected to describe its basic role in society and contain a statement of its overall objectives. In addition to its area of operations, the mission might provide a statement of the culture, its reasons for existence, its aims and the stakeholders served.

The *Ashridge College* model identifies four features of a successful mission:

(i) **Purpose**: Why does the organisation exist? Who does it exist for?

(ii) **Strategy**: the competitive position and distinctive competence of the organisation.

(iii) **Policies and standards of behaviour**: the policies and behavioural patterns underpinning its work.

(iv) **Values**: what the organisation believes in which is replicated in employees' personal values.

These can be used to assess CTE's mission statement:

Purpose

CTE's mission statement has addressed this feature. It identifies its purpose as 'to promote the relief of poverty and suffering'. The choice of words is quite emotive. There is a lack of clarity concerning the definition of 'poverty and suffering' and in addition it is unclear whose poverty and suffering CTE is concerned with. The second part of the mission would suggest that this relates to the poverty and suffering experienced by the local producers, farmers and presumably their workers.

CTE has defined its area of operation as 'arising in connection with the conduct of trade in any part of the world.' This creates a very wide and as such, it might be argued, unachievable remit.

The mission goes on to acknowledge one group of stakeholders – the disadvantaged producers and workers – but does not explicitly consider the objectives of other groups, including for example employees, licensee companies, donors and sponsors. As the only group mentioned, there is an implication that the need of the producers and farmers take priority over all others.

Strategy

CTE has outlined its strategy for promoting relief: 'This will be achieved by providing assistance to disadvantaged producers and workers' and provided some opportunity for measuring the success of the strategy by stating its desire 'to help improve their social and economic position'.

Again there is no explanation of what constitutes 'disadvantaged' and if performance were to be assessed, CTE would need to consider how social and economic position might be measured.

The charity does not have direct competitors for its core activity, so in some ways its competitive stance is of less relevance, however it will be competing for people's time and funds.

One of the distinctive features of the charity is its use of the CTE logo as a consumer guarantee and some reference to this might reinforce the charity's unique position.

Policies and values

While CTE's mission addresses its purpose and strategy, it makes no real reference to policies, standards of behaviour and values.

The function of a mission statement is to:

(i) Communicate the nature of the organisation to its stakeholders

(ii) Help instil core values in the organisation

(iii) Provide a basis for control and evaluation of an organisation ie managerial and operational goals can be set on the basis of them and performance can then be reviewed

In its current form, CTE's mission statement is likely to achieve the first of these only.

At present it appears that the mission statement is largely a public relations exercise. The general nature of it would make it hard to tie down specific strategic implications or to develop meaningful strategic objectives. It is not clear to what extent the mission statement has been taken into account by those responsible for formulating or implementing the charity's strategy.

Suggested improvements

To make CTE's mission statement more effective it should:

(i)   Incorporate references to a wider range of stakeholders and their goals

(ii) Include the core values of the organisation eg transparency

(iii) Refer to the unique nature of the CTE logo

(iv) Be more specific about the area of operations so that the remit is not impossibly wide eg refer to target countries or specific types of farmer/producer

(v)   Define the terms 'poverty', 'suffering' and 'disadvantaged'

(vi) Refer to the charity's policies and standards of behaviour

(c) **Stakeholder analysis**

Note: The answer provided covers the range of possible stakeholders that might have been identified, although candidates were only expected to focus on a few key ones in their answers.

Stakeholders: groups or persons with an interest in what the organisation does, what resources the organisation may have and what is to be achieved. They are affected by, and feel they have a right to benefit from, or be pleased by, what the organisation does.

All stakeholders will have an element of power in their dealings with an organisation to a greater or lesser extent and this will affect the way that CTE chooses to deal with that particular stakeholder or stakeholder group.

Stakeholder	Interests	Power and Influence
Founder members/ patrons	Achievement of aims/ greater good Political power Image of charity in the media/wider environment	Significant. May depend on the size of their annual contributions and the status/reputation of the organisation they belong to. They may well have power as a result of their areas of expertise and network of contacts.
Charity employees	Job satisfaction, security, pay, experience	Power is primarily resource based – they will provide services and time often for relatively low reward. The board will have a greater degree of influence over the day-to-day running and direction of CTE.
Government funding agencies	Value for money Promote the good name of the UK or EU	Depending on the proportion of funding they provide their power could be quite considerable. May have to balance the interests of the charity with the interests of large retailers, producers etc. Will have network power to influence other governments and funding agencies to assist CTE.
Donors	Proper use of funds, recognition or confidentiality as appropriate, satisfaction of having done the right thing	Power is not just about the size of any donation but also based on an individual's ability to raise the profile of CTE eg if a well known celebrity.
Corporate sponsors	Improved image, brand awareness, transparent and cost effective operations, reputational capital by association	Power depends on the value of sponsorship and possibly also on the value to CTE of any expertise that they can provide.

Stakeholder	Interests	Power and Influence
Farmers/ producers	Adequate and sustainable income, long-term contracts, ensure premium gets to farmers	Power virtually non existent unless they have unique products to offer.
Licensee companies	Produce commercial products, increase sales, reasonable margins, enhanced image	Given that the charity's success relies on persuading companies to take out licences, they may have some collective power to influence CTE as a group.

CTE's primary stakeholders can be analysed by considering Mendelow's power-interest matrix as follows:

Stakeholder	Interests	Power and Influence
Retailers	Wider range of products, increased sales/market share by being seen to adopt ethical stance	Again may have some power due to the relative size of the organisations and CTE's need for them to stock the products.
Consumers	Feel virtuous, increased range of products available, reasonable prices	Little power as individuals.
Consumer groups and others, eg World Trade organisation	Lobby govt/organisations to promote and stock goods Interested in the performance/success of the organisation	May have network power to influence other bodies to assist CTE with funding or expertise.
Supporters/ volunteers	Proper use of funds, ethical activities, governance, wide range of merchandise available, organise events	Little power as individuals.
Press/media	Coverage of topical and emotive issues may increase circulation	Need to be kept on side as they have the power to increase publicity or damage the reputation of CTE.

(d) **Governance issues**

The following are the main issues that Ellen should be concerned with in respect of the governance of CTE:

Accountability and openness

This is fundamental to the corporate governance of the charity, with regard to both the proper stewardship of public and donated funds and the increasing demand for stakeholders to be involved in decision-making.

The trustees of CTE should be as open as possible about the decisions and actions that they take. They should give reasons for their decisions and restrict information only when the wider public interest clearly demands.

The Board of CTE must be prepared to submit to an appropriate level of scrutiny. This will lessen the risk of being accused of acting improperly.

Stakeholders

Since CTE has a wide number of stakeholders (as discussed in (a) and (c) above), issues of accountability are not clear-cut and conflicts can arise, eg the charity trustees have a legal duty to act in the interests of their beneficiaries, but this may not always coincide with the priorities of the founder members or the wishes of corporate sponsors.

Such conflict is illustrated by the founders' concerns regarding the marketing expenditure. On the one hand this may be seen to raise CTE's profile with consumers and retailers and increase the effectiveness of CTE as an organisation. On the other, since any direct link between marketing spend and effectiveness is hard to prove, it could be argued that this money would be better going directly to alleviate the poverty of the farmers or improve the conditions of their workers.

The board must have a clear policy statement about the amount of investment in and the purpose of the CTE logo.

Actions of the board

Board members must take decisions in line with the objectives of the charity and in the interests of its beneficiaries (the disadvantaged producers and workers). They should not do so to gain financial or other material benefits for themselves, their family or their friends. Nor should they place themselves under any financial or other obligation to outside individuals or organisations that might influence them in the performance of their duties.

The board have a duty to declare any private interests relating to their duties and to take steps to resolve any conflicts of interest.

Ellen has expressed concern regarding the acceptance of donations and sponsorship from certain multinationals. In considering such sponsorship CTE needs to take into account the likely benefits of increasing the funding available, the interests of its beneficiaries and the impact that this will have on the charity's image.

The trustees should draw up transparent and public guidelines about the source of grants and sponsorship.

The board would be advised to satisfy themselves as to the current trading practices and ethics of the prospective sponsors. They should provide as much information as possible about the reasons for accepting such money and ensure that they have complied with the principles set out above regarding transparency, honesty and self-interest.

Monitoring performance

The board needs to implement an effective system of performance measurement as this demonstrates to external stakeholders that the charity's mandates and objectives are being met (see (e)).

(e) **Assessing performance**

When assessing CTE's performance, three important issues must be taken into account. These are:

(i)   There is no profit motive objective so many of the traditional financial performance indicators cannot be applied eg the ROCE.

(ii) No particular stakeholder group dominates, unlike say the shareholders of a limited company.

(iii) It may be difficult to find other, similar organisations that can be used as benchmarks for assessing the performance of CTE.

Despite these difficulties it is important that CTE maintains control by setting performance standards and implementing a system of monitoring, feedback and reporting on performance.

In order to assess whether CTE is achieving its objectives, key performance indicators need to be established, and actual performance measured and monitored for each of those indicators.

CTE will need to establish targets, thereby enabling measurement of the extent to which objectives have been achieved. A significant number of these are likely to be of a non-financial nature and as a result the balanced scorecard approach to performance measurement is likely to be particularly relevant.

The BSC approach looks at four perspectives in order to provide operational control so that the organisation's mission and objectives can be met. These perspectives are financial, customer, internal, and learning and growth. They are balanced in the sense that managers are required to think in terms of all four perspectives to prevent improvements being made in one area at the expense of another.

Financial perspective

In profit-making organisations this would be expressed in terms of shareholder value and return; however the financial perspective is still relevant to a non-profit organisation such as CTE.

Here the financial perspective will be in terms of economy and efficiency: allowing the available resources to be put to best use to add value to society, providing value for money for the sponsors and fund providers.

Appropriate KPIs include:

(i)   Average donations
(ii)   Sales of CTE merchandise
(iii) Licence fees received
(iv)   Level of marketing spend
(v)   Costs of producing/sourcing merchandise
(vi)   Costs involved in setting up and monitoring licence agreements

Customer perspective

A not-for-profit organisation such as CTE needs to know what its users and beneficiaries feel about its services. CTE aims to ensure that the licensee businesses offer farmers and producers a guaranteed income and to make money available for community projects.

Appropriate KPIs include:

(i)   Actual income received by farmers/producers compared to guaranteed income promised
(ii)   Increase in average wages received by workers/wages received in comparison to other workers
(iii) Amount contributed by CTE to producers/workers as a proportion of total funding received
(iv)   Increase in number of beneficiaries and/or number of regions/areas covered by CTE aid
(v)   Amount spent by CTE/licensee companies on community projects

Internal business process perspective

This perspective asks the question what processes must CTE excel at to achieve our financial and customer objectives and it aims to improve internal processes and decision making.

CTE must assess how it goes about delivering its services and what impact this has on its effectiveness.

Appropriate KPIs include:

(i)   Number of new licences

(ii)   Percentage of revenue spent on admin

(iii) Percentage of revenue that is spent on the publicised cause (eg rather than on advertising or administration)

(iv)   Speed of processing of licence applications

Learning and growth perspective

This considers CTE's capacity to maintain and grow its position through the acquisition of new skills and the development of new products or services.

CTE will benefit from learning from the past (both successes and failures), to enable processes to improve over time leading to improved user satisfaction.

Ellen has identified a need to raise the profile of the charity and so might look at innovative ways to raise awareness, attract new funding, or bring in new products to the CTE logo.

Appropriate KPIs include:

(i)   Number of new products carrying the CTE mark
(ii)   Increase in range of products available
(iii) Amount of training undertaken by staff
(iv)   New fundraising initiatives undertaken

The introduction of a new performance measurement system may create fear and uncertainty among staff since it raises their visibility and accountability. It will be important to implement an appropriate programme of consultation, communication and training.

Information requirements

The following information may be useful in assessing CTE's performance:

Strategic information: Derived from both internal and external sources and summarised at a high level

(i) Activities of other charities engaged in similar activities
(ii) Government (and in some cases overseas government) policy on trade
(iii) Public and retailer attitudes to equitable trade

Tactical information: Primarily generated internally (but may have a limited external component). Prepared on a regular basis to help monitor and control performance

(i) Percent of revenue spent on admin
(ii) Average donations
(iii) 'Customer' satisfaction statistics
(iv) Statistics regarding awareness of CTE brand/mark

Operational information: Derived from internal sources. Prepared on a very frequent basis to help track the organisation's specific and day-to-day operational activities

(i) Households collected from/approached
(ii) Banking documentation
(iii) Number of new licences
(iv) Licence fees received
(v) Sales of CTE merchandise

General comments:

This scenario is a charitable company engaged in promoting the relief of poverty through the conduct of fair trade. Its primary activities are the certification of products, via a fair trade logo and the granting of licences to companies wishing to operate under this logo. The newly appointed director, who has no experience of the charitable sector, wants to raise awareness of activities and extend the range of certified products on offer. She has asked for help in measuring performance but also needs to address concerns raised by the founder members about spending money on promotional activities and accepting donations from large multinationals who have previously adopted unfair trade practices.

Many attempts at this question were marginal. Some scripts were very weak due to poor performance on the requirements concerning mission and objectives, a failure to answer part (d) on governance and possible overall time pressure at the end of the exam.

Requirement (a) requested candidates to discuss the extent to which the objectives of the charity will differ from those of a typical profit-focused organisation. Answers to this requirement were disappointing. Weaker answers simply stated that the objective of a trading organisation is to maximise shareholder wealth whereas a charity aims to provide aid for its beneficiaries. Better answers related their points to the scenario, identifying the need to balance the interests of a much wider range of stakeholders and commenting that as a result objectives might be less easily measured. The best scripts identified similarities to the extent that both organisations would be aiming to maximise returns from limited resources and went on to say that increasingly there is a need for even profit-focused organisations to consider corporate social responsibility and its wider group of stakeholders.

Requirement (b) asked candidates to critically evaluate the content of CTE's mission statement and to suggest improvements. Most candidates explained that a mission statement should identify the general purpose of an organisation and that CTE's mission statement did indeed do this. Better candidates commented on the use of unspecific terms such as 'poverty and suffering' and pointed out that CTE's mission is very far reaching in terms of remit and as such potentially unachievable. Some candidates failed to make recommendations for improvements, despite this being specifically requested. A number attempted to apply the 'SMART' principles but in doing so, seemed a little confused by the distinction between a mission statement and the objectives of an organisation.

Requirement (c) asked candidates to identify the key stakeholders of CTE and explain their interests and likely influence. Candidates were clearly well prepared for this part of the question, with most demonstrating a good knowledge of Mendelow's matrix and an ability to apply it to the scenario in question.

Requirement (d) requested candidates to advise Ellen on the specific governance issues arising as a result of the concerns raised by the founder members. Many candidates did not attempt this requirement at all and those that did often discussed whether the concerns of the founders were valid, without advising Ellen on the implications for governance. Better scripts addressed the need for the board to apply principles such as transparency, ethical behaviour and accountability to the stakeholders.

Requirement (e) asked candidates to explain how Ellen might measure the performance of CTE. In addition to suggesting appropriate key performance indicators, candidates were also required to describe the information that would assist in the measurement process.

Many candidates did not attempt the first element of the requirement at all and those that did tended to make a brief comment on the need for both financial and non-financial measurement. Only the better candidates identified that a balanced scorecard approach would be appropriate in these circumstances and explained the benefits that this would bring. The section on performance measures was normally well answered and it was pleasing that these were on the whole tailored to the scenario. Most candidates were able to give some examples of useful information and some discussed benchmarking as a means of comparing CTE's relative performance in the charitable sector.

15 Embury Ltd

Marking guide

			Knowledge	Skill	Marks
(a)	PESTEL		2	8	
	Maximum full marks				8
(b)	(i)	Capacity planning/procurement	3	4	
	(ii)	Outsourcing benefits and problems/risks	2	5	
	Maximum full marks				12
(c)	Ethical procurement		2	4	
	Maximum full marks				5
(d)	Change management problems/how to address		5	8	
	Maximum full marks				11
(e)	Pros and cons of product development		2	6	
	Maximum full marks				6
			16	35	42

(a) **PESTEL analysis**

Political

(i) Current and future restrictions imposed by governments and/or the water companies on the use of water eg for garden purposes may limit demand for garden equipment

(ii) Legislation or changing attitudes of overseas governments may affect the availability of low cost labour in other countries

(iii) Any future restrictions placed on imports by the UK government or exports by overseas governments would affect costs and possible competition

Economic

(i) Changes in interest rates and the state of the economy will affect disposable incomes and hence demand for gardening products which are discretionary purchases

(ii) Rising charges for water services will reduce the amount that individuals are prepared to spend on non-essential water such as for gardening purposes

(iii) Changing exchange rates may affect the cost of manufacture and hence margins on the outsourced products

(iv) Recession in the housing market may affect the number of households and the size of gardens. An increase in the proportion of people choosing to rent for example is likely to mean less interest in gardening

(v) Availability of low cost resources in other economies means increased pressure on margins for UK manufacturers

Social

Demand for gardening equipment is derived from the demand for gardens and gardening:

(i) Increasingly busy lifestyles may reduce people's desire to have a garden and hence decrease the need for gardening equipment

(ii) Modern housing developments with small gardens decrease the need for gardening and equipment

(iii) Alternatively increasing concerns about the quality of the environment may stimulate demand for an outdoor lifestyle and hence garden products. If market research is to be believed, a desire for a better quality of life may increase demand for natural surroundings and gardening as a form of leisure

(iv) An increasingly ageing population may mean there are more retired people with time on their hands for leisure and gardening

(v) Peer pressure may mean that consumers do not want to be seen watering their gardens or washing their cars. Conversely this may boost demand for water conservation measures and other environmentally friendly products

Technological

(i) Technological developments may mean cheaper products become available to E or its competitors

(ii) Alternatively modern technology may allow the production of more efficient watering equipment to bypass restrictions

(iii) As developers are forced to become more ecological, all new houses may be built with underground rainwater tanks and garden irrigation systems, avoiding the need for gardening equipment or offering companies like E an opportunity to sell its new product range to developers

Environmental

(i) Climate changes and the weather are uncontrollable factors which may increase or decrease the demand for gardening equipment

(ii) Increased environmental concerns may cause households to reduce the non-essential consumption of water for leisure purposes thus reducing the demand for hosepipes and sprinkler systems

(iii) An increased desire to be sustainable may cause households to switch to alternative approaches to irrigate their gardens or alternatively to plant different types of trees and shrubs which do not need so much watering

(iv) May be an increase in environmental groups lobbying for sustainability, which widens the stakeholder groups that need to be considered

Legal

(i)   Legislation regarding the environment, the use of water etc may affect production processes or demand. It might also influence the types of product E is able to offer

(ii) E will need to comply with minimum wage legislation and other Health & Safety issues

(iii) E will also need to ensure it complies with any legislation regarding factory closures and redundancies which could increase costs

(iv) The water industry is regulated by law in the prices it can change (by OFWAT) and thus changes in regulatory policy may affect water prices as well as the pricing policy of the water companies. This will affect the amount of the charge, but also the form of the charge (eg compulsory water metering)

(v)   Penalties for breaching water use regulations might be both public and quite severe

Summary

Demand for garden equipment is significantly affected by factors outside the control of the industry, such as the weather. This is exacerbated by the increasing cost of water, the drive for water conservation and the restrictions on water use imposed by governments. Certain demographic factors are favourable but a key threat for UK-based manufacturers such as Embury is the increasing competition in the industry (as evidenced by GZ's entry to the UK market) and the pressure on margins as a result of the availability of other lower cost products.

(b)   (i)   **Capacity planning and procurement**

Capacity planning

Capacity planning involves consideration of E's capability to supply both existing and future demand but with an understanding of the costs of providing spare capacity as a buffer for uncertainty and a buffer for seasonality.

Capacity planning also links to supply chain management since supplier capabilities and reliability will affect E's own capability.

- **Variations in demand**

  The key issue for Embury is the fact that demand will vary considerably with the time of year and also the weather conditions.

  Embury has always faced the fluctuations of seasonality for watering products leading to spare capacity or tight periods. However while E is likely to be able to predict that demand for its products is higher in the spring and summer than autumn and winter, within these periods demand is subject to unexpected climate changes or problems created by restrictions placed on water use. Hence E faces issues of overstocking and stock-outs which are largely caused by factors outside its control.

  Longer term trends are also affecting demand:

  –   The new generation of gardeners and the generally predicted shift to increased demand for gardening and leisure products

  –   The nature of products in the mix may change as water saving products are demanded more in the longer term and at peak times due to drought and government restrictions on water use

- **Balancing capacity and demand**

  The major retailers will expect E to respond flexibly and quickly to changes in demand.

  There is a significant problem with capacity utilisation. Unit costs are likely to be high as facilities and staff will be underutilised in off-peak periods. Hence the proposals to reduce the number of factories and staffing levels would appear to make sense.

  The MD has identified the need to move to more flexible manufacturing. E must try to anticipate variations in demand and alter its capacity accordingly, eg by having minimum numbers of full time staff and taking on part time staff or working overtime in peak demand periods.

Variations in equipment levels might also be necessary, perhaps by means of short-term rental arrangements.

Embury needs information and data to support forecasting and modelling of the future and possibly IT models to assist in analysis. Models may need to link to integrated ERP and supply chain management systems with data sharing backwards and forwards in the supply chain. Inventory control systems may be required to control buffering costs.

Embury may have opportunities to expand market share through marketing and will need to build these potential increases in demand into its planning and procurement models.

E may be able to smooth production and pass some of the risks of weather on to the retailers, for example by negotiating fixed early season orders at off-peak prices.

Procurement

E needs to decide on a strategy for sourcing materials and or products.

From a business perspective Embury will need greater access to supplies to lower risk of procurement shortages.

Also E as raw material prices increase, E needs to be able to compete with companies who are able to produce lower cost products.

Procurement issues would include whether to buy in raw materials and components, part assembled products or to sub contract the whole manufacturing process for certain products (see discussion below on outsourcing).

Additionally E needs to decide whether to choose one or more different suppliers.

The advantage to E of creating a long term, single-source strategic relationship with a supplier is that it facilitates economies of scale and can increase competitive advantage by affording cooperation and flexibility. However, E would need to choose the supplier carefully as reliance on a single company exposes E to possible disruptions in supply.

(ii) **Benefits of outsourcing**

- Faced with increasing raw material costs and low cost products from competitors, outsourcing production of certain products may enable E to reduce costs because the external supplier can source raw materials cheaper overseas, gain access to lower costs of labour or take advantage of economies of scale.

- E may also gain access to cheaper products due to exchange rate advantages.

- This may improve competitive advantage and hence improve sales and performance. The MD's comments imply that competitors have benefited from this and it is particularly important given the entry to the UK market of GZ, together with the existing presence of competitively priced own-brand products.

- Given the variability of demand and the seasonality of the product, E may want to reduce operating gearing by making its cost base more variable.

- Risk may be managed better by outsourcing, eg may pass risks on to the supplier such as overproduction in the face of a sudden drop in demand but this will depend on the flexibility built into the outsourcing contract in terms of a minimum level of demand.

- There may also be scope to shift legal liability to the supplier and levy charges for breakdowns in performance or delays in delivery that will mitigate losses.

- Gain from outside expertise or competence – an external supplier may have better or different knowledge in relation to certain product lines eg the new water conservation range. This may improve E's ability to differentiate its product from competitors and/or lead to increased product innovation.

- E may shop around and choose to use different suppliers for different products according to their competences, flexibility, costs and so on.

- E can improve its competitive advantage by creating a network of long-term relationships with the suppliers in its value chain. Some of these benefits may be lost if E only outsources certain product ranges.

Problems and risks

- Choice of partner – E is exposed to risks if the supplier is unreliable/unstable or the product produced is poor quality.

- May be problems in controlling supply chain: there will be admin costs and time spent in co-ordination.

- May be harder to guarantee supply eg delays in delivery may arise if products are being imported from overseas locations.

- May be harder to control quality, particularly with a variety of suppliers. E will need to ensure that there is an appropriate contract and performance measures.

- There may be hidden costs eg impact of 'kick backs' required to do business in certain countries.

- Costs will also be affected by exchange rate fluctuations. A relatively weak pound would increase the costs for E, despite these being manufactured in low cost countries.

- There is a risk that E's learning & intellectual property is being transferred. The in-house operation may be a source of significant learning leading to product and process improvement. E may face direct competition from the supplier after any contract comes to an end.

- Closure costs may be prohibitive: redundancies, exit penalties etc and will lead to bad publicity. If the outsourcing agreement fails, E may find it hard to source alternative supplies but will no longer have the production facilities in house.

- Managing this change will require considerable time and effort on the part of management.

(c) **Ethical procurement**

An ethical procurement policy is an attempt by E to fulfil its own Corporate Social Responsibility commitments by demanding similar commitments and standards of behaviour from suppliers.

As an ethical approach becomes increasingly popular with customers and investors, it may also contribute to E's longer term business success.

E may however be accused of being hypocritical if while demanding ethical behaviour from suppliers it attracts adverse publicity for the way its own employees are being treated as a result of the factory closures.

E is likely to expect all suppliers to comply with the policy and may choose not to do business with companies that are not prepared to comply or to take corrective action.

An ethical policy is likely to lead to:

(i) Reduced choice/range of suppliers
(ii) Increased costs of the product
(iii) Requirement to monitor compliance and costs incurred as a result
(iv) Additional terms in outsourcing agreement

However it might also be used as a USP to differentiate E from competitors such as GZ.

When E is considering its choice of suppliers and the drawing up of contracts, ethical procurement would have an impact in the following areas:

(i) **Working in partnership with suppliers**

E's policy may cover the need for fair contracting terms and conditions with suppliers and transparency of negotiations.

This would include fair prices, adherence to reasonable payment terms and having a grievance procedure to deal with suppliers' grievances. It would also make clear timescales for contract re-tendering and award/non-renewal.

(ii) **Human rights**

The human rights of workers within supplier firms must be protected so that:

- Employment is freely chosen and no child labour is used
- Working conditions are safe, hygienic and humane
- Working hours are not excessive and reasonable wages are paid
- No discrimination is practised

(iii) **Health and safety**

There would be an expectation that proper health and safety standards should be maintained in operations that may affect employees and the general public.

(iv) **Environmental protection**

E is likely to have objectives for sustainable development which would mean that suppliers are expected to comply with all relevant local and national environmental regulations and to work to minimise the harmful effects of their activities.

(v) **Fraud and corruption**

There will be zero tolerance of the offering of gifts and inducements by suppliers and also of conflicts of interest.

(d) **Change management**

There are two separate change management issues:

(1) The leaked e-mail
(2) The planned closures

(1) **Leaked e-mail**

The leaked e-mail may have put information into the public domain prematurely or even when it was never intended to be public information. There are risks of inaccuracy and of escalation of rumour.

The leaked e-mail gives rise to issues for shareholders and wider stakeholders who may use information to advantage or react to information from their stakeholder view, commercially or emotionally. There are political implications and social issues.

The press describe the potential closures of two factories as 'shocking' and talk of 'lost' jobs in an emotive way. The implication is that there was no proper consultation and that maybe profits come before people. The news report also 'mocks' the reason as if it is all down to water shortages.

The MD of Embury has been quoted addressing only his shareholders and not all stakeholders. His response appears economically rational. He also uses the opportunity to mention outsourcing that has positive economic benefits to shareholders but potential social issues for other stakeholders. Longer-term job losses may be implied.

His final reported comments appear to say that job losses are just collateral damage in the pursuit of return and growth and management of risk the implication is that there is an opportunity as well as a threat.

Embury may need to consider some additional PR communications to reduce the negative social messages and internally will need to manage the rumour and people issues. There is potential for resistance to change and local protest from staff and the community. There is a risk of broader reputational damage.

(2) **Planned closures**

All changes tend to be resisted by employees. The nature of the changes such as E are proposing which involve downsizing and redundancy will be resisted even more strongly –

particularly if, in the first instance, employees find out about the proposed changes as a result of the leaked article.

(i) **Cultural barriers**

The new proposal puts forward fundamental changes that will affect the culture of the organisation. Power structures within E may be threatened by the redistribution of decision-making authority or resources, or the changing of lines of communication.

This will in particular affect management and thus management may be reluctant to implement changes which will be against their own interests eg the managers of the two factories that are to be closed.

(ii) **Stakeholder groups**

Group inertia may block change where the changes are inconsistent with the norms of teams and departments, or where they threaten their interests.

Examples from E might include:

- Strikes and other forms of resistance to change implementation by E staff to be made redundant

- UK raw material suppliers taking legal action for contract termination if the business is now to be switched to overseas suppliers

- Shareholders selling shares as a result of the changes

(iii) **Individuals**

There are also barriers which affect individuals and result in them seeing the change as a threat to earnings and job security. This may affect not only the UK factories that are to be closed but also the employees in the remaining consolidated site where there are likely to be substantial changes in work practices and also redundancies of old skills in favour of new skills.

Addressing the issues and managing the change

Change management will involve two project levels a technical project and a people project, the two are interlinked:

Technical

(i) Shifting production and technology to one site
(ii) Liquidation of old sites
(iii) Redesign of processes for efficiency
(iv) Redesign of supply chain processes
(v) Setting up of new departments for R&D

People

(i) Managing the rumour internally and externally
(ii) Ensuring the need for change is understood
(iii) Dealing with redundancy announcements, implementation and exit support
(iv) Building new teams to implement the change
(v) Getting staff onside and positive for the change
(vi) Getting staff ready for the additional work and pressure of change
(vii) Building the new culture internally and across the supply chain
(viii) Managing news to motivate
(ix) Managing investor relations issues

A change agent should be appointed to oversee the change process. Ideally someone from outside who can clearly communicate the benefits of change and where possible involve the remaining staff in the process. This will help strengthen the forces for change.

E needs to identify key stakeholders and encourage them to support the change.

Communication will be an essential part of the process:

(i) Shareholders will be interested in the impact on share price and profitability and dividends. E will need to provide reassurance re the state of their investment and how strategy will benefit them/improve results.

(ii) Key customers (retailers etc) will need reassurance about quality and reliability and availability of supply. They will also be interested in any impact on prices.

(iii) Unions and staff must be consulted and the case for change to ensure the long term survival of the company made clear. Participation in the process may improve motivation. If staff are to be made redundant, they may be motivated by making negotiation of redundancy terms, references and assistance with alternative employment contingent on smooth transition.

(iv) E will need to preserve PR by communicating information to the financial press and analysts about how and why has decision been made and how will it be implemented.

Once the changes have taken place Lewin would argue that it will be necessary to refreeze the new methods. This will involve ensuring that the remaining staff adapt to the new business model and are motivated to work within it.

Techniques such as introducing new reward systems and changing the way in which activities are carried out should help embed the model.

(e) **Product development**

Advantages

(i) E would benefit from having a range of products to reduce dependence on any one product and ensure a balanced portfolio of products that smooths out cashflow. It appears to have devoted too little attention in the past to developing products that will be the future of the company.

(ii) Introducing water conservation products widens the product base and reduces total reliance on products that require plentiful water supplies.

(iii) Water conservation products would appear to be a growing market and E can establish an advantage if it can be first to the market with these types of product. Market research should be undertaken to assess demand.

(iv) A different balance of products may lessen some of the supply chain pressures by spreading demand more evenly.

(v) The current proposal still links to existing area of expertise so within E's competence.

(vi) Being seen to be environmentally friendly may enhance the company reputation and image and may help it be looked on more favourably by government/legislators and environmental groups.

(vii) May help compete with GZ and protect market share in UK.

Disadvantages

(i) New products may be expensive to purchase or install and as a result demand may be limited.

(ii) The products still rely on the availability of water which is subject to factors beyond E's control.

(iii) Use of household waste may be unsanitary and lead to litigation claims and/or bad publicity.

(iv) Given the size of GZ and its reputation for innovation, E's technology and products may be superceded.

(v) Current proposals represent only limited diversification of the product range. Thus there will only be a limited reduction in the impact of the weather on the seasonality of revenues and cashflow.

Conclusion

The development plans probably do not go far enough. Larger businesses all produce across the whole range of gardening equipment which is likely to reduce the risks of their portfolios and extend the season of demand for their products eg leaf blowers in autumn and sprinklers in summer.

Perhaps Embury needs to consider additional new products eg pond and water equipment or selling its products to markets where the seasons are opposite to those in the UK.

General comments:

The scenario is based on the UK's leading manufacturer of garden watering equipment which is facing unpredictable demand due to environmental issues. It is also confronted with increasing raw material costs and competition from a multi-national garden equipment company that is expanding into the UK. As a result it intends to widen its product range to reduce dependence on seasons. The company has recently suffered bad publicity when its previously unknown plans to reduce costs by closing two factories and outsourcing certain product manufacture to China were leaked to a local newspaper.

This question is the mini case and, at 42 marks, was the longest question on the paper, although the requirements were broken down to help candidates in developing answer headings and assessing mark allocation.

Overall good scores on (a), (b)(ii) and (d) made up for poorer scores in (b)(i) and (c). Part (e) tended to be variable in quality.

Requirement (a) asked candidates to prepare a PESTEL analysis on the garden equipment industry. Most candidates found this requirement reasonably straightforward as the bulk of the points could be discerned from the text of the scenario. A number applied their analysis to the company rather than the garden equipment industry as a whole and weaker candidates restricted their marks by producing tables or lists of undeveloped points. Some candidates wrote far too much here for the marks available, leaving themselves short of time for later requirements. Only the best candidates indicated the relative importance of the various factors or attempted to summarise the overall implications of their analysis for the industry.

Requirement (b) (i) asked candidates to describe the capacity planning and procurement issues currently facing the company and (ii) to explain the benefits and risks involved in the outsourcing proposal. The subject of capacity planning and procurement is new to the learning materials and many candidates seemed to lack specific knowledge here. As a result many did little more than repeat the information from the question regarding the unpredictability of demand and the issue of stock-outs/overstocking; often failing to discuss procurement at all. Better candidates explained the implications for fixed cost recovery and the value chain, commented on the need for a more flexible manufacturing strategy (as highlighted by the managing director) and discussed the importance of reducing fixed costs and developing closer relations with suppliers.

Candidates were better prepared to discuss the pros and cons of outsourcing in b(ii). Most scored well here, although higher skills marks were earned by those who applied their points to the case eg pointing out that most of Embury's competitors were already adopting this strategy. Only the stronger candidates linked their discussion back to the issues in b(i), explaining that outsourcing might help to reduce fixed costs and transfer some of the risks of variable demand to the supplier.

Requirement (c) involved ethics. Candidates were asked to explain how the company's proposed ethical procurement policy might affect any outsourcing agreement. Answers were quite poor on the whole. Most candidates appreciated that such a policy would probably increase the cost to the company and limit the available suppliers, but only the better ones went beyond this to explain fully what such a policy would cover (labour, environmental issues, raw materials) and how the agreement would be drafted (monitoring, sanctions, termination etc). A number were highly critical of the likely ethics of a Chinese manufacturer and the impact this might have on the company's reputation but seemed to ignore the fact that the recent press article cast a shadow on Embury's own ethical behaviour.

Requirement (d) asked candidates to explain the change management problems that are likely to occur as a result of the newspaper article and the planned factory closures and to discuss how these might be addressed. As usual the majority of candidates showed good knowledge in this area but often failed to earn the skills marks available for applying this to the scenario. Weaker candidates either made general points without reference to any theory or discussed barriers to change and possible change management approaches including Lewin's 'unfreeze/move/refreeze' model, in generic terms. Weaker answers tended to focus solely on the employee aspects of closure, rather than considering also the wider commercial issues and the other stakeholders. Many completely ignored the effect of the change being announced by the newspaper article.

Requirement (e) requested a discussion of the advantages and disadvantages of the plans for product development and was reasonably well attempted by the majority of candidates.

Skills marks were earned by those who linked their discussion back to the PESTEL analysis and the impending competition.

16 DT Ltd

Marking guide

		Knowledge	Skill	Marks
(a)	SWOT	1	8	
	Maximum full marks			8
(b)	Evaluation of expansion proposals	4	10	
	Maximum full marks			12
(c)	Business model/basis of competitive Advantages/benefits for a franchisee	3	10	
	Maximum full marks			12
		8	28	32

(a) **SWOT ANALYSIS**

Strengths

(i) DT has a successful business model that has delivered a profitable and rapidly expanding business in just a few years.

(ii) David has been prepared to reinvest profits and not just run a 'lifestyle' business.

(iii) David's technical expertise has allowed him to develop an innovative training product which appears to have attracted customers.

(iv) Training requires less time, costs less and results in improved success rates – part of the core competence in attracting trainee drivers – which will give DT a competitive advantage.

(v) DT is able to compete with both types of business – self-employed driving instructors based on time and quality and large schools based on time and cost.

(vi) Proprietary knowledge is protected by patent which restricts competitors copying the product.

(vii) Well known brand name locally – the brand name seems to have become well known and is thus recognisable. This reinforces reputation and allows DT to capitalise on referrals.

(viii) Extended life of product and wider potential market – ability to use the simulator for more experienced and commercial drivers widens DT's target market and hence increased sales opportunities. It also means that DT can continue to sell to existing customers once they have a licence.

(ix) Ability to use simulator in winter months reduces seasonality of revenues and cashflow.

(x) May appeal to environmentalists due to reduced costs.

Weaknesses

(i) Reliance on David – much of the control and culture appears to depend on one person. David also is the real innovator with software. There is thus a risk if David leaves or is ill.

(ii) There is also limited capacity for one person to control expansion as the business grows.

(iii) Rapid growth may have put pressure on systems and led to overtrading.

(iv) Profits and cashflow affected by seasonality (though this may have been minimised by the use of the simulator).

(v) Lack of further debt finance – expansion is constrained by lack of financial resources.

(vi) David has a high level of personal debt which needs servicing – the high debt creates financial risk.

(vii) Expansion has been limited to the known London geographical market, where the company has a reputation. Wider geographical expansion may be outside management's experience and the business may take time to develop a reputation and customer base outside London.

Opportunities

(i) Provincial expansion – there is an opportunity to expand in other cities/ areas of the UK.

(ii) Further organic growth eg raise share capital via friends and family.

(iii) New investors such as IMS appear to be available to supply new resources for expansion.

(iv) Brand name and proprietary software mean the business is capable of being franchised.

(v) Develop the commercial driver training element of the business eg through corporate contracts.

(vi) Expand the concept of training for extreme conditions.

(vii) Develop complementary products eg DVDs/CD Roms or simulator products for other industries.

Threats

(i) Contestable market – there are few barriers to entry and competition is intense. Eventually David's patent will expire and in the meantime rivals may develop other innovative training methods and compete away DT's profits. The patent will only protect the specific programme used rather than the idea of driving simulation as such.

(ii) There is a threat to the personal control of David if more shareholders are needed – David may eventually lose control of the company under strategy option (ii). Thus while the business may succeed, David's investment may not if this source of external finance is used.

(iii) There is a need to change organisational structure as the business grows – this may affect the business model. If David's 'hands on' approach is making the business succeed this may not be available as the business expands and new management is brought in.

(iv) Any bad publicity would damage reputation and lose clients and referrals.

(v) Inability to service high debt costs if business declines or over-expands.

(vi) A fall in pass rates would affect demand.

(vii) The product is IT-based and as such open to the inherent risks of system failure, malfunction, viruses etc.

(viii) Takeover by a national chain (could be seen as an opportunity).

Key issues

David's technical expertise has allowed him to develop an innovative training product which has given DT a competitive advantage. However, the business is heavily reliant on David and has limited resources for expansion. In view of this and given the low barriers to entry and the intense competition in the industry, organic growth is likely to be difficult to achieve. DT's brand name and proprietary software make it attractive as a partner and thus offer a good opportunity to expand either through franchising or in partnership with another business such as IMS.

(b) **Evaluation of expansion proposals**

Proposal 1 – Franchising

Under a franchise a firm grants other firms the right to use its brand, its product or its know-how. There is also likely to be some degree of central control and support. In return, the franchisee will normally provide a lump sum, share of earnings and specific payments.

In the current context, a franchise is likely to be on a geographical basis in order to segregate the markets of the individual franchisees.

Governance and control

DT maintains some general contractual control over franchisee but loses some operational control.

If franchising is to be taken up by many small operators, then DT is not dominated by its business partner(s).

There is a need to monitor franchisees and there may be quality control issues. Franchisees must be chosen carefully and contracts need to be drawn up to ensure DT's reputation is protected.

Risk

Reduced financial risk by having franchisees' own capital.

There are fewer risks from franchisee losses as cost of failure is shared with franchisee. This reduces the maximum potential loss from the failure of an outlet but also provides an increased incentive for the franchisee to succeed.

Poor quality franchisees may harm brand name eg lower quality instructors may have an impact on success rates.

May be more difficult to change the strategic direction of the business in the future if franchisees have a degree of autonomy in the running of their outlet.

There is a need to monitor the franchisees as they may have different objectives, approaches and abilities compared to DT. David may find he is overburdened as the number of franchises grows.

Franchisees gain access to intellectual property and may misuse or copy the software or break away and set up in competition.

May invite national competition.

Franchisees may not want to take up the opportunity – there needs to be some incentive to purchase a franchise and without successful establishment in the market outside London this may be unlikely.

Resources

This method offers quicker business expansion than using DT's own financial resources as the franchisees offer a new source of capital.

David will be required to provide training in the use of the simulator. Franchisees may also expect support with marketing. DT may need to take on additional manpower to provide training and support and manage the franchisees.

Franchisees are likely to be individuals so unlike IMS will not be able to provide any large scale expansion or financial support.

The need to share profits with franchisee means fewer profits can be reinvested in the expansion of the business than if DT were to grow organically.

DT gains access to the local knowledge/reputation of the franchisee which may attract candidates, increase awareness of the brand and increase referral rates.

Proposal 2 – New share capital via IMS

IMS offers economies of scale in two respects: increased financial capital and access to IMS driving schools across Europe as a wider market.

Governance and control

Initially David retains control of the business because of his majority stake, although IMS will have a significant stake and may interfere in the day to day running of the business.

Control of the business will remain centralised and David may have more influence over instructors than under a franchise arrangement.

After five years, David may lose control of the company if IMS takes up the option to increase its shareholding. He will become more dependent on IMS who may decide to change the control and reporting structure. David is likely to have reduced influence on the board of directors and this may lead to stalemate for important operating decisions.

Risk

The brand name may be unknown outside London and thus needs to be established in each individual city. This may not be easy or quick.

IMS has no experience of the UK and there may not be the local knowledge and core competences within DT to operate successfully in provincial cities.

Expansion outside UK may not be as successful, or may be more uncertain. Competition for the simulator training product may already exist.

Simulator may need modification eg for right hand driving.

Rapid expansion may carry the risk of overtrading and loss of David's investment in the event of failure.

Requirement for dividend or exit route by IMS may limit future availability of funds.

The terms of which IMS can expand its shareholding from 33% to 50% need to be clear or there is a risk that resources input may not compensate for the loss of control by David.

IMS may not fulfil their promises in respect of resources or finance.

May reduce risks as effectively a venture which eliminates competition.

Additional equity capital will lower financial risk through reduced gearing (although this depends on the extent to which DT takes advantage of the loan finance offered by IMS).

The additional debt represents increased gearing risk.

Resources

If significant new capital is provided by IMS then growth could be rapid in terms of the number of outlets.

The sites in provincial cities are likely to be lower cost than London thus enhancing profitability.

DT will be able to benefit from access to IMS expertise in the market place.

IMS will be able to provide DT with support for advertising, training etc, which is the inverse of the franchise situation.

Conclusion

Before deciding on which option to pursue David should carefully consider his and DT's objectives in expanding and his eventual plans for exit. Both options address the issue of limited resources and share the risk of expansion but also require David to share the control and the future profits of the business.

The deal with IMS gives DT access to a large pool of funds and expertise and is likely to offer more opportunity for significant growth; however David's control will be greatly diluted. Contractual protection may be needed if and when IMS gain a 50% shareholding.

Franchising offers a slower growth route, with DT providing the expertise, but David is much more likely to retain control of the direction of the business and may benefit from the local knowledge and reputation of franchisees. More detail is required regarding the terms of the franchise and the number of interested franchisees.

David's key skill is the development of the software, rather than the management of an expanding business. Thus developing the business under a license system may free him up to concentrate on further product innovations.

(c) **Extract from business plan to attract franchisee**

(i) **DT Limited: Business model**

DT's mission is 'to provide high quality, convenient and comprehensive driver education courses at the lowest cost'. We operate five successful driving centres in and around the London area, which provide training for learner drivers, via a virtual reality driving simulator, similar to those used in airline pilot training. The simulator is used in addition to traditional road-based instruction and learning.

Three years ago, when the company was founded, David Thomas (the founder and sole shareholder) realised that there was an untapped opportunity in the driver education industry.

No company was providing what the customers truly demanded, high quality driver education at the lowest possible cost. Large companies were charging too much for their services and the local companies were not providing enough programmes and services or they were poor quality.

DT is at the cutting edge of driver training by instituting the use of computer simulators. The technological revolution in computers has enhanced our abilities to teach.

Simulator training widens the market opportunities as it can be offered to:

(1) Learner drivers
(2) Existing drivers wanting refresher courses or needing advanced driving skills
(3) Commercial drivers

The company will continue to seek new ways to provide a better and more convenient teaching environment through technology.

DT's steady growth in a mature market is a sign of the firm's viable business strategy and our success in the London area has proven that our product works. Now the company is ready to expand and is seeking like minded individuals who want to participate in our success.

Through franchising, DT aims to create a national network of driver instructor centres providing cheap, effective driver training at the forefront of technology.

In return for an initial capital investment, DT will provide franchisees with the necessary equipment, training and ongoing support to establish themselves as the premier instructor in their region. Franchisees will retain the profit from their business, after paying a percentage to DT to cover ongoing costs.

(ii) **DT's competitive advantage**

The driver education industry is highly competitive. Each company within this field has high capital and running costs, low margins, and a high intensity of competition.

In addition buyer power is also very high. Buyers are willing to search for the most favourable combination of price and acceptable service. Also under the conventional model there is a lack of opportunity for repeat business.

DT's unique, patented driving simulator has allowed us to create a new low cost position while still being able to compete with the larger driving school companies on quality.

DT believes that the critical success factors for this industry are all met by our new and innovative training approach:

(1) Excellent reputation which will stimulate referrals
(2) Improved driver success rates which provides sustainable competitive advantage
(3) Minimises time commitment required from the learner
(4) Reduces cost of training for trainee
(5) Lowest possible cost base for instructor

(iii) **Benefits to you as a franchisee**

    (1)   An innovative training product that is patent protected and a unique selling point compared to other instructors in your area

    (2)   The benefits of running your own business but with the initial training, advice and ongoing support to establish yourself as a driving instructor

    (3)   Risks of set up are shared with DT, as are some of the initial costs

    (4)   Lower running costs for your business – less vehicle wear and tear, lower repairs, reduced fuel costs

    (5)   A better return on your time since using the simulator four drivers can be trained at any one time 'off road'

    (6)   Increased market potential as you can extend your services to existing and commercial drivers and extend the revenue from learners by offering them advanced driving courses via the simulator

    (7)   You will benefit from national advertising and awareness of the DT brand

    (8)   Reduces the seasonality of your business as the simulator can be used to maintain driver training and hence income in the winter months and for non daylight hours

General comments:

This question involves a relatively new UK business providing training for learner car drivers, via a virtual reality driving simulator. The business is keen to expand but the owner is unsure whether to achieve this by offering franchise arrangements to would-be driving instructors or an equity stake to a European driving school wishing to expand into the UK.

Marks on this question were polarised. There were some very good attempts but it was also noticeable that candidates who had mismanaged their time allocation failed to score well on this question.

Requirement (a) requested candidates to prepare a SWOT analysis of the current strategic position of DT. This was reasonably well done although many candidates failed to indicate the major issues, despite a specific requirement to do so. Some weaker candidates mixed up the internal nature of strengths and weaknesses with the external nature of opportunities and threats, and candidates who used a grid presentation with undeveloped bullet points scored limited marks.

Requirement (b) asked candidates to evaluate the key factors to be considered with respect to the two proposals for expansion. Candidates did well here, with almost all clearly distinguishing the governance/control, risks and resource requirement issues of each of the two proposals. Better candidates linked their comments back to the key issues identified in (a) and skills marks were awarded to those who recognised that there were two parties involved in the expansion. Thus for example, while DT might need to provide resources for franchisees, it would also benefit from the sharing of risk and reduced exposure should the franchised business fail.

Requirement (c) asked candidates to produce three sections of a business plan to attract potential franchisees, covering DT's business model, the basis of DT's competitive advantage and the benefits for a franchisee.

Weaker candidates failed to appreciate that the business plan asked for in part (c) was specifically aimed at attracting potential franchisees, and so should be couched in appropriate terms, not in overly academic ones; also that a discussion of the 'cons' of DT's strategy would be inappropriate. Some struggled to distinguish adequately between DT's business model and its competitive advantage, repeating the same points under both headings and a significant minority limited their mark by concentrating on the benefits for DT rather than the franchisee.

17 Taylor-Thorne plc (TT)

Marking guide

			Knowledge	Skill	Marks
(a)	(i)	Value chain	2	8	
	(ii)	Description & how creates value	3	3	
					13
(b)	(i)	Strategies – benefits and problems	4	8	
	(ii)	Recommendation	1	3	
					14
			10	22	27

General comments:

Taylor-Thorne (TT) operates in the luxury handbag market, selling under the Timy brand. It makes high margins on its bags, but sales volumes are restricted by the high price, as only a few people can afford them.

In order to leverage the brand over a wider market, the company is considering three strategic options: (i) license the brand to an upmarket fashion house; (ii) engage in a strategy of brand diffusion by launching a lower priced handbag with a variant brand name (Miss Timy) through different distribution channels; (iii) vertical integration through the acquisition of a fashion retailer.

Candidates are required to prepare a value chain for TT; explain the benefits and problems of each of the strategies; and recommend one strategy.

Overall candidates performed well on this question.

(a)

FI	Company HQ – Hands on management, local control culture				
TD	Personalised ordering systems Low tech inventory control and creditor management	Low tech, skilled production	Internet based delivery systems		Basic receivables systems
HRD	Skills training	Skilled production	Internally staffed delivery systems		
P	Preferred supplier buying, managing supplier relationship			Advertising agency Product placements and celebrity promotions	
Primary activity	Supplier owned delivery system sourcing high quality leather	Non capital intensive factory Hand made product Skilled labour	Direct delivery to customers in own vans with own staff	High advertising to support brand Restricted to quality retailers	10 year guarantee Lifetime 'repair and care'
	IL	O	OL	M/S	S

A value chain identifies the relationships between the company's resources, activities and processes that link the business together and create a profit margin.

The value chain can be used to examine linkages between activities and processes where value can be created using the resources of a business to generate strategic options. Non added value activities can be identified and reduced or eliminated.

The primary activities are those that create value and are directly concerned with providing the product/service. The support activities do not create value of themselves, but enable the primary activities to take place with maximum efficiency.

TT is pursuing a differentiator strategy within Porter's generic activities and should thus focus upon high quality resources and processes to produce a high quality product which is valued by customers who will pay a price premium. This is reflected in the high labour and materials costs in the supply side and operating activities of the value chain and the personalised delivery chain to customers, which provides a quality and reliable service.

There is also high quality after sales service to customers in the latter stages of the value chain to enhance consumers' perception of quality.

Examiner's comments:

Requirement (a) asked candidates to prepare a value chain and to explain how it creates value for TT.

The value chain diagram was well done in most cases, with many candidates including a good number of relevant notes in the different parts of the diagram. An alternative, and equally acceptable, approach was to label the cells in the diagram (eg A, B, C etc) then provide corresponding notes in narrative form. In a few cases, presentation was poor.

In (a) (ii) most candidates found it difficult to explain how TT's activities were linked together to add the high value that it displayed as a differentiator in the market. Most talked about differentiation in some way, but not that many addressed the specific value drivers, or the key linkages within the chain and externally to TT.

(b) **Strategy 1 – Licensing**

A licence grants a third party (Lume plc) the right to exploit an asset (in this case the brand name, Timy) belonging to the licensor, TT.

The main advantages to TT are:

(i) It creates a revenue stream without any up-front investment

(ii) Financial risk is low

(iii) Lume does not have its own well-known brand name, so it may be prepared to pay a premium to use the Timy brand

(iv) Revenue will be based on the number of units sold and Lume has existing production facilities

Problems:

(i) Controls are needed so the Timy brand is not damaged:

- Control needed in the licensing contract over volumes, so do not flood the market

- Control needed over quality so the reputation damage is limited. This may be more difficult to control contractually and may need visits to Lume sites

- Control over advertising image presented

(ii) There may be confusion of Timy bags and Timy clothing in consumers' minds if the clothing is pitched outside the existing price/quality range

(iii) Formula for royalty payments needs to be agreed and included in the contract so minimum amounts can be guaranteed

(iv) A break date or exit route from the contract needs to be established in case the relationship fails within the contract period

(v) Controls measuring sales volumes are needed so Lume does not exploit the contract and underpay on the licence royalties

Strategy 2 – brand diffusion

Brand diffusion attempts to exploit a core brand by using a variant. Normally this involves taking a brand downmarket, so lower prices and higher volume sales can be attained, while maintaining some differentiation from the main upmarket brand.

In this case the MT bags would sell at around 13% of the average price of the Timy bags.

The advantages are:

(i) High volume sales can be attained
(ii) Keeps control of the marketing and production internally (unlike strategy 1)
(iii) There are some (limited) common costs in head office costs

The disadvantages are:

(i) There are few common resources so little core competence or economies of scale

(ii) Outlets are different so there are few distribution economies or economies of scope

(iii) There may be brand confusion resulting in damage to the main Timy brand

(iv) A significant initial investment is required so if the venture fails there are high exit costs

(v) The disparity in the product/price relationship between MT bags and Timy bags is huge, giving significant scope for brand confusion and damage to the main Timy pricing

(vi) The scale of the MT sales needs to be predictable. If MT sales, and the profit from those sales, is much greater than from Timy then there may be greater tolerance of damage to the Timy brand. If MT sales are small by comparison to Timy the brand damage is more of an issue

Strategy 3 – Acquisition of Skin-Deep Ltd

This is an example of downstream vertical integration where a manufacturer acquires a retailer.

Advantages include:

(i) Diversifying into retailing so not dependent on manufacturing
(ii) An outlet for the sales of Timy bags where the retailer does not take 25%

Disadvantages

(i) No core competence in retailing

(ii) No core competence in jewellery and clothing

(iii) Price paid for Skin-Deep is a major investment with a risk of exit strategy and exit costs

(iv) Limited distribution benefits. TT already sells to these outlets so no advantage of obtaining additional outlets (which appears not to be a problem anyway as outlets are vetted)

(v) Limited overlap benefits as only a small proportion of sales relate to Timy bags so capturing the 25% retailers' margin has limited benefits

Recommendation

Strategy 3 appears to be the weakest as it offers few benefits, but is high risk in terms of capital investment and the lack of core competences in the operations.

Strategy 1 is dependent on the contractual terms, but tends to sacrifice control to a third party where there is a danger of brand damage on the main product long into the future even from a short term licensing agreement.

Strategy 2 therefore appears to be the preferred option as control of operations and marketing is maintained internally. Nevertheless, it is not without risk as there is significant outlay and there may be significant brand damage to Timy given the disparity in prices.

Changes to Strategy 2 to consider are:

(i)   Sell MT bags at a price and quality closer to Timy (say £1,000)

(ii) Outsource production at first, or assess feasibility of hand making internally, to avoid immediate initial investment before establishing whether there is a significant market

Examiner's comments:

Requirement (b) asked candidates to explain the benefits and problems of the three proposed strategies and to recommend, with reasons, which strategy should be adopted.

Most candidates tackled the requirement competently ensuring, as a minimum, that they considered each of the three strategies in turn, and the key benefits and problems that each presented to TT.

The advice section was answered reasonably, with nearly all candidates actually making a recommendation, but only the better ones coming up with clear supporting arguments that related well to their previous discussions. Even some very good candidates however were let down by failing to explain any cogent amendments to the selected strategy, which was part of the requirement.

(Note: There were no marks awarded for selection of any particular strategy. The marks for skills related to how the candidate's chosen recommendation was justified.)

18   CWI International Ltd

Marking guide

		Knowledge	Skill	Marks
Report format		1	–	
(a)	Data analysis/explanation/financial and non-financial	2	9	
	Other information	2	4	
				14
(b)	Barriers and overcoming them	3	4	6
		8	17	20

General comments:

This was the data analysis question. CWI International Ltd (CWI) operates a chain of English language schools in a range of African, European and Asian countries. Each CWI school offers course for two types of qualification leading to an external exam: International Baccalaureate Diploma (IBD) and Test of English as a Foreign Language (TOEFL). These are aimed at 16-18 year old students and entrance is selective. CWI are in the process of applying for accreditation by the English Language Board (ELB) and as a result need to introduce a new performance measurement system (covering tutors, results, class sizes, materials and management), since the current approach is simply to monitor pass rates against world-wide averages. The chief executive believes this will also help identify underperforming schools and tutors and might be used to differentiate CWI when talking to prospective students. Candidates were provided with some financial and operating data for the company as a whole, together with recent statistics on pass rates for both qualifications.

Overall, candidates performed fairly well. Some candidates started off badly on this question by failing to produce it in the required report format.

To: Chief Executive of CWI Ltd
From: AN Consultant
Date: XX March 2009
Subject: CWI – Performance measurement system

This report sets out the issues to consider in implementing the proposed performance measurement system in order to gain ELB accreditation.

(a) (i) **Performance analysis**

> **Examiner note:**
>
> Here are potentially a lot of different figures that could be calculated by candidates in answering this question, given the richness of the data provided. The skill here is analysing and discussing the key data and not crunching all available numbers. It is suggested that candidates include the key figures in an Appendix to the report.
>
> Here, in addition to the suggested appendix, which contains the analysis discussed in the report, a separate schedule of possible calculations has also been included at the end of the answer, for marking purposes.
>
> Where different approaches to calculations are possible, and acceptable, candidates are advised to show their workings or explain their method eg candidates adopted a number of different approaches in calculating gross profit and some chose to include grant income in calculating gross profit margin.

Key indicators of the financial and non-financial performance of CWI during 2007 and 2008 are set out in Appendix 1 to this report.

Commentary on performance

There has been a significant growth in fee income over the period (31%), which as course fees have remained constant, must relate to the increased volume of students (56% for IBD courses and 14% for TOEFL).

However as the revenue per school has only increased by 5% year on year, a substantial amount of the increase is presumably a result of the increase in the number of schools from 8 to 10. More information would be needed as to when these came on stream in 2008 and how many courses each was offering.

The fact that revenue has increased because of expansion in the number of schools rather than improved efficiency is underlined by the fact that while sales have increased by 31%, expenditure has increased by 36%.

Allowing for the increase in the number of schools, it is clear that whilst IBD revenue has gone forward, TOEFL revenue has gone backwards. This is reflected in the sales mix, with IBD income increasing from 41% sales in 2007 to 48% in 2008.

IBD courses

The average figures per school suggest that the growth in IBD revenue appears to have come from CWI schools offering additional courses (an average of 3 per school in 2008 compared to 2007). However it is unlikely that all schools have increased the volume of IBD courses on offer.

Instead it is possible that CWI has acquired two additional schools during the year whose focus is IBD courses, although if there has been no organic growth within the existing 8 schools, then the additional schools would need to be very sizeable to account for the additional 14 IBD courses. The reality is likely to be somewhere in between.

Certainly the increase in revenue appears to have come at a price, as the average class size has dropped from 20 to just fewer than 17, leaving CWI with spare capacity, although this may be looked on favourably by the ELB.

Whilst the reduced class size might be expected to lead to improved pass rates, this has not happened. In fact the IBD pass rate has dropped and is now only 7% above the worldwide average (compared to 10% in 2007). This could mean that CWI have had to accept less able students in order to fill places or that the new schools are not as successful as the existing ones. However as the IBD is a 2 year course it is likely to be the end of 2009 before the true impact on results can be seen.

Overall the impact of the change in sales mix and the spare capacity created in the IBD classrooms is to reduce the gross profit margin from 60% to 56%. A breakdown of staff costs is required in order to assess the margins made on each type of course, as well as the breakdown of the financial results by school to assess the profitability of each school.

TOEFL courses

Although the average figures suggest that the existing schools have reduced the number of TOEFL courses they are offering, as mentioned above, more information is required about the number and breakdown of the courses offered by the two new schools to properly assess the position.

If the majority of courses offered by the new schools are IBD courses then the existing schools have managed to grow their TOEFL revenue organically.

These courses are likely to have been more profitable in 2008 due to the increased class size (12.8 students compared to 12).

TOEFL pass rates have remained largely consistent across the two years and are considerably above the worldwide average. It is possible that IBD get the best quality students and the pass rates are therefore higher because of the ability of the students rather than the quality of the courses. Also the courses could be more intensive and costly than the opposition so the pass rates are higher as a result. (Other students could be self taught which lowers the general pass rate.)

Expenditure

Key resources within the school are staff costs and premises which accounted for 64% of fee income in 2008 compared to 62% in 2007. This increase is likely to be due to the additional staff and rooms associated with the increase in the number of courses.

Other expenses have remained largely consistent as a percentage of fee income, with the exception of marketing which has increased from 7 to 10% of revenue. This is likely to have been incurred to market the new schools and to generate demand for the additional IBD courses.

Net profit

Since the schools are largely a fixed cost business they will have high operating gearing and need to operate courses at full capacity to ensure a good overhead recovery rate. Thus despite the significant increase in revenue, the reduction in the gross profit margin and the increase in marketing expenses has led to a net profit margin of 7% compared to 12 % last year.

Without the grant income, CWI would have made a loss in 2008 and more information is required as to the nature of the grants and the extent to which this is regular, recurring income.

(ii) **Additional information and performance measures**

Examiner note:

This answer is longer than a candidate would have been expected to produce but a variety of different points have been included below for marking purposes.

Detail on individual schools

The analysis above is based on data for an average school. In reality the 10 schools may be different sizes and offer a different mix of courses. Depending on the nature of the staff and/or the student catchment, some may have more success at one qualification than another.

In order to assess each individual school, a breakdown of revenue, costs, staff and pass rates by school is required.

Comparative information

In order to interpret performance, information is needed regarding budgets and targets, competitors and industry norms, so that CWI can benchmark performance not just between its schools but against others in the industry. This would help CWI assess which schools are performing well and which are not, both currently and with respect to changes over time.

The stated ELB criteria covers teachers, results, class sizes, materials, management, student welfare and premises. CWI need to obtain information regarding the targets which will be set by the ELB in each of the performance areas and specifically any restrictions that they are likely to place on class sizes which will affect CWI's flexibility and efficiency.

It is also important to distinguish the performance of the school from the performance of the manager. A badly performing school could be improved by changing the manager or it could be the inevitable consequence of its local market, additional competition or other non-controllable factors.

Internal benchmarks – comparisons of pass rates, resource utilisation, revenue growth and profit compared to the best performing school in CWI. The problem with this measure is that the performance of any school might be a function of its location, as well as its management, nevertheless, perhaps some lessons could be learned.

External/Competitive benchmarks – compares to the industry leader in the sector and the locality. Information might be hard to come by for competitive language schools, however, indicators are: fees charged, courses offered, pass rates.

In looking at performance, revenues are generated throughout the world. The ability to charge high fees in say Africa is different to a prosperous nation (eg Germany) and this will impact performance. Expenditure if incurred locally is also likely to be lower.

Exchange rate volatility is a further issue in measuring performance consistently.

Multiple performance measures

As the ELB will use a range of assessment measures, any system implemented by CWI should use as wide a range of measures as possible, both financial and non-financial.

One tool by which this can be achieved is the balanced scorecard which looks at the following perspectives:

- Financial
- Customer
- Innovation and learning
- Internal business
- Thus in addition to the analysis above, other useful information would include:

  - Financial – staff costs split by IBD/TOEFL to assess profitability by course

  - Customer – customer satisfaction surveys/student feedback forms regarding standards of tuition, facilities, pastoral support etc

  - Innovation and learning:

    - External recognition of student/tutor achievements
    - Qualifications held by staff
    - No of staff undertaking extra training/qualifications
    - No of candidates accepted for Further education

- Internal business:
    - Staff turnover
    - No of staff whose teaching is assessed as satisfactory and above
    - No of student drop outs
    - No of applicants vs. no of places available
    - Value added by school ie actual pass rates vs. predicted pass rates
    - Extracurricular activities offered
    - Details of the course materials used by CWI

Future performance

Other useful information would be budgets for the forthcoming periods and the assumptions on which the budgets are based.

Projections of eg student numbers, staff and premises costs, fee income, capital expenditure would be useful.

It would also be useful to know the basis on which grant income is awarded and the extent to which this is recurring income.

Market research could indicate whether the data that is available for past periods can be projected into the future with any reasonable degree of reliability.

Appendix 1: Analysis of financial and non-financial performance 2007/08

	2008	2007
Financial analysis		
Sales mix:		
IBD	48%	41%
TOEFL	52%	59%
Profitability:		
Gross profit margin (tuition fees – tutor costs)/tuition fees	56%	60%
Net profit margin (PBIT/total income)	7%	12%
Resources: expenditure as a % of total tuition fees		
Staff costs and premises	64%	62%
Marketing	10%	7%
Performance indicators		
Tuition revenue per school	£744k	£708k
IBD		
No of courses per school	3	2
Ave class size	16.7 students	20 students
Percentage points above worldwide average pass rate	7%	10%
TOEFL		
No of courses per school	24	28
Ave class size	12.8 students	12 students
Percentage points above worldwide average pass rate	15%	15%

	% Increase between 2008/07
IBD tuition fees	56.25
TOEFL tuition fees	14.29
Total fee income	31.36
Total expenses	36.04
Revenue per school	5.08

Requirement (a) was the data analysis section of the paper which has been indicated as a regular feature of Business Strategy papers. It asked candidates to evaluate the financial and non-financial performance of CWI, based on the data and other information provided. They were also asked to identify and justify any additional information required to better assess the performance of the individual schools.

Most candidates coped reasonably with the analysis of performance and were engaged with the financial and non-financial data and understood the links. Most were also happy to try to explain why changes in performance had come about, not just describe what had come about, and appeared to have spent about the right amount of time calculating ratios. Some weaker candidates only provided qualitative analysis or only made a nominal quantitative attempt by just repeating data from the question. Where candidate did address the data, some set out their quantitative analysis at the beginning of their answer, then provided the discussion. Others interspersed calculations and comments throughout their answer. Either approach was acceptable, although better candidates normally tended to use the first of these methods.

It was somewhat disappointing that the majority of candidates failed to appreciate that the ELB was looking at particular indicators such as class sizes, and therefore the company may have been seeking to reduce class sizes in order to gain accreditation. However, in the course of their analyses a pleasing number of candidates did pick up on the importance of performance by school and by course, which informed their suggestions for other information that would be useful. Whilst clearly prepared for the requirement to specify additional information, weaker candidates lost marks by failing to justify their answers or by merely listing further information in the context of performance measurement in general rather than in respect of individual schools.

(b) **Barriers to change and approaches to overcome**

Barriers to change

All changes tend to be resisted by employees. The nature of the changes such as CWI are proposing may be resisted strongly by staff or schools that feel they are underperforming – particularly if employees find out about the CEO's plans to use the new system to help identify and address this.

(1) **Cultural barriers**

Structural inertia: the existing system of performance measurement that is focused purely on exam results may act as a barrier to change to a new wider measurement process.

Power structures within CWI may be threatened if it becomes clear that a particular school or particular members of staff are more important or more successful than others. This will in particular affect management and thus management may be reluctant to implement changes which will be against their own interests.

Group inertia may block change where the changes are inconsistent with the norms of team working and departments, or where they threaten their interests. Thus schools may resist comparison with each other as they are not used to working within a competitive environment. CWI may also face resistance from unions which are common in the teaching profession.

(2) **Personnel barriers**

There are also barriers which affect individuals and result in them seeing the change as a threat eg to earnings and job security. Teaching staff may be worried by what they see as implied criticism of past performance. They may resist the new appraisal system as a result of their fear of the unknown or use selective information to justify their position. As they are not used to being appraised in this way, the new system is likely to make them feel uncomfortable.

(3) **Psychological contract**

Pressures will arise if the changes affect the current set of expectations between the employee and the employer. In this case the staff may perceive a change in the way in which they are being managed.

Approaches to overcome the barriers

Staff are likely to get used to the new performance measurement system if given sufficient time to do so.

Information about the proposals should be freely circulated and staff should be given an opportunity to talk about their concerns.

The change must be sold. Staff need to be convinced that accreditation by the ELB is a good thing and that the measurement system is a necessary step to achieve this. Rather than focussing on the more threatening angle of identifying the underperformers, the positive aspects of the change need to be encouraged eg the ability to differentiate the school using these measures, the ability to rewards schools and staff for good performance, CWI should provide learning/training opportunities for staff. They will need help to adapt and reassurance about the impact of the system on pay and job security.

Resentment and fear is likely to be lessened if staff feel that they have been involved throughout the change process.

The project manager will need to act as a change agent in order to drive the new system through.

The Lewin/Schein three stage (Iceberg) model could be used to summarise the necessary approach:

1. Unfreeze existing staff behaviour by selling the reasons for change (eg the need for accreditation to attract more students)

2. Move the attitude by communicating the new norms and encouraging staff to welcome and adopt the new measurement culture (through learning and participation)

3. Refreeze the new behaviour eg by offering incentives/reward system to motivate staff to pursue the accreditation targets

Examiner's comments:

Requirement (b) asked candidates to explain the barriers that may be encountered in implementing the new performance measurement system and to indicate how these might be overcome. As usual, the majority of candidates showed good knowledge in this area, but often failed to earn the skills marks available for applying this to the scenario. Weaker candidates either made general points without reference to any theory or discussed barriers to change and possible change management approaches including Lewin's 'unfreeze/move/refreeze' model, in generic terms. Better candidates made reference to the nature of the staff and the context of accreditation. It was evident that quite a number of candidates simply equate 'change' with 'redundancies', an assumption that was not really supported by a scenario based on amending a performance measurement system.

19 Kemmex Ice Cream plc (KIC)

Marking guide

			Knowledge	Skill	Marks
(a)		Barriers to entry	3	6	8
(b)		Market share evaluation and definition	2	5	6
(c)	(i)	Data analysis and explanation	3	9	
	(ii)	Price reduction – strategy 1	2	5	
					17
(d)	(i)	Risks	3	4	
	(ii)	Marketing strategy	3	4	
					12
			16	33	43

General comments:

The scenario in this question looks at a listed company which manufactures ice cream in the 'economy' sector of the market. The company has attempted to expand recently by lowering its selling price in order to increase sales volumes. While sales revenues have increased, profits have fallen and there is a dispute between the finance director and the marketing director as to whether it is appropriate to continue with this strategy. An alternative strategy has been put forward by the marketing director which is to enter the premium branded sector of the market using a licensing agreement to utilise a brand name of a large confectionary manufacturer.

(a) **Economies of scale and capital investment**

The lowest barriers to entry are in the 'economy' sector of the ice cream market which is characterised by smaller manufacturers. The smaller scale of production and lower quality levels mean that the production process is less capital intensive and thus the direct entry costs of capital investment are lowest in this sector. As a result, economies of scale would be less significant as a barrier to entry than in other sectors of the ice cream market.

Moreover, as this ice cream is not branded, then there is not the requirement for marketing expenditure which is necessary in other sectors to compete with larger producers.

In the premium branded sectors, economies of scale are more significant as large scale production is needed to cover significant capital investment and brand advertising. Smaller new entrants may therefore find it hard to compete. Existing small ice cream companies in the 'economy' sector could also find it difficult to enter the premium sector from their existing market position (see notes below concerning KIC's *Strategy 2*).

Product differentiation and switching costs

There is little branding in the economy sector of the market, thus there is little brand loyalty by consumers. This means that switching is possible by consumers so it is less difficult for a new entrant to enter the 'economy' market.

In the premium sectors there is more branding and thus loyalty may be significant, making switching more restricted and thus new products would take longer, and at greater cost, to become established.

It would appear there are near zero switching costs for a consumer to transfer from one brand to another so this is unlikely to be a barrier to entry.

Access to distribution channels

The requirement to deliver ice cream to retailers in chilled conditions adds greater costs. Larger incumbent operators are likely to have the advantage of economies of scope with a larger distribution chain.

Small new entrants can avoid the initial capital cost of delivery vehicles if they outsource deliveries, but this may increase operating costs and reduce flexibility of supply.

Distribution barriers can also include access to retailers.

Tutorial note:

A practice of restricting access to manufacturer-owned freezers located at retailers would have been a major barrier to entry. It is an advantage that this practice is now illegal but there remains the issue of attracting retailers, as customers, as well as appealing to consumers.

Cost advantages to incumbents irrespective of scale

These may include:

(i)   Access to suppliers of ingredients on favourable or exclusive terms
(ii)   Knowledge and expertise on health and safety issues
(iii)   Knowledge and expertise on production processes
(iv)   Brand rights

These are all more likely to occur in the premium ranges where the skills and ingredients are less generic.

Response of incumbents

Large incumbent companies may defend their market positioning by aggressive marketing to counter new entrants. This might include targeted advertising in the product or geographical sector of the new entrant. Similarly, targeted price cuts or discounts may prevent new entrants gaining a foothold.

These are more likely to occur in the premium ranges where larger incumbents are more likely to defend specific brands where there is a similar new entrant launching a product in similar price-quality space, rather than for more generic ice creams.

Examiner's comments:

Candidates' answers were generally of a good standard. The two most common approaches were either (i) to structure answers according to the barriers existing in each market segment or (ii) to consider each type of barrier to entry sequentially and explain how it affected the different market segments. Either approach was acceptable.

Better answers considered the relative strengths of the barriers to entry in the individual segments. Weaker candidates described the relevant barriers but did not explicitly state why they would deter entry.

(b) **Market share**

If the UK ice cream market is £1,000 million and the quarter ending 31 May is typical for KIC then a full year's sales would amount to £41.4m (£10,350,000 x 4). This means the market share is 4.14% (£41.4m/£1,000m). Alternatively this would be 4% based on the quarter to 28 February 2009 in applying the previous strategy.

This is fairly small, but the market can be redefined in terms of the take-home market as KIC only operates in this market. The size of this market is 72% of £1,000m which is £720m. This gives KIC a market share of the 'take-home' market of 5.75% (£41.4m/)/£720m), which is far from insignificant.

The market share could, however, be further refined to the take-home regular/economy sector. More information would be needed for this purpose.

The market share of KIC by comparison to smaller competitors is illustrated by the average size in the UK market. Total sales are £1,000 million and there are 200 manufacturers of varying sizes so the mean annual sales achieved per company in the industry in the UK is only £5m. By comparison KIC has sales of over £40m. Given that the industry is characterised by two large companies then the median size is likely to be much lower than the mean. Similarly, the average size of the manufacturers is lower in the economy sector. KIC is therefore quite large for this sector.

KIC is clearly at the low cost end of the market and with its narrow portfolio of products (currently) it is entirely dependent on this sector. Its size within this sector makes it a reasonable sized player in the market, particularly in its focussed geographical region.

The product is commodity type and largely undifferentiated so competition is in the form of distribution, service and price through cost leadership.

The above discussion excludes the European market, given the problems of transportation, although it could be argued that market share needs to consider the import/export market.

Examiner's comments:

This requirement was poorly attempted in general. Many candidates did not perform a calculation of market share but just discussed the different ways of segmenting the market in general terms. There was a lot of repetition of the facts in the question, often with little analysis. The stronger answers were those which attempted to compute market share under different market definitions and drilled down further by redefining size. Only the best answers assessed market share in relation to the likely share of most other competitors.

(c) (i) **Evaluate and explain performance**

	3 months to		
	28 February 2009 £'000	31 May 2009 £'000	% Change
Sales	10,000	10,350	+3.5%
Production costs			
Variable	5,000	5,750	+15%
Fixed	2,500	2,500	–
Distribution costs			
Variable	500	750	+50%
Fixed	250	250	–
Administration and other fixed operating costs	1,250	1,250	–
Operating profit/(loss)	500	(150)	
Number of customers	2,500 outlets	3,000 outlets	+20%

Sales prices have been reduced by 10% thus, comparing the two quarters on a constant price basis, growth in sales volumes can be determined:

$$\frac{10,350}{10,000 \times 0.9} = 15\%$$

Alternatively:

$$\frac{10,350/0.9}{10,000} = 15\%$$

This increase in sales volumes is consistent with the objective of increasing market share.

Variable production costs have therefore changed in direct proportion to sales volumes.

Despite the sales volumes increasing by 15% and sales prices decreasing by only 10% this has had an adverse effect on profits. The reasons for the fall in profits are best analysed in the first instance prior to distribution costs.

The changes can then be analysed according to the impact on the existing customer base and the impact of the new customers.

In terms of the existing customers, the loss of contribution is just the loss of 10% of sales revenue (as 'sales volumes to existing customers have been consistent with those in the quarter to 28 February 2009').

As a consequence, controlling for the price change and comparing sales to existing customers, the profit before distribution costs would be:

	3 months to	
	28 February 2009	31 May 2009
	£'000	£'000
Sales	10,000	9,000
Production costs		
Variable	5,000	5,000
Fixed	2,500	2,500
	2,500	1,500

There is therefore a loss of contribution of £1m of sales to existing customers as a consequence of the price reduction.

Sales to new customers are therefore the remaining sales. Thus the profit before distribution costs for new customers would be:

	3 months to 31 May 2009
	£'000
Sales	1,350
Production costs	
Variable	750
Incremental fixed costs	–
	600

Overall therefore the contribution prior to distribution costs has fallen by £400,000 from £2.5m to £2.1m (£600,000 + £1.5m). The extra contribution of £600,000 from sales to new customers, is insufficient to compensate for the lost revenue from existing customers due to reducing selling prices to them (£1m).

The increase in distribution costs of £250,000 reduces the contribution from new customers further to £350,000 (£600,000 – £250,000).

This means an overall reduction in profit of £650,000 (£400,000 + £250,000) which explains the reduction in operating profit from £500,000 to an operating loss of £150,000.

The fact that distribution costs have risen by 50% while sales volumes have risen by only 15% is a matter for concern. This may be due to the following:

- The new sales are to 'retailers well beyond the 100 mile limit that we used to have and this is where most of our new customers have arisen.' The distribution costs are therefore greater due to larger distances.

- The new customers cover a wider area so are likely to be more spread out giving diseconomies of scope.

- The new customers are smaller on average than existing customers. At the new prices average quarterly sales to existing customers are £3,600 (£9m/2,500). Average sales to new customers are £2,700 (£1.35m/500). If order costs are fixed per delivery, then smaller deliveries are (for the moment at least) being made to new customers so there is less profit per sale to cover delivery costs.

Overall, therefore, short term financial performance has been poor as a consequence of the price reduction. It may be, however, that the marketing director is correct is saying it is too early to judge, as there may be other effects not considered:

- Lagged effects – customers and consumers may take a while to react to the new prices (eg terminating existing contracts with other ice cream suppliers may take a while before they can buy more from KIC).

- Competitor reaction – if competitors do not copy the price reduction then sales volumes may increase substantially in future. If, however, competitors follow the price reduction, then the market sector may be locked into lower prices with lower profits in the industry sector.

(ii) **Evaluate the price reduction strategy**

A reduction in price should generate more sales, but the extent to which it does so will depend on the elasticity of demand. Current evidence suggests that demand is elastic as sales volumes have increased by 15% in response to a 10% price reduction. However, while this indicates an improvement in revenue, it has already been demonstrated that profits may fall due to the increases in variable production costs and distribution costs.

The source of the increase in sales volumes is also important. Potentially it could increase the sales volumes to existing customers, but it could also generate new customers. To date, the new strategy only appears to have achieved the latter of these two goals. To the extent that early data is reliable, this would suggest that the policy of reducing all prices by 10% was inappropriate as the price reduction to existing customers yielded no benefits and was just a deadweight loss of £1m.

A policy of price discrimination on a geographical basis may therefore have been more appropriate. Assuming no leakage between the two markets, this would have generated an incremental contribution from new customers of £600,000 while maintaining the existing operating profit of £500,000. This would have given an overall operating profit for the quarter of £1.1m.

If this price discrimination is not possible, through market leakage or alienation of existing customers, then the new policy may be justified despite short term losses, as part of a strategy of price penetration. This is where price in a new market starts low in order to penetrate the customer base and gain market share (ie in new geographical markets for KIC). Having gained some customer loyalty, prices can then be gradually increased again. If market research deems this to be feasible, then the low initial price may be an appropriate sacrifice, notwithstanding the short-term reduction in profit.

If price discrimination and/or price penetration are not possible then the price reduction policy needs to be judged on its longer term financial merits of increasing sales volume at the new lower prices on a more permanent basis.

Taking Jane's assumption of an increase of 25% this would yield the following quarterly results in steady state (assuming all new growth is out of the 100 mile radius and thus distribution costs for new customers are similar to that occurred in the last quarter).

	Workings	*3 months to* *31 May 2009* £'000
Sales	10,350 × 1.25	12,938
Production costs		
Variable	5,750 × 1.25	7,188
Fixed		2,500
Distribution costs		
Variable	500 + 250 + (250 × [43.75 − 15]/15)*	1,229
Fixed		250
Administration and other fixed operating costs		1,250
Operating profit/(loss)		521

* Given a 10% price reduction, sales volumes have risen by 15% (10,350/9,000). However, at the margin, variable distribution costs have risen by 50% from £500,000 to £750,000. This is because the new customers are located further away from the factory than existing customers. If sales volumes increase by a further 25% then these are also likely to be to more distant customers. Assuming that the additional variable costs for the 25% increase will be similar to the 15% increase then the overall increase is 1.15 x 1.25 = 43.75%.

On this basis profit would increase from £500,000 to £521,000, but only if Jane's assumption of 25% growth is correct.

Examiner's comments:

This requirement was the data analysis section of the paper which has been indicated as a regular feature of Business Strategy papers. Part (i) asked candidates to assess and explain the performance of KIC in the most recent quarter using the available data. Part (ii) asked candidates to evaluate the price reduction strategy (Strategy 1). In general, answers to this requirement were weak.

For part (i), typically the data analysis was poor – often only amounting to quantifying the movement year on year, with a commentary of what had happened, rather than an explanation of the causal factors giving rise to the changes in the figures (ie why it had happened). Many candidates did work out sales or contribution per customer, but it was disappointing how few worked out that the volume increase was 15% which was a fundamental part of the answer. As a result, many candidates incorrectly talked about variable production costs being out of control and rising disproportionately to sales. Many recognised the significant rise in distribution costs and provided reasonably good explanations for this in terms of the location of new customers. Better candidates linked evaluation to the stated objective to increase market share. Those who prepared a table of calculations at the beginning of their answers generally produced a more coherent analysis than those who made occasional, and sometimes random, calculations within their narrative. Some candidates seemed determined to produce a long list of additional info (possibly having clearly learnt this by rote!)

In part (ii) there was not much numerical analysis, although a few candidates did talk about elasticity. Some candidates briefly mentioned price discrimination and market penetration. A significant minority evaluated strategy 1 through the use of SFA (Suitability, Feasibility, Acceptability) analysis, but the discussion tended to be descriptive as opposed to analytical. Answers were awarded good marks where price elasticity of demand and break even analysis were explained.

(d) This is a new product being sold in a new market, so it would be regarded as diversification in the Ansoff matrix. As it is in a related area of ice cream it would be regarded as related diversification.

(i) **Risks**

Break-even risks

If the price is set at the equivalent of competitors at around 50p then break-even is:

Contribution per unit is £0.50 – £0.20 – £0.05 = £0.25

Annual fixed costs are £3m + £1m = £4m

Thus sales of 16 million Chocnuts would be needed per year to break even.

This would generate annual sales of £8m (quarterly sales of £2m assuming no seasonality) just to break even.

This is an increase of 20% based on existing sales (at pre reduction prices).

There is clearly a significant risk that the break even level of sales will not be achieved and thus the new product will not make a profit.

Operating gearing

The level of fixed costs is high by comparison to the existing products. Indeed, although sales are only 20% of the existing sales (at the break-even point) the incremental fixed costs are equal to the existing level of fixed costs at £4million. In compensation, the contribution margin ratio is high for the new product at 50%. (25p contribution per 50p sale).

As a consequence, if sales are around break-even level then operating gearing is very high, making changes in profit very sensitive to changes in sales.

Exit costs

There is a high level of initial investment, both in terms of manufacturing capability, but also in terms of an up-front royalty to the holder of the 'Chocnut' brand name rights. If the launch fails there may be high exit costs from the loss of the royalty payment and low realisable values for the machinery.

Royalty relationship

If the brand rights are short term or renewable on different terms then, if the product is a success, the owner of the brand, Yocolate, may increase the royalty to take up any excess profit.

New market

This is a new product being launched in a new market and there are therefore significant risks of product acceptance in the market and production learning for a new product.

Exchange rates

If the 'Chocnut' is to be sold in Europe then exchange rate variation provides an additional risk.

Reversal of price increase

It has been assumed that the reversal of the 10% price decrease will reassert the status quo before the change. However, the changes in price may have altered customer and consumer perceptions and there may be an unfavourable response to the restoration of the original prices applying prior to 1 March 2009.

(ii) **Marketing strategy**

Marketing strategy can be considered using the 4Ps model:

Price

The price of the product needs to be determined according to the estimated market willingness to pay and the prices of competitors for similar products. This clearly needs to be achieved through market research in order to establish the viability of the launch and this should be before any capital commitment is made.

A price penetration strategy may help establish an initial market, but may damage consumer perception about the quality of the product and therefore make it difficult to raise prices at a later date.

Product

Product marketing includes the nature of the actual product, but also the customer perception of the product that needs to be managed.

The product needs to be of high quality to achieve premium pricing. The low quality perception of the existing ice creams will need to be overcome.

The appearance of the product also needs to be appropriate in addressing consumer perceptions.

Branding is a key issue and the use of the Chocnut brand is key as it uses the instant recognition of a well know product (at a price). Using similar packaging, similar outlets and making the appearance of the product the same as the Chocnut chocolate bar will reinforce the branding image.

Brand recognition of the Chocnut brand in the rest of Europe will need to be tested by market research and the rights to use the brand outside the UK will need to be established in any contract.

Place

'Place' includes the whole issue of distribution. The existing distribution area of 100 miles appears inappropriate but this then raises similar issues of cost and economies of scope as those noted above with respect to strategy 1.

The issue of distribution into Europe is more significant, not just in terms of cost, but for communications, currency and knowledge of markets. The extent to which a viable launch is dependent on significant European sales needs to be established and separate market research carried out.

Place refers not just to the geographical area, but also to the distribution channels used. The new product appears suitable both for the 'take home' market in the form of multipacks and for the 'impulse' purchase market.

There may be some overlap of distribution channels with existing products in the 'take home' market but this is only in a limited geographical area. The impulse market is likely to require a strategy to set up an entirely new customer base.

Sharing distribution channels with Yocolate may save costs and help access their customer base. The need for chilled distribution of ice creams may however prevent or restrict this.

Promotion

In order to support the brand, significant advertising is likely to be needed, or at least enough to match competitors. Joint advertising with Yocolate may be possible but this would assume they are willing to do this and there may be additional cost.

Promotion would need to be to both the customer (retailers) and the consumer to obtain both a push and a pull effect.

Larger customers would be a major advantage and may be the target of any promotion strategy. This might include supermarkets but also the use of intermediary wholesalers who may widen distribution through their own networks more efficiently than could be achieved by KIC directly.

20 Evara Electrical Engineers Ltd (EEE)

Marking guide

			Knowledge	Skill	Marks
(a)		Structure	3	3	
		Information systems	2	4	
					10
(b)		Ethics	3	4	6
(c)		Memo	1	–	
	(i)	New structure and recommendation	2	5	
	(ii)	Outsourcing v new staff	2	5	
	(iii)	Advice re contract	1	4	
					16
			14	25	32

General comments:

The scenario in this question involves an electrical contracting company with one large customer and a number of small commercial customers. It has a flexible pricing policy with respect to small customers which gives rise to some ethical issues. Following an acquisition of the largest customer there is the possibility of taking on the work for the entire new group under a proposed new contract, which will very significantly expand the scale of EEE's activities. A key question is whether the company can cope with the new level of activity and the most appropriate organisational structure to do so.

(a) Organisational structure

EEE has an entrepreneurial structure where all the key decisions are centred around one person.

In terms of Mintzberg's organisational forms, Eric is at the strategic apex as a single owner-manager who exercises direct control over the operational core below him. Other functions are reduced to a minimum and are fulfilled by the two administrative employees and external professional assistance.

The organisational structure is very flat as there is only Eric and then the team leaders and general employees. There is no middle management layer and no internal technostructure. Co-ordination is achieved through direct supervision, so the structure is flexible and suitable for a dynamic environment.

The small size of the business and its geographical concentration means that it is feasible for Eric to devote adequate personal time to mange the jobs and staff personally without being unduly distracted from managerial tasks and managing the wider strategy of the business.

Eric's ability to control the operations of the business is enhanced by his technical knowledge of electrics. His control over purchases and pricing also means that significant direct control is exercised over key functions without delegation.

Information systems

Eric needs information for a number of purposes. These include:

Strategic planning: internal information includes knowledge of which are the most profitable elements of the business to develop in future (eg BB or other work) and external information about competitors and markets. Also information about future regulations that may constrain the business or provide new opportunities.

Tactical planning: Resource utilisation, staff planning; overall customer satisfaction; average recovery rates.

Operational issues: management of individual assignments; pricing and costing individual jobs; customer needs and feedback; resolving operational issues and customer needs.

A particular need may be to have information systems that are capable of producing data that can be evidenced in order to support the cost plus pricing nature of the contract with BB. Audit and verification by BB seems likely. Informal systems may be difficult to support the contract information needs for BB.

In terms of managing the business, the day to day involvement of Eric reduces the need for formal detailed information as he is likely to be aware of the labour time and materials being used on each job given his personal involvement. As the business expands, whether through one of the two suggested strategies, or otherwise, the level of detailed personal involvement becomes less and less thus more formal information systems are likely to be needed, irrespective of any contractual obligations for verifiable information to third parties.

Examiner's comments:

The identification of an entrepreneurial structure and the advantages and disadvantages associated with this was generally reasonably well done. Well prepared candidates discussed Eric's control and direct management style. Weaker candidates tended to describe the structure rather than evaluate whether it was suitable.

The information systems part was normally rather briefly answered, with some candidates omitting it all together. Candidates did note that systems were very simple and may cause problems for pricing and job cost identification.

(b) Ethical issues exist at the level of the business and the individual. In the case of Eric however the interests of the business and the individual are closely aligned as he is the sole shareholder and managing director.

Ethics may also relate to the society and to corporate responsibility. In this case of pricing however the primary issue relates to Eric's dealing with one particular stakeholder group – the smaller customers.

EEE does not currently appear to have an ethical code thus the ethics of the company tend to be the personal ethics and morals of Eric – especially in relation to pricing, where Eric has sole responsibility.

In terms of ethical constraints Eric does not belong to a profession so there is no issue of abiding by a professional ethical code. Clearly, his dealings with customers must be legal and thus comply with the law relating to fraud and misrepresentation.

The policy of pricing on a 'willingness to pay' basis is legitimate and does not appear to be in breach of any major ethical principles, even though some customers are paying more than others for the same work. This is a common business practice of price discrimination, and is normally ethical as the customer is not forced to accept the contract and could obtain alternative quotes from other electrical firms.

The key issue is that of variations in price once the contract has commenced and it is then more difficult to go to an alternative contractor.

The ethical issues that arise are:

(i) **Honesty** – there appears to be an attempt to exaggerate faults and charge a substantial premium of 10% for a minor change to the agreed work by falsely claiming it to be major.

(ii) **Transparency** – there is a lack of transparency as the customers do not have the technical knowledge to determine the extent of the variations to ascertain a fair price. EEE appears to be exploiting the lack of transparency to further its own ends.

(iii) **Equity** – there is a lack of fairness in the pricing of variations compared to the main agreed work by EEE exploiting its superior technical knowledge.

Aside from the procedures of pricing variations, there is the ethical dilemma of making gifts to the budget holder. Depending on the value of the gifts, there is the potential for deception and fraud in this case. There is a potential conflict of interest as budget holder may gain personally from the gifts and, as a consequence, authorise payment of funds by his/her employer to EEE. The key ethical issues here are:

(i) The size of the gifts and whether they are sufficient to strongly influence a decision

(ii) Whether the gifts are conditional upon favours being received by EEE or whether they are just given in the hope of influencing the budget holders' behaviour

(iii) Whether there is transparency and the budget holders' line managers are aware of the gifts

Overall, the key ethical issue is whether the price variations are carried out openly and honestly in accordance with normal business practice. In this respect the customers have a responsibility to protect themselves (eg by limiting price variations in the contract or by obtaining third party verification of major variations). It is not an ethical obligation by Eric or EEE to do this on the customers' behalf.

Note. This may have been different if the customer had been an individual consumer who is more vulnerable.

A further ethical issue arises in respect of the SS contract. If it is signed, there is an obligation for EEE to comply with the ethical code of SS for all customers. If the pricing of variations falls outside this code then it may be misleading not only to the smaller customers, but also to SS, in dishonestly claiming compliance with its ethical code when it does not do so. If discovered, this may also have commercial consequences for EEE.

Examiner's comments:

Most answers to this requirement were rather disappointing. Many did not distinguish the three different issues – pricing policy, variations and gifts. Most commented about the tickets as gifts being a bribe but many seemed to think it was unethical, rather than normal business practice, to charge different customers different prices. Better candidates mentioned price discrimination and linked the ethical issues to the new contract demands.

Many candidates failed to state explicitly the ethical issues involved eg honesty or conflict of interest. Instead, they merely described the actions that had occurred and asserted they were unethical, as if it were self evident. Some candidates appeared to believe that the ICAEW code applied to electricians and were all for contacting the ICAEW to report Eric's behaviour!

(c) (i) **Organisational structure**

With the SS contract there would be a number of fundamental changes in the nature of the business which would require reassessment of the organisational structure. These include:

- The scale of the business would increase by 350% from revenue of £1 million to £4.5 million

- The business would be geographically dispersed, not just throughout the UK, but throughout Europe

- The complexity of the operational tasks is likely to increase requiring new skills
- Possible management of outsourcing

Personal management by Eric therefore seems unfeasible with the new contract as he is unlikely to have the time or expertise to manage operations personally, as he has done in the past. Therefore the entrepreneurial structure would probably be inappropriate for the new needs with the SS contract.

Features needed in the new structure are likely to be:

- More non operational managers in the business, perhaps as an additional layer within the organisational structure
- Greater technical expertise
- Flexibility as the SS contract may be temporary
- More formal reporting and control lines
- More support and administration staff

This is likely to lead to a taller organisational structure than EEE has at present with a narrower span of control for Eric.

Options for organisational structure include:

- *Customer or market segment divisionalisation*

  This would have a separate division responsible for each type of customer. This may however only require two divisions: SS group and other smaller customers. Key advantages are that it:

  – Focuses on customer need and customer service
  – May enable profit centre responsibility

  A key disadvantage is that the division responsible for SS is 8/9ths of the entire company and thus the divisional manager would have many of the same control problems as already cited for an entrepreneurial structure. To manage this he or she may need sub divisions (eg for the UK and Europe; or for different aspects of the work).

  Even with divisionalisation there may need to be some functional responsibility eg for finance, administration, human resources, purchasing).

- *Geographical divisionalisation*

  This could be similar to the above but based on geographical areas. Such as each region within the UK and one for continental Europe.

  A key advantage is that it could focus on local resources (eg staff located in an area) a key disadvantage is that it may lack a customer focus and require some centralisation (eg a company-wide safety inspection for SS).

- *Functional structure*

  This would divide the company according to work specialism, with departments defined according to functions. For example: operations; finance; purchasing; human resources; outsourcing management.

  Problems for EEE would include:

  – A lack of customer focus
  – Does not reflect business processes of individual assignments
  – More difficult to attribute profits and losses

General issues

(1) Within any of these structures, the apex would be likely to require a board of directors rather than just Eric as an individual. The board is likely to need a range of skills (finance, technical, HRM) as well as responsibilities (eg divisional managers in a divisionalised structure). The apex would then be given a greater capacity for strategic planning and operational control.

(2) While there is a need to manage the increased size of the business there is a danger that the SS contract may be lost after a year and EEE revert to a smaller organisation with a revenue of only £0.5 million from smaller customers (as work for BB would also be lost under the new regime). If this is the case, then an entrepreneurial structure may again become appropriate. Any new structure should therefore be flexible and capable, as far as possible, of reversal. The probability of losing the contract needs to be assessed as early as possible.

(3) A different type of management structure may be needed according to whether the additional capacity is acquired through outsourcing or with new staff (see below).

(ii) **Outsourcing or new staff**

A significant increase in the size of the business means that new capacity is essential. Key issues in acquiring the new capacity are:

(1) The scale of the increase relative to the existing size of the business is immense (350%) therefore the new work will dominate the existing work. There may be problems in hiring sufficient employees with the right skills, in the right locations in should a short period given the scale of the labour increase.

(2) There is a need, not just for more staff, but for greater skills, including some which the existing staff do not possess. Outsourcing may provide more immediate, more flexible and more reliable access to these skills than attempting to employ individuals. This is particularly the case if these skills are only needed occasionally.

(3) While greater human resources is a key need, there is also a requirement for additional support services for these people. If new electricians are employed then there is likely to be the need also to acquire the additional support services to manage these employees and the operations that they will carry out. With outsourcing some of the support services may come with the additional human resources (eg equipment, training, technical support). If new electricians are employed then there is likely to be the need also to acquire the additional support services to manage these employees and the operations that they will carry out.

(4) There is a risk that the new contract with SS will not be renewed after a year or, if it is, then it may not be renewed at some stage in the near future if there are annual contract reviews. Given that this contract will make up 89% of the revenue of EEE, then there will need to be major downsizing if the contract is lost. These exit costs are likely to be significant if 100 new employees are hired in terms of redundancy costs and disposal of support assets. Outsourcing is likely to be more flexible in this respect if the duration of the outsourcing contracts match those of EEE's contract with SS.

(5) Cost is likely to be a major factor. Outsourcing is likely to be much more expensive than employing individuals as the outsourcing companies will charge a significant premium over the wage costs of their employees.

(6) Both outsourcing and employment of additional staff raise quality problems of different kinds. Outsourcing would require contractual control over quality with penalties for any shortfall. Nevertheless, while some control over technical quality can be exercised, the control over service delivery and customer satisfaction can be more difficult.

Similarly, however, staff recruitment and training to obtain so many new, good quality employees in such a short period may be difficult.

(7) The cost plus pricing formula with SS needs to be considered for the impact on the contract price of (i) outsourcing (where most of the costs are direct) compared to (ii) internal hiring of more staff (where support costs may be largely overheads).

It should not be assumed that any costs incurred can be recovered in full from SS with a profit mark up. Nor should it be assumed that the price to SS under the formula will be the same irrespective of whether outsourcing takes place.

Summary

The key issues appear to be:

- Immediacy of the requirement, being in only 6 months' time
- Cost
- Flexibility as the need may be temporary
- Impact on contract price

A possible decision may include:

(1) Employ staff on temporary contracts where possible (although this may influence the quality of the staff that can be acquired).

(2) Obtain a mix of new staff and outsourcing, where outsourcing provides the flexible top slice and the technical skills, with temporary employees providing the core.

(iii) Decision to accept the contract

The status quo of having the small customers plus BB does not appear to be an option that is on offer. Therefore some significant change is required.

The choices are:

- Significant downsizing to have only smaller customers with a revenue of £0.5 million (ie half the previous size)

- Scaling up to £4.5 million revenue by accepting the SS contract but taking on the risk annually of losing the contract

One view may be that the SS contract would make more profit in one year than downsizing would make in many years thus accepting the contract would be advantageous even if it is only temporary. This, however, ignores the initial investment in assets and new procedures to engage in the contract and the exit costs to be incurred if, and when, the SS contract were to be terminated.

The key issue therefore is to determine the likelihood of renewal. This depends partly on EEE's strategic capability of delivering on the contract and the intentions of SS. Given that at least some of the new contract appears to be beyond the current core competences of EEE, then significant risks are apparent and there is significant reliance on the ability of EEE to engage successfully in change management and on the ability to acquire new key skills and resources in the next 6 months.

Examiner's comments:

Answers to this requirement were good overall. For part (i), there were some rather generic answers. Most candidates concluded in favour of restructuring on a divisional or functional basis. There was also some support for matrix structures and Handy's shamrock. The inappropriateness of continuing with the entrepreneurial structure and the point of Eric being unable to maintain direct control over activities was well recognised.

In part (ii), knowledge of outsourcing was good. A pleasing number identified key points including the volume of employees, skills required, contract renewal issues, control of staff, standard of work and availability/influence over staff. A number of candidates seemed to think Eric would outsource the whole contract to one company which is unlikely to be the case and only better candidates realised a mix of employees and subcontractors could be an option. The impact of the decision on the cost plus contract pricing formula was considered by some better candidates.

In part (iii), some did a full SFA (Suitability, Feasibility, Acceptability) analysis despite the 'briefly advise' requirement. Better candidates discussed the need for change management and talked about Eric's future objectives. Few made the point that the status quo was not an option and that refusal of the contract would mean the loss of a major customer. Only a minority of answers were linked to, and flowed from, the points made in other parts of the question.

21 Rugeley Tableware plc

		Knowledge	Skill	Marks
(a)	SWOT	1	9	8
(b)	Ansoff	3	6	8
(c)	Decentralisation	3	3	
	Change management issues	3	3	
				10
(d)	Benchmarking	3	5	7
(e)	Corporate governance and NEDs	4	4	7
		17	30	40

General comments:

The scenario in this question looks at a listed company which is a niche manufacturer of quality ceramic tableware, based in UK. The company has attempted to address competition from cheaper imports by outsourcing some of its manufacturing operations to Asia, however this has not halted the decline in sales and profitability. The institutional shareholders have been openly critical of Belinda Rugeley (the Chairman and Chief executive) who runs the company in an authoritarian manner and has refused to appoint non-executive directors. The board is considering the future strategic options. The marketing director has suggested a strategy of both market and product development to attract a wider range of consumers. The production director on the other hand believes the lack of sales is a result of supply chain issues and the centralised management structure. He has identified a consumer electronics company that could be used to benchmark the supply chain and has also suggested changing the decision making structure of the company.

This question was the mini case and, at 40 marks, was the longest question on the paper. The requirements were broken down to help candidates in developing answer headings and assessing mark allocation. Overall candidates performed reasonably well, with good marks in the earlier requirements making up for relatively weaker attempts at parts (d) and (e).

(a) (i) Swot analysis

Strengths

- Long established business with a previously good record of growth and profitability
- Prestigious brand image and reputation and client base includes top hotels and restaurants
- High quality exclusive luxury product (may be recession proof as truly wealthy unaffected by credit crunch)
- Reputation for innovation (although not clear if this is still true today)
- Move to outsourcing is evidence that management are prepared to change
- Listed company therefore should have access to finance

Weaknesses

- Falling profits and negative operational cashflow are a cause for concern
- Unfashionable product, hence limited market with focus on older generation which restricts sales
- Poor customer service and high level of overdue orders may lose business
- High inventories lead to increased costs including obsolescence
- Long lead times due to overseas manufacturing will lead to dissatisfied customers

- Inflexibility and slow response times due to centralised structure and Belinda's authoritarian approach may mean alternative strategies are not fully considered

- More expensive than alternative products offered by cheap imports and retailers own brands

- Lack economies of scale of global ceramics manufacturers and presumably also can't match their marketing budget

- Not diversified so no spread of risk

- Lack of compliance with principles of good corporate governance

- Institutional shareholders have been openly critical of Belinda Rugeley which will undermine confidence in the company and its management

Opportunities

- New product ranges eg designer everyday tableware
- New markets eg Asia, younger generation
- Expand into related products eg glassware, crystal, gifts
- Get taken over by one of global manufacturers
- Take over a competitor
- Re-engineer supply chain
- Change the structure of the company and the decision making

Threats

- Changing dining trends mean product has reached end of life cycle

- Credit crunch means further sales decline is likely

- High levels of competition from cheap imports, large global retailers and more diversified competitors may further reduce market share

- Liquidation as a result of poor cash position

- Dissatisfaction of institutional shareholders may cause them to force change

(ii) **Key issues**

The key issues are:

- The declining financial position raises questions over the long term viability of the business

- The long term change in dining habits which has significantly impacted on R's sales and means that its core product appears to be at the end of its life cycle, as a result R urgently needs to pursue other opportunities for growth

- Poor customer service which is inconsistent with premium product

- The centralised authoritarian structure and the dissatisfaction of the institutional shareholders which needs to be addressed as a matter of priority

(b) **Strategic options proposed by marketing director**

The following matrix, developed by Ansoff, can be used to analyse the possible growth strategies available to Rugeley.

	Existing product	New product
Existing market	Internal efficiency and market penetration	Product development
New market	Market development	Diversification

(i)   Internal efficiency and market penetration involve attempts to reduce cost or further penetrate existing markets by taking market share from the competition. The outsourcing of some manufacturing in 2000 was presumably an attempt at increasing internal efficiency in order to match competitors through low cost manufacturing, but this does not appear to have generated additional sales. Thus to achieve market penetration, it may be better, as the marketing director suggests, to focus on differentiating itself from its competitors on a quality basis.

A marketing campaign aimed at emphasising the traditional English heritage might achieve this, although the problems identified by the SWOT analysis (and the marketing director) suggest that this approach may not be viable given the change in dining habits, the narrow customer base and the credit crunch. Indeed given that Rugeley are operating in a niche market, their market share/level of penetration may already be high and there may be little scope to increase this, unless they can persuade customers to buy multiple dinner services for different occasions or increase penetration of sales to hotels and restaurants eg through links with Melinda James.

Hence increased sales growth is likely to necessitate other strategies.

(ii) Product development involves selling new products to existing customers and normally requires research and development expenditure.

The introduction of the Melinda James everyday designer tableware range could be said to represent product development, although it is also possible to view this as simply an extension of the existing product range.

The fact that R intends to introduce this by way of a joint venture would be deemed 'External domestic development' according to Lynch's expansion matrix. This shares some of the risk and may allow R to save on marketing as it will enjoy additional publicity from the association with Melinda.

Alternatively, as this product is not going to be targeted at existing customers, who are in the older age range and may not associate with the celebrity chef, it could be argued that it is a means of market development (see below).

Other possible product development opportunities include: increased R&D to make innovations in patterns and designs; own brand ranges for large retail chains; giftware, glassware and other associated items for dining.

(iii) Market development involves selling existing products to new customers and involves investment in marketing.

In this case the marketing director is proposing two elements of market development:

Domestic expansion in terms of targeting a new market segment of younger customers (discussed above).

Overseas expansion in the context of exporting to the Asian market. According to Lynch this could be achieved organically or through some form of JV/licensing agreement. The fact that the marketing director is keen to emphasise the English heritage may mean that use of a 'local' partner is inappropriate.

R could also consider overseas development of other markets eg India.

(iv) Diversification involves making new products for new markets. It can be vertical (backward or forward in the firm's existing production chain), horizontal (acquisition of competitors) or conglomerate (a move into a totally different area). R does not appear to be considering diversification at this point in time.

Possible diversification opportunities include wider ceramics manufacture for bathrooms and kitchens. As they have no experience of this, it would be sensible to use 'external development' methods eg JV/acquisition

Note: It is possible to argue that the JV with Melissa James (everyday tableware for the younger market) is related diversification (new product and new market).

Examiner note:

In requirement (b) candidates were asked to use Ansoff to analyse the marketing director's proposals. Candidates tended to score well here. Not all candidates depicted the Ansoff matrix and provided an explanation of the framework but most were able to explain where the marketing director's strategies would be positioned on the grid. Better candidates went on to discuss the appropriateness of each growth strategy in light of their SWOT analysis and the risks involved, pointing out that the risk of introducing a new designer range of everyday tableware might be reduced via the joint venture with a celebrity chef.

(c) **Decentralisation and change management issues**

Decentralisation proposals

Currently it appears that Belinda Rugeley has adopted a very authoritarian, centralised management structure, with all key decisions being taken at Board level. The structure of the business does not appear to have changed despite growth.

The production director suggests that this has stifled innovation, and led to inflexibility and slow response times. He also implies that the sales forecasts produced centrally may have been inaccurate causing problems of overstocking and at the same time outstanding orders.

Decentralisation involves granting greater decision making powers and autonomy to a wider range of managers within the company.

Benefits of proposed changes:

*   Increases speed of response to changes in local markets and local conditions

*   May facilitate supply chain changes and hence improved customer service. Individual managers are likely to have a better idea of customer requirements and can stock the products the customers actually require, reducing levels of incorrect inventory

*   Local knowledge and expertise eg in respect of sales planning might improve quality of information and decision making and allow production to be driven by demand

*   Less rigid structure may foster a different culture and promote innovation re methods and designs. This may help extend the product life cycle or attract a wider range of customers

*   Would free up the Board to focus on strategic rather than operational decision making, therefore allowing Belinda and the other directors to address the declining profitability

*   Increased responsibility may motivate more junior managers and create a career path/ on job training for senior management

Disadvantages:

- Belinda and they other board directors may be reluctant to relinquish control

- Lack of experience may lead managers to make incorrect decisions, exacerbating the issues of overstocking etc. May also lead to incongruent decisions if local managers have differing objectives

- Would not reduce lead times as these are a result of basing production in Asia

- Increased need for coordination and communication as decision makers will be spread across the business

- Likely to require training of junior managers, some of whom may not want the added responsibility

Change management issues

Type of change

The restructuring change here might be said by Johnson, Scholes and Whittington to be 'Adaptation' (incremental and reactive).

It is incremental in that it is likely to be a gradual process rather than a sudden major, transformational change. It is also reactive in the sense that it appears to be in response to continued declining results and poor customer service, so R is being forced to make adjustments to adapt to its environment.

The focus of the change is at the organisational structure and system level, since it involves redesigning the approach to planning and decision making to facilitate changes in the supply chain.

Given the recent poor performance, change may be fundamental to R's survival.

Barriers to change

Change management involves managing people's expectations and attitudes since all changes tend to be resisted by employees. The key staff affected here will be the Board and the management, rather than the general employees. The change will not be successful unless Belinda can be persuaded of the need for change.

(1) **Cultural barriers**

Power structures within R may be threatened. This will in particular affect senior management, who may be protective of their current decision making authority and be reluctant to implement changes which will be against their own interests.

Structural inertia: the existing systems of planning and decision making may act as a barrier to change to a new decentralised approach. It appears that Belinda has favoured an authoritative centralised approach in the past and the management may find it hard to believe that she will support a new structure.

Group inertia may block change where the changes are inconsistent with the norms of team working and departments, or where they threaten their interests. The local sales managers may feel that they lack the necessary skills or rewards to take on additional responsibility.

(2) **Personnel barriers**

There are also barriers which affect individuals and result in them seeing the change as a threat. Here habit and fear of the unknown may mean some individual managers are unwilling or reluctant to take on the additional responsibility involved.

Approach to change

A mixture of the adaptive and coercive approach is likely to be appropriate. Adaptive change alone may be too slow, and R's management may need to emphasise that it is vital that changes are made if the company is to survive. Some participation will be appropriate however, particularly given that the new structure is to involve more decentralisation.

Belinda will need to actively demonstrate a willingness to delegate and adopt a more hands off approach to the management of the company. Otherwise local managers may perceive that their involvement is simply a token and that the substance of decision making has not altered.

Managers will need educating that the existing systems are insufficient to allow successful improvements to the supply chain. R will need to provide local managers with training and support to increase their confidence in their ability to make sales planning decisions.

Conclusion

Decentralisation would appear to be sensible and is likely to help address the supply chain issues and facilitate growth of new markets, however this will only be successful if Belinda can be persuaded of the need for change.

Examiner note:

Requirement (c) asked candidates to evaluate the production director's proposal to decentralise decision making and to explain the change management issues that might need to be addressed as a result. Most candidates were well prepared to discuss the pros and cons of decentralisation and showed good knowledge of change management (types of change, barriers to change and Lewin's 'unfreeze/move/refreeze' model). Weaker candidates failed to earn the skills marks available for applying this knowledge to the scenario however, simply providing a text book list of generic points, with little or no reference to the issues facing the company. Better candidates identified the fact that the current authoritarian structure – the cause of several of the company's problems – had been in place for some time and needed to be changed quickly to facilitate a turnround of the company's fortunes. Thus decentralising decision making was likely to improve some of the supply chain and customer service issues identified in (a), but the authoritarian chairman/chief executive would represent a key restraining force in the drive for change. A minority of candidates limited their marks by concentrating solely on either decentralisation or change management, and/or by concentrating on 'employees' in general rather than directors and managers in particular as being most affected.

(d) **Benchmarking**

By suggesting that Rugeley might use PCE's experience, the production director is referring to the activity of benchmarking.

Benchmarking is identifying, understanding and adapting business best practices and processes to lead to superior performance.

This can lead to changes which may improve productivity, reduce costs or increase competitive advantage. In Rugeley's case it appears that a key aim is to improve its supply chain in terms of responsiveness, reliability and relationships and hence improve customer satisfaction.

There are four bases for benchmarking:

- Internal – comparisons within the business over time, or between business units
- Competitive – comparisons with other firms in the same industry/sector
- Best in class/Activity – best practice in a completely different industry
- Generic – against a conceptually similar process

Internal and competitive benchmarking would involve making comparisons within R's own industry. To an extent R has done this in the past, as competitive benchmarking led it to outsource some of its manufacturing in 2000.

When a company or its whole industry is performing badly or losing out to other industries, there is a case for the wider perspective offered by 'best in class' and generic benchmarking. This would involve identifying suitable benchmarking partners.

The production director is thus correct that there may be lessons to learn from PCE's experience in re-engineering their supply chain and this would be in the context of activity/best in class benchmarking.

Whilst the industry is different, they both sell consumer products and the concepts of lead times, responsiveness, overdue orders and inventories would still apply. Also PCE may well have experience of outsourcing production to Asia.

The chairman's concerns that PCE operate in a different industry might in fact be an advantage rather than a constraint, as it could encourage R to think more widely and be more innovative in its approach, rather than being limited by the way things are normally done within the industry. This might lead to an approach which is different from competitors and hence generates competitive advantage (something that the outsourcing in 2000 appears to have failed to do).

One approach does not preclude the other, so R could identify the competitor with the best supply chain in the ceramics industry at the same time, although it may be harder to get the necessary information. PCE may be more inclined to share information as it will not feel the need to be protective of trade secrets and some data has already been published.

The Chairman is correct that PCE's targets may not be appropriate for R, but benchmarking is more than just collecting data or setting targets. R needs to identify the drivers of good performance. So comparisons with PCE might indicate the areas of the supply chain that R needs to focus on and may give R an insight into the problems that were experienced by PCE in managing the changes. This may help R obtain better results or facilitate the implementation of the change.

In addition to improving the efficiency of operations, benchmarking may also enable R to identify scope for improving its management structure and decision making processes eg the need to decentralise the system of sales planning and decision making.

A possible downside of benchmarking is that managers may feel their role is reduced to copying others and thus any benchmarking programme would need careful management.

Conclusion: R urgently needs to establish or regain its competitive advantage and benchmarking the supply chain against PCE may help it do so. It might also consider other forms of benchmarking and perhaps undertake a value chain analysis.

Examiner note:

In requirement (d) candidates had to discuss the differing views expressed in the scenario about the relevance of using a company (PCE) in a different industry to benchmark Rugeley's supply chain. Answers were varied. Some candidates failed to spot that this requirement was about benchmarking and limited their marks by discussing the potential comparison only in general terms. Better answers explained the different types of benchmarking available to Rugeley and went on to consider whether PCE plc was an appropriate choice for benchmarking. Many also provided consideration of supply chain issues. Candidates who discussed the use of value chain analysis as a means of identifying improvements to the supply chain and increasing competitive advantage were awarded credit.

(e) **Corporate governance and NEDs**

Corporate governance involves the set of rules which governs the structure and determines the objectives of a company and regulates the relationship between a company's management, its Board of directors and its shareholders. It is not about the day-to-day management of operations or the formulation of business strategy.

Key aspects of good corporate governance involve the transparency of corporate structure and operations; the accountability of managers and boards to shareholders; and corporate responsibility towards employees, creditors, suppliers and the local community.

The UK Corporate Governance Code 2010 issued by the FRC sets out best practice which R currently does not comply with:

- There should be a separate chairman and chief executive, whereas Belinda currently does both roles

- The Board should consist of sufficient non-executive directors to prevent domination by the executive directors

- Non-executive directors (NEDs) should establish a remuneration committee to decide on directors' remuneration and an audit committee to work with the external auditors. As there are no NEDs it is assumed that R does not have either of these currently

The Code is only a legal requirement for premium listed companies so non-compliance by R in some ways is not an issue, as there is a 'comply or disclose' policy. Thus as a condition of its continued listing R is simply required by the Stock Exchange to disclose the areas where it has not followed the Code. However a bigger issue may be that the institutional shareholders are becoming increasingly unhappy with the situation.

Belinda would be advised to appoint NEDs and form a remuneration committee as this would protect her and the other executive directors from the criticism/accusation that the company is being run for their personal benefit.

NEDs would provide a better balance of power on the Board and may encourage Belinda to delegate some of the decision making to others.

NEDs could also help improve the efficiency and effectiveness of the remuneration system and act as a buffer between the Board and the auditors.

The benefit to Belinda of the NEDs is that they would be seen by the institutional investors and other shareholders as independent, which would improve the perception of the company.

In addition they may bring skills and experience that improves the quality of decision making which could lead to better performance. NEDs would also be able to help R appoint new directors should the need arise.

Overall the appointment of NEDs may increase institutional shareholder confidence in the running of the company, and if they are reassured by the move they are less likely to demand that the company seeks a buyer.

Examiner note:

Requirement (e) asked candidates to explain the principles of good corporate governance and the ways that non-executive directors (NEDs) might be of benefit to the running of the business. A disappointing number of candidates failed to explain the concept of corporate governance and restricted their answer to a discussion of NEDs. Better candidates considered corporate governance in the broader context of agency theory, talked about the applicability of the Code and the need for a separate Chairman and CEO, discussed the issue of directors' remuneration being linked to performance and highlighted the need for better governance given the concerns of the institutional shareholders.

22 Pitstop Ltd

Marking guide

			Knowledge	Skill	Marks
(a)	(i)	Strategy 1 analysis	2	6	
	(ii)	Assumptions/overall	2	6	
					12
(b)	(i)	Strategy 2 calculations	1	4	
	(ii)	Impact of strategy 2	2	5	
					10
(c)		Future profitability	1	5	5
			8	26	27

(a) (i) **Evaluation of forecast for Strategy 1**

Appendix 1:

	Actual 2009	Forecast 2010
Food as % of turnover	35%	35%
Labour % of turnover	33%	33%
Gross profit margin	32%	32%
Net profit margin	0.1%	8.1%
No of customers pa (Revenue/Ave spend)	54,000	72,000
No of customers per day (based on 360 days pa)	150	200
Turnaround of tables (daily customers/50)	3	4
Gross profit per customer (gross profit/no of customers)	£2.88	£2.88

	% Increase 2009-2010
Revenue	33.3%
Gross profit	33.3%
Overheads	Nil
Net profit	9,969%
Customers per day	33.3%
Ave spend per customer	Nil

Commentary: Impact on current position of an average restaurant

Currently the 'average restaurant' is making a contribution of £155,520 but only just breaking even (net profit of £520) after its allocated share of the rent, marketing and other overheads. This appears to be consistent with the suggestion that results have suffered as a result of significant rent increases.

Overall the new strategy would therefore appear to significantly improve the situation, with the 33% increase in customers generating a £51,840 increase in gross profit and hence PBIT.

Assuming there is no change in fixed costs, and that gross margins remain at 32%, any increase in customer volumes will increase capacity utilisation and hence lead to extra profit.

On the face of it, the sales director's forecasts suggest the proposal is a good one, however this depends on whether the sales director's forecast of both volumes and cost behaviour is realistic, and whether the increased customer numbers can be achieved across the chain in the manner suggested. Given the FD's absence, it is possible that the sales director lacks the necessary experience to produce accurate forecasts and this is examined further in a(ii) below.

(ii) **Reasonableness of forecast and assumptions for predicting company-wide results**

Customer numbers

The sales director has assumed that widening the target market will increase the number of customers by 50 per day or 33.3% overall. The implication is that these will come from the new target market.

This target seems quite ambitious and equates on average to an extra sitting a day, as the turnaround of tables increase from 3 to 4 times. Whether the planned increase is achievable will depend to an extent on the location of the restaurant and the competition in the surrounding area.

In reality the increase is unlikely to be spread evenly across the week – business customers are more likely to use the restaurant Monday-Friday, whereas local families may be more inclined to visit at weekends. The restaurant may encounter problems if, for example, the additional custom is all generated at lunch time, when the tables may already be full.

Also in view of the strong competition, if Pitstop continued with its existing strategy customer numbers may decline between 2009 and 2010, requiring even more customers to be generated from the new target market.

It would be helpful to break the forecast down, to more clearly identify the forecast revenue and customer numbers under both the existing and new strategies.

Average spend and margins

The forecast is based on average spend remaining constant at £9 per customer and gross margins continuing at 32% or £2.88 per customer. Thus the 33.3% increase in customers leads directly to a 33.3% increase in overall gross profit. The forecast does not appear to take account of the fact that the new target customers may have a different spending pattern. Business customers who use the restaurants for meetings are likely to occupy a table for longer but may spend less if they only purchase several cups of coffee.

The introduction of a new snack menu may attract increased volumes of travellers but is likely to lead to a reduction in the average spend. This type of food may require little preparation however, so it is possible that margins will increase on these menu items as there is less labour cost involved if the product is offered on a self service basis.

Average spend is thus likely to vary by type of customer and time of day and margins will vary by menu dish, thus more information would be required to make a more accurate prediction.

Overheads

The sales director has assumed that allocated overheads will remain constant. In reality overheads are likely to increase for the following reasons:

- Pitstop will need to raise awareness of its new strategy and menu. This will necessitate promotion to business customers and local families, and printing of new menus. Widening the target market will therefore involve increased marketing costs unless Pitstop believes that it can attract sufficient coverage via articles in local newspapers and word-of-mouth.

- Pitstop will incur capital costs to fit out part of the restaurant as an office area and ongoing IT costs to support and maintain this strategy.

- Certain costs may be subject to annual price increases eg rent and utilities.

Extrapolation of results company-wide

As the gross profit margin is broadly the same across all Pitstop restaurants and all other costs incurred by the business are split equally across the 65 restaurants, the only variables are customer numbers and average spend.

In order to properly predict the results for the chain as a whole, the customer numbers and average spend for each individual restaurant would be required and these could be amalgamated to create a group forecast.

In the absence of such information, the sales director's forecast for the average Pitstop restaurant could be extrapolated.

With the average restaurant only just breaking even after allocated overheads, the company's PBIT for year ended August 2009 could be estimated at £33,800 (65 × £520) which is unlikely to be a sufficient return for investors after interest and tax payments.

Leaving aside the inaccuracies noted above, then the overall forecast group PBIT for year ended August 2010 under strategy 1 would be estimated at £3,403,400 (65 × £52,360) – a substantial improvement.

Range of possible results

To get a better idea of the variation in performance, the range of individual restaurant results could be considered:

Actual 2009

Gross profit:

Worst: 95 customers × 360 days × £7.50 × 0.32 = £82,080

Best: 245 customers × 360 days × £10.50 × 0.32 = £296,352

After deducting overheads at £155,000 this means PBIT in 2009 ranged from a loss of £72,920 in the worst restaurant to a profit of £141,352 in the best.

Forecast 2010

Assuming the worst and best restaurants were also forecast to increase their customer numbers by 33.3%, 2010 forecast profits under strategy 1 would range from:

Gross profit:

Worst: £82,080 × 4/3 = £109,440

Best: £296,352 × 4/3 = £395,136

PBIT

Worst: £109,440 – £155,000 = Loss £45,560 (a reduction in the loss of £27,360)

Best: £395,136 – £155,000 = £240,136 (an increase of £98,784)

Thus the new strategy would increase profits in the average and best restaurants but would still result in Pitstop's worst restaurants being loss-making after the allocation of overheads.

The competition is likely to vary from one restaurant to another and this will affect the results and whether the planned 33% increase in customer numbers will be achievable uniformly across all Pitstop restaurants.

Also some restaurant locations may be more suitable for business/family trade than others. It may not be appropriate to convert all restaurants for business use for example.

Conclusion:

Strategy 1 may be feasible but requires more market research and competitor analysis. Pitstop could attempt to assess the impact of this strategy by running it as a trial in certain restaurants before phasing it in across the whole chain.

(b) (i) **Strategy 2**

Customers required to maintain 2009 PBIT

Calculation of new contribution per customer

	Average restaurant £
Current average spend	9.00
New average spend (85% × current spend)	7.65
New contribution (20% × new spend)	1.53

Customers required to maintain profits:

	Average restaurant
Total 2009 Contribution	£155,520
New Contribution per customer	£1.53
Customers required per annum	101,647
Hence customers required per day	282
Increase in customers per day (282-150)	132

Alternative approach to calculations:

Contribution per customer

Gross profit per customer at existing prices (a(i))	£2.88
Reduction in gross profit due to price decrease	15% × £9.00 = £1.35
New contribution per customer	£2.88 – £1.35 = £1.53

No of customers required:

Lost contribution = lost revenue from price reduction = 150 × 360 × £9.00 × 15% = £72,900

Thus increase in customers required = £72,900 / £1.53 = 47,647 pa or 132 per day

(ii) **Likely impact of Strategy 2**

Impact on average restaurant

Unless there are potential savings in staff and food costs, the 15% reduction in price causes the gross profit margin to fall from 32% to 20% for an average restaurant. The calculations in b(i) show that to compensate for this, the average restaurant would need to attract 282 customers per day. This is more than the best performing restaurant currently attracts and for an average restaurant represents an additional 132 customers per day (an increase of 88%).

This looks unobtainable and even if it were successful in doing this, the average restaurant would only be operating just above breakeven. In reality such additional volumes may also necessitate an increase in marketing expenditure or other fixed costs which would further reduce profitability.

Thus the sales director's confidence would appear to be misplaced unless demand is very price elastic.

Impact on the company as a whole

In 2009, using the existing pricing strategy, after allocating fixed costs, the worst restaurant made a loss of £72,920, the average restaurant was just breaking even, and the best restaurant made a profit of £141,352.

The operations director is worried about the downside risk of the price reduction strategy.

In the worst case scenario, if the price reduction failed to attract any additional customers, the calculations in Appendix 2 show that the worst and average restaurants would become loss making (£115,773) and (£72,380) respectively and the best restaurant would only make a small profit of £18,489. Thus the likely effect on the company as a whole is a significant deterioration in profitability, which would render it loss making.

Impact on breakeven point

An alternative way to assess the risk of the strategy is to consider the impact of the 15% price reduction on the breakeven point:

Compared to the actual number of customers in 2009, with the 15% price reduction the worst performing restaurant would need to generate an extra 280 customers a day just to break even – almost 3 times its existing customers and more than the number of customers of the best performing restaurant in 2009!

The average performing restaurant would require 131 customers and the best performing restaurant would have a margin of safety of 26 customers.

Conclusion

The price reduction of 15% proposed in strategy 2 would not appear to be viable and without significant increase in numbers or major cost reductions is likely to increase the chain's losses. Rather than reducing all prices by 15%, Pitstop could consider implementing price discrimination strategies eg offering senior citizen or early bird discounts to smooth out the peaks and troughs of trade.

Appendix 2 of possible calculations:

	Worst	Ave	Best
New contribution per customer	£	£	£
Current Ave spend	7.50	9.00	10.50
New ave spend (85%)	6.375	7.65	8.925
New contribution (new spend × 18/20/22%)	1.147	1.53	1.963

Impact on profits of the price reduction if there were to be no increase in customer numbers:

	Worst	Ave	Best
Existing customers per day	95	150	245
New contribution per customer	£1.147	£1.53	£1.963
Annual Gross profit	£39,227	£82,620	£173,137
PBIT (after £155,000 overheads)	(£115,773)	(£72,380)	£18,137

	Worst	Ave	Best
Existing 2009 PBIT (see (ai))	(£72,920)	£520	£141,352
Reduction in profitability	(£42,853)	(£71,860)	(£123,215)

Impact of price reduction on breakeven point

	Worst	Ave	Best
Overheads	£155,000	£155,000	£155,000
New contribution per customer	£1.147	£1.53	£1.963
Break even no. customers	135,135	101,308	78,961
Breakeven customers per day	375	281	219
Actual customers per day 2009	95	150	245
Increase in customers required to break even	280	131	(26)

Examiner note:

Requirement b(i) asked candidates to prepare calculations showing the additional number of customers per day that would be required to maintain the gross profit of an average restaurant if prices were reduced by 15% in accordance with Strategy 2. Overall this was poorly attempted and it was disappointing to see many candidates failing here, despite the simple nature of the calculation (a variant of break-even). The most common error was to calculate the number of customers required per day in an average restaurant to maintain revenue rather than gross profit. Those that correctly performed the calculation in terms of profit often assumed that, despite the 15% price reduction, the GP margin would be maintained at 32%, when the scenario clearly stated that margins would fall and indeed, the new estimated margin of 20% was provided in the exhibit.

In requirement b(ii) candidates were then required to discuss the likely impact of Strategy 2 on the profitability of the company as a whole and to provide any supporting calculations. Most fared a little better here, with many performing calculations of the impact on profit if the price reduction failed to generate an increase in customer volumes, although only the better candidates referred back to their calculations in b(i). Better candidates pointed out that the sales director's assertion that any increase in revenue would more than compensate for the reduction in price depended on the price elasticity of demand. There was some confusion on the part of weaker candidates regarding elasticity however, with many stating that as the price reduction had led to increased volumes, then demand must be elastic (therefore failing to recognise that this is the case for all downward sloping demand curves and that elasticity requires the increase in volume to be more than proportionate to the reduction in price). Only the best answers included comments about the need to consider the impact of this strategy on the other restaurants in the chain and the possibility of applying price discrimination rather than a universal price cut.

(c) **Additional considerations for future strategy**

Note: this answer includes a complete range of points for marking purposes and is far more than would be expected in the time available.

In order to decide on the future direction of the business Pitstop needs:

(i) To more accurately evaluate the proposed strategies

(ii) To assess the current position of each individual restaurant in order to identify the underperforming restaurants

(i) **To assess the proposed strategies**

Budgets – Predictions of customer numbers, average spend and overheads for 2010 if Pitstop continued with the existing strategy would be useful as a baseline to assess the impact of the new proposals.

Capital expenditure – More information is required regarding the cost of fitting out the restaurants as a business centre.

Competitor analysis – This needs to be done on an overall company and individual restaurant basis to establish the appropriate target market and strategy for each restaurant.

Market research – Pitstop needs to carry out some market research:

(1) Regarding the target market (local families, business users) and the new snack menu to accurately predict increased customer numbers and average spend for strategy 1.

(2) To assess the likely impact of reducing prices and the price elasticity of demand for strategy 2. Each Pitstop restaurant should also compare their prices to those of the local competition.

(ii) **To assess underperforming restaurants**

Detail on individual restaurants

Pitstop's reporting system assumes constant gross profit margins and an equal allocation of overheads. In reality not all restaurants will successfully keep to the target for food and labour costs. Also the actual rents are likely to vary depending on the restaurant location eg those near London or on prime routes are likely to pay more rent than those in more rural areas. By allocating overheads evenly Pitstop is likely to be overstating the profit in some restaurants and understating others.

In order to assess each individual restaurant, a breakdown of revenue, costs and staffing levels is required. Pitstop also needs to make an attempt to split overheads between those that are traceable per restaurant eg rent, utilities and other premises costs, and those that are central costs eg marketing and management that need to be reallocated.

Seasonality

Trade is likely to be seasonal and the clientele is likely to vary at different times eg:

Time of year – the summer may be busier because of tourists

Time of week – more trade at weekends from families

Time of day – more business trade in the earlier part of the day

More information is required about the utilisation of the tables in order to assess when a restaurant needs to generate additional trade eg is the restaurant usually full on weekday lunchtimes but empty between 9.30am and 11.30am? This would help identify the type of clientele to be targeted.

Popularity and profitability of menu items

Some meals will be more popular than others and the profitability of the various menu items will differ. This information would help assess which menu items should be offered.

Comparative information

In order to interpret performance, information is needed regarding budgets and targets, competitors and industry norms, so that Pitstop can benchmark performance not just between its restaurants but against others in the industry. This would help Pitstop assess which restaurants are performing well and which are not, both currently and with respect to changes over time.

It is also important to distinguish the performance of the restaurant from the performance of the manager. A badly performing restaurant could be improved by changing the manager or it could be the inevitable consequence of its local market, additional competition or other non-controllable factors.

Multiple performance measures

Pitstop might consider using a wider set of assessment measures to identify the drivers of an individual restaurant's success or failure, including non-financial areas such as level of customer complaints, waiting times, staff turnover. One tool by which this can be achieved is the balanced scorecard.

Conclusion

Pitstop may be unable to return to profitability unless it has sufficient information to identify and either turn around or close underperforming restaurants.

Strategy 1 may be feasible but requires more market research and competitor analysis. The price reduction of 15% proposed in strategy 2 would not appear to be viable and without significant increase in numbers or major cost reductions is likely to increase the chain's losses.

Other possible strategies to consider include:

- Offer takeaway or drive through service
- Get taken over by another chain
- Sell franchise to one of the fast food chains

Examiner note:

Requirement (c) asked candidates to explain any other factors that the company should consider before making a decision about how to improve the company's profitability. A wide range of points could be made here (identifying the worst restaurants with a view to closure, considering the impact of the competition, undertaking market research to provide better information for decision making etc). Most candidates made sufficient sensible comments to make up at least in part for weaknesses elsewhere in the question.

23 Somborne Zoological Park Ltd

Marking guide

		Knowledge	Skill	Marks
(a)	Report format	1		
	(i) Strategic planning benefits	1.5	2	
	(ii) Objectives (2 per goal)	1	4.5	
				8
(b)	Allocating limited resources	2	5	6
(c)	(i) Costs and benefits of sustainability initiative	2	4	
	(ii) Impact of staff/key stakeholders	1	3	
				9
(d)	Information system	3	3	
	Performance measures	2	4	
				10
		13.5	25.5	33

This scenario involves a charitable, not-for-profit company which is engaged in animal conservation and research, as well as operating a well-known zoo in the UK. The organisation has set itself a number of strategic goals including maximising the impact of its conservation activities, promoting the zoo and developing alternative income streams. It has recently decided to seek accreditation from the global industry body for sustainability and environmental management and has appointed a new Chairman to assist with this.

Candidates were not expected to have any specialist knowledge of these topics and additional information was provided in the scenario about the nature of environmental management and also to explain the zoo's aims for sustainability in four different areas: financial, environmental, HR and social.

NFP organisations and sustainability are far from being peripheral syllabus areas (a point suggested in tutor feedback), indeed both these topics are introduced in early chapters of the learning materials and are developed throughout. The concept of sustainable development is a key consideration for businesses today and for the ICAEW and its members.

There were some very good attempts at this question and no obvious evidence of time pressure. A sizeable number of candidates attempted the exam out of order and did this question first or second. Some candidates did start off badly however by failing to produce it in the required report format.

Report

To:	Chairman of Somborne Zoo
From:	A.N.Other
Date:	September 2009
Re:	Proposed Sustainability Initiative

(a) (i) **Strategic planning – benefits**

Strategic planning involves setting goals and then designing strategies to meet them.

Purpose and benefits of planning:

- To ensure Somborne meets the needs of its diverse stakeholders. A strategic plan will help communicate the purpose and values of the zoo to staff, visitors and sponsors, and help identify the priorities for the zoo

- Attract and maintain funding and public support, avoiding over-reliance on any particular source of income. The availability of a plan may help sell the zoo to the public and sponsors in particular

- Ensure optimum use of resources which, as with most NFP organisations, are likely to be limited

- Ensure day-to-day operations are consistent with the long term goals of the zoo. As part of its strategic planning process Somborne has already identified four strategic goals. The strategic plan needs to set out in more detail how each of these goals will be pursued and will consider areas such as financial strategy and the raising of funds, marketing, visitor services, the organisation and scale of the site and exhibits, development of the animal collection, intentions for breeding, forming strategic partnerships for conservation and research

- Guide the development and evolution of the zoo – coordinate the growth and ensure coherency of the site plan and exhibits. May help increase chances of gaining IZF accreditation

- Relate the zoo to its external environment

- Improve performance of zoo and its chances of survival

- Help to identify and manage risks

(ii) **Objectives**

Whilst the zoo's goals may be stated quite generally, the specific objectives need to be SMART (specific, measurable, achievable, relevant and with a timescale attached):

Goal: To maximise the impact of conservation and research activities

- Ensure at least 5 research papers are published during the year
- Secure x number of new animals from threatened species within 5 years
- Gain recognition from conservation bodies for activities eg be cited for or win awards, press coverage/ media accolades within one year
- Ensure x animals born per year under the zoo's breeding programme

Goal: To promote the zoo and provide learning opportunities

- Increase the number of return visitors to 20% of total over three years
- Increase admissions revenue by 15% per year
- Complete the development of the panda exhibit by July 2010
- Introduce a quarterly 'Friends of Somborne' newsletter in 2010
- Upgrade the zoo's café and restaurant facilities by May 2010
- Appoint a schools coordinator by Dec 2009 and visit 5 schools a month to promote the zoo's school programme
- Ensure the zoo is featured in local press and current affairs programmes at least every month

Goal: To develop alternative income streams

- Have approached 20 potential corporate/sponsors by Dec 2009
- Attract 5 new benefactors in 2010
- Increase the annual membership of the 'Friends of Somborne' by 15% by summer 2010
- Promote the zoo as a venue for corporate events and hospitality such that this forms 10% of the income in 2010
- Increase the sales of zoo merchandise by x%

(b) Allocation of resources

In common with other not for profit (NFP) organisations, Somborne is likely to face the following issues in making decisions:

- Multiple objectives (driven by diverse stakeholder needs)
- Conflicts between stakeholders
- Need to take a long term view of the impact of short term decisions
- Not always easy to measure results or to quantify the impact of decisions
- Requirement for greater awareness of corporate responsibility and sustainability issues
- Financial and other resource constraints
- Operations in the public eye

In view of its limited resources, Somborne therefore needs to prioritise its goals, audiences, and activities.

In order to make a decision on how best to use resources and what projects the zoo can afford to carry out each year, Somborne first needs to identify the resources available, not just in terms of finances but also staffing and space. Potential projects will be constrained by any physical limitations of the actual site. Increasing Somborne's use of volunteers will help increase the resources available.

In making a choice as to which exhibits and programmes to allocate funds and space to, Somborne must strike a balance between the needs of the animals, visitors and staff.

Somborne's licence may require resources to be dedicated in certain areas and the desire for accreditation will affect the zoo's priorities. There may also be conditions attached to certain donations which restrict what the funds can be used for.

The mission statement acknowledges the dual role of the zoo as a visitor attraction and as an organisation engaged in animal conservation.

Thus it may appear that there is competition for resources between Somborne's revenue-producing activities and its conservation desires and needs eg the zoo may face a choice between dedicating more money for conservation and spending this on visitor facilities.

An improved entrance or a new exhibit may bring extra visitors and increase the number of returning visitors. This in turn may generate more funds for conservation and research activities.

Conversely good conservation or recognition of successful research may enhance the zoo's budget by attracting funding. This would then allow development of the zoo's visitor attractions.

Thus the two roles are not necessarily in conflict.

Having decided to spend money on either conservation/research or its commercial activities, Somborne still faces competing choices.

Resources for research are finite and must be carefully targeted. In choosing between potential research or conservation projects, priority must be given to research that has clear implications for saving species, populations and habitats.

If Somborne decides to spend money on new visitor features, then it will need to consider how best to spend this. Thus it may need to consider choice of location within the zoo, order of construction of exhibits, amount of space to be allocated to visitors/staff/animals.

There is also a distinction between short and long term goals. Somborne needs to focus on the ultimate goal of conservation, but also on meeting the immediate day-to-day needs of the living creatures for which it is responsible. Thus in allocating funds it needs to consider how to provide the best possible conditions for the animals in its care and whether funds will be available in future years for projects to continue.

One of the problems facing Somborne is how to measure the return on its investment. It is likely that the spending on projects within the zoo, rather than conservation research, will have a more direct impact which is easier to quantify – eg if a new gorilla exhibit is created, Somborne can measure the impact in terms of number of visitors, press coverage, increased admissions revenue, adoption of the animals etc.

It may take much longer to assess the impact of conservation and research activities and this is also likely to be affected by wider and possible uncontrollable influences eg climate change, natural disasters eg fire and floods, other parties engaged in similar research.

Examiner note:

Requirement (b) asked candidates to identify the issues the zoo is likely to face in deciding how to allocate resources. Answers here were polarised. Most candidates identified the issue of limited resources in the context of funding and the need to choose between conflicting objectives, sometimes referring back to the wide range of goals identified in (a). Better candidates recognised the dual role of the zoo – as an organisation dedicated to conservation and as a visitor attraction – and the trade-off between allocating resources to animal welfare and research and spending on marketing and promotion to attract more visitors to the zoo. They also noted that the zoo's licence and its sponsors may impose certain constraints and that resources were not limited to cash but extended to labour, both paid staff and volunteers.

(c) (i) **Sustainability**

Costs and benefits of sustainability

Sustainability involves using natural resources in a way that does not lead to their decline. In the context of the zoo, sustainability has been identified as having an impact not just on the environment but also in other areas: financial, human resources and social.

Costs of implementing a sustainability programme

In the short term this may lead to:

- Increased costs eg using greener energy sources, buying fair trade products, paying higher wages to workers
- The environmental audit will take time and money, as may the accreditation process
- Increased admin time in screening suppliers and contractors, and reduced number of parties available
- Possible reduced income eg no donations from non-ethical sponsors
- Additional management considerations eg regarding the ethical HR policies

Benefits:

- Sustainable activities will help to improve the environment and will fulfil the zoo's moral obligation to be involved in such practices
- Accreditation by IZF for its sustainable activities may enhance the reputation of the zoo particularly if, as a result, it qualifies for official awards and recognitions
- If Somborne stresses sustainable activities as a basis for promotion and marketing it may become a more attractive option to visitors, donors, investors, and strategic partners and thus increase net income. Accreditation may help attract ethical investors
- Green practices adopted by the zoo may lead to cost savings through eg reduced costs of utilities such as water and energy
- This strategy will improve employees' awareness of environmental issues and responsibilities, enhance employee morale and help to ensure that Somborne is seen as a desirable employer
- Somborne will stand as a model for sustainable practices, encouraging others, especially in the same community, and setting an example for 'greener' governance
- The sustainability initiative will improve their image as champions for environmental responsibility, enhance compliance with environmental principles and, even better, help to inform and shape future legislation

(ii) **Impact on staff and one other key stakeholder**

Stakeholder group	Area of interest	Impact
Staff	Financial	Will want the zoo to operate as a going concern to safeguard jobs
	Environment	Can enhance sustainability through own personal convictions eg view on environment. May contribute to change and innovations or may resist change due to extra workload
	HR	Will be interested in development opportunities, HR practices, health and safety
	Social	May feel rewarded through participation in educating the local schools and community
Suppliers/contractors and other business partners	Financial	Will be concerned about the potential impact on their contracts and working practices which could lead to additional costs
	Social	May be concerned about the cost implications eg if required to use recyclable packaging
		May welcome ethical procurement if it increases their chances of winning work or the price that they will receive

Candidates may have instead analysed any of the following which were deemed to be key stakeholders:

Visitors	Environment Social	May have a genuine concern about the welfare of the animals, the environment and the sustainability of the zoo's performance
Investors/ sponsors/ donors	Financial	May contribute if they believe that the zoo's activities and its financial position is sustainable
		May want to ensure funds given are allocated for specific causes
Local community	Social	Will expect the zoo to provide socio-economic development through jobs, links with the schools, cooperation with local business

(d) **Use of information to assess sustainability initiative**

Somborne needs to implement a system which provides the appropriate type and amount of information for managers to implement and control the sustainability initiative and assess its success.

The current information management system may need to be enhanced to allow collection of new types of data, eg may need to first measure energy usage before can implement policies and procedures to reduce it.

In addition certain specific information may be required by IZF to demonstrate achievement levels and in order for Somborne to acquire accreditation. Thus S needs to establish any specific performance criteria that will be used by IZF in order to decide what indicators need to be measured and monitored in each of the four areas identified.

Some of the information that needs to be gathered may be qualitative as well as quantitative, eg impact on visitors' willingness to adopt a sustainable lifestyle will be hard to measure and may be based on responses to surveys/conversations etc.

Somborne may make use of exception reporting eg to highlight problem areas where energy or water usage has overrun, breaches of relevant guidelines.

One purpose of an information system is knowledge management so that best practice with regard to sustainability can be shared. Staff may need training to formally record data/information necessary if such records have not been kept in the past.

Once the environmental audit has been conducted Somborne will have information about the current level of achievement in various areas. Baseline performance can be defined and targets set for future achievement.

On an ongoing basis performance can then be measured against these targets/budgets and deviations from the plan can be investigated. S may benchmark performance targets against other zoos (IZF may be able to provide appropriate information).

The zoo will need to undertake staff training, communicate the new system and establish procedures for cost control.

Baseline performance measures:

Overall impact

- Increase in positive zoo/conservation news stories or features
- Increase in partnerships with other conservation bodies

Financial

- % of revenue from zoo based activities
- Retail revenue per visitor

- Increase in number of visitors per month.

- Funds received from research and development activities

- Donations received

- Responses to pledges and petitions

- Increased zoo membership numbers and increased sponsorship schemes, especially those prompted by support for conservation/sustainability

- Deficit/surplus of income over expenditure

- No. of suppliers/contractors subject to screening

- No. of suppliers meeting sustainable criteria

- % procurement from fair trade countries/suppliers

Environmental

- Volumes of waste disposed of vs. recycled
- Monthly levels of energy consumption
- Monthly water usage
- Volume of recycled water
- Methods of visitor travel to and around zoo
- No. of fair trade and organic products in the shop and cafe
- No. of new environmentally friendly initiatives implemented
- CO_2 and other emissions
- % of energy from alternative sources

Human resources

- Staff and volunteer injury rate
- Hours and expenditure on sustainability training
- Number of certificates awarded to staff and others trained at the zoo
- Percentage of staff receiving recognition from professional organisations
- Percentage of staff who have completed their professional development plan each year
- Percentage of staff walking/cycling or using car share schemes to get to work

Social

- Number of training programmes offered by Zoo staff covering topics related to sustainability

- Number of presentations and publications that connect and inform the general public and the professional community about sustainability

- Attendance figures at specific education projects

- Assessments of the educational effectiveness of different exhibits via surveys and questionnaires, observations of visitor behaviour, conversations

- Number of research programs, citations, no. of papers published

- Number of news stories that cover sustainability initiatives at the zoo

- Records of media coverage, and teacher feedback on formal programmes

- Records of sales of products in the zoo that have been associated with particular messages or campaigns

24 Green Cards Ltd (GC)

Marking guide

			Knowledge	Skill	Marks
(a)	(i)	Power of suppliers	1	4	
	(ii)	Substitutes	1	3	
					7
(b)	(i)	Competitive position/threats	3	7	
	(ii)	Performance and comparison	2	9	
					18
(c)		Withdrawal – ethical and business	2	5	6
(d)		Briefing note format	1		
		Strategy 1	1	4	
		Strategy 2	1	4	
		Advice	1	2	
					12
			13	38	43

General comments:

The company in this scenario owns a chain of shops retailing greeting cards. Green Cards Ltd is positioned towards the quality end of the market, but it is small by comparison to the market leaders. The company recently introduced a range of environmentally friedly cards but it is now seeking to withdraw from this market. Two strategies have been proposed to improve performance. Strategy 1 is to allow a confectionary company some floorspace where the fee is to be based either on the square meters occupied or on a share of revenue generated. Strategy 2 proposes to cut costs by reducing staffing.

(a) (i) Power of suppliers

The key suppliers to the retail greeting card industry are card publishers (ie manufacturers).

The fact that the card manufacturing industry is concentrated, with 88% of the UK market being controlled by the largest 19 publishers, means that on average the producers are of significant size by comparison to all but the largest retailers. This may indicate that they have some power over smaller retailers to negotiate high prices and extract profits from the retail card industry.

There are however other factors which would affect the power of the publishers.

- There is a sufficient number of UK suppliers at 19 for there to be competition

- The card publishing industry is international so this generates further competition from overseas and weakens the power of UK suppliers over UK retailers

- The publishers may be reliant on the greeting card industry if they specialise in this type of printing and thus their power is reduced as they have nowhere else to sell their output other than to greeting card retailer

- The suppliers' product is a major cost for retailers (GC has a margin of 25% and even Mood only a margin of 40%). There will therefore be greater resistance to price increases

- There is low (but some) differentiation between suppliers' products, so switching is fairly easy for retailers, thereby lowering the power of suppliers

- In a recession there may be surplus production capacity for producers thereby increasing the power of retailers

Producers may be able to sell directly to consumers (mail order; internet) which would increase the suppliers' power by cutting out the retailers as intermediaries if the gap between wholesale and retail prices becomes too large.

Other suppliers to the retail card industry should also be considered – for example, lessors of high street retail properties. In a recession their power may be significantly reduced as many properties become vacant and retailers have more choice at the end of contractual rental periods.

(ii) **Substitutes**

The most obvious substitute for the traditional greeting card is the e-card which may be sent more cheaply and can have additional features (eg sound, personalised photos). This will limit the prices that consumers are willing to pay for traditional cards but may also increase the demands made from the format of traditional cards. It would be easy for consumers to switch to the e-card.

The fact that producers may be able to sell directly to consumers could also be seen as a substitute for the service that greeting card retailers offer.

Other forms of communication on a special occasion may substitute for greeting cards if prices rise too much (eg text messages, e-mails, telephone calls, letters, delivered presents such as cakes/flowers/wine etc).

One of the major threats to the card industry is that it is a non essential purchase which may be forgone in a recession or as a response to using paper which is an environmentally unfriendly activity. In this case some consumers may cease purchasing cards and substitute this with not buying any form of greeting or communication.

Examiner's comments:

Requirement (a) asked candidates to provide an analysis the industry using two of Porter's Five Forces: the power of suppliers and threats from substitutes.

Nearly all candidates were able to discuss the power of suppliers. However a large majority only discussed the card manufacturers and failed to mention any of the other suppliers to the business. As required, answers were generally industry focussed, with only weaker candidates discussing company specific issues. Candidates were reasonably good at using the information in the scenario to explain the card manufacturers' position and mentioned issues such as switching cost, and differentiation. Few candidates picked up on the threat from overseas suppliers. Stronger candidates included a conclusion on the power of suppliers.

With regards to substitutes, a majority of candidates only mentioned e-cards as a possible substitute. Hardly any candidates picked up on the issue raised in the question about the manufacturers supplying directly to the public. Stronger candidates thought more broadly and mentioned text messages and social networking sites as substitutes. Stronger candidates included a conclusion.

(b) (i) **Competitive position**

GC is a small participant within the greeting card retail industry. It cannot therefore compete on cost with larger companies such the 'big five' and with Mood in particular. This is due to the fact that larger companies have economies of scale. These may include:

- Large orders with publishers giving discounts

- Ability to have power over suppliers (per Porter's Five Force Model) to negotiate superior terms of trade. This includes not just suppliers of cards but other major costs such as rental agreements with leaseholders

- Greater customer awareness

- Larger shops with a wider range of cards to attract customers

- Better financing terms

- Fixed administration costs on a larger scale spread over more units of output

GC does not attempt to compete on the basis of cost. Instead it differentiates the products it sells by selling good quality cards and providing a high level of service. Given that the quality card market is 10% of the total market, it could be described as competition in a niche market, although this description might be more appropriately applied to retailers selling hand-made cards.

Within this market, GC is growing its market share. However this increase is very minor and is only being achieved through more investment in more outlets rather than through generic growth (see below).

Even though GC's market share is growing slowly, the market itself is growing by 4.5% in 2008 and 2.8% in 2007. This may, at first sight, be indicative of a reduction in competition in the industry. However it is clear that there are few barriers to entry as set up costs are low, and this is evidenced by 'small retailers constantly leaving and joining the industry'. As a consequence, if the market continues to grow, then this may draw in new entrants and increase competition. Conversely however there appear to be few barriers to exit so if the recession becomes more severe then retailers exiting the industry may reduce the impact on remaining participants.

One caveat is that the growth in the overall market may not be reflected in a growth in the 'quality' market. It would only be growth in this sector that would benefit GC and here there are fewest barriers to entry, so there may be little benefit as new entrants are drawn in. However, it is at the higher end of the market that the effects of the recession are most acutely felt, and this will serve to deter potential new entrants.

More generally, a product can be positioned in a number of ways eg via a price or emphasis on a particular characteristic or set of characteristics. In other words, positioning means giving a product or service a place relative to its competitors on factors such as quality, price, image, providing status, etc. The price-quality trade-off is therefore just one aspect of market positioning.

The overall market could be seen in the diagram below.

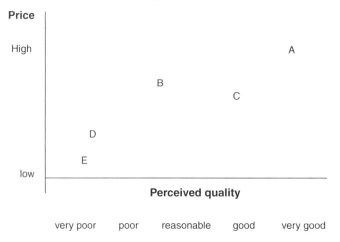

In the diagram:

C represents GC where price and quality are maintained at a high level

D represents Mood and other big retailers where price and quality are mid market ranges

B could represent strategy 2 (see below) if service was cut and price increased

E represents Cardworld Ltd

A represents the specialist retailers with hand-made cards charging high prices

Within this mapping, one might regard any of the positions on the price-quality trade off as acceptable, other than **B** (which is dominated by GC's position C which offers better quality at a lower price). However:

- Quality is a question of perception where it is not always readily observable by the customer.

- The relative price difference between companies is more observable than quality.

- Short term and long term price/quality effects may be different as reputation may ultimately be affected.

One further issue is the profit margin achieved by GC which is only 25% compared to 40% for Mood. This is despite being a differentiator where one would normally expect greater profit margins. In terms of competition by price if there were to be a price war then there is limited scope for GC as once other operating costs are deducted the operating margins are much lower.

Threats to GC's competitive position

- If the recession deepens then there may be more pressure on the 'quality' market as consumers may substitute cheaper cards for quality cards.

- If the larger participants in the industry are suffering reductions in sales then they may attempt to become more broad-based by selling across the range of quality rather than focussing on up-market and mid-market sales.

- There is the threat of substitutes with competition from internet and mail order sales and from e-cards. This may increase in future even though e-cards in particular have not yet had much impact.

- Exchange rates variations with the £/euro may make supplies more expensive and GC only has one significant supplier, which is in the eurozone. Increases in costs may not be able to be passed on in full. Other retailers appear to be mainly UK-supplied, so they will not experience similar problems to the same extent.

(ii) **GC's performance**

Superficially, GC has experienced growth in sales and operating profits of around 5% in 2009 and 6% in 2008. However this growth can be attributed largely to expansion in the number of outlets. The increase in profit is not therefore, of itself, evidence of improved performance. The business was expanding over this period and an element of the increase in profitability was due to larger scale activity rather than increased efficiency or improved market conditions.

Indeed, the data analysis shows that over the period 2007 to 2009 there was a reduction in performance after allowing for scale differences in terms of the increase in the number of new outlets. Specifically, the above table shows that the revenue per shop fell by around £10,000 per annum in each year, which is about a 4% pa reduction. Similarly, operating profits per shop fell by around 4.7% in 2009 and 3.6% in 2008.

This is also reflected in floorspace, as the data shows, the average floorspace per shop is unchanged following the opening of new outlets. So, controlling for shop size, the average revenue and operating profits per sq metre will parallel the figures per shop.

Overall therefore, while there has been some growth in sales and profits this cannot, with any certainty, be attributed to improved performance. The major contributory factors in improving sales/profits appear to be a larger scale of activity from an increased number of shops. This would be reflected in a greater investment (even if the shops are leased) and thus a greater overall expected return.

The increased in market wide sales may have also benefited GC.

It should however be recognised that, while the performance of the company may not have improved, the results have been achieved with the onset of the recession. The performance of management may therefore have been reasonable. Nevertheless, market growth would indicate that the recession has not, as yet, affected the overall UK industry significantly.

Comparison with Mood Cards

Caution needs to be exercised in comparing the performance of GC and Mood Cards as:

*   The scale of activities is so significantly different that the nature of the operations and financing is unlikely to be comparable

*   Whilst the two companies operate in the same industry, they address different sectors of the market and thus their fortunes may have been affected differently by different factors

Notwithstanding these reservations about making comparisons, it is clear from the data that Mood is performing rather better than GC. This is clearly true in absolute terms but also, adjusting for scale in terms of outlets, Mood appears to significantly outperform GC.

The comparison of revenue/profit per outlet is not valid as Mood has a larger average floorspace for each of its outlets. The data for sales per sq metre of floorspace is a more valid comparison and this shows Mood generating revenues of £2,500 per sq metre (£460m/184k sq metres) compared to £1,533 per sq metre (£10.58m/6,900 sq metres) for GC (which is 63% greater).

Examining the change in performance of the two companies over the period 2007-2009 it appears that while GC is expanding the number of shops, Mood is contracting its shops. Despite this, Mood it still expanding sales by over 10% and operating profits by 22.3% and 23.7% in 2008 and 2009 respectively.

When adjusting for scale, in terms of the number of shops, Mood is increasing operating profits by 25.0% (£40,430/£32,340) and 23.7% (£50,000/£40,430) in 2008 and 2009 respectively. This is far greater than GC.

One comparison with Mood is using the BCG matrix which looks at the relative market share (market strength) compared to the market leader or major competitor (Mood) and the overall market growth rate (market attractiveness).

Relative Market share

Market growth		High	Low
	H I G H	STAR	QUESTION MARK
	L O W	CASH COW	**GC** x DOG

Examiner's comments:

Requirement (b) was the data analysis section of the paper which has been indicated as a regular feature of Business Strategy papers. Part (i) asked candidates to analyse GC's competitive position and explain any threats to that position. Part (ii) asked candidates to evaluate the performance of GC and draw comparisons with the market leader.

Most candidates used the data available to help them in their discussion of competitive position and performance. Stronger candidates set out the information coherently in a table format and included data relative to the size of the business (eg revenue or operating profit compared to floorspace/shops/employees). However, only a minority fully explained cause and effect relationships based on this relative data analysis.

Most candidates identified Green Card's position in the overall market, a number using the BCG matrix to assist them in their discussion. Stronger candidates went on to discuss Green Card's position in the niche market. A fair number used a SWOT analysis to discuss Green Card's position. Most candidates gave suitable specific threats for Green Cards. Candidates who had planned their answer well, could analyse the performance of Green Cards and compare it to Mood. Again, those who had considered size relationships were able to give stronger explanations.

Weaker candidates demonstrated a lack of planning in their answer and used the data randomly on an ad hoc basis in the main body of their writing, with a surprising number of candidates failing to relate the data to floorspace/shops/employees. Some weaker candidates also failed to distinguish clearly between parts (i) and (ii) of the requirement and produced a merged answer. Also, some very weak candidates produced a largely, or entirely, descriptive answer with little, or no, use of the data.

(c) **Ethical aspects**

An ethical issue that arises is whether the company is sacrificing profit/sales (and therefore self interest) in favour of promoting a more environmentally friendly and sustainable product.

In this context, corporate responsibility is concerned with the ways in which an organisation exceeds the minimum obligations required of it through the law and other regulations. This can relate to internal aspects of the business and related stakeholders or to external aspects and external stakeholders.

In the case of the environmentally-friendly cards there are a number of ethical and CSR issues.

Positive aspects:

- The decision to sell these cards offers consumers a choice of using cards with at least some recycled paper which is better for the environment than normal cards

- A (small) donation is made for each card sold to an environmentally beneficial charity

Negative aspects

- Transparency – it is not clear from the heading 'Made with Recycled Paper', that only part of the card is recycled. If a large percentage is from recycled paper then this may not be an issue. If it is a small percentage then it may amount to dishonesty and deceit.

- Motivation – while the consequences of selling these cards may be ethically beneficial, the motivation for doing so by GC does not appear to be based in ethics. This may be indicated by the fact GC is withdrawing from the market due to the fact that they are not making enough profit.

- Motivation can also be challenged on the basis that the additional price charged to the customer (£1.00) is far greater then the money handed over to charities (£0.01). GC is therefore making an additional profit of £0.99 per card, which means that it is exploiting consumers' ethical values for its own profit.

- The sale of these cards uses a significant amount of non recycled paper and therefore does some damage to the environment.

Business aspects

- The profit per card is almost double that of normal cards, so if customers substitute buying recycled cards for normal cards then a greater profit will be made

- New, environmentally conscious customers may be drawn into shops, thereby increasing revenues

- The higher price may deter customers, so volumes sold may be small

- There is loss of 5% of floorspace in accommodating ethical cards, so if volumes sold are low it may not justify the floor space occupied in terms of opportunity costs, despite a higher contribution per unit

- There may be additional fixed costs in dealing with a different type of card

- There may be reputational damage if it becomes known that such a small contribution is made per card or that the proportion of recycled paper is low

Withdrawal from the market would negate the above costs and benefits. It may also send a particular signal that the company was never serious about environmental issues. It also demonstrates uncertainty in applying strategy, given that entry into, and exit from, this market are within a short period.

Examiner's comments:

Requirement (c) asks for a discussion of the ethical and business issues of participating in the environmentally friendly cards market and the withdrawal from that market. Most answers discussed both ethical and business issues. Weak candidates confined their answer to how it could be unwise from an ethics and business point of view to withdraw from such a market, as it may damage reputation. Only strong candidates discussed the issues highlighted in the scenario in relation to the profit margin on the cards compared to the size of donation, and the fact that they were made from a small amount of recycled paper, despite the claim that they were 'made from recycled paper'.

(d) **Strategy 1**

In concept, the strategy of cross-branding may have a number of benefits. These include:

- Generation of additional income
- Drawing more people into the shops (higher 'footfall')
- Improve reputation of the GC brand by linking it to another quality brand

Disadvantages include:

- Reduced floorspace may mean fewer sales of the primary product (eg smaller range of cards could be displayed, although some floorspace is already being freed up by pulling out of ethical cards)

- There is reputational risk if C4O is unpopular

- GC may be tied into a contract giving up floorspace with little benefit if C4O does not prove popular

Fee options – data and numbers

The fee of £100 per sq metre would generate a total fee of £138,000 (6,900 sq m × 20% × £100).

If operating profit is taken to approximate contribution then 20% of total operating profit would be £169,200 (£846,000 × 20%). Thus if operating profit is reduced pro rata to floor space then the contract would not be worthwhile.

However, the income would be low risk, as it is not dependent on market conditions, but only on C4O fulfilling the contract.

The revenues from C4O could also be compared to the cost of renting additional floorspace to replace that lost. This might not always be possible close to the original floorspace but would represent a measure of comparison.

The 10% contingent fee has a number of problems:

- GC would be assuming part of the business risk of C4O. This means that the amount of the fee income would be unknown and dependent on C4O's success.

- If C4O withdrew from a shop it may have a contractual right to leave floorspace vacant with GC having no fee from it.

- If C4O can generate as much revenue per sq metre as GC then this would (assuming pro rata to floorspace) be: £2.116m (£10.58m × 20%). This would then generate £211,600 revenue for GC (£2.116m × 10%). It is however a major assumption that C4O can generate the same revenue as an established business.

Strategy 2

The cost reduction strategy could be beneficial if costs can be reduced without affecting the service given to customers. If, however, costs can be cut only by reducing service quality, then there may be lost sales in both the short run and the long run. The contribution lost from the sales reduction may outweigh any cost reduction.

Lost service may include:

- Damaging GC's quality reputation in the long run.
- Long queues at tills putting customers off buying in the short term.

Comparing the staffing of GC to Mood then:

	2009 estimated
Employees per shop	
GC	10
Mood	10
Sq m of floorspace per employee	
GC (6900/460)	15 sq m
Mood (184000/9200)	20 sq m
Revenue per employee	
GC (£10.58m/460)	£23,000
Mood (£460m/9,200	£50,000

While GC's staffing per shop is the same as Mood, this is not comparable as Mood's shops are one third larger. Once this is considered, then GC appears to have more staff per 1,000sq m of floorspace, ie they have only 15 sq m each to cover rather than 20 sq m as for Mood.

Mood staff also generate more sales per employee.

The key question however is about the marginal impact to GC of reducing staff as it has a higher quality ethos than Mood.

Also the comparison may not be valid, as some staff may not be employed in the shops but in head office. Due to economies of scale Mood may have proportionately fewer than GC.

Recommendation

Overall a review of staff is needed before any decision is taken but if there is evidence of overstaffing this is likely to be the better option as it retains the core competences of GC and does not concede operating capacity to an unknown partner for uncertain benefits.

Examiner's comments:

Requirement (d) asked for an evaluation of the two proposed strategies with clear and reasoned advice. A majority presented their answer in briefing note format.

Strategy 1 was generally well attempted with candidates discussing how it could affect the reputation (positively or negatively) and that there could be an opportunity for cross branding. Only strong candidates utilised the data provided in the scenario to discuss the fee and compared the two fee-based options. Those that did this scored highly on this requirement.

For scenario 2 most candidates discussed quality and reputational issues, however, again only strong candidates utilised the data provided in the scenario. Many answers tended to focus on the effects of redundancies on staff morale and the costs of redundancy. Better answers concentrated on the lack of fit with the service-related strategic position of the firm, but very few made the link back to any per-employee analysis produced in requirement (b).

The majority of candidates gave a recommendation, but in many cases the reasoning was thin, or was just an assertion of the best course of action.

25 Efficiency Systems Ltd (ES)

Marking guide

			Knowledge	Skill	Marks
(a)	(i)	Critical success factors	2	3	
	(ii)	Mission statement	1	3	
					8
(b)		Business plan assessment/additional information	4	12	15
(c)		Key risks	3	7	9
			10	25	32

General comments:

The scenario in this question involves a small, recently formed enterprise with two entrepreneurial owner/directors. The company develops and markets software to improve the operational processes of organisations. The directors are seeking additional finance and they require assistance in drawing up a business plan to present to the bank is support of a loan application. An assessment of the key risks facing the business, assuming that the loan is granted, is also required.

(a) (i) **Critical success factors**

For ES the critical success factors in seeking to expand the business may include:

- Successful development of the Z-Info system in a reasonable period of time at reasonable cost

- Z-Info and existing Comax software must be constantly developed so they continue to outperform similar products from closest rivals in terms of delivering cost savings to clients

- The service delivery and support must outperform rivals in combination with software

- Winning an adequate number of tenders to secure new larger customers at a reasonable tender price that generates adequate profit

- Securing adequate finance to develop the Z-Info and employ the new staff required to install and operate the system for clients

- Appointing and retaining key staff to deliver the core competences of the business

- Retain sufficient agility compared to competitors, in a fast moving industry in terms of products and skills of staff

(ii) **Mission statement**

To develop and supply our software products and to provide supporting services in order to deliver significant cost savings to our customers. This will be achieved by developing staff's skills and other resources to compete with the market leaders in our sector of the industry.

(b) **Introduction and background**

Management

There is insufficient detail about managerial skills and background. The respective roles of the two directors need to be explained in more detail.

More information may be required to assure the bank on the following matters:

- Dependence of ES on the two directors for skills and finance

- Lack of skills and experience outside IT for the two directors (eg management or finance experience)

- The age of Mike is a concern as he is 62 and nearing retirement, in particular because he is developing the new software and customising the existing Comax software. His knowledge, as program writer, would be difficult to replace

Products and services

More detail is needed on the nature of Comax, the existing software. For example:

- How software works in relation to clients' systems

- The amount of work needed to turn the standard Comax program into one customised for a client's needs

- More evidence than one case study of how existing clients have been helped by existing software (evidence of satisfaction, such as repeat business)

In respect of Z-Info, much more information and evidence of its current and future operational capability is needed. Specifically:

- Detailed specification of the software, what it is intended to achieve and how it differs from existing software in the industry

- Comparisons to other commercial software available (industry standard)

- Evidence of field tests

- Trial runs with clients' systems

- Project plan for Z-Info development and time-line for completion

Fees

A more detailed description of each of the activities is needed including how much revenue each has generated in the two years of business.

A list of clients is also needed, perhaps with revenues generated for each and contracts in place with each.

Marketing

A much more detailed marketing plan is needed which specifies the nature and size of the market that the business is in. Detail is needed about target companies and the process about how the right to tender will be awarded.

More detail on pricing is needed. How are prices set generally and particularly the strategy for tender pricing? Winning a tender needs to be distinguished from making a profit on a contract. Cost analyses are therefore also needed.

The aim of achieving a high success rate needs to be supported by marketing evidence. Also evidence is needed from any past tender experience.

A policy on relationship marketing for existing customers is needed.

Competitors

More details of competitors will be needed, eg:

- The names of the entities that are likely to be in the tender process with you
- The nature of their products
- An outline of their programs for developing new products, to the extent this may be known
- A summary of the customer base of main rivals
- Evidence to support claim that Comax is a 'superior' product

Financing requirements

A detailed financial history is needed including financial statements and cash flows for the years of operation.

The assumptions underlying the forecasts need to be spelt out and justified. Full forecast financial statements are needed, including cash flows, for perhaps three years ahead.

Show separately the impact of:

(i)   existing contracts (highly certain)

(ii)   probable contracts (eg under final negotiation or repeat business with existing customers) and

(iii)   more speculative future contracts that may be won with new customers

A success rate of 'one in three' on new contracts is very high if the number of tendering companies is large. This needs to be justified but is likely to be viewed as unduly optimistic. Some sensitivity analysis is needed to explore risks and the consequences of over-optimism.

A more detailed explanation of what borrowed funds will be used for is also necessary.

Given the level of profit being earned, the directors' remuneration totalling £80,000 seems high for a growing business as it is taking much-needed cash out of the business.

Additional information

Also needed in the business plan are:

- Detailed business strategy
- Executive summary
- Supporting documentation

The supporting documentation in appendices may include:

- Tax returns of ES since incorporation

- Statement of personal wealth of Jon and Mike (eg independent valuations of directors' houses)

- Copies of Jon and Mike's personal tax returns

- Copies of any key contracts

- CVs of Jon and Mike

- The bid documentation from the company offering £500,000 to acquire ES

Summary

As it stands, there is little in the business plan to support a loan of the size being requested. Specifically:

- The profit projections appear uncertain as they depend on a new product not yet fully developed

- The projections appear optimistic as they depend on a one in three success rate for tenders when there are three to five tenders expected for each contract

- The key corporate asset is the software which is poor security on a loan

- The cash flows appear to be weak even with optimistic sales predictions

A major positive point, however, is that the bank may still lend based on the fact that the directors' houses provide sufficient security to cover the loans requested, provided that the valuations are credible given reductions in house prices in the recession.

Examiner's comments:

Requirement (b) asked candidates to critically assess each section of the draft business plan and identify any additional information. This requirement produced mixed responses. The majority of candidates presented their answer with structured headings as per the question. A minority of candidates did not take this approach, which often resulted in disjointed and weaker answers. Stronger candidates thought about the user's needs and focussed on information that the bank would want to know. In asking for additional information some answers were too vague just noting 'more detail' was needed while others seemed unrealistic in asking for almost every possible piece of information. The best answers addressed all sections and indicated, selectively, the need for key additional information, both in the body of the answer and in a section at the end.

(c) **Risks:**

- Failure of the business may lead to loss of directors' homes

- Failure of Z-Info to outperform competitors would mean there is no competitive advantage and winning new substantial business would be unlikely. (Given it is in development stage its feasibility may even be in doubt)

- Reliance on few products (existing software) means there is no diversification of risk if one product fails

- Reliance on two key personnel. Risks of them leaving, retiring, having conflicts, illnesses may put the entire future of the business into doubt

- High fixed costs in developing Z-Info mean high operating gearing and volatility of profits

- High debt finance means high financial gearing and volatility of profits with interest needing to be paid. Jon and Mike initially invested a total of £200,000 in equity. The current borrowing request at £250,000 is greater than this amount. Even if there are some retained earnings, financial gearing is around 50%

- Intellectual property rights over software may be questioned if it was developed while working at University of Northern England

- The industry is rapidly changing and any competitive advantage that does exist can be eroded away quickly

As the business grows, there needs to be reliance on new staff rather than the owners themselves carrying out all the work. Staff selection and retention is a key risk in this respect.

Examiner's comments:

Requirement (c) asks candidates to explain the key risks assuming that the bank loan was to be made available. This requirement also produced a mixed response.

Good answers gave detailed specific risks relating to the scenario. Weaker candidates took a text book approach and presented risks that any business could face without relating them to the circumstances facing the company in the specific scenario. Sometimes this approach appeared to arise from the use of a form of the PESTEL framework to analyse risks, and thereby tended to provide rather generic analysis which was insufficiently focused on the firm. This highlights the more general problem of over-reliance on frameworks in an inflexible manner, often resulting in very generic discussion.

26 Total Equipment Hire Ltd (TEH)

		Knowledge	Skill	Marks
(a)	Divestment and cost reduction	2	7	8
(b)	Closure, measuring performance	3	6	8
(c)	Joint venture	3	7	9
		8	20	25

General comments:

The company in this scenario hires out plant and equipment to other businesses in the building and construction industries. It has three divisions: heavy equipment, small equipment and scaffolding. Due to the recession the building industry has suffered significantly and TEH has similarly suffered a significant reduction in trade. As a consequence, there is doubt over the company's liquidity and going concern as it may be unable to make a forthcoming interest payment. In order to improve liquidity a number of proposals have been put forward; first, to sell off about 20% of equipment and to reduce labour and other costs; second, to close a division; and third, to enter into a joint venture to hire equipment at deeply discounted price to an overseas development project.

(a) **Divestment**

The divestment of equipment would release £60 million cash. However operating capability would be downsized significantly by 20%. If the operations director is correct in stating this cash is only half what the equipment is worth, then this would mean that to restore operating capability in future would be possible only at significant cost. There is therefore a significant risk that, in order to attain short term liquidity in this way, the company will be smaller for some time to come.

This may have effects on costs and efficiency as economies of scale (eg better utilisation of support activities over more output, spreading of fixed costs, ability to satisfy large orders) and economies of scope (eg simultaneous deliveries to common sites or common regions) would be reduced.

Although the suggestion is that disposals will only be made where there are multiple items held, there is still likely to be an impact on the marketing strategy of having available for customers a wide variety of equipment at all times. If utilisation rates are (even in a recession) 70%, then a reduction of 20% in equipment would put average utilisation at around 87.5% (70/80). Minimal daily or weekly usage variability – and variability of usage between different items of equipment – would mean customers could not be supplied reliably with the items they wish. This is likely to have an impact on TEH's 'quality' market positioning.

As the economy recovers and underlying utilisation rates improve, this problem is likely to become more pronounced.

The reductions are likely to affect each division differently. For instance in the heavy equipment division the cost of losing a sale from hiring will include the loss of hiring out operators who may need to be made redundant.

The amount of cash raised from the sale is much greater than the half yearly interest payments. This may be a financing issue to give more liquidity than immediately necessary. Also however it may give more strategic flexibility to discount prices or invest in some new, but different, items more suitable to demand during a recession.

Cost reduction

The cost reduction exercise may have strategic consequences as TEH has positioned itself as a provider of a differentiated product (per Porter's generic strategy). If costs are cut, and as a consequence the service quality is reduced, then the marketing message may be confused with that of cost leadership. This may result in long term damage to the brand.

Other criticisms of this approach would be that it may increase cash over time, rather than immediately, as with the sale of equipment. It may also be that, in net terms, it is not cash generating if customers are put off by the change in service levels. This would mean that the changes could be revenue reducing which may offset any cost savings.

The case in favour of cost reductions is that if equipment is scaled down by 20%, then support costs to maintain, deliver and operate equipment could also be reduced (eg administration and maintenance costs and heavy equipment operators). In this respect, the two aspects of the finance director's strategy may be seen as consistent.

It would also appear that hire charges have been reduced. Utilisation has fallen by 12.5% (from 80% to 70%) while revenue has fallen by 25% (from £60m to £45m). This would imply that prices have fallen by 14.3% . [where i = price change then $(1 - i) = 0.75/0.875)$]

This may mean that this is a strategy to become a low cost provider and cost reductions are consistent with this pricing policy. However, this would be a hasty conclusion as the key issue is relative prices compared to competitors. If all sectors of the market are reducing prices in the recession then the relative position of TEH as a quality provider may be maintained in terms of its relative pricing strategy. Service reductions would not therefore necessarily be consistent with price reductions.

Examiner's comments:

Requirement (a) asked candidates to explain the impact of the proposed strategy to divest equipment and reduce costs.

Most candidates made a reasonable attempt, but a significant minority did not refer directly to the fundamental cash flow problems facing the firm.

Stronger candidates answered both parts of the question and included headings for divestment and cost reduction. Nearly all candidates mentioned the effects the strategies would have on quality and reputation and most mentioned that this was moving away from their core strategy. Some noted the need for a major cultural change in the organisation if the cost reduction strategy is pursued, questioning whether or not this was feasible. Most focussed upon the downside of the suggestions with little focus in the fact that it would actually solve the immediate problem of paying the interest and the threat this was posing to going concern.

Very few candidates used the data given in the scenario to calculate revised utilisation rates, or that hire prices have fallen. Weaker candidates largely ignored the cost reduction element of the requirement and focused mainly, or solely, on divestment issues.

(b) **Financial performance**

The financial performance of the divisions is likely to be difficult to determine as, although they are controlled separately, they are not operationally independent. In particular:

Interdependence of revenues – customers come to TEH for a comprehensive range of products which can be delivered simultaneously. Thus, for instance, scaffolding is requested alongside other items of equipment and delivered together. The closure of (say) scaffolding might therefore have an adverse impact on the revenues of small tools. The converse would also be true if the small tools division was closed.

The extent of this interdependence of revenues needs to be determined.

As the heavy equipment division and the small tools division have few, if any, common customers there is likely to be less interdependence of revenues in this case.

Interdependence of costs – there are likely to be a number of costs incurred jointly between the divisions which may have been allocated. Also, there may be some scale economies for storage and maintenance of equipment and administration, so closure of one division would impact on the costs of the other divisions. As already noted, there are likely to be efficiencies of delivery costs in terms of economies of scope.

The impact of closing a division might be slightly different than 'across the board' cost savings as suggested by the finance director. Specifically, if the cost drivers relate to a product line the costs may be saved but, more likely, the cost drivers are likely to relate to functions which cut across the three product divisions. In this case, performance is difficult to identify as the costs are common and the cost savings from closure may be limited due to these interdependencies.

Non-financial performance

Given the recession and the significant impact on the building industry, poor financial performance may be viewed as inevitable in the short term. If the divisions, however, are still satisfying customers and outperforming competitors then the company may be well positioned to improve performance with the recovery. Some divisions may, in this respect, be better than others and this may form the basis of any performance assessment and closure decision rather than financial data. Possible approaches include:

Benchmarking – This may be internal, where the divisions are benchmarked against each other but this is not likely to be helpful in determining closure where there are many common functions between the divisions (eg delivery).

Competitive benchmarking may be more helpful in assessing performance against competitors (eg delivery times, range of products, prices).

Activity benchmarking (generic) could be fairly close to existing activity and look at say specialist scaffolding firms. More generally, for the function of delivery it could be compared against couriers and specialist logistics companies.

KPIs – These could be developed from benchmarking or internal measures but may include customer satisfaction, delays in availability of request products, delivery time once product is available, collection times, product failures/breakdowns per 100 hires.

The Balanced Scorecard could form a framework for these KPIs but would need to be focused on the closure decision, rather than measuring performance generally.

Examiner's comments:

Requirement (b) asked candidates to explain the issues to be considered in measuring financial and non financial performance in order to determine which division should be closed.

Again, the biggest criticism is that the immediacy of the liquidity issue was ignored and most candidates failed to talk about this being a longer term solution. Most candidates split their answer between financial and non-financial issues. Joint costs were mentioned by most, but only stronger candidates discussed the interdependence of revenues and costs.

Many candidates discussed performance generally without relating it to the immediate purpose of deciding which division to close. Many of the candidates taking this approach used the Balanced Scorecard framework rather too inflexibly and thereby tended to miss many of the key issues concerning closure. This again highlights the problem of the inflexible use of frameworks and their application in an uncritical manner.

(c) **Benefits**

- Cash is raised without selling off the assets

- The assets will be available to restore growth to the business when the recession is ended

- While the prices are discounted below UK levels, some revenue would be generated from underutilised equipment

- The joint venture structure would share the risks of the project without needing to establish any permanent relationship with the other party

- The JV would allow incentives for both parties to exploit the rewards, while contributing their (very different) core competences. A mere transport contract may just provide a fixed reward for ITT and not the incentive for it to seek further opportunities for the mutual benefit of both parties

Problems

There will be a significant reduction in the availability of equipment in the UK if there is a commitment to it being used overseas on the new project. In this respect many of the problems noted above for the finance director's strategy of 20% divestment would be repeated here. There are however some key differences:

- 40% of the heavy equipment could be unavailable and, as this makes up 70% of total equipment held for hire, this would be a reduction of 28% in operating capability compared to 20% with the FD's proposal

- The focus of the reductions is even more significant in the heavy equipment division and these customers may be disproportionately affected

- The upfront cash amount is lower than with the FD's proposal and does not cover the interest payment. Thus, the immediate liquidity issues may not be resolved by this venture as they were by the FD's proposal

- The JV agreement requires equipment to be made immediately available if requested. This means that they may need to be withheld from longer term hire in the UK. This could create a situation where equipment is not rented out in the UK at relatively high rates, but is only being reserved for use overseas so is not actually earning any fees

- The JV arrangement is for three years so it may extend into the recovery period after the recession when utilisation rates increase and there may be a much greater opportunity cost in lost UK revenues

- The joint venture structure may give rise to conflict as it relates to the conduct of an entire project rather than just a contract for specified transport services. There is therefore a need for independent assurance over the parties (eg over fees collection and sharing)

Issues for clarification include:

- There may be a risk of damage or loss of equipment in transport or overseas. It is not clear who bears this risk (eg who stores the equipment while it is not being used overseas)

- The heavy equipment requires a skilled operator in the UK and who incurs the cost of providing this needs to be established

- As ITT is dealing directly with the client, any additional benefits arising from the contract may accrue to ITT rather than jointly with TEH

- The hire days need to be defined, as days in transit will not attract revenue but will be days out of use for TEH

- The fee split seems unreasonable given that ITT are merely transporting the goods and supplying the client contact. In effect, if ITT is getting half and the fee is 75% of the UK fee then this is only 37.5% of the UK fee coming to TEH. The basis of the split needs to be justified and may be renegotiated

- Is there exclusivity or could ITT also be using rivals and leaving TEH products largely unutilised but held in reserve in case they are requested

- There may be reputational damage if ITT does not provide a good quality of service – although the impact in the UK may be restricted given the location and specialised nature of the contract. The need for a service level agreement needs clarification

Requirement (c) asked candidates to evaluate the benefits and problems of the proposed joint venture and to identify any matters to be clarified. This part of the question resulted in the weakest answers.

The majority of candidates discussed generic issues relating to joint ventures. Only stronger candidates related their answer to the specific points in the question. Most seemed to think that the joint venture was a good idea – better candidates discussed the shortfall of £5 million for the required interest payment, and the fact that the contract may not be a good deal after assessing the costs and benefits involved. Again, only the better answers attempted any data analysis or recognised the change in the situation likely to be faced by the company as the economy emerges out of recession, together with the implications for the other proposed strategies.

27 Blazing Bicycles Ltd (BB)

Marking guide

		Knowledge	Skill	Marks
(a)	Industry and product lifecycle	3	5	7
(b)	International competitive advantage	3	5	7
(c)	Calculations	–	8	
	Evaluation of performance and competitive position	2	6	
				12
(d)	External risk factors	3	6	8
(e)	Evaluate strategies 1 and 2	2	7	8
		13	37	42

General comments:

The scenario in this question involves an independent bicycle retailer which operates a chain of ten shops across the UK, selling high quality bicycles and bike accessories. Information was given in the question about the development of the UK bicycle retailing and manufacturing industry since the 1930s, together with detail regarding the nature of the competition and relevant environmental and market factors. The company's recent financial results (which were provided) are giving some cause for concern, with profits falling despite a number of new stores being opened. Candidates were also supplied with a risk analysis prepared by the Managing Director which listed the key commercial risks currently facing the company. Two alternative strategies are being considered to address these issues: expand the product range to offer other sporting and outdoor equipment or set up specialist in-store bicycle workshops to offer repairs and servicing.

This question was the mini case, incorporating some data analysis and, at 42 marks, was the longest question on the paper. The requirements were broken down to help candidates in developing answer headings and assessing mark allocation. Overall candidates performed reasonably well on this question, showing good knowledge of the models tested and on the whole demonstrating improved data analysis skills.

(a) Industry and product life cycle analysis

The concept of life cycle analysis is used to describe the phases of development that an industry or product goes through.

The key stages of the life cycle are:

- **Introduction** – a newly invented product or service is made available for purchase and organisations attempt to develop buyer interest.

- **Growth** – a period of rapid expansion of demand or activity as the industry finds a market and competitors are attracted by its potential.

- **Maturity** – a relatively stable period of time where there is little change in sales volumes year to year but competition between firms intensifies as growth slows down.

- **Decline** – a falling off in activity levels as firms leave the industry and the industry ceases to exist or is absorbed into some other industry.

Some industry life cycles are identical in pattern and timing to that of their product (eg the steel industry). Others have longer life cycles than the particular products, eg the music industry which has endured from sheet music till MP3 and downloads, merely releasing (and re-releasing) its music as new products as the format changes. This appears to have been the case with the bicycle retailing industry which has seen a variety of products come and go within the industry life cycle.

Thus the cycle has been influenced by two factors:

(i) Changes in the usage to which bikes are put (transport, leisure etc). Such changes lengthen the industry life cycle but may not necessarily involve a new or separate product.

(ii) Changes in the types of bike (products).

The industry appears to have followed a traditional pattern of introduction, growth, maturity and decline from 1800 through to the mid 1960s, when the product was essentially a bicycle as a means of transport.

Thus it took a while for sales to develop after the introduction of the bicycle in its modern form in the late 1800s. Then from 1930 onwards the industry experienced a period of growth and expansion as bicycles became a popular form of transport. After a short period of stability, the industry can be seen to enter decline in the 1950s with the advent of more affordable motor car transport, lasting to the mid 1960s.

From the mid 1960s the industry appears to enter a different phase, with the bicycle becoming a leisure rather than transportation product.

In terms of the product life cycle it is common within an industry for products to overlap. As one product declines, another is in maturity and another is growing (either because of changes in consumer demand or technological change). This can be seen in the bicycle industry from the mid 1960s onwards where the product life cycles of individual products such as small wheel bikes or mountain bikes have overlapped at different times. It could however be argued that these are design modifications to the same basic product, rather than different products themselves.

The overall trend from the mid 60s to 2010 is one of growth (sales of 0.75m increasing to around 3.25m per the graph), punctuated by periods of rapid expansion then slow-down as a variety of products have come and gone. Hence the small wheeled bicycle and children's version accounted for much of the growth in the late 60s and 1970s, then there was a period of relative stability until the industry developed the mountain bike in the mid 80s, leading to another rapid expansion.

The apparent slowing down in the 90s is likely to have led to intensified competition but changing attitudes to health and the environment have seen the bicycle reinvented as a mode of transport again, leading to another period of growth in the 2000s.

Hence the concepts of both product and industry life cycle do appear to apply in the bicycle industry, which has managed to extend the life of its product by continual innovation and to revitalise its product by responding to changes in the external environment (such as technological developments) and consumer preferences.

Examiner's comments:

In requirement (a) candidates were asked to consider the extent to which the concept of the industry and product lifecycle could be applied to the bicycle retailing industry and to sales of different types of bicycles. Most candidates scored well here, demonstrating appropriate knowledge when describing the lifecycle in its different stages, often with an accompanying diagram. It was pleasing that the majority were able to apply this knowledge well to the scenario. Most candidates distinguished between the industry and product lifecycles, pointing out that the lifecycle of an individual type of bike, eg BMX was typically much shorter than that of the industry and that continued product innovation had allowed the industry lifecycle to be extended. Weaker candidates wrote about the lifecycle in overall terms or incorporated lengthy comments about the impact of the various stages of the lifecycle for a manufacturer, which did not answer the question.

(b) **Competitive advantage and international trade**

> **Examiner note:**
>
> Candidates were not necessarily expected to use two models but both are produced here for marking purposes.

The International Trade Life Cycle suggests that many products pass through a cycle during which high income, mass-consumption countries are initially exporters but subsequently lose their export markets and ultimately become importers of the product from lower-cost economies. This is consistent with the information in the scenario where the UK moved from a net exporter to a net importer of bikes.

From the perspective of the initiator high income country, the pattern of development is as follows:

- **Phase 1. The product is developed in the high income country** – here the UK which was the source of innovation for the modern version of the bicycle. There are two main reasons for this.

    - High income countries provide the greatest demand potential.

    - It is expedient to locate production close to the market during the early period so that the firm can react quickly in modifying the product according to customer preferences.

- **Phase 2. Overseas production starts.** Firms in the innovator's export markets (such as mainland Europe) start to produce the product domestically. Thus, for example, the European market is then shared by the innovative UK firms as well as local manufacturers. This has the effect of reducing the level of exports.

- **Phase 3. Overseas producers compete in export markets.** The costs of the other producers begin to fall as they gain economies of scale and experience. They may also enjoy lower costs of labour and materials than the UK firms (this is particularly true of China and Taiwan). These firms now start to compete with the UK producers in third-party export markets such as, say, the USA.

- **Phase 4. Overseas producers compete in the firm's domestic market.** The new firms become so competitive, due to their lower production costs (the scenario refers to wages in China and Taiwan being less than a third of UK costs), that they start to compete with the UK firms in the UK domestic market. In the bicycle market this eventually led to all major bike manufacturers ceasing production in the UK by 1999 and the majority of bikes and parts being imported from China and Taiwan.

Porter's diamond also provides a framework for assessing the relationship between location and competitive advantage and could be used to explain the UK's historic dominance of bicycle manufacturing:

Factor conditions – the resource inputs needed by the business. Since the UK was instrumental in the development of bicycles a workforce will have developed with the necessary knowledge and skills to design and manufacture bikes.

Home market demand conditions – these shape a firm's priorities and the way it responds to buyer needs. Thus UK manufacturers were successful in places such as USA and mainland Europe which are generally similar to the UK market.

Supporting local industries – manufacturers of gears, brake cables, frames and tyres will have grown up around UK bike manufacturers. Thus the metalwork and engineering expertise of the sewing and armaments industries helped the UK become a world leader in cycle manufacture.

Firm strategy, structure and rivalry – emergence of firms with strong competitive characteristics which are then able to dominate worldwide markets. Since the UK was credited with developing the modern bicycle it had a strong presence in the industry until the later part of the 20th century.

Using this framework the competitive advantage may have passed to China and Taiwan for the following reasons:

- Factor conditions – the availability of a large pool of low cost labour means bikes can be manufactured at a much lower cost

- Home market demand – a large population with a very strong cycling culture

- Supporting local industries – major steel industry and a reputation for expertise in electronics and technology will have supported the development of new carbon fibre frames etc

- Firm strategy, structure and rivalry – the UK has witnessed the decline of its manufacturing base and as it has moved towards service businesses, China and Taiwan have increasingly benefited from the outsourcing of manufacture

Examiner's comments:

In requirement (b) candidates were asked to use models of international trade to explain why the UK had a historic competitive advantage in bicycle manufacture and why this had now passed to countries such as Taiwan and China. The majority of candidates tackled this using Porter's Diamond. Less frequently applied, though also relevant, was the concept of the International trade lifecycle. Most answers explained the UK's historic advantage in terms of its role in developing the modern bicycle, the knowledge and resources available from the sewing machine and armaments industries, and the sophistication of demand. They also identified the key point from the scenario that as a result of low labour costs this advantage had now passed to China and Taiwan. Better candidates developed their answers further, referring to the change in focus in the UK from manufacturing to service industries such that now only 5% of bicycles are manufactured in the UK, China's increasing experience of outsourced manufacturing and technological innovation and its strong cycling culture.

(c)   Refer to appendix for supporting calculations

    (i)   **Competitive position**

        Market positioning

        The information suggests that in 2009 BB had around 1.4% of the UK bicycle retail market (7.178/ 510).

        It is clearly a small player relative to Benhonda (30% share) and the other large retailers which between them account for 25% of the market. However it is probably reasonably large in terms of the independent cycle retailers which between the 2,000 of them hold 45% (or an average share of just 0.0225%). This is further borne out by the fact that BB has 10 shops whereas a large number of the independent retailers are local owner managed businesses with a single shop.

        Each BB outlet has a market share of 0.14% (1.4%/10). An average BB outlet is therefore over 6 times (0.14/0.0225) larger than the average independent outlet.

Competitive stance

Although BB stocks a range of bicycles, it focuses on the sale of high quality bikes and employs staff with specialist knowledge and expertise. This (and its premium pricing discussed below) suggests that it is a differentiator according to Porter's generic strategies.

Pricing

BB's average price is significantly higher (£398 in 2009) than the retail industry average of £150+. This could mean that BB charges more for similar models than competitors but is more likely to be a result of the types of bike sold by BB, which focuses on the higher specification models and may exclude children's bicycles.

The overall market could be seen in the diagram below:

In the diagram:

BB represents BB where price and quality are maintained at a high level

ML represents Benhonda and other big retailers where price and quality are mid market ranges

S represents specialist retailers selling high performance competition bikes

(ii) **Performance**

The key issue here is that although the additional four stores appear to have led to an increase in sales revenue of 32%, this is not sufficient to cover the 61% increase in admin and distribution costs and as a result, overall profit before tax has fallen from £1.1m to £1.089m despite the increase in sales revenue.

Sales volumes

The MD suggests that BB has recently been affected by increased competition as a result of the recession. Although the number of bikes sold has increased from 9,200 in 2007 to 11,000, four additional stores have been opened in this period. Thus the number of bikes sold per store has fallen from an average of 1533 in 2007 to 1100 in 2009.

More information is required to assess the cause of this, as some of the stores may only just have opened or may be smaller than the original six stores. Alternatively the drop in sales could be due to consumers trading down or delaying the purchase of new bikes as a result of the recession.

The average price per bike has increased by £45 from £353 to £398. Since this is an average price for all ranges, BB might have changed the mix of bikes sold. Alternatively if this is due to BB raising prices, it could have resulted in a decrease in volume.

Sales mix and margins

The proportion of bicycle sales has remained largely consistent at 60-61% of total revenues. This is significantly higher than the average retailer, where bikes amount to just under 47%, but again could be accounted for by the fact that BB sells items of higher individual value.

BB's margin on bicycle sales is lower than the industry average of 37% and disappointingly has dropped from 34 to 30%. This is perhaps surprising given BB's focus on higher quality bikes, as it might expect to make better margins, but the decrease could be due to increased import prices as a result of changing exchange rates.

The higher margin sales of accessories and servicing account for only 39% of BBs sales in 2009, compared to 53% for the average retailer. This suggests that there is scope for BB to improve overall margins by increasing this side of the business, as proposed by the Sales director under Strategy 2.

Profitability

As discussed above, overall profits have fallen, as have profits per store (£109k 2009 compared to £183k 2007).

The increase in admin and distribution overheads is not unreasonable given the additional operating leases for the four new stores, so the key to understanding BB's profitability lies with its sales figures.

Allowing for certain one-off set up costs and assuming the new stores take a while to achieve the same level of sales as existing ones, BB's future performance may improve. Alternatively BB may have opened stores too close together which are competing for sales, or in poor locations.

Further information

As the figures are summarised for the business as a whole, more detail is needed on a shop by shop basis to identify those shops that are doing particularly well or underperforming.

A breakdown of prices and sales volumes by type of bicycle, for BB and the average retailer, would allow for a better analysis.

Appendix of calculations:

Examiner note:

Candidates were not expected to produce the full range of calculations which are included here for marking purposes.

	2007	2009	Mkt Average 2009
Sales mix			
Bikes %	60	61	47
Access. and servicing %	40	39	53
Margins			
Bikes %	34	30	37
Access and servicing %	42	45	48
Total GP margin	37.3	36.0	
Total PBT margin	20.2	15.2	
Store performance			
Sales/store £000s	907	718	
GP/store £000s	338	258	
PBT/store £000s	183	109	

	2007	2009	Mkt Average 2009
Analysis per bike			
Average price per bike	£353	£398	£150
Bikes sold per store	1533	1100	
GP per bike	£119	£119	£55.50
Market share			
BB market share		1.4%	Market leader = 30%
Share per outlet		0.14%	
Share relative to market leader (1.4/30)		4.67%	
Ave independent share 45/2000			0.0225%

Examiner's comments:

Requirement (c) was the first of two requirements in this paper that required some data analysis, which has been indicated as a regular feature of Business Strategy papers. Candidates seemed well prepared for the requirement in this question which asked them to evaluate the company's performance and competitive position based on historic results. Most, but not all, candidates used the data available to help them in their discussion.

Stronger candidates set out the information coherently in a table format, included data for both position and performance, and made calculations of revenue and profit on a per shop or per bicycle basis. However, only a minority fully explained cause and effect relationships based on this relative data analysis and made full use of the industry information that had been provided for benchmarking purposes. A number concentrated on revenue growth, without identifying the key point that whilst revenue had increased, probably as a result of opening four new stores, overall profits had fallen.

In terms of competitive position, most candidates identified BB's competitive strategy in terms of Porter's differentiation and a significant number produced a price/quality diagram to show BB's relative positioning. Typically BB's market share was calculated in relation to the overall market. Stronger candidates related this to the share of the market leader, Benhonda, and the average share of an independent retailer and went on to discuss BB's position within its niche market.

Candidates who had planned their answer well analysed both performance and competitive position. Those who had produced analysis on a per bike or per shop basis were able to give stronger discussions. Weaker candidates demonstrated a lack of planning in their answer and used the data randomly within the main body of their writing. Some very weak candidates produced a largely, or entirely, descriptive answer with little, or no, use of the data, or limited their data analysis to a long list of the % movements from 2007 to 2009. A number of weaker candidates only showed numerical analysis relating to performance and omitted completely any numerical analysis of the competitive position.

(d) **External sources of risk**

> **Examiner note:**
>
> Models such as PESTEL or 5 forces might have been used to help generate ideas here but whatever approach is adopted, it is important to consider the implications of such industry factors for BB and explain why they might be considered to be sources of risk.

Economic and industry conditions:

Political – changes of attitude by the government or differing levels of support may affect demand for bikes. The attitude of the current government appears favourable for the industry but spending priorities may change as a result of the recession or a new government. This will have an impact on the industry as a whole but may affect some product ranges more than others. The government may be more likely to subsidise basic ranges rather than the higher quality bikes offered by BB.

Economic – the economy has a major influence on levels of spending. Recession may have both positive and negative effects. The downside risk is that consumers could cut back on spending, or trade down to lower quality bikes which may adversely affect BB as they appear to be operating at the higher end of the market. Alternatively people may keep bikes longer, thus delaying spending on new bikes but increasing the likelihood of sales of parts and servicing. BB's sales and profits may be at risk unless it caters for this additional demand, as suggested by Strategy 2.

In an attempt to save money eg on fuel people may use bikes in preference to cars for short journeys and commuting. As far as BB is concerned the risk is that this may change the mix of products being demanded.

Technology – BB may experience price deflation caused by technology development or radical developments could render existing stock obsolete. This is particularly likely to affect the high end of the market and the competition bikes.

Competition

The industry is highly competitive and has become more so as a result of the recession. BB faces competition from a variety of small independent UK retailers, as well as international companies and internet-based operators. Failure to compete with competitors on areas including price, product range, quality and service could have an adverse effect on BB's financial results. The market share calculations in (c) suggest that BB is small compared to Benhonda and other big retailers. There is a risk that if they choose to offer similar ranges to BB, it will be unable to compete on price.

Responsiveness to changing market preferences

The history of the bike market demonstrates that over time consumer tastes have changed rapidly. There are also a wide variety of substitutes both for bicycles as a form of transport and also as a form of entertainment eg interactive games consoles. If BB fails to offer products that reflect the changes in demand, there is a risk that its sales will decline. In addition it may be left with high levels of unsold stock.

Reliance on foreign manufacturers

A significant amount of parts and bikes are imported. This gives rise to risks associated with international trade including exposure to different economic conditions, regulatory requirements, trade restrictions and changing foreign government policies.

Transportation problems may affect BB's ability to meet customer demand, which is a problem given low customer switching costs.

Given the majority of bikes are imported, the weak sterling exchange rate may have a significant impact on the costs of the business and hence erode margins.

(e) **Evaluation of Strategy 1 and 2**

Strategy 1: Expansion of product range

This represents a new product for BB and may attract a different type of customer or alternatively may offer BB the chance to increase the amount spent by existing customers, since bike enthusiasts may also need sporting and outdoor equipment.

This may increase sales per shop provided that BB has unutilised floorspace in its stores.

Development of the product range will reduce the company's reliance on the difficult bicycle industry and hence reduce risk.

However BB lacks experience in this area and there is a high level of existing competition from companies which are much larger. As a smaller player BB would find it hard to get economies of scale and may lack purchasing power with new suppliers.

This strategy does not focus on BB's core competences, as staff are cycling experts and may lack knowledge in other areas.

Strategy 2: Integrated workshops

Servicing and parts is the higher margin business so this strategy should improve results and may increase customer retention as BB can try and tie in customers with after sales plans.

The specialist workshops build on existing expertise and provide BB with an added differentiation factor. Given its knowledgeable staff, BB may be able to achieve this with relatively low investment.

This strategy is also consistent with environmental conditions where consumers are retaining bikes for longer and therefore spending more on repairs and servicing. The fact that BB has already trialled this in the Manchester store reduces the risk of failure and suggests it may be successful.

This strategy does not however reduce reliance on the bicycle industry although it helps diversify within it, and avoids competition with larger retailers.

Other options

Strategy 2 is the most obvious one for BB to pursue in the first instance. The strategies are not necessarily mutually exclusive however and BB might consider testing strategy 1 in certain stores, as it has done with the workshop in Manchester.

BB should also consider whether it is losing out on sales by internet/mail order.

Performance may be improved by identifying which shops are performing well and why, as it may be worth closing some down. Similarly some product ranges may be better than others and it may be worth specialising in certain bike ranges only.

Examiner's comments:

In requirement (e) candidates had to discuss the merits of the two options set out in the scenario. This was typically well done. The better candidates related their points back to the risks identified in (d) and attempted to reach a conclusion as to which strategy was more viable, in some cases recommending other options to be considered.

---

28 Deeshire Council (DC)

Marking guide

		Knowledge	Skill	Marks
(a)	Briefing note	1		
	Calculations		11	
	Implications for strategy		5	
				13
(b)	Change management issues for each	4	7	10
(c)	(i) Principles and action	3	4	6
	(ii) IS to monitor performance	2	7	7
		10	34	36

General comments:

This question asked candidates to play the role of an employee working in the strategic planning and policy department of a local council. Domestic waste collection and disposal services are currently operated 'n-house' by the council. Estimates of the council's waste management costs for the latest financial year were provided. Under pressure from the government to reduce landfill and increase recycling rates, the council is considering two proposals to reduce costs and avoid the government's landfill tax penalties:

Option 1: Reduce the number of general refuse collections from weekly to fortnightly in the hope of improving recycling rates

Option 2: Outsource the recycling element of the waste collection. The council have received two tenders for the four year contract: Contractor A based on a variable price per tonne and Contractor B which is a fixed annual sum. Councillors face and ethical dilemma since the chief executive of Contractor A has offered to fund life membership of the local golf club if they support his tender.

This question, which also incorporated some data analysis, was the least well attempted on the paper with reasonable performances on part (b) often failing to make up for poor attempts at either (a) or (c). A disappointing minority did not produce their answer in the style of a briefing note.

It appears that where the data analysis is anything other than financial analysis of performance, which has clearly been well rehearsed on revision courses, candidates are less comfortable manipulating data in order to produce some simple calculations highlighting key issues. This is an important skill for a chartered accountant and will continue to be tested in Business Strategy by way of progression for the Advanced Stage.

A number of candidates made only a brief comment on part (c) (i) or (ii), which appeared to be due to a lack of knowledge rather than time pressure. Candidates should be aware that the mark plan for such an openly worded requirement is extensive and that the examiner is keen to award marks for sensible relevant points. In the event that a candidate lacks detailed knowledge from the learning materials, a common sense approach is likely to gain some credit whereas no marks can be awarded for the requirements that are left unattempted.

(a)   **Evaluate financial implications of options**

Briefing Notes

To: Deeshire Councillors
From: Strategic planning and policy group
Date: March 2010
Re: Waste management strategy

The attached notes set out the financial implications of the proposals under consideration and other issues that Councillors need to consider in deciding on an appropriate waste management strategy.

Option 1: reduce collections and promote recycling

General refuse becomes $0.8 \times 1.5m = 1.2m$ tonnes and hence recycling = 0.8m (0.5+0.3 converted from refuse).

NB. This is within the limit for recyclable waste of 1m tonnes

Financial implications

(i)   **Incremental approach:**

The primary saving is the £2.5m reduction in fixed costs as a result of the once per fortnight general refuse collection.

In addition the Council saves £1.50/tonne by getting households to convert general refuse to recycling (VC of general refuse collection are £3/tonne, recycling costs a net £1.50 per tonne – £4 less £2.50 revenue generated), so the saving is $£1.50 \times 0.3m$ tonnes = £0.45m.

Thus the total saving is £2.95m.

The maximum amount of current waste that can be recycled is $0.5 \times 2m = 1m$ tonnes, so the total potential saving if recycling rates increase from 09/10 levels would be an additional 0.5m recycling at £1.50 = £0.75m.

(ii) **Alternative approach: Calculation of total cost**

		£million
General refuse		
Variable costs	1.2m tonnes @ £3/tonne	3.6
Fixed costs	6.5-2.5 saving	4.0
		7.6
Recycling		
Variable costs	0.8m tonnes @ £4/tonne	3.2
Fixed costs		3.2
less		6.4
Revenue generated from sale of		
recycled waste	0.8m tonnes @ £2.50/tonne	(2.0)
		4.4
Other overheads		2.7
Total waste management costs		14.7

Since existing costs are £17.65m, option 1 would save the Council £2.95m per annum once established. The increase in recycling rates may also help the Council avoid the government's proposed landfill tax.

Further information required:

- Can further general refuse fixed costs be saved if more waste is recycled?

- Alternatively will the FC of recycling increase as limits of existing capacity are reached?

- What are other overheads and how will these be affected?

- Are any inflationary price increases expected or changes in rates at which recycling can be sold?

- Projections for number of households and levels of waste over next 4 years?

- Any additional fixed costs as a result of campaign to promote recycling?

Option 2: Outsource recycling

Financial implications

(i) **Incremental approach:**

	Contractor A £m	Contractor B £m
In house costs saved	3.95	3.95
Contract management costs	(0.1)	(0.1)
Contract price	(2.5)	(4.0)
Net saving/(cost)	1.35m	(0.15)

(ii) **Alternative approach: Calculation of total cost**

	£million
Existing general refuse costs	11.0
Contract management	0.1
Other overheads	2.7
Total waste management costs excluding contract price	13.8

Total cost with contractor A = 13.8 + (0.5 × £5) = £16.3m

Total cost with contractor B = 13.8 + 4 = £17.8m

Comments

Contractor A is cheaper assuming the current level of recycling is maintained, but overall Option 2 is more expensive than Option 1.

However the options are not necessarily mutually exclusive, so the Council could outsource recycling and switch general refuse collection to once per fortnight, to increase recycling rates.

If Option 2 is combined with Option 1, total cost becomes:

	£million
Option 1 general refuse costs	7.6
Option 2 outsourced costs for 0.8m tonnes	4.0
Contract management	0.1
Other overheads	2.7
Total waste management costs	14.4

Overall it appears that this is the best decision from a financial point of view.

Choice of contractor

Contractor A: has tendered a price of £5 per tonne, hence total cost of contract increases as quantity of recycling increases. Thus it is in the contractor's interest to promote increased recycling (which benefits the Council as far as the government targets are concerned but costs it more).

Contractor B: fixed price of £4m, hence cost per tonne for the Council is reduced as amount of recycling increases. There is less incentive for the contractor to promote recycling but it will be in the Council's interests to do so as it reduces cost and helps meet government targets.

Contractor A is significantly cheaper at the current levels of recycling. If the Council can increase recycling as planned to 0.8m tonnes, then both contractors are the same price. B becomes cheaper if either the number of households or the levels of recycling increase substantially.

There are however ethical issues surrounding the golf membership offered by Contractor A – see later notes (c).

Summary of total annual costs for various options:

Option	Quantity recycled	Total cost £		Saving £m
Current	0.5m	17.65m		
1 only	0.8m	14.7m		2.95
2 only	0.5m	A: 16.3m	B: 17.8m	A:1.35
1+2	0.8m	A: 14.4m	B: 14.4m	3.25
Max recycle	1m	A: 14.8m	B: 13.8m	B: 3.85

Other issues:

The quantity of recycling achieved by the external contractor will impact on the costs of general refuse collection for the Council. This would affect the decision if it is felt that one contractor is likely to achieve different recycling rates than another.

It is possible that other overheads may be reduced if all recycling is outsourced.

Contractors will pursue a profit maximisation objective which may cause them to ignore or reduce unprofitable activities eg waste collection in rural areas, reduction of number of collections.

As the Council remains responsible for the services, poor performance on the part of the contractor will reflect badly on the Council. It may also result in risks to health and the environment and give rise to claims for damages.

Redundancies of in-house workers may cause dissatisfaction and damage the Council's reputation. The Council may need to consider the degree of unionisation (see notes on change management).

Outsourcing may not improve recycling rates as a private contractor may be less likely to be joined up with other Council activities in this area.

It will be hard to go back to in-house provision if the decision proves to be the wrong one.

Examiner's comments:

Requirement (a) asked candidates to evaluate the impact of the two proposals in financial terms and to comment on the implications for the council's waste management strategy. This was one of the least well attempted requirements on the paper and many attempts were marginal.

Most candidates were able to produce sensible calculations for options 1 and 2, either by recalculating the total costs for each option, or by calculating the cost savings on an incremental basis. Either approach was acceptable, although the incremental approach would have been faster. Common errors included: calculating the additional amount to be recycled as 20% of the current recycling, instead of 20% of the current volume of general refuse; ignoring the additional £100,000 monitoring costs for outsourcing; treating the contractors' bids as revenue for the council, rather than costs.

Comments on the implications were less insightful and often amounted to a statement of the overall cost saving for each option. Only the better candidates discussed the accuracy of the estimates and questioned whether the residents would be satisfied with fortnightly collections or whether the promotional campaign would achieve the necessary increase the recycling. The stronger candidates also realised that given the government's desire to increase recycling rates and avoid landfill taxes, the volumes of recycling were likely to increase in future. As a result, the fixed price offered by Contractor B might become a more attractive option during the four years of the contract. Any attempt at sensitivity analysis here to identify the volume of recycling at which the council would be indifferent between the two contractors was awarded credit.

Disappointingly few candidates picked up on the fact that, as the two options were not mutually exclusive, combining the proposal for fortnightly collections with the outsourcing of recycling would potentially lead to the biggest savings. There were sufficient marks available for candidates to pass the requirement without addressing this higher skills issue, but those who recognised the possibility and produced calculations to prove it, scored very highly.

The weakest candidates tended to avoid numerical analysis almost entirely and instead discussed the impact of the proposals in more general terms, selecting one or two figures from the question to back up their comments. This approach typically failed to generate sufficient marks.

(b) **Change management issues**

The following issues are relevant when changing the way in which waste management is operated:

(i)   Pace, manner and scope of change
(ii) Barriers to change
(iii) Ways to implement and manage the change process

(i) **Pace, manner and scope of change**

The change may be incremental (building on existing methods) or transformational (a new model of waste management) and may take place gradually or require a rapid one-off change. Option 1 is more likely to involve incremental change whereas Option 2 is more transformational.

Here outsourcing is new in the context of waste management but the Council may already have experience of managing outsourced contractors in other areas of service provision. The government is putting pressure on Councils to improve recycling rates and some funding may be dependent on reaching appropriate targets, so the changes will probably need to be introduced relatively quickly. The switch to outsourcing is likely to be done in one go rather than being gradually phased in.

(ii) **Barriers to change**

A very important aspect of successfully implementing the changes required will be identifying all the factors that could hinder change and then reduce them. At the same time it is important to identify those factors that will promote change and strengthen them.

The capacity to undertake change must be considered in terms of the resources the Council have available and whether there are any cost or time constraints which could prohibit change.

The barriers to change need to be considered by looking at the stakeholders who will be affected by it – specifically here the Council employees who currently operate the waste collection services and the residents who are used to a certain level of service. Their readiness to change or their resistance to it will have a significant impact on the success of the new recycling strategy. Other important stakeholders might include the local media who have the power to support and promote the Council or alternatively damage its reputation.

Given the size of the county there will be a wide variety of communities and issues will differ from one to the other.

For Option 1, the greatest barriers to change are likely to come from the residents who will be used to a weekly collection and will have ingrained habits concerning the disposal of waste which are difficult to change and may prevent recycling targets being achieved.

For Option 2, the barriers to change are likely to be highest among the Council workers, who may well be unionised. These will be split into two groups – those who are to be made redundant, who will no longer be involved, and their colleagues in general refuse who will continue with the current ways of doing things but may feel their job security is threatened (either because of a reduction in number of collections and less volumes of waste or perhaps because ultimately the Council may decide to outsource all aspects of waste collection).

(iii) **Implementing the change**

The way in which the changes are introduced will be very important in them being implemented successfully.

Resistance needs to be acknowledged and discussed and can be lessened by involving both the employees and residents in the planning and implementation. The change needs to be sold to all those involved and communication will be key to this.

Within the Council work force employees must be helped to change their attitudes and behaviours.

Lewin/Schein's 3-step iceberg model of change would prescribe the following approach:

- Unfreezing standard operating procedures (identifying the restraining forces and overcoming them)

- Changing to new patterns of behaviour (carrying out the change and switching to the outsourced contractor) and

- Refreezing to ensure lasting effects ie reinforcing the new system and behaviour

The **Gemini 4Rs** framework could also be used here:

Reframe – create the will and desire to change (the Council may focus on the need for a sustainable environment and the benefits to the environment and future generations of reducing landfill).

Restructure – redesign the structure and culture to facilitate the new approach. This may involve holding meetings with residents, setting up appropriate targets and measures and creating a culture of teamwork between the contractor and the Council's own staff to promote recycling.

Revitalise – ensure an appropriate fit with the environment eg issue promotional literature regarding the Council's plan.

Renewal – ensure the change is supported on an ongoing basis and that individuals involved have the necessary skills eg education of residents as to what is recyclable, reward systems for contractor's achievement of new recycling targets.

Candidates were clearly more comfortable with requirement (b) which asked them to explain the change management issues that might need to be considered by the council under each option, referring to change management models where appropriate.

Most candidates showed good knowledge of change management (types of change, barriers to change and Lewin's 'unfreeze/move/refreeze' model) although relatively few mentioned Gemini's 4R approach. Weaker candidates failed to earn the skills marks available for applying this knowledge to the scenario, simply providing a text book list of generic points. Better candidates identified the fact that the nature of the change, the size of the barriers and the stakeholders affected was different for each option, with the greatest resistance likely to come from households in option 1 and employees to be made redundant in option 2. A minority of candidates limited their marks by writing about change management in general, rather than for each option separately, and/or by only discussing 'employees' in each case, which tended to result in some repetition of points.

(c) (i) **Principles of public sector governance**

Examiner note:

This answer is quite long to cover all possible angles a candidate may adopt, but not all points would need to be made to score maximum marks.

Corporate governance in the context of Deeshire County Council will be concerned with the way in which the Council manages and applies public funds in providing services to the community and its relationship with its various stakeholders. It incorporates the Council's responsibilities and mandate, its decision making processes, and accountability.

The Nolan Committee set out 7 Principles of Public Life which apply to public sector governance: selflessness, integrity, objectivity, accountability, openness, honesty, leadership.

- **Selflessness**: Holders of public office should take decisions solely in terms of the public interest. They should not do so to gain financial or other material benefits for themselves, their family or their friends.

- **Integrity**: Holders of public office should not place themselves under any financial or other obligation to outside individuals or organisations that might influence them in the performance of their duties.

- **Objectivity**: In carrying out public business, including making public appointments, awarding contracts or recommending individuals for rewards and benefits, holders of public office should make choices on merit.

- **Accountability**: Holders of public office are accountable for their decisions and actions to the public and must submit themselves to whatever scrutiny is appropriate to their office.

- **Openness**: Holders of public office should be as open as possible about the decisions and actions that they take. They should give reasons for their decisions and restrict information only when the wider public interest clearly demands.

- **Honesty**: Holders of public office have a duty to declare any private interests relating to their public duties and to take steps to resolve any conflicts arising in a way that protects the public interest.

- **Leadership**: Holders of public office should promote and support these principles by leadership and example.

The offer of lifetime golf membership would appear to directly conflict with the principles of **selflessness** and **integrity** and threatens the **objectivity** of the relevant Councillors.

To comply with the **honesty** principle, Councillors would need to declare the offer that has been made and it is likely that the appropriate response would be to withdraw from the decision-making process.

Were the Councillors to be involved in awarding the contract it is possible that the media and the electing public might question the reasons for their decision on the basis of personal interest. The Council needs to be seen to apply the decision criteria fairly and not leave itself open to appeal by unsuccessful contractors.

In making a decision, the remaining members of the Council must review each case against the criteria set down by local government and award the contract on merit ie based on:

- Contract price
- Capability of contractor to provide services
- Financial strength

As members of the Council will be accountable for the decision they need to consider whether they have sufficient experience to select and manage the best contractor. If not they may need to engage external advice or support.

They also need to consider whether the process has attracted sufficient suitable responses. It is possible that the Council may feel none of the applicants is suitable.

The Council may struggle to elicit sufficient information from their own in-house contractors in order to specify the performance terms of the contract as they may fear for jobs.

Aside from the Nolan principles, there are general ethical issues involved here (where ethics are defined as the moral principles governing or influencing conduct).

The Institute of Business Ethics suggests that 3 questions be applied in deciding whether a situation raises ethical issues:

(1) Transparency – do I mind others knowing what I have decided? It is likely that the Councillors involved would not wish the information regarding golf membership to come to light as it suggests a conflict of interest.

(2) Effect – whom does my decision affect or hurt? In this case it might be the unsuccessful contractors, or the local community if it transpires that the best contractor has not been appointed.

(3) Fairness – would my decision be considered fair by those affected? The public and media are likely to question Councillors' motives in awarding the contract.

There are also ethical issues surrounding the behaviour of the waste management contractor's chief executive which would give the Council general cause for concern about the organisation's corporate responsibility. Even if this organisation were to meet the various decision making criteria, it may be inappropriate for the Council to engage this contractor because it is not the type of company that the Council wants to be involved with.

Examiner's comments:

Requirement (c) which covered public sector governance, ethics and information systems, was poorly attempted by many. In part (i) candidate were asked to explain the principles of public sector governance that the councillors must apply when choosing between Contractors A and B and to recommend any appropriate action that the councillors should take. Few candidates seemed to be familiar with the Nolan seven principles of public sector governance set out in the learning materials. Despite this, candidates who applied their corporate governance and ethics knowledge to the public sector were able to gain marks. Sensible comments regarding the non-profit making nature of the council, its need to consider wider stakeholders and the requirement for transparency, honesty and accountability in decision making were sufficient to score a pass. Weaker candidates referred to Deeshire as if it were a company rather than a council and some completely failed to discuss the ethical issue involved with the lifetime golf membership being offered by Contractor A. Those that did tended to state that the golf membership offer was essentially a bribe which should be rejected. Better candidates identified that given this threat to objectivity, the councillors concerned should declare it and remove themselves from the decision making process. They also pointed out that the behaviour of Contractor A called into question its suitability to work with the council.

(ii) **Information system to monitor performance**

An information system can be used for monitoring and control purposes, to check adherence of the contractor to the service level agreement, but also for decision-making in respect of contract renewal and future waste management strategy.

The Council can collect data in order to measure actual results in relation to the promised standards set out in the contractor's service level agreement and in relation to any specific targets the Council are required to meet eg by the government.

Data might be collected in different ways, eg using electronic chips in bins to measure volume and type of waste being disposed of/recycled, or via contractor reports and customer satisfaction surveys.

Exception reporting may help to highlight areas of concern in terms of cost overruns, resource utilisation, customer dissatisfaction, or failure to meet recycling targets.

- Compliance with legislation/environmental standards
- Quality control procedures
- HR policies and employment issues (diversity, training etc)
- Effectiveness of contractors' own monitoring and reporting systems

Measures of delivery standards would include:

- Number of collections weekly
- Number of collections made on time
- Number of vehicle breakdowns
- Number of complaints received from residents
- Rates of recycling
- Number of litigation cases/damages claims
- Employment record
- Compliance with legislation and other environmental standards

Financial stability will affect ability to resource the contract now and in future. This can be evidenced by recent accounts, bank references and credit ratings, all of which should be monitored closely.

Comparatives

The Council will need benchmarks to assess performance. In addition to specific comparatives eg Council targets and standards agreed in the contractor's SLA, the Council may be able to compare itself to other Councils which have achieved high rates of recycling.

As a minimum the Council will need to monitor performance in the following areas, against the three decision making criteria:

- Contract price (ie costs incurred)
- Capability of contractor to provide services
- Financial strength

Price

The actual costs incurred may not reflect the original price tendered, either because the contractors lack the detailed information to provide a realistic price or as a result of later variations in service requirements.

In establishing whether the outsourcing decision has been a success, any price must be compared to the cost of in-house service provision but calculations of cost savings should factor in any exit costs for the current arrangement eg redundancies.

Measures: Annual spend vs budget, Cost overruns.

Provision of services

The Council will need to consider :

- Standards of service delivery

- Contractors' capacity to continue to resource contract and flexibility to cope with increased volumes in future (information about vehicle fleet, staffing levels, working partnerships, disposal facilities)

Examiner's comments:

Requirement c (ii) asked candidates to describe how the council could use an information system to monitor the performance if an outsourced contractor is appointed. Most were less well-prepared for this topic, which came into the syllabus for the new Business Strategy paper and which has not yet been examined in any depth. Many answers were limited to a brief discussion of the use of systems to monitor costs and service levels, with one or two basic performance measures suggested. A small minority made some good points about the use of IS to check adherence to targets specified by the council or the government; assess resident satisfaction, monitor recycling trends; benchmark the contractor and council's performance and make decisions regarding contract renewal. Stronger answers made imaginative suggestions about methods of data collection (eg electronic chips in wheelie bins), identified a range of relevant KPIs that could be used (sometimes involving a balanced scorecard) and discussed the use of exception reporting to identify specific areas of underperformance.

29 NP Ltd (NP)

Marking guide

			Knowledge	Skill	Marks
Report format			1	–	
(a)	(i)	Market research	2	4	
	(ii)	Segmentation and targeting	2	4	
					10
(b)		Joint development/CDT/Eco/Licensing relative merits	5	9	12
			10	17	22

General comments:

This question involves a small manufacturing company which currently operates in the steam cleaning industry. It is owned by a former research scientist, Nilesh Patel, who has recently been granted worldwide patent for a new energy-efficient washing machine technology which uses nylon beads to reduce the energy and detergent required and significantly lowers water consumption. The company faces a choice of whether to develop the technology for the domestic or commercial laundry markets and also how to structure the business to exploit the new technology. Options under consideration are a company offering venture capital style funding and support, a strategic alliance with an environmentally friendly dry cleaning company that has a chain of businesses across the US or a licensing agreement(s) with manufacturers of domestic and industrial washing machines.

There were some very good attempts at this question and a number of candidates chose to attempt this question first on the paper. A disappointing minority did not produce their answer in the report format requested.

(a) (i) **Market research**

Report

To: Nilesh Patel
From: A.N.Other
Date: March 2010

Re: Exploiting proposed new washing machine technology

This report sets out the issues to be considered when selecting a market for the new technology and the relative merits of the joint development strategies under consideration.

(a) **Selecting the best market**

Market research can help in identifying the potential size of specific markets and provide information about customer characteristics, needs and wants, attitude to price and quality, and competitors' products. Market research may also help in defining appropriate elements of the marketing mix (product, price, place, promotion).

Desk research would involve gathering and analysing existing (secondary) data to ascertain which customers might be interested in the new washing machine technology. This is usually cheaper as the data is already published eg by governments, trade journals and commercial companies but as the technology is new it may not provide all the information required.

External databases may help identify customers in prospective markets eg the major manufacturers of industrial and domestic washing machines, and any competitors with similar products or similar technologies. It might also provide factual information about the economy, legal and political considerations, environmental protection standards etc.

Desk research may be a useful initial step in identifying certain markets as unattractive or lacking in profit potential. It may also assist in setting prices eg by ascertaining how much people could save on overheads by using the new technology.

More detailed information can be obtained by **field research** which involves the collection of new data from respondents. This might be in the form of surveys, interviews, focus groups and discussion with company heads.

Field research can be used here to determine which markets are likely to have the highest demand and also what price different users are prepared to pay for the new technology:

- Who is the target market and who is the decision maker in the purchasing process?
- What product features must the product incorporate?
- What benefits will the product provide?
- How will consumers react to the product?
- How will the product be produced most cost effectively?
- Will the product be profitable when manufactured and delivered to the customer at the target price?

In selecting the best market relevant factors will include:

- Where the most profits can be made
- The sustainability of these profits into the future
- How barriers to entry can be preserved or raised to discourage competition

Market research may also help NP in identifying other applications of the technology beyond those already decided.

Having undertaken the necessary research, NP must:

- Estimate likely selling price based upon competition and customer feedback
- Estimate sales volume based upon size of market
- Estimate costs to produce, profitability and breakeven point

Segmentation and targeting

Market segmentation is the practice of identifying homogeneous sub-groups within a market, which can then be marketed to in different ways. Here NP can segment the market for the new washing machine technology based on the type of customer, their needs and also possibly their geographic location.

It would be normal practice to divide consumer and industrial markets – the two distinct markets available to Nilesh – particularly since these will have very different buying characteristics and product requirements.

	Consumer (Domestic)	Industrial
Buying frequency	Rare (low volume, high value)	Often
Reliability	Recommended	Essential
Size of machine	Small	Large
Load	Light	Heavy
Economy	Relatively important	Very important

Within the market for consumer durables (low volume, high value purchases) NP's new technology is likely to be attractive to innovators who typically are the first to try various new products (relatively young, intelligent, socially and geographically mobile and of a high socio-economic group).

A key characteristic for NP to focus on is the growing eco-awareness of consumers. NP would be best identifying those markets which are most environmentally aware – this may be a particular group of consumers or a particular geographic location.

Issues to consider in deciding on whether to target consumer or industrial markets:

Targeting involves selecting the best market segments. This will depend on:

- The sales potential (market size and growth forecasts)

- The ability to manufacture and distribute the product according to customer requirements

- The likelihood of the segment providing a stable income stream

- The profits available given the capital investment required

- How defendable the market is from competition eg the barriers to entry in the form of the patent may prevent competitors developing similar products initially

NP may decide to concentrate on a single market segment eg domestic washing machines, or adopt a multi-segment strategy, offering smaller machines for the domestic market and much larger machines for industrial purposes. Given the size of the existing company and the limited resources available to NP, it is likely that if it grows organically, a single market segment would be advisable (see part b below).

NP could adopt a price skimming strategy, targeting those who are keen to be early adopters of the new technology, then lowering the price later to develop the market further.

Test marketing might involve a trial run of all elements of the marketing mix in a sample market segment that is small, self-contained, representative and with adequate promotional facilities.

Examiner's comments:

Requirement (a) asked candidates to advise Nilesh on the issues to address when selecting the best market for the technology, considering (i) market research and (ii) segmentation and targeting. As usual, candidates were well-rehearsed in the marketing knowledge required and in most cases applied this to the scenario. As well as giving examples of both types of research, better candidates pointed out that desk research might be less relevant for a situation involving new technology but also that the cost of field research might be an issue for Nilesh. Most answers identified the need to segment the market between domestic and industrial buyers and good answers went on to explain the differences that were likely to arise between the two markets. Only the strongest candidates pointed out that given the size of the company, it may not have the resources available to target all segments successfully, hence the need to consider some form of joint development strategy.

(b) **Joint development strategies**

NP is facing two issues:

(1) Can NP successfully commercialise the new technology?

The patent and the initial testing suggest that the new technology has a number of possible successful applications.

(2) Would it be better doing so independently or in co-operation with a larger partner?

Desirability of a joint development strategy

The need for a joint development strategy stems from the inability of NP to exploit the full potential of the new technology using existing resources or those that could easily be acquired, and NP's lack of experience in the laundry market. Development in association with a third party would provide access to their core competences – here NP requires the other party to be able to engage in large scale production and to have access to a wide distribution market.

Another important issue is that the new product is subject to a high degree of risk and the impact on the existing business needs to be considered.

The key advantages of combining with a third party are as follows:

- Growth can be achieved more quickly and efficiently as expertise can be shared eg third party may have experience of overseas operations.

- A partner may provide access to countries or companies that it would otherwise be impossible for NP to access (eg America).

- Will increase access to resources and/or capital for growth, both of which are likely to be limited but critical at the start-up stage.

- Third party may bring purchasing power and economies of scale which are unlikely to be available to NP due to its limited size.

- Risks are shared and it reduced the risk of failure due to Nilesh Patel's inexperience and possible inability to control growth.

- May provide access to existing supply and distribution chains, on an international scale.

- May allow NP more time to ensure that the existing business does not suffer because with organic growth all the focus may have to be on the new technology.

Third party may add value to the brand if it is an established brand name

However:

- NP will suffer a loss of control

- If the venture is successful NP will make less profits since these have to be shared

- May lose rights to intellectual property which in this case is of fundamental importance

- Change may happen too fast (inefficiencies, inability to control, lack of appropriate systems). Organic growth may be easier to control

- Association with the wrong third party may devalue the brand

Relative merits of the joint development strategies under consideration

Option 1: Offer from CDT

Benefits:

- Established business with experience of converting ideas into commercially viable businesses
- Provide financial investment for promotion and marketing
- Greater network of contacts and bargaining power
- Help in choosing outsourcing partners for production and distribution
- Prestige and rewards from flotation which offers NP an exit route

Drawbacks:

- Loss of controlling equity stake and introduces another key stakeholder as a 50% shareholder. Also CDT will help 'identify appropriate commercial partners' which may further dilute control.

- CDT likely to be major player and therefore dictate to NP; it may interfere in the day-to-day running of the existing business.

- Differing objectives and priorities may be a source of potential conflict. CDT may be looking for a fast return on their investment, rather than being interested in NP in the long term.

- Differences in culture.

- May be problems after exit when NP is on his own.

NP needs to ascertain the exact nature and form of the financial and commercial support and clarify certain issues eg how the patent rights will be affected, the impact on the existing business, and whether CDT will expect to be involved/share returns from this business too.

Option 2: Strategic alliance with EcoLaundry

Nature and terms of the alliance need to be negotiated and this will depend on the relative strengths of the two parties – EcoLaundry is likely to be the stronger party in this respect with more commercial experience so NP, as the smaller partner needing access to economies of scale and a wide distribution network, may be disadvantaged.

Benefits include:

- Faster growth than would be possible organically.

- Access to capital provided by Eco and to marketing expertise.

- Synergy from the fact that the Eco brand name is well-known and linked to environmentally friendly laundry.

- Will give access to wider geographical markets internationally. Eco has a chain of businesses across the US with an established customer base of both companies and consumers.

Disadvantages:

- Unclear who will be responsible for manufacture
- Gives away a share of the benefits of the innovative technology
- Likely to lead to some loss of control since Eco wish to sell the technology to other companies
- Disputes may arise over the rights and obligations of the parties involved
- Access to know-how is given away
- Exchange risk affecting the remittance of NP's share of profits from the US

Option 3: Licensing

NP can license to one or two large companies or many smaller companies. The form of licence would need to take into account the geographic spread or could be on a product basis eg the right to manufacture domestic machines rather than industrial ones.

There needs to be some incentive for the companies involved to purchase the licence.

The technology is patented so competitors will therefore be restricted in their ability to copy, but prospective licensees may need some more evidence of commercial viability beyond initial testing of technical functionality.

Advantages of licensing

- Will offer faster expansion than using own resources
- Affords opportunity for much greater worldwide coverage
- Reduce risks for NP
- May enhance recognition of NP brand name and stimulate sales of dry-steam cleaners
- Depending on strength and life of patent, it may guarantee revenues for a significant time

However:

- Growth is likely to be slower than the other options as NP will need to convince others about the potential of the new technology

- Involves sharing profits and know-how with larger companies which may exploit this when licence period ends

- Multi-nationals with economies of scale and distribution networks are likely to have much greater bargaining power than NP so may drive down terms

Conclusion

If NP wants to retain control of the business and his intellectual property, then he could segment the market and exploit his patents on a worldwide basis by implementing Option 3. The options are not necessarily mutually exclusive so one possibility might be to undertake the strategic alliance in respect of the American industrial laundry market and then use licensing as a strategy for the domestic market and for countries other than USA.

Examiner's comments:

Requirement (b) asked candidates to discuss the desirability of pursuing a joint development strategy and the relative merits of the three options being considered. This was a relatively straightforward requirement and most candidates demonstrated good understanding of the differences between the options. Once again the distinction between a strong and weak answer tended to depend on the candidates' ability to apply this knowledge to the scenario, thereby prioritising the points of relevance to Nilesh which centred around control, retention of intellectual property, risk and resources. Weaker candidates tended to ignore the requirement to consider the desirability of a joint development strategy and simply assess the three options, sometimes only listing the advantages of each option, without considering any downside. The strongest scripts identified that as a small company, NP was likely to need help to exploit the full potential of the technology and having considered the relative merits of the options, made a recommendation as to the best course of action.

30 Executive Travel Ltd (ET)

Marking guide

			Knowledge	Skill	Marks
(a)		Evaluation of performance of ET		18	16
(b)	(i)	Likely effects of pricing policy	3	4	
	(ii)	Likely impact of incentives	1	5	
					11
(c)	(i)	Benefits and risks	1	4	
	(ii)	How the risk can be managed	1	4	
					8
(d)		Ethical issues and action that should be taken	3	5	
					7
			9	40	42

General comments:

The company in this scenario (ET) owns a chain of 21 upmarket travel agent outlets. The company has been significantly affected by economic downturn and, as a response, it has introduced more flexible pricing methods, with greater discretion given to branch managers to offer discounts. Also, performance incentives have been given to branch managers based on sales volumes achieved. Data was provided on the performance of both the company and the industry. The company has recently had a crisis board meeting to review the price discounting policy and consider a contract with a hotel company for a guaranteed minimum number of booking next year. Ethical issues have arisen at the company's Outlet21, which is based in an investment bank. These issues arise from a letter sent to the chartered accountant FD from an ex-employee, concerning gifts received by ET staff in return for upgraded bookings, and the charging of business expenses against a charitable trust which is supported by the bank.

(a)

	2007	2008	2009
Industry			
(per question)			
Value of trips	36,500,000	35,800,000	35,300,000
Commissions	4,380,000	3,938,000	3,530,000
Trips	68,600	65,200	64,100
Company			
(per question)			
Value of trips	90,000	84,000	78,000
Commissions	9,000	7,560	6,240
Trips	30	27	24
Sundry Commissions	8,000	9,000	10,000
Analysis			
Industry			
Value per trip (£)	£532	£549	£551
% Commission/value	12%	11%	10%
Commission per trip	£63.85	£60.40	£55.07
Growth in value of trips		(1.9)%	(1.4)%
Growth in commissions		(10)%	(10.4)%
Growth in number of trips		(5.0)%	(1.7)%

ICAEW

Business Strategy answers 315

Company

Market share (value)%	0.25%	0.23%	0.22%
Market share (comm)%	0.21%	0.19%	0.18%
Commission per trip (£)	£300	£280	£260
Value per trip (£)	£3,000	£3,111	£3,250
% comm/value	10%	9%	8%
Growth in value of trips		(6.6)%	(7.1)%
Growth in commissions		(16.0)%	(17.5)%
Growth in number of trips		(10)%	(11.1)%

ET Performance

ET is trading in difficult market conditions, hence the decline in performance must be judged against this background. In common with many industries, companies operating in upmarket sectors are suffering more than those in mid-market and downmarket sectors as people 'trade down' in the recession.

The market demand for the services of travel agents is a derived demand from the market demand for holidays/tours. Performance can therefore be explained, in part, by the changes in market demand for holidays/tours.

The industry data provided indicates that there was a modest decline of 1% to 2% in the value of trips in both 2008 and 2009. Unusually for industry data there is also a measure of volume in the travel industry in terms of the number of trips. This shows a more severe decline of 5% in 2008, although the 2009 fall of 1.7% is broadly in line with the fall in value. The discrepancy between the fall in value and volume in 2008 is explained by the increase in the value per trip from £532 to £549 (3.2%).

By contrast, the data for ET indicates that there was a more substantial decline of 6.6% in 2008 and 7.1% in the value of trips in 2008 and 2009 respectively. This may indicate that ET has performed poorly in attracting new customers compared to the industry average or it may indicate that the upmarket sector is performing poorly as a whole by comparison to the industry. A more valid comparison might be how well ET is performing relative to upmarket competitors (ie in the same sector of the travel market).

For any given level of demand for holidays, travel agents face competition, not only from each other, but also from direct on-line bookings between the consumer and the tour operator. In a recession, when market conditions are difficult, the level of competition is likely to be more severe and this may take the form of price competition, putting pressure on travel agents' commission levels.

In terms of the industry, % commissions have fallen from 12% to 11% then to 10% over the period 2007-2009. This means there have been reductions of around 10% in each year in commission, which amplifies the fall in volumes of trade already considered.

The percentage commissions (ie commissions to trip value) of ET were lower than the industry average at the start of the period and they have maintained this gap, falling broadly in line, from 10% down to 8% over the same period. The lower level of the commissions to value % is likely to be due to the fact that the value per trip for ET is far greater than the industry average. Thus, for instance, the average value per trip in 2007 was £3,000 for ET compared to the industry average of £532 (ie 5.6 times greater). The commission per trip booked is therefore far larger for ET than the industry average, despite the lower commission to value %.

Nevertheless, the significant fall in volumes, combined with the reduction in % commission rates, has caused a very severe reduction in the overall absolute value of commission income for ET. Overall commissions from holiday sales have fallen from £9 million in 2007 to £6.24 million in 2009 – a 30.7% reduction in primary income in two years.

Two areas where there is a better performance are 'Outlet21' and sundry commissions.

Outlet21 has a flat level of performance of £3 million each year. This means it has not suffered from the recession. More detail is need on commission rates and volumes, but if these have changed the changes have compensated each other. Whilst performance in these conditions can therefore be regarded as good, and has a stabilising effect on overall revenue, there is a risk that such a high proportion of income now comes from one source (at £3 million it is almost half of the core commissions on holidays of £6.24 million generated by the other 20 outlets).

Sundry commissions have performed very well with a 10% increase in 2008 to £1.1 million and maintaining revenues at this higher level in 2009. The performance has been all the more creditable as it has been achieved against a reducing volume of trips on the core business. Thus, for instance, in 2008 the number of trips fell by 10% and sundry commissions rose by 10%, so the sundry commissions per trip increased by 22%.

Overall the table below shows that revenue has fallen by 10.3% in 2008 and 11.3% in 2009. The sundry commissions and Outlet21 have moderated the reduction in core commissions but dependency on these areas in future is uncertain as they depend on the core business to generated customers for sundry commissions and to enhance reputation.

£000s	2007	2008	2009
Commissions	9,000	7,560	6,240
Outlet21	3,000	3,000	3,000
Sundry	1,000	1,100	1,100
Total	13,000	11,660	10,340
% change		-10.3%	-11.30%

Thus the poor performance in terms of revenues may be due to market conditions, in whole or in part, but in assessing the performance of the business, as opposed to the performance of the managers of the business, there has been a very severe reduction in trade and a poor performance.

Additional key information

- Details of performance of rival companies in the same sector as a benchmark

- Breakdown of performance for each branch

- Detailed analysis of costs. Given that all the 20 outlets have high fixed costs and are maintained in operation, then the impact of a downturn on profit is likely to be much more severe than that on revenue as operating gearing is high

- Breakdown between sectors (eg business and leisure)

- Industry projections

Examiner's comments:

The performance on the data analysis section showed general improvement from previous sittings and this was reflected in a majority of candidates' answers to this question. Nevertheless, there continues to be some variability in the quality of answers. The better candidates were able to calculate meaningful ratios which focussed on both the company and industry changes with appropriate evaluation of performance in explaining the data and identifying causal relationships, both for ET and for the industry. Better candidates also tended to set out a structured table of calculations at the beginning of their answer, then provided a narrative commentary which evaluated this data.

Weaker candidates tended to provide random calculations intermingled within a general narrative. Weaker answers also tended to focus merely on the company with little or no coverage of the industry, despite this specifically being required in the question. More generally, weaker answers tended to describe what has happened to various ratios (eg increased or decreased) rather than attempting to address how it has happened (eg analysing the data in more detail) or why it has happened (eg identifying underlying factors discussed in the scenario which may have caused the changes in the ratios/data). Weaker answers were also very repetitive and more often than not attributed all aspects of the declining performance to the worldwide economic recession. Some weaker answers also omitted any mention of Outlet21.

The additional key information from the weaker students was the usual list of cash flows, balance sheets and management accounts. However, the highest scoring answers produced excellent lists of additional information, including other companies specialising in luxury holidays, costs, performance on a branch by branch basis and sector information.

(b) (i) **Discounting pricing policy**

ET is an upmarket provider and therefore prices of travel are high. While, in most industries, upmarket sectors tend to be less price sensitive and more quality sensitive than downmarket sectors there is significant competition in travel. For simple products such as a first class flight or a specific hotel the product is homogeneous between providers and price comparisons can easily be made. These conditions may therefore force discounting in order to match competitors.

More generally, however, where there is a bespoke package of travel arrangements the price is less comparable and the level of service may be more important.

A key point also is that the travel agent is only able to discount its commission, which has only a marginal impact on the overall cost of the holiday cost. Thus, if commission is £100 and this is 10% of the holiday value then a 50% reduction in this commission to £50 is only a 5% reduction in the overall cost of the trip to the customer.

It should also be noted that price is a signal of quality. If, as the FD suggests, discounting indicates a perceived cheapening off the service provided then this may have a long term reputational effect.

Overall, the elasticity of demand is key, in that if discounting increases the volume of sales significantly then it may be advantageous.

The policy of discretionary discounting does seem more appropriate than a general overall discount. This is because it enables price discrimination on a customer by customer basis as the manager can make an assessment of the price resistance of each individual. If however the discounting becomes more or less automatic by the manager, or expected by the customer, then the policy moves de facto from discretionary to general discounting.

In terms of the evidence available, it should be noted that, despite discounting, the number of trips has continued to fall. Clearly, without discounting it the number of trips may have fallen more sharply but the success of the policy may nevertheless be questioned.

(ii) **Managerial incentive policy**

The policy of rewarding managers on the basis of volumes sold and, at the same time, giving them the discretion to discount may cause a conflict of the managers' personal interests with ETs underlying objectives. The incentive for managers could be to discount to maximise sales volumes rather than to maximise commissions from revenues or profits.

Some sales that could be made at full price may be needlessly discounted by managers who are over-anxious to make the sale even if it reduces ET's revenue unnecessarily.

The policy also ignores costs. Although variable costs tend to be low, the manager may incur search costs for holidays (staff time, international telephone calls etc) which are out of line with the value of the commissions generated.

Managers would also have the incentive to promote small trips rather than the high value large trips if they are rewarded on a volume count as these incur less staff time and generate the same bonus. This may lead to key, high value customers not receiving the level of service that they require and the high commissions that they pay would warrant.

Examining the evidence however the value per trip has risen from £3,000 in 2007 to £3,250 in 2009, so there is no evidence to support the notion that incentives have caused lower value trips to be sold. Further scrutiny is needed but one possible explanation is that very high value holidays are more resistant to the recession.

Examiner's comments:

Most answers in (i) focussed on the impact on the image of ET and recognised that customer perception could be adversely affected. Better candidates discussed the price elasticity of demand and were able to link their answers to the data. This was very encouraging and demonstrated good knowledge and application of skills. Price discrimination between individuals, given the management discretion, was surprisingly not discussed by many candidates. A minority pointed out that despite the drop in commission per trip for ET, demand had decreased rather than increased.

In (ii) answers to this section were generally good and recognised the motivational issues involved and that there could be a potential conflict of interest for managers. Given that managers are rewarded on volume rather than value, answers focussed on managers' tactics to sell lower cost holidays which were heavily discounted. Some answers went one step further and suggested alternative policies for management incentives such as value of booking and performance of their particular branch. Few answers referred back to the data to evaluate whether there was any evidence to support a falling value of per trip arising from these incentives.

(c) (i) **Benefits**

- The proposed arrangement with Snooty Hotels offers accommodation that is appropriate to the customer base (as it has been used previously) but this year is offered at a significant discount

- There is a cross branding facility whereby the luxury brand of Snooty Hotels is linked with that of ET as an upmarket provider of leisure services

Risks

- The key risk is that the price reduction will not be sufficient to increase demand from last year's level of 1,000 room nights to 1,600 room nights. As a consequence, ET will need to pay for the shortfall

- At 1,600 room days at £200 the total cost is £320,000. At last year's rate it would be 1,000 room days at £300 per day which is £300,000. This may imply a maximum probable exposure of £20,000. However, with declining sales volumes, it would be wrong to assume that last year's sales volumes could be sustained. The risk exposure could therefore be far greater than £20,000

(ii) **Managing the risks**

SHC operates in a number of cities and resorts. If ET has in the past recommended alternative accommodation in these locations then it may be advisable to push customers towards SHC instead. This would ensure that the minimum target was achieved, and thus no penalties would arise.

More generally, given the potential exposure to low demand, ET could attempt to persuade customers to take trips to these locations instead of other locations.

If closer to the departure date there were excess rooms with SHC then they could be sold off down to cost price of £200. Indeed, ultimately even a price below £200 at the last few days would yield some contribution rather than ET pay the full guaranteed price.

Examiner's comments:

In part (i), the benefits and risks section, coverage was good on the whole. The main points discussed centred on the compatibility of SHC and ET with the luxury holiday label being retained. The main risks noted were that ET may fail to let out all 1,600 rooms and that SNC's reputation was not well known to ET, in turn potentially having an impact on the overall business. Better candidates used numerical data to illustrate the relatively small increase in annual commission and the extent of the risks.

In part (ii), on managing risks, performance was generally poor with many candidates struggling to come up with reasonable approaches to mitigate risk. Answers were typically too general and often asserted that ET could transfer or reduce the risk but did not elaborate further on how this might be achieved. Some of the methods suggested for risk mitigation, for example taking out insurance, were unreasonable and showed a lack of commercial reality. A number of candidates produced generic descriptions of different approaches to risk management, and thereby scored some knowledge marks, but low marks in terms of skills.

(d) The issue of ET staff receiving rewards from the bank's staff represents a potential conflict of interest between promoting ET's goals, promoting the bank's goals and promoting the staff's own personal goals. The disbursement of the bank's resources in order to gain personal benefits may also be fraudulent. However given that discretion and judgement are involved this may be difficult to demonstrate. A policy of transparency of gifts received or a prohibition of any significant gifts may prevent such behaviour, or at least make it more apparent.

The issue of senior bank staff travelling at the charity's expense would depend on the agreement with the charity, the charities internal rules and disclosure of administration costs compared to donations would be appropriate. If such expenditure was contrary to the charity's basic trust terms then this may be not only an ethical breach but a fraudulent act which would make any excess cost repayable.

If the charity is being charged with travel costs which should properly be due to the commercial activities of the bank then this may be fraudulent and may amount to money laundering.

As Carol is a chartered accountant then she is bound by the ICAEW ethical code for accountants in business. This could require the disclosure of fraudulent activity, notwithstanding the general duty of confidentiality. There may also be a duty not to act for the bank although as Carol does not work for a firm of chartered accountants this would not be a duty on the other directors. Carol may therefore need to resign her position where there is fraud and the fellow directors continue to act for the bank.

Examiner's comments:

This requirement was not well answered. Many candidates addressed the issues in terms of a lack of controls by the company to limit these actions, rather than the ethical implications that were asked for in the question. Similarly, some candidates pointed out the commercial consequences of the actions, rather than their ethical implications. A number of candidates failed to acknowledge the fact that Carol was a Chartered Accountant and was therefore bound by the ICAEW code of ethics. More generally, candidates failed to apply their knowledge of ethics to the situation provided. Most candidates did address the two ethical issues individually, drawing separate conclusions, although did not always go on to suggest actions, even though this was a specific part of the requirement.

31 Hutton Haulage plc (HH)

Marking guide

			Knowledge	Skill	Marks
(a)		SWOT analysis	2	8	10
(b)	(i)	How outsourcing can improve supply chain efficiency	3	5	
	(ii)	Actions to enhance environmental sustainability	2	4	
					12
(c)		Factors to be considered - acquisition	3	7	9
			10	24	31

(a) **SWOT analysis**

Strengths

- High efficiency leading to low cost service provision due to volumes, IT system, shared loads, and drivers sleeping in cabins

- A large customer in Goonhill giving volume and reputation

- Wide general customer base

- Strong core assets in modern trucks

- Specialisation in chilled food (market leader)

- Operating in an essential industry

Weaknesses

- Solely in road transport and therefore undiversified
- Comparative disadvantage compared to EU haulage companies on diesel costs
- Road congestion compared to rail and water transport
- Low profit margins in the industry

Opportunities

- Acquisitions to increase size and maintain economies of scale and economies of scope
- Diversification opportunity into rail with RailTrans
- Freshco agreement is near finalisation

Threats

- Potential loss of Goonhill as a large customer with the existing five year contract finishing next year

- Failure to enter into agreement with Freshco by not satisfying new conditions

- Volatility in diesel fuel costs reflecting oil price volatility and fuel tax changes

- Further economic downturn would be reflected in a decline in industry volumes and increased competition

- Increased EU regulations opening up UK market to European competition

- Increased general pressure on carbon emissions and specific pressure from Freshco

- Competition from water, rail and air transport may increase if road transport becomes slower (eg congestion) or more expensive (road pricing or taxes)

- Low barriers to entry may increase competition when recession ends

- Even if Freshco agreement is signed it may withdraw or reduce volumes as it is a 'pay as you' go basis

- Exchange rate volatility with euro changing competitive position with EU haulage companies

Summary – key points

The key points would seem to be:

- The high utilisation and operating efficiency giving a competitive advantage in terms of low cost and quality service

- Potential loss of Goonhill on contract renewal

- Diversification opportunity into rail with RailTrans

Examiner's comments:

The SWOT analysis was well done in general. Candidates did struggle to state weaknesses other than the fact that there was only one large major contract. Some candidates thought that weaknesses were the same as threats and vice versa, when weaknesses identified should be internal to the company and threats should be external factors. Most, but not all, addressed the requirement to provide a summary, although in the case of the weakest candidates this tended to be a generic comment about building on strengths to counter threats.

(b)

From: A. Candidate
To: HH Board
Date: 14 June 2010
Subject: Outsourcing and sustainability

(i) **Outsourcing and efficiency improvements for Freshco**

HH needs to provide a more efficient transport service for Freshco, than the company is currently providing internally. It also needs to charge a price which is lower than the costs currently being incurred by Freshco, but still makes a profit for HH.

HH is a long established road haulage company with a core competence in the industry. Freshco is a supermarket and does not necessarily have the core competences in road distribution. These core competences do not just arise in the road transport industry generally, but in the specific function that is the subject of current negotiations between HH and Freshco – the transport of chilled and frozen food in the supermarket industry. This has arisen most obviously with the Goonhill contract over a four year period but also this is an area 'where HH is a market leader'.

In addition to greater experience in the industry compared to Freshco, HH also has advantages of scale and scope. HH serves a range of customers and therefore deals with large volumes giving economies of scale with fuller loads, fewer empty loads, more networked journeys, fewer simple return journeys, and a larger fleet of trucks giving flexibility of size, availability and specification.

Economies of scope are achieved through servicing several customers simultaneously in a given area (eg shared load).

Other issues include:

- The high specification modern fleet will give a more reliable delivery (eg fewer breakdowns, less service time and repair time off the road)

- The IT system can enable monitoring of trucks, but may also facilitate data transfer from Freshco to HH on a real time basis

- More frequent deliveries may be possible as the fleet is more heavily utilised and can operate viably by dual loading which is often not possible with a single customer internal provider

- Multimodal travel from Europe may soon be possible with the acquisition of RailTrans. This gives a faster, more rapid and more reliable supply chain over distance

- The 'pay as you go' system enables Freshco to use HH's services without a long term binding commitment. Service improvement therefore needs to be demonstrated quickly to retain the contract even in the short term

Overall the efficiencies and cost savings can enable a better service to be delivered at lower cost but clearly much will depend on how Freshco determines its costs internally (eg Full cost with allocation of overheads? Are the old trucks fully depreciated?). A focus on service improvement rather than cost reduction may therefore be appropriate.

(ii) Environmental sustainability

Environmental sustainability relates to environmental policies that meet the needs of the present without compromising the ability of future generations to meet their own needs. In so doing it considers the inter-relationship between the environment, society and business.

The proposed acquisition of RailTrans is a transparent and clear signal of carbon reductions. Rail transport has much lower carbon emissions than trucks and the acquisition would signal a major commitment towards rail and away from road only transport.

Moreover, if the volumes increase with the Freshco contract, then the train becomes an even lower producer of carbon emissions, for instance on the Spain route where containers may be shared with Goonhill.

Other possible environmental sustainability contributions from carbon savings:

- Increase the proportion of modern fuel efficient vehicles by a replacement programme for old vehicles

- Use of larger vehicles with full loads as volumes increase

- Use of cleaner, high grade diesel fuel even where this is more expensive

- Improve utilisation to decrease the number of 'empty load' journeys which waste fuel without benefit (more IT, more common loads, greater flexibility in drivers' contracts)

- Better refrigeration to reduce emissions from this source

- Compliance with EU regulations in advance of implementation

Examiner's comments:

In (i) most candidates performed well. There were good discussions centred around the fact that there were differences in HH's and Freshco's core competences, the provision of up to date vehicles and alternative transport routes and the opportunity to diversify into other areas. Candidates identified the main issues and made reference to cost savings because of the ability of drivers to sleep in their vehicles, new routes and modes of transport which would open, plus access to more sophisticated IT systems which would in turn, lead to efficiencies.

Application skills on this requirement were generally good, and high skills marks were accordingly awarded.

In (ii) environmental sustainability was not answered as well as expected. This was surprising as it is very topical. Many candidates tended to cite 'trucks fitted with green technology' but did not elaborate further nor give any other points. Many also failed to answer this in the context of the Freshco contract. This was quite disappointing.

Only a minority attempted to provide some generic definition of environmental sustainability, and those who did tended to provide only weak definitions. Only a significant minority mentioned the contribution of RailTrans.

(c) Potential acquisition of RailTrans

Benefits

The acquisition of RailTrans is a major diversification away from road transport and therefore reduces dependence, to an extent, on the road transport industry. Thus, fuel cost increases, more adverse regulation, road congestion, road pricing may all put pressure on the viability of the road haulage industry. In this case, access to rail transport may give some alternative if only at the margin.

The access to rail transport gives HH the chance to offer multimodal transport which may combine the benefits of multiple methods in a single journey eg long distances or large loads by train (eg from Spain to the UK), then shorter distances to multiple destinations (onward transport within the UK).

Observable and clear carbon reductions to meet Freshco's requirements and more generally.

Compete more effectively with EU road haulage.

Reduced variable costs.

Potential to use rail for two major customers, Goonhill and Freshco, if these contracts are retained and entered into respectively. Common usage on the Spain route will give scale benefits.

Expansion into Europe to give greater European presence. May be benefits for integrated rail and road transport for acquiring new customers in Europe.

Problems

High initial cost which:

- Increases operating gearing with high fixed costs

- Damages liquidity if it is a cash acquisition which may be a particular issue in a recession

- Increases sun costs if venture fails (eg lose Goonhill contract and/or Freshco contract not entered into)

HH has no core competence in rail transport.

Integration costs may be high with two separate sectors.

Synergies may be low given different sector unless a degree of co-ordination and integration can be achieved through multi-modal transport. What HH can add to RailTrans's existing business may need to be significant to make the acquisition viable.

Rail transport may be leased rather than acquiring an entire company to enter this sector of the market.

Overall much will depend on the acquisition price as to whether this would be viable.

Examiner's comments:

This section was generally well answered with candidates noting the obvious benefits and risks, with some application to the scenario. The better candidates presented their answers in terms of acceptability, feasibility and suitability or (less frequently) Porter's attractiveness framework. This enabled them to produce more structured answers. Weaker candidates produced largely generic lists, with minimal application, and which could been applied to almost any acquisition.

32 Cutting Edge Ltd (CE)

Marking guide

			Knowledge	Skill	Marks
(a)		Advantages/Disadvantages of options 1 and 2	6	10	15
(b)	(i)	Prepare balanced scorecard	3	6	
	(ii)	Discuss whether balanced scorecard is the best method of monitoring performance	2	3	
					12
			11	19	27

(a) **Option 1 - Direct control by Jane**

This would mean a wide span of control for Jane with significant centralisation.

The current organisational structure of ET was entrepreneurial with key decisions being taken by the main shareholder. Jane has replaced that role as ET is now a division within Cupitt.

This proposal is very centralised, with Jane taking most of the key decisions, not just at divisional level but for the key operations at the level on the individual salon (pricing, staffing, inventories of products).

The managers therefore have little strategic or even operational autonomy in the day to day affairs of the salon. All these will be imposed by Jane with little responsibility for managers.

The **advantages** of central control for ET include the following:

- If managers are of poor quality (as suggested by Jane's initial review) then they may not be capable of making good decisions if they had autonomy. While good local managers may add benefits with knowledge of local conditions, poor local managers may be worse than good a central manager.

- The close geographical proximity of the salons in Northern England enables close personal control by Jane (eg frequent personal visits).

- There is effective communication and monitoring of the salons using the new IT system so Jane can readily monitor performance at each salon.

- Co-ordinated decisions can take place so a coherent brand image is presented.

- The decentralisation of key strategic decisions would be important where rapid responses are required in a changing and dynamic environment. However, hairdressing is a reasonably stable environment which is suitable to slower, more considered centralised decision making.

- ET is a small division where the span of control is wide, but reasonable, so Jane is not overburdened in making centralised decisions and can have reasonable knowledge of each salon.

- The more diverse the organisation, the greater the need for lower down decision making and specific expertise. In the case of ET however there is a large degree of homogeneity between salons so centralised control of decisions may be more appropriate.

The **disadvantages** of central control for ET include the following:

- Individual managers cannot be held directly accountable for the profitability of individual salons. They may be able to improve the service and motivate more customers to visit the salon but this is limited if there are poor quality staff who are not properly trained or if prices are too high.

- Salon managers may become demotivated with their lack of control an inability to influence performance. This may increase if they are to be held responsible for performance.

- Highly centralised structures tend to stifle innovative strategic solutions and result in less flexibility to react to changing marketplaces or requests of individual customers.

Option 2 - Franchise

Under a franchise a firm grants other firms the right to use its brand, its product or its know-how. There is likely to be central control and support, advertising of the brand. In return, the franchisee will provide a lump sum, share of earnings and specific payments.

In the current context, a franchise could be on a geographical basis (eg one for each city) in order to segregate the markets of the franchisees. Alternatively each salon could be franchised out individually.

The **advantages** of franchising ET include:

- Attract better new managers than ET's current managers

- If ET's current managers took over a franchise they would take on the risk

- Enables new salons to be opened to expand the ET business, so there would be quicker business expansion than using Cupitt's own financial resources alone

- Reduced risk by having franchisees' own capital

- Generates incentives with franchisees' keeping residual rewards and using local knowledge

- Maintains some control over salons

- If franchising is temporary then ET could retake control of the business after salon's have been improved

- Ultimately could abandon the ET brand to the franchisees and expand using the Cupitt brand

The **drawbacks** of franchising ET include:

- The need to share profits with franchisees

- The need to monitor franchisees

- Poor franchisees may harm ET brand name but given problems with previous this risk is small and brand may actually be improved by enthusiastic franchisees

- There needs to be some incentive to purchase a franchise and with the poor performance recently under Peter this may be difficult.

- Risks of operational and contractual disputes with franchisees

- Increased monitoring costs which may vary depending on the perceived risk of the franchisee

Examiner's comments:

Candidates identified the main points on both centralised and franchised structures. Good answers included the fact that a centralised structure would be demotivating for managers of salons, there would be overall goal congruence and control but it would limit management being able to have independence, which could in turn stifle ideas and adaptation to the local conditions facing each salon. In addition candidates identified that Jane was not experienced in this sector and was also a very young manager with no knowledge of how the salons were run in practice, and with a very wide span of control.

The points on franchises which were commonly made centred on the loss of control for Jane, problems with branding, maintaining standards across salons, risks to reputation and lack of consistency of products.

(b) (i) **Financial perspective**

Goals	KPIs
Profitability	Operating profit per salon
	Profit from each activity (hairdressing, beauty treatments, sun tanning)
	Gross margin %
	Net margin %
Revenue	Revenue growth
	Revenue from each activity
	Annual revenue per customer
Shareholder value	Return of capital employed
	Projected profit growth
Liquidity	Operating cash flows
	Projected cash balances

Customer perspective

Goals	KPIs
Overall Customer satisfaction	Scores on customer surveys (satisfaction)
Customer acquisition	% of sales from new customers
	New customers taking up offers
	Growth in customer numbers
Reliability of service	% of customers commenced on time
	% of customers completed on time
Customer dissatisfaction	Number of written complaints per salon
Market share	Revenue as % of sector revenue
Competitive Price	Comparison to competitors
	Price based complaints
	Response of customers to price changes

Internal perspective

Goals	KPIs
Quality of service	Number of repeat bookings
Quality of assets	Average age of facilities
Utilisation	Appointments made/total available appointments
Quality of staff	Hairdresser training expenditure
	Qualifications achieved

Innovation and learning perspective

Goals	KPIs
New hairstyles and treatments	% of revenue from new styles
	% of profit from new styles
Employee satisfaction	Staff turnover
	Staff complaints
Technology capability	Customer complaints concerning IT booking
	Use of new equipment
Widening of services	% of profit from new services
	% of revenue from new services
	Growth in revenue from new services
	Growth in profit from new services

(ii) **Balanced Scorecard**

The BSC approach seeks to develop a range of measures that are linked to strategic objectives and the operations to achieve those objectives. As such, it has the following advantages:

- It emphasizes long term strategic business development rather than just short term financial achievement (eg customer satisfaction this year may determine profits in future years)

- Financial measures alone may ignore strategic goals

- A range of financial and non financial objectives are addressed which balance strategic and operational goals

- Short term financial measures only offer a single perspective on performance

- Short term financial measures can be subject to distortion

Overall a BSC approach enables Jane to measure whether key strategic goals are being achieved.

A disadvantage is that BSC may have too many goals which may conflict or lack prioritisation and this may confuse managers.

Alternative measures could include: financial measures only and benchmarking.

If the performance of managers, as opposed to the performance of the salons themselves is to be measured using a balanced scorecard then it is important that managers have control over the factors affecting the KPIs. This appears to be the case under the new suggested organisational structure where managers have significant autonomy.

Examiner's comments:

In section (i), candidates' performance was surprisingly disappointing. Even in terms of the knowledge of the format and structure of the BSC, many candidates where unable to demonstrate these basics and hence lost many of the knowledge marks. There was even confusion as to the nature of basic goals and KPIs. Some answers were little more than a general narrative, while others grouped a series of goals together, then grouped a series of KPIs, without ever relating individual goals to individual KPIs. The KPIs were often very general and sometimes not relevant to this particular business. However, some answers were excellent and showed skills by applying the BSC very specifically to the scenario and using KPIs such as profit from different treatments within the salons, number of repeat customers, number of additional products (such as shampoos etc) bought by customers, number of complaints, staff retention and ability to attract experienced stylists. This type of answer was however all too infrequently produced by candidates.

In (ii) better answers evaluated the BSC both generically and in terms of its applicability to CE. A minority ignored the BSC almost entirely and devoted most of the answer to a discussion of benchmarking as being more appropriate.

33 Supaspeed Ltd (Supa)

			Knowledge	Skill	Marks
(a)	Industry evolution		2	7	8
(b)	Value chain/key drivers		4	7	10
(c)	(i)	Calculations		9	
	(ii)	Evaluation of new strategy, including other info		11	
					18
(d)	Stakeholders		2	6	7
			8	40	43

General comments:

The company in this scenario (Supa) specialises in the home delivery of parcels for the Business-to-Consumer market. The market is highly competitive, with a wide variety of choice in terms of different companies and different delivery services. The industry has been significantly affected by free trade and globalisation, technological advances and the development of the internet/online shopping. This has led to a wider customer base, changed the nature of delivery services and increased customer expectations. Having found it hard to compete with the major players, Supa decided to exit the non-urgent delivery market and invest heavily in technology in order to offer a time-guaranteed next-day delivery service. It is now carrying out a post investment audit to decide whether the strategy, implemented at 2008, has been successful. The operations director has suggested Supa could improve results further by closing half of its depots and creating a new centralised sorting facility.

Overall candidates performed well on this question.

(a) Evolution of parcel home delivery industry

Examiner note:

Models such as PESTEL or 5 forces may have been used to generate ideas. Use of the industry life cycle model to explain the development of the industry was also acceptable.

Evolution of parcel home delivery industry

Development of global distribution networks

Reduced protectionism and increased global trade have widened cross-border trade and increased the trend for businesses to outsource. Business customers need to send parcels to customers in many different countries. This requires parcel companies to have a global distribution network and has led to consolidation within the industry as the leading companies grow by acquisition. It has also led to increased co-operation as a business model, with smaller companies creating global networks through the use of strategic alliances or partnerships.

The economic development of countries such as China and India also provides new customers from different cultures who may need dealing with in different ways from the traditional domestic customers. Using local partners helps to address this.

Finally the development of partnerships as a business model is facilitated by the ease of communication and technology which allows the sharing of data/information between business partners.

Range of services offered

Historically the industry offered a standard delivery service for mail-order businesses. A wide range of services has now been introduced to address the changing expectations of customers:

- Development of express service due to customers' reduced tolerance of delays (want speed of delivery to match speed of ordering on the internet)

- Significant reduction in time for non-urgent deliveries (2-3 working days compared to the previous 14 days for mail order customers)

- Introduction of specified time/date deliveries – facilitated by technology which allows better logistical planning

- Automated tracking service for customers to address their need for visibility

- Premium priced environmentally friendly (carbon neutral) services

Customer base

A big increase in internet trade has widened the target market for delivery companies and reduced their reliance on mail order customers. Also new market segments have developed due to the use of online marketplaces such as eBay and this may lead to an increasingly significant C2C market.

Delivery methods

Increased focus on the environment has led to a change in packaging materials offered to ensure they are recyclable, and the development of carbon neutral delivery services.

There has been a reduced focus on air transportation methods due to rising costs and security concerns. Higher fuel prices have increased costs and put pressure on margins.

Pricing and competition

The internet has made pricing structures more transparent.

The industry has become increasingly competitive with companies constantly differentiating themselves by offering different service features.

Impact of technology

The internet and IT have already been mentioned as having had a major impact on the industry in a number of areas:

- Increased demand as the use of e-commerce provides a wider geographic market and new customers

- Greater ability of customers to compare prices and services between competitors and increased expectations concerning speed of delivery

- Use of IT to improve logistical planning and efficiency of distribution, and also to increase levels of customer service through delivery reminders and tracking

Examiner's comments:

Requirement (a) asked candidates to explain how the parcel home delivery industry has evolved in the face of changing consumer demand and other key external factors. Answers were of a good standard, with most candidates extracting the key information from the scenario. High marks were awarded to those who structured their answers so as to distinguish between consumer and external factors, and who demonstrated clearly the impact of those factors on the industry. A number of candidates applied strategic models such as PESTEL and/or Industry life cycle to help them develop a balanced answer.

(b) **VCA**

Value chain

A value chain is the sequence of business activities by which value is added to the products or services produced by a company. Primary activities create value and are directly concerned with providing the product/service. Support activities do not create value in themselves, but enable the primary activities to take place with maximum efficiency.

VCA recognises that it is the way that a company's resources are organised that ensures that its products or services are valued by its customers. Thus it is the relationship or linkages between the company's resources, activities and processes that are important and which create a profit margin - the margin being the excess that the customer is prepared to pay for the service over the cost of providing it. Competitive advantage is sustained by linkages in the chain and the wider value system that extends to a company's various business partners. VCA can also be used to identify activities in the chain which are not adding value.

Supa's value chain consists of the following:

Primary activities:

Inbound logistics – collecting the parcel from the customer (or receiving it at the depot)
Operations – sorting, storage and transportation scheduling

Outbound logistics – delivering the parcel to the end customer

Marketing and sales – advertising and promotion

Service – handling of redeliveries, lost or damaged parcels, complaints

Support activities

Infrastructure (the way the company is organised, its management structure etc)
Technology
HR
Procurement

Competitive advantage for a parcel delivery company centres on providing an excellent service, which involves two key aspects: the physical collection and delivery of a parcel and the management and utilisation of the information relating to that delivery.

In terms of Porter's generic strategy, Supa is a focussed differentiator and the key value drivers within Supa's value chain include:

Use of technology to

- Increase cost efficiency of collection and distribution through better logistical planning due to real time information provided by GPS system, notebook computers etc

- Increase likelihood of first time delivery (use of chosen time slots and delivery reminders means customers are more likely to be in), reducing costly redeliveries and the risk of lost parcels

- Provide better customer service due to enhanced visibility/automated tracking facility

- Share information with JV partners in the distribution network thus generating a more seamless service

Customer service

- Ability to specify timed delivery slots
- Automated tracking facility
- Text/email messaging services
- First to introduce carbon neutral delivery option

HR

- People treated as a valuable resource not a commodity

- Strong customer service ethos

- Investment in training and development, particularly with reference to using the technology and customer service

- Corporate uniform generates strong cultural identity

Marketing

Distinctive company branded purple uniform, vans and packaging

Extended value system

Use of strategic partners which provides global coverage and better understanding of local customers' needs. Again this is facilitated by technology and sharing of information

Examiner's comments:

Requirement (b) asked candidates to analyse Supa's value chain and describe clearly its key value drivers. Most candidates demonstrated a good understanding of the components of the value chain and were able to explain them in the context of Supa's parcel delivery. A disappointing number failed to highlight the key value drivers and, when they did so, often focussed simply on trivial issues such as the use of purple vans and uniforms. The best candidates identified that Supa was a focussed differentiator and that, as such, its use of technology to improve speed of delivery and customer service was key to its competitive advantage. Despite an instruction to the contrary in the question, a minority of candidates produced a value chain diagram.

(c) **Evaluation of performance**

(i) **Exhibit 2 missing figures:**

Revenue growth:

Note. to assist with interpretation the figure for 2008-20 10 could be annualised.

Budget 2008-2010 = 42.3-35/35 = 20.86% , annualised = 10.43% (simple) or 9.94% (compound)

Actual 2008-2010 = 46-35/35 = 31.43%, annualised = 15.71% (simple) or 14.64% (compound)

Operating profit margin:

Budget 2010 = 2.1/42.3 = 4.96%

Actual 2010 = 1.6 1/46 = 3.5%

Appendix of financial performance indicator

	Supa Budget 2010	Supa Actual 2010	Supa Actual 2008	Mkt leader 2010
BSC missing financial measures				
Annualised revenue growth	10.43%	15.71%	n/a	n/a
Operating margin	4.96%	3.5%	3.00%	4.47%
Parcel stats				
Average revenue per parcel	£9.00	£10.00	£7.45	£9.05
Operating profit per parcel	£0.45	£0.35	£0.22	£0.40
Operating costs £m	40.20	44.39	33.95	363.00
Operating costs per parcel	£8.55	£9.65	£7.22	£8.64
Depot stats				
Parcels handled per depot (m)	0.235	0.230	0.235	0.840
Average revenue per depot £m	2.12	2.30	1.75	7.60
Operating cost per depot £m	2.01	2.2195	1.6975	7.26

(ii) All calculations are provided in the supporting appendix.

In assessing whether the implementation of the new strategy has been a success we can consider:

- Whether actual performance has improved since 2008 (actual 2008 to 2010)

- Whether the performance achieved is as good as Supa intended (actual 2010 compared to budget 2010) and compares favourably with that of the market leader

- The non- financial perspective provided by the other BSC indicators

Intended impact of strategy

A review of the budget suggests that in the first two years of the new strategy Supa intended to maintain the volume of parcels handled at 4.7m but increase revenue and profit, by more than doubling the operating margin per parcel from 22 pence to 45 pence. Further analysis indicates that this was to be achieved by increasing the average revenue per parcel from £7.45 to £9.00. This can be explained by Supa's decision to pull out of non-urgent deliveries market (the most price sensitive market) and focus on overnight deliveries with a specified time slot, which are likely to command a price premium. Supa has had to invest heavily in technology to offer this service and is likely to have had to increase the frequency of deliveries given the number of time slots it is now offering. This is reflected by the budgeted 18% increase in operating costs from £33.95 to £40.2m.

2010 Actual performance (new strategy) in relation to Actual 2008 (old strategy)

The change in strategy appears to have resulted in revenue increased by over 31% from £35m to £46m (or 15.7% per annum). This has been achieved by a marginal reduction in the volume of parcels handled (4.6m compared to 4.7m) and a significant increase since 2008 in the actual average revenue per parcel from £7.45 to £10, reflecting the change in strategy towards the higher value deliveries.

Operating costs per parcel have increased significantly from £7.22 to £9.65. This is likely to be due to the increased frequency of customer deliveries and the additional costs incurred for the new technology required in order to offer guaranteed time slots, provide delivery reminders and track parcels.

The increase in the prices charged to the client more than outweighs the increased cost however, so operating profit has increased from £0.22 to £0.35 per parcel, resulting in an increased operating margin (3.5% compared to 3% in 2008).

2010 Actual performance in relation to budget

2010 revenue is 8.7% more than budgeted despite the volume of parcels being slightly down at 4.6m compared to the budget of 4.7m. The fact that the average revenue at £10 per parcel is higher than the budget of £9 may reflect a difference in the product mix compared to that forecast eg relatively more deliveries than expected being undertaken during the most expensive 7am-9am slot. Alternatively Supa may have been forced to increase prices in an attempt to cover the increase in operating costs and this could have reduced demand.

Overall operating costs are 10% higher than budgeted and, at £9.65, significantly more expensive per parcel than the budget of £8.55. Since a high proportion of Supa's costs are fixed, an increase in the volume of parcels handled would reduce the average cost per parcel. If total costs were to remain at the 2010 level of £44.5m, Supa would need to handle 5.2m parcels in order to achieve the target cost of £8.55. Alternatively it needs to reduce its operating costs and this may be what has motivated the operations director's suggestions regarding the rationalisation of depots.

Comparison with market leader

It is hard to compare Supa directly to the market leader (ML). Supa's market share is only 21% of theirs. The ML has 30 more depots and the appendix shows that these are significantly larger, handling an average 840,000 parcels per depot (Supa 230,000), generating 3.3 times the amount of revenue (£7.6m compared to Supa's £2.3m) and incurring average operating costs of £7.2m (Supa £2.2m).

In terms of market positioning, Supa's target implies they intended to price themselves just below the market leader at £9, although in practice they have achieved average revenue of £10 per parcel. This may be because of a change in pricing strategy or alternatively because Supa has different types of customer or product mix.

The ML is likely to have greater international coverage than Supa and so it may be more relevant to compare Supa's performance with the ML results for the UK deliveries, if they were available.

Balanced scorecard indicators

The balanced scorecard indicators may be viewed as a vertical hierarchy, with the quality of the processes (as measured by innovation and learning) leading to increased business efficiency (internal business) and hence customer satisfaction. Conversely the failure of internal processes may explain inefficient operations or lower customer satisfaction.

Looking at the innovation and learning perspective, Supa has successfully implemented employee training with respect to the new IT systems which reinforces its commitment to HR as a valuable resource. It is however falling short of its target in respect of IT downtime.

The new service with specified time slots relies on technology, hence delivery problems may have arisen as a result of the system being unavailable (eg an inability to text or email the parcel recipient to remind them about the delivery), resulting in a failed first attempt. As we can see from the internal perspective, Supa has only managed to achieve a first attempt delivery rate of 65% against a target of 70%. The other internal measure is the number of trips made per vehicle. Utilisation rates will be a key factor in driving operational efficiency and lack of system availability may have caused scheduling problems and hence delivery failures.

This could explain why both the customer perspective measures are less than the target, and also explain why costs per parcel are relatively higher. Failed attempts at delivery potentially increase the chance of the parcel going missing or having to be returned to the sender as undelivered. They also lead to Supa incurring additional administration and transport costs associated with the redelivery, for which there will be no additional revenue. Certain customers may have built targets into their service level agreements allowing them to claim discounts or refunds if Supa fails to meet these targets, making failed deliveries even more costly as a result of a negative impact on revenue as well as increasing cost.

Quality and standard of budget/targets

When considering performance it may be that the 'budget' rather than the 'actual' is at fault. It is possible that the targets set were too ambitious, given the changes in system and strategy, and failed to take into account teething problems/learning curve issues. Alternatively the targets may have been deliberately ambitious in order to motivate staff to aim for the top and management may be very pleased with the results.

What is not clear is how Supa has performed in comparison with previous years or competitors, and more information is required to do this (see below).

Further information required

Breakdown of results

- Detailed breakdown of operating costs to assess areas of over-/under-spend and scope for rationalisation

- Analysis of revenue, costs and profit for 2008 by type of service would allow us to see how Supa's performance has improved in the speed sensitive delivery market

- Analysis by depot – to assess performance of individual depots/managers

- Analysis of pricing structure and revenue by time slot (pre 9am or weekends are priced more highly than afternoon deliveries)

- Results for 2009 in order to consider year on year performance. 2009 was the transition year

- Monthly management accounts to assess any seasonality impact

- 2008 and 2009 balanced scorecard measures for next day deliveries to assess whether the service has improved as a result of introduction of the new technology

Comparatives

- Details of the industry average prices for the different services on offer

- Benchmarks for the other indicators in the BSC to assess how Supa is performing in relation to the best overnight parcel delivery company (competitor benchmark) and also any other market leaders in distribution or companies renowned for their fleet management/distribution capabilities

- Could also do internal benchmarking by comparing individual depots with Supa's best depot. This might help the operations director decide which depots to consider for rationalisation

Objectives/budgets/targets

- In order to assess performance fully, details of the aims and specific objectives for the change in strategy would be helpful (eg increase market share by x%, retain more customers)

- Part of a post-investment audit would include assessing the quality and accuracy of the forecasts and budgets. In order to do this more information would be required about assumptions made

- Details of management expectations regarding the appropriate level of achievement of the target would also be useful

Preliminary conclusion

On the face of the initial analysis, the strategy appears to have been a success, having grown both revenue and profit, but there is more scope for Supa to increase its operational efficiency. Comparisons with the market leader would suggest that one way of achieving this is to reduce the number of depots but increase the size of each.

Examiner's comments:

Requirement (c) was the data analysis requirement and dealt with whether the implementation of the new strategy had been a success. Candidates were provided with actual company results for 2008 and 2010, a budget for 2010 and relevant data for the market leader. They were then asked (i) to prepare two specific calculations (revenue growth and operating margin) together with other relevant financial performance indicators; and (ii) to use their calculations in (i) and the balanced scorecard indicators provided in the scenario to evaluate the impact of the new strategy. An indication of useful additional information was also required.

Almost all candidates were able to calculate the two specific performance indicators requested, although very few recognised that to aid interpretation it might be sensible to annualise the figures for revenue growth. There was some variability in candidates' ability to calculate other meaningful ratios, and those that were weak in this area then struggled to provide a meaningful interpretation of financial performance in (ii), as they had little on which to base their discussion.

The better candidates were able to identify the need for calculations on a per parcel basis such as average revenue/operating profit/cost per parcel, and also to provide comparisons between Supa's 2010 actual results and the figures for 2010 budget, 2008 and the market leader.

Weaker candidates tended to focus only on revenue calculation, or only considered the comparison between 2010 actual and budget, producing relatively few calculations for the 8 marks available. Those candidates who focused on calculations per depot appeared to have given little thought to the figures that would be relevant in determining Supa's performance, since the number of depots had remained static throughout the period.

In part (ii) most candidates produced a reasonable evaluation of the financial impact of the strategy and the non-financial performance measures provided, and a larger proportion of candidates seemed well-prepared for the balanced scorecard than at the previous sitting. Some weaker candidates did however ignore the balanced scorecard measures. Better candidates linked their discussion, using the increased system downtime to explain the failure to meet certain delivery targets and then suggesting that this might explain the increased operating costs. Stronger candidates also questioned the accuracy of the initial budget, and/or identified that it was still very early to judge the success or otherwise of the strategy.

As in the past, weaker answers tended to describe what had happened to various figures (eg increased or decreased) rather than attempting to address how it had happened (eg analysing the data in more detail) or why it had happened (eg identifying underlying factors discussed in the scenario which may have caused the changes). The additional useful key information from the poorer students was also the usual generic list of cash flows, balance sheets, management accounts and competitor information.

(d) Depot closure

Power/interest matrix

The impact of the proposed depot rationalisation on the employees can be assessed by the Mendelow power-interest matrix.

The interest of the employees will certainly be high. The extent of their power may be less so.

Interest

Interest will be high due to:

- Concerns about job security and possible loss of jobs

- Impact of any proposed relocation for example to the new central sorting hub

- Inability to find replacement work locally due to economic slowdown and general level of unemployment

However if the redundancy payments offered are sufficiently high, some employees may favour voluntary redundancy to continued employment and thus have a positive interest in closure of the depot (eg if they were going to leave anyway or were close to retirement).

Power

The power of employees to stop or moderate any decision is limited. As individuals the employees have low power, however their collective power will partly depend on the extent to which the workforce is unionised. It will also depend on the level of support for the depot staff from the rest of Supa's workforce. If the entire UK workforce is united, then significant costs can arise from disruption. Once the decision is announced and implemented however, then the remaining employees who are to retain their jobs have a much lower negative interest in the decision.

Where depot employees may have some power is in resisting the change and therefore increasing the costs involved. In this respect the threat of action may make the perceived exit costs higher, particularly when the costs of damaging the brand are taken into account. Employees may expect to have more power/influence as Supa has historically treated them as a valuable resource and they are a key factor in providing good customer service.

Examiner's comments:

Requirement (d) asked candidates to explain how the depot sorting staff, as key stakeholders, would be affected by and have the power to resist the operational director's proposal to rationalise the depots. A significant number of candidates used Mendelow's matrix, and may considered staff on both an individual and a group (unionised) basis. Stronger candidates identified both positive and negative consequences of the rationalisation proposals and the fact that staff resistance might disrupt the process or increase the company's costs, but would be unlikely to prevent closure.

34 e-Parts Ltd (EP)

Marking guide

		Knowledge	Skill	Marks
(a)	Relevance of risk management/contents of BCP	3	4	6
(b)	Key IT risks and management	4	5	8
(c)	Outsourcing to implement IT strategy	3	5	7
		10	14	21

(a) **Risk management and business continuity planning**

Risk management is the process of identifying and assessing the risks facing EP's business and the development, implementation and monitoring of a strategy to respond to those risks, in order to reduce threats to acceptable levels.

When running a business, risk is unavoidable and will include financial, strategic, operational and hazard risks arising from both internal and external sources. Risk management is a corporate governance issue as there is the danger that directors of companies might take decisions intended to increase profits without giving due regard to the risks. They may also continue to operate without regard to the changing risk profile of their organisation.

The point of risk management is that risks can be mitigated if management have plans to deal with problems if they occur. Risk management should be carried out by all businesses and involve all levels of staff and management. The aim is to prioritise the risks according to the ones that threaten the business most and then to take action to reduce or otherwise address the risk.

In addition to the general risks faced by all businesses, as a retailer EP faces additional risks because it carries large volumes of stock and also because business is largely done online (see (b)). A key issue for an online business is that technical failure has a significant and immediate impact. Problems with the ecommerce site are immediately visible and it is easy for customers to switch to a competitor if the website is unavailable. Thus it is important for EP to take action to prevent/reduce losses due to excessive risk exposure that may include theft, fraud and data insecurity.

Kamal must ensure that all staff are trained and fully aware of ecommerce security issues and fraud risk.

Whether EP thrives or fails will partly be dependent on how as a business it manages risk and exploits opportunities. The aim is to reduce the probability and/or consequence of failure but retain as far as possible the benefits of success. Thus effective risk management is integral to EP's competitive advantage and will help ensure EP's survival in the longer term.

Business continuity planning is the process through which a business details how and when it will recover and restore operations interrupted by the occurrence of a massive (but rare) risk event eg natural disaster such as a warehouse flood or fire or a major breach of security causing the website to be down for an extended period.

Where risk management is largely pre-emptive, BCP is designed to deal with the consequences of a major realised risk. The difference is also linked to the extent of the impact – for instance the difference between website disruption due to a temporary loss of internet connection and a denial of service attack that places the business's existence in jeopardy.

A BCP is concerned with crisis management and disaster recovery. It must specify the actions to be taken in order to recover from any unexpected disruptive event. Factors that should be considered by a BCP include:

- Securing interim management and staff
- Inventory replacement
- Restoration of data and other IT systems
- Securing interim premises
- Management of the PR issues

Methods of recovery might include:

- Carrying out activities manually until IT services are resumed (eg via the call centre)

- Moving staff at an affected building to another location

- Agreeing with another business to use each other's premises in the event of a disaster

- Arranging to use IT services and accommodation provided by a specialist third-party standby site

All members of ES staff should be aware of the importance of business continuity planning, training should be given and the plan tested regularly.

Examiner's comments:

Requirement (a) asked candidates to explain the relevance of risk management to the business as a whole and to identify the main factors that would be covered in a business continuity plan. Overall answers were of a poor standard with many candidates failing this requirement because they were uncertain about the nature and content of a business continuity plan, despite the clear hint given in the scenario about ensuring the business could continue to function in the event of a major incident. Explanations of risk management tended to be extremely generic and only the best candidates pointed out that risk management was critical given the risks faced by EP as a result of its inventory levels and the e-commerce nature of the business. Weaker candidates often mentioned Turnbull, which demonstrated a lack of understanding of its application.

(b) **Risks of ecommerce and how to manage them**

EP must take steps to minimise the risk of systems failure, protect the integrity of its systems, safeguard information and ensure the continuity of its operations.

Risks may be transferred, avoided, reduced or accepted.

Specific risks arising for EP and recommendations for risk management:

- Inaccessible website/Website too slow/payment system for ecommerce website goes down. This is critical given that 90% sales are online and is likely to result in frustrated customers and lost sales as they can easily switch to another online competitor.

  Risk can be reduced by ensuring appropriate systems development and maintenance takes place and by having back-up servers. EP could also reduce the risk by providing other channels to market and ensuring that customers are directed to alternatives such as the call centre in the event of system delays or failures.

  EP could transfer the risk by outsourcing the provision of the website to a specialist provider (see (c)).

- Identity theft/credit card fraud arising due to online payments – this would damage EP's reputation and may result in lost customers.

  EP should ensure it reduces the risk by having access controls, appropriate payment verification software, firewalls and secure communication.

- Loss of critical data, particularly given there are 2m customers on the database and 100,000 different products to control. Failure of stock control system may cause inaccurate information to be provided regarding stock levels or wrong products to be despatched. Failure to comply with the Data Protection Act could also result in penalties/litigation.

  EP should reduce the risk of inadequate or inaccurate information by performing regular physical stocktakes and reconciling these to computerised records.

  EP must ensure the stock system and customer database are kept up-to date, backed up regularly and hard copies kept off site. It must have systems in place to monitor compliance with data protection regulations and ensure all data held is secure (eg via encryption).

Reduce the risk by ensuring all feedback is screened regularly and ensuring appropriate security features are in place to control access and content.

- IT system becomes out-of-date or is less capable than that of online competitors.

  Systems need to be upgraded regularly to ensure they are capable of providing the necessary capacity, particularly given the growth EP has experienced.

Where risks cannot be reduced or eliminated it may be possible for EP to transfer them via:

- Insurance (however this may be costly and it may be problematic to quantify the extent of business loss from a security incident)

- Contracting out the management of ecommerce to a third party who can host the system (see (c)). The loss may still occur and impact on the business, but the service level agreement can stipulate penalties

Other more generic IT risks include:

- Virus attacks and/or hackers exploiting vulnerabilities in the system (steal data, damage system or corrupt information)

- Website defacement (impact on reputation/brand image)

- Denial of service

- Infrastructure failure eg loss of internet connection

- Software/hardware systems malfunction

- Loss of key IT personnel eg website designer/IT manager

- Risk to corporate information/intellectual property

- Human error

- Deliberate sabotage

- Fraud

- Natural threats (fire, flood, electrical storm)

More generally EP can reduce vulnerability and increase its level of confidence in its technical environment by:

- Installing firewalls, using strong authentication processes and secure communication

- Implementing policies to manage activities eg internet and email usage

- Setting standards for firewalls, servers and procurement of PCs

- Establishing a high level of Information security and access controls, and measuring to detect unauthorised access

- Ensuring there are regular back-ups

- Undertaking appropriate systems development and maintenance

- Ensuring physical and environment security

- Complying with relevant legislation

Examiner's comments:

Requirement (b) asked candidates to identify the key risks arising for EP as a result of its reliance on IT and to recommend how they could be managed. Answers were quite variable. Good answers concentrated on relevant IT risks for EP, including the possible failure of the website, loss of customer database information, identify theft and the possibility of damaging reviews on social networking sites. The best candidates tended to set out their answers in the form of a table, clearly identifying, for each risk identified, the way that it could be managed. A significant number of answers discussed IT risks and the TARA model for risk management in very generic terms. The weakest candidates failed to concentrate on IT risks, mentioning any types of risk they could think of.

(c) **Considerations in outsourcing the provision of the website and inventory control system**

EP is considering outsourcing all its systems relating to the website and stock control.

Factors to consider include the following:

- EP has experienced substantial growth and its current systems may no longer be able to cope with the increasing volume of transactions. Outsourcing may reduce the chance of system breakdown and give EP access to back-up servers and systems.

- Outsourcing would provide access to specialist IT knowledge and allow Kamal to concentrate on the strategy of the company.

- As specialists, with the potential for economies of scale, an outsourcer may be able to provide better, more efficient systems for EP at a lower cost. They are also more likely to be able to keep the systems up-to-date and develop new applications which may help EP maintain its competitive advantage.

- By outsourcing, EP can transfer the risk of systems failure to the IT provider and may have recourse to compensation in the event of financial loss.

However:

- EP has a database of 2m customers. Outsourcing would require it to share confidential information with the IT provider, who may also work with competitors.

- Any problems experienced when transferring the systems over may disrupt EP's business and cause it to lose sales/customers.

- Once EP has decided to outsource it may find it difficult to switch suppliers and is unlikely to be able to revert to in-house provision as it will no longer have its own web designers/IT experts.

Other factors to consider:

- Fees charged by contractor
- Costs currently incurred in own service provision
- Potential redundancies of staff no longer required
- Time and cost involved in agreeing and monitoring service level agreement
- Attitude of influential stakeholders
- Previous incidence and consequence of system breakdown

Conclusion: If EP does decide to outsource it will need to choose a partner carefully, and assess their financial stability and track record of delivering suitable services elsewhere.

It must then agree a series of performance targets and penalties in the event of the contractor's failure to deliver.

Examiner's comments:

In requirement (c) candidates were asked to explain the factors that should be considered by EP in deciding whether to use outsourcing as a method of implementing its IT strategy. Candidates were clearly well rehearsed for this requirement in terms of knowledge but many weaker candidates failed to obtain the available skills marks. This was due to the fact that they produced largely generic lists of pros and cons, with minimal application of EP and its IT strategy, which could have been applied to almost any outsourcing scenario. Better answers focussed specifically on the factors that would influence the choice between in-house and outsourced IT provision and the impact on risks for EP.

---

35 Marcham plc

			Knowledge	Skill	Marks
(a)	Report format				
	(i)	Info system benefits/competitive advantage	3	6	
	(ii)	SFA banking strategy	3	10	
	(iii)	Organic growth v joint development	3	6	
					28
(b)	Ethical issues		3	6	8
			12	28	36

General comments:

This scenario relates to a major supermarket chain which is proposing to take advantage f the recent turmoil in the banking sector by launching its own banking services (rather than as a joint venture with another bank). Marcham has a 30% share of the supermarket sector and was the first supermarket to introduce a loyalty card. Along with an EPOS and inventory control system the loyalty card forms part of an integrated information and knowledge management system and is to be a key driver of competitive advantage for the expansion into banking. Candidates were provided with an extract from a national newspaper which has recently criticised Marcham for using its loyalty card to spy on customers and for abusing its suppliers.

Overall the performance on this question was quite good, although weaker candidates struggled with the requirement on ethics.

(a) Report

To:	Operations Director
From:	AN Other
Date:	September 2010
Re:	Information systems and proposed expansion into banking

(i) Benefits of and use of information system for competitive advantage

- Increased revenue (from customers and also from sale of data to suppliers)

- Reduced costs (better stock control)

- Increased customer service and hence improved customer retention – effectively the loyalty card acts as a barrier to exit for the customer

- Improved decision making (forecasting, scenario planning, market analysis)

- Existing database for direct marketing

- Targeted discount coupons as a form of price discrimination

- EPOS system facilitates better stock control, allowing for a Just-in-Time approach which reduces costs and wastage

Marcham's competitive advantage (CA)

In the supermarket industry, most players have EPOS systems and loyalty card schemes. In order for CA to arise, Marcham not only needs to be better at capturing information than competitors but also better at using it.

The loyalty scheme is a form of relationship marketing whereby Marcham is trying to build a long-term relationship with the customer. Marcham's CA arises because in terms of capturing the information:

- It was the first of its kind to introduce the scheme and therefore captured (and retained) an initial loyal customer base, obtaining first-mover advantage

- Its dominance within the market (60% of the UK population shop at a Marcham store at least once a month and 1 in 4 adults in the UK belong to its customer loyalty scheme) means it has a more extensive database than any other competitor (data about more customers and also collected for longer)

In terms of its ability to use the information:

- It has reduced costs by increasing the frequency and accuracy of ordering, leading to lower levels of inventory and wastage

- It has more effective marketing which facilitates market segmentation and targeting, so low price goods can be promoted to certain customers and high quality ones to others

- It has better price discrimination and hence increased margins

- It can to trade up sales by targeting promotions

- The percentage of customer spend can be extended by identifying products customers are likely to buy but may currently be buying elsewhere

- It has higher margins – it is cheaper to keep existing customers and to sell more to them than it is to attract new ones

- It is likely to result in a higher success rate for new product lines as it has already identified what customers want

- It shares this with suppliers, generating revenue from the sale of the database, promoting better captive relationships with the supplier and improving the matching of products with demand

Within the financial services sector none of the competitors has loyalty cards so Marcham will have first mover advantage if it uses the loyalty card within the banking sector.

Examiner's comments:

Requirement (a) asked candidates to write a report which (i) explains the potential benefits of an effective information system for a supermarket and discusses how Marcham has used its information systems to create competitive advantage in the supermarket industry (ii) assesses the suitability, feasibility and acceptability of Marcham's proposed expansion into the banking sector and (iii) discusses the relative merits of Marcham's intention to expand into banking via organic growth rather than having an established bank as a business partner.

A minority of candidates did not use the report heading which was disappointing.

In (a) (i) most candidates were able to discuss the benefits of an information system in a retail environment citing better inventory control and improved supply chain management to help minimise costs and prevent wastage. In addition, if buying habits of customers could be tracked then market segmentation, targeted marketing and price discrimination could be undertaken.

The better candidates considered the benefits for the industry and then the reasons for Marcham's competitive advantage separately. Weaker candidates tended to simply discuss information systems in the context of Marcham but in doing so did not explain clearly the reasons for the firm's potentially sustainable competitive advantage. Thus they failed to recognise that most supermarkets have EPOS systems and many have loyalty cards, and that the benefits for Marcham arise because of it being the first to introduce a loyalty card, its dominance in the market and its integration with suppliers – all of which allow it to capture more data and be better at using it than competitors.

(ii) **Suitability, feasibility, acceptability**

Suitability (strategic logic and fit)

There is a precedent as Marcham would not be the first major retailer to get involved in financial services (Tesco, Sainsbury, M&S) although it would be the first to set up a full banking service.

Strong brand name – timing is good given some people's loss of faith in the banking sector and perceived lack of transparency surrounding banks' behaviour. The issue is whether Marcham will be seen by consumers as a credible provider of banking services, although the fact that they have been granted a licence suggests the FSA believe they are.

Both banks and supermarkets are about serving personal customers and Marcham already possesses core competence in customer service and responsiveness.

There is also a strong link between retail spending and the need for credit.

Both banks and supermarkets require a presence on the high street and Marcham can use existing infrastructure.

The loyalty card scheme offers exposure to a large number of customers and the opportunity to increase share of customers' spend.

However:

- Are financial services a core competence for retailers?

- It is a very competitive market

- Relatively Marcham will be a very small player faced with large competition

- Core competences in procurement and logistics would be less relevant in banking than if it expanded into other retail areas

- There are onerous compliance requirements related to data protection, identity confirmation, regulatory compliance and money laundering of which Marcham has limited experience

- Many customers now use online banking so Marchambank's presence in stores may not be that attractive to them

Feasibility (can the strategy be implemented?)

This looks at whether Marcham have the necessary resources.

Marcham has already been granted a licence which demonstrates government support.

Branches will be located in existing stores which reduces the overhead costs associated with the operation.

Cash appears to be available although there is an opportunity cost if it is not invested in other new stores.

The loyalty card provides instant access to a database for direct marketing and profiling information which will allow Marcham to tailor products to different groups of customer.

Marcham already has systems in place to collate data about customers and process applications, so credit assessment would simply be a bolt-on.

Marcham would need to hire new staff and management with appropriate financial services knowledge – there is likely to be a big training requirement.

The pricing of financial services and processes are much more complex than individual retail transactions eg selling a loaf of bread.

The banking sector will entail onerous compliance requirements related to data protection, identity confirmation and money laundering.

Financial services are long term in nature so Marcham will need to commit resources for a significant period. It will take time to recoup initial set-up costs and for the venture to become profitable.

Acceptability (to stakeholders)

This considers the likely benefits to stakeholders (returns) and the likelihood of failure and its associated consequences (risk).

Returns

More information is required to assess the proposed financial impact of the strategy. Here we are told that it will offer access to higher margins at a time when the retail business is under pressure, so it may result in increased profitability for shareholders. The core retail business is mature and growing slowly so this offers an opportunity for continued growth.

The government grant reduces the cost of setting up the call centre.

Customers may perceive the strategy as enhancing the service on offer which may help retain/attract new customers for the retail business.

Given the government's stated aim to increase competition they may well look favourably on the venture by Marcham.

It may provide additional career opportunities for some employees.

Risk

The biggest risk is that management have no experience/expertise in financial services products, which are complex.

From a risk point of view, adding financial services spreads the risk profile of Marcham's business. However according to Ansoff this strategy would be classed as unrelated diversification and as a result is a high risk approach to increasing profits. Given recent events, banking is no longer the safe and secure business that it was once deemed to be. Institutional shareholders will already have well diversified portfolios and it could be argued that if shareholders wanted ownership of a bank then they could just buy shares in one themselves.

Shareholders may be concerned that management will be distracted from the core business.

There is a big reputational risk for the existing business if Marcham gets it wrong and it would need to ring fence this area of the business as a separate company.

Marcham may lose customers from the retail business if it rejects applications for loans or credit cards.

Conclusion:

The fact that a number of other supermarkets have launched financial services products suggests that the strategy is viable, although further consideration needs to be given to the best method of implementing the strategy (see (iii)).

Examiner's comments:

Answers to (a) (ii) were generally of a good standard, with many candidates scoring well on the skills marks. The strong candidates clearly knew the difference between 'suitability, feasibility and acceptability', describing how these would be judged more generally, before assessing each in relation to Marcham's expansion into banking. Weaker candidates tended to blur the distinction between the three areas.

The best answers were extremely well-balanced and contrasted the positives (Marcham's brand name, loyal customer base and loyalty card, the grant of £5m, the FSA licence) with the negatives (no experience, increased regulatory requirements, high competition and the fact that space would be taken up in supermarket branches by the banking section which could impact on Marcham's core business.

Some candidates did appear to struggle with the 'acceptability' part of the question and there was a distinct lack of recognition that whiles the proposal had to be acceptable to a variety of stakeholders (investors, customers, government) the impact on risk and return for shareholders was likely to be of critical importance.

(iii) **Organic growth versus joint venture**

Arguments against organic growth (in favour of joint venture)

Gaining competences via organic growth takes time. Marcham does not have any expertise in financial services so will need to buy it in. A partnership with an existing bank would ensure rapid access to the relevant expertise.

There are significant regulation and compliance issues in the banking sector, including barriers to entry such as the licence. Although Marcham has already been granted a licence it will lack expertise and systems to ensure compliance in areas such as money laundering legislation.

The FSA may be more favourable in the long term towards a venture that has already demonstrated financial expertise and compliance.

Most other retailers have chosen to move into financial services through partnership with banks, thus combining banking expertise with the retailer's brand strength and reputation.

Risk is shared.

Arguments in favour of organic growth (against joint venture)

Organic growth gives Marcham full control over the venture and avoids the need to share profits.

Having to buy-in operational expertise from a bank may restrict the scope for Marcham to do banking in a different way, which is a key driver for its strategy.

An alliance with a bank would not address the issue of the public's mistrust of the banking sector. Marcham's loyalty card provides access to existing customer base.

The government grant may not be available if Marcham expands with a partner.

The available choice of partner would be limited as there would be relatively few options available to choose from in terms of a bank with a reputation still intact.

It avoids placing reliance on the future reputation of the chosen partner.

Organic growth avoids any potential clash of strategy or disagreement - banking partners may be reluctant to sanction new financial services products that are critical of their own service provision or that overtly compete.

It saves the time and cost of negotiating terms of a JV agreement, profit share, exit options etc.

Conclusion:

Other supermarkets have chosen to enter financial services with banking partners for a reason and Marcham needs to consider carefully the risks involved in pursuing this strategy alone.

Examiner's comments:

In part (a) (iii), candidates were well prepared to discuss the merits of organic growth vs. joint venture in terms of cost/time/risk. However a disappointing number of answers tended to repeat the learning materials and were not in the context of the scenario. Those candidates who scored higher marks highlighted relevant factors such as the regulation required by the FSA, Marcham's lack of expertise, its information systems and loyalty card and customers' generally poor perception of existing banks.

(b) **Ethics**

Examiner note:

This answer includes more points than is necessary for the marks available but a full range of points has been provided for marking purposes.

Loyalty card:

The issue concerning the loyalty card is really one of ethical marketing and relates to the collection, use and sale of the data gathered in this way. Is Marcham behaving in a fair and transparent manner and what is the likely effect on its customers?

It is partly a question of boundaries – how much data is it reasonable to collect, what is acceptable use and is it legitimate to sell the data on?

Collection of data

The ethical argument is that collection of the data is an invasion of privacy and that it could be abused if it falls into the wrong hands.

Effectively consumers who join the loyalty scheme trade information for product savings. Customers have a choice as to whether to shop at Marcham and whether to join the loyalty card scheme. The fact that 1 in 4 adults belong implies they do not have a problem, or perceive that the benefits are sufficient to compensate for the lack of privacy.

The Data Protection Act (DPA) strictly regulates the confidentiality, storage and use of personal information and Marcham is likely to have sophisticated security and access systems to ensure it does not fall into the wrong hands.

Marcham will also have a stated policy explaining what data is collected and how it is used/shared with preferred partners (transparency) plus an option for consumers to tick a box if they don't want their data shared.

Critics might argue that consumers know what data they have given when they apply to take out a card but lack awareness of how much data is subsequently captured and how it is used. The key ethical issue here is therefore transparency and whether informed and willing consent has been given by consumers to Marcham to utilise data in an agreed manner in return for the benefits of the scheme.

Use of data

Issues concern motives and transparency.

The debate about marketing centres on whether it is about meeting people's needs and expectations or selling people things they don't need.

It could be argued that Marcham uses the loyalty card to better identify the specific needs of different groups of customers and so wastes fewer resources because marketing is targeted. As a result it becomes more efficient at stocking shelves with products consumers want, and can therefore pass the savings on in lower prices, although some argue that this is at the expense of higher prices paid by non-loyalty card holders (lack of fairness/negative effect on some).

Marcham could use data captured to promote healthy food and provide improved education re healthy diets, hence offering a benefit to society.

Profiling could however also be used negatively to exclude undesirable customers (eg recent case of the customer wearing pyjamas whilst shopping at Tesco) or to concentrate on a wealthier class of customers, and this would be regarded as unethical.

Sale of data

The potential issue regarding the sale to third parties (suppliers, direct mail companies, telemarketers) is that Marcham has less control over it and has also made money from it.

DPA means it is illegal for companies to sell on people's details without their consent or for uses other than those they were originally told about. Thus Marcham will give consumers an option on the loyalty card application form to tick a box if they don't want their data shared. This is standard practice engaged in by most retailers.

It is not in Marcham's interests to breach DPA as it will face consequences in terms of damaged reputation and lost customers.

Conclusion

Ultimately Marcham is no different than a whole host of other retailers also operating loyalty card schemes and consumers have the choice of whether to belong to the scheme or not. They can also shop elsewhere if they don't like it.

Treatment of suppliers

Business ethics covers the way a firm as a whole behaves and thus any victimisation of suppliers by Marcham would contravene this. Corporate responsibility would also suggest that Marcham owes a responsibility to society and its wider stakeholders and that a balance needs to be struck between making profits for the shareholders and treating suppliers fairly.

Marcham is being blamed, like a number of other supermarkets and large retailers in the press recently, for exacerbating the poverty of farmers and other weak suppliers.

The issue centres on whether Marcham is merely implementing good supply chain management or is guilty of unethical treatment due to exploitation.

Marcham's ability to dictate terms and conditions to suppliers is evidence of its bargaining power as a customer (Porter) – the bigger the company the greater its likely power to push prices down and demand better payment terms. Lower prices achieved from suppliers may benefit consumers if they are passed on. Thus terms and prices may differ between suppliers depending on their relative bargaining power in relation to Marcham.

The policy of extending payment terms is good cash flow management and could be argued to be in the interests of shareholders.

Even if it adopted standard payment terms, Marcham would be a relatively cash rich business - cash sales mean it has few receivables and JIT policies keep inventories relatively low, leading to an effective cash operating cycle.

The argument against extending payment terms is that Marcham's monopoly position in the market allows them to exploit suppliers by driving prices down, which can force smaller suppliers out of business. Marcham's terms could be compared to the industry average and to other organisations of its size to assess whether they are reasonable. Marcham might be said to be being unfair if it significantly differentiates terms between large and small suppliers, thus abusing its position of power, or if it is not adhering to Industry codes of practice.

However it is unlikely to be in Marcham's interest to drive suppliers out of business as it would then be faced with disruptions in supply or emergency supplies at premium prices. As a major player in the market and a successful plc, Marcham will not want to risk damaging its reputation. Outwardly at least Marcham it is likely to argue that that it supports local businesses and works in partnership with suppliers, adopts ethical procurement policies with transparent payment terms and conditions agreed in advance, and has grievance procedures available to unhappy suppliers.

A lack of personal ethics might lead individual managers to abuse their position or make threats to suppliers and Marcham must ensure it creates an ethical culture and has procedures in place to deal with such inappropriate behaviour.

Note that the OFT has the power to act if it believes that a firm in a dominant position within an industry is abusing its monopoly power.

Finally it is worth pointing out that the newspaper article may be guilty of sensationalism and some of the criticisms may be unfounded.

Examiner's comments:

Requirement (b) asked candidates to discuss the ethical issues raised by the newspaper article in respect of Marcham's customer loyalty card and its treatment of suppliers. This requirement was often not well answered. Weaker candidates failed to apply their knowledge of ethics (in terms of transparency, fairness and corporate responsibility) to the situation provided and a significant number addressed the issues in terms of the commercial consequences of these actions and/or how to manage bad publicity, rather than the ethical implications.

Many answers were extremely one-sided. Weaker candidates adopted the approach that Marcham was acting extremely unethically, was breaching the Data Protection Act in using customer data for other purposes and was intimidating suppliers with its behaviour. Whilst there was merit in some of these propositions, better candidates contrasted this with the fact that customers do have some choice in providing their data and can choose whether they wish their information to be shared with third parties. In addition, Marcham does have significant bargaining power and influence and, whilst there is an obligation for Marcham to act responsibly, what it was doing with suppliers was not illegal and not uncommon within the industry.

The strongest candidates questioned the reliability of the newspaper report.

36 Quantum Agencies Ltd

Marking guide

		Knowledge	Skill	Marks
(a)	PESTEL	4	7	11
(b)	Evaluate performance of QA compared to 2007	-	12	12
(c)	Merits and problems of strategic alliance (Proposal 1 GTA)	2	5	7
(d)	Proposal 2 (Terra)			
	(i) Performance comparison	2	5	7
	(ii) Benefits and problems	3	4	7
		11	33	44

General comments:

This scenario related to a medium-sized, upmarket estate agency, QA with 20 branches. After a number of years of growth in the industry, the recession in the property market has made trading conditions for estate agents difficult. The performance of QA has deteriorated and the two owner-directors are considering two proposals to improve matters. Proposal 1 is to close some branches and enter into a joint venture with a local firm of solicitors, GTA. Proposal 2 is to merge with a rival firm of estate agents, Terra, then rationalise the branch network. Performance data was provided for QA is respect of 2007 and 2010 and also for Terra in respect of 2010.

Candidates were required to:

- Prepare a PESTEL analysis for the UK estate agency industry

- Analyse the performance of QA in 2007 and 2010 explaining the key factors that caused profit to decline

- Discuss the merits and problems of the strategic alliance with GTA in Proposal 1

- Consider Proposal 2 by (i) comparing the performance of QA and Terra in 2010; and (ii) explaining the benefits and problems of the merger and giving advice

(a) **PESTEL**

Political

Political influences relate to the extent to which it is government policy to support the housing market (social housing, owner occupied housing, increased 'new builds') for example in the form of local and national governments' incentives (taxes, grants) and reductions in regulations which are a deterrent to house purchase.

Also, however, given the dependence of the housing market on the prosperity of individuals, the success of a government's economic policies is likely to impact on the housing making.

Economic

The factors affecting the estate agent industry are very closely linked to prosperity and activity in the residential housing market.

One of the major factors that has influenced the industry was the recession, as estate agent sales are strongly dependent on house sales, which in turn are closely correlated with economic prosperity.

The housing market has suffered severely in the recession as disposable incomes have fallen and economic confidence to make major financial commitments has been reduced (eg through redundancies, pay freezes, and general economic uncertainty).

Adverse credit market conditions have meant obtaining mortgage credit is more difficult, although lower interest rates have reduced the cost of credit with some low borrowing rates in evidence.

Social

The increasing population and the change in demographics have expanded the long run potential growth of the housing market. Social trends can also affect the types of houses (eg single dweller or large houses) and the balance between purchased and rented accommodation.

Technological

Increased usage of the internet, and other electronic means of communication, is a threat as a substitute sales channel for direct transactions between buyer and seller without the need for an intermediary estate agent.

Also however internet technology is an opportunity to advertise the stock of each estate agent more effectively to a wider audience.

Ecological/environmental

The requirement for increased energy efficient homes can be both a capital cost to new buyers but also a potential cost saving in energy bills. This may change both the quantity and types of housing sold, but also require estate agents to become more knowledgeable about energy issues.

The continued regulation for an energy efficiency certificate makes buyers and sellers conscious of the environmental factors in addition to energy costs.

Legal

Legal issues can be both a benefit and a cost to the industry. Legislation may directly affect the practices of estate agents, but also impact upon the housing market.

The energy efficiency certificates have been a cost to sellers and thus may have deterred them from putting their houses on the market. However the certificates may have encouraged buyers by reducing uncertainty.

Examiner's comments:

This requirement was generally well answered, with most candidates covering all six elements of the PESTEL framework and generally including appropriate factors under each heading. However, some candidates did not relate their comments specifically to the estate agency industry and discussed only the property market. Some discussions were very well developed, with candidates identifying the issues in the question and being able to explain their impact. Some answers missed out the ecological and environmental impacts completely, even though the new energy efficient certification procedures were mentioned in the question. Poorer answers did not cover all six elements individually, sometimes combining political and legal and/or including wrong content under certain headings. Poorer answers were also characterised by a lack of detail, with only one or two brief points under each heading.

(b) **Data analysis**

	Quantum		Terra	Industry	
	2007	2010	2010	2007	2010
Average value per property (000s)	300	250	250	203	162
% fees earned	75	69.2	69		
% fees from other services	25	30.8	31.0		
% profit/sales	16.7	1.5	–5.7		
Branch costs (000s)	8,500	5,000	7,200		
Total costs (000s)	10,000	6,400	9,200		

QA change data

% change in fees	(45.8)%
% change in profits	(95)%
% change in sales transactions	(25)%
% change in branch costs	(41)%
% change in total costs	(36)%

Data per branch

Fees from sales (000s)	450	225	200
Other fees (000s)	150	100	90
Total fees (000s)	600	325	290
Costs (000s)	425	250	240
Profit per branch (000s)	175	75	50
Number of sales made	100	75	83.3
Number of employees	7	6	5
Number of properties on books	30	35	40

Data per sale made

Total fee per sale (000s)	6	4.3	3.48
Sales fee per sale (000s)	4.5	3	2.4
Branch cost per sale (000s)	4.25	3.33	2.88

Other data

Sales made: average prop held	3.33	2.14	2.08		
Sales revenue per employee (000s)	85.7	54.17	58		
Sales made per employee (no. of properties)	14.3	12.5	16.67		
House price per sale (000s)	300	250	250	203	162
% commission on sales	1.5%	1.2%	0.96%		

Tutorial note:

The detail of the data analysis is more than would be expected from any one candidate but reflects the range of data that may be used by candidates generally.

There is clearly a very substantial deterioration in Quantum's overall company performance between 2007 and 2010.

The fall in fees of almost 46% was a very significant reduction in the level of trade. Due to the fixed nature of many costs, the total cost fell by only 36% resulting in a fall in profit before tax of 95%. In comparing the performance at branch level with the overall picture for the company there is little additional information provided as the branch network was maintained at 20 branches and thus it is a linear picture of the overall situation.

A factor in the reduction in performance is the fall in the number of properties sold of 25% from 2,000 to 1,500. However, this reduction needs to be compared to the fall in the volume of transactions in the UK industry generally, in order to isolate industry effects.

In terms of obtaining houses under contract (ie on its books) QA has done well as the average number of houses available for sale has increased by 12.5% from 600 to 700. However, in terms of the company's ability to sell these houses, performance has been poor as properties sold have declined by 25% from 2,000 to 1,500. This implies that in 2007 it took on average about 110 days to sell each house ([600/2,000] × 365days). However in 2010 it took about 170 days ([700/1,500] × 365days).

Also the fall in the volume of sales is less than the fall in fees generated so there has been pressure on pricing as well as on volumes.

The key assessment in measuring performance and assessing its causes is therefore to measure the extent to which the decline in the performance in QA can be explained by the decline in the industry performance, which is uncontrollable, and how much it may be due company specific factors.

There is clearly an industry effect on QA in terms of the general fall in sales volumes, but there has also been an industry effect in falling house prices. For QA the average property sold has fallen by 16.7% from £300,000 to £250,000. Whereas, for the industry, the average property sold has fallen by 20.2% from £203,000 to £162,000. This may reflect the local housing market for QA or may be a failure to continue to attract higher value house sales.

While QA has, along with the rest of the industry, suffered a decline in sales volumes, it appears to have done so despite reducing its effective commission charges below 1.5%. In 2007 its average commission was 1.5% implying there were no discounts. In 2010 however the average commission was 1.2% (a 20% reduction) as a consequence of the discounting policy.

The adverse impact in the fees reduction % is magnified by the fall in the average property price such that the fall in commission per sale made fell by one third from £4,500 in 2007 to £3,000 in 2010.

Fees from other services remain around the same proportion of total fees in 2007 compared to 2010. This appears to have suffered in the same way as may be expected if the property sales are falling which is likely to be the revenue driver for other sales.

Examiner's comments:

This requirement was well answered on the whole, showing continued improvement in candidates' ability to deal with data analysis. Most answers included sufficient quantitative analysis of the data to assist in making some relevant comments on the decline in performance. The best responses focused on the relationship between sales volume decline, decreases in house prices and the decrease in the percentage commission earned. Poorer answers tended to ignore cause and effect relationships in that they provided a commentary on what had happened to key figures, but failed to provide further computations (such as ratios) to break down how it had happened or to provide any detailed explanation of why it had happened.

(c) **Merits and problems of a merger with GTA – Proposal 1**

The strategic alliance with GTA offers the opportunity to save most of the costs of maintaining five branches while attempting to link the QA brand with that of GTA.

The disadvantages are that one third of the commission would be lost and the volume of trade may be lower if vendors are not able to visit the estate agent's premises and receive the level of service which was previously provided.

In pure financial terms, assuming a best case scenario that no customers are lost under the new arrangement, if the new arrangement would 'save about 75% of our branch costs' then the saving per branch would be £187,500 (£250,000 × 75%). The loss of fees would be £108,333 (£325,000 × 33.33%) assuming the agreement applies to all fees.

An alternative calculation would be to assume they only give away the commission and that as the average commission for 2010 is 1.2% they are giving away 0.5 and keeping 0.7:

The loss then becomes 0.5/1.2 × £225,000 = £93,750

However there is also a significant risk that there will be a loss in trade volume arising from QA not maintaining its own premises. Market research would need to be carried out to assess the magnitude of this potential loss.

The fee sharing agreement allows a half percent to GTA, but if there is a discount to the customer this would appear to be out of QA's 1% in full, thereby representing a disproportionate reduction in fee.

A source of revenue may be that GTA should pay to QA a percentage of the legal fees it earns from QA clients.

Other issues to consider are:

- The need to build a working relationship with a different, but complementary, type of business

- An alliance can be reversed beyond a contractually agreed period if the market recovers, unlike a merger

- There are likely to be exit costs (eg redundancies, lease termination costs) but also some minor exit benefits from the sale of surplus assets arsing from branch closures (note as the properties are leased they will not be surplus assets)

Examiner's comments:

Most answers provided a general qualitative evaluation of the merits and disadvantages of the proposed strategic alliance, often relating discussion to generic features of such alliances. Only a minority of candidates addressed, in any detail, the specific terms of the arrangement in the scenario by attempting financial calculations of savings and fee loss arising from the alliance and indicating the disproportionate drop in commission for QA arising from the fee sharing proposal.

(d) (i) **Comparison of the performance of QA and Terra**

Key differences between QA and Terra which make performance comparisons more difficult are: the larger branch network of Terra; and its different business model of low price, low cost service provision.

In terms of size it therefore appears more valid, initially at least, to compare performance at the branch level in order to compare like with like.

Both companies operate in a similar geographical market, but also appear to operate in the same sector of that market as they both have an average property sales price of £250,000.

In financial terms the fees per branch are greater for QA at £325,000 compared to £290,000 for Terra. Terra has some cost advantage with cost per branch of £240,000 compared to QA's £250,000. Nevertheless, the profit per branch of £75,000 for QA is greater than the £50,000 per branch for Terra.

In operational terms, Terra appears to be more successful in attracting new properties onto its books with 1,200 in all (40 per branch) compared to only 700 for QA (35 per branch). This may be a reflection of the lower effective commission rate of 0.96% for Terra compared to 1.2% for QA.

In 2010 Terra also made more sales per branch at 83.3 compared to QA at 75. However this is only 11% more sales per branch compared to 71.4% more properties on the books available to sell. As a consequence, Terra appears to sell a lower proportion of the properties on its books than QA. However the figure of average properties on the books may be misleading as it depends on the time taken to sell and the realism of the prices being asked by vendors.

The proportion of fees from other services is around the same for each company and thus does not appear to impact on an assessment of relative performance in any significant way.

In overall financial terms, the branches of QA generate a profit of £1.5m (£75,000 x 20) which, after head office costs of £1.4m, reduces overall profit to £100,000.

The branches of Terra also generate a profit of £1.5m (£50,000 x 30) but, after higher head office costs of £2m, there is a loss of £500,000.

It is clear therefore that in pure financial terms QA has overall outperformed Terra, but nevertheless there are serious questions about the performance of both companies.

(ii) **Benefits and problems of a merger with Terra. Advice on merger.**

Both QA and Terra operate in the same industry and therefore share many of the same core competences.

The business models are however significantly different. QA purports to operate in the upper end of the market, in terms of service provided, while Terra is a low cost provider. If a merger takes place there is therefore the potential for brand confusion with customers as to the positioning of the new company. A clear strategy will be needed for the new firm in terms of pricing and quality of the provision.

There are some synergies that would be gained from a merger. Potentially the closure of one head office would save significant costs as many activities would be duplicated. Similarly, in the towns where there are two branches, one may be closed to save costs. However, it does not follow from this that all the sales will be transferred from the previous businesses to the new branch. Each of QA's branches 'is located in towns where there are normally two or three branches of other estate agents'. Where one branch is closed some potential customers may be attracted to the rival estate agents.

Also, although the branches are held under operating leases, these may be of significant duration and there may be exit costs in terminating the lease either by a period of vacant possession or in terms of a sub lease on adverse terms.

In terms of a best case scenario, one head office could serve the new company at the existing cost of Terra's head office of £2m. If all customers are retained in the ten towns where one branch is closed then there could be a saving of £2.4 million (£240,000 × 10 taking the lower average branch cost of Terra).

The best case scenario would then be the existing contributions from branches:

QA	£1.5
Terra	£1.5
Branch cost savings	£2.4m
Head office costs	(£2.0m)
Profit before tax	£3.4m

In terms of cost savings this is optimistic, but nevertheless even with more modest savings there is potential for the merged entity to make significant profit. Economies of scale in a number of functions are likely to exist, but not to the extent that the head office or a branch could be closed with costs maintained at the previous level of only one entity.

While Terra is a larger estate agent chain than QA this appears to yield little benefit as it is loss making. Also, while it is larger, there do not appear to be significant assets in either company as branches are held under operating leases. Indeed, if branches held under operating leases were originally entered into at the peak of the market, the company may be bound into excessive and onerous rental contracts representing an effective liability rather than an asset.

If the general UK industry is about to recover, then there is more potential for revenue generation and further increased profit, but positioning within a merged entity may not be ideal, particularly given the different business models.

Governance is a key issue as the shareholders would be split 50:50 and this may make decision making difficult where the coalition is split evenly in this way. Overall the most important issue is integrating the two companies' strategies where market positioning and business models are so different. This will be important in establishing the new brand.

Advice

Overall, in concept, an alliance or a merger may yield benefits given the reduced volume of activity in the recession. In each case however the terms of the agreement and the proposed partners may be worth further consideration and negotiation. As it stands neither proposal seems particularly favourable either in the current downturn or in terms of strategic positioning for a recovery.

37   SkinDeepe plc

Marking guide

		Knowledge	Skill	Marks
(a)	Mendelow	2	7	9
(b)	Barriers to change	2	6	8
(c)	KPI	2	4	6
(d)	Response to Tatton	3	7	10
		9	24	33

General comments:

The scenario in this question relates to a company which manufactures and markets skin creams and lotions. 75% of sales are under the SD brand but the remaining 25% are to a single large retailer customer, Tatton, using its own brand. Difficult trading conditions have caused the company to implement a cost reduction plan. This involves, in phase 1, closing one UK factory and outsourcing production to a Chinese company, Huang, with immediate effect. If this is successful then in one year's time phase 2 will be implemented which involves closing the other UK factory and also outsourcing packaging and distribution to Huang. After being informed of these proposals, Tatton has written to SkinDeepe expressing concerns about quality assurance and the reliability of delivery times.

Candidates were required to:

* Identify and justify the positions of key stakeholders in the Mendelow power-interest matrix, in respect of the proposed changes

* Explain how barriers to change may differ between phase 1 and phase 2

* Identify and explain key performance indicators to monitor the performance of the outsourcing company, Huang, in phase 1

* Provide a response to the letter from Tatton raising concerns

(a)   **Factory A employees**

Power – Low

Interest – High negative

Factory A employees have high negative interest as they are under immediate threat of losing their jobs.

The power of Factory A employees to stop or moderate any closure decision is limited. If the entire UK workforce is united, then significant costs to SD can arise from disruption. Given however that sales and marketing jobs are not under threat then there may be limited co-operation in industrial action from these employees – unless they perceive themselves to be under threat from unannounced changes.

Once Phase 1 is implemented, Factory B employees are likely to be affected, but have a year to find alternative work, so they may not support Factory A employees in resisting closure during Phase 1.

Given that Factory A workers have short term contracts they have little contractual protection or other powers to resist change.

Perversely, if the redundancy payments are sufficiently high, some employees may favour redundancy to continued employment and thus have a positive interest in the plan (eg if they were going to leave anyway).

Factory B employees

Power – Moderate

Interest – High negative

Factory B employees have high negative interest in phase 2 of the plan as they are under threat of losing their jobs when it is implemented in one year.

They are also likely to have a high negative interest in Phase 1 as this may be perceived as being a very probable stepping stone to Phase 2.

The power of Factory B employees to stop or moderate any closure decision is very limited, but is probably slightly greater than Factory A employees. Once Phase 1 is implemented SD still needs Factory B employees for a year until Huang is in a position to carry out packaging. This gives them slightly more power but ultimately there may be little to be achieved.

The individuals making up the 30 employees transferred to head office will be less resistant to the change once it has been announced who they are.

Tatton

Power – High

Interest – Moderate

Given that 25% of SD's sales in volume terms are with Tatton they have considerable power over SD and are likely to be in a position to influence the decision to source production in China. The cost savings from transferring production are unlikely to compensate for losing 25% of sales. As their letter specifies, they will, as a minimum, need assurances, if products are to be manufactured overseas, as to quality and delivery schedules.

Tatton is only moderately interested in the production transfer as skincare products manufacture is a competitive market, with a range of alternative suppliers being available if Tatton fails to deliver. Nevertheless, SD is currently Tatton's preferred supplier for presumably good reasons, so there may be a moderate wish to continue the relationship, despite the concerns expressed in their letter.

The uncertainty over quality and supply may mean that they have a negative moderate interest in the proposal. However, Tatton may also be positively interested in the decision, if part of the cost savings made by SD are to be passed on to Tatton.

Examiner's comments:

This requirement was well answered on the whole. Most displayed a good understanding of Mendelow's framework. The application part of the question was quite variable with candidates producing a range of positionings within the matrix for each stakeholder's power and interest. This variability in the conclusions drawn by candidates is acceptable if it is supported by appropriate reasoning.

(b) The closure of a factory is an extreme form of change where the barriers that can be put in place by individuals and groups are limited.

A key difference between Phase 1 and Phase 2 is timing. Irrespective of differences in the nature and culture of Factory A and Factory B, Phase 2 comes one year later so there is greater opportunity for employees in Factory B to resist change over time.

Aside from timing, a series of cultural barriers may exist to resist change. There are to be fundamental changes in the structure of SD as it moves from a manufacturer of its products alongside marketing, to become a leaner marketing organisation that outsources most other key functions, including production and distribution.

This threatens power structures by the redistribution of decision-making authority and resources, and the changing of lines of communication. This will impact on the roles of employees in head office as well as in the factories (though perhaps not so fundamentally). Phase 1 is likely to give people an insight into the changes and determine whether they are favourably or adversely affected. Phase 2 is more likely to extend the established trend of structural change so there may be less fear of the unknown.

Group inertia may block change where the changes are inconsistent with the norms or where they threaten stakeholder interests. In this respect Factory B appears a more organised and cohesive group to resist change and is closer to the norms of head office (if only in geographical proximity and length of service).

Examples of group resistance include:

- Strikes and other forms of resistance to change implementation by staff.
- Suppliers taking legal action for contract termination.
- Gathering the support of other groups to resist change.

There are also personal barriers which affect individuals and result in them seeing the change as a threat. This may affect not only the factory that is closed but also the employees in head office where there are likely to be substantial changes in work practices and also redundancies of old skills in favour of new skills.

Phase 2 will demonstrate a significant period of uncertainty for many individuals (eg if they will be part of the group offered alternative positions in head office or in China) hence there is more scope for individual resistance and disruption. Phase 1 is much quicker and hence the period of uncertainty and opportunity for resistance is less.

Examiner's comments:

Answers to this part varied in standard significantly. There were mainly two approaches. One was purely knowledge based and explained, in general terms, the various barriers to change such as group inertia, cultural barriers and structural barriers, defining what each meant. The second approach was very scenario focussed and discussed barriers such as skills of the workforce, the impact of moving production to China and the problems with the distribution network. The best responses related the scenario discussion to generic barriers, drawing comparisons between the phases as well as recognising the importance of the sequencing of events and timing.

(c) **Quality of product**

Maintenance of quality is a key factor in making the outsourcing successful. Any cost advantage gained would be quickly eroded if reduced quality leads to reduced sales. It is therefore important to provide metrics to measure various aspects of quality.

- Number of defective batches delivered (measures the proportion of batches of unacceptable quality)

- Consumer satisfaction surveys with the smell, texture and effectiveness of products (measures the extent to which consumers are happy with average quality, perhaps by comparison to the results of any previous surveys that are available from when products were made in the UK)

- Satisfaction reports from Tatton (feedback from the major customer which may survey its own consumers, or sales levels)

- SD quality management procedures satisfaction levels compared to previous in-house production (looking at internal measures of quality control within the factory)

Distribution

- Number of late deliveries (pre ordered) (measure fact, length and reason for delays)

- Ability to respond to short term orders (assess the minimum lead times. This may vary by product but also by volume – eg small volumes could be flown from China if this was key to a customer's relationship such as Tatton)

- Number of goods damaged or perishing in transit (measure amount, cost and reason for damage)

Price

- Correct invoicing (number of errors discovered)
- Conformity with contracted prices (measure variances)

Examiner's comments:

This part was surprisingly poorly answered, overall, particularly given the broad clues provided in the question in the memo from Tatton regarding costs, quality and reliability of delivery. A significant minority did not provide specific measures and merely talked around the subject. Also, those who attempted to produce a Balanced Scorecard often missed some key measures.

(d)

To:	Tatton plc
From:	Skin Deepe plc
Date:	13 December 2010
Subject:	Outsourcing plans

Product quality assurance

Quality assurance procedures are being put in place to ensure there is no loss in product quality from the outsourcing arrangement. Specifically:

- Care and due diligence has been undertaken in selecting Huang as a quality provider of our manufacturing needs.

- A service level agreement provides benefits and costs to Huang from the quality of the product delivered which will lead to strong incentives.

- SD staff in the UK and China will be appointed to new quality management positions to monitor the quality of Huang's processes and output.

- Our approach is one of quality assurance which focuses on the way a product or service in produced. Procedures and standards are devised with the aim of ensuring defects are eliminated (or at least minimised) during the production process, rather than detected and corrected afterwards.

- Once the goods arrive in the UK there will be additional quality checks made by newly appointed employees.

Distribution

It is recognised that there will be a delay in transporting manufactured goods from China to the UK such that short term orders cannot be directly supplied from China within a reasonable period.

We have 33 product lines and it is our intention to hold all 33 lines packaged with the Tatton branding in the UK sufficient to satisfy a wide range of variable quantity demands by Tatton.

To this end, from next year we are outsourcing our distribution systems and inventory holdings to a reputable distribution company in the UK, Fell plc. They will hold and deliver inventories on SD's instructions at short notice to meet your needs.

Statement of relationship

Overall our view is that our relationship with Huang is one of strategic procurement and is therefore the development of a true partnership between SD and a supplier of strategic value. The arrangement is intended to be long-term, single-source in nature and addresses products, materials, development, capacity and delivery.

This recognises that the need for, and benefits of, establishing close links with companies in the supply chain. This has led to our view of an 'integrated supply chain' with Huang.

I hope this reassures you that we will continue to deliver the highest quality of product and level of service.

Examiner's comments:

The communication style adopted by candidates was generally good, adopting the format and approach of a letter to a major customer. However, answers were often brief and sometimes did little more than mention that a service level agreement was in place and that existing staff would move. There was frequently no explanation provided of assurance of quality or due diligence.

38   Heaton Home

Marking guide

		Knowledge	Skill	Marks
(a)	Mission statement and beliefs of a mission statement	2	4	6
(b)	Risks and managing risks	4	6	10
(c)	Ethical issues	3	4	7
		9	14	23

General comments:

This scenario relates to a not-for-profit charity (HH) which operates a residential care home for elderly people who have lived locally. The house was gifted by a rich individual, with the gift be subject to conditions for resident care and eligibility, and for maintenance of the property. The home is run by trustees, but is partially funded by local government. The number of residents has dropped recently which is placing the viability of the home in question. Possible withdrawal of local government funds as a consequence of decreased resident numbers is a major issue. There are also problems of deterioration of the property. A new manager has been appointed and reviewed the position of HH. The local government trustee has also proposed: an increase in fees; wider geographical eligibility; and reduced staffing to save costs.

Candidates were required to:

* Prepare a mission statement for HH and explain why this might be useful

* Identify the home's key risks and describe how these might be managed

* Discuss the ethical issues of the proposals of the local government trustee.

(a) (i) 'To offer high quality, affordable, residential nursing care in a safe and caring environment to elderly residents of the town Northport.

The board and its managers will work together with staff, volunteers, local government and the local community to deliver this service and to provide finance to reduce the cost for residents.'

(ii) A mission statement is a useful formal document for incorporating the objectives and values of an organisation and to communicate these to internal and external stakeholders.

They can include: purpose, strategy, policies and values

For a not-for-profit organisation, such as HH, where there is no clear profit motive, the mission statement can provide clarity as to the objectives of the organisation for key stakeholders and how these may be achieved.

Examiner's comments:

This requirement was generally well answered. The majority, but not all, provided an attempt at a mission statement and were able to give appropriate reasons as to why one would prove useful for HH. Poorer efforts produced mission statements which were either too brief, being little more than advertising slogans, or far too long. Better answers referred to the need for the inclusion of purpose, strategy, policies and values, particularly in the context of a not-for-profit organisation, often with conflicting stakeholder interests. Weaker answers provided only a general justification for a mission statement without referring to the nature and circumstances of HH.

(b) **Key risks**

The fall in demand for places in the home represents a key loss of income to HH both from the residents themselves and the per capita fee paid by local government.

The table below indicates that a surplus of £50,000 is made at current fees levels when all the places are full. However, at the current level of occupancy of 45, a deficit of £25,000 per annum is being made. It is not immediately clear whether this deficit on an accruals basis is equivalent to the cash deficit but, if so, the cash reserves of £100,000 would only last 4 years.

More significantly, if occupancy declines further to 40 residents, then the local authority will withdraw one third of its lump sum funding. In these circumstances HH would not be viable.

Management of risk

The reasons for the fall in demand need to be established. A key feature could be the increase in price two years ago. While this was intended to raise more funds, it may not have done so if the price change was the sole cause of the reduction from 50 to 45.

Under this assumption, the gain in revenue was £67,500 (45 × £1,500) from the residents who stayed and paid the additional fee. The loss in revenue was also £67,500 (5 × (£5,000 + £8,500)). Given that the costs are 'are almost entirely fixed costs' there was therefore no net revenue gain.

In managing this risk, the sensitivity of the residents to price needs to be explored to aim, as far as possible, to the fill the 50 beds while earning some fee from the marginal residents (eg waiving of some fees for needy local residents).

Alternative, non-price, explanations for the reduced number of residents also need to be explored (eg reductions in service levels through fewer volunteers, decaying of the fabric of the building, competition, local reputation).

At the margin of 40 residents the risk is significant of losing £100,000 of local authority funding. At the margin this could be controlled by (in the extreme) giving away a few free places to lift the average above 40.

The clause in the gift limiting the home for the benefit of 'elderly people who have lived in the local town for ten years or more' could be explored with the trustees. The definitions of 'elderly' and 'local town' could be explored to see if the potential resident base could be widened. (see (c) below).

The building

A condition of the original gift was that the mansion should be 'maintained in good order'. There is a risk that the 'deterioration in the fabric of the building affecting its appearance' may be in breach of this element of the gift conditions and there may be consequences for HH for its rights over the continued use of the building.

Management of risk

The terms of the gift need to be clarified to see if there is a definition of 'maintained in good order'. Discussions could be held with the trustees to establish their view and the likely course of action they would take.

The necessary repairs to meet the conditions of the gift should be fully costed and perhaps a special appeal for donations could be launched that had a focus of maintaining the building.

Volunteers

The reduction in the number of volunteers is not only a financial risk in needing partially to replace them with paid employees, but also a risk in terms of the quality of the service provided. It may also be a reflection of the esteem with which the home is held in the local community. If the support of the community is reducing this may have a significant impact on the home's role, charitable contributions and wider support.

Management of risk

- Exit interviews could be held to explore the reasons why people have ceased to volunteer or reduced their hours

- The role volunteers play and how they are treated by paid employees could be explored

- A recruitment drive in the local town and local schools could be carried out to raise awareness of the voluntary scheme and promote the home

Current Full capacity 40 residents

	Current	Full capacity	40 residents
Residents (45 × £10,000)	450,000	500,000	400,000
Local authority (45 × £5,000)	225,000	250,000	200,000
Local authority	300,000	300,000	200,000
Donations	250,000	250,000	250,000
Costs	(1,250,000)	(1,250,000)	(1,250,000)
Surplus/(deficit)	(25,000)	50,000	(200,000)

Examiner's comments:

Answers varied in quality. Better candidates identified most of the key risks and attempted to provide guidance as to how they should be managed. Others often only listed the risks without any attempt at consideration of their management. Answers which provided numerical analysis and/or considered price elasticity of demand were in a minority. Only a minority made reference to generic risk management techniques, often using TARA, but often not applying this very well to the scenario.

(c)   The ethical issue of raising the price to residents is that some may not be able to afford the increase and therefore may need to leave the home. Also many potential residents may not be able to take up a place in future. This may be in conflict with the charitable aims of HH providing 'reduced cost' places for the elderly in the area.

There may be an additional ethical issue in terms of the conflict of the objectives of the terms of the gift between maintaining the building and providing care to elderly residents. If the proposed scheme is an appropriate means of funding the repairs then ethically it may discharge the duty of the directors to fulfil this element of the terms of the gift.

The additional funding may also be ethically defensible if it is a means of sustaining the financial viability of HH and ensuring that it can continue to operate as a going concern and fulfil its intended charitable purposes.

Given the evidence of price elasticity (see (b) above) raising prices may not secure the additional revenues desired if occupancy levels fall. The local government director has suggested expanding the age range and the geographical area where HH can target residents. The ethical question here is whether this is in accordance with the terms of the gift by Lady Heaton by which managers are bound in using the property.

If the definitions of age and geography are unclear in the terms of the gift then the ethical issue is whether the directors can act against what are perhaps the implied wishes of the founder in order to promote their strategy, even if there is no legal constraint in doing so.

Examiner's comments:

In general, this requirement was not well answered. Many poorer candidates were unable to produce balanced discussion and only delivered a one-sided analysis which asserted unethical behaviour as self evident following a statement of facts. No ethical principles were identified in many answers. The best answers balanced the discussion and couched it in terms of ethical issues and principles.

39 Family Entertainment Company

Marking guide

		Knowledge	Skill	Marks
(a)	Five forces	3	5	8
(b)	Benefits and risks	2	5	7
(c)	Data analysis	–	15	15
(d)	Market segmentation and pricing	3	5	8
(e)	Ethical issues	3	4	7
		11	34	45

General comments:

The company in this scenario (FEC) is a UK-based company which operates a chain of family-oriented theme parks throughout Western Europe. As its existing market is mature and profitability is under pressure, it is considering expansion by opening up a new theme park in India and is in the process of assessing the potential benefits and risks of this strategy; approaches to marketing and pricing; and issues concerning health and safety. The operations director has suggested that one benefit of the Indian park would be lower annual running costs, especially for labour, and that in addition, because of limited regulation, FEC can reduce its normal expenditure on park safety and ride maintenance.

This question was the mini case, incorporating some data analysis and, at 45 marks, was the longest question on the paper. The requirements were broken down to help candidates in developing answer headings and assessing mark allocation. This was the best attempted of all three questions, with the majority of candidates performing well, showing good knowledge of the models tested and with many demonstrating good data analysis skills. Disappointingly the requirement on ethics (e) was poorly done by a significant minority.

(a) Porter's Five Forces is a model that considers the level of competition in an industry. In addition to the three forces below, there are two others, bargaining power of customers and suppliers.

Threat of entry

The barriers to entry to the theme park industry in Western Europe are high due to high capital cost for rides and also the expense of the site. In addition the potential sites for park development are limited due to scarce supply of land. Finally the maturity of the market, the major brand names and domination by existing multi-national entertainment corporations such as Disney would act as a barrier. The economic climate may also act as a barrier currently since consumers are inclined to spend less and have more constraints on their disposable income. Overall the threat of new entrants in Western Europe is probably low.

Competitive rivalry

Global competition is great in the industry. There are major international players and national / local smaller scale parks. The mature market in Western Europe means competition is intense, companies have to spend money to maintain state of the art rides, sites are difficult to come by (other than through acquisition) and only the most powerful players will survive. The economic climate means companies must fight even harder as consumers spend less money. Many of the multinationals are better placed to withstand competition as they gain marketing benefits from linking rides to TV/film characters, have access to wider resources and are more diversified – offering a wide range of entertainment (TV, films, retail outlets, parks). As a result of all these factors competitive rivalry is intense.

Threat of substitutes

There is a wide variety of other tourist attractions, cultural and entertainment offerings, all competing for a share of household leisure spend, thus the threat of substitutes offering an alternative 'day out' is quite high. Some of these alternatives are less affected by poor weather and the impact of the recession may be to encourage some people to switch to cheaper alternatives for a day out.

However there is an element of thrill/risk associated with theme parks which may mean these other leisure pursuits are not perfect substitutes.

Conclusion

The forces examined suggest that the theme park industry in Western Europe is fiercely competitive and that there is pressure on its long-run profit potential.

Examiner's comments:

Requirement (a) asked candidates to prepare three sections of a Porters Five Forces analysis for the theme park industry in Western Europe – threat of entry, competitive rivalry and substitutes.

Answers were of a good standard, with most candidates extracting the key information from the scenario and using it to assess the strength of each particular force; the majority concluding that the threat of entry was relatively low but competition was fierce and there were many substitutes for a 'day out'. High marks were awarded to those who, in addition, summarised the overall impact of the three forces on the potential for long term sustainable profits in the theme park industry in Western Europe. Some weaker candidates confused competitive rivalry and substitutes and a very small minority answered the wrong question by applying the analysis to the theme park industry in India. It was noticeable that some weaker candidates wrote far more than was necessary for the 8 marks available, causing themselves unnecessary time pressure on other parts of the paper (normally question 3).

(b) **Proposed expansion strategy**

Benefits of expansion:

- Mature market in UK/US so opportunity to expand into market at different stage in product life cycle

- Lack of further development opportunities in existing markets due to scarcity and cost of land means FEC needs new markets such as India

- Availability of land in India reduces barriers to FEC's entry

- Indian government policy appears favourable and there may be incentives to invest

- Increasing economic growth and wealth of local population provides a ready market

- No existing international competition – existing parks are small and often simple, so FEC would be a dominant player and have competitive advantage, particularly as a first mover

- FEC's values fit with the family culture in India

- Better spread of risk as diversified business worldwide so not just exposed to macroeconomic factors in Europe. Also the business is seasonal but the seasonality in India may differ from that in Europe, creating better smoothing of cashflows

- May improve earnings/profits to keep shareholders happy

Risks of overseas expansion

- Significant investment required in infrastructure

- Opportunity costs of funds required to invest overseas

- European/US theme park model is untested in India. FEC may need to adapt product model culturally to ensure local success (global v local) but may lack knowledge to do this. Existing parks are quite different and appear to have a local cultural/historical theme. Appropriate food, beverage and merchandise may be quite different from European parks

- FEC may lack experience/knowledge of how to do business outside Europe and there may be hidden costs of which it is currently unaware

- Impact on profitability of factors/risks outside FEC's control – foreign exchange, government policy

- The government may remove its support and/or the licence to operate if it believes FEC are compromising on health and safety (see (e))

- Indian climate is very different from Europe. There is a possibility of natural disasters – floods, monsoons – so FEC may not be able to operate all year round

- High exit barriers

- Threat of expropriation of assets – may mitigate via possible JV/government equity stake and also by demonstrating local wealth generation via employment etc

- Sensitivity of tourist industry to strikes/war/exchange rates/terrorism

- Other multinationals may not have entered the market either because they believe it is not viable or because the risks are too high

- Lucrative emerging market may attract other major players increasing competition in the longer term

- If the Indian venture fails this may have a damaging effect on FEC's reputation and European parks

Conclusion

The industry in Western Europe is highly competitive and FEC is under pressure from its shareholders to address falling EPS. The fact that a number of other operators are expanding in Asia and South America suggests expansion outside its traditional markets may be a suitable strategy. It needs to consider the financial projections to determine whether the Indian venture is likely to generate sufficient returns to compensate for the additional risks and uncertainty involved.

Examiner's comments:

Requirement (b) asked candidates to discuss the benefits and risks of the proposed expansion. Again answers were of a good standard with most candidates extracting information from the scenario and explaining the implications for FEC in the context of benefits and risks. Better candidates used their knowledge of overseas expansion to generate additional points and concluded that, subject to appropriate financial returns, the strategy seemed a sensible one, given the challenges faced in Western Europe and the shareholders' concerns about falling EPS. Weaker candidates merely regurgitated points from the scenario or discussed generic risks, such as cultural and foreign exchange risk, without applying them to the specifics of the scenario.

(c) (i) **Profit forecast**

Attendance	Number of Months	Visitors	Total Attendance
High Season	3	90,000	270,000
Mid Season	5	75,000	375,000
Low Season	4	50,000	200,000
Visitor numbers pa			845,000

Revenue	$
Admission 845,000 @$10	8,450,000
Food and merchandise @$10	8,450,000
Total revenue	16,900,000

Variable costs	
Admission 8.45m @$2	1,690,000
Food and merchandise (8.45m × 0.5)	4,225,000
Total variable costs	5,915,000

Contribution	
Admission (8.45m × 0.8)	6,760,000
Food and merchandise (8.45m × 0.5)	4,225,000
Total contribution (16,900 − 5,915)	10,985,000
Less	
Fixed costs	(9,000,000)
Net profit	1,985,000

(ii) **Break-even calculations**

Annual fixed costs	$9,000,000
Total revenue per visitor (10/0.5)	$20
Contribution per visitor (0.8 × 10) + (0.5 × 10)	$13
Break-even visitors (9m/13)	692,308 visitors

(iii) **Sensitivity**

To fixed costs

Annual fixed costs	$9,000,000
Current estimated net profit	$1,985,000
Fixed costs can increase by 1.985m/9m	22.06%

To admission price

Admission revenue	$8,450,000
Current estimated net profit	$1,985,000
Admission revenue (and hence price) can drop by 1.985m/8.45m	23.5%

Note: Assumes each visitor continues to spend $10 a head on merchandise and food/beverage.

Note: the attendance fee is calculated on an average basis. In reality FEC may not charge the same fee at all times of the year or to all visitors (see (d)).

(iv) **Commentary and further information**

Commentary on figures

On the basis of the estimates the park looks set to make healthy profits, with an average contribution margin of 65% and a net profit of £1.985m once the park is up and running, which represents an 11.7% margin. However it will take a while for the park to be established, considerable investment is required and there may be losses in the first months/year(s) of operation.

In terms of sensitivity to the estimates: The breakeven attendance figure is 692,308 so the estimated attendance of 854,000 gives a margin of safety of 18% (845,000 - 692,308/845,000).

Fixed costs can increase by 22% before the Indian venture becomes loss-making, which would seem to be a reasonable margin of safety. This does however assume that the other estimates for attendance, admission and other revenue and margins are achieved.

Similarly the admission price could fall by 23.5% assuming that other revenues for food and merchandise and other costs remained constant.

Note: figures given assume that once the park is up and running attendance will be static. As the market is new, the annual attendance is likely to grow whilst the park is being established. It would be more accurate to prepare forecasts of demand year by year.

FEC also need to prepare projections for capital expenditure and set-up costs. Typically given the size of investment FEC would probably use a 10-15 year time period to evaluate the theme park and a cash flow forecast will also be required.

Information to assess accuracy of assumptions

Need to compare results to the performance of FEC's existing parks.

Need to know whether the assumptions are based on European parks or have been tailored to the Indian market – the entrance fee at $10 would probably suggest the latter as even though it is an average, it looks low. However the Indian market may spend a different proportion on food and merchandise than Western Europeans for example.

Fixed costs are high and profits depend on admission numbers and revenues. The key to accurate assessment of prospects is the ability to predict demand. Need results of any market research undertaken to ascertain where estimates have come from for the seasons and the attendance – are these figures based on competitors in India or FEC's experience in Europe? How likely is the attendance to drop below the break-even figure of 692,308?

Park may not be able to be open for 12 months of the year – many parks find it is not viable to open for the low season as operational costs may outweigh the revenues in this period. The seasonality is also likely to be different from Western Europe.

Admission price is an average and in fact may vary depending on age and nature of visitor and time of visit (see (d)). The amount spent on food/beverages and merchandise per head is also likely to vary. Could benchmark these figures against the prices charged by existing Indian parks.

No detail is given about what is included in fixed costs – is it just the cost of running the park or does it also include depreciation on equipment, interest charges on finance?

Need to also consider:

- Tax
- Exchange rate differences
- Any compliance fees

Examiner's comments:

Requirement (c) was the data analysis requirement. Candidates were provided with assumptions regarding estimated attendance figures, admission price, other revenues, and costs in order to produce some financial projections for the Indian park. This requirement was broken down into four clear parts covering: (i) calculation of the park's estimated annual profit (ii) break-even analysis in terms of attendance figures (iii) sensitivity to fixed costs and admission price and (iv) a commentary on the significance of the calculations together with any additional information required. The calculations were designed to highlight that, with high fixed costs and seasonal attendance, profits would be highly dependent on estimated attendance numbers and revenue per visitor.

This requirement tested candidates' ability to apply basic data analysis skills in the context of forecast data. Answers to the calculation elements of this requirement ((i) – (iii)) were quite polarised, with a significant number of candidates scoring full marks, but a small minority failing to make all but the briefest attempt.

The performance on the data analysis section of the paper has shown general improvement over recent sittings, although it appears that some candidates were unable to apply their skills in this context, having perhaps been led to expect that data analysis equates to the analysis of historic business performance which, the learning materials are clear, is only one possible area that might be examined.

Almost all candidates attempted the calculation of projected profit, the most common errors arising in the calculation of revenue and costs for food and merchandise. Where candidates made an error with the cost structures or profit figure at this point, they were awarded full credit for using their figures in the subsequent calculations and commentary. There was some variability in candidates' ability to calculate the break-even attendance figure, the most common errors being to base the calculation on revenue rather than contribution, or to ignore the contribution from food and merchandise.

A number of candidates correctly calculated the sensitivity of the profits to estimated fixed costs but were unable to assess the sensitivity of the proposed admission price.

Marks were awarded to those sensible candidates who, despite being unsure of the exact calculation, adopted a 'what if approach' by calculating how much profit would vary for a given change in the relevant estimate.

Even if they had found elements of the calculations demanding, most candidates produced a reasonable commentary on their figures, with many pointing out that the profit projections were highly dependent on the assumptions made and on exchange rates. The strongest candidates also pointed out that, as the figures related to revenues and expenses once the park was fully established, it would take some time to reach this point and that the initial capital expenditure to acquire land and build rides would be considerable.

The additional useful key information from the poorer students was the usual generic list, including requests for breakdowns of cost, cash flows and competitor information. However, the highest scoring answers produced excellent lists of additional information, typically including the need to understand whether the assumptions had been based on a typical European park or tailored to the Indian market, the benefits of market research to confirm seasonality and attendance figures, benchmarking of the admission price and other data against existing Indian parks, and the need to produce forecasts for the set-up period.

(d) **Market segmentation and pricing**

Market segmentation is the division of the market into homogenous groups of potential customers. In FEC's case this is likely to be:

- Local residents
- Tourists (domestic and foreign)

FEC may then also choose to sub-divide these groups by income level or age.

The benefit of market segmentation is that FEC can adjust components of the marketing mix to improve returns from each group according to spending potential, location, needs and tastes.

Foreign tourists to India – can capitalise on existing brand, will have sophisticated expectations of rides, attractions, food and merchandise based on prior theme park experiences.

Domestic tourists and local residents – may need or expect a product experience which is more tailored to local culture. Alternatively the attraction of FEC's park may be its Westernised nature.

Tourists are probably prepared to pay more than residents but will offer less opportunity for repeat business and the tourist business is likely to be more seasonal.

Pricing

In the theme park industry there are two approaches to pricing – Pay as you go tickets may work better for one group than another.

(i) Pay as you go

This involves visitors paying a small fee on entry to the park then, once inside the park, a separate amount for each ride/attraction. The cost of each ride/attraction is based on its popularity, with the most popular costing up to four times the price of the least popular.

Advantages

- May be more attractive to less wealthy customers as they only pay for what they experience

- Can vary prices etc to cater for changing demand

- More scope for price discrimination

Disadvantages

- People are more conscious of what they are spending so they may limit it
- Need more staff to sell tickets/take money round the park
- Visitors may spend less on food/beverage and merchandise

(ii) Single price

This involves visitors paying a single large admission fee for which they receive unlimited use of attractions and rides. Some specific high value attractions may not be included in the price or may incur a premium.

- Easier for customers to budget
- Don't need as many staff at park to take ticket money
- But customers have to pay for rides and attractions they don't want to experience

Price discrimination means setting different prices for a similar product in different markets. The reasoning behind this is that a universal price may be lower than some people eg foreign tourists would be prepared to pay (losing revenue) and higher than others (local residents) can afford (losing volumes). Thus the best strategy is to charge each group the maximum they are prepared to pay. Successful price discrimination relies on segmentation and differing price elasticities of demand.

FEC could operate differential pricing by:

Market segment – eg loyalty schemes for locals who are regular visitors or who purchase annual passes Timing eg peak/off peak – seasonality around festivals/ tourist periods; weekdays vs weekends.

Dynamic pricing – according to levels of demand compared to normal patterns.

Captive product pricing eg for food, beverage and merchandise once in the park.

Other options: loyalty cards, discounts for groups or families, seasonal pricing of admission fee.

Recommend: Suggest a multi-tiered pricing structure to take account of ride popularity, attract customers for repeat visits and increase business during quieter periods.

Examiner note:

Consideration of the 3 Cs would also be an acceptable approach for discussing pricing.

Examiner's comments:

Requirement (d) asked candidates to explain how FEC might segment the market as part of its approach to marketing and also to discuss appropriate pricing strategies.

Most candidates discussed segmentation in terms of domestic residents and tourists and better candidates went on to identify opportunities for breaking these markets down further eg by income or age. Candidates seemed well prepared to talk about pricing and many referred to the benefits of adopting price discrimination to maximise revenues. The highest marks were scored by those candidates who linked their discussions on price to the market segments they had identified.

(e) **Ethics and stakeholder conflict**

> **Examiner note:**
>
> Candidates could either have used the three levels of ethics (personal, business, corporate responsibility) or the three tests (Transparency/Effect/Fairness) as an approach to discuss the ethical issues. This answer covers both for marking purposes and is longer than candidates would have been expected to produce in the time available.

Ethical issues

Ethics are the moral principles governing or influencing conduct which is deemed acceptable in the society or context in question. Ethics exist at three levels: personal, business and corporate.

> **Personal ethical behaviour** eg the suggestions of the operations director to keep maintenance costs low because the market is not yet developed perhaps calls into question his personal ethics.
>
> **Business ethics** – the way FEC as a firm behaves. FEC's management needs to consider the ethical implications of its proposed strategies before implementing them. Customers and employees have a right to expect certain standards of ethical behaviour. As a business FEC has an obligation to maintain proper health and safety standards and it is unlikely to be acceptable to take advantage of lower standards or lack of procedures in one country compared to another.
>
> **Corporate responsibility** is the belief that the firm owes a responsibility to society and its wider stakeholders, not just its shareholders. This links to the discussion of stakeholder conflict below.

In deciding whether the operations director's suggestion raises ethical issues, FEC could adopt the Institute of Business Ethics tests:

- **Transparency** – would FEC mind others knowing that it had decided to reduce maintenance expenditure?

This may depend on whether health and safety is compromised because of the planned level of expenditure. FEC may be planning to spend what they believe is necessary to maintain good health and safety, albeit that this is lower than the levels enforced on them in Europe. If however the motivation was because the current lack of safety standards allowed them to get away with it, then it is likely that FEC would not want the reason for this to come to light.

- **Effect** – Who does the decision affect/hurt?

From a health and safety angle, lack of maintenance may increase the risk of workplace injury to employees and also customer injury in the event of a ride breakdown or accident.

An accident would also have financial consequences for FEC – increased costs of insurance, compensation payments, legal costs – as well as reputational consequences: lost customers, loss of employees, possible loss of licence, knock on effect on image and attendance at European parks.

- **Fairness** – would the decision be considered fair by those affected?

This partly depends on whether the actual level of expenditure is seen as a justifiable business decision, which might take into account cost/benefit analysis, risk assessment and the normal level of expenditure in European parks.

Stakeholder conflict

Stakeholders are groups of people who are interested in what FEC does. In the case of FEC's approach to health and safety this would include internal stakeholders (employees, management), connected stakeholders (shareholders, customers) and external stakeholders (government/regulatory bodies).

Here the issue of maintenance costs highlights the potential for conflict within and between various stakeholder groups:

Shareholders want profitability – indeed the Indian venture is partly to address their concerns about falling EPS – so some may prefer FEC to only spend what is absolutely necessary on maintenance.

The theme park employees, customers and local government may value safety more highly however.

Whilst only local regulation exists at present, the national regulator may publish standards that are more onerous if it feels that FEC is not taking its responsibility for employee and customer safety seriously. Also any safety incident may lead to the withdrawal of government support/licence.

Which stakeholders' interests determine FEC's actions will depend to an extent on their relative power. Clearly FEC's primary focus is to maximise shareholder wealth. However in the context of a new park, customers are very important to success and may choose to go elsewhere if they think their safety is being compromised. Also shareholders may acknowledge that higher levels of expenditure on health and safety in the short term will establish FEC's reputation and ensure government and public support, giving FEC a competitive advantage and higher profits in the long term.

Examiner's comments:

Requirement (e) asked candidates to discuss the ethical issues raised by the operations director's comments on health and safety and the potential for stakeholder conflict that might be present. As has been the case with most previous papers, the ethics requirement was often not well answered. Some candidates failed to discuss the ethical issues and simply restricted their answers to stakeholder analysis. Weaker candidates who did cover both areas often failed to demonstrate any knowledge of ethics (in terms of transparency, fairness and corporate responsibility) and addressed the issue in terms of the commercial consequences of cutting back on health and safety and the likely effects in terms of bad publicity and litigation, rather than the ethical implications.

Whilst there was merit in some of these comments, better candidates pointed out the fact that the operations director might be operating legally, within the scope of the existing Indian regulations, but went on to discuss the impact of the proposed strategy in terms of transparency, effect and fairness and whether FEC might be better served by applying a higher standard of corporate responsibility. They then went on to consider the likely interest and influence of various stakeholder groups, including visitors, employees and the Indian government and regulatory authorities.

Many weaker answers were extremely one-sided with a number of candidates implying that all shareholders would be happy to make profits at the expense of the safety of visitors and employees. The strongest candidates concluded that there may not in fact be conflict as shareholders might recognise that setting high standards of health and safety would establish FEC's reputation, capture market share, and ensure government support, leading to long term sustainable profits for the shareholders.

40 MPW Ltd

		Knowledge	Skill	Marks
(a)	Evaluate comments (inc. report)	4	9	13
(b)	Supply chain and performance	4	6	10
(c)	CSFs and KPIs	3	5	8
		11	20	31

(a) **To:** The Board of MPW
From: A N Other
Date: March 2011
Re: Growth strategy

The purpose of this report is to consider whether MPW's growth strategy has been successful and to make recommendations for improvements in the supply chain, performance measurement and incentive schemes.

Directors' comments

The wholesale phone business is very competitive with narrow margins. In order to be successful MPW needs to operate with high sales volumes, hence the growth strategy would appear in the first instance to be sensible, as is the focus on improved customer service to penetrate the market. Also the board's attempt to gain commitment to the strategy and motivate employees via incentive schemes appears to have led to happy staff and the company has recognised the need to monitor strategy by using KPIs.

In the context of these KPIs, the managing director is right that the strategy has been successful, however achievement of these KPIs has not led to an increase in overall profitability since, according to the MD, net profit has in fact fallen, and MPW needs to understand the reasons for this.

Sales Director's comments

The sales director believes the purchasing strategy is at fault.

MPW's new strategy involves guaranteed next day delivery which will necessitate large amounts of stock, but if this stock is not sold quickly it risks becoming obsolete which will reduce profitability.

The fact that the purchasing manager's bonus is based on manufacturer discounts seems to have encouraged the buying of handsets that do not appear to have matched demand – a point raised by the sales director. This is partly due to the fact that the manager may have bought excessive quantities in order to achieve a bulk-buy discount but it is also likely that manufacturers are offering the best discounts on older handset models or models that they know are soon to be upgraded.

It is in the purchasing manager's interests to maximise their bonus by buying the cheapest stock in large quantities which demonstrates a lack of goal congruence. This has the following impact:

(i)   Bulk buying may have generated discounts but will involve increased stockholding costs (cost of capital tied up, insurance, warehousing) and have a negative effect on profitability and cash flow.

(ii)   If the discounted handsets can be sold at normal prices then the discount obtained will improve the gross margin. However the fact that over 40% of MPW's stock is over 2 months old means that the firm will suffer reduced margins on these models, if indeed it is able to sell them at all. Thus, as highlighted by the MD, it is likely that MPW are making money on some handsets and not others.

The sales team, whose bonus is based on % gross margin, will ensure they only sell items with positive margins (as the sales director comments) and will have little incentive to push sales of these older models if they will at best just recover cost. The longer the stock is held, the more it is likely to become unsaleable and the write-off of such stock, particularly if it has been bought in large quantities, will significantly reduce future gross profits.

(iii) Stock that the sales director believes the company could sell (newer, more popular models) is probably not being purchased, since manufacturers are unlikely to be willing to offer discounts on such items. Given the competitive nature of the market and the fact that there are low switching costs for buyers, it is likely that MPW will lose customers to competitors if it consistently fails to meet demand for such items.

Also the more popular items may earn lower margins, but if retailers prefer a one-stop shop, the newer models may act in the same way as a 'loss leader', forming part of a larger order for a range of different, more profitable handsets.

Purchasing director's comments

The purchasing director believes the issue is with the sales strategy. According to the purchasing director the existing customer base has changed its purchasing strategy to take advantage of next day delivery and this has had a damaging effect.

By focussing its attention on gross margin the business is not taking all costs associated with selling the product into account, particularly the costs of processing and distributing orders.

If we consider the financial results for sales to existing customers, MPW may be making the same level of revenue and gross profit as before but, unless it has passed on the extra charges to its customers, MPW will almost certainly have seen a reduction in net profit due to the costs involved in handling more frequent, smaller volume orders and in distributing to retailers daily. This is not just a short term issue and, in answer to the MD's question, MPW may well be losing money on customers placing small orders, if the costs of ordering and distribution outweigh the gross profit per order.

As a result of the sales growth and the sourcing of new retailers, the volume of orders will have increased but the increase in custom may not have been sufficient to offset the increased administration and delivery costs.

Finance Director

Although the targets MPW set are both financial (sales growth and gross margin) and non-financial (% deliveries on-time), they are not looking at the whole picture, which is what the new FD is concerned about.

Ultimately for long term financial success, as well as sales and gross margin, overall profitability is important and the KPIs do not currently take this into account. They also do not consider MPW's internal processes or the company's innovation and learning capabilities. Use of a wider set of measures may have helped the board understand sooner that the strategy was not as successful as first hoped and the reasons behind this (see (c) for more details).

A large proportion of MPW's costs are likely to be fixed overheads and these will have increased with the new warehouse facility. As the new strategy has only recently been implemented, it is possible that it will take time to achieve the increase in volumes necessary to cover the additional fixed costs, so the lack of profitability may be a short term issue.

The new FD has also raised the issue of incentives. Incentives are a good way to gain commitment to a strategy and motivate staff but, as discussed above, the current incentives may be causing a lack of goal congruence. For example, if the incentive scheme for the sales team is based on % gross profit then they may go for high price and low volume which could be entirely contrary to the growth strategy.

Conclusion

In the context of the existing KPIs, the strategy has been successful, however the growth in sales and the improved customer service levels have been at the expense of overall profitability. MPW needs to ensure it sets targets that are consistent with the overall objectives of the business and which promote long-term as well as short-term interests.

Examiner's comments:

(b) **Recommended improvements to supply chain**

Supply chain management (SCM) is the management of all supply activities from the suppliers (in this case the phone manufacturers) through to the customers (the phone retailers).

Key aspects of SCM are:

- Responsiveness – ability to supply customers quickly with the goods they want
- Reliability – ability to meet agreed service standards
- Relationships – better integration between MPW and its suppliers

MPW may want to address the following issues in order to improve its supply chain efficiency and performance:

Co-ordinate purchasing with demand

- MPW need to move to a demand pull rather than cost push system

- Use forecasting for handsets with predictable demand in order to reduce stocks of these items

- Identify which phones are most popular and in short supply and focus efforts accordingly

- Ensure communication and co-ordination of effort between sales and purchasing departments, so they don't buy stock at a special price unless MPW believes it can market and sell it

- Ascertain minimum order volumes required to make next day delivery viable or pass on increased costs to customers

- Adopt different pricing strategies for fast and slow moving items

Reduce stock levels

- Co-ordinate pricing and stock – use promotional pricing, discounts etc to manage fluctuations in demand and to reduce excessive stock holdings/sell off aged stock

- Levels of stock required will depend on lead times for receiving orders from manufacturers and the predictability of demand. There may be scope for JIT system to reduce stocks so that MPW only order from manufacturers in response to retailer demand

Reduce costs

- Use value chain analysis to ascertain cost and value drivers. Profitability can then be improved by focussing on these. Here a key cost driver appears to be the number of orders placed, so MPW should investigate ways of reducing the costs of order processing eg implement an e-procurement system to automate order processing and reduce costs through online ordering, payment and invoicing eg impose a minimum order size/value on customers to ensure that gross profit from the order is sufficient to cover costs of processing and distribution

- Another factor that has increased costs is the new warehouse. If stock levels are reduced and purchasing is more in line with demand, MPW may find that they do not need so much space. If exit costs in the form of lease penalties and redundancies are high then one possibility may be to sub-let space

Increased use of technology

- Increased use of technology for forecasts and then to track actual demand, orders placed, inventories etc

- Possible use of Enterprise Resource planning (ERP) software to manage the key aspects of the supply chain: product planning, purchasing, stock control, order tracking

- Consider linking computer systems with those of phone manufacturers/retailers to reduce paperwork and administration

Customer relationship management

- Use of relationship marketing to build longer term relationships with retailers, thereby increasing loyalty, minimising chance of losing customers if MPW does not have stock, sharing information with customers concerning expected demand

- Emphasis on improving profitability through customer retention as well as new customer attraction

- Identify the best and most profitable customers eg reduce number of customers served and concentrate on those customers placing larger volume orders with high margin products

Examiner's comments:

Requirement (b) asked candidates to advise on the steps that MPW could take to improve the efficiency of its entire supply chain and hence its performance.

This requirement was often badly done. Only the strongest candidates demonstrated a clear understanding of the fact that the supply chain covers all the activities from acquiring stock from suppliers through to delivery of the product to the customers. Few discussed supply chain management in terms of responsiveness, reliability and relationships. Many candidates confused supply chain management with value chain analysis and whilst the latter was worthy of consideration, it was not the sole focus of the requirement. Candidates who used their analysis in (a) to make sensible suggestions about coordinating purchasing and demand, reducing stock levels, controlling costs (eg by setting minimum order sizes for next day delivery), and using information systems to improve stock control and assess customer profitability scored well.

(c) **Performance measurement and incentives/CSFs and Revised KPIs**

Critical success factors (CSFs) are the areas that are vital if MPW is to achieve competitive advantage. These should guide KPIs, the setting of targets for incentive schemes and the reporting of information for control and decision making.

CSFs are likely to include:

- Ability to meet customer demand (availability of wide range of handsets)
- Ability to offer high level of customer service (guaranteed next day delivery)
- Good relationships with retailers to retain customers and encourage repeat purchase
- Good stock control to encourage fast turnaround and minimise stock obsolescence/write offs
- Efficiency and cost of order processing

Improvements to performance measurement

MPW is currently looking at performance from two angles: financial and customer. It needs to use additional measures in these two areas but also to widen its system of performance measurement.

A balanced scorecard approach may be useful to MPW, since in addition to KPIs covering the financial and customer perspective, this would have highlighted the need to consider internal business processes and decision making, and innovation and learning.

MPW may also improve its approach to performance measurement by benchmarking performance with competitors/other wholesalers.

Incentives

Changes in the incentive scheme would encourage staff to take decisions which are in line with the overall company objectives and hence improve performance.

MPW needs to make the sales team aware of the overall costs of meeting orders so it is important that any bonus offered takes into account net margin per order, not just gross margin.

In awarding the purchasing manager a bonus, MPW needs to incentivise the manager to purchase the right stock at as good a price as possible – currently the only factor being considered is price. Thus the purchasing manager needs to be encouraged to consider MPW's ability to sell the items purchased and the incentive could perhaps be based on gross margin per order. In this way the purchasing manager will only get a bonus if the sale is made and will get a bigger bonus if they have negotiated a good supplier discount as the margin earned will be higher. Any bonus could be restricted by taking into account aged stock levels, stock write offs etc.

To ensure co-ordination of the purchasing and sales team's efforts, an element of everyone's incentive should be based on the overall results of the business.

Additional measures

> **Examiner note:**
>
> Only four are required and a prioritised list addressing CSFs raised above will score more highly than a generic list.

Four additional measures that could MPW usefully use to widen its KPIs are:

(1) Overall profitability: operating and net profit margins. MPW should also report profitability per order and per product.

(2) Since the MD is concerned that MPW may be losing money on some customers it should consider customer profitability – both gross and net of selling and distribution costs, number of orders per customer and average order value.

(3) The purchasing director has highlighted the importance of considering the efficiency and cost of order processing. MPW could do this using a measure such as average processing cost per order.

(4) Stock management is also critical and appropriate management information here would include an aged stock analysis. MPW could measure stock write-offs/write-downs as a percentage of stock held.

> **Examiner note:**
>
> Alternative approach for marking purposes.

As an alternative, candidates may adopt a balanced scorecard approach when discussing how MPW could improve its performance measurement, which is set out below:

Financial perspective

MPW is already measuring sales growth and gross margin but has failed to consider overall profitability.

Additional measures should include looking at:

- Cost control eg overheads as a percentage of revenue

- Overall profitability: operating and net profit margins and also profitability per order, per customer and per product

- Market share

- Revenue mix
- Cash flow

Customer perspective

MPW are currently measuring satisfaction based on on-time delivery. It would also be useful to monitor satisfaction in terms of number of products demanded that are out of stock.

In addition to satisfaction, MPW should also measure customer profitability, both gross and net of selling and distribution costs, number of orders per customer and average order value.

Since it typically costs more to attract new customers than to keep existing ones it could also measure customer loyalty in the form of retention rates and assess whether it is a preferred supplier based on its share of the key retailers' spend.

Internal business processes and decision making

The purchasing director has highlighted the importance of considering the efficiency and cost of order processing, using measures such as average processing cost per order, time taken to process each order.

Stock management is also critical and appropriate management information here would include:

- Product profitability analysis
- Sales vs inventory reports
- Weekly stockholding
- Aged stock analysis – eg % stock held over 2 months
- Stock write-offs as a percentage of stock held
- Exception reporting of aged stock and small order values

Innovation and learning

This looks at whether MPW can continue to improve and create value. For example they may consider the number of new products added to the range as this might encourage them to include more captive products such as mobile phone accessories.

They could assess employee satisfaction, particularly given the potential changes that may take place in the incentive schemes. They could also assess productivity of employees in terms of sales and order processing.

Examiner's comments:

In requirement (c) candidates were asked to identify MPW's critical success factors and discuss how it can improve its performance measurement. The issue here was that the company needed to widen its KPIs, linked also to changing the incentive targets. Most candidates were able to suggest appropriate critical success factors for MPW although these were sometimes too narrow, focussing exclusively on customer needs and failing to take account of the internal need for operational efficiency and better stock control as identified in the earlier requirements. The best candidates went on to link their suggested performance measures to the CSFs they had already identified. A minority did not provide four specific measures (as per the requirement) and some confused KPIs with goals. Candidates who used the Balanced Scorecard as a framework to identify a key performance measure for each of the four areas (financial, customer, internal and innovation) tended to produce wider answers and score more highly than those who gave a range of measures for the customer perspective. A number of candidates restricted their marks by suggesting KPIs that the company was already using.

41 SPV plc

			Knowledge	Skill	Marks
(a)	(i)	Structure	2	3	5
	(ii)	Operational culture	2	3	5
(b)		Sustainability	3	5	8
(c)		Joint venture	2	4	6
			9	15	24

General comments:

The scenario concerns a manufacturer of solar energy panels, which uses a unique patented thin-film technology. Demand for solar energy is unpredictable and dependent on a variety of external factors, including government incentives for renewable energy (detailed background information was provided in the scenario for those candidates who were unfamiliar with the technology and the nature of the industry). SPV is considering how to maintain its competitive advantage in the face on an uncertain industry environment and increasing competition from Asia. One strategic option is a joint venture with a major utility company in the USA.

Overall the performance on this question was very variable with too many poor answers. The weaker candidates performed poorly on the skills-bases elements of this question (requirements a(ii) and (b). Although there was no general evidence of time pressure (all but one of the candidates attempted every question), some weaker candidates who spent far too long on the Q1 mini case made a very truncated attempt at Q3. As a result there were a number of very low marks for this question which is reflected in the question average.

(a) **Structure and culture for success**

    (i) **Structure**

        Organisational structure defines how the various functions in an organisation are arranged. A successful strategy requires effective organisation of people and decision making.

        The contingency approach takes the view that there is no one best structure and emphasises the need for flexibility. The most appropriate structure depends on the stage of development of the organisation and the nature of its competitive environment.

        SPV needs a structure which is quick to change but which can cope with the levels of growth anticipated.

        Entrepreneurial structures can be flexible and quick to change but would not be suitable here as SPV is likely to be already too large and such structures tend to limit expansion capability.

        Highly centralised structures or bureaucratic structures tend to stifle innovation and the rigidity makes them unsuitable for the unpredictable environment of the solar power industry.

        SPV needs to be able to respond to rapidly changing demand from country to country and technological developments on the part of Asian competitors. In a complex, dynamic environment such as that faced by SPV, Mintzberg recommends an adhocracy/innovative configuration which is essentially a matrix structure. In this type of business the operating core who work directly on the product are the key building block of the organisation, and work autonomously. Whatever co-ordination is necessary is achieved by mutual adjustment which involves interaction and informal communication.

        The matrix can be a mixture of functional, product and territorial organisation and is most suitable for complex/hi-tech industries. Such a structure offers great flexibility and is ideal where, as in the case of SPV, there are many geographic areas with distinct needs but the firm needs to exploit economies of scale to keep production costs low. The use of multi-skilled teams where employees are trained to undertake a variety of tasks would further enhance flexibility.

Burns and Stalker identified two extremes of structure – mechanistic or organic. Organic structures are flexible and adaptive and suitable for fast-changing environments and would therefore be appropriate for SPV.

(ii) **Culture**

A successful company is often one that is outward looking, and has accepted the reality of constant change and the necessity to review its product-market policy continuously. It places emphasis on vigorous initiative, always looking to the future towards new markets, innovative products, better designs, new processes, improved quality and increased productivity.

SPV has developed and patented thin-film technology but needs to continue to innovate if it is to maintain competitive advantage. It can help foster a culture of innovation by:

- Recruiting and retaining the best talent – innovative organisations tend to attract and retain higher quality staff, who want to gain experience with the market leader and want the opportunity to contribute to the development of a forward-looking organisation.

- Getting the best from its employees. Cross-disciplinary teams allow employees to be more involved in the development of new products or processes, to move around and experiment with fresh ideas. Training and development will also be key.

- Creating a culture that promotes and rewards creativity and inventiveness and supports individual and team abilities. This is evidenced by the adoption of the employee suggestion to offer leasing to customers.

- Implementing a management style and structure designed for innovation: praising new ideas, encouraging staff to explore off-beat possibilities, and giving them a high degree of autonomy.

- Being aware of and making use of common information/resources available to industry. Certain managers can be made responsible for obtaining information about innovative ideas from outside and disseminating it throughout the organisation.

- Spending on R&D and market research and risking capital on new ideas.

- Using multiple sources of innovation – R&D, employees, customers, suppliers, partners, outsourcing and joint ventures, working with government or other public sector initiatives.

- Going beyond product innovation to consider how they can innovate their processes, their structure, their business model and even their market.

Examiner's comments:

Part (ii) was less well done, with too many failing this part of the requirement. Weaker candidates overlooked the requirement to focus on operational strategies and instead discussed Porter's generic strategies of cost leadership and differentiation or focussed on high level strategic options. Better candidates identified that innovation and flexibility were critical success factors and discussed ways that SPV could promote this internally eg recruiting and retaining talent, empowering employees with a high degree of autonomy, promoting/incentivising creativity and innovation, collaborating on research and development.

(b) **Sustainability and control**

Sustainability and SPV's strategy

Sustainability is about maintaining the world's resources rather than depleting or destroying them. The Bruntland report defined sustainability as 'the ability to meet the needs of the present without compromising the ability of future generations to meet their own needs.'

Sustainability is not limited to the environment and encompasses social, environmental and economic issues.

Protecting the environment and preserving its resources are at the core of SPV's activities. It is engaged in the provision of sustainable energy where the source of the energy is sustainable and there is little disruption to the environment. Such energy will help promote worldwide sustainability by reducing dependence on fossil fuels and mitigating the effect of greenhouse gases. Thus sustainability is integral to SPV. The world's increasing consciousness of the need for sustainability offers SPV a wide range of opportunities but also presents it with considerable risk.

There is a clear need for SPV to be a sustainable enterprise (a company that generates continuously increasing stakeholder value through the application of sustainable practices). The payback period for its panels can be up to 10 years and customers want confidence that the panel manufacturer will stay in business for the duration of the panel warranty period.

Ability to control success

SPV's established reputation and track record help to reduce the risks it faces, as it will be seen as a stable business partner, which is critical given the long term nature of the product. As the market expands, SPV may therefore be more attractive as a partner for utility companies who are typically risk averse (see (c)).

SPV has used patents to protect its proprietary technology which will reduce the risk of copycat products for a period of time until newer, cheaper products are developed. We discussed in (a) how SPV can help ensure success through careful design of its structure and culture and this could facilitate ongoing innovation to stay ahead of the market.

In addition to SPV's use of cheaper thin-film rather than the more expensive silicon, its vertically integrated process and economies of scale mean that it can provide relatively affordable panels. Compared to traditional silicon, the panels also have a high energy yield in the absence of sunshine, making them more suitable for a wider range of climates and countries. Thus if demand exists, SPV is likely to capture market share, at least in the short term.

However demand for SPV's product is heavily dependent on the level of industry demand, which is itself dependent on the political framework and also the economic climate, both of which are outside SPV's control. Thus SPV may choose to invest in certain countries, only to find that a change in government or financial position render the market unattractive. This is evidenced by the case of Spain reducing green energy subsidies due to budget constraints.

In the absence of government subsidies, sustainability may become less popular when levels of disposable income fall and consumers and businesses are either unprepared to pay the price premium to be green or alternatively cannot wait so long for the payback.

To an extent SPV can mitigate against this risk through careful choice of markets, operating in a range of different locations, and cultivating appropriate networks and relationships for lobbying purposes but ultimately if alternative cheaper forms of renewable energy are developed/become widely available or governments worldwide stop supporting sustainable energy initiatives then SPV's long term success is largely outside its control.

Examiner note:

Candidates may also approach the discussion of controllability by using the 5 factors listed in the scenario as drivers of demand as a structure for their answer (climate/price of electricity/public awareness/economy/government).

Requirement (b) asked candidates to explain how the need for sustainability influences SPV's strategy and assess the extent to which its success is driven by factors outside its control. Weaker candidates struggled with the first part of this and had little to say other than quoting the Bruntland Report definition of sustainability and discussing fossil fuels. Better answers appreciated that sustainability is wider than just the use of green technology, picking up on the points raised in the scenario about the need for SPV to be a sustainable business given the long payback period for its panels and the fact that customers want confidence that SPV will be in business for the duration of the panel warranty period.

Many candidates extracted the information from the scenario about the drivers of demand for panels (climate, price of traditional power sources, state of economy, government attitudes and public attitudes) and noted that in the main these were uncontrollable by SPV. The stronger candidates went on to produce a more balanced answer by discussing the fact that SPV has already managed to create a market leader position through its use of unique patented technology and that by having an appropriate structure and culture and strengthening its position, eg with the proposed joint venture, it will be able to create sustainable competitive advantage. Thus when the demand drivers are favourable it will be able to profit more than most.

There is a high emphasis on skills in the Business Strategy paper because it is a fundamental part of the preparation for Advanced stage. Thus in certain parts of the paper candidates are expected to be able to apply their knowledge and exercise judgement. Where a requirement is more skills-based, as this one was, those candidates who recognise that a lot of the necessary information is provided in the scenario and have the confidence to use their knowledge of the learning materials in that context can score well even if they struggle to use their skills fully. Candidates who fail to produce an answer to a requirement because, to quote the tutor commentaries it is 'not widely practised' or 'a regular requirement', cannot be awarded credit for a blank page.

(c) **Joint venture with UTILCO**

A joint venture is a contractual arrangement whereby two or more parties undertake an economic activity which is subject to joint control. Here SPV's solar panels will be attached to UTILCO's existing telephone and electricity poles throughout the USA.

Attractiveness to UTILCO

- Need to comply with government policy and the 33% target for renewable energy, so is going to be forced to increase renewable energy

- Does not have the technology itself and is unlikely to have the expertise to develop it in-house

- SPV is a well-established, market-leading company with tried and tested technology therefore likely to be a preferred partner

- Longstanding track-record and financial stability of SPV will reduce risk

Attractiveness to SPV

- Utilco have access to a very large distribution network and an extensive customer base

- Will be able to take advantage of the growth opportunities arising from the government policy, without having to find all the finance/ bear all the costs

- May be further scope to collaborate eg on the development of major solar power plants

- Likely to have access to resources and capital which are critical to the development of the solar powered industry and may help facilitate further technological development

- Will help raise awareness and demand for solar power which may further stimulate demand for panels by households and businesses

Conclusion

The joint venture looks to be beneficial for both parties and, subject to the ability to agree appropriate terms and conditions, should be pursued.

42 Cauldron Cereals plc

Marking guide

			Knowledge	Skill	Marks
(a)		Analysis competitive position	3	9	12
(b)	(i)	Analysis performance	-	9	9
	(ii)	Risks	3	4	7
(c)		Ethics	3	5	8
(d)		FoodSave contract	2	6	8
			11	33	44

General comments:

This is the mini case and data analysis question. The scenario relates to a manufacturer of healthy eating breakfast cereals, Cauldron Cereals (CC). CC is at the higher end of the quality spectrum, but it has performed poorly in recent years. In 2008, a new CEO was appointed and, in an attempt to improve profits, he cut costs by lowering grain quality. At the same time, he entered into a 2-year contract with a supplier to fix the price of grain. Demand fell so the CEO, with the agreement of only a few directors, increased the salt and sugar content, without internal or external disclosure, in order to improve taste. Profits at first increased, but then discovery of the undisclosed change in salt and sugar cased a fall in sales and the removal of the CEO. An ethical issue is that the finance director discovered the undisclosed change, resigned and disclosed this to the newspapers. A new board is considering a contract to sell to a supermarket under its own label at a lower price, while the core product reputation has time to recover.

(a) Average revenues using Exhibit 1:

CC average sales	£35.0m
Industry average	£7.4m (£980m/132)
Big three average	£178m ((295+127+112)/3)
Average of non-big 7	£2.144m (£268/125)

CC's market share (by value ie sales revenue) 3.57%(£35m/£980m)

CC's sales are only 11.9% of Astra's sales and only 19.7% of the average of the big three companies. Despite this, CC is one of the larger companies in the UK industry with revenue 16.3 times the average of the smaller companies outside the 'big seven'.

In order to assess the competitive position of CC it may however be more appropriate to view it as competing in a niche market with the general industry. Its niche appears to be defined by both the type of cereal (healthy) and by the quality-price relationship. In this latter context it can be seen from the other information available that the average price per box is £3 for CC ($35m/11.67m) and £2 for the industry average (£980m/490m). The contention is therefore that in selling £2 boxes of cereals there is a rather different market segment than for £3 boxes of cereals and thus they are not, in normal circumstances, in direct competition. (Care must be taken in using this data as the average size of a cereal box is assumed to be constant for companies in the industry. The assumption will be made that boxes are approximately the same size but more information would be required to verify this.)

This is not to argue however that there is no competitive effect outside the market niche. In recession, cheaper cereals may be a substitute for expensive cereals as people trade down. Similarly, there may be a competitive effect from outside the breakfast cereals industry from substitutes (eg other type of health food for (say) lunch, or other types of breakfast eg croissant).

However, taking a primary view of competitive position as within the market niche then the main competitors appear to be:

- 'The wide product range of the "big three" includes the full spectrum of price and quality choices, as well as market niches such as healthy-eating and children's cereals.' This means that at least a segment of the big three are in direct competition with CC. More information is needed about the extent of the activities of the big three in the healthy eating sector and the manner of pricing within that sector. Nevertheless, the advertising budgets and economies of scale and scope are likely to mean that big three brands are major and direct competitors with CC products, significantly affecting the company's competitive position.

  Rival 1 is a direct competitor of CC in terms of producing primarily healthy cereals. Its sales are almost double those of CC in value terms, and more than double in volume terms so it would benefit from greater economies of scale.

  However, in terms of price and quality it does not appear to be in direct competition with CC as it has an average price of £2.25 compared to £3 for CC. There is therefore likely to be some limited impact in terms of competitive position and this is likely to be greater in a recession where substitution of Rival 1's lower price products, but still within the 'healthy' sector, may be common.

- Rival 2 is closer to CC in terms of size and average price than Rival 1, but it seems only to compete in a niche within a niche, as it specialises in children's healthy cereals. It therefore appears to be a prime and significant competitor to CC within this sub-sector. The impact on the overall competitive position of CC would depend on the proportion of sales falling within the children's healthy food sector. More information is needed on the sales mix of CC in respect of adult cereals and children's cereals to evaluate the competitive risk from Rival 2.

- Despite being a similar size to CC, Rival 3 does not appear to be a primary rival in the context of healthy breakfast cereals. It does however compete with CC in the quality market with an average price of £3.50 compared to £3 for CC. The difference in price however may be regarded as fairly significant and therefore is probably the least direct competitor for CC of the three similar-sized rivals.

- Other smaller companies are not likely to be major competitors individually but, collectively, groups of smaller companies may have competitive impact on CC. The smaller companies may, if successful, grow sufficiently in the longer term to be more substantial competitors to CC and similar companies in the industry.

Using Porter's Five Forces model, CC's competitive position can be seen as not only being affected by competition within the industry, but also by relationships with suppliers and customers. The relative power of larger buyers (such as supermarkets and other large multi outlet retailers) over CC is likely to be substantial as most sales by CC are to these groups. If there is pressure on prices from powerful buyers this affects CC's profitability and price competitiveness compared to large competitors who may have more bargaining power with buyers such as large supermarkets. If the 'big 3' are better able to resist price pressure from supermarkets then this would strengthen their competitive position compared to CC.

As a general indication of buyer power in the industry, the profit margin of retailers is given by comparing total retail sales of £1,200 million to wholesale sales of £980 million. This is a healthy margin for retailers of over 18% on a basic food product. In 2008, before the changes by the new CEO, CC only had a profit margin of 11.1%. This may be an indication of CC's lack of competitiveness in the market, but other explanations such as cost inefficiencies may also be contributory.

A similar argument could be made with respect to power over suppliers but international grain markets are likely to be robust even for the big three to obtain and advantage.

Competitive threats from overseas manufacturers are significantly reduced 'due to the low-cost, high bulk-volume of breakfast cereals, which make transport costs high.' This may limit new entrants which would need a UK manufacturing base to compete effectively, rather than just export into the UK.

In terms of changes in competitive position, it would appear that the market share of CC is worsening. Long term industry sales have increased by 3% whilst CC has not shared in this growth.

Tutorial note:

Candidates may also use a BCG matrix approach using the data that CC's sales are only 11.9% of the market leader, Astra, and there is currently zero market growth.

Examiner's comments:

Requirement (a) asked candidates to use the industry data provided and other information to evaluate CC's long term competitive position. Any additional information needed was also requested. Answers to this part varied in standard.

There were few calculations produced, other than the 3.57% market share, which most candidates correctly determined. The most common model used was Porter's Five Forces and salient points were normally made using this framework. The better answers focussed on CC's immediate competitive position in comparison to its rivals and also in relation to the 'big 3'. Good discussion was seen in terms of CC's position in the niche market and as a differentiator. Some candidates, however, chose to do a SWOT analysis for this part of the question, which did not tend to bring out the key points. It was surprising to note that most candidates produced no calculations on CC sales, compared to the industry average or the average of the big three. Some candidates produced price/quality trade-off diagrams to depict the relative strategies of CC and its close rivals.

The request for further information led to a standard shopping list in many cases. It was quite apparent that candidates approached this element of the question very generically and did not really think about what further information would be useful. For example, there were some requests for information which has already been given in the question itself.

(b)

	2008	2009	2010	
Revenue	£36m	£34m	£35m	Per question
Grain cost	£16m	£13m	£13.4m	Per question
Operating profit	£4m	£5m	£5.6m	Per question
Volume	12m	11.33m	11.67m	Per question
Price	£3	£3	£3	
Grain cost per cereal box sold	£1.33	£1.15	£1.15	
% change in revenue	-	(5.5)%	2.9%	
% change in volume	-	(5.6)%	3.0%	
% change in total grain cost	-	(18.75)%	3.0%	
% change in grain cost per box	-	(13.5)%	Nil	
% change in operating profit	-	25%	12%	

(i) **Performance**

Financial performance

In pure financial terms, the operating profit has increased substantially by 25% and 12% in 2009 and 2010 respectively.

Looking at factors which may have given rise to this improvement, it does not appear to be the selling price as this has remained constant. Similarly, fixed operating costs have remained constant. Neither does it appear to have been sales volumes, which have decreased and therefore have had the opposite effect in reducing overall sales revenue and profit.

The key causal factor driving the increase in operating profit therefore appears to be the reduced cost of grain. There are three interrelated factors in respect of the change in grain cost which need to be understood to evaluate their impact on financial performance. These are changes in total grain cost due to:

- Lower unit costs due to lower quality
- Lower total volumes of usage
- Contract pricing effects

Unit costs and volumes

2009

Ignoring the contract pricing effects for the moment, in 2009 the overall grain cost has fallen by 18.75%, but the cost per box sold has only fallen by 13.5% this is due to the fall in volumes of 5.6%. At a constant volume of 12 million boxes then the profit at the new grain prices for 2009 would have been £6.2m (£36m – £16m – (£1.15 × 12m). To the extent that the deterioration of grain quality has impacted demand, then this is a harmful effect as, at constant quality, profit would be £6.2m. Thus the unfavourable profit impact of the quality deterioration (assuming all the volume change is attributable to this) is £1.2m. However, this is outweighed by the cost saving resulting in an overall increase in operating profit in 2009 of £1m.

2010

In 2010 there has been no change in selling prices, fixed operating costs or grain prices per box. The increase in operating profit of £0.6 million is therefore attributable to the increase in sales volumes. This can be demonstrated by the change in total contribution of £1m – (£1.15 × 0.34m) (subject to rounding).

This financial gain appear to be attributable to the increase in salt and sugar content which 'helped to improve the taste a little and, as a consequence, demand recovered slightly in 2010'. To the extent that this is true there has been a short term narrow financial benefit to the decision to include more salt and sugar content, but ideally we need to estimate what would have happened in 2010 in the absence of this action rather than assume that the 2009 performance would automatically have been repeated.

Fixed price contract

The final element of financial performance has been the fixed price contract. This has enabled the acquisition of grain at artificially low prices compared to its fair value on world commodity markets. Performance can therefore be analysed between (i) operating activities and (ii) financial contracts.

In terms of assessing sustainable business operating performance, the financial contract performance can be separated out (as it is unlikely to be sustainable that the commodity market can be predicted in the long term). This can be achieved by charging the fair value of grain, which 'unexpectedly increased by 10% each year', rather than the artificially low cost attained in the contract.

In this case grain prices would be:

2009	1.1 × £13m	=	£14.3m
2010	1.1 × 1.1 × £13m	=	£15.7m

Profit would then be as follows:

Financial data for CC

	2008	2009	2010
	£m	£m	£m
Revenue	36	34	35
Fixed operating costs	(16)	(16)	(16)
Variable operating cost (grain)	(16)	(14.3)	(15.7)
Operating profit	4	3.7	3.3

Reviewing the revised figures shows that profit has now fallen and the company's performance has deteriorated. This is not to suggest however that the management has, of necessity performed badly as profit would have fallen anyway under the old strategy of high quality grain due to the global grain price increases (see below).

The value of the contract over two years has been the difference in profit of £3.6 (5 + 5.6 – 3.7 – 3.3).

Strategic performance

Overall there has been an improved financial performance in the short term.

This is largely due to a fortuitous raw material hedging contract that has generated significant profit.

If the existing strategy has been maintained with the grain price increases as follows:

2009	$1.1 \times £16m$	=	£17.6m
2010	$1.1 \times 1.1 \times £16m$	=	£19.36m

then the following would have arisen assuming no other changes in volumes:

Financial data for CC

	2008	2009	2010
	£m	£m	£m
Revenue	36	36	36
Fixed operating costs	(16)	(16)	(16)
Variable operating cost (grain)	(16)	(17.6)	(19.36)
Operating profit	4	2.4	0.64

These profits are lower than those that would have been achieved above of £3.7m and £3.3m under the new strategy in the absence of hedging. This could superficially lead to the conclusion that the change in strategy was advantageous.

A key problem is that the policy is unsustainable as once the salt and sugar changes became transparent to the consumer a new level of demand based on fuller information was established which is only at 80% of the previous level, at which point the company makes a loss (see (d) below).

Thus the strategic cost of a short-term financial gain has been:

- Loss of reputation
- Damage to the healthy eating brand characteristic
- Reduced sales and profit in the longer term

This impacts on CC's market positioning and its future long-term viability.

(ii) **Risks**

A key risk facing CC has been its long-term decline compared to the industry average. Note:

'… long-term annual volume growth in UK retail sales of over 3% until the end of 2008' 'Despite the growth in sales in the UK breakfast cereal market as a whole up to 2008, CC sales have not grown for some years'

Therefore, despite the risks in the new strategy adopted from 2009 there were also risks in doing nothing and continuing with the old strategy.

Aside from any particular business strategy adopted, the volatility of grain prices is a key risk. The magnitude of the changes is illustrated by the calculations above indicating the impact on profit that would have occurred had the hedging contract not been in place.

This risk has been effectively managed by CC in the period 2008-2010 through the fixed price contract. However, to the extent that long-term grain prices have remained high, then CC became exposed to the higher prices and future volatility when the contract expired at the end of 2010. The contract was only therefore a temporary means of risk management.

The risks from the market appear to be relatively stable as it is a long established company in a mature industry where prices and volumes appear to be stable and, despite the maturity, there appears to be longer term growth in sales outside the recession period. This is not therefore a highly contested market.

Moreover, the size of the market leaders and their advertising spend tends to create barriers to new entrants which restricts future competition, albeit that the big 3 are better able to do this rather than CC.

A key short-term risk is the recession where high quality producers are at particular risk of falling sales through consumers trading down.

Change in consumer tastes, particularly with respect to healthy eating, is another key risk. In the case of CC it is also a potential benefit although a reduction in health consciousness in the population may have a dramatic effect on sales as it directly impacts the core values of CC's marketing.

In addition to the above market and industry risk there are also a number of risks that apply specifically to CC as a consequence of their recent decisions. These include:

- Reputational risk. The reputation risk of the company has been damaged by the public disclosure of salt and sugar content and grain quality. Future decision making needs to consider the possibility of further reputational damage.

- Alongside harm to the company's reputation, there is likely to be impairment of the overall brand and the brand names of individual cereals. This mainly relates to the quality of the product which, to the extent it may vary in future, represents an additional risk to which consumers are likely to be sensitised. Consumer goodwill is therefore likely to be fragile.

Examiner's comments:

Requirement (b) requested candidates to: (i) analyse the financial and strategic performance of CC using the data provided; and (ii) explain the risks facing CC in 2011 and beyond.

Candidates produced a range of calculations in answering part (i). The recurring calculations were operating profit margin, % change in revenue and % change in costs of grain. The better answers recognised that although there was an improved profit in the short term, this was not sustainable in the longer term as, strategically, the reputation of the business had been damaged by the change in grain quality and increase in salt and sugar content. The weaker answers merely focussed on trying to explain the reasons for the increased short term profit without acknowledging that financial performance will deteriorate as the full impact of the change in strategy was felt. A minority considered the 'same taste at lower cost' tactic as a conscious change of strategy towards cost leadership in the niche although, at the same time, not reflecting on the fact that the price had not been lowered. Only a minority recognised the favourable, and fortuitous, impact on profit of the long term contract fixing grain prices. Even fewer attempted to extract the impact of the grain contract quantitatively, in order to assess the underlying operational performance in financial terms.

Part (ii) on risk was generally done quite well, with most candidates discussing the reputational risk to CC, the damage to the brand and the loss of consumer goodwill. The higher scoring answers highlighted various types of risk bringing in wider economic impacts and discussing recession.

(c) (i) The key ethical issues in this case are transparency and honesty. Despite the increase in salt and sugar content, the action of adding more of these ingredients to improve flavour in not, in itself, illegal or unethical as levels remain well below the industry average and are not therefore a material or unacceptable risk to health in the view of the consumers who continue knowingly to purchase these products.

The issue of transparency is both internal to CC and external to customers.

Internally, this is a question of corporate governance. An important decision has been made, not by the board in a formal meeting, but by a subset in an informal meeting where the decision was deliberately not communicated. This was a breech of good faith and an improper process of decision making. Its legality may be called into question.

Externally, the communication of 1% and 3% rather than 1.49% and 3.49% could be regarded as a lack of transparency and deliberately misleading the customers. The ethical implications would depend largely on the industry norms as to the level of accuracy with which these ingredients are disclosed. The magnitude of the changes is however significant, being a 49% increase in salt and a 16.3% increase in sugar. A phrase such as 'to the nearest whole percentage' may have gone some way towards a defensible ethical position but transparency in line with rival companies and consumers' expectations would have been a preferable position.

(ii) The ethical issues with respect to Jenny are confidentiality and whistleblowing. In terms of confidentiality, there is a presumption that private information acquired from within a company by employees and officers should not be outwardly disclosed to the public without authorisation. This presumption can however be overturned and whistleblowing can be ethically justified where there has been an illegal act committed.

As it stands, it is unclear whether the CEO has deliberately attempted to deceive the public or has acted within acceptable norms of accuracy of disclosed data. To the extent that he may have acted illegally then the breach of confidentiality by whistleblowing can be justified on ethical grounds within the ICAEW Code of Ethics. Authoritative guidance should have been obtained by Jenny however prior to public disclosure.

Examiner's comments:

Requirement (c) asked candidates to explain the ethical issues arising from: (i) the CEO's decision to increase salt and sugar content without disclosure, either internally or externally; and (ii) the FD's decision to resign and publicly disclose the decision.

Weaker answers tended to adopt extreme ethical positions, for example by regarding the increase of the salt and sugar content as illegal so on this basis the FD had acted in the public interest and her actions were correct in amounting to whistleblowing. The better scoring answers adopted a more balanced approach and identified the key ethical issues using ethical language. In terms of the FD's actions, better candidates identified that Jenny could have potentially breached confidentiality and should have sought further advice before making a disclosure to the press.

(d) **To:**   Cauldron Cereals plc Board
From: An Accountant
Date: 13 June 2011
Subject: FoodSave Contract

The contract with FoodSave is fixed price. A significant risk therefore arises to CC from volatility in grain prices over the two year contractual period which has a minimum quantity clause as costs may increase significantly without any corresponding ability to increase selling prices to FoodSave.

In simple financial terms the new contract creates a positive contribution per year as follows:

First year		
Sales	(400,000 × £2)	£800,000
Grain costs	(£1.77 × 400,000)	£708,000 (see note 1)
Contribution		£92,000
Second year		
Sales	(400,000 × £2)	£800,000
Grain costs	(£1.95 × 400,000)	£780,000 (see note 1)
Contribution		£20,000

Note 1

The original grain quality has been restored. In 2008 the cost of grain per box is £1.33; by 2010 this has increased by 10% per year and so is £1.61 per box. The contract is being considered in July 2011 and we know: 'Further increases in grain prices are now expected from 2011 onwards'.

As a working assumption it has been assumed that grain prices will increase by a further 10% in the first year of the contract which would be £1.77 per box.

In the second year of the contract if (say) grain increases by a further 10% then the price of grain per box is £1.95.

There may be further benefits:

- There is significant slack capacity as sales are only 80% of their previous levels so this keeps staff and other resources employed while the company tries to recover its reputation and volumes

- The 400,000 volume is a minimum and sales to FoodSave may be much higher

- Other supermarkets may offer similar contracts if CC can show it can satisfy FoodSave's needs

- The reputational damage of the old board may be limited by the vote of confidence by FoodSave

Disadvantages may be:

- If it becomes known by consumers that the FoodSave cereal is the same, in substance, as the CC cereal they are likely to buy the FoodSave version for £2 rather than the CC version for £3

- There may be further reputational damage as a quality provider if it becomes known that CC is supplying a low cost supermarket

- The contract is small relative to the size of CC so the balance between reputational damage and financial benefit leans towards rejecting the contract

- There is a risk that volatility in grain prices outside the assumed 10% may create a negative contribution, particularly in year 2 where the margin in thin. If this is the case, CC's cereals may be the lowest cost that FoodSave can obtain and it may demand large quantities from CC thereby magnifying the negative contribution

Examiner's comments:

Requirement (d) asked candidates to produce a report which provides advice on whether to accept the FoodSave supermarket contract, including supporting calculations.

Many candidates produced few, if any, calculations, despite the specific request in the question to do so. A significant number of candidates appeared to assume that the additional cereals could be sold without any additional costs being incurred such that the full £800,000 revenue was added to profit each year. Amongst those who did address costs, there was frequently a misconception that grain prices would remain stable. Few addressed risks in any detail.

43 Henford plc

Marking guide

			Knowledge	Skill	Marks
(a)	(i)	BCG	2	4	6
	(ii)	Life cycle	2	5	7
(b)	(i)	Organisation chart	2	4	6
	(ii)	Function to new structure	2	5	7
(c)		Barriers to change	3	5	8
			11	23	34

General comments:

The scenario in this question relates to a manufacturer of traditional toys and games, Henford, which has become a conglomerate in recent years through expansion by acquisition into diverse industries, namely paper and medical containers. A decision has been taken to change the organisational structure of Henford from a functional basis to a divisional basis. As part of the change management procedures, the company is facing resistance from marketing managers who are resisting the new divisionalised arrangements. Some brief numerical information is provided for each product and the market in which it operates.

(a) (i) The relative shares of the three products compared to the major competitor are:

Toys   5.0
Paper   0.10
Pharmaceuticals   1.10

Toys

The traditional toys section is trading in a zero growth market. Its sales are also only half that of the largest competitor so market share is relatively low. Operating cash flows are modest.

Toys may have been a cash cow in the past but as a result of increasing competition from IT-based toy manufacturers it has suffered new entrants in a competitive market.

As a consequence, the BCG matrix is likely to view toys as a 'dog' product with limited potential for growth and development.

Paper

Henford's paper products section has high growth but the market share is small relative to the main competitor, being only 10% of its size by sales.

The paper products could therefore be regarded as a question mark (or problem child). This means that there may be a case for additional capital expenditure to expand the product in order to gain critical mass.

With a portfolio of products as a conglomerate, the cash cows could help finance the question marks to stimulate early growth.

Pharmaceuticals

Henford's pharmaceuticals section is a market leader with a high market share. There is low growth at 3% as this is a mature market so new entrants are less likely. There is a limited need for new investment in production assets as expansion is low and there is little need to defend market position from new entrants. As a consequence there is high positive cash generation.

As a consequence, Pharmaceuticals could be viewed as a cash cow within the BCG matrix.

(ii) **Product life cycle (PLC)**

The product life cycle can be adapted to use the same market growth, market share and cash generation classification as the BCG matrix. The PLC however tries to explain these factors as sequential over the life of the product.

Traditional toys

This product is between the maturity and decline phases of the life cycle. This is characterised by low market share and zero growth, with modest cash flows. Within the PLC this places it between a dog (as in the BCG matrix) and a dodo. The key issue however is not the exact position in the PLC but the direction of movement. This is a product which is past its peak and is now struggling to compete, with poor cash generation.

The next phase would be to cease production at the end of its PLC as cash flows may move to be negative.

Paper

Paper is classified as a question mark in the BCG matrix with high growth, low market share and poor cash generation. Within the PLC this is explained as a product still trying to establish itself in the growth phase of its development. If successful it can move to the next section of maturity and possibly become a cash cow. There is however uncertainty over its development and progression along the life cycle hence the title question mark.

Pharmaceuticals

Pharmaceuticals are in the mature phase of the PLC with established products having high market share, low growth with good cash generation. There is no inevitability that mature products will go into the next phase of the PLC of decline. Cash cows are often sustained for many years. However at the moment the PLC would consider the cash cow in the BCG matrix as mature and mid life.

Examiner's comments:

Requirement (a) asked candidates to use the industry data and other information provided to: (i) explain and justify its positioning within the BCG matrix; and (ii) explain where each product is located within the product life cycle model.

In part (i) most candidates performed relatively well and sound knowledge of the BCG matrix was demonstrated in qualitative terms. However, while a majority of candidates correctly positioned each product in the correct quadrant, the numerical data relating to market growth and market share percentages were not discussed in much detail or used to position products within a quadrant.

In part (ii), the majority of candidates were able to discuss the phases of the product life cycle in general terms and accurately link each product to the correct phase. However parts (i) and (ii) of the question were often answered in isolation and many candidates failed to make linkages between the product life cycle and the BCG matrix. High marks were awarded where the linkage and understanding of the interaction between BCG and the product life cycle were demonstrated.

(b) (i)

Old structure: functional

Tutorial Note:

The senior managers of only one division have been included for illustrative purposes.

New structure: Product divisionalisation with some centralised functions

Tutorial note:

Different versions of this diagram were acceptable provided the reporting lines and the distinction between the operating divisions and the centralised functions were clear.

ICAEW

(ii) There is no one universally correct structure. Rather, the contingent view argues that the structure should be appropriate to the circumstances of the organisation.

In the case of Henford the original functional structure was presumably suitable for the company when it only made a single product, toys. In this case there was no need for separate profit centres as there was only one type of toy being made. Also, the market and technology used at that time appeared stable. The size of the company was also not too large at £25 million (to the extent that current sales reflect historic sales).

As the organisation has changed however the functional structure has become less suitable in a number of respects.

- The size of the organisation has increased from around £25 million to £140 million. This is more than a five-fold increase. This means that functional managerial tasks are larger and wider. There may be benefits of economies of scale for functions but there is also a risk that they could be less efficient in dealing with an increase in scale of activities across functions.

- The environment is more dynamic and changing. Toys was a stable product but, for instance, the paper section is high technology, in its infancy, based on R&D changes and expanding. Functional structures tend to be bureaucratic and may not cope will with changes particularly in co-ordinating changes for a product across functions and may therefore hamper creativity and future change.

- There is now greater diversity in the range of products, as Henford is a conglomerate. Functional structures are not normally best suited to dealing with this diversity as the nature of the function could vary. Thus production technology for paper is different to that for toys and uniting them in one function may have few shared skills and benefits.

The new structure is a movement towards divisionalisation but it retains a functional element in finance and HRM.

The structure is one of product divisionalisation but, as the factories are in separate locations, it can also be regarded as geographical divisionalisation.

The new structure enables a divisional manager to take holistic responsibility for the performance of a product by coordinating a range of functions and resources. This enables profit centre responsibility to be implemented.

The fact that Henford is a conglomerate makes the product lines largely independent of each other and therefore segregated management of each product is facilitated.

Advantages for Henford are:

- Managers are held accountable for profitability so the objectives of the reporting unit parallel those of the company

- Functional product specialisation can be developed within divisions, eg marketing pharmaceuticals may be different to marketing toys

- Coordination of functions is facilitated

- The focus of managerial goals is outputs in terms of performance and achievements (profits), rather than inputs in terms of carrying out functional activities

Disadvantages for Henford are:

- The divisional managers may not have the competencies and skills to run a division as their experience and background is in managing a specialised function.

- There may be some duplication of effort and tasks within functions.

Requirement (b) addressed changes to the organisational structure of Henford. It required candidates to: (i) draw organisational charts for the new and old structures; and (ii) evaluate the changes.

In part (i) most candidates produced reasonable diagrams. There were some omissions in relation to the new structure, mainly around the lower level senior managers within each function/division. A minority of candidates incorrectly considered the new structure to be a matrix structure as opposed to divisional.

In part (ii) the discussions on the new structure compared to the old structure were very general but the key principles of autonomy and lack of specialist knowledge were reflected in most answers and candidates appeared to be very comfortable with this element of the question.

(c) Marketing managers appear to dislike the change, which for them is transformational since all their reporting lines and even their location have changed.

They 'are still in communication' so clearly identify themselves with the culture of their previous group as a function rather than their new group as a division. The marketing managers appear to have their own culture based on the old function of marketing which may have been built up over many years.

Cultural barriers include:

Group inertia: Barriers to change may take the form of cultural barriers to change based on group resistance despite their recent geographical separation. The changes make the group dispersed and perhaps their professional skills less understood. Performing less well may be a means of emphasising their role especially when this appears to be a coordinated effort to make the case.

Structural inertia: this is the cumulative effect of the systems and processes. These include promotion and reward systems. These can act as a barrier to change in resisting the new systems by lack of cooperation and the seeking of further changes through board representation with Alan.

In addition to the group of marketing managers resisting change, individuals who are affected by the change may have individual resistance. This may arise because marketing managers have moved geographically (if not working in the Toys division) or there may be a change in role position or rewards.

Barriers to change may be deliberate attempts to resist change but may also be genuine difficulties in coping with the new system or dealing with different people with dissimilar backgrounds.

Individual barriers may include:

- Working less efficiently when reporting to a non-marketing line manager who may not fully understand a marketing role and cannot therefore easily observe or monitor marketing staff

- Failing to interact appropriately with non-marketing staff

- Leaving the organisation (eg to seek a job locally without moving house)

- Lacking appropriate skills in a multi-discipline environment

- Declining morale and motivation

Examiner's comments:

In requirement (c) candidates were asked to consider the barriers to change that the senior marketing managers could potentially create.

Many answers were very generic in describing barriers to change from the learning materials with limited application to the scenario. At the opposite extreme, some candidates commented on the specific changes made by just adopting common sense and without relating the suggestions to relevant models. Those candidates adopting a more balanced approach performed well, although some answers drifted from discussion of the marketing managers to the more general impact on all marketing personnel or all staff.

44   Felan Fashions plc

Marking guide

		Knowledge	Skill	Marks
(a)	Marketing Mix	4	8	12
(b)	Compare two strategies	2	8	10
		6	16	22

General comments:

The scenario in this question concerns a company which designs, produces and retails upmarket ladies' fashion clothing. Felan has a wide coverage of stores in the UK and is seeking to expand into Europe. It is considering two alternative strategies. The first strategy option is to open independent stores across Germany, France, Spain and Italy. The second strategy option is to expand only into France using an agreement to take floor space within a chain of French department stores.

(a)   The marketing mix is the set of controllable marketing variables that a firms blends to produce the response it wants in a target market.

Product

In the marketing mix, 'product' refers to the qualities of the product as perceived by potential customers. This relates to the product's benefits to the consumer and its suitability for its stated purpose including aesthetic factors, durability, brand and associated services.

What is particularly important is not how well these factors are satisfied as such, but how they are perceived in comparison with the key competitors in the market niche selected. The low market recognition for FF of 20% represents a problem in this respect as presumably domestic brands in target countries have higher recognition than FF.

With respect to the product itself, FF has expertise in manufacture, retailing and service delivery in the UK that has proved to be successful. A key question is whether this can be replicated in European countries which may have different tastes, even where there is recognition of the FF brand. Whilst the business model was 'to base her latest designs on current trends set by the major international fashion houses', Tanya attempted to 'tailor FF products to UK market tastes' and may not have the core competences to adapt fully to European tastes which themselves may vary across the target range of countries.

The FF brand name is part of customer product perception. Although it is not widely recognised, a key issue is what it is recognised for. If it develops a good reputation and recognition widens, then the perceived value of the product may increase in customers' perceptions.

The test of success of the product will be in consumers' reaction to the product and this could be revealed in market research, market testing or initial market entry.

Place (distribution)

The use of FF's own shops under Strategy 1 controls the quality of the immediate environment within which FF's clothes are sold. This environment can then be made consistent with the marketing image and the supporting personal service can also be provided.

Unfortunately, FF may not benefit from economies of scope if it uses stores spread across western Europe and it may be unable to take advantage of common distribution channels with its products assuming they continue to be made in the UK. The high value and low volume/weight is likely to reduce this problem as clothes can be sent by courier if needed urgently.

Price

The pricing policy needs to be appropriate to the wider marketing strategy. A low price may penetrate the market and achieve recognition more quickly, but it also sends a signal about the quality of the product. Once established as below the designer range in market positioning, it could be difficult to improve its image and increase the price later.

- Costs

    There may be greater costs of operation and distribution in Europe than in the UK and the influence of costs on price needs to be considered alongside marketing issues. In the long term, price should be expected to cover average costs. However this in turn may depend on the volumes sold in Europe and the economies of scale achieved.

- Customers

    Customer tolerance of prices may vary from country to country for the target group according to how important clothing expenditure is in an individual's budget. Market research will be needed to assess price resistance in this sector of the market. A key issue in this respect is price elasticity.

- Competitors

    The prices charged by competitors may be different than UK competitors as cost structures may vary, as may the intensity of competition. Also there may be some variation, as the £:Euro exchange rate may alter, possibly significantly.

Promotion

Promotion is about communication – informing consumers about the product and enhancing their perception of the product in a manner that persuades them to buy it. The means and method of promotion needs to be appropriate to the product and its positioning. The cost of promotion also needs to be considered in relation to the benefits.

In terms of promoting to consumers, there is a range of methods including: advertising; sponsorship, offers, discounts. Not all these are likely to be appropriate in an upmarket context.

Advertising is likely to be the most important means of sales promotion for FF. If the brand is to be up-market then this needs a significant marketing effort to promote this image compared to maintaining the brand image in the UK. If a new local European market is to be accessed, a greater initial marketing effort will be required, perhaps reflected by the use of outside marketing specialists with local knowledge and a significantly larger marketing budget.

Whilst it normally takes significantly more resources to establish a brand image in a new market, there may be enduring benefits once brand reputation and recognition are established.

Market research may reveal a particular market segment where FF clothes most appeal in terms of their attributes, image and appearance. This may mean that more effective advertising could take place as efforts could then be targeted using a segmentation strategy. Each target country may be different to the UK and to each other.

The 7Ps

The 4Ps model can be expanded into the 7Ps model and this is particularly relevant in the marketing of services. While FF sells goods, a high level of FF customer service is important and may be as much of a key feature in marketing FF in Europe as the clothes themselves.

People

Recruiting appropriate staff in Europe would be a key feature of the service element of the marketing plan. The people working for an organisation which has an interface with customers often say more about that company than the product being sold. In the case of FF, this may include the ability to sell clothes as well as knowledge of local fashions and tastes in advising customers. It may also include skills of altering and fitting the clothes. Assessing the nature and extent of staff recruitment and training will be an important feature of the marketing plan.

Physical

Physical refers to items that give physical substance surrounding the delivery of a service, such as logos, staff uniforms, carrier bags and packaging, and store layout/design. FF's clothes are upmarket and the physical evidence of the quality of the stores in which they are sold is an important part of the image and context within which the clothes are sold. The marketing plan therefore needs to consider the size of the stores and decor etc.

Processes

The ways in which the clothes are sold and customer service is delivered have an impact on the way in which FF customers perceive the organisation. As part of a customer service, efficient administrative processes underpin a high quality of provision. For instance if a customer cannot obtain the size or colour of clothes they want then they may go elsewhere. Efficient processes for FF would include: maintain an appropriate level and type of inventories; ordering services for customers where an item is not held in inventory; and an efficient fitting service.

Examiner's comments:

Requirement (a) asked candidates to set out the factors to be considered in a marketing plan for strategy 1 using the marketing mix.

Most candidates produced answers which used the 4Ps marketing mix model. Although points made specifically in relation to Felan were brief, some good application skills were demonstrated. A minority extended the analysis to 7Ps or, at least, considered 'people' as an extra factor in addition to the 4 Ps. Most candidates were able to state the main points in relation to the fact that FF is an unknown brand outside the UK, moving abroad meant migrating into a different market with different consumers and that distributing the unknown product abroad may be difficult. Some excellent answers were produced which focussed on different fashion tastes, other established brands in the market and the fact that the alternative strategies would have an impact on how and where the product was to be distributed. The higher scoring answers focussed on consumers, competition and push/pull pricing. Some poorer answers were also produced in this part which did not even discuss the 4Ps.

(b) **General issues of overseas expansion for both strategies**

Lynch's Expansion Method Matrix identifies the proposed strategy as 'international development'. The two options of acquisition and direct investment are identify in Lynche's Expansion Method Matrix as 'Organic Growth' (or internal development) in an international market.

Core competencies

The core competencies that have allowed FF to prosper in the UK may not exist in an overseas country. Specifically, core competencies may relate to design and production.

Within this framework, Kay's sources of core competencies are:

Architecture

- Internal architecture – is the relationship with employees. These are likely to be entirely or largely new employees where a new relationship needs to be established.

- External architecture – this includes relationships with external stakeholders such as suppliers and customers. There is likely to be a need to establish some new local suppliers as entire supply from the UK is unlikely to be feasible.

- Network architecture – collaboration between businesses and local networks needs to be established from scratch.

Reputation

It is likely that FF will need to establish a new reputation locally. This may prevent it from initially charging a price premium as in the UK.

Innovative ability

Innovation in design is likely to be able to be 'transported' from the UK to the overseas markets but it is an industry where tastes vary across countries and thus is unlikely to give the same competitive advantage.

Risks

The risks are substantial from the overseas venture and include:

- Foreign currency translation, as revenues would occur in Euros. This is however partially naturally hedged by the fact that costs are also partly being occurred in the same currency.

- Lack of knowledge of overseas markets.

- High level of sunk costs in entering the new market with associated high exit costs if the venture fails and there is a need to withdraw from the market.

- This is a strategy of market development within the Ansoff Matrix. In order to penetrate this new market it is necessary to have core competencies that at least match established local competitors. This is uncertain given the established positions of local competitors.

- The fact that the expansion will reduce dependence on the UK market and the UK economy may reduce risks but only if the other countries are not correlated with the UK in terms of its economic cycle.

Comparison

Issues in favour of Strategy 1

- There are fewer limitations on the scope of development compared to Strategy 2 as there are only 10 UneShop stores. Strategy 1 has no such limits.

- With Strategy 1, FF can develop its own independent market positioning, whereas with Strategy 2 it is questionable whether UneShop has a reputation consistent with FF as it is mid to upper market.

- High street space is likely to be at ground level and prime locations. UneShop floor space may be less prime space (perhaps a corner of the top floor).

- There may be greater operational independence with Strategy 1 than with Strategy 2 in operating with UneShop eg regarding opening times, presentation, staff and other shared facilities.

- Greater scope to choose prime locations in major European cities rather than be restricted to only 10 French cities.

Issues in favour of Strategy 2

- Greater initial impact as 10 stores can open immediately whereas under Strategy 1 it may take time to find and develop 10 new sites

- There is cross branding between UneShop and FF so greater initial market recognition is achieved

- There is more immediate footfall from existing UneShop customers who would visit FF

- Rentals may be lower than high street space depending on the location

- Economies of scope as geographically is more condensed from operating in France alone

- May be able to use UneShop distribution channels and joint marketing

- Greater initial market recognition in France at 25% with Strategy 2 compared to 20% elsewhere in Europe with Strategy 1

- Less range of culture and tastes by focusing in one country

Recommendation

The recommended course of action will depend largely on the terms of agreement with UneShop (eg the cost of renting the floor space, restrictive conditions etc). Assuming, however, that there is no significant difference in rental cost or other conditions between the two strategies, then Strategy 2 appears to offer much better long term scope for expansion and gives more control and autonomy.

The above recommendation is of course provisional and will depend on market research demonstrating evidence of viability of the project. It may be that the evidence demonstrates the opposite, in which case neither strategy should be accepted.

Examiner's comments:

Requirement (b) asked candidates to compare and evaluate the two alternative strategies and to provide appropriate advice. Answers to this part focussed on organic growth compared to a joint venture. Many answers lacked detail and focussed on: Felan's lack of knowledge of overseas markets, exposure to foreign currency risk, the fact that fixed costs would likely remain constant and that there would be an established customer base with strategy 2. Although it was apparent that candidates had understood the key advantages and disadvantages, it would have been encouraging to see development of these points and an assessment of the impact of the strategies on business, customers, strategy and performance of FF.

Weaker candidates tended to list advantages and disadvantages of each of the two strategies as two separate propositions, while stronger ones compared and contrasted them. The majority provided recommendations, with most opting for strategy 2. Some suggested that use could be made of an emergent strategy approach, starting with strategy 2 and then possibly moving on to wider expansion.

45 Brownroll plc

Marking guide

		Knowledge	Skill	Marks
(a)	Separate brands	3	3	6
(b)	(i) Market share and financial performance		8	8
	(ii) Benchmarking	3	3	6
	(iii) Results without CP		8	8
(c)	Future direction	3	9	12
		9	31	40

General comments:

This is the mini case and data analysis question. The scenario relates to a listed company (Brownroll) operating in the UK leisure industry. It has two separate divisions trading under different brand names: a chain of upmarket coffee bars – Cafe Premium (CP) – and a chain of budget hotels – Value Lodge (VL). Despite the presence of a major competitor, Budgetbeds, the hotel side of the business has performed well in the recession, attracting an increased proportion of business travellers and a large share of the tourist market due to very competitively priced room rates. Although CP's financial performance has also been strong, revenue growth has slowed during the recession as the UK coffee bar market, dominated by 3 large chains, approaches saturation.

There is currently some dispute about the future direction of the company. VL's director is considering expanding hotel coverage in the UK and has suggested selling CP to provide the necessary funds (Brownroll has been approached by an international food and beverage company which is interested in the acquisition). CP's director on the other hand believes that the best option is to expand CP in Europe by franchising. Finally the FD has suggested that given the very different markets and strategies of the two divisions demerger may be the best option for the shareholders.

(a) Separate brands

Brands add value to a business by making its products recognisable and creating associations with a particular market segment. They may help customers to distinguish competing products. A company may choose to adopt single company brand name 'Brownroll' or different brand names for each product, as in this case: 'Value Lodge' and 'Café Premium'.

According to Michael Porter a company can adopt one of two generic strategies: cost leadership or differentiation, and this can be done on an industry-wide or a focussed basis. Here Brownroll has chosen to focus on two different market segments within the hospitality industry (budget hotels and branded coffee bars) and is adopting different generic strategies for each – cost leadership in the case of the hotel division and differentiation in the case of coffee bars. This is reflected in the fact that VL's hotels conform to a standard design and layout, whereas CP's coffee bars are tailored to each individual location.

Brownroll's two brands are positioned differently in perceived price and quality terms.

CP's brand name suggests it is aiming to be a premium brand. This is reinforced by the fact that it markets itself as selling high-quality unique Italian blend, tailors each coffee bar to its location and invests heavily in customer service training for all its staff.

VL is more likely to be positioned somewhere between Economy and Bargain, offering reasonable quality for a low price.

Conclusion

As there is limited scope for synergy between the two and as the attributes of the two brands are quite different, like many companies which produce a number of products with significantly different positions in the market place, Brownroll has chosen to use different brand names.

Examiner's comments:

Requirement (a) asked candidates to explain why Brownroll operates its business under two separate brand names. This requirement was generally well done with almost all candidates pointing out that the separate brands were a probable consequence of the two divisions operating different strategies in different industry sectors. However, some candidates produced a slightly more balanced argument by providing examples of some successful company-wide brands such as Virgin. Good discussion was seen in terms of the generic strategies of the two divisions with CP as a differentiator and VL a cost leader. The better answers used the information in the scenario to illustrate this and also discussed price/quality positioning and the use of the brand as a marketing tool. Some answers had a limited focus, with discussion almost entirely relating to differences in market positioning.

(b) (i) Data analysis

Market share

Hotels

Budgetbeds: (BB) £208m = 31% of market
Hence market = 208/0.31 = £671m
So VL share = 290/671 = 43.2%

Therefore VL is currently the market leader in a budget hotel market which is dominated by VL and BB, with the remaining third of the market being fragmented.

The size of the market has grown in the recession as more business customers have switched to budget hotels. VL's scope to grow further will depend on the rate of growth in the market and its ability either to steal market share from BB or to attract customers who are currently using the independent hotels.

Clearly in terms of the wider hotel market, VL will have a smaller market share as it will be competing with a variety of different hotels which are positioned differently in terms of price/quality.

Branded coffee bars

3 major chains have 2,015 outlets out of a total of 3,500 = 57.6% share in terms of number of outlets.

In terms of revenue, the 3 chains hold a 72.5% share of £1.2bn market, which amounts to £870m.

CP holds 370/3500 = 10.6% share by number of outlets
CP has £116m or 9.7% share of revenue

Therefore relatively CP is a much smaller player in its market place than VL. Assuming the 3 major players are of similar size (which is practice is probably unlikely) this would amount to around 24% of the market revenue each, which means that CP has less than half the share of the market leaders. This may be a problem as the market becomes saturated since this is likely to lead to consolidation and CP may find it harder to compete.

CP is however following a differentiation strategy so it may be more reasonable to assess its position within the premium segment of the market.

Financial performance of divisions

A table of performance measures is set out in Appendix 1.

Both divisions have done well and have continued to make profits despite the recession.

CP is the smaller division, accounting for less than one third of the company's revenue but in 2011 it generates 41.2% of the contribution, so would appear to be the more profitable business.

Results for 2011 suggest CP's revenue growth is limited compared to VL (6.4% compared to 19.3%) which is consistent with the explanation that the UK coffee bar market is approaching saturation.

However, it is making a significantly bigger increase in contribution (24% to VL's 10.6%) and this is reflected in the fact that between 2010 and 2011 CP's margins (contribution: sales) improved from 16.8% to 19.6%, whereas VL's reduced from 12.1% to 11.2%. This may be due to the fact that VL is having to keep room rates very low to attract customers. Also VL is pursuing a cost leadership strategy whereas CP is a differentiator. This probably explains why CP's contribution margin is generally higher than VL's.

CP is generating significantly better ROCE than VL. This could however be because its assets are of different ages or that it has significant assets under operating leases which are therefore not reflected. More information is required to assess this.

One of the problems when assessing divisional performance is the allocation of central costs. In order to appraise the performance that is attributable to the division/its manager the comments above have focussed on divisional contribution. Ultimately however the existence of the divisions gives rise to central costs such as marketing and accounting which Brownroll needs to cover.

Here, if we compare the divisional contribution and reported operating profit we can see that these costs have been allocated equally between the divisions as follows:

	2010	2011
VL	8.7	9.1
CP	8.7	9.1
	17.4	18.2

Given that it is the smaller division, CP incurs more than its proportionate share of central costs and this explains why, despite generating 41.2% of Brownroll's contribution, it is only providing 36.9% of its operating profit.

Examiner note:

A range of calculations has been provided in the appendix to offer guidance for markers. Candidates were not expected to produce the full set of calculations in order to score the maximum marks available.

Appendix 1

Comparison of performance

	2010		2011	
	VL	CP	VL	CP
Contribution: sales ratio (using divisional contribution)	12.1%	16.8%	11.2%	19.6%
Divisional ROCE (using divisional contribution)	19.7%	34.9%	20.2%	39.7%
Reported operating profit margin	8.5%	8.8%	8.0%	11.7%

	Change 2010 - 2011		
Change in:	VL	CP	Brownroll
Sales	19.3%	6.4%	15.3%
Contribution	10.6%	24.0%	15.8%
Operating profit	13.1%	41.7%	22.2%
Net assets	8.0%	9.0%	8.2%

Examiner's comments:

Requirement (b) requested candidates to: (i) compare the current market share and financial performance of Brownroll's two divisions; (ii) explain the usefulness of benchmarking for Brownroll and recommend two specific KPIs for each division that would help benchmark performance and (iii) ignoring strategic considerations, evaluate the VL director's comment that the company's financial results would look much better without CP, stating any assumptions and suggesting further internal information that would be useful.

Candidates produced a range of calculations in answering part (i). The recurring calculations were market share, operating profit margin, and % change in revenue which most candidates correctly determined. However, some candidates used 2010 figures to determine market share rather than 2011. Stronger candidates also recognised that, having been provided with net assets, some form of ROCE measure would be useful. Relatively few picked up on the hints in the question about central costs and the impact of these on reported performance. The narrative element was more disappointing with weaker answers merely providing a commentary on VL's figures compared to CP without explaining the reasons for the differences in the results of the two divisions. A minority of weaker candidates provided entirely quantitative answers, with no discussion of the numbers. The better answers addressed both market share and financial performance, linked the performance to the different strategies and markets and concluded that although CP had a lower overall market share and lower revenue growth than VL, it had actually performed better in terms of asset utilisation and contribution to profits.

(ii) **Benchmarking**

By comparing performance with others, Brownroll can learn how to reduce costs/improve quality in order to increase its market share in the branded coffee bar market. Alternatively benchmarking may help Brownroll better understand how it is achieving competitive advantage and superior performance in the budget hotel market, in order to maintain this.

Bases:

Historic or internal – internal benchmarking would be at the level of comparing individual hotels or coffee bars with each other to determine those that are under- or over-performing when considering the same brand, price, etc.

Brownroll could also compare performance over time or compare the divisions with each other. However CP and VL operate in different markets so this comparison may not be helpful. Therefore wider benchmarking may help Brownroll get further insight into how each division is performing and also assist in deciding whether or not to sell CP.

Competitive – compare performance with other firms in the same industry or sector. This may assist Brownroll in ascertaining ways to improve performance – eg comparing the performance of the hotel division with Budgetbeds, and the coffee division with other branded coffee bars. If the whole domestic industry is underperforming, international comparisons may be more useful so comparisons.

Activity (best in class) – compare with best practice in whatever industry can be found eg could compare VL's online booking systems with an online booking system for airline seats to ascertain whether there is scope for improved efficiency.

Generic – against a conceptually similar process eg compare a hotel's guest management with a hospital's patient management, or compare a coffee bar's customer service with the customer service of another organisation that has a good reputation for the way it deals with the public eg a bank or filling station. *Could also be made with hotels and coffee bars in other markets.*

KPIs to benchmark divisions (only two required for each)

Coffee bars

As CP is following a differentiation strategy, measures that focus on customer service and quality would be important. These might be benchmarked in relation to other premium branded coffee bars and/or the Big 3:

- Number of customers served per hour
- Level of repeat business (maybe difficult to measure though could use loyalty card information)
- Average transaction value
- Revenue per day

Hotel industry

As VL is following a cost leadership strategy, measures that focus on cost and price would be important. These could be benchmarked against Budgetbeds and might include:

- Occupancy rates
- Average room rate
- Level of repeat bookings
- Average length of stay
- Conversion of initial enquiries into bookings

Examiner's comments:

Part (ii) on benchmarking and KPIs was generally done quite well, with most candidates demonstrating appropriate knowledge. The higher scoring answers applied this knowledge to the scenario, realising that a comparison of CP to VL may not be that useful as the divisions were in such different industries. Better candidates were selective in choosing the most appropriate forms of benchmarking for Brownroll and also in selecting and justifying specific KPIs that linked to each individual division's strategy and competitive position. Weaker candidates produced some unusual KPIs which were unlikely to be controllable at divisional level or which were broad objectives, not capable of being easily measured.

(iii) **Results without CP**

Financial impact of the sale of CP

In addition to the calculations in Appendix 1, further calculations of the impact of sale are provided in Appendix 2.

Brownroll's results, taking the two divisions into account, show improved performance between 2010 and 2011. Sales are up by 15.3%, operating profit margin has increased from 8.6% to 9.1% and ROCE has improved considerably from 15% to 17%. In the context of an economy emerging from the recession, shareholders are likely to be happy.

The sale of CP, which is contributing 28.6% of sales and 41.2% of divisional contribution, would make Brownroll a much smaller company. On a basic level, the CP division is making a positive contribution to the group results (£22.7m) and without it absolute profit would decrease as at least some of the allocated central costs would presumably remain in place.

Although the VL direct is correct that revenue growth at 19.3% would be better without CP, it was clear in b(i) that in 2011 CP outperformed VL in terms of all other measure (margins, ROCE and profit growth). Therefore the company as a whole would be worse off without CP (ignoring any benefits from reinvesting the cash raised from its sale) and in addition would show a decline in performance relative to 2010.

The exact results would depend on the extent to which central costs can be saved.

To properly assess financial impact, we would need to consider any interdependency between the divisions (although the suggestion is there is very little) and the impact of any sale on the results of VL.

Further internal information

Additional information that would be useful includes:

- The extent to which central costs would be saved by closing the CP division

- Information regarding the age and current value of the assets used by each division and the extent to which each division is using assets held under operating leases, as this will affect ROCE

- Likely exit costs arising from redundancy, lease penalties etc

It is not just historic performance but future performance that is relevant for the purpose of deciding whether to keep a division open, therefore details of budgets/plans for both divisions beyond 2011 would be useful.

In addition to profit-based performance, investors are likely to use other measures to assess the company. This would include measures such as the EPS and other market-based measures derived from share price eg PE ratio. Information regarding the relative shareholdings of key investors, together with their preferred targets, eg for sales growth, ROCE, growth in share price etc would be useful to assess whether all investors are likely to view Brownroll in the same way.

Also to make a complete assessment, wider measurers of performance for the divisions should be considered, based on financial and non-financial criteria.

Conclusion

On the basis of the financial results the VL director's assertion that Brownroll's results would be better without CP appears to be purely based on revenue growth and his suggestion, which may be motivated by personal interest, appears to be incorrect. There are also wider strategic issues to be considered, such as the impact on Brownroll's portfolio and its brand, which are discussed further in (c).

Appendix 2: Impact of sale of CP

	2010		2011	
	VL	CP	VL	CP
Share of revenue	69.0%	31.0%	71.4%	28.6%
Share of divisional contribution	61.6%	38.4%	58.8%	41.2%
Share of operating profit	68.2%	31.8%	63.1%	36.9%

£m	Brownroll 2011	VL only with all central costs	VL only – if half central costs saved
Total revenue	406	290	290
Divisional contribution	55.1	32.4	32.4
Allocated HO costs (see (b))	18.2	18.2	9.1
Reported operating profit	36.9	14.2	23.3
Net assets	217.4	160.2	160.2

	Brownroll 2010	Brownroll 2011	Brownroll 2011 without CP (all central costs)	Brownroll 2011 without CP (CP's central costs saved)
Sales growth	n/a	15.3%	19.3%	19.3%
Operating profit margin	8/6%	9.1%	4.9%	8.0%
ROCE	15.0%	17.0%	8.9%	14.5%

Examiner's comments:

Answers to part (iii) about the financial effect of selling CP were variable and weaker candidates appeared to struggle here. Some made no reference to the data analysis that they had undertaken in part (i) which suggests a tendency to take a silo view of the individual parts of questions, rather than linking the findings together to reach a conclusion. Those who simply made comments of a strategic nature (which they often went on to repeat in part (c) restricted their marks, given the specific instruction to ignore strategic considerations. Stronger candidates identified from their analysis in b(i) that although CP's revenue growth was worse than VLs, other performance measures such as margin, ROCE and profit growth were better and some then went on to produce results for the group as a whole to prove that Brownroll would be worse off without CP. As a result the VL director's comments, which were likely to involve a degree of bias, only considered part of the story. A critical issue here was the allocation of central costs and whether these would be avoided if CP were sold, but a very significant number of candidates failed to make any reference to this. Some weaker candidates provided entirely descriptive answers with no numerical analysis at all. Another common mistake was to provide a long list of generic additional information including industry and competitor data, despite the instruction to focus on internal information only.

(c) **Future direction**

Sale of CP division (divestment) to fund expansion of VL

A divestment would involve Brownroll disposing of the CP division in order to concentrate on its hotel activities.

One reason for doing this may be to improve the overall company performance. The rationale for divestment is normally to reduce costs, or to increase return on assets by deploying resources to activities with a higher return on invested capital, or to return capital to shareholders. This is particularly true if a division is loss-making, which is not the case here – CP's managing director comments that its margins are excellent. It has been seen in (b) above that, based on the 2011 figures, divestment of the CP business will not necessarily improve the company's results, other than with regard to sales growth. Brownroll has to decide what constitutes core activities and where the next growth opportunities exist. VL's managing director believes the growth prospects in the UK coffee market are disappointing, so Brownroll may feel that growth opportunities can be best realised by concentrating on the core hotel business. An alternative, suggested by CP's managing director and discussed below, is to pursue growth in other markets eg by franchising coffee bars overseas.

In deciding whether to sell off CP, the amount of cash being offered by the international food and beverage company will be a key factor in the decision. If as a result of the offer on the table Brownroll can sell the division at a good price, then it may consider doing so if it is short of cash for the expansion of hotels or in order to protect the rest of the business from takeover. However CP may be a cash cow division, generating day-to-day cash for the group and the loss of this would need to be taken into account.

Another option would be for Brownroll to sell CP to its management, although they may find it difficult to make an offer which is competitive in the light of the price being offered by the food and beverage company.

Expansion of VL

VL's managing director suggests that it needs to buy more hotels to consolidate its position. From (b) we can see that VL is the market leader with 36% of the market compared to BB's 31%. Clearly it is important that VL takes action to maintain this position of competitive advantage. VL could open hotels in areas that are not currently covered by either VL or BB, or open hotels in direct competition with BB in certain places. With occupancy rates at 80% there is some existing spare capacity so VL would need to be sure that demand exists and that it can achieve good occupancy rates in the new hotels.

Demerger

The finance director is correct that ultimately Brownroll needs to consider what is best for its shareholders. Brownroll is a plc and in theory its objective is to maximise the wealth of the shareholders. There may however be conflict between different groups of shareholders as to the direction they wish Brownroll to take.

One way to resolve the conflict would be to demerge the two divisions so the shareholders can then decide for themselves which of the two businesses they want to retain shares in.

A demerger is the opposite of a merger. It is the splitting up of Brownroll plc into two separate, independently operating companies, VL plc and CP plc. The existing Brownroll shareholders are given a stake in each of the new separate companies. In a demerger, shareholders would exchange shares in Brownroll for shares in the two separate companies, therefore the demerger will not raise any cash for expansion of either division. If seen as worthwhile by the market, however, it can result in two businesses with greater market capitalisation than the original group.

VL's managing director comments that there is little synergy between the two divisions and there appears to be little in the way of interdependency. Therefore there may be no strategic logic for running the businesses together. The fact that the businesses operate different competitive strategies under different brand names (see (a)) may further support this argument and would facilitate a demerger. Indeed if the public are aware that both businesses are owned by Brownroll, this may affect perceptions of CP, who may be struggling to be seen as a differentiator because of its association with VL.

Disadvantages might include overall increase in overhead costs as a result of the fact that, instead of benefiting from central services, VL and CP will now need to provide their own marketing, accounting etc. Also each individual company will have lower revenue, profits and net assets than the previous group. This may affect its status and ability to raise finance.

There will be transaction costs associated with the demerger. Finally some shareholders may have invested in the group precisely because it has a varied mix of businesses, diversifying risk to some degree, so these shareholders will possibly oppose the demerger.

Expansion of CP via franchise

Product life cycles vary from country to country. Often a reason put forward for global expansion is that if the domestic market is saturated, other markets may be growing. This is what CP's managing director is suggesting and if Brownroll's shareholders expect growth then this may be a good way of continuing to deliver it.

Another possible benefit is that if competition in the oversaturated domestic market is intense, rivalry may be less keen in overseas markets. CP is however unlikely to be the only branded coffee bar chain considering such an expansion. A number of branded coffee chains such as Costa and Starbucks are currently expanding into markets such as China and India.

CP may also benefit overseas because it will not be associated with the conflicting image and strategy of VL, which only operates in the UK.

According to Lynch, a business can expand organically (internal development) or via an external partner. CP's MD indicates that within the UK CP has grown organically by opening new outlets but this strategy may not be appropriate for overseas markets. Many businesses choose to expand internationally via franchise. This is often a suitable method as it allows the business to grow faster, requires less capital and shares the risks involved. It may help reduce risk as CP would benefit from the knowledge and expertise of a local partner. Given its emphasis on differentiation and tailoring its coffee bars to the local neighbourhood, this may be very successful.

Other issues to consider with overseas expansion through franchising include whether the CP brand, which is UK-based, would be sufficiently strong to attract franchisees in Europe, the need for CP to manage the franchises in unfamiliar markets, cultural differences in taste and the risk of exchange rate movements.

Conclusion

The strategies being put forward by the directors are not necessarily mutually exclusive. Thus Brownroll could choose both to expand the hotels and franchise its coffee bars, provided it can access sufficient finance. Alternatively Brownroll might consider opening CP coffee bars within VL hotels, although there may be some issues due to the conflicting brand image.

Examiner's comments:

Requirement (c) asked candidates to evaluate the comments made at the Board meeting with respect to the three options being considered for the future direction of the company: sale of CP to fund expansion of VL; demerger; and expansion of CP outside the UK by franchising. Candidates on the whole made a good attempt at discussing the sale of CP and whether expansion of VL was worthwhile, although rarely made any comment on how much cash might be obtained from the sale. They were less comfortable discussing demerger. Whilst most candidates broadly understand that a demerger would result in a splitting of VL and CP, they did not really show a detailed knowledge of the impact on the shareholders and the fact that there would be two new separate companies, with the shareholders being given a stake in each. Most showed a good knowledge of the pros and cons of franchising, but only the better scripts linked this to the risks of overseas expansion and the fact that Brownroll has little knowledge of overseas markets. Surprisingly few candidates made any attempt at a conclusion.

46 Dearman Cranes plc

		Knowledge	Skill	Marks
(a)	Porter's Diamond	2	4	6
(b)	Risks	2	4	6
(c)	Joint venture	3	5	8
(d)	Governance and risk management	3	5	8
(e)	Ethical issues	2	3	5
		12	21	33

General comments:

The scenario in this question relates to Dearman Cranes, a family owned business based in Scotland that manufactures mobile cranes. Dearman was established to meet local demand for shipbuilding and background information was provided on the development of Scotland's industries. The crane industry has in recent years been dominated by a few large Japanese and American manufacturers but competition from China is rapidly increasing. Dearman operates in a niche market and has developed an excellent reputation and a loyal international customer base. Product development in terms of capacity and technology is key to Dearman's success. Dearman is currently considering an AIM listing to raise more funds for research and also a joint venture with a major Scottish university to establish an engineering research centre. Rob Price, Dearman's MD, has recently received a request from a major customer, YXL ltd, asking Dearman to fit additional safety mechanisms to its cranes in light of new regulations in the city where it operates. YXL is unhappy about the restrictions on weight that the new regulations involve and has asked Dearman to fit the necessary mechanisms to comply with the regulations but then to install a bypass switch to allow YXL to circumvent them. In return YXL has promised Dearman a large future order. The Board is concerned that this raises legal and ethical issues.

(a) Porter's Diamond

Porter's Diamond provides a framework for assessing the relationship between location and competitive advantage and can be used to help explain why clusters of industries arise due to the existence of common technologies, skills and knowledge or the linking of buyers and suppliers.

In the case of Scotland, during the 19th and early 20th centuries Scotland enjoyed a strong market presence in heavy engineering, in particular shipbuilding. Later in the 20th century this clustering was evident in the petro-chemical industry when Scotland became a key location for the oil industry.

According to Porter, the clustering of the shipbuilding industry in Scotland may have arisen for the following reasons:

Factor conditions – the resource inputs needed by the business. Since Scotland had a thriving shipbuilding industry, a workforce will have developed with the necessary knowledge and skills for heavy engineering: welders, platers, electricians etc.

Home market demand conditions – these shape a firm's priorities and the way it responds to buyer needs. Thus demanding customers in the shipbuilding industry helped to establish qualities required for market dominance outside the UK. Also Scotland's heavy engineering was driven by demand for ships and aero-engines for the defence industry.

Supporting local industries – competitive success in one industry is often linked to success in related industries. At the time that Scotland was leading the market in shipbuilding, it was also doing well in other heavy industries such as marine and aerospace engineering. A number of these industries relied on the proximity of port facilities and the availability of labour. Raw materials were also available from the neighbouring steel industry.

Firm strategy, structure and rivalry – firms emerge with strong competitive characteristics which are then able to dominate worldwide markets. Large volumes demanded then enable companies to develop economies of scale.

It may also be argued that government played a part in attracting investment to Scotland as a result of grants and loans available.

Now the UK as a whole has witnessed the decline of its manufacturing base and moved towards service businesses as other countries benefit from the outsourcing of manufacture and this may have explained the decline in heavy engineering. However the advent of oil means that, in Scotland, this has been replaced to an extent by petro-chemicals.

Examiner's comments:

Requirement (a) asked candidates to use Porter's Diamond to explain the reasons for the clustering of the shipbuilding industry in Scotland. Most candidates performed relatively well here, demonstrating sound knowledge of Porter's Diamond and extracting the relevant information from the scenario to illustrate the reasons for Scotland's historic dominance. A small minority did not know the four headings in the model and were restricted to providing common sense answers based on the information in the scenario. Others failed to read the requirement carefully and incorrectly focussed on the crane industry.

(b) **Risks of current position**

Strategic risks – include

- Lack of competitive advantage due to failure to stay ahead of competitor's products and undertake successful research and development into new cranes

- The danger that new Chinese competitors enter Dearman's market niche and take market share

- The failure to safeguard intellectual property and proprietary knowledge

- Risk of technical obsolescence of existing cranes due to technological developments

- Risk of produce obsolescence in certain markets due to changes in road regulations eg if Japanese road regulations tighten, some of Dearman's cranes may become too heavy to use

- Lack of available finance to pursue research

- Risk to reputation if safety incidents arise with Dearman cranes. The nature of the product mans such incidents are likely to be high profile and may have fatal consequences – this would have major consequences for Dearman's reputation

- Over-reliance on the Price family/lack of succession planning

Operational risks – include

- Risk that Dearman cannot recruit sufficient skilled labour given changing market place, or that imported labour does not provide the same quality

- Risks arising from lack of compliance with health and safety issues and other laws/regulations that govern occupational health and safety in Dearman's production facilities

- One issue for Dearman is that regulations vary considerably from one location to another and cranes may be needed to ensure that are aware of safe product design and safety features, and the provide appropriate guidance re safe useage etc

- Risk of inadequacies or failure of Dearman's management and control structures

Examiner's comments:

Requirement (b) required candidates to identify the major risks arising from Dearman's current strategic position. Most candidates recognised that Dearman was operating in a market niche and that technological change, increased regulations, labour issues and increased competition from overseas could potentially be issues for the company, although this was often presented as a shopping list of unprioritised or undeveloped points. Better candidates structured their answers, eg under the headings strategic and operational risks, and explained clearly (often using a grid) how the particular issue identified would result in a risk for Dearman. Others used Porter's Five Forces Model as a basis for structuring risks.

(c) **Joint venture – implications for stakeholders**

Jane Price has suggested that the company consider a joint venture with a major Scottish university to establish an engineering research centre.

Benefits for the university

- Revenue from sale of any intellectual property (IP) – provides university with a route to market for intellectual capital

- May help attract further funding/investors/grants

- Increase number of academic papers published

- Attract more students to come to the university

- Publicity for the university/recognition in terms of academic community esteem

- Placements for university students may increase success rates in finding work and improve position in university league tables

- Practical commercial applications for scientific research

- Technology transfer from private sector

- Access to company knowledge and resources

- New ideas for teaching and training

- May allow research to continue in a climate of funding cutbacks

- New opportunities for staff in terms of personal development

Benefits for Dearman

Dearman's main aim will be enhanced product differentiation and therefore competitive advantage.

Benefits include:

- Cheaper R&D than if it hires its own staff

- May increase speed of product development

- May increase the value of R&D output

- Access to wider pool of inter-disciplinary, cross-industry and cross-national expertise, knowledge and ideas

- May learn about new areas of research

- Fresh outlook (younger, less constrained) may bring new ideas

- Shared costs/risk

- Help provide replacements for products whose obsolescence is being accelerated

- May help benchmark the quality of Dearman's in-house research

- May help retain research staff by offering them development opportunities within the university

- Offers a pool of talent for the future – easier to recruit the right people with the right skills

- Promote positive image of commercial company with a wider pool of stakeholders

- Satisfy some corporate responsibility objectives

- May access government funding available for private/public sector collaborations

- May be beneficial for Dearman's image in the context of corporate social responsibility which may become more important in view of the AIM listing

Potential Issues for the two stakeholders

These arise because of the potential for conflicting goals, cultural differences, financial disagreements, disputes over the ownership of intellectual property and differing degrees of accountability.

A key issue here is how the intellectual property rights will be divided between Dearman and the university in future in terms of access, exploitation and payment.

Dearman is a profit-making entity which primarily exists to maximise shareholder wealth.

The university is a public sector organisation which has to take account of the multiple objectives of a wider range of stakeholders. It may have concerns over whether the research will benefit wider society or only be applied for the benefit of the commercial partner.

The university is probably more interested in longer term research that benefits the whole industry whereas individual companies like Dearman are more likely to pursue research that delivers more focused company benefits. Shareholder pressure for Dearman to produce short term results may increase if the AIM listing is achieved.

Culturally the university researchers may not be used to operating under the same type of commercial constraints as Dearman or being accountable on a short term, regular basis for performance. Dearman is likely to want to control and monitor the project using KPIs.

Typically academics will want to publish their research as this brings credibility and recognition. Dearman may want to limit publication of results for fear of loss of competitive advantage and is therefore more likely to want to patent or protect findings.

Examiner's comments:

In requirement (c) candidates were asked to identify the benefits for both Dearman and the university of pursuing a joint engineering research venture and the issues that might arise. Most clearly understood how a joint venture operates and were able to identify the key benefits for each party but often did not develop the issues beyond a comment that agreeing profit share may be difficult. Weaker candidates omitted to consider the specific benefits for the university in addition to Dearman. Better candidates recognised that the key issue would be the ownership of IP and the benefits arising from it, and that the motives of the university as an entity may conflict with those of a commercial company such as Dearman.

(d) **Stakeholders' expectations of governance and risk management as a result of listing**

Dearman has to date been 100% family-owned. As a result of listing on AIM it will become a part publicly-owned company with a wider range of shareholders, from private individuals to institutions. This gives rise to possible agency issues since the owners and managers of the business will no longer necessarily be the same people.

Rob has indicated that the main purpose of the AIM listing is to gain access to finance for research and this will probably result in some institutional shareholders. These shareholders are likely to have expectations concerning the corporate governance of Dearman – where corporate governance is about the relationship between Dearman's Board and these external stakeholders, rather than the day-to-day operational management of the company.

In recognition of their size, AIM companies are not specifically required to comply with the UK Corporate Governance code. However adopting good corporate governance best practice is likely to increase investor confidence and help with risk management. One of the challenges for

Dearman is to stay ahead of its competitors. By going beyond minimum regulatory requirements and adopting a strategy of good corporate governance, Dearman is likely to be more successful in satisfying the needs of its investors and wider stakeholders (employees, customers, suppliers), thereby increasing its competitive advantage. There may also be benefits for Dearman in terms of reduced financial vulnerability.

The reality is that most business cannot grow beyond a certain size and continue to be effective without having already applied some of the principles of corporate governance. This is likely to be what Rob means when he says 'I've always made sure we had processes in place that add value to the business, and attitudes that help build our reputation and ensure long-term success.' This may have included creating a culture of innovation, adopting a strategic planning process that takes into account the opportunities and risks facing the company, and developing internal control and management information systems.

If it lists on AIM, Dearman should ensure that it adopts basic principles of leadership and effectiveness by splitting the roles of Chairman and Chief Executive and ensuring clear division of responsibility between running the Board (Chairman) and running the company's business (Chief Exec). By splitting the Board into teams to work on individual projects, Rob can concentrate on the strategic direction of the business.

It would also be sensible to appoint some independent non-executive directors who will help ensure that the Board has the necessary skills to govern effectively and can improve decision making.

Sustainability and corporate responsibility

Corporate responsibility is about the actions, activities and obligations of a business in achieving sustainability, where sustainability is the ability to meet the needs of the present without compromising the ability of future generations to meet their own needs (the Brundtland report). To achieve sustainable success businesses must balance economic, social and environmental issues.

Although the UK corporate governance code places greater emphasis on the long-term sustainable success of the company based on its business model there are no such specific mandatory requirements for listed companies to implement sustainable business practices.

However, many companies whether listed or not, choose to pursue sustainable development for reasons of competitive advantage or to avoid the adverse publicity that may arise if they do not.

Risk management

Rob is concerned that by going public Dearman isn't allowed to take the same risks.

If the directors take decisions to increase profits without due regard to risk then the shareholders may stand to lose some or all of their investment. As a result external shareholders need to have confidence that the Board is aware of the risks a company faces and have systems in place for monitoring them.

This does not mean avoiding risks but determining the nature and extent of the risks that Dearman is willing to take to achieve its objectives and ensuring good practices in risk management.

Thus Rob needs to ensure that there are systems in place to identify the strategic, operational, financial and hazard risks faced by the business. It can then assess the scale of the risks and the likelihood of loss, in order to set priorities for risk mitigation. Risks can then be dealt with according to the TARA model – transfer, avoidance, reduction or retention.

For example Dearman can take steps to reduce the hazard risks associated with the cranes by ensuring sound construction and design and by using technology to prevent such hazards eg alarms and automatic cut-outs if a crane is overloaded.

Deciding how certain risks are to be addressed will depend on the costs and benefits of doing so, stakeholder views and other legal requirements. In the context of Dearman's business, risk management will need to take into account any legal requirements such as health and safety legislation.

Requirement (d) dealt with the potential AIM listing. Candidates were asked to explain the impact that such a listing would have on stakeholders' expectations of the company's governance and risk management. Some answers were very brief and simply focussed on the fact that an AIM listing would result in additional regulation, and more need for compliance. Risk management, if covered, was often discussed in the most generic of terms. Better candidates linked their answers to the quote in the scenario from Rob Price, discussing the agency issues arising from having non-family shareholders and going on to explain the concept of governance and the need to consider wider stakeholders in the context of corporate social responsibility. The best candidates pointed out that the listing may not require radical change but rather a slightly more formalised approach with increased communication and stakeholder engagement. They went on to point out that risk management did not mean that Dearman would 'not be allowed to take risks' and discussed attitudes to risk in the context of the scenario and the investors in the company.

(e) **Issues arising from email**

Ethics pertain to whether a particular behaviour is deemed acceptable in the context under consideration. Here the issue is that Abbeyville's local government has introduced new regulations for the cranes which will restrict their operating capacity. Initially the obligation to comply is on the crane operator (YXL) rather than the crane manufacturer (Dearman). Dearman becomes involved however because YXL, a key customer, is asking for help to circumvent the new regulations which it perceives to be unnecessary.

Rob should take legal advice regarding the legality of the action being considered.

In making a decision as to how to proceed, Rob may also find it helpful to apply the Institute of Business Ethics three tests:

- Transparency
- Effect
- Fairness

Transparency – would Rob mind other people knowing that, in addition to fitting the required alarm, Dearman had fitted an override switch. This test is partly about whether the action required contravenes Rob's personal ethics and belief in 'doing the right thing' – it is not about whether he can get away with the behaviour provided he is not found out.

Effect – who does the decision affect/hurt? YXL stand to gain competitive advantage if they are able to flout the rules and keep margins higher by controlling operating costs.

In the short term Dearman would gain by winning the additional contract for 5 new cranes. However Dearman also risk reputational damage if it came to light that it had accepted this proposal and effectively colluded to contravene the regulations – there may be repercussions in terms of fines etc and this would almost certainly affect the future sustainability of the business. The losers would be the regulator, anybody who gets hurt in the event of a safety incident which could involve the crane operator, other construction workers, passers-by etc.

Here Dearman needs to recognise that as a business it has an obligation to society and its wider stakeholders to behave responsibly. There may also be certain industry codes of conduct that apply.

Fairness = would the decision be considered fair by those affected? The issue for Dearman is that they are being asked to fit the override in the knowledge that this might be used inappropriately by the client, YXL. Should someone be badly hurt as a result of YXL's actions, it is unlikely that they would perceive Dearman's actions in fitting the override to be fair, particularly if Dearman was seen to have gained by winning more business.

The promise of future orders is a threat to Rob's integrity and objectivity in terms of decision-making. If Dearman says no then they may lose YXL's future order and possibly lose them as a client. However Dearman may feel that it is not in its interests to continue to do business with clients of this nature.

In the context of business ethics, YXL's behaviour, which could be seen as bribery or intimidation, would be deemed bad conduct.

Conclusion:

What YXL are asking Dearman to do would appear to be unethical and quite possibly illegal. Rob might want to seek advice regarding the legality of such an action but as Dearman has a duty to ensure that its products do not cause harm to workers, customers, the environment and wider society, Rob should agree to fit the alarms but decline YXL's request to fit the over-ride switch.

Examiner's comments:

Finally in requirement (e) candidates were asked to discuss the issues arising for Dearman as a result of YXL's email request. The standard of answers varied here. Higher scoring answers were well-structured and considered the legality of the request before discussing the ethical implications, either in terms of personal, business and corporate ethics, or by applying the business ethics tests of transparency, fairness and effect, or by considering how YXL was essentially threatening the company's business ethics (especially integrity) by intimidation. Weaker answers were restricted to issues of legality and reputation and some cited the ICAEW code of ethics which was not directly relevant to the scenario. Candidates often concluded that what was being offered was essentially a bribe although many did not offer a conclusion as to whether Dearman should undertake the work or what Rob's response should be. Other weaker answers attempted to address ethical issues without considering legality.

47 Happy Valley Yoga Centre

Marking guide

			Knowledge	Skill	Marks
(a)	(i)	Benefits of a business plan	2	2	4
	(ii)	Content	3	5	8
(b)		Weaknesses and threats	2	5	7
(c)		Pricing policy	3	5	8
			10	17	27

General comments:

The scenario in this question concerns an individual who wishes to set up her own yoga centre. Samantha Bikram used redundancy money from her job as a gym manager at a local hotel to train as a yoga practitioner. She has been working as a yoga instructor for a local recreation and leisure facility on a self-employed basis. Sam intends to set up Happy Valley Yoga Centre (HVYC) on a large business park offering group and individual sessions to employees of the various offices and businesses. Sam has discussed the idea with her local bank manager who has asked her to prepare a business plan using the banks proforma headings but she has little knowledge of how to go about it. Candidates were provided with background information and estimates in the form of a letter from Sam and asked to produce a report to assist her in responding to the bank's request.

Answers to this question were usually of a reasonable standard although the need to apply knowledge to the scenario and to focus on the needs of the user of the business plan (ie the bank) appeared to be a challenge for the weaker candidates.

(a) **Report**

To: Sam Bikram
From: A N Accountant
Date: September 2011
Re: The Happy Valley Yoga Centre (HVYC)

This report sets out the issues we recommend you consider in respect of the business plan for the Happy Valley Yoga Centre (HVYC).

(i) **Benefits of business plan for Sam**

The purpose of producing a business plan is to help demonstrate the viability of your business proposal for HVYC. A business plan:

- Will help put forward a case for funds and convince Bourne Bank to back the venture

- Can be used to attract other potential investors who may be needed as your yoga business expands

- May demonstrate the viability of the business to major employers on the business park and hence help you win corporate contracts

- Will assist you in assessing the resource requirements of the business eg the number of classes and the number of other instructors required

- Will provide a good starting point for the development of budgets for planning, control and decision making

- May incorporate possible exit strategies

(ii) **Content**

The presentation of a comprehensive business plan is an important step towards obtaining the finance you need to launch HVYC. Bourne Bank (BB) has a standard template so it is important that the plan you submit conforms to this:

Executive summary

This should provide the Bank with an overview of the most important points in the document. It should include a summary of each of the sections of the plan. It is important that the summary is tailored to the requirements of the user – Bourne Bank. Banks generally make lending decisions based on a range of criteria – the summary needs to allow the Bank to form an initial opinion regarding the suitability, feasibility and acceptability of an investment in HVYC.

When making a decision about the business plan, key things Bourne Bank is likely to be concerned with include:

- Market opportunity – whether HVYC has the potential to be a profitable venture

- Credibility and capability of management – BB will want to know about your business background not just your yoga qualification

- Returns and repayment schedules – they will expect to see realistic financial projections to demonstrate how you can service interest and also generate cashflow for future loan repayments

- Security available – as HVYC will have limited assets, they are likely to require personal guarantees from you

Detailed description of the business

- Start with a statement of the nature and commercial purpose of your business. The bank will want to understand whether there are any unique selling points (USPs) that distinguish HVYC from the competition, which in your case would include the convenience of location

- The plan should then go on to give a more detailed account of strategy, target markets and marketing plan. This might include the marketing mix: product, price, promotion, place, people, processes and physical evidence. This allows the Bank to get a clear picture of the business goals and the strategy to achieve them. You should include market information and details of competitors, their services and prices

- As far as BB is concerned the risk of the venture will be lessened if you can provide evidence of demand eg provisional contracts with customers; indications of willingness to buy from existing yoga clients; letters of intent from prospective corporate clients

- Your personal history will be important to the bank in making the credit decision. This is not just about your yoga qualification, which demonstrates your competence to provide the service, but also a summary of your previous experience at the gym, managing budgets and people. This will reassure the Bank about your ability to manage the business. As well as your personal involvement they will also want to see financial commitment from you, so you should include the fact that you are investing £20,000 of your own funds. They will also want to know about your credit history

Financial data

- You need to include details of how much money is required and for what purpose – BB will be keen to ensure that HVYC has an adequate level of both long- and short-term funding. You are likely to require an overdraft facility as well as the £10,000 loan.

- The bank will expect to see forecasts of profitability and cashflow, including the assumptions on which they are based. Your forecasts for HVYC will be based on your past experience in the hotel gym and running classes for the leisure centre, so you must establish the credibility of this.

- The cashflow forecast should be broken down by month, and should indicate to the bank how you intend to service interest and future capital repayments.

- The bank will be interested in the sensitivity of the business to changes in demand/price and may want some form of break-even analysis to help assess risk (see (d) for more information).

Supporting documents

You should include copies of

- Your CV
- The other instructor's CV
- Any contracts with companies on the business park
- Lease agreement for premises
- Personal tax returns
- Credit history

This will help to provide the Bank with evidence to substantiate the rest of the plan.

Examiner's comments:

Requirement (a) asked candidates to (i) explain the benefits for Sam of producing a business plan and (ii) provide a brief overview of what the bank might expect to see under each heading and explain why such content would be important to the bank.

Candidates demonstrated excellent knowledge in this area and were clearly well prepared for a question of this type. Most produced reasonable answers but those that answered generically restricted their scores. A fair amount of detail is provided in the scenario and to secure high skills marks it is important for candidates to extract the relevant information, to use it to apply their knowledge and to communicate it appropriately to the recipient of the report. Higher marks were scored by those who showed these skills.

In part (i) a surprising number of marginal candidates failed to produce the answer in the required report format but most recognised that the plan would provide structure and direction for Sam and allow her and the bank to assess the viability of the business. In part (ii) most candidates were comfortable with the presentation and content of the plan but only the better answers used information in the scenario to illustrate to Sam the specific nature of the content she should include. A reasonably significant number of candidates failed to recognise that the executive summary should provide an overview of the rest of the plan, with some weaker candidates believing that this section should focus on the executives running the business. Better candidates concentrated on the reasons why the content would be important to the bank, spotting that financial projections and sensitivity would be key to assessing the viability of the business and the ability to secure, service and repay the loan.

(b) Weaknesses and threats

Key issues for BB are likely to be:

Key Weaknesses (internal factors)	Mitigating factors
High reliance on Sam both for provision of the yoga classes and for marketing/business development	• The fact that you are enthusiastic and committed and have experience in running classes which have developed a loyal clientele • The fact that you intend to have a second instructor to run classes which will free up some of your time
Sam's lack of financial awareness	• Involvement of us as your accountant to provide advice and support • Your previous experience of managing budgets in the context of your hotel gym job
Resource constraints for the business as most classes will be required before/after work and at lunchtimes	• Additional instructor • Pricing to try and spread demand

Threats (external factors)	Mitigating factors
Competition • Not just in the form of other yoga classes but also a wide range of alternatives – gyms/fitness classes/sporting activities • Other corporate fitness schemes on offer eg gym membership	Mitigating factors here are your USPs • One of the key points is the location which will allow clients to attend in their breaks/lunch hours • You have build up a devoted clientele at your existing classes and this suggests that you are a high quality instructor who is likely to attract clients. It will be important to ensure that the co-instructor is of similar quality • Evidence the HVYC has attracted corporate sponsors
Limited market appeal – lack of business at weekends	This may be addressed by discussing your pricing strategy (see (d))
Closure of the business park may affect demand	Ensure a range of corporate contracts and an appropriate balance of business and personal clients

Examiner's comments:

Requirement (b) asked candidates to identify and explain the key weaknesses and threats for HVYC that are likely to be of concern to the bank and any mitigating factors. Most were comfortable coming up with weaknesses and threats, with answers centring on Sam's inexperience, the business park location, the limited client base, the lack of marketing and the range of competition. Candidates who separated the weaknesses (internal) from the threats (external) generally scored more highly. The mitigating factors were often not covered or were done quite poorly by weaker candidates. Again, the key to a good answer was to recognise that the bank would be concerned about risk and would be looking for reassurance about the steps that Sam might take to reduce or limit its exposure. Candidates who used a tabular structure, linking the mitigating factors to the risks, created an opportunity to score well on skills marks.

(c) **Pricing strategy**

Prices for classes should be set with regard to costs, customers, competitors and corporate strategy.

Costs

The business may make losses initially during the start-up phase, but in the long term you will need to set prices in order to cover costs and provide you with sufficient income to make it worth your while taking on the additional risks and responsibilities of running your own business. You have commented that you do not want to be any worse off than you are currently.

Major fixed costs are rent £15,000 and interest on the £10000 loan which at, say, 10% pa would amount to £1,000 = £16,000 pa. Ignoring other expenses, at a price of £6 per person per class, you need to sell 16,000/£6 = 2,667 sessions a year, or just under 52 people attending a week to cover these costs.

If you use an additional instructor then, at a price of £6 per person per class, the business will need to attract at least 5 people per class to cover the cost of hiring the instructor at £30 per class (assuming that the rate you were paid at the leisure centre is the market rate).

Competition

Your price will be influenced by the price of other yoga classes in the area (competitors) and the price of alternative leisure/fitness activities (substitutes).

The local leisure centre is charging participants £6 per one hour class – your yoga sessions will be 15 minutes shorter but they are more conveniently located. They are also in a bespoke yoga centre and as a result the environment is likely to be superior, so you can probably charge at least this amount.

Your working clients may well be more concerned about time than cost and as a result may be prepared to pay considerably more for classes in a convenient location at peak times.

Customers

Price discrimination means setting different prices for the same product or service in recognition of the fact that different customer segments have different attitudes to price. You can maximise revenue by attempting to charge each customer or customer segment the maximum they are prepared to pay.

Such a differential approach to pricing is common within the leisure industry where, for example, gyms may offer different rates for peak and off-peak membership and where it is cheaper to sign up for a number of classes rather than pay for each individually on a drop-in basis.

For this to be successful it is important that the different groups of customers have different price elasticity's of demand (that is, they are willing to pay different prices) and that there is some way of ensuring the different groups remain separate for pricing purposes.

This requires you to segment the market and to understand clients' likely reaction to price, perhaps by undertaking market research.

Your two main target markets are

- Corporate clients
- Individuals

You have already been approached by one possible corporate client. These customers will have stronger buying power as they are likely to provide you with guaranteed block bookings for larger numbers. As well as being good for future business reputation, such potential contracts may help demonstrate the commercial viability of your business to the Bank.

As far as individuals are concerned, the focus should be on people employed on the business park who are likely to be physically active and interested in health and well-being. Many may well have attended yoga sessions before. This market may then be further subdivided by age/gender or income level; for example, those in high income brackets for whom time is at a premium may be prepared to pay for one-to-one tuition, particularly if the timing of this can be flexed to suit their needs.

In setting the price for one-to-one sessions you need to recognise the cost involved. There is a direct cost in terms of the instructor but also an opportunity cost if this prevents you or the other instructor from running a group session at the same time.

Corporate strategy

Your pricing strategy should take into account the perceived quality of your product and the fact that you are operating in a niche market. As a result, setting prices too low may detract from the image of HVYC that you want to create.

Constraints

Your core clientele are employees working on the business park. Assuming standard office hours, peak demand is likely to occur on weekdays between say 07:30-9:00, 12:00-14:00 and 17:00-19:00 and so prices should be highest for classes at these times. Outside these hours and at weekends demand is likely to be much more variable and lower rates could be offered eg to encourage retired or non-working clients to attend.

When deciding on the price you also needs to bear in mind that there is likely to be a limit to the number of people who can be accommodated in each class and therefore there will be a cap on the maximum amount of revenue that can be generated. To facilitate planning it would be better to charge for peak time classes in blocks (eg a course of 10), but to offer drop-in rates for classes outside these hours which are less likely to be full.

It is not clear how many studios are available – at the moment there are only two instructors, including yourself, but as demand grows presumably the yoga centre can offer more classes by sourcing additional instructors.

Discounts

You have raised the issue of offering discounts.

Offering a discount may increase sales volumes but comes at a cost in terms of lost revenue. Thus you need to ensure that there is some benefit to compensate for the cost involved so you are not simply offering discount to clients who would have paid full price.

For example a class of 10 clients paying £6 each generates £60 revenue. Were you to offer an introductory discount by charging £5 per person per class, then the discount needs to attract 2 additional clients in order for revenue to be maintained. One possible approach would be to offer a discount to clients who commit up-front to a full course say of 10 classes as this gives you some guaranteed income. Alternatively a loyalty system, eg pay for 9 classes and get the 10th free, may help create repeat business.

You might also consider offering 'Recommend a friend' schemes where clients are offered a discount if they introduce additional clients who are prepared to commit up-front for a series of classes.

Additional services

Once clients are on the premises they are a captive audience and you can adopt captive product pricing for food, beverages and merchandise.

Recommendation

It is recommended that you adopt a multi-tiered pricing structure to take account of the needs of different clients and to increase business during quieter periods.

In requirement (c) candidates were requested to advise Sam on the factors to consider when deciding on a pricing policy, including relevant supporting calculations. Most candidates had the relevant technical knowledge but approaches varied considerably. Those who used a model such as the 4Cs tended to produce better structured answers. Most candidates were able to discuss different approaches to pricing and considered the opportunity for price discrimination but again there was a tendency for the weaker scripts to be quite generic, for example simply stating that prices should cover costs or not be higher than competitors. The better answers identified the fact that Sam would be looking for earnings commensurate with her previous job and considered the fact that discounts might be offered to encourage membership. Disappointingly few picked up on the fact that there were two separate groups of customers (individual and corporate) and that different pricing strategies might be appropriate for each.

Many candidates produced few, if any, calculations in requirement (c), despite the specific request in the question to do so. Those who used the data provided in relation to fixed costs and competitors' prices and performed some form of break-even calculation generally scored well. Again weaker candidates need to take note that data is provided in the scenario for a purpose and that the numbers provided can be used as a peg on which to hang a discussion.

48 KoganAir

Marking guide

			Knowledge	Skill	Marks
(a)	(i)	Analyse operating profit	1	14	15
	(ii)	Forecast profit and working assumptions	2	7	9
(b)		Risks PESTEL	3	7	10
(c)		Marketing director and Porter	3	6	9
			9	34	43

General comments:

This is the mini case and the data analysis question. The scenario relates to the airline industry. The company in the scenario, KoganAir, is a low-cost airline operating routes within Europe. The company has expanded the number of routes this year and increased revenue. Despite this, profits have fallen and losses are expected in the current year. Data is provided to show changes in key financial and operating elements of the business. KoganAir is evaluating the impact of future fuel cost increases. It is also examining a strategy of repositioning itself in the market between the low cost airlines and the national airlines by increasing prices and service quality.

(a) (i)

	2010	2011	% change
Basic analysis of operational data given in question			
Available passenger seats (millions)	6.4	7.0	+9.4%
Actual passenger seats	5.4	6.0	+11.1%
Load factor %	84.4%	85.7%	+1.5%
Number of aircraft	49	50	+2.0%
Routes operated	62	64	+3.2%
ASK (millions)	7,271	7,868	+8.2%
Revenue analysis			
Revenue	313	337	+7.7%
Revenue per passenger	£57.96	£56.17	(3.1%)
Revenue per available seat	£48.91	£48.14	(1.6%)
Revenue per aircraft	£6.39m	£6.74m	+5.5%
Revenue per route	£5.05m	£5.27m	+4.4%
Revenue at 2011 prices (ie 2% inflator on 2010 revenue)	£319.26m	£337m	+5.6%
Cost analysis			
Operating costs per aircraft	£0.51m	£0.52m	+2.0%
Total cost per passenger	£57.8	£58.2	+0.7%
Fuel cost at 2011 prices (ie 17% inflator on 2010 fuel cost)	£88.92m	£96.0m	+8.0%
Fuel cost per 1 million ASK	£10,452	£12,201	+16.7%
Fuel as a % of total cost	24.4%	27.5%	
Operational analysis			
ASK per aircraft	148.4m	157.4m	+6.1%
ASK per route	117.3	122.9	+4.8%
Load factor	84.4	85.7	+1.5%
Average flight length (ASK/available passenger seats flown)	1,136	1,124	(1.1%)

Revenue

Overall the data shows an operating profit of £1m in 2010 being turned into an expected operating loss of £12m in 2011. This is not due to a reduction in the level of revenue or number of passengers, both of which have increased.

Revenue has increased fairly significantly by 7.7%. Part of this increase is due to an average increase in prices of 2%. The real terms increase is shown in the above table as 5.6%. This could be explained by (i) an increase in the volume of sales (ii) a change in the mix of sales or (iii) changes in exchange rate where tickets are sold in a foreign currency.

The number of passengers and ASK have increased by 11.1% and 8.2% respectively so this suggests that the sales mix has changed with a greater number of lower value journeys and/or there have been unfavourable currency movements with the £ strengthening relatively against other European countries where tickets are sold overseas.

These factors (mix and currency) are demonstrated in a fall in revenue per passenger of 3.1% despite the overall increase in prices and volumes. It may be that the new routes introduced are shorter, lower value routes (the average flight length has fallen by 1%, for instance) or just an overall shift away from higher price flights.

Fuel costs

Fuel costs have risen substantially in 2011 compared to 2010, by 26.3%. This is significantly in excess of the revenue increase and increases in other costs and is therefore a major reason for the decrease in operating earnings.

The increase can be divided into a price increase and a volume increase. Prices increased by 17% according to the chief executive. ASK increased by 8.2% (the determinant of volume of fuel used according to the CEO's working assumptions). This gives an imputed change in total fuel spend of 26.6% (1.17 × 1.082). The actual increase in fuel spend is 26.3%. The difference in actual and imputed fuel spend could be due to fuel efficiencies arising perhaps from the increased load factor. (The relationship with ASK is only approximate according to the working assumptions.)

Overall, fuel makes up a significant proportion of total costs and this has increased from 24.4% in 2010 to 27.5% in 2011. The increase in fuel price is therefore significant in affecting profit in terms of its importance in the cost structure and the % increase.

In absolute terms, fuel spend increased by £20m which is greater than the change in operating profit of £13m.

Other costs

Other costs changed broadly in line with the change in revenue. They reflected capacity increases (aircraft and routes) but also inflationary increases.

Operating efficiency

Operating efficiency in terms of asset utilisation appeared to have improved in 2011 compared to 2010.

The ASK per aircraft increased by 6.1% which may reflect better utilisation (quicker turnaround or more demand). It might have reflected longer flights but the data does not support this as the above table shows that the average flight length has fallen by 1.1%.

Similarly, the load factor increased from 84.4% to 85.2% showing that the proportion of occupied seats was greater in 2011 than in 2010. This is important as it generates revenue at the margin, but the marginal cost of an additional passenger on an existing flight is likely to be minimal.

Examiner's comments:

Requirement (a)(i) was fairly well answered on the whole, however the main drawback for the majority of candidates was an inability to distinguish correctly between volume and price effects on the growth of revenue and fuel costs between 2010 and 2011. Many did not recognise any volume effect at all. Thus, when attempting to explain the difference between KoganAir's increase in fuel costs of 26% and that of the industry as a whole (17%), many incorrectly explained this as being due to, for example, inefficient operations, old planes etc. The poorest answers made little if any attempt at explaining changes, merely describing what percentage changes occurred, without suggesting how, why or when these may have arisen. Many weaker answers did no calculations of their own and merely repeated calculations which had been given in the question, such as the 7.7% revenue increase, without adding any analysis or explanation. The rise in fuel costs tended to be the major factor which candidates picked up and discussed in detail – bringing in global oil prices generally. The best answers understood the volume change effect, and the possible impact of changes in the sales mix. Additionally, only a very few candidates explicitly referred to the importance of load factor improvements, given that the marginal cost of an extra passenger is virtually zero.

(a) (ii)

	2011 Estimated	2012 Forecast	Comment
Total revenue (£m)	337	364.1	Prices are constant so revenue varies in accordance with ASK £337m × (8,500/7,868)
Fuel costs (£m)	(96)	(134.8)	£96m × (8,500/7,868) × 1.3 Increase related to the price per tonne increase of 30% and the increase in ASK

	2011 Estimated	2012 Forecast	Comment
Operating costs of aircraft (£m)	(26)	(26)	Assumed constant despite three new aircraft. This may imply that larger aircraft have been replaced by a larger number of smaller aircraft or other cost efficiencies made (eg leasing contracts renewed on better terms given recession in industry)
Other operating costs (£m)	(227)	(233.8)	Increase only 3% – more info needed on these assumptions
Operating (loss) (£m)	(12)	(30.5)	

With a 30% price rise assumed, the total increase in fuel costs in 2012 would be 40.4% (in 2011 there was a 26.3% increase). In absolute terms this is £38.4m which is larger than the increase in the forecast operating loss of £18.5m. The fuel price increases are therefore driving the increase in operating losses.

This analysis of fuel spend however needs to be considered both in terms of increased usage of fuel (assumed to vary according to ASK) and increases in the price of fuel per tonne.

If fuel prices per tonne were constant in 2012 compared with 2011 then total fuel spend would rise to £103.7m (£96m × (8,500/7,868)) ie an increase of £7.7m (£103.7m – £96m).

In terms of basic sensitivity analysis therefore it would take a total fuel spend of £116.3m to achieve the same overall operating loss of £12m as in 2011. The maximum fuel price increase would be 12.2% (£116.3m/£103.7m) to maintain the operating loss at its current level.

To achieve break even overall, fuel spend would need to be £104.3m (£134.8m – £30.5m). This would require an increase in price per tonne of fuel of only 0.58% (£104.3m/£103.7m).

These calculations of course depend on the validity of the working assumptions but a limitation of sensitivity analysis is that it only considers one factor at a time while holding all other factors constant.

Working assumptions

Fuel prices – the assumption of a 30% increase is a possibility and may be a worse case scenario for scenario planning purposes, but it is unlikely to be the most probable scenario as oil is a traded commodity and is likely to be priced efficiently. If a 30% increase next year is the most likely estimate then this would lead to speculation, thereby immediately forcing up current fuel prices.

Average price per passenger – in a recession, constant prices appear reasonable as a prudent assumption. It may however be the case that prices need to fall if competitors reduce prices.

Fuel and revenue vary according to ASK – fuel varying according to ASK seems a reasonable assumption if there are no major changes in the fleet of aircraft such as size of aircraft or fuel efficiency. Revenue varying according to ASK may not be a reasonable assumption as the price of a flight is unlikely to vary in direct proportion to distance travelled (ie twice the price for twice the distance). However, if the portfolio of routes remains similar in 2012 then ASK appears a reasonable short term measure of activity against which to evaluate revenue changes.

Operating costs will remain constant – this assumption seems unlikely as three new aircraft are to be acquired in 2012 which will increase leasing costs and/or depreciation.

Other costs will increase by 3% – this assumption seems a reasonable approximation of inflation (eg of wages) given that the recession creates downward pressure on wages and other costs. However, this assumes that 'other costs' are fixed, whereas there is likely to be a variable cost element which will increase with the predicted increase in activity for 2012 (eg ASK is estimated to increase by 8% in 2012).

Examiner's comments:

Answers to requirement (a)(ii) tended to be highly variable in quality, with some scoring virtually full marks while others struggled to achieve a pass mark for the question. The key discriminating factors were whether or not candidates could provide correct calculations for the 2012 forecast, and make a reasonable attempt to calculate and explain the sensitivity of operating profit to changes in the cost of fuel.

The most common errors in the calculations for 2012 were to arrive at a revenue figure of £376m, rather than £364m, and a fuel cost figure of £125m rather than £134.8m. The £125m ignores the volume effect ie simply increasing £96m by 30%. The revenue figure of £376m uses forecast passenger seats sold as the driver rather than basing the projection on ASK (as stipulated in the key working assumptions of the question itself) which reflects the length of journeys in addition to just the number of journeys.

Sensitivity analysis was ignored by many candidates and also tended to vary in quality amongst those who did attempt it. Poorer efforts merely provided some form of calculation, often just fuel costs as a percentage of profit or revenue, with little attempt at interpretation. Most candidates did recognise profits to be sensitive to fuel price changes. The comments on the working assumptions were quite weak with many candidates focussing their answers purely on the fuel price rise, without taking into consideration the impact of other costs on overall profit.

(b) **PESTEL**

Risk and impact	Risk Management
ECONOMIC	
Fuel costs Sudden sustained and significant changes in fuel prices would unexpectedly increase costs	Buy fuel on forward market (hedge) Fuel is a common cost in the industry and so may be covered by common price rises Scenario analysis and planning Contingent fuel surcharges on tickets (ie charge passengers extra if fuel prices increase, even on tickets already sold)
Currency movements Changes in exchange rates which reduce the sterling value of revenues (eg ticket sold overseas) or increases the sterling value of costs (oil is priced in US$)	International diversification Hedging
Recession Lower passenger demand and more price resistance leading to lower revenues	Sensitive and flexible prices Flexible operations (eg short term leases on aircraft)
Industrial action Loss of flights leading to uncertainty and lower reputation. Increased wage costs	Human resources policy Regular employee engagement Appropriate wages for the industry
ECOLOGICAL	
Environmental issues Impact on consumer perception and reputation. Increased environmental compliance costs Pollution from aircraft	Sustainability policy Environmental public relations policy Use of modern fuel efficient aircraft Recyclable materials

Risk and impact	Risk Management
LEGAL	
Security (illegal acts)	Checking of baggage
Terrorist incident or accident leading to loss of reputation and direct financial cost	Liaison with authorities and airports
	Regular maintenance checks
	Passenger safety procedures
Regulatory intervention	
Increase of costs or reduced flexibility due to new laws affecting the industry or one jurisdiction	Lobbying of governments
	International diversification
Taxation	
Increases in general tax, fuel tax or industry specific tax (could also be classified under economic)	Monitoring of budgetary proposals
	Lobbying

Note: many of the risks are industry wide (eg fuel prices) thus while they may have an impact on the competitiveness of the industry, they will have a limited effect on the competitiveness of individual companies within the industry as the effects would be common to most airlines.

Examiner's comments:

Requirement (b) requested candidates to explain the key risks for KoganAir that arise from factors within the economic, ecological and legal sections of the PESTEL framework and to explain how these risks might be managed.

This requirement was generally well answered, with the majority of candidates displaying a good understanding of the PESTEL framework and correctly categorising risks between Economic, Ecological and Legal. Most candidates considered how the firm could manage risks but the risk management techniques were not always linked to the specific risk to which they related. Many better candidates used a columnar format to link risks to the relevant risk management technique, but other methods of providing this linkage were also acceptable.

Some of the risk management techniques were very general and not really appropriate to the risk identified. For example, for Ecological issues, most candidates identified that there were pollution issues with the use of aircraft. However, instead of using their knowledge on sustainability or CSR and applying it to the airline industry, some candidates chose to offer development by KoganAir of alternative means of transport, such as diversifying into coach and sea travel, which was entirely unrealistic for an airline operator.

Also, despite being specifically instructed in the question to deal only with Economic, Ecological and Legal matters, some candidates wasted time outlining the political, social and technological risks, which were not required and received no additional marks.

(c) Porter argued that competitive pressures are such that only two competitive strategies will deliver competitive advantage (ie superior ROI).

- **Low cost**: a firm following this strategy will withstand the shrinking margins better and so, as rivals fall away, may be left as a major player with enhanced power against the power of suppliers and buyers.

- **Differentiation**: a firm presenting itself as a superior provider may escape price pressure by avoiding straight-forward price comparisons with rivals.

Porter's generic strategies can be represented as follows:

Porter's generic strategies

	LOW COST	DIFFERENTIATION
BROAD	COST LEADERSHIP	DIFFERENTIATION
NARROW	COST FOCUS	DIFFERENTIATION FOCUS

COMPETITIVE SCOPE

Cost leadership

As a low cost airline KoganAir is attempting to adopt a (focused) cost leadership strategy whereby it is seeking to achieve the position of lowest-cost airline in its sector of the industry (ie European short haul). By operating at the lowest cost, KoganAir has been able to compete on price with every other airline in its sector of the industry, and still earn profits.

Key factors in cost leadership may include

(a) Economies of scale as operations increase (aircraft/routes).

(b) Use the latest technology to reduce costs and/or enhance productivity (eg online booking).

(c) High utilisation of aircraft (quick turnaround, high load factors).

(d) Concentration on improving productivity.

(e) Minimise overhead costs.

(f) Get favourable access to sources of supply (fuel discounts).

KoganAir has suffered high fuel costs but these are a common cost in the industry. They affect costs and profit but would not directly affect KoganAir's competitive position. If other costs can be controlled, then rival companies, with less efficient cost structures, are less likely to survive and the survivor companies many pick up their customers.

A significant price increase of 10% is likely to cause confusion about the brand as it would no longer be a low price airline and customers would require additional services for the extra price.

Porter regarded this as a *stuck in the middle* strategy. This means that the firm has sought to attract many segments at different price points and so is seen as not being as differentiated as the market leader but, perhaps because of the costs of serving the differentiated segment, not able to make good profits at the cost leader's prices.

One alternative model to consider this issue is Bowman's Clock

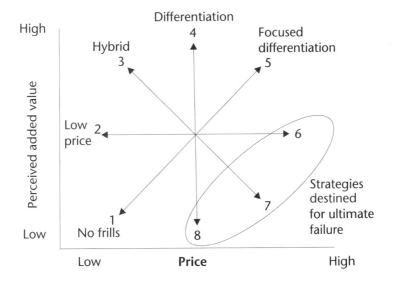

Price-based strategies

Strategies 1 and 2 are price-based strategies.

*   A **no frills** strategy (1) has been used by KoganAir aimed at the most price-conscious consumers. This strategy has been used for market entry, to gain experience and to build volume.

*   A **low price** strategy (2) offers better value than competitors. This can lead to price war and reduced margins for all. Porter's generic strategy of **cost leadership** is appropriate to a firm adopting this strategy.

If however KoganAir increases its price it is moving more towards a hybrid strategy which may have a valid position in price-quality space, or it may create uncertainty in the minds of consumers.

A similar model is in the diagram below. This diagram shows that a brand can be positioned in a number of ways, eg via a price or emphasis on a particular characteristic or set of characteristics. In other words, positioning means giving a product a place relative to its competitors on factors such as quality, price, image, being exotic, providing status, etc.

Positioning can be facilitated by a graphical technique called perceptual mapping, various survey techniques and statistical techniques like multi-dimensional scaling and factor analysis.

Even such a rather simple product positioning matrix as shown above may give valuable insights in the relative positions of the various brands.

In the case of KoganAir an increase in price without an increase in service would move its positioning upwards vertically. This would make it less competitive in price quality terms compared to its rivals.

The exception would be if rivals also increased prices by a similar amount in order to compensate for common increases in costs. If so, KoganAir's positioning within the industry might be constant, but the competitiveness of the industry compared to alternative forms of consumer expenditure made be reduced (eg consumers may choose to buy a car rather than go on holiday if the prices of flights increase).

Examiner's comments:

Requirement (c) requested candidates to evaluate the suggestion of the marketing director to reposition KoganAir upmarket, by referring to Porter's generic strategies and any other appropriate strategic models. There was more or less an equal split between those candidates who only used Porter's generic strategies framework, and those who additionally introduced other frameworks to enhance their analysis eg Bowman's clock; Ansoff; Price-Quality framework.

Those candidates using only Porter's generic strategies framework tended to conclude that the marketing director's suggestion would lead to KoganAir being 'stuck in the middle'. There was however little analysis or use of any other model to justify this conclusion. Where alternative models were offered with reasoned analysis and recommendations, more rounded conclusions were normally drawn.

49 Universal Office Supplies

Marking guide

			Knowledge	Skill	Marks
(a)	(i)	R&D bus strategy	2	4	6
	(ii)	R&D recharging	2	5	7
(b)		Current divisional structure (performance measurement and transfer pricing)	3	9	12
(c)		New divisions restructuring & new performance measurement	3	5	8
			10	23	33

General comments:

The scenario in this question relates to a company (UOS) which manufactures office equipment of two types (i) communication systems (including videoconferencing, audio conferencing and data sharing) and (ii) office furniture. The two products sell to many of the same customers but the production technology is very different (ie similar markets, different industries). The communication systems industry and market are dynamic and rapidly changing and dependent on new developments in technology and usage. The office furniture market and industry are more stable. The company has a number of operating divisions which are currently vertically integrated: (i) procurement (ii) manufacturing (iii) marketing. The company attempts to maintain autonomy of the operating divisions by arm's length transfer pricing. There are also three support divisions: R&D, Human Resources and Finance. The company intends to engage in a restructuring from functional divisional to be product-based divisional. The manner in which the R&D function is charged to divisions will also change.

(a) (i) R&D can improve products and processes and can be an important element in the strategy of the business. However it is likely to be of greatest value in a dynamic changing environment such as communications, where it can be a source of innovation and competitive advantage, rather than in a lower value, stable environment, such as the manufacture of office furniture.

A key point is that the R&D strategy should be appropriate to the broader corporate strategy.

In the Communications Systems Division, *product innovation* could be a source of differentiation by giving competitive advantage over rivals' products.

Process innovation may enable differentiation or cost leadership. In the Office Furniture division, although it competes on price, it appears not to be a cost leader and does not use R&D. This may be due to the basic and standardised nature of the processes for furniture manufacture, such that the costs of R&D would not be justified by the benefits.

Other strategic aspects of R&D for UOS include:

- **Porter's value chain**: R&D is included within all parts of the value chain including support activities of *technology development*. It can be harnessed in the service of lower costs or improved differentiation.

- **Ansoff matrix**: R&D supports all four strategic quadrants. Strategies of Market Penetration and Market Development can be served by product refinement. Product Development and Diversification will require more significant innovations.

- **Industry and product lifecycles**: the obsolescence of existing products can be accelerated by industry wide product R&D, and so company specific R&D is required to provide the firm with replacements. In UOS's case the communications products are likely to have very short life cycles due to the dynamic nature of the industry hence R&D is essential.

Despite the potential benefits, the new product development process must be carefully controlled. While new products can be a major source of competitive advantage they can cost a great deal to bring to market. A screening process is necessary to ensure that resources are concentrated on projects with a high probability of success.

Examiner's comments:

Requirement (a) related to the R&D function and asked candidates to: (i) explain how R&D can contribute to the business strategy of UOS; and (ii) compare and evaluate the current and the proposed structuring and recharging arrangements for R&D.

Part (a)(i) was well answered on the whole. Most answers considered the effect of R&D on product innovation in the context of the Communication Division's differentiation strategy, and also R&D's support for process innovation through the value chain for the Furniture Division in order to deliver a generic strategy of what most candidates considered to be cost leadership. In this respect, there was some excellent knowledge displayed on how R&D was included in value chain analysis and how its relative importance was dependent on where a product was in the product lifecycle.

(ii) **Existing R&D structure**

There appear to be two key issues:

- Who initiates and determines the nature of the R&D projects to be undertaken?

- How, if at all, are the costs of R&D to be accounted for in divisional performance measurement?

On the demand side, under the existing structure, R&D is a free good for the communications section, which is the sole internal customer. It therefore has incentives to make excessive demands as it receives the benefits of R&D without incurring any of the costs. Under the current arrangements however it appears that the communications section has limited formal influence over the number or nature of the R&D projects taking place.

On the supply side, the R&D division appears to be setting its own agenda without reference to the communications section (the internal customer) or to those with best knowledge of the needs of the external customers (ie the Marketing Division).

The risk is therefore that new R&D is technology driven by engineers in R&D rather than being driven by customers' needs and desires. This may lead to additional features on the products which incur costs to UOS, but do not give benefits to customers who will not therefore pay a price premium for these new features.

Proposed R&D structure

Under the proposed structure, the R&D projects appear to be demand led because they are initiated by the Communications Systems Division. The fact that the new head of the Communications Systems Division is a marketing person is likely to improve the extent to which new products are market driven, rather than technology driven.

In terms of costs, the R&D Division has no incentives to control costs as these are passed on to the Communications Systems Division. However, it may be that overheads are recharged on a budgeted basis, in which case if there is an insufficient volume of R&D projects demanded by Communications Systems Division then there may be an under-recovery.

The recharging of costs may also act as a disincentive for the Communications Systems Division to demand R&D services, as short term divisional profit is damaged, while the benefits may only be longer term. This may therefore give incentives only to take on R&D projects which give short term benefits (eg by enabling short term cost reduction or immediate and substantial product improvement).

Conclusion

Overall, the new structure seems preferable in terms of how the R&D projects are identified and initiated as it depends on customer needs and benefits in the marketplace.

The recharging of costs, however, needs further consideration in terms of the disincentives for Communications Systems Division to demand R&D services. One alternative may be to amortise the recharge of R&D costs in the divisional budget of Communications Systems Division (eg the current year R&D costs to be spread over (say) the next 5 years in the divisional accounts of Communications Systems Division). This would enable costs incurred by the Communications Systems Division to be matched against the profile of R&D benefits over time.

Examiner's comments:

Part (a)(ii) answers were highly variable. Many candidates misread the question and provided an evaluation of the existing and proposed structure overall for the whole firm. This was despite the question explicitly stating that the current and proposed structure should be discussed only in respect of the R&D function. The best answers only focused on an evaluation of R&D and recharging arrangements under the current and proposed structures and these candidates tended to perform reasonably well.

(b) The current structure is a functional structure of vertically integrated operating divisions, with separate support divisions, which are also defined on a functional basis.

Functional structure

A functional structure enables specialisation of skills and economies of scale in coherent groups of: procurement, manufacturing, marketing, R&D, HR and finance. However, where there are significant interdependencies between divisions (eg procurement and manufacturing) then such a structure may lead to bureaucracy as tasks are not always separable.

Conversely, while manufacturing is considered as a single function then the skills needed to produce office furniture are likely to be largely independent of those required to produce communications systems equipment. As a consequence, there may be few benefits of retaining these in the same division.

The combination of functions in manufacturing, without much synergy, seems likely to cause conflict and dispute as it is difficult to allocate costs to each product and thus determine the profitability of each product in order to make pricing and output decisions. It also makes it more difficult to control costs as allocation of responsibility is less clear within a division than it is between divisions given common costs and common tasks.

Transfer pricing

Transfer pricing between procurement and manufacturing divisions

Transfer pricing between procurement and manufacturing divisions provides incentives for the procurement division to minimise purchase costs below budget as much as possible. This has a number of problems:

- Obtaining the lowest cost item may mean lower quality which may damage reputation

- The larger discounts may only be available on older parts and materials. In a rapidly changing environment this many mean less functionality compared to the current industry standard

- If budgets are set at the beginning of the year then, in a rapidly changing environment, they may become irrelevant during the year as prices fall with technological change. This enables the Procurement Division to make profits without much skill or effort

The fact that the nature and quantity of the required purchases are determined by the Manufacturing Division prevents excessive ordering by procurement to obtain quantity discounts. The extent to which the Manufacturing Division can precisely define the type of product required may further limit the ability of procurement to obtain low quality, low cost items and materials.

An additional concern over the transfer price relates to the inclusion of overheads by the Procurement Division in addition to the purchase price. The apportionment of overheads on the basis of purchase price may not reflect the level of effort or achievement by the Procurement Division in making the order. For example, the purchase of wood or metal to make office furniture may be relatively straightforward with a limited number of local suppliers. The sourcing of silicon chips or other small electronic items may however involve a global search of many suppliers requiring significant incremental search costs.

Transfer pricing between manufacturing and marketing divisions

In principle, the setting of transfer prices by negotiation based on market prices preserves autonomy. However there seem to be a number of factors mitigating against the validity of such an approach in the case of UOS:

- Furniture may be an active market, hence the prices of similar items of office furniture can be observed to set transfer prices. However Communications Systems is less likely to be an active market as the products are differentiated, specialised and rapidly changing. The market prices may therefore be a poor guide and it may be expensive to keep up to date information for like-for-like market comparisons.

- The government contract may be a poor guide and the price set is contractual and may be out of date. The price may also not be competitive for the private sector.

- The transfer price is a wholesale price but the gap between wholesale and retail prices may not be justified by the efforts of the Marketing Department. The added value by marketing therefore needs to be questioned.

Divisional performance measurement

To the extent that transfer prices are distorted, the performance measures based on profit centres will also be distorted.

The Marketing Division appears only to be breaking even but it includes installation which is not really a marketing function and it may not therefore possess the necessary core competences.

The profit of the Manufacturing Division does not attempt to distinguish between the profitability of the two separate products. If for instance one of the products was not viable but the other was profitable this would not necessarily be revealed by the profit centre reporting system.

An additional problem is that allocations of overheads with the Manufacturing Division are not required yet may further hide the profitability of each individual product.

The performance of the Procurement Division is as much dependent on the setting of budgeted prices as it is on the actual discounts achieved. Moreover the discounts, as already noted, reflect market movements as much as they reflect effort and searching by the Procurement Division staff.

Examiner's comments:

Requirement (b) asked candidates to comment on the merits and problems of the company's current divisional structure in respect of the three operating divisions. Candidates were required to evaluate performance measurement and transfer pricing arrangements.

This requirement was well answered on the whole. Most candidates correctly considered the existing structure to be a functional one and provided discussion of its advantages and disadvantages.

Performance measurement and transfer pricing issues were less well addressed, although many did explicitly recognise the limitations of the existing structure in evaluating the performance of the two separate product lines.

(c) The new structure is one of product line divisionalisation for the two operating divisions, with support divisions (R&D, HR and Finance) remaining as functional divisions.

Under this system, operating division managers are responsible for products, but also each controls personnel working in a range of functions (procurement, manufacture and marketing).

The advantages of this method of divisionalisation are:

- The focus is on the profitability of individual products

- Managers can be held responsible for product performance

- Product specialisation can be linked to functional specialisation with learning over time (eg marketing of office furniture)

- The different functions involved in making and selling each of the two products can be co-ordinated under a single span of control

- Separation of control over manufacturing of the two products reflects the separate and different nature of the production processes

Disadvantages include:

- Functions are under the control of divisional leaders without expertise in that function (eg Pauline's control over furniture marketing and Andy's control over communications manufacturing).

- The divisions are likely to be larger with a wider span of control for each divisional head.

- Pauline has not previously managed a division and is now in charge of an expanded division with multiple functional activities.

- Change management may cause barriers to change. For example Jim, who previously headed communications systems manufacturing, was not promoted to be communications divisional head, unlike Pauline. This may cause individual demotivation. There may also be group demotivation where functional divisions such as Marketing are split within the new divisional structure with possible loss of security, status or remuneration for some groups or alternatively a change of role.

- The Communications Systems Division shares many of the same customers as the Furniture Division. There may therefore be increased distribution costs and reduced economies of scope if these customers are serviced independently by each division.

Divisional performance measurement

As all the operations for each product now fall within the one division, transfer pricing between operational divisions is no longer necessary. There may be some recharging of support division costs to operational divisions, but this is less of an issue where there is no profit upload (see previous R&D discussion for example).

The absence of transfer prices means that the relevant pricing is with outside parties and is thus market driven. This makes divisional profit more relevant as a measure of divisional performance measurement as there is less need for arbitrary transfer prices. However, there remain some issues:

- The Communications Systems Division shares the same factory as the Office Furniture Division. As a consequence, there are likely to be common overhead costs which need to be shared between the two divisions. As costs are interdependent, then this jointness causes a degree of arbitrariness in divisional profit.

- The Communications Systems Division shares many of the same customers as the Office Furniture Division and there is therefore some interdependence of revenues. If one division treats the customers well (or badly) then there may be benefits (or costs) to the other division.

- The recharging of support division costs (or the absence of such recharging) is also likely to distort profit as an adequate divisional performance measure.

Conclusion

The new structure based on product divisionalisation has many benefits compared to the old functional structure in terms of control, accountability and performance measurement. Most significantly, a clearer idea of the performance of the two products will enable each to be managed more coherently and independently.

Examiner's comments:

Requirement (c) asked candidates to evaluate the proposed restructuring of the three operating divisions and suggest the most appropriate method of divisional performance measurement.

This was one of the weakest requirements on the paper for many candidates, although most achieved a pass mark. Often, even with good responses, there tended to be too much focus on change management at the expense of structure, performance measurement and transfer pricing. There was also a tendency to include a fairly lengthy discussion of the use of the Balance Scorecard for performance measurement, but often with little direct relevance to the central issues as depicted in the scenario. Better answers offered very specific observations on the potential splitting of overhead costs and the potential distortion of profits from the absence of recharging.

---

50 Conchester Theatre

Marking guide

		Knowledge	Skill	Marks
(a)	Ethics	3	5	8
(b)	Market segmentation; database; pricing	5	11	16
		8	16	24

General comments:

This was the smallest question on the paper but includes some basic data about revenue generation. The scenario relates to an independent, regional theatre which is a not-for-profit organisation. It currently has income from three major sources (i) ticket sales (ii) membership donations (iii) government grants. The mission of the theatre is to promote traditional, high quality drama and musicals in the local community while breaking even financially. Grants have been very significantly reduced by the government this year which has caused a crisis in funding. A rich individual has offered to provide finance to compensate for the loss of government funding, but he requires control over the nature of some performances, which may be contrary to the type of performances in the mission statement. An alternative means of generating revenue would be to use more flexible pricing for tickets using a database of members and those attending the theatre. An ethical issue arises as the trustees would be personally liable if the theatre makes a loss.

(a) From the perspective of Henry, he is offering a significant sum of money in return for some control over the performances and a role on the board as a trustee. From Henry's point of view this seems an open and transparent offer to the board of trustees which they can accept or reject in accordance with their normal procedures. From Henry's perspective therefore there does not seem to be any major ethical issue based on the information provided.

From the perspective of the board of trustees there is a potential conflict of interest between their role as trustees in protecting the mission and culture of CT and their personal risk in assuming liability for the debts of CT.

Their role of protecting the culture and mission of CT of putting on 'traditional plays and musicals with high artistic merit', may be compromised by the ten plays selected annualy by Henry. This also appears to be contrary to the wishes of at least one stakeholder, the members. It may also be contrary to the wishes of other stakeholders, such as local government, who may be unwilling to offer a subsidised rent to a populist commercial theatre.

The conflicting interest is that if they maintain the culture and refuse the money, the ticket sales may be insufficient to cover costs, debts would accumulate and the trustees may become personally liable. There is therefore the personal incentive to accept the £250,000 to reduce personal risk, even though the mission of CT could be damaged.

There is a further conflict between two objectives within the agreed mission statement – financial break even and the objective of putting on 'traditional plays and musicals with high artistic merit.' In the absence of the government grant, these two objectives may be in conflict and therefore the directors face an ethical dilemma in choosing between them.

However, it may be that the ten plays selected by Henry may fall within this remit of artistic merit, although there is a significant risk that they will not.

The proposed arrangement with Henry would also be a breach of the corporate governance structure as, under the current regime, the board decides which performances take place and the members decide who sits on the board. This would need to be resolved transparently with the members who appear to have the power not to appoint Henry.

Examiner's comments:

Requirement (a) asked candidates to discuss the ethical issues for CT's board of Trustees arising from the offer from Henry Strong.

It was reasonably well answered by most candidates. The main structure which candidates adopted in answering this question was to use Transparency, Fairness and Effect. This led candidates to conclude that the Mr Strong was attempting to 'bribe' the trustees and the acceptance of the offer would lead to a breach of the mission for which the theatre was originally established.

Other candidates used ethical language and principles to structure their answers. Some candidates questioned the motives in Mr Strong's offer and therefore questioned his integrity – they concluded that Mr Strong was attempting to make a personal gain by increasing profit from populist theatre productions. This showed that candidates still have a habit of jumping straight to a conclusion and be highly suspicious of any hint of an ethical issue, without reference to the evidence available or analysing the situation from both sides.

Poorer answers tended to ignore the conflict of interest for the trustees regarding their potential personal financial liability and the objectives/mission of the trust, concentrating only on the ethics of Henry Strong.

(b) (i) Market segmentation is the division of a market into homogenous groups of potential customers. In CT's case it is only information about customers that enables classification into a range of overlapping groups.

The purpose of market segmentation for CT is that it can adjust components of the marketing mix to improve returns from each group according to, for example, spending potential, age, location, needs and tastes.

Thus, for instance, advertising can be targeted at the relevant segment for each performance eg for a drama with appeal to older age groups advertising could be targeted at those who are retired. This may in part come from the database, but could also be widened into magazines and clubs for older people living in the Conchester area.

Similarly, geographical targeting of those living closest to the theatre may be appropriate for performances mid-week when many theatre goers would be unwilling to travel.

Perhaps the most important purpose of segmentation is to set prices according the price elasticity of demand of each segment group. This aspect is dealt with below.

(ii) The database retains details of customers' characteristics and their preferences with respected to attending the theatre.

The classification permitted by the database includes:

- **Age** – may give an indication of whether the person is employed and thus available during daytime hours for matinees. It may also give an indication of income and likely preferences in drama and music.

- **Postcode** – may show how far the person has to travel to attend a performance and thus the willingness to attend performances during weekdays. It may also indicate the affluence of the area where they live and thus the degree of price resistance.

- **Profession** – may give an indication of social class and income and thus the degree of price resistance. If, for instance, they are students, this may indicate low income, some daytime availability and youthful tastes.

- **Past attendance** – this indicates the type of performance they are likely to attend, and the frequency of attendance may indicate the extent to which they are worth targeting as a future customer with discounts for regular attendance.

There are however limitations to the database in that only the 'Friends of CT' (including members) are available. Other theatre goers do not appear to have made available their details to CT so only 4,000 of the potential customers can be specifically targeted using this information set. During 2011, 100,000 tickets have been sold (£1.5m/£15). While this will include multiple attendances by some individuals, it seems likely that there are many more customers than there are 'Friends of CT'.

Note: capacity is: 800 × 5 × 50 = 200 000 seats [therefore only 50% utilisation has been achieved]

(iii) The current pricing strategy treats all segments as one homogeneous group. Moreover, it treats all seats as homogeneous and all performances as homogeneous.

Segmented customers

A policy of price discrimination involves setting different prices to different groups for the same product/service. To succeed, this pricing policy requires two conditions:

- That segmented groups have different price elasticities of demand.

- There is limited leakage between markets such that tickets intended to be sold to a low income group at a low price, cannot be accessed by high income groups.

Examples of price discrimination arising from market segmentation include:

- Students and senior citizens can obtain discounts when buying tickets if they produce status identification when buying and when attending the performance.

- Discount voucher could be sent to local postcodes or to low income postcodes to encourage attendance.

- High income groups (eg by profession or postcode) could be targeted for sales of premium seats or packages at premium prices.

Differentiated performances

Some performances are likely to be more popular than others (eg with well-known actors or well-known plays). If, in the past, these have filled the theatre with some people unable to obtain tickets, then extra revenue could be raised by increasing price beyond £15 until demand equates to supply.

Conversely, if some performances are poorly attended (eg afternoon matinees) then prices could be lowered if demand is price elastic in order to attract lower income groups and sell more seats.

Also, weekend performances could be priced more highly than weekday ones as there is more demand, and perhaps more demand from lower income groups during the week.

Differentiated seating

All seats at any given performance are currently priced the same. The best seats are therefore obtained by members and early bookers, without any price premium being paid. If the better seats are more highly valued, then this means a price premium could be obtained from these seats and more revenue generated.

Conversely, if £15 is too much for some customers, they may be willing to sit in poorer seats in order to be able to see the performance at all. If these seats would otherwise be empty (eg because nobody would pay £15 to sit in them) then incremental revenue would be generated.

Examiner's comments:

Requirement (b) asked candidates to explain: (i) the purposes of market segmentation for CT; (ii) how the CT database may be used to segment the market; and (iii) how different prices may be set by CT in order to increase revenue.

This part was generally well answered. The knowledge displayed of market segmentation and pricing strategies was good and candidates were very comfortable applying their knowledge to the facts of the scenario. The use of the database produced some very good answers with many candidates recognising both the benefit of being able to segment customers by age, profession, address and attendance type and how this information could be utilised to help Conchester Theatre.

In terms of pricing, answers were well structured and suggestions included: giving discounts for students and retired people; charging lower prices for less popular productions; attempting to do some research into competitive pricing; and using differential pricing throughout the year. Some candidates made calculations from the data given in the question, which showed a good skill in using relevant information.

51 Debt Crisis Aid

Marking guide

		Knowledge	Skill	Marks
(a)	PES factors	3	5	8
(b)	Stakeholders	2	6	8
(c)	(i) Centralisation of shared services	2	5	7
	(ii) Change management	3	5	8
(d)	Info system outputs	2	5	7
(e)	Ethical and governance issues	3	3	6
		15	29	44

General comments:

This is the mini case study. The scenario relates to the personal debt advice sector. DCA is a government funded organisation, run by Trustees, that provides support and assistance to individual clients with financial problems. It does this though 12 regional offices which assess a client's needs and then refer them to an approved external expert (accountant/solicitor) for the relevant advice. Advice costing less than £2,000 is allocated to the most appropriate approved expert at the discretion of DCA employees, in all other cases two competitive quotes must be obtained. DCA's core budget is under pressure due to government funding cuts. As well as needing to achieve a range of balanced scorecard targets set by the government, from 2012 DCA will be subject to an annual cost and quality compliance audit. To cut costs and improve efficiency the trustees are considering making 50% of the regional staff redundant and creating a central shared service centre to handle the screening, approval and payment of experts. They will also introduce a new information system with a central database to assist in measuring performance and gathering the information required by the government. A potential ethical issue has arisen because Mary Bourne, the managing partner of a national chain of solicitors, has recently approached the trustees to suggest that DCA allocates all legal advice work under £2,000 directly to her firm in return for a single consolidated monthly invoice.

This question was the highest scoring on the paper and was very well attempted by most candidates.

(a) **PESTEL extract**

There are a range of external factors that DCA needs to take into account when setting objectives and deciding on a strategy for how best to serve clients. Here the key political, economic and social factors are considered, although there will also be technological, ecological and legal influences

Political factors include government policies, targets, funding

- DCA has to operate within the framework of funding and targets set by the government. It is using taxpayers' money so they have a right to know how it has been spent and therefore there will be certain minimum reporting requirements that the trustees need to comply with.

- A change of government could result in different focus/policies so objectives/funds may be altered which makes planning difficult. DCA will also have to compete with other public sector organisations for central government funds. If there are public sector cuts, funds could be diverted away from DCA elsewhere, so the trustees may need to try and increase the level of donations.

- Government policies will also have an impact on some of the social, legal and economic factors that influence DCA. There are a range of regulations to ensure sustainable borrowing and lending and to protect the consumer. These may dictate the options available to clients for repaying or consolidating debts/declaring bankruptcy. DCA's advisors may also need to consider whether credit has been fairly extended in first place.

Economic includes changes in economy, market factors such as interest rates, people's spending patterns and general level of wealth

- The volume of work for DCA depends on the state of the economy – an economic downturn is likely to increase level of unmanageable debts. Conversely DCA may not need so many staff in upturn. Thus resource planning needs to take into account the forecasts of the number of people facing financial difficulty.

- Increases in interest rates increase the cost of credit and make it more likely that people will face financial difficulty, leading to more people for DCA to serve.

- It may be hard to balance the budget if it is a fixed amount annually as DCA is likely to spend more providing professional services in years of a downturn. This may involve DCA in difficult choices – who to help and who to turn away.

Social includes changes and trends in society

- The growth of the internet, changes in consumer spending patterns, and the cultural move away from saving to spending is likely to continue to increase the number of clients needing advice from DCA.

- DCA needs to focus on the individual customer and put their needs first unlike the commercial debt agencies – one consideration will be the extent to which clients are aware that a charitable debt management organisation exists. The trustees might make more use of the internet to raise profile and increase awareness.

- Sustainability – as well as sorting immediate financial problems for clients DCA also needs to take a long term approach to financial health by providing education.

- DCA will be expected to have ethical work practices – again unlike some of the commercial operators.

Conclusion

A better understanding of PESTEL forces and how they affect its work will help DCA plan resources effectively and deliver a better service.

Examiner's comments:

Requirement (a) asked candidates to explain the political, economic and social factors that DCA's trustees need to take into account when developing strategy.

Most candidates performed very well on this requirement and were comfortable extracting the relevant information from the scenario and using it to highlight the key external issues under the given headings. Better candidates went on to clearly demonstrate how these factors would affect the trustees when developing strategy eg the fact that they would face difficult decisions allocating a restricted level of funding between clients if tough economic conditions led to increased volumes of work. Some weaker candidates spent too much time here and produced answers that were far longer than necessary for the marks available.

(b) Stakeholder analysis

Mendelow suggests that DCA can position stakeholders on a matrix of power and interest which helps define the relationship that DCA should then seek with them:

Level of interest

	Low	High
Low *Power/influence*	Quadrant A Minimal effort	Quadrant B Keep informed
High	Quadrant C Keep satisfied	Quadrant D Key players

Government – high power and interest

The government's power will be high because of their role as initial founder and fund provider. The government controls the majority of DCA's income and sets key targets which will now be monitored through a cost and compliance audit.

Interest: This might also be considered high due to the following:

- The government will be concerned about the impact of debt and financial issues on the economy – it wants to be seen to be doing something through DCA.

- The government wants to ensure sustainable borrowing and lending – DCA will be a source of information regarding this.

- There is a need to promote responsible consumer spending. DCA will have a role to play in educating clients to help promote future financial health.

- The government may have a desire to avoid other indirect costs of debt issues.

DCA will need to ensure that it complies with government regulations and monitors performance in the light of the government targets and cost/quality compliance audit.

External experts – medium interest, low-medium power

There will be a wide range of accountants and solicitors working with DCA. Their position may depend on their relative size and the importance of the work to them.

Power: Low – medium

There are likely to be a wide range of experts for DCA to choose between and once approved, switching costs are likely to be low. National chains may have more power and influence than individual offices. The policy of not allowing any one provider to account for more than 10% of total advice work should help ensure that no single supplier is in a position of undue influence.

Interest: Medium

DCA work may be a good source of regular income for experts, though this will depend on the rates of pay offered. Clients initially picked up via DCA may lead to further work in future or recommendations for work. Firms who are concerned about sustainability and ethics may want to be associated with helping the vulnerable in society.

Experts should be kept informed about DCA's strategy and plans eg the proposed move to the SSC.

Clients – high interest, low power

Power: Low

Collectively the clients are the reason for DCA's existence and DCA has an obligation to focus on their best interests, however, as individuals they will have relatively little ability to influence, particularly as they are not paying for the service.

Interest: High

Most are vulnerable and may not be able to afford to pay for advice, therefore they will be heavily reliant on DCA, particularly if they feel that commercial companies may not have their best interests at heart. Clients may feel that as DCA is a government funded body they are more able to trust them.

DCA needs to monitor client satisfaction since this ties in with some of the government's annual targets.

Examiner's comments:

Requirement (b) asked candidates to use Mendelow's matrix to identify and justify the position of three key stakeholders: the UK government, external experts and clients. Candidates were well prepared for this requirement, showing a sound grasp of the model and tended to produce answers that scored very highly. Many reproduced Mendelow's diagram, using it to identify the position of the various groups. Almost all candidates acknowledged the role of the government as key players because they control DCA's income and monitor performance via targets and a cost and quality compliance audit. The better candidates recognised the fact that national chains of solicitors/accountants might wield more power than sole practitioners but discussed the fact that the rule preventing any expert providing more than 10% of advice work would limit their power. Some weaker candidates failed to recognise that as clients were not in a position to pay for DCA's services they would be unlikely to hold much individual power although collectively they are the reason for DCA's existence.

(c) **Centralisation of services – Advantages and disadvantages and change management issues**

(i) **Advantages of centralisation of services:**

- Economies of scale – having a shared central service centre may allow larger volumes of work to be done with the same or fewer resources and reduce the unit cost of the work. For example, a group of people handling supplier applications in one place may take more calls and give more standard responses than individuals working in separate offices.

- Applies the same standard to the approval of all potential suppliers which is more likely to result in similar quality of service delivery across the country and ensure consistency of service for clients.

- Avoids duplication of processes between regional offices. As a number of professional services firms are regional/national DCA can approve the firm once rather than having to process and approve 12 different applications.

- Greater efficiency resulting from having standardised processes. All staff will know what to do in any given situation. Systems across the organisation will be more consistent whereas before staff in the different regional centres may have created their own processes to implement policies. This is more cost-effective and fits with the governments drive for efficiency.

- Reduced staff costs in the long run due to redundancies. There may also be some savings in rent, overheads etc if the regional offices can be down-sized.

- New information systems mean some manual processes may be carried out electronically reducing time and costs.

Disadvantages

- Staff at the central service centre may lack local knowledge of potential suppliers that could be gleaned from the local marketplace.

- Loss of relationships built up with professional advisers – some professional advisers may feel the loss of the personal element if they do not always deal with the same local admin person.

- The service centre may experience difficulties handling workload at peak times leading to delays and local staff may no longer have the experience to take work on/support them. This may damage the service offered to the client.

- Local staff may feel they have lost control and become demotivated as a result. There may be heavy resistance to the change (see below).

- The level of redundancies may attract negative publicity for DCA – it could be accused of causing financial difficulty for its own staff.

- There may be cost and time issues implementing the new information system and any disruption will affect client service.

Overall however in the context of the drive to cut costs and increase efficiency it appears that there are more advantages than disadvantages and the Trustees plan to move to a shared service centre should be implemented.

(ii) **Change management**

The type of change will strongly influence the way in which change is managed. Change may be incremental (a gradual process, undertaken as a series of small steps) or transformational (a major significant change) and may take place gradually or require a rapid one-off change.

Here the change is to the structure of the organisation and also involves the introduction of new information systems and processes, so is likely to be viewed by the employees as transformational.

The way in which the changes are introduced will be very important in them being implemented successfully. There will be cultural and individual barriers to change. Resistance needs to be acknowledged and discussed and may be lessened by involving the employees in the planning and implementation. Clearly there are three groups of employees here and they will need to be managed differently:

- Those required to transfer to the new service centre
- Those required to leave the organisation
- Those who will retain their roles at the regional office

The experts and clients are also likely to be affected by the change. Experts will need to deal with the central SSC rather than local staff. If this increases the efficiency with which applications and payments are handled then they may be powerful advocates for the change.

Clients are likely to continue to deal with their local office and assuming DCA is successful in resolving their financial difficulties, clients are likely to represent one-off business and therefore be unaware of how things have been managed previously.

The change needs to be sold to all those involved and communication will be key to this.

Lewin/Schein's 3-step iceberg model of change would prescribe the following approach:

- Unfreezing standard operating procedures (identifying the restraining forces and overcoming them)

- Move to new patterns of behaviour (carrying out the change and switching to the shared service centre) and

- Refreezing to ensure lasting effects ie reinforcing the new system and behaviour

While these phases may be appropriate to employees moving or retaining roles within DCA, clearly they will not apply to those who are to be made redundant, as they will not have to accept a new structure or culture.

The **Gemini 4Rs** framework could also be used here:

Reframe – create the will and desire to change (the Trustees may focus on the need for cost cutting and increased efficiency in the light of central government budget issues)

Restructure – redesign the structure and culture to facilitate the new approach. This may involve holding meetings with employees, asking for volunteers to relocate to the service centre or to take redundancy, setting up the new teams and processes

Revitalise – creating a culture of teamwork between the shared service centre and the employees who are to remain regional, designing appropriate targets and measures

Renewal – ensure the change is supported on an ongoing basis and that individuals involved have the necessary skills eg training in the new information systems, recognition for achievement of government targets

The *coercive change* approach is where change is forced without participation. This requires the ability to push through the change without co-operation In this context, the creation of the shared service centre could be promoted as the only alternative in convincing the government to continue to support DCA or it could be argued there may be wider repercussions for DCA's long term position.

Examiner's comments:

Requirement (c) concerned the Trustees' plans for the shared service centre (SSC). In c(i) candidates were requested to discuss the advantages and disadvantages of the Trustees' plans to centralise shared services. Requirement c(ii) asked them to explain, with reference to relevant models, how the trustees should manage the change, assuming the plans for the SSC went ahead.

In the case of weaker answers to (c)(i) it was not always clear from the generic nature of the points made exactly what was being centralised. Better answers offered specific benefits and disadvantages in the context of the Trustees need to increase efficiency and reduce costs and discussed the pros and cons in relation to the screening of experts, processing of payments and monitoring of service levels. Many candidates made some good points regarding the possibility of bad publicity arising from the redundancies and the potential time and cost issues associated with implementing a new information system. Those candidates who did provide a conclusion tended to suggest that in the context of possible government funding cuts the move to an SSC was likely to be sensible.

As usual candidates demonstrated good knowledge of change management in c(ii) and it was pleasing to see an improvement in the ability to relate this knowledge to the scenario. Most discussed Lewin/Schein's iceberg model of change although the Gemini's 4Rs framework could also have been used. The best scripts recognised the change is likely to be transformational and then went beyond a discussion of the impact of the change on the employees (50% of whom were being made redundant) to also consider the impact of the change on experts and clients.

(d) **Use of information system to measure performance of DCA and of its suppliers**

To date the government has assessed DCA using a 'Balanced Scorecard' approach to report against key indicators which include: the number of clients DCA helps each year, how quickly and successfully they are helped and how efficiently the budget has been managed.

The new performance monitoring system can be used to compare actual results with government targets for the various Balanced scorecard measures. In setting up the system DCA's Trustees need to ascertain what additional cost and quality measures the new annual compliance audit will focus on.

Costs

DCA's fixed annual budget is awarded in two lots: an amount to cover DCA's employment and administration costs and a separate budget to pay for the cost of services and advice provided to clients. DCA will need to monitor these costs separately.

DCA supplements the government funding with donations from other organisations – large retailers, banks and building societies. It would be useful to track the amount and timing of these funds, since this may allow DCA to spend more on services than the fixed government budget.

The system should monitor:

- Spending levels against budget and over time
- Spending per regional office
- Costs incurred by the shared service centre
- Amounts paid to employees
- Amounts paid to each supplier by region (to ensure compliance with the 10% policy)
- The cost of advice split between legal and accounting

The system can help with cost control by ensuring that the amounts invoiced by suppliers are within the agreed budget. The system should only approve suppliers for payment if they have complied with all the terms and conditions of service and met their service targets (see below).

Quality

A large element of the quality of DCA's service depends on the services provided by the approved suppliers. DCA does not currently appear to monitor supplier performance and there is no review process once the suppliers have been approved, so they can remain on the approved list indefinitely.

The new system can be used to implement the monitoring and review of suppliers. As part of the supplier approval process DCA needs to ensure there are service level targets in place for each supplier.

In line with existing government targets it should track for each supplier: the number of clients helped, the nature of advice given, how quickly they are helped (eg time between approaching DCA and meeting professional advisor), how successfully they are helped (no of clients successfully repaying debts, time taken to repay debts, number avoiding future debt problems).

DCA can make use of exception reporting to prompt action and to facilitate decision making eg reporting suppliers who have missed deadlines and/or whose service levels have fallen below those necessary for approval.

Also to highlight suppliers who consistently outperform targets since employees should be encouraged to direct work towards these.

The system can also be used to assess the performance of the shared service centre eg in terms of the number of supplier applications processed, the time taken to process applications, the number approved etc.

One of the things the compliance audit is likely to check is that work is being allocated in accordance with DCA's stated policy and the system needs to monitor this.

Examiner note:

An alternative but equally acceptable approach to this requirement was to consider output in the context of various KPIs for each of the four balanced scorecard headings.

Examiner's comments:

In requirement (d) candidates were asked to explain the outputs that will be required from the information system to enable DCA to measure performance.

Answers here were quite variable. Those candidates who discussed DCA's need to monitor a range of KPIs in the context of the Government's balanced scorecard targets and cost and quality compliance audit typically scored well. The best answers made it clear that the system would need to produce different data to monitor the experts, DCA's use of the funding budget and the provision of service to clients and that exception reporting would be useful. The weakest candidates failed to make the link with DCA's need to monitor performance in the context of the government requirements and discussed the requirements of information in generic terms (relevance, reliability etc).

(e)   **Ethical and governance issue**

Ethics and corporate governance in the context of DCA will be concerned with the way in which the Trustees manage and apply public funds in providing debt advisory services. It incorporates the Trustees responsibilities and mandate, decision making processes, and accountability.

The Trustees will need to operate in accordance with DCA's objects and must ensure that any decision regarding Longparish is in accordance with the stated policies concerning approved suppliers:

- Work likely to cost under £2,000 should be allocated to the most appropriate approved supplier at the discretion of the DCA employee. In all other cases at least two competitive quotes must be obtained.

- A single supplier cannot carry out more than 10% of the total advice work (by value) provided by a DCA regional office in any financial year.

This issue could be considered using the three tests of Transparency/Effect/Fairness or alternatively by considering the Nolan Committee's 7 Principles of Public Life which apply to public sector governance: selflessness, integrity, objectivity, accountability, openness, honesty, leadership.

Using the three ethical tests:

Transparency: would the Trustees mind the government, public and other professional advisers knowing that they have awarded the contract for services under £2,000 to Longparish?

This may depend on whether there has been any inducement to do so (the offer from Mary Bourne would not appear to give the Trustees a personal conflict of interest since as individuals they do not stand to gain personally or financially from the decision) and whether they can justify the decision as benefitting DCA on the grounds of reduced cost and increased efficiency.

Effect: who does the decision affect or hurt?

The effect on DCA would be to reduce the admin costs associated with allocating work to suppliers and processing payments. The service provided may also be more uniform.

The decision will affect other suppliers who would previously been allocated work by the regional office.

Clients may be affected positively if the service is more consistent and higher quality or negatively if the service is not good enough (not all Longparish's suppliers are currently on the approved list which could either be because they have not applied for approval or because the regional office has felt they were not up to the standard required).

Fairness:

The clients are unlikely to be overly concerned about who provides the service so long as they receive appropriate free help. The other suppliers who miss out on work are likely to perceive this as unfair. Allocating all the work to one supplier may also contravene government policies for procurement by public sector organisations.

Alternative approach using the Nolan Principles:

The 7 principles are selflessness, integrity, objectivity, accountability, openness, honesty, leadership.

The Trustees need to consider how they apply in the context of this situation:

Selflessness: Holders of public office should take decisions solely in terms of the public interest. They should not do so to gain financial or other material benefits for themselves, their family or their friends.

Honesty: Holders of public office have a duty to declare any private interests relating to their public duties and to take steps to resolve any conflicts arising in a way that protects the public interest.

The offer from Mary Bourne would not appear to give the Trustees a personal conflict of interest since as individuals they do not stand to gain personally or financially from the decision. Thus there does not seem to be an issue with Selflessness and Honesty.

Integrity: Holders of public office should not place themselves under any financial or other obligation to outside individuals or organisations that might influence them in the performance of their duties.

Objectivity: In carrying out public business, including making public appointments, awarding contracts or recommending individuals for rewards and benefits, holders of public office should make choices on merit.

Here the Trustees need to ensure that all Longparish's offices meet the approved supplier criteria. If so then awarding work to Longparish could be argued to fall within the stated policy that 'work under £2000 should be allocated to the most appropriate approved supplier at the discretion of the DCA employee'.

They must also not breach the condition that 'a single supplier cannot carry out more than 10% of the total advice work (by value) provided by a DCA regional office in any financial year'. This will ensure that Longparish is not able to exert undue influence on DCA or its Trustees.

Accountability: Holders of public office are accountable for their decisions and actions to the public and must submit themselves to whatever scrutiny is appropriate to their office.

Openness: Holders of public office should be as open as possible about the decisions and actions that they take. They should give reasons for their decisions and restrict information only when the wider public interest clearly demands.

This depends on whether the Trustees can justify the decision as benefitting DCA on the grounds of reduced cost and increased efficiency. The effect on DCA would be to reduce the admin costs associated with allocating work to suppliers and processing payments. The service provided may also be more uniform and therefore benefit clients.

Thus provided the Trustees are open and honest about their reasons there may be no issue.

Leadership: Holders of public office should promote and support these principles by leadership and example. Again there does not seem to be a question here about the ethics or behaviour of the individual Trustees.

Conclusion

The Trustees need to ensure that all Longparish's offices meet the approved supplier criteria. They must also not breach the condition that 'a single supplier cannot carry out more than 10% of the total advice work (by value) provided by a DCA regional office in any financial year'.

If they can do this and can demonstrate that there are cost and efficiency benefits for DCA of using one supplier and that the individual clients will continue to receive the best advice then there may not be an ethical or governance issue.

Examiner's comments:

Requirement (e) required candidates to discuss the ethical and public sector governance issues arising from Mary Bourne's proposal to the trustees. As in previous sittings the answers to the ethics requirement were quite variable in standard. Weaker answers ranged from stating that Mary Bourne was clearly unethical and attempting to bribe the trustees, to believing that there was no problem accepting the offer given the trustees' need to save costs. Better candidates adopted a framework for their answer (eg transparency, effect, fairness or Nolan principles) and produced a balanced argument rather than a one-sided discussion. Those who discussed the offer in the context of the requirement to provide the best advice to clients and DCA's policy on allocating work to experts and who recognised that not all Longparish's offices are currently approved, tended to score reasonably well. Most candidates showed some awareness of public sector governance requirements either by quoting some of the key Nolan principles or recognising the need for the Trustees to demonstrate integrity and accountability.

52 Bootwear

Marking guide

		Knowledge	Skill	Marks
(a)	Strategic fit	3	7	10
(b)	Financial performance/issues	2	12	14
(c)	Future risks	2	4	6
(d)	Conclusions	–	4	4
		7	27	34

General comments:

This is the data analysis question. The scenario in this question relates to a company (Bootwear) which produces high quality long-lasting waterproof protective footwear, sold to men aged 25-35. Bootwear places great emphasis on corporate responsibility and sustainable business. The business is profitable but needs to expand its customer base and is currently considering two mutually exclusive acquisition targets: BHC and MK. BHC is an online retailer of premium-priced sports style fashion clothing aimed at affluent 18-25 year olds. It has grown rapidly, apparently unaffected by the recession but has received adverse publicity in newspapers for being an over-priced disposable fashion brand. MK is an established family owned and managed company producing a range of climbing equipment, known for its technical attributes and safety. It has an ethical procurement policy which results in a higher cost base than competitors. Key financial data was provided for Bootwear and both target companies to facilitate a preliminary appraisal of the acquisition strategy.

Candidates were asked to prepare a report comparing the two target companies, clearly identifying further information required. The report (and mark allocation) was broken down into four separate headings: strategic fit; financial performance and other relevant financial issues; future risks; preliminary conclusions and recommendations. This question was well attempted by the majority of candidates.

Report

To: Board of Bootwear plc
From: A N Accountant
Date: March 2012
Re: Possible acquisitions

This report sets out the issues we recommend you consider in respect of the potential acquisition of either BHC or MK and highlights any additional information required.

> **Examiner note:**
>
> Additional information could have been noted within each section of the report or as a separate section at the end. Either approach was acceptable and attracted full credit.

(a) **Strategic fit**

Growth objective

Bootwear's product is designed to last, so the time between replacement purchases will be quite long. Also the nature of the product means that customers are unlikely to buy more than a couple of pairs of boots. With such limited potential for repeat business, Bootwear needs to attract new customers or reach different market segments if it is to grow. The market in which Bootwear operates is likely to be mature, with strong competition, so acquisition may be a faster way of securing the desired growth. Bootwear will need to weigh up the costs of developing new products or markets organically with the costs of acquisition.

Generic strategy

Porter believes there are two ways to create long-term superior profits: Cost leadership or Differentiation. The chosen strategy can then be adopted industry-wide or focussed on a particular market niche.

All three businesses appear to be adopting a differentiation strategy where competitive advantage is gained as a result of perceived product differences:

Bootwear's 'Footwear for life' is long-lasting and does not need to be replaced regularly; BHC has created a perception of a luxury lifestyle brand, based on its classic British heritage; MK is recognised in the climbing industry for its technical attributes and safety and as a result it has a loyal customer base. Therefore the generic strategy of all three companies is consistent.

Target market

Bootwear's current market is predominantly males aged 25-35, working outdoors or engaging in outdoor leisure pursuits.

MK's products are also targeted at those enjoying outdoor activities although MK has focussed on a smaller specialist market niche – climbing and mountaineering. There may be some degree of overlap between the two customer bases, since many of MK's customers may be males aged 25-35. It is possible that they already purchase Bootwear footwear. As a result MK may help Bootwear increase its market share but will probably offer limited potential for targeting new market segments.

BHC operates in a different market, targeting affluent 18-25 year olds interested in traditional sporting and country pursuits (polo, hunting and shooting, rugby and rowing). It would be useful to know the split between male and female customers. There is some similarity to Bootwear in that they are interested in outdoor activities, but the nature of the product they are purchasing is different and has a much shorter life. Some BHC customers may buy Bootwear footwear but they would only represent a small proportion of Bootwear's current market. Thus there may be an opportunity for Bootwear to reach a new market via BHC's website or to introduce new ranges of footwear targeted at younger consumers eg deck shoes, riding boots.

Industry information in relation to the size of the various markets, expected growth and the size and market share of competitors would be useful.

Core competences/Operations

Bootwear manufactures and sells waterproof outdoor footwear. MK also operates in the outdoor clothing and equipment market, albeit in a more specialised niche. Both company's products are stocked by specialist outdoor retailers. As a result Bootwear is likely to have the necessary knowledge and experience to run MK. There are also likely to be synergies available in terms of distribution and marketing.

BHC is an internet based fashion retailer with a high turnaround of products. This is very different from Bootwear's long-lasting durable products and is likely to require very different management skills. Bootwear would probably need to run BHC as a separate business.

Sustainability and corporate values

As a business, Bootwear places great emphasis on corporate social responsibility and sustainable business practices. The company is known to be openly committed to reducing its environmental impact and to adding value to the communities in which it operates. MK's approach to business would appear to fit well with this. Although it results in an increased cost base, MK has an ethical procurement policy and insists on strict contracts to ensure appropriate working conditions and fair terms for suppliers. Since the two companies have the same values there should be fewer integration difficulties.

It could be argues that BHC on the other hand is less influenced by the need for sustainability – through its lifestyle magazine and viral marketing it appears to actively encourage customers to buy new items on a 'want' rather than 'need' basis, just because they are the latest colour or design. There may be a clash of values with Bootwear in this respect which as well as damaging the Bootwear brand could mean that it is harder to integrate post acquisition.

Examiner's comments:

Requirement (a) related to strategic fit. Most candidates were comfortable discussing strategic fit in terms of competitive strategy and target markets, however several seemed to overlook the fact that Bootwear has limited opportunity to grow organically and that whilst there might be some clash of ethos with BHC, it might offer more scope to target new markets by reaching a wider customer base through online sales. Candidates who widened their discussion to consider the core competences of the various businesses and the scope for operational synergies gained high marks. It is surprising that a small minority of candidates continue to miss out on the format mark available for producing the answer in the style of a report.

(b) **Financial performance and other relevant financial issues**

Appendix:

Note: A wide range of calculations have been produced here for marking purposes – candidates were not expected to calculate all of them.

	Bootwear	BHC	MK
Gross profit margin	35%	47%	22%
Operating profit margin	12%	25%	4%
Net margin (PBT)	11.3%	24.2%	2.9%
Return on investment (PBT/NA)	27%	58%	9%
Revenue/NA	£2.37	£2.39	£3.10
Interest cover	12	33	5
£ Debt (NA x Debt/Equity)	4.6m	0.6m	1m
Revenue as a % of Bootwear		29.8%	51.5%
Net assets as a % of Bootwear		29.3%	39.4%
PBT as a % of Bootwear		63%	15%

Profitability

Gross margin of BHC (47%) is much higher than Bootwear (35%) reflecting the perceived value pricing strategy that it has have applied in the niche market. BHC has created a must-have brand that consumers are prepared to pay a significant premium for and this appears to be more about the brand name than a substantive difference in quality or design.

MK's margin is significantly lower at 22%. This is consistent with the fact that the ethical procurement strategy gives rise to a higher cost base and as manufacturing is outsourced also reflects the deterioration in sterling exchange rates, giving rise to margin pressure.

Sales for all businesses have grown between 2010 and 2011, although it is clear that with an 18% increase year on year, BHC is growing fastest. This is probably due to the fact that it is the youngest business, having been launched in 2005 and is still penetrating the market. Both Bootwear and MK are more established businesses and their growth rates reflect this. Bootwear's growth at 6 % could be due to an increase in prices or an increase in volumes and more information is required to determine this. This is also true of MK which may have increased prices to compensate for the increase in manufacturing costs.

BHC has managed to minimise operating expenses by not having a shop presence and by using viral marketing techniques. MK's operating expenses are likely to be higher because they spend significant amounts on marketing and sponsorship of high profile climbers.

Return on investment

At 58% BHC's return on investment is a function of its high profitability and low investment in non-current assets. It is hard to see that this rate of return is sustainable in the long term.

MK's relatively low return reflects the pressure on its profits but means that there is likely to be scope for improvement in the future and because of the scope for synergy discussed in (a) above, Bootwear may be in a position to raise this nearer its own 27% return in future.

Finance structure

There does not appear to be any major cause for concern with the finance structure of either target. Both companies have lower gearing ratios than Bootwear. As a relatively new internet-based business BHC may have lacked the non-current assets to secure high levels of debt finance. It has clearly had no problem meeting interest payments in 2011. MK is a well established family company and the family may have tried to avoid having excess debt. At 5 times, MK's interest cover is acceptable but further pressure on margins could lead to finance costs becoming an issue for the company.

Size and financial prospects

MK is a bigger company than BHC. In revenue terms MK is just over half the size of Bootwear, with approximately 40% of its Net Asset value. It is currently underperforming due to pressure on margins. As the businesses are quite similar and have complementary products there may be scope for reduction in costs to improve profitability: eg by using one distribution network, joint marketing and the need for only one management team.

Cost of acquisition

A key issue for Bootwear is going to be the likely cost of the prospective purchase. Neither business is listed – both appear to have at least some shareholders who are keen to sell therefore it is unlikely to be a hostile takeover.

Some of MK's family shareholders want to retire and there is little succession planning in place, so they may be more open to negotiation on price. Particularly as the business appears to be underperforming in terms of operating margin and return on investment.

BHC's key shareholder is also likely to be open to an approach if she is keen to realise her investment. However as the company is currently growing rapidly and proving to be successful the price can be expected to be significantly higher and a premium is likely to be payable for control.

Bootwear will also need to consider how they intend to finance any acquisition and what cash is available to them. Whilst the target shareholders may be prepared to receive some of the consideration in the form of shares they may also wish to realise some of their investment in the form of cash. In the case of MK's retiring family members Bootwear may be able to negotiate some form of earn out based on future profits which may help motivate them in the integration period.

Further information required

There is only one year of results for each of the targets. More information is required on past performance to establish how the businesses have fared through the recession and to put the current results into perspective.

Budgets and forecasts are required to assess the future prospects of the two targets which will be a key factor for Bootwear in assessing the chances of a return on its investment. Cashflow information would also help to assess liquidity.

Information about the size of the various markets in which the company's operate would allow market share to be calculated. An analysis of competitors would provide more information on the likely sustainability of the two company's competitive advantage.

Industry benchmarks would also allow better assessment of how each company is performing relative to its market.

Valuations of comparable business and details of the likely prices that the current owners are looking for.

Examiner's comments:

Requirement (b) asked candidates to consider financial performance and any other relevant financial issues. Candidates had been given gearing ratios and revenue growth but were required to produce a range of further calculations. The recurring calculations produced by most candidates were gross margin, operating margin and interest cover, which most candidates correctly determined. Stronger candidates also recognised that, having been provided with net assets, some form of ROCE measure would be useful. A minority of weaker candidates produced no calculations of their own and merely repeated figures given in the scenario, or simply restated their calculations in narrative form without adding analysis or explanation. The better answers compared the results for the targets to Bootwear to assess the impact an acquisition might have on the overall results. Most candidates showed some ability in using the information in the scenario to explain the reasons why BHC, which is a smaller business in terms of net assets and revenue, is outperforming MK in terms of revenue growth, profitability and return on investment.

The discussion of other financial issues tended to be limited to comments on gearing and interest cover with only a small minority of candidates referring to the issue of price/consideration which was mentioned in the scenario. Some candidates missed out this element of the requirement altogether. Most candidates produced a reasonable list of further information although this was not always prioritised and many failed to recognise the importance of projections in assessing the future potential of the two targets.

(c) **Future risks**

BHC

The success of BHC depends on social trends and its products remaining in fashion with consumers. Many internet fashion retailers are very successful whilst they are the latest brand but their success may be short-lived. If this is true of BHC, Bootwear may end up paying lots of money for a business at the peak of its life cycle which then matures and declines quickly.

Reliance on social networking sites means that BHC is not in control of its marketing and brand image. Adverse content could spread rapidly and the high levels of growth BHC has experienced could be quickly reversed.

Association with BHC's disposable consumer brand image may damage Bootwear's brand and sales.

MK

MK may lose the long term contract with Whiteout plc to supply own brand goods – further information is required to assess what % of sales and profitability is attributed to this.

MK's faces exchange risk as a result of outsourcing production. Although they may undertake hedging, any long term movements in exchange rates could lead to further increases in cost of sales.

MK's business may rely on the contacts held by the MK family. Customers may be loyal to the family members and may go elsewhere if they retire. Retention of the contract with Whiteout plc may depend on existing relationships.

MK's marketing is heavily reliant on sponsoring high profile climbers. If any of them are involved in negative publicity this could adversely affect MK's brand.

Climbing is a dangerous sport – any quality or safety problems with MK's equipment would also significantly damage its reputation.

MK has made an issue of the fact that it is an ethical procurement company – should this prove to be a PR exercise only (eg if any of their suppliers are found to be using unethical working practices) then they may lose their loyal customer base.

Other

Acquisition of BHC probably diversifies risk more than MK because it is a different product and market. However the business itself may be inherently less stable than Bootwear or MK.

Size, strength and reaction of competitors in the market will affect the sustainability of earning streams.

Examiner's comments:

Requirement (c) asked candidates to evaluate future risks.

This requirement was reasonably attempted although weaker candidates tended to produce a shopping list of points without any sort of structured approach. Most candidates discussed the risk that BHC might pose to Bootwear's reputation and the issues for MK in terms of exchange rate risk and the cost of ethical procurement.

Better candidates recognised that BHC might be at the peak of its life cycle and that Bootwear might end up paying a premium for a business that reaches maturity/decline quickly. They also discussed the fact that MK's future profitability might rely on retention of the Whiteout contract.

(d) **Preliminary conclusions and recommendations**

In MK, Bootwear would be buying a business that is potentially underperforming currently. There is scope for synergies, the business would probably be relatively easy to integrate and Bootwear has the potential to use its own management team to run the company. If the business is currently underperforming Bootwear may be able to acquire it at a reasonable price and then make a return on its investment.

It is likely to have to pay a high price to acquire BHC given its current success and the key shareholder's desire to capitalise on this. Once acquired, given the greater potential for a clash of brand and culture it is hard to see how the business could be integrated. Without integration the potential for synergistic cost savings is limited. BHC would almost certainly deliver high growth for Bootwear in the short term but Bootwear would be buying earnings growth at a premium.

On the face of it MK appears to be the better choice. Clearly more information is required before a decision can be made and due diligence would need to be carried out once a target is chosen.

Examiner's comments:

In requirement (d) candidates were requested to make some preliminary conclusions and recommendations. Most candidates did make some attempt at a conclusion although in the case of weaker candidates they tended to sit on the fence rather than making a preliminary recommendation in favour of one or other acquisition, based on their answers to (a)-(c). The majority of candidates tended to conclude that MK was a better strategic fit for Bootwear but that BHC was outperforming it financially. Surprisingly few candidates seemed to realise however that the price for BHC might be inflated as a result and that MK might offer a better deal and more scope to improve future performance through synergies.

53 Vicaro Ltd

Marking guide

		Knowledge	Skill	Marks
(a)	Evolution of PC industry	2	6	8
(b)	Development methods	6	8	14
		8	14	22

General comments:

This is the shortest question. Vicaro is a small research and development company set up in India by a group of entrepreneurs. It develops new business ideas which it normally commercialises by granting licences to other companies to use its intellectual property within India and the rest of Asia. Vicaro's latest development is aimed at making a low-cost tablet PC (the Sibal) accessible for the first time to the domestic Indian population. It is currently considering three different options for the financing and commercial development of the Sibal: a joint venture with a global PC manufacturer which will provide manufacturing and distribution facilities in return for Vicaro's intellectual property; its usual practice of granting a licence to use the technology to companies wishing to manufacture and sell the tablet in Asia or the creation of a new company, financed by private investors. In the case of the latter option, the company might be able to seek some government sponsorship because the Sibal will contribute to the education and growth of the Indian economy.

Answers to this, the last question, were quite polarised and this is reflected in the average mark. There were some excellent attempts. A minority of weaker candidates who mis-managed their time and wrote too much on either the mini-case or the data-analysis question produced a truncated attempt at question 3 or in the case of a couple of candidates, no attempt at all.

(a) Life cycle/Evolution of PC industry

The concept of life cycle analysis is used to describe the phases of development that an industry (or product) goes through:

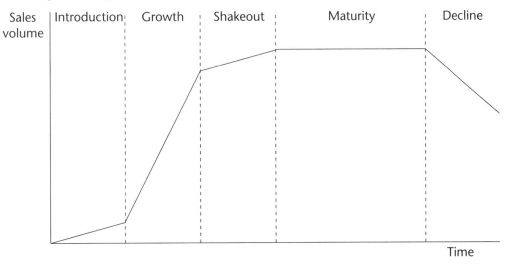

The key stages of the life cycle are:

- **Introduction** – a newly invented product or service is made available for purchase and organisations attempt to develop buyer interest.

- **Growth** – a period of rapid expansion of demand or activity as the industry finds a market and competitors are attracted by its potential.

- **Maturity** – a relatively stable period of time where there is little change in sales volumes year to year but competition between firms intensifies as growth slows down.

- **Decline** – a falling off in activity levels as firms leave the industry and the industry ceases to exist or is absorbed into some other industry.

The development of the microprocessor in 1971 led to the introduction phase of the PC industry with buyers at that stage being largely drawn from technical computer specialists.

Developments in the 1980s made PCs attractive to less technical users and product standardisation also made them more accessible in terms of price, leading to the growth phase of the industry. The advent of the internet stimulated a period of rapid expansion which continues today.

Some industry life cycles are identical in pattern and timing to that of their product. Others have longer life cycles than the particular products. This appears to have been the case with the personal computer industry which has seen a variety of products come and go within the industry life cycle.

As one product declines, another is in maturity and another is growing (either because of changes in consumer demand or technological change). Thus although the PC industry appears to be still growing, certain products within the industry are at a later stage in their lifecycle. Desktops might be considered to be in decline, laptops at maturity and tablets somewhere between introduction and growth.

In terms of the product life cycle it is also common within an industry for products to overlap. This can be seen in the computer industry where the product life cycles of individual products have overlapped, such as desktops and laptops and now laptops and tablet computers.

Thus the cycle has been influenced by various factors:

(i)   Technological developments which have led to changes in the nature of the products eg the introduction of the micro-processor facilitating the development of smaller scale personal computers in contrast to the giant mainframes; the development of graphics leading to more interactive, user-friendly machines.

(ii) Technological developments which have stimulated demand and changed the nature of computer usage eg the development of the internet and e-commerce means that most people use a computer in their home as part of their day-to-day life.

(iii) Lifestyle changes which have meant that consumer demand has evolved – the desire for immediate access to data and for media consumption leading to the introduction of smaller handheld gadgets and the development of phones that can also behave as computers.

Hence the concepts of both product and industry life cycle do appear to apply in the personal computer industry, which has managed to extend the life of the industry by continual product innovation and by responding to changes in the external environment (such as technological developments) and consumer preferences.

Examiner's comments:

Requirement (a) asked candidates to explain, with reference to the industry and product life cycle models how the personal computer industry has evolved. The vast majority of candidates were familiar with the life cycle model although a small minority chose to incorrectly apply Porter's 5 forces or Ansoff's product/market development matrix. Most candidates were able to use the information in the scenario to identify and discuss the various phases of PC industry development (introduction, growth, maturity, decline) with many drawing a diagram to illustrate. The better candidates made a clear distinction between the lifecycle of the industry and the shorter, overlapping lifecycles of its various products, recognising that whilst desktops might be considered to be in decline, laptops are probably at maturity and tablets somewhere between introduction and growth. The strongest pointed out that the PC industry has managed to extend its life by continual product innovation and by responding to changes in the external environment (such as technological developments) and consumer preferences.

(b) Methods of development

Examiner note:

This requirement could alternatively have been approached by considering each method of development in turn and then discussing resources/control/risks and returns within that.

Vicaro is currently considering three options for the development of the Sibal:

(1) **Joint venture (JV) with a global PC manufacturer**

(2) **Licensing**

(3) **Creation of a new company**

Each option has different implications for resources, control and risk/return.

Resources: Financial

If Vicaro decides to go it alone, significant finance will be required for final development of the tablet, market research and marketing, production and distribution (although production and distribution are likely to be outsourced). Depending on their personal wealth the entrepreneurs may be able to contribute some of this but will almost certainly need to seek additional investors. There may be a number of private investors who are willing to invest on ethical grounds if they are convinced about the viability of the tablet. The entrepreneurs also need to consider how likely the Indian government are to sponsor the project in view of the benefits to the Indian economy and what form this sponsorship will take – grants, loans or equity investment? Short term or long term?

Less finance is required if some form of strategic alliance is considered and some of it may be provided by the JV partner. If the JV is undertaken with an existing PC manufacturer then the use of existing facilities will reduce the capital investment required.

Continuing with its normal model of licensing would minimise the financial and other resources required from Vicaro and will offer scope for faster and wider market expansion than if Vicaro were to undertake commercial development of the Sibal alone.

Resources: Other

The prototype has been successfully developed but there are two issues here:

(i) Whether the entrepreneurs can successfully bring the prototype to market:

- Is it feasible to generate the volumes of production necessary to keep the costs down?

- Will demand exist at the anticipated price?

- Will other tablet manufacturers have access to similar technology and be able to bring out rival products before or shortly after Sibal is launched?

(ii) Whether this is better done independently or in cooperation with a larger partner due to issues of scale

- How easily can large scale production and distribution be established?

- Significant marketing will be required to establish sales and promote customer interest.

- Large scale commercial production will also require support processes: procurement, HRM, IT.

Cooperation is likely to yield advantages in the form of existing resources and infrastructure. A joint venture will provide access to competences in production, distribution and marketing that the entrepreneurs may not possess.

However if the entrepreneurs set up their own company it would also be possible to make use of the core competences of other businesses by outsourcing these activities.

Again as Vicaro's normal approach to commercialisation is to grant licences, this approach should already be within the scope of its current resources and competences.

Control

Control can be discussed in relation to strategy and day-to-day operations, intellectual property (IP) and profits.

The entrepreneurs who currently own Vicaro will retain greatest day-to-day control of operations if they set up a separate company. However the involvement of the government as a key sponsor may limit freedom to pursue own strategy. IP will be retained by the company and profits will be available for the shareholders, who are likely to consist of the entrepreneurs and private investors and possibly the government. The entrepreneurs will need to consider the objectives and exit plans of the other investors.

In a JV, the global PC manufacturer is likely to be bigger than Vicaro and provision of production, distribution and marketing facilities would probably give the chosen partner greater control of day-to-day operations. It would also put them in a strong negotiating position regarding share of profits. IP would be shared and would need to be protected or the JV partner may seek to leave the venture and produce the tablet alone once in possession of the necessary technology. The JV contract would need to be carefully negotiated. Control can be exercised by ensuring that there are clauses in place regarding branding, marketing and pricing.

In relation to licensing, there is a similar risk as with the joint venture in terms of loss of control of IP. The extent of Vicaro's control over the licensee and the quality of the product will depend on the constraints imposed via the licensing agreement. Again Vicaro may dictate branding and pricing issues.

Risks and Returns

A wide range of global PC manufacturers exist with well-known brand names. Despite them being higher in cost, consumers with sufficient income may prefer to purchase PCs from these companies since they are tried and tested.

The tablet market is dominated by a single player and a number of its competitors have already introduced tablet PCs. Given their size, resources and research capacity it is likely that they will be able to imitate the Sibal or because of better access to economies of scale develop their own rival tablets at lower cost.

Given the rate of technological change in the industry (as discussed in (a)) there is also considerable risk that new innovations will appear which supersede the tablet PC.

The technological infrastructure in India may not support the wireless connection necessary for the Sibal. If there are system problems when the product is launched it may fail quickly.

If the entrepreneurs set up their own company then they bear all these risks but they also retain all the rewards, so they have unlimited potential to enjoy the success of the Sibal.

The JV would be better placed to withstand the risks associated with competition because of access to a global brand name and resources. The remaining risks would be shared and may be diversified if the JV allows the Sibal to be sold in other emerging markets. Any profits would however be shared with the global PC manufacturer, which may be in a position to insist on the greater proportion.

If Vicaro adopts licensing, it will transfer the majority of risks to the licensee but in return only receive a proportion of the sales revenue.

Conclusion

Licensing is tried and tested but may limit Vicaro's potential to benefit from the potential success of the Sibal.

Whilst it is harder to control, and benefits are shared, joint development with an established company will provide access to existing resources and infrastructure and give faster market entry than the creation of a company. A JV may allow the Sibal to become the established market leader in India before other rival low cost tablets are developed. An alliance with a global PC manufacturer may also permit wider geographical coverage by giving access to other emerging markets.

The nature of the industry and its history suggests that product life cycles are often quite short and as a result Vicaro needs to exploit the opportunity as quickly as possible so a JV would seem to be the sensible option. Care will need to be taken in selecting the most appropriate partner.

Examiner's comments:

Requirement (b) asked candidates to explain the issues that Vicaro needs to consider when choosing an appropriate method of commercial development for the Sibal using three given headings: Resources, Control, Risks and Returns.

Most candidates had sufficient knowledge of the various methods of development to score a pass on this requirement although some comments were surprisingly uncommercial – eg a number of candidates made sweeping comments implying that licensing relinquishes all control and carries a high reputational risk when this is Vicaro's preferred current model and clearly therefore has some attraction. Better candidates related their knowledge to the issues presented in the scenario. Discussions of control and risk/return were normally quite well done although comments on resources were more varied. The key issue was to recognise that whilst Vicaro has the intellectual property it will need significant financial and other resources for the marketing, production and distribution of the Sibal. Given the dynamic nature of the industry and the relatively short product life-cycles identified in (a), Vicaro needs to exploit the IP as quickly as possible, making some form of co-operation attractive.

June 2012 exam answers

54 Palladium Printing

Marking guide

		Knowledge	Skill	Marks
(a)	Competitive forces in UK printing industry	3	7	10
(b)	Performance of PP	–	15	15
(c)	Draft letter	3	5	8
(d)	Strategic review	2	10	12
		8	37	45

General comments:

This question is the mini case and also the data analysis question. The scenario relates to a small company operating in the printing industry. The question provides details of the processes, products and markets relevant to the UK printing industry and sets out the competitive conditions within that industry. The company in question, PP, provides digital printing services and, to a minority of clients, graphic design services. PP has performed poorly in recent years, despite a boost to sales from the 2012 London Olympics. Financial and operating data for PP is provided. As part of a strategic review, a large potential new contract is being negotiated with a university where digital printing, using data management, can provide an added value service for the client. A further element of the strategic review is considering the closure of the graphic design function.

(a) **Power of suppliers**

Where suppliers are powerful then the prices of inputs can be forced upwards, thereby squeezing industry profits.

The key external suppliers to the printing industry are paper manufacturers as this makes up half of the variable operating costs (assuming that PP is typical of the industry).

The fact that paper manufacturers 'tend to be large, highly mechanised companies' means that the industry is concentrated, and that they have significant size and power by comparison to all but the largest printing companies (eg the 'few very large printing companies [which] generate annual revenues in the range £100 million to £500 million').

This may indicate that paper manufacturers have significant power over smaller printing companies to negotiate high prices and extract profits from the printing industry. The fact that the increase in transportation and energy costs incurred by paper companies appears to have been passed on in full to printing companies in the form of a 15% increase in paper prices appears to support the proposition that paper companies supplying the print industry have significant power.

There are however other factors which would affect the power of the paper companies:

- Given the size of the European paper industry there is a sufficient number of suppliers, at over 50, for there to be competition, despite needing to export to the UK and incur distribution costs. However, they may act in unison to pass on cost increases, particularly where they are systemic across the paper industry (eg energy costs)

- The paper manufacturers are reliant on the printing industry as a major customer group and thus their power is reduced as they may have few other industries to sell their output to other than print companies

Business Strategy answers   455

- The suppliers' product is a major cost for printers. There may therefore be greater resistance to paper price increases by printers as paper costs are a significant factor in determining profitability

- There is low differentiation between different suppliers' paper products as it is like a commodity, so switching is fairly easy for printers, thereby lowering the power of suppliers

- In a recession, there may be surplus production capacity for paper producers, thereby increasing the power of printers

- Ecological concerns mean the overall level of demand for paper is contracting, thereby further increasing the power of printers

Other suppliers to the printing industry may also need to be considered (eg machinery, land and buildings) but these are more generic and more information would be needed.

Substitutes

Substitutes are alternative products that can perform similar functions to those supplied by the industry in question.

The ready availability of close substitutes limits the demand and the price for the outputs of the printing industry. This drives down industry profits.

The most obvious substitute for printed output is electronic communication which may be provided and distributed more easily than printed materials and can have additional features (eg sound, real time updates, variations). This will limit the prices that consumers are willing to pay for traditional printed material, but may also increase the demands made from the format of printed output. It has been increasingly easy for consumers to switch to electronic communications as the internet has become more available in portable form, more sophisticated and more flexible. The variable cost of providing and distributing electronic communications is also extremely low.

Power of customers

The greater the power of customers the more they can put downward pressure on prices and reduce the UK printing industry's added value. The following factors are relevant:

- There are many printers in the industry (almost 14,000). While there may be differences of quality and service there are many choices available to customers so switching costs are likely to be low, giving customers' significant power over printers to negotiate price.

- There is significant variation in the size of printers (from very small to almost £500 million revenues) and in customers (from governments and large companies to individuals) so it is difficult to generalise about the effects of the relative size of customers on the printing industry other than to note that it is likely to vary significantly in various sectors of the industry.

- Purchases of printing services may represent a material part of some customers' costs (eg publishers) but a low proportion of other customers' costs. Again therefore there may be variation in resistance to industry price increases by customers.

Overall, industry profits are driven down by the power of some major customers and by their sensitivity to price increases.

Threat of entry

Threat of entry means that where companies can easily enter a profitable industry then high industry profitability can be competed away by increased supply and increased competitiveness.

A factor increasing the threat of entry is that the industry has relatively low differentiation of output and service (other than the digital or lithographic distinction) making switching to new entrants easier, as there may be little brand loyalty given the degree of commonality.

The low initial capital cost of digital printing makes the barriers to entry low in this sector, although they may be higher in the lithographic sector of the market where the costs of entry are greater (see below). The required skills to operate the machinery are likely to provide some additional barriers initially.

The barriers to entry for litho printing are much greater partly because of the high initial capital cost but also because of the ongoing fixed operating costs arising from long print runs.

Other factors decreasing the threat of entry:

- Low prices and losses in the market at the moment provide disincentives to entry
- Customer loyalty reduces switching

Overall, the entry barriers might appear to be low as there are disincentives to entry. Indeed the key question currently appears to be barriers to exit, rather than barriers to entry.

There is, however, a key distinction between the UK industry and the UK market. There may be low barriers to entry into the UK industry, but the barriers to the UK market are even lower when there can be imports from low-cost overseas producers, particularly the large scale, efficient producers in the Far East.

Competitive rivalry

Factors increasing competition:

- There are exit barriers where fixed costs are high or machinery is highly specialised. This may be true of the lithographic sector of the industry, but the fact that 'approximately 16% of UK printing companies ceased to trade in 2011' and that these were small companies is indicative that exit barriers are low for smaller digital printers.

- Industry demand has fallen, which means there is slack capacity, thereby increasing competition amongst existing companies for a reduced total market.

- Some of the printing companies are large, with economies of scale enabling them to compete strongly compared to smaller companies.

Examiner's comments:

This requirement requests candidates to evaluate the competitive forces in the UK printing industry using Porter's Five Forces model. The majority of candidates correctly identified all five forces and many provided conclusions as to the relative strengths of each force. The best answers also provided an overall conclusion regarding the relative attractiveness of the industry as a whole. A small minority incorrectly focused as much on the firm itself as the overall industry. A common weakness was to give equal importance to each of the five forces, rather than determining the key forces in this particular industry. Better candidates used the information (qualitative and quantitative) in the question to draw inferences about each force. For example the 15% price rise in paper indicated that paper suppliers were sufficiently powerful to pass on their own price rises in full, despite there being over 50 suppliers to choose from. Many candidates failed to distinguish between the competitive forces in the two sectors of the industry – litho and digital printing. Thus for instance the barriers to entry, and therefore the threat of new entrants, are very different in these two sectors.

(b)

	2010	2011	2012 (6 months)
Increase in printing revenue (annualised)		4.2%	6.4%
Change in variable operating costs (annualised)		7.0%	8.9%
Increase/(Decrease) in op profit (annualised)		(12.5%)	14.3%
Op profit %	3.3%	2.7%	2.9%
Revenue per print run £	2,050	1,969	1,700
Op profit per print run £	66.7	53.8	50
Revenue per million pages £	37,846	37,647	32,381
Op profit per million pages £	1,231	1,029	952
Paper cost per million pages £	12,154	12,426	10,952
Pages per print run	54,167	52,308	52,500
Revenue per employee (annualised)	82,000	85,333	90,667
Op profit per employee (annualised)	2,667	2,333	2,667
Increase in print runs (annualised)		8.3%	23.0%
Increase in pages (annualised)		4.6%	23.5%
Increase/(decrease) in paper cost (annualised)		2.2%	(11.9%)

Overall performance

In assessing performance over the period of 2.5 years there are a number of factors to consider in the case of PP and the information available:

(1) In comparing the reporting periods the final period is only 6 months so the data needs to be annualised to make valid comparisons. The processes of annualisation makes no assumption about what will actually happen in the second half of 2012, it is merely an arithmetic adjustment of a short accounting period in order to make a like-for-like comparison with an annual accounting period.

(2) There have been two random and exogenous events in the final two periods – one favourable and the other unfavourable – being the London Olympic Games and the increase in paper prices. In order to assess underlying performance it is necessary to attempt to view the performance in the absence of these events, or at least separately identify the contribution of these events, so a better notion of sustainable performance can be ascertained.

Tutorial note:

Performance appraisal involves not just explaining **what** has happened, but **how** it has happened and **why** it has occurred. A fuller explanation may also require identification of **when** events occurred in order to isolate their effect to sub-periods.

Printing revenues

Annualised printing revenues were £2.4 million in 2010, a period during which there was no benefit from the Olympic games. These revenues increased by 4.17% in 2011 and 6.4% (annualised) in the half year to 30 June 2012.

The increases may have been due to increases in sales volumes, perhaps in part arising from the Olympic Games which will not be sustained. Similarly the additional temporary demand in the industry may have meant that sales prices could be increased.

An alternative explanation for possible sales price increases is that there was a common increase in costs in the industry from increases in paper prices and some, or all, of this has been passed on to customers in the same way as paper manufacturers have passed on their cost increases to their customers in the printing industry. This explanation is consistent with the increase in variable costs and the decrease (from 2010 though not 2011) in net margin for PP despite the increased revenue.

In testing these propositions, the data indicates that there has been an increase in volumes both in terms of the number of print runs (8.3% in 2011 and 23% in 2012 annualised) and the number of pages printed (4.6% in 2011 and 23.5% in 2012 annualised).

As the increase in volumes exceeds the increase in revenue we see that revenue per print run and revenue per million pages have fallen. This may imply decreasing sales prices, but as the number of pages per print run has fallen in 2011 compared to 2010, it could also imply a change in product mix with a higher proportion of small print runs being taken on.

The data on revenue per employee reflects the fact that the increases in volumes and in sales revenues have been achieved with a workforce of constant size, thus demonstrating improved efficiency per employee.

Operating profit and costs

Operating profit fell in 2011 compared to 2010 (down 12.5%) but then recovered substantially in 2012 (up 14.3%) when the data is annualised.

In 2011 variable operating costs increased by 7% which is higher than the increase in revenue and, as a consequence, operating profit fell, despite the increase in revenue. To explain this increase, there are two key factors: the increase in volumes produced and the significant increase in paper prices. The price increase occurred 'at the beginning of 2011' so in identifying **when** this factor occurred it can be assumed that the cost of paper was higher for almost all the year.

Despite the increase in paper costs of 15% by suppliers, the cost of paper used only increased by 2.2% per million pages in 2011 compared to 2010. In 2012 the cost of paper per million pages actually decreased by 11.9%. This needs further investigation but possible reasons might be: purchasing poorer quality paper, less wastage, reduction in average size per page.

Estimating the impact of the paper cost increase, in order to isolate the effect, the following calculation can be carried out which takes into account (1) that paper is only 50% of variable costs and (2) that paper rose in price by 15% at the start of 2011:

	2010	2011	2012 (6 months)
Total revenue	2,460,000	2,560,000	1,360,000
Fixed operating costs	800,000	800,000	400,000
Variable op cost without paper price increase (W1)	1,580,000	1,580,000	860,000
Op profit ignoring paper price increase	80,000	180,000	100,000
Annualising 2012			200,000
% change		125%	11.1%

(W1)

2010   Unchanged
2011   (£845/1.15) + (£845k) = £1,580,000 (rounded)
2012   (£460k/1.15) + (£460k) = £860,000

Once the paper price increase effect has been stripped out, there is a 125% increase in underlying operating profit in 2011. Possible explanations are:

- Variable costs have decreased despite increases in volumes. This may be due to:

    - Smaller print runs (eg Olympic Games) or increased efficiency

    - Paper cost increases for PP may have been lower than the industry average

    - Use of opening inventory (eg if paper cost increase had been foreseen by PP and inventories accumulated at the previous cost levels then, particularly on a FIFO basis, this would lower cost of sales in the period)

- Increased revenues

Excluding the paper price increase (which is uncontrollable) then, subject to the above factors, there has been a significant increase in performance in 2011 compared to 2010. The temporary nature of the impact of the Olympic Games may however mean that this improvement is unsustainable, but no data is available to quantify this effect.

The improved performance in 2011 has been sustained in the first half year of 2012. After eliminating the paper price change, and annualising the 2012 data, profit improved by 11.1% in 2012 compared to 2011. Operating profit increased by 14.3% if there is no adjustment for paper prices.

Looking at the underlying causes of the improvement in 2012 there has been an increase in printing revenues of 6.4%, but also an increase in variable costs of 8.9%. The improvement in operating profit therefore means the company has benefited from high operating gearing. As a consequence, increasing sales volumes generated a high additional contribution and fixed costs remained constant.

While the Olympic Games affected both 2011 and 2012, it could be an explanation for the improvement in 2012, as there may have been a greater impact as the Games approached. However, any improvement in operating profit may have been temporary and unsustainable in the period after the Olympic Games, when there will be no further exogenous boost to demand.

Examiner's comments:

This requirement asks candidates to use the data provided to analyse and explain the performance of PP. Whilst most candidates calculated a few very simple ratios, a lot of answers were very brief and extremely general and did not go into sufficient detail, given the number of marks available. As in previous sittings, the weakest answers occupied the extremes of being either almost entirely qualitative or almost entirely quantitative in their approach. The better answers not only gave a balance of the two approaches but also linked them together by developing quantitative issues with appropriate narrative explaining causes and consequences. Many candidates failed to link the increases in volume and increases in revenue/costs together. Calculating revenue/cost per print run or revenue/cost per page printed would have assisted them in this. Hardly any candidate attempted to strip out the effect of the paper cost increase from other factors. Credit was given where some obvious attempt was made at this, even if the numbers were not always correct. Many candidates failed to deal well with comparing performance in a 6 month period with performance in a 12 month period. The weakest candidates either concluded that revenues/profits had decreased significantly in the 6 month period or just failed to deal with the issue. Other candidates recognised the issue but only in terms of comparison to the expected results for a full year after the remaining 6 months had elapsed. This slightly missed the point of making a comparison of historic performance during periods of unequal length, irrespective of what may occur in future. A number of candidates made no mention of the impact of the Olympic Games, despite this being highlighted in the question.

(c)

Palladium Printing Ltd
Address

11 June 2012

Dear Admissions Service

PP is pleased to make available to its clients the benefits of the latest variable data printing (VDP) software. We believe that Southern University will benefit particularly from this technology in the printing and distribution of its prospectuses to applicants.

Cost benefits

As you will be aware, your current printing suppliers use large scale lithographic printing. In the past, such a choice has been understandable as this delivered low cost per unit of output for large volume print runs compared to digital printing for comparable output.

However, lithographic printing is inflexible and can only print identical prospectuses, without tailor making to individuals' needs. If a student is only considering two or three courses then he/she only needs a small proportion of the total prospectus. PP's VDP technology enables only the relevant pages to be printed for each student and thus significantly fewer pages can be printed. As a consequence, there are significant cost savings for your university as:

- Paper cost savings enable competitive pricing for our clients
- Recent increased costs of paper magnify this effect
- There will be lower storage and handling costs at the university with smaller physical volumes
- Lower postage costs in sending prospectuses to student applicants
- Lower wastage as there are no unused prospectuses
- No need for short print runs after August to make up for poor initial estimation of quantities each year

Marketing benefits

Our VDP technology enables us to print a different prospectus for every individual applicant. This enables your university to market itself to particular students to maximise the probability that they will select your institution for their future education. The marketing benefits for your university include:

- No irrelevant materials describing courses or issues that the applicant is not interested in.
- Given the reduced size of the prospectus, there is opportunity to provide more detail on relevant courses which would not be practical in a single prospectus covering all courses.
- An opportunity to tailor-make other aspects of the prospectus. For example: highlight selected social activities where the applicant has already indicated that he/she has an interest; overseas or home-based student fees and concerns; accommodation details for non-local students only; gender specific issues.
- Opportunity to personalise each prospectus for each applicant (eg with their name or some other personal details declared on their application).

Environmental benefits

Many of the university's stakeholders will be aware of environmental issues and the carbon footprint involved in producing large quantities of printed paper. The scaled-down prospectus that could be produced by PP compared to lithograph printing would be a significant response to this concern given the large volumes of paper necessary in producing a prospectus.

Client service benefits

The use of PP's digital printing enables quick turnaround for urgent work and production of supplementary publications to applicants, which is not offered by lithographic printing. If small print runs are required for a small sub-set of applicants, this is also possible using digital printing.

Also, in the past, all prospectuses were printed in one print run. In future, the smaller monthly print runs lend themselves to digital printing, rather than lithographic printing, as the set-up time is lower and short-term adjustments can be made.

Conclusion

PP's digital printing using VDP technology offers a flexible product that can be tailor-made to your needs and avoids producing irrelevant material, thereby reducing paper costs and protecting the environment.

Yours sincerely,

Haraj Harris

H Harris
Marketing Director
Palladium Printing Ltd

Examiner's comments:

In this requirement candidates need to draft a letter to the university which explains the benefits to them of changing their printing supplier to PP. This part was attempted reasonably well, with candidates using the facts from the scenario and recognising the key advantages for SU. It was also extremely encouraging to see candidates digesting the requirements of the question fully and the presentation of answers together with the language and tone used was appropriate for the type of communication requested. Most candidates described in detail how the VDP system would benefit the university by allowing a more personalised approach. However a number of candidates produced narrow answers by failing to make many, or any, additional points (eg cost, environmental sustainability). Cost benefits to the university were less often referred to than marketing benefits.

(d) (i) **Price**

The total incremental cost of the contract would be:

$$[(20{,}000 + 32{,}000 + 35{,}000) \times £1.60] + (3 \times £11{,}600) \quad = \quad (87{,}000 \times £1.60) + £34{,}800$$

$$= £174{,}000$$

The average incremental cost per prospectus = break-even price to the university

$$= £174{,}000/87{,}000$$

$$= £2$$

(ii) **Graphic design proposed closure**

A firm decision on proposed closure seems difficult to make given the poor financial information available which appears to trace neither costs nor benefits directly to the graphic design function.

In terms of revenues, there appears to be interdependency between graphic design revenues and printing revenues as these services are supplied jointly on all graphic design contracts. PP appears to use an arbitrary rule of thumb of 10% of total contract price. This seems unlikely to be universally applicable and fails to discern a cause and effect relationship.

However, to the extent that revenues, as recognised, are valid, then the graphic design function only appears to be just covering its employee costs (assuming graphic design employees are paid the average for the company) ie:

Average salary   = £600,000/30 = £20,000 pa.

Graphic design wages =   3 × £20,000   =   £60,000 pa.

Graphic design revenue   = £60,000 pa

The financial viability of graphic design also depends on the other variable costs created by this function. This excludes the major variable costs of paper (solely used in printing) and wages (already considered) but other variable costs generated by graphic design need to be reviewed.

Even if graphic design does make a loss, there may still be reason to keep it open if other printing work is won based on PP's ability to deliver printing and graphic design together. The closure of graphic design may therefore lead to a lost contribution from printing.

As graphic design is 10% of joint revenues, then the printing revenues generated on joint contracts is £540,000 (9 × £60,000), so joint contract value is £600,000. This is a substantial proportion (23.4% in 2011) of total revenue which may be put at risk if graphic design is closed.

Conclusion

A better accounting system to identify costs and revenues with the graphic design function is required in order to make a more informed choice on closure. Even then, a good understanding of customer requirements is needed. It may well be that graphic design should remain open as a loss leader given the dependence of a significant amount of printing revenue on contracts requiring graphic design input.

Examiner's comments:

Requirement (d) has two parts. In (i) candidates need to calculate a multi-period break-even price for the university contract; and (ii) an explanation is required of the factors that PP should consider in determining whether it should close the graphic design section. In (d)(i) a reasonable number of candidates calculated the break-even price correctly, but many arrived at a figure of £1.93, which just looked at one year in isolation.

Answers to (d)(ii) varied in standard quite remarkably with the better candidates considering both the pros and cons of closing the graphic design department, considering employees, interaction effects with printing revenue, the fact that PP was regarded as a differentiator and the impact on costs in terms of interdependency or jointness. The poorer answers did not really get to grips with the requirements of the question and focussed on resistance and barriers to change, which did not answer the question posed. The poorest answers did not recognise the problems associated with the arbitrary calculation of the graphic design department's revenues.

55 Flambard Foods

Marking guide

		Knowledge	Skill	Marks
(a)	Value chain	5	9	14
(b)	Factors for FF board consideration	3	7	10
(c)	Market research	3	5	8
		11	21	32

General comments:

The scenario in this question relates to a company which is a low cost producer of frozen ready-made meals. The company, FF, is vertically integrated, owning a chain of retail outlets to sell the products it manufactures. The industry has become increasingly competitive recently and, as a result, FF is considering diversifying into the manufacture of chilled ready-made meals. In order to be distinctive in a crowded market FF intends to focus on three food styles in the chilled ready-made meal market: Polish, Lebanese and Vietnamese.

(a) (i)

FI	One factory, freezer warehouse, 50 shops, founder/main shareholder on board, tight operational and financial controls, low cost minimalist culture				
TD	Simple ordering systems, limited inventory control and payables management	Basic, old technology, simple automated systems	Own lorries used 24 hours per day		
HRD	Limited training (unskilled); employees replaced; minimum wage, strict rules	Limited training; employees replaced; minimum wage, strict rules	Limited training; employees replaced; minimum wage, strict rules	Limited training; employees replaced; minimum wage, strict rules	Own staff n shops
P	Bulk buying, low quality, managing supplier relationships, simple payables management	Machines: automated but simple processes	Purchased own vans		Few receivables (cash sales) so no admin for credit control
Primary activity	Constant amounts delivered, organised by suppliers, simple delivery systems	Simple automated machinery, low cost unskilled labour, small product range	Direct delivery to own warehouses by own fleet	Collected by customers; no advertising	Health and safety
	IL	**O**	**OL**	**M/S**	**S**

(ii) A value chain identifies the relationships between the company's resources, activities, functions and processes that link the business together and which create a profit margin. In essence it combines the firm's functional strategies necessary to achieve a business' overall strategy in order to create value.

The value chain can be used to examine linkages between functions and processes, where value can be created using the resources of a business to generate strategic options. Non-added value activities can be identified and reduced or eliminated.

The value chain can also be used to examine where value can be created using the resources of a business to generate strategic options. It can also help identify the cost drivers behind FF's least cost strategy.

The primary activities and functions are those that create value and are directly concerned with providing the product/service. The support activities do not create value of themselves, but they enable the primary activities to take place with maximum efficiency.

FF is pursuing a least cost strategy within Porter's generic activities and should thus focus upon low cost resources to produce a low cost product. This is reflected in the low labour and materials costs on the supply side and operating activities of the value chain and the delivery chain to customers via FF's own shops.

Low cost features are built in throughout the value chain including:

- Automated but simple production processes
- Low cost labour at the minimum wage for production and support staff
- Low cost produce which is mainly imported from Eastern Europe
- Costs of inbound logistics shifted to suppliers
- Small product range so longer production runs
- Efficient distribution system

FF can use the value chain to examine whether all activities (primary and supporting) are contributing to its least cost strategy and hence identify inconsistencies eg if the machinery is old and necessitating increased repair costs with production disruption, thereby reducing margins. In so doing it helps identify FF's source of competitive advantage.

The value chain can also be extended to the whole supply chain to ensure suppliers also contribute to the least cost strategy.

The value chain can assist in identifying further scope for cost reduction eg increase the number of potential suppliers so the company can shop around for best price or to invest in technology to make for more efficient production.

Examiner's comments:

Requirement (a) asks candidates to (i) prepare a value chain diagram for FF and (ii) explain the FF value chain and describe how FF creates value. Whilst it was apparent that most candidates understood and were well prepared for a value chain question, the standard of the actual value chains produced was quite disappointing. Most candidates made some attempt to relate the value chain to the firm's cost leadership strategy but for many this was very general. For weaker candidates, the value chain cells merely described what each of the headings related to, without applying it to FF specifically. Comments which were then provided often just repeated the facts from the question, without showing an appreciation of where each activity should properly fit or how it linked into the value chain. For example, in respect of procurement, candidates often just stated that low cost ingredients were purchased and then did not link that to how they were used in operations, the low cost machines used for production, and the fact that this then linked to the outbound logistics point with the fleet of lorries.

Of even more concern was the fact that some candidates appear to have totally overlooked part a(ii) and were unable to recognise the appropriate value and cost drivers or how FF created value. It was apparent that candidates had spent too much time and got far too involved in the actual presentation of the diagram for the value chain and had not focussed on using the information in the question and applying it to the analysis. The best answers provided an applied description of the value chain cells and a good discussion of the coherence between primary and support activities in delivering the firm's cost leadership strategy.

(b) Within the Ansoff matrix, the proposed commencement of production and sale of chilled meals is product development (ie same market but a different product).

Favourable factors

- **Higher margins** – chilled foods have higher margins than frozen foods so a similar level of sales will generate more profit.

- **Growing market** – chilled foods is a growing market in the UK, while frozen foods is a declining market. With a small market share, frozen foods could be seen as a 'dog' product in the BCG matrix, being in the declining phase of the product life cycle. Conversely chilled foods could be seen as a 'question mark' or 'problem child' in the expansion phase of the product life cycle.

- **Common suppliers** – there may be cost savings as the food needed for chilled and frozen meals is similar and thus there are common suppliers and efficiencies.

- **Common customers** – if chilled meals are to be sold through FF shops then there are likely to be common customers and thus common marketing opportunities built on access and reputation.

- Common production facilities prior to chilling/freezing are likely to lead to some cost savings through economies of scale.

- **Distribution** – the distribution network from factory to shop is common for frozen and chilled meals. This generates economies of scope. This is particularly the case if FF lorries can be adapted to take both chilled and frozen meals.

Unfavourable factors

- **Capital investment** – there is a risk that, if the venture fails, the realisable value of assets purchased will be low and therefore there is a risk of high exit costs.

- **Core competences** – it is questionable whether the core competences established in frozen meals will be appropriate for the manufacture, distribution, storage and marketing of chilled meals.

- There may be brand confusion between a least cost product in frozen food and a high margin chilled product in chilled meals.

- The new storage and distribution technology may not easily transfer to chilled food and it may displace capacity for frozen meals whose operating efficiency may suffer.

- **Sales displacement** – if customers buy FF chilled meals, these sales may displace sales of FF frozen meals thereby limiting the benefit of market entry.

- **Competitive market** – although chilled meals is a growing, high margin business at the moment, there is evidence that it is increasingly competitive, with low cost offers available from existing market participants.

- **Floor space displacement** – space in the FF factory and shops, currently occupied for the benefit of frozen foods, may be displaced by chilled meals. This may reduce frozen meals' operating efficiency.

- Inventory management may be a much more complex issue given the disparity in shelf life of frozen and chilled products.

Examiner's comments:

Requirement (b) requests candidates to explain the factors that the FF board should consider before deciding whether to enter the chilled ready-made meals market. In this requirement, a significant number of candidates failed to structure their answers or use models from the learning materials to assist them in evaluating the proposed strategy. Some answers were particularly one-sided and only assessed the benefits or the problems of the venture. Most candidates commented that this was a growing market but there was lots of competition and finance would be needed. Often, answers were not developed beyond that. Higher marks were awarded to the candidates who used suitability, acceptability, feasibility, Ansoff or the BCG matrix. Some good points were made on the problems faced in entering a new market and how there may be some brand confusion. Good marks were also awarded for candidates who took a resource based or core competence approach highlighting for example capacity, skills of staff, storage and distribution.

(c) Market research is the systematic gathering, recording and analysing of information about problems relating to marketing of goods and services. Market research therefore involves gathering information about the 4Ps of marketing.

The particular focus of market research for FF is whether there is a demand for the three particular types of ethnic cuisines proposed (ie Polish, Lebanese and Vietnamese cuisines).

In particular, the key objective for market research in this case is to determine the likely volume of customers and the most appropriate prices. Relevant to this objective are the following:

Place: There may be varying demand for the three cuisines in different parts of the UK eg where there is a high Polish population then this type of cuisine may be more popular. This means that any market research is only likely to be valid with respect to a particular location. The idea of assessing a national demand may be too abstract without specific locations and therefore is likely to be largely invalid.

Price: The price that potential customers are willing to pay is clearly a specific objective of the exercise of assessing viability. Again this may vary throughout the UK according to demand and income levels.

Product/service: In this case, there are three separate products so they need to be evaluated separately not as a composite whole. It needs to be considered in terms of the attributes that are likely to generate demand (eg convenience, taste, shelf life, volume). This may vary not just between the three cuisines, but within them, according to cooking styles and regional variations with the three countries.

Promotion: As a new venture, the initial impact of advertising and other promotion on price and demand should be considered.

Market research types

The two broad areas of market research are:

- Desk research
- Field research

Desk research

Desk research is the gathering and analysis of existing or secondary data. This is likely to be of background significance in establishing the characteristics of the potential market identified, but is nevertheless important.

In particular, this might relate to the total size of the market: for the UK; for a particular city; or for the region around a specific FF shop.

Data sources for total market size may include:

- Industry publication of market size and growth of similar ethnic cuisines including prices

- Data on popularity of restaurants selling each of these cuisines (trade magazines)

- Existence and extent of market for these three cuisines by supermarkets already, including prices

- Ethnic population and distribution statistics for three relevant groups (government statistical sources)

Field data

Data sources may include:

- Surveying local supermarkets for volume of sales of ethnic food of these three types or similar types

- Observing prices of ethnic ready made chilled meals

- Questionnaires of existing customers (tastes, volumes, price resistance)

- Questionnaires of local potential customers (tastes, volumes, price resistance)

- Sample tastings for existing customers

- Sample tastings for local potential customers

Examiner's comments:

Requirement (c) asks candidates to describe the market research that should be undertaken before entering the chilled ready-made meals market. Candidates were very familiar with desk and field research and the differences between the two. Answers again were often very general and merely gave an outline description of the types of research. Only a minority focused on the stated objective for the market research ie determining the likely volume of customers and appropriate prices. Similarly only a minority discussed market research in any detail with respect to the three proposed cooking styles as required by the question.

56 Keeler Kinetics

General comments:

The listed company in question, KK, manufactures small electrical appliances for use by consumers, having been spun off from a large multinational electronic company. KK's business model is to make products with attractive designs, rather than leading edge, technologically advanced products. The company believes it is doing the right thing strategically but has made losses in the first year of trading and is facing questions from analysts. It is therefore seeking ways of measuring its performance that do not solely rely on financial measures. An ethical issue has also arisen whereby a new employee, Jack, who had previously been a business adviser in the industry, is offering to make possibly confidential information from previous clients available to KK.

(a) **Financial perspective (how does the company look to shareholders?)**

CSF/goals	KPIs
Operating losses (stability)	Changes in operating losses
Revenue (growth)	Revenue growth Revenue from each product
Shareholder value (added value)	Return of capital employed Share price changes
Liquidity (survival)	Operating cash flows Projected cash balances

The recognition that losses will be made in the next few years does not prevent an assessment of the financial perspective in terms of the scale of the losses and how they are changing over time.

For a loss-making company, liquidity is an important financial measure. Liquidity needs to be controlled if the company is to survive a difficult period and return to profitability in the longer run with the new strategy.

Customer perspective (how do customers see the company?)

KK's new business model attempts to present a changed product and a changed brand image. KPIs need to measure whether the company is being successful, over time, in changing customers' perceptions of the company/brand/products. This is particularly the case as the same brand name is being retained. A favourable brand image will lay the foundation for future profitability and sustainable competitive advantage.

Internal perspective (what must the company excel at?)

CSF/goals	KPIs
Quality of service	Delivery lead times
Employee utilisation	Productivity per employee
Quality of staff	Training course (number, type) Results from training courses (qualifications, skills attained, new procedures introduced)
Quality of product	Number of returns inward Number of claims on guarantees

Reliance on design does not mean that technology can be ignored. Customers are likely to require acceptable levels of technology (including reliability, quality and durability) even if they do not need the latest features.

Similarly production efficiency is important in terms of labour productivity particularly if cost control is a key element in returning to profit as suggested by the CEO.

Innovation and learning perspective (how to continue to improve and create value?)

CSF/goals	KPIs
Design leadership	Number of design awards Time to develop next generation of design Market recognition (surveys, industry articles, questionnaires)
Employee satisfaction	Staff turnover Staff complaints Employee ideas used
Impact of innovation	% of sales from new designs or products
Technology capability	New features on products – time lag behind first introduction by market leader (compare to 2-year target)

The new business model no longer requires the company to achieve technology leadership in the market place. Design leadership is however essential if products are to appeal to customers above rival products. The response to, and consequences of, new designs are therefore vital (financial and non-financial) as this is the new core competence to give competitive advantage.

Examiner's comments:

Requirement (a) asks candidates to prepare a Balanced Scorecard for KK and explain why each of the four perspectives and the KPIs within this scorecard are important to KK. This part was quite poorly done by many candidates. Some candidates tended to explain each of the perspectives but did not actually set out a balanced scorecard for KK with relevant KPIs and CSFs. Conversely other weak candidates prepared a balanced scorecard but did not explain each of the perspectives. It was apparent in this section that candidates found it difficult to apply their knowledge to the scenario. Where KPIs were produced, they were often non-specific and demonstrated a failure to consider the facts which were given in the question. For example, the question explicitly informed candidates that KK had, and would continue to experience, operating losses, yet one of the KPIs offered was often operating profit %. Hardly any candidate stated that an appropriate KPI would be to look at changes in operating losses or indeed the liquidity of the company. When KPIs were offered, there was a notable absence of CSFs or goals for each KPI which was very disappointing. In terms of the customer perspective, CSFs and KPIs described could have been those for any business and it was not obvious that the candidate was discussing KK specifically. Whilst customer satisfaction is relevant to all businesses and customer feedback is vitally important, there was much information in the question regarding the brands, type of product and the general market that could have been used to produce some high quality answers. The internal perspective was generally acceptable, but KPIs were written without linkage to CSFs. With innovation and learning, some facts from the question on the technology and appetite for new designs and products could have been used, but answers again tended to be very general and merely focussed on employees' satisfaction which resulted in some very restricted KPIs.

(b) In general terms, ethics are 'the moral principles governing or influencing conduct'. From the perspective of business ethics, this is a system of behaviour which is deemed acceptable in the society or context under consideration.

Professional bodies have specific ethical codes which bind members (eg ICAEW) but there is no suggestion that Jack is a chartered accountant and is thus not bound by this code.

Ethics can also be viewed at the individual level (Jack) and the corporate level (KK). The consideration here is with respect to KK.

A key ethical issue is that of legality.

This relates not just to whether KK is acting legally, but whether Jack has acted illegally and whether KK will knowingly take advantage of Jack's actions. KK therefore has an ethical obligation to make itself aware of the legality of the actions of its employee, albeit that they occurred before he became an employee.

If Jack has been an independent adviser then he will have been acting under a series of consultancy contracts. Almost certainly these will have contained confidentiality clauses.

Copying of company data therefore seems likely to be in breach of the contract (a civil transgression) but may also be criminal act.

The use of wider knowledge gained seems less likely to be an issue in terms of KPIs, as this is general industry knowledge. Company data is more of an issue as it is specific but probably cannot be remembered without reference to the copied files.

Legal advice should be taken but, if Jack has acted illegally, KK should not benefit from those actions and may consider dismissing Jack.

To the extent that Jack has acted legally, then additional ethical considerations apply. The key ethical principle here is confidentiality and whether, even if there is no legal duty of confidentiality, there is an ethical duty to keep confidential information obtained as part of a private agreement.

In making a decision as to how to act, KK may refer to the Institute of Business Ethics three tests:

- Transparency
- Effect
- Fairness

Transparency – would Jack's consultancy clients mind other people knowing the details of their KPIs and data of achievement? This test is partly about whether the action required contravenes business ethics principle of confidentiality and whether it is 'doing the right thing' – it is not about whether Jack can get away with the behaviour, provided he is not found out. In this case, if the information is private and confidential then transparency may not be appropriate in terms of making files available. General unattributable use of knowledge by Jack however seems implicit and acceptable in any contract.

The other issue of transparency was whether it was known and acceptable to Jack's clients that he copied and retained the files and whether Jack has, or could obtain, any evidence of permission.

Effect – who does the decision affect/hurt?

In this case, the rival companies whose data has been extracted may suffered a comparative disadvantage if Jack reveals not just the data itself but the source of the data. Moreover, it could be argued that KK will obtain an unfair competitive advantage over all rivals by illicitly obtaining better measures of strategic control.

It should be noted that Jack is not asking to benefit by direct payment, but he may hope to benefit indirectly as a more effective employee.

Fairness – would the decision be considered fair by those affected?

The issue for KK is that they are being asked to benefit from confidential information. In the context of business ethics, KK's behaviour, if they accept the information, is to gain an unfair advantage over rivals.

Conclusion

What Jack is offering KK to his employers is access to information that is not otherwise readily available in the public domain and was gained by virtue of confidential agreements.

CC might want to seek advice regarding the legality of such an action.

There does however appear to be a difference between (i) detailed copied file information being made available which appears, without evidence to the contrary, to be a breach of confidentiality and (ii) general use of knowledge and experience acquired as an adviser which clients would have perceived Jack would probably use in general terms on other advisory clients.

Examiner's comments:

Requirement (b) asked candidates to assess the ethical implications for KK of accepting either of the offers from Jack. The structure of answers often looked at transparency, fairness and effect. However, this structure was sometimes applied rather inflexibly thereby limiting the scope of candidates' answers to look beyond these three issues. What was needed was an appreciation of the facts and issues first. The transparency, fairness and effect structure is a valuable approach in assisting in making a decision on how to act. What was missing from the answers was the preceding step, where the issues should have been identified. The key issue in this question was that of confidentiality of data and whether there was a breach of that confidentially and consequently if the use of the data was legal. Some candidates did spot the issue and some good answers were produced, but others focussed on Jack's integrity overall. There was also a lack of distinction between the two proposals. The second proposal of using experience to set KPIs was not as contentious as the first proposal to use other firms' actual data. Candidates, however, treated both very suspiciously and advised often against either proposal.

57 Bigville Council

Marking guide

			Knowledge	Skill	Marks
(a)		Key stakeholders	2	5	7
(b)	(i)	Breakeven	–	4	4
	(ii)	Implications	–	9	9
(c)		Business case	3	11	14
(d)		Key risks	2	6	8
			7	35	42

General comments:

This is the mini case and also the data analysis question. Bigville's rugby club is in need of a new stadium with greater capacity as a result of its recent league success (the current stadium is leased from the local council). The local football club is in a similar position. The city council have been approached by the rugby club to consider the creation of a community stadium which could be partly funded by sale of the existing stadium land to a developer for a retail site. The council has undertaken an initial feasibility study and is considering the high level business case for the venture. There is demand for a shared stadium with facilities for rugby, football and athletics, plus a range of additional commercial and community uses on non-match days. Land has been identified which would meet the necessary planning criteria. Either a basic stadium can be constructed, with a shared pitch for rugby and football and community sports facilities, or the Council can spend more on an enhanced stadium with a hotel and conference centre. Additional funding would be available in terms of grants provided certain criteria are fulfilled and a sponsorship deal could be sought with a large credit card company, Finanex, whose HQ is in the city. The stadium is likely to be run by a joint stadium management company (SMC) created by the Council and the two clubs.

Candidates were provided with a range of data concerning the build cost, capacity, forecast revenue and costs for each element of the stadium, and attendance figures for comparable rugby/football clubs.

This question was well attempted by most candidates.

(a) Stakeholder conflict

The clubs and the Council will have different objectives, which will themselves be linked to their different stakeholders. Key stakeholders for the clubs will include the players, the fans and the governing body. Key stakeholders for the Council will be residents, local businesses, the wider community and central government.

The Council as a Not For Profit (NFP) organisation has a wider range of stakeholders and is likely to have to balance the use of limited resources to ensure it provides the best possible services and maximises benefits for the wider community. The clubs are likely to have two main aims:

- To achieve the best sporting success possible in order to retain/attract new fans
- To generate as much profit as possible in order to be able to acquire better players

In certain cases these aims may coincide with the Council's eg if the clubs achieve sporting success, this will generate additional attendance and income which will increase the wealth of the stadium and facilitate the Council's objectives. However there is also scope for conflict between the individual clubs and between the clubs and the Council:

Construction of the stadium:

The clubs are likely to be predominantly interested in the main stadium and pitch. There may be conflict between them as to the best layout and surface of the pitch for their particular requirements. Each club will be interested in any stipulations or health and safety regulations set out by its ruling league body. Since the football club is contributing more capital, it may expect priority over decisions.

The Council will also be interested in the additional community facilities and there may be conflict between the Council and the clubs if the siting or construction of these is seen to negatively affect anything in relation to the main stadium eg a running track around the pitch may cause the fans to feel separated from the game. Similarly the environmental sustainability of the stadium is of key importance to the Council whereas this may be a low priority for the clubs, particularly if it affects the visibility of fans or anything to do with the playing surface or training/changing facilities. The clubs may also be reluctant to pay additional capital costs for community facilities.

The two clubs may also conflict on the seating capacity if for instance there is little prospect of the rugby club ever being promoted and filling a larger stadium but there are realistic prospects of the football club achieving the new capacity. The clubs may also disagree over the size and nature of the playing surface.

Operation of the stadium:

Again the clubs are likely to have their own interests at heart. Although the clubs typically play matches on different days there may be conflict between them over scheduling of training and cup match scheduling.

Similarly if the rugby club has a big championship match on a Sunday they may not take too kindly to the football club having churned up the pitch on the previous day.

The clubs are likely to want priority over the use of the stadium on match days and for weekday training sessions (unless, like some professional clubs, they have access to separate training pitches). Weekday use may conflict with the Council's desire to make the stadium available for the community. Also the Council may want to use profits generated by the stadium to cross-subsidise the use of the community pitches for example, which may conflict with the clubs' profit motives.

Similarly the Council may want to hire out the stadium for events such as concerts. These may benefit the clubs by attracting a wider audience however the clubs may be concerned about the impact that such events might have in terms of damage to the stadium or the playing surface.

Sharing of joint costs between the Council and the clubs is also likely to be an issue.

Operational Issues for the Council will include: crowd safety and security; noise, lighting, energy, waste management, traffic and transport. In respect of these issues the clubs will be focussed on the needs of the clubs and their fans, whereas the Council will also need to take into account the needs of the wider community which may conflict with those of the fans/clubs.

Clearly the arrangements for the SMC will need to be carefully established and agreements drawn up to minimise the potential for conflict between the parties and to protect the interests of the Council.

Examiner's comments:

Requirement (a) requested candidates to assess the potential for conflict between the three key stakeholders (Council, rugby club and football club). On the whole this was very well done. The majority of candidates recognised that the Council was a not-for-profit organisation and were able to discuss the potential for conflict between the clubs – who were likely to be focussed on commercial and league success – and the Council's need to satisfy the wider community (and possibly the stadium sponsor). Better candidates also pointed out that in addition to this conflict, there was also likely to be conflict between the two clubs over the type of pitch, match scheduling etc, and that the football club might expect to have priority given that it was contributing a larger share of the capital. In their desire to apply models, candidates must be selective – a number of weaker candidates had learnt and churned out Mendelow's matrix which tended to result in too much focus on power and interest rather than on conflict between stakeholders. Some weaker candidates also dwelt exclusively on the stakeholders' objectives and did not get round to conflicts at all.

(b) **Break even**

    (i) **The break even attendance is as follows:**

Contribution per visitor

Football   £640,000/(25 × 3,200) = £8

Rugby   £270,000/ (15 × 3,000) = £6

Break even

Football £644,000/£8 = 80,500 visitors p.a which with 25 matches = 3,220 per match

Rugby £214,000/£6 = 35,667 visitors p.a which with 15 matches = 2,378 per match

    (ii) **Discussion**

Implications of calculations

The BE attendance for the football club is marginally higher (by 20 visitors per match) than the attendance figure used in the forecast, which explains the predicted loss (20 × £8 × 25 = £4,000).

The BE figure is 12.5% higher than the current attendance enjoyed by the football club and 5.6% higher than the average for the league. Thus the projections may be quite optimistic and if the initial attendance is below this figure then the football club will make a bigger loss than predicted. (It can be seen from the appendix that there is a loss of £71,400 based on current attendance and a loss of £34,000 based on the average for the current league.) It would be useful to know what the capacity of the existing football ground is and whether, like the rugby club, it is already at full capacity.

In respect of the rugby club the BE figure is 6.4% higher than the current attendance (which would result in a loss of just under £13k) but 16.3% lower than the average for the league. As the club's existing ground appears to be at capacity there is likely to be an implied waiting list of fans wishing to attend and so the estimated attendance level of 3,000 seems reasonable and provides a margin of safety of 20.7% (3000 – 2378/3000).

Variability of attendance levels

The attendance and financial performance of any sports club is heavily dependent on its team's performance. Thus the financial success of both the football and rugby club will depend on their ability to retain their current league position or the chances of being relegated/promoted, which can be seen from exhibit 1 to significantly affect attendance levels.

(On average, attendance levels for football clubs are 64% higher in the league above and 41% lower in the league below.)

As the break-even levels of attendance for both clubs are above the average attendance for either club in the lower league, then relegation of a club would lead to significant losses or the need to curtail costs. The financial impact of promotion/relegation is set out in the Appendix, based on the figures for a typical club in the league. These calculations make it clear that the profitability of the football club is much more at risk than the rugby club because of the high level of traceable fixed costs (discussed further below). As a result the potential results for football range from a loss of £284k if relegated to a profit of £356k if promoted, which compares to a loss of £43k and a profit of £146k for the rugby club.

In addition to variations in attendance, success in non-league tournaments during the year would lead to more matches, further increasing profits. Each additional football match would contribute an additional £25,600 on projected attendance levels, with an extra rugby match generating £18,000. Using the expected attendance levels provided, it can be seen from the appendix that 26 football matches and 12 rugby matches would be more than sufficient to break even.

To better assess the accuracy of the forecasts and the likelihood of profitability, it would be useful to know each club's position in the current league to assess the likelihood of promotion/relegation. Also the attendance levels and number of matches for the previous two or three seasons would indicate any trend – in reality the attendance is likely to vary between matches depending on the recent success of the team and who the opposition is.

Revenues and costs

The calculations of break-even attendance depend on assumptions about the average spend per visitor, contribution and traceable fixed costs. If the forecasts have been based on existing ticket prices and spending on merchandise/catering, these may increase with the new stadium, in which case the contribution per visitor might increase and the required attendance would be lower. A breakdown of the average spend per visitor between ticket price and merchandising and details of the different ticket prices, which presumably include concessions for the young and elderly, would be useful.

One of the reasons the football club is predicting a loss is because its traceable fixed costs are significantly higher than those of the rugby club leading to a greater variability of profits if relegated/promoted. This may be because of the level of wages in the market place for footballers but more information is required here.

Appendix: Financial analysis

Estimated profits at various attendance levels: £'000

	Current attendance	If relegated	League average	If promoted	Per forecast
FOOTBALL					
Attendance	2,863	1,800	3,050	5,000	3,200
	£	£	£	£	£
Contribution	572.6	360	610	1,000	640
Fixed costs	644	644	644	644	644
Profit	(71.4)	(284)	(34)	356	(4)
RUGBY					
Attendance	2,234	1,900	2,840	4,000	3,000
	£	£	£	£	£
Contribution	201.06	171	255.6	360	270
Fixed costs	214	214	214	214	214
Profit	(12.94)	(43)	41.6	146	56

Sensitivity to number of matches

	Fixed costs	Forecast contribution per match	BE no of Matches (fixed cost/contribution)
Football	£644,000	640,000/25 = £25,600	25.16
Rugby	£214,000	270,000/15 = £18,000	11.89

Examiner note:

A variety of calculations were possible and other sensible approaches involving marginal increases/contribution would have attracted credit.

Requirement (b)(i) asked candidates to calculate the breakeven attendance figure per match for both rugby and football and then (b)(ii) to discuss the implications of the variability of attendance on the forecasts, providing supporting calculations.

Answers to b(i) were good with a large number of attempts scoring full marks. The most common mistake was to provide the answer in the form of annual attendance rather than per match. Only a small minority seemed unfamiliar with the breakeven formula or divided fixed costs by revenue instead of contribution.

Answers to b(ii) were slightly more disappointing ranging from a discussion with very little use of supporting data, to a set of calculations with no discussion. The key issue here is that the breakeven attendance for football is in excess of that currently forecast, whereas rugby has some margin of safety, although it is not clear how the traceable fixed costs (which are considerably higher for football than they are for rugby) have been arrived at. The calculation also makes assumptions about the number of matches and is based on average spend per visitor which will almost certainly vary. Using the data provided for the 'average' club to estimate attendance, it is evident that the forecast for match profits will not be realised if either club is relegated since they will be loss making, and conversely that league promotion would considerably increase the profits available. Also the risks arising from variability in attendance are higher for football than rugby. This was capably demonstrated numerically by the better candidates. Candidates would be well advised to note that when supporting calculations are asked for, it is very hard to produce a high-scoring discussion without reference to at least some numbers.

(c)

Report
To: Bigville Council
From: A N Consultant
Date: September 2012
Re: Community stadium

The council has identified three criteria which it will use to assess the high level business case:

(a) Ability to raise finance
(b) Commercially sustainable venture
(c) Alignment with council's overall strategic priorities

(1) **Ability to raise finance**

The costs of the proposed stadium are as follows:

	£m
Stadium construction	6.75
Community facilities	3.25
Basic stadium	10m
Additional level	1.1
Expanded stadium	11.1m

Currently the following funding appears to be available:

	£m
Sale of council land	6
Club contributions	3
Finanex payment for naming rights	1
	10m

Thus the Council would appear to have sufficient funding in place for the basic stadium, with a shortfall of £1.1m if the additional conference and events facilities are built. The forecasts suggest that an enhanced stadium would increase profits by £250,000 p.a. which means the additional investment would payback in less than 4.5 years (1.1m/250,000) and therefore appears on the face of it to be worthwhile.

It would be useful to know what information the build costs have been based on and whether these make any allowance for potential overruns which are often incurred on this type of project. The amount budgeted and actually spent on comparable stadiums would help assess whether the costs being put forward by the Council fall within the range of other stadiums.

If a 10% allowance was made for overruns and the Council wished to build the enhanced stadium then they would need to find around £2m extra finance. It appears that some grant funding may be available and the Council needs to ascertain the amount that is likely to be forthcoming and the relevant conditions attached (which appear to be quite closely linked to the Council's own priorities in terms of employment, participation in sports and environmental sustainability).

A significant element of the finance is to come from the sale of the land so any uncertainty over the price or timing of this would need to be considered. For example work may need to start on the new stadium before the old one is demolished and the Council will need to ensure sufficient finance is available. In addition the Council is likely to have limited resources and therefore has a duty to consider the opportunity cost of using the money for the stadium in terms of the other projects that require funding.

Overall the initial findings suggest that there is a viable funding proposition provided the Council can find a suitable buyer for the land and receive some grant income. If this is not forthcoming then the Council would need to draw on any existing reserves or use debt finance. An alternative might be to consider the costs of building a smaller stadium since at 6,000 seats the capacity exceeds the maximum attendance for either club if promoted to the league above.

(2) **Commercially sustainable venture**

Basic stadium	Football	Rugby	Non-match	Total £
Club income				
Current profit/(loss) from clubs	(4,000)	56,000		52,000
Other income				
Community pitches/sports facilities			50,000	
Stadium advertising/sponsorship			200,000	
Revenue from non-match day activities			187,000	
			437,000	
Costs				
Stadium running costs			(375,000)	
				62,000
Overall surplus				114,000

Enhanced stadium		
Incremental costs/revenues		
Non-match day activities (537 – 187)	350,000	
Advertising (250 – 200)	50,000	
Stadium running costs (525 – 375)	(150,000)	
Additional income generated		250,000
Total surplus (114,000 + 250,000)		364,000

The financial projections suggest that the basic stadium would generate £114,000 of annual surplus, increasing to £364,000 for the enhanced stadium (this is before the interest cost associated with any borrowing requirement, and assumes the forecasts of revenue and costs from the clubs are achieved).

This equates to a ROCE of 1.14% (114k/10m) for the basic stadium and 3.3% for the enhanced (364/11.1m). More importantly the additional tier generates a return of £250,000 on an investment of £1.1m (22.7%) and would therefore seem to be a sensible option.

The commercial viability of the venture is quite heavily dependent on the ongoing sponsorship to be received from Finanex. Without this the basic stadium would generate a loss (ignoring match revenues/costs) of £138k, with the additional commercial activities from the enhanced stadium leading to only a small profit of £62k. If the venture fails however the Council will still be in the position of owning the land on which the stadium is built.

One of the considerations for the Council will be the extent to which it shares in the profits generated by the stadium. Were the clubs to keep their own profits/losses then the predicted income for the Council would be £62,000 from the basic stadium and £312,000 from the advanced. However it appears that the suggested agreement is for the SMC to pay rent to the Council for the stadium and for the members of the SMC (of which the Council is one) to then share the profits/losses from its operation. It is not clear whether the costs of the lease are included in the forecasts provided and what the nature of the profit sharing agreement between the three parties to the SMC will be. To better assess the commercial viability from the Council's perspective it would be useful to compare the Council's share of the incremental costs and revenues of the proposed stadium with the current situation where the Council receives lease payments from the rugby club for its existing ground.

(3) **Alignment with council's overall strategic priorities**

Bigville Council's recently stated strategic priorities are:

- To maintain and develop Bigville's successful economy and provide suitable employment opportunities for residents

- To ensure accessible opportunities for all to engage in culture, leisure and recreational activity

- To promote and provide support for local people to make healthy lifestyle choices

- To create, enhance and maintain cleaner, greener and safer environments

Basic stadium

A shared community stadium should provide job opportunities and if the stadium is used for events on non-match days eg concerts this may attract more visitors to the area, thus stimulating the economy. However the existing football and rugby grounds are likely to employ local people currently and amalgamation of two grounds into one may actually lead to a reduction of jobs in some cases.

Providing a new and improved stadium is consistent with the Council's aims of ensuring accessible leisure and recreational activities and promoting healthy lifestyle choices. The all-weather sports pitches and athletics track will be of benefit to Bigville's clubs, schools and colleges, thus increasing the opportunities available in the area for local people to have a healthy lifestyle. Concerts and other events on non-match days may also increase the cultural activities available.

Finally the design of the stadium appears to focus on environmental sustainability. However, it would be necessary to assess in more detail the impact on the environment of the construction activities and then the ongoing running of the stadium in terms of pollution, noise, use of resources etc.

Enhanced stadium

The extension of the stadium to provide a conference and exhibition centre is likely to significantly increase local employment opportunities, attract more visitors to Bigville, provide opportunities for its businesses and provide more economic benefit than the basic stadium.

In addition it will widen the scope of the activities available in the area. There may also be operating synergies which help the Council to minimise the costs involved in the provision of services or cross-subsidise the community activities from the profits generated by corporate hospitality etc.

Thus the plans for the community stadium do appear to be aligned in overall terms with the Council's four stated priorities and the enhanced stadium is likely to improve rather than worsen the strategic fit.

Conclusion

There does appear to be a positive high level business case for the shared stadium and the preliminary indications are that the enhanced stadium would be the most commercially viable and more likely to help achieve the Council's strategic priorities. The Council should arrange a meeting with the key stakeholders to discuss the project, their requirements and their potential involvement and then create a steering group to take the project forward and undertake a more detailed financial analysis and feasibility study.

Examiner's comments:

In requirement (c), candidates were required to write a report to the Council assessing the high level business case for the stadium using the Council's three stated criteria from the scenario: ability to raise finance; commercial sustainability and alignment with strategic priorities. Generally candidates made a good attempt at assessing the ability to raise finance. The vast majority produced calculations showing the estimated costs of construction and the amount of finance already secured, recognising that cash was available to fund the basic stadium but that government grants would be required to build the enhanced version. The better answers pointed out the risk of over-runs and also the fact that there may be some uncertainty associated with the sale of the land to the developer. The evaluation of commercial sustainability was less well done, with the weaker candidates concentrating their discussion on the environmental aspects of the stadium (thereby overlooking the commercial element of sustainability) or merely reiterating their discussion of the variability of match profits, already addressed in (b)(ii). Using the projections in the scenario it is clear that the enhanced stadium increase profits significantly and that the additional £1.1m investment would be worthwhile. The best candidates pointed this out, some producing ROCE or payback calculations which were encouraging, and a number recognising the reliance on income from the sponsor. Only a few candidates pointed out that the Council has a dual role – as lessor of the stadium (which will guarantee a fixed rental income) and as a partner in the SMC (which will entitle them to a share of the profits (losses). Candidates felt more comfortable evaluating whether the stadium met the Councils' strategic priorities, although surprisingly few discussed whether these were better met by the enhanced rather than the basic stadium. The weakest candidates simply made passing reference to the stated priorities and failed to analyse whether and how the stadium would achieve these. Disappointingly some candidates continue to ignore the presentation mark available for formatting their answer appropriately (in this case as a report) and the marks available for further information and a preliminary conclusion (both of which were specifically asked for). Better marks were scored by those candidates who attempted to tailor their request for further information to the scenario.

(d) **Risks**

The risks for the Council in relation to the construction of the stadium and its operation by SMC include the following:

Construction

Funding requirement

Risk arises because of the uncertainty regarding the level of capital requirement and the funding available, especially in terms of grants. Should there be a shortfall then the Council may need to find more capital by diverting it from other needs or by borrowing.

The Council may not find a developer willing to buy the land on which the existing stadium is built or one who is prepared to pay the asking price for it. Even if the sale can be arranged there is a risk that it takes time and that construction of the new stadium needs to be started before the finance from the sale of the land is available. Local residents may also decide that the money would be better spent on services such as health and education.

There are uncertainties regarding stakeholder commitment to the project. It is unclear how the football club for example would react to a shared stadium and to the fact that they are contributing more capital than the rugby club. In the current economic climate Finanex may face budget constraints and decide that it has higher priorities to spend its money on.

A major capital cost overrun, which is not uncommon in such projects, would leave the Council with the residual funding risk.

Location and planning

It appears that a site has been earmarked but a potential risk is that it turns out not to be suitable. Planning permission for the new venture is critical. There is a risk that issues arise during the construction period in relation to the environment eg protestors complaining about the impact on the landscape or local residents unhappy about the noise/traffic etc.

Timing

Any delays in construction, as well as increasing costs, could result in adverse publicity for the Council if the clubs do not have a stadium to play in at the start of the season.

Construction company

The council will need to ensure that the building contractor is carefully selected in accordance with policy to avoid the risks associated with the work not being done properly.

Operation by SMC

The current plans are for an SMC jointly controlled by the Council and the clubs. The joint venture potentially reduces risks for the Council (as does the receipt of an annual lease payment) but an agreement will need to be carefully drawn up to minimise the potential for conflict between the parties and to specify profit sharing arrangements, contributions to ongoing costs etc.

Financial

As discussed in (b) and (c), the financial models are dependent on a number of assumptions and estimates. The Council should undertake more detailed sensitivity analysis/scenario planning to get comfort regarding best and worst case scenarios. Should the venture be loss-making, or Finanex decide to cease their sponsorship, the Council is likely to have to provide further ongoing support/financial assistance.

It appears that the profits of the whole venture will be shared between the three parties but this needs to be clarified. If one or other club starts to perform poorly and/or gets relegated this would cause the stadium to become financially unsustainable and would affect the SMC's ability to make the lease payments.

Alternatively the clubs may be expecting to retain match-day profits in which case the SMC may only share the profits from the rest of the stadium and conferencing. This may reduce the amount of community activities that can be undertaken as the Council is likely to need a share of the profits from the clubs to subsidise such initiatives.

Legal

There is likely to be a range of regulations affecting the Council, its role and powers and, in particular, the Council's legal position if the revenue targets are not achieved.

Changes in regulations of the rugby and football governing bodies may also affect the stadium and/or the number of matches eg there is a risk that increased pitch specifications or health and safety requirements increase the running costs.

Other stakeholders

As commercial entities, the clubs may have more in common with each other than they do with the Council and, if the objectives conflict, the Council may find itself in a minority over certain decisions, resulting in the venture not achieving its strategic priorities.

There is a risk that the clubs fall out or that one of them becomes insolvent and that, as a result, the Council loses one of the parties to the joint venture. Any change in ownership and/or management of the clubs may significantly affect the venture. For example if the football club is acquired by a wealthy investor it may decide that it wants a stadium for its own use.

Examiner's comments:

Requirement (d) requested candidates to consider the risks for the Council associated with the construction of the stadium and its operation by the stadium management company (SMC). This was the least well done element of question 1. Most, but not all, candidates split their discussion between construction and operation, although some candidates chose instead to structure their answers by using a model such as PESTEL and as a result sometimes lost focus on the specific requirement. A common weakness was to produce a list of risks that would be faced by all parties rather than specifically the council and to make only passing reference to the SMC. In this regard better answers were produced by those candidates who clearly appreciated the dual role of the council (referred to above) and their position as stakeholder within the SMC.

58 Beauty Soap

			Knowledge	Skill	Marks
(a)	(i)	Strategic models	3	4	7
	(ii)	Appropriateness of BB's plans	2	6	8
(b)		Standardisation v adaptation	2	3	5
(c)		Merits of the two options	3	5	8
(d)		Ethical marketing	2	3	5
			12	21	33

General comments:

The scenario in question 2 concerned Beauty Soap (BS), a large UK based company which manufactures and sells personal care products throughout Europe. BS was established in the 1900s as a soap producer. It grew organically by investing in research and development to expand its product range, then later by the acquisition of a number of competitors and also a European dental care company. BS wants to reduce its dependence on the European market which is mature and where margins are under pressure. It is keen to expand into Latin America, as forecasts suggest there is considerable growth potential, particularly in countries like Brazil. BS is considering two options: organic expansion using a direct selling model of local workers, or the acquisition of Gomera, a local personal care business with existing product range and supply chain/distribution networks. Preliminary research has suggested that the local market needs smaller products sizes and lower prices than BS's European product model. BS has also recently announced plans to launch an education campaign, in conjunction with the governments in the countries in which it operates, promoting the regular washing of hands with BS soap to reduce infection and disease.

The question provided scope for a limited amount of data analysis as candidates were given brief information about sales revenues in the European personal care industry as a whole, together with those for BS and the market leader.

This question was also well attempted by the majority of candidates.

(a) (i) **Growth strategy**

Lynch expansion matrix is a two by two matrix of company growth (internal and external development) and geographic location (home/domestic and international).

Under this model BS's initial growth was carried out internally in its domestic market – the UK. After establishing itself initially as a household soap manufacturer BS used research and development to generate internal organic growth through new products such as shampoos and face creams. BS's growth then continued externally through acquisition. This occurred first domestically with the acquisition of the UK based dental care business and then internationally with the acquisition of other European companies making personal care products.

BS is now proposing further international expansion in respect of Brazil, but has not yet decided whether it will undertake this by internal or external development.

The Ansoff matrix is another two-by-two matrix, of products (existing and new) and markets (existing and new). Relating product opportunities to markets gives rise to four possible strategies:

Market penetration – involves selling more existing products to existing markets. In the case of BS it started as a household soap manufacturer and quickly penetrated the market due to the range of sizes and fragrances on offer.

Product development – selling new products to existing markets. BS did this initially by investing in research and development to expand its product range from soap to shampoos, face creams etc. Later BS further developed its product range in the UK by acquiring a company specialising in dental care products – an area where BS perhaps lacked expertise to develop the product itself internally.

Market development – new markets for existing products, usually requiring an investment in marketing. BS pursued this via acquisitions of personal care product manufacturers in Europe. It is likely that this route offered a faster method of entry to the market and potentially got round barriers to entry. The proposed expansion to Brazil is another example of market development.

Diversification: new products for new markets – BS does not specifically appear to have done this, however an example might be the acquisition of a perfume manufacturer based in America. Since the single-use products proposed for Brazil are already being sold to a European hotel chain this does not really constitute diversification.

(ii) **Current position and appropriateness of targeting new markets**

Current market position

BS is currently operating in Europe, a market which appears to be mature. If we consider the data provided, the overall market for personal care products in Europe has shrunk by 6% between 2010 and 2011. Since prices are under pressure this could be due to a fall in average selling prices rather than sales volumes. BS's share of that market was maintained at 3.8% in both 2010 and 2011 but the 6% reduction in the size of the market has led to a 27m euro drop in BS turnover.

Relative to the market leader BS has performed slightly better, generating 30% of their revenue in 2010 and 32% in 2011.

More information is needed to ascertain the European market trend and exactly where personal care products are in the industry life cycle. At this stage of the life cycle the European market may still offer good profit and cash generating opportunities and it is likely that people will continue to buy personal care products so the market decline may take some time. However for a sustainable future and growth opportunities, BS may need to look elsewhere.

Under the BCG matrix, BS's UK and European business might be deemed a cash cow (or possibly a dog) and its desire to expand in Latin America could be seen as an attempt to create a star.

Appropriateness of targeting emerging market:

- Reduces dependence on core European market and spreads risk given threat to margins

- BS may face less rivalry initially in developing markets such as Brazil compared to mature markets and hence enjoy better margins

- The stage of the industry life cycle will be different in Brazil etc where markets are still developing, which offers opportunities for better cash flow and profits over a longer period

- Western brands may be very attractive in this market so it could be a good opportunity to increase sales volumes

- Economic growth will boost demand and industry forecasts for personal care products are promising

- Expanding internationally outside Europe widens brand and image so BS becomes a more global company – this may also help strengthen its position in Europe

- It may help address any seasonality in terms of revenue and cash flow

- Competitors are doing this elsewhere (eg the three multinational companies already in Brazil)

- There may be financial arguments for setting up eg grants/incentives from local governments

However BS should be aware that there may be some downsides:

- Increased risk of operating in unknown, emerging markets. BS will need to invest time and money to understand the needs of the local market

- Political and legal risk eg as demonstrated by the Brazilian government attitude to foreign owned companies creating value; any quotas/tariffs/restrictions on free trade; any specific regulations to comply with

- Economic and transaction risk – to date BS has only exported to Europe and been exposed to exchange rate risk in terms of the Euro

- Existing competition – multinationals will be large with economies of scale; domestic competitors have the advantage of local knowledge. Will BS have any distinct competitive advantage over these players? Also as other markets are predicted to grow other companies may be considering expanding

- Will BS have sufficient resources and management skills to exploit the opportunity eg language skills, ability to recruit local workforce?

- BS needs to consider the extent to which it needs to adapt products/marketing for other markets – these costs, when taken with the additional distribution costs and the exchange movements, may mean the margin is no better but the risk is higher

  If expansion is deemed appropriate, the method of expansion chosen may help to reduce some of the risks/downsides

Examiner's comments:

Requirement (a) was split into two parts. Part (i) asked candidates to use relevant models to analyse the ways in which BS has chosen to expand historically and its plans for Brazil. Part (ii) went on to request a discussion of the appropriateness of its strategy to move away from the European market and target other international markets. Overall this requirement was answered very well. There were a number of ways to approach an answer to (a)(i) – as a discussion of organic growth/acquisition; products and markets; or domestic and international expansion. Those candidates who used Lynch's model and/or Ansoff's product/market development matrix to structure their answers tended to achieve higher marks. It was pleasing to see that the majority of answers were very specific to the scenario, identifying how BS had initially used R&D to expand organically through product development and then used acquisition to target other products and markets. In (a)(ii) most candidates used the data in the exhibit to identify that whilst the European market had declined between 2010 and 2011, BS has retained its market share, which has increased in relation to the market leader. Whilst further information would be necessary to confirm the trend, this suggests that the European industry may be reaching the mature stage of its lifecycle and that other markets, at an earlier stage of development, might offer more potential for future growth. Quite a lot of candidates identified the scope to use either the BCG matrix or life cycle model here as a starting point for discussion. The better candidates realised that this was not a case of BS immediately leaving the European market, rather that to ensure future prosperity it should continue the expansion strategy discussed in (a)(i) by finding new markets and/or products offering better potential. Some weaker candidates let themselves down by applying the BCG model very literally and concluding from the data that 'BS should shoot the dog.' Better answers were less categorical, recognising that there is some degree of uncertainty within the BCG categorisation. Sadly, some candidates wasted time here by starting to discuss the methods of expansion being proposed for Brazil, despite a specific instruction to ignore these for this requirement.

(b) **Standardisation v Adaptation**

Products can be classified according to their degree of or potential for global marketing:

Local products – suitable in a single market

International products – have the potential to extend to other markets

Multinational products – adapted to the perceived unique characteristics of national markets

Global products – designed to meet the needs of global market segments

The global/local dilemma refers to the extent to which products and services can be standardised across national boundaries or need to be adapted to meet the requirements of specific national markets because of different social and cultural conditions. Adaptation may involve changes to the actual product (involving changes in production) or to the method of promotion (brand, price etc) or some combination of the two.

Whilst standardisation tends to bring benefits in terms of economies of scale it may fail to target the market needs appropriately. Conversely adaptation is likely to involve greater costs, as a minimum in terms of R&D and marketing, but may increase competitive advantage.

The multinational personal care companies have expanded into Brazil using their existing globally branded products. Gomera on the other hand is currently producing a product which is only being sold in a single market – Brazil. It appears that for the market in Brazil, BS believes it has no choice but to adapt its product for financial reasons because its standard European product is not affordable for a significant element of the domestic population. It would be interesting to see how BS products compare in size and cost to the existing products in the market place and to what extent this view is backed up by further market research. BS does however have the advantage that it already produces single-use products for the European hotel chain which should help to reduce the costs involved in adaptation.

The other choice available to BS (and other international companies) is whether to retain its manufacturing in a limited set of locations so as to exploit economies of scale and then distribute a standard product internationally, or whether to set up production facilities in South America.

Examiner's comments:

Requirement (b) requested candidates to discuss the need for global companies to consider standardisation/adaptation of products. On the whole this requirement was poorly attempted and answers here were polarised. Some candidates clearly appreciated the nature of the problem and produced good answers discussing the trade-off between economies of scale in production and marketing on the one hand and satisfying the needs of different consumers and market places on the other. Others appeared to confuse this with Porters generic strategies and discussed cost leadership vs differentiation, and some weaker candidates missed this requirement out completely.

(c) **Method of market development**

Lynch's expansion method matrix would identify the two options of acquisition vs. direct investment as external development (acquisition) vs. internal development (organic growth).

Acquisition of Gomera, the local company, comes with the following advantages:

- Existing knowledge of the environment and local market providing useful initial expertise

- An instant skill base in terms of resources, employees etc is likely to mean faster growth

- It provides access to existing supply chain and distribution networks reaching into remote parts of Brazil

- A locally known established brand and reputation with an existing customer base – this may be viewed more favourably by the Brazilian government and consumers than a foreign owned brand. Once the acquisition has occurred BS can then start to introduce its other products.

- Acquisition buys out a potential competitor and better enables BS to compete with the other two domestic companies

- There are likely to be synergies as BS can provide the advertising and product innovation that Gomera is lacking

- Gets round any barriers to entry in terms of resistance from the Brazilian government

- Capitalises on the market opportunity more quickly, which may be important if other European companies are also considering expansion in Brazil

Direct investment offers the following merits:

- Gomera may not be an ideal partner in terms of size or market positioning and there may be a conflict between strategies if BS is seen as a premium producer compared to Gomera. With direct investment BS is free to pursue its own strategy.

- The price BS is required to pay for Gomera may not be appropriate. Organic growth avoids paying for goodwill therefore BS can acquire a larger tangible asset base for the same cost as acquisition.

- May offer a chance for more gradual expansion and an opportunity to test the market by exporting products from Europe to be sold locally under the direct selling model before then investing in production facilities in Brazil.

- Organic growth creates a business with the same culture as BS thereby avoiding any conflict etc on integration.

- The Brazilian government may look favourably on the direct selling model proposed by BS and there may be grants or other incentives available.

- Avoids any hidden or unforeseen losses that do not come out as part of due diligence on Gomera.

On the face of it, it would appear that acquisition is probably preferable, however the final decision as to the most appropriate method of expansion will probably depend on the price that BS is likely to have to pay for Gomera and the premium on acquisition.

Examiner's comments:

Requirement (c) asked candidates to discuss the relative merits of the two methods of expansion being considered for Brazil. This was very well done. As usual candidates were well prepared for a discussion of organic growth vs acquisition and the majority undertook this in the context of the scenario. Only the better candidates picked up on BS's proposed use of the direct selling model and questioned where BS was planning to produce the products. Those candidates who attempted to reach a preliminary conclusion as to the better method of expansion attracted higher skills marks.

(d) **Social and Ethical marketing**

The marketing concept suggests that a commercial organisation's goals are best fulfilled by identifying customers' needs and providing products which satisfy those needs efficiently and profitably.

The concept of social or ethical marketing extends this idea to see marketing as a social force that reflects and influences cultural values and norms. Thus marketing can extend beyond economic considerations and be used to promote the welfare of society as a whole. Here the social aim of BS's campaign is for improved education and hence better health, thus BS could argue that through marketing it is providing information and helping people make informed choices.

Marketing of BS soap to promote a healthier way of life is designed to instil awareness of the need for hygiene and then to create a behaviour change whereby people wash their hands more often – educating people re standards of hygiene could be argued to eradicate disease and enhance the benefits to society. Thus BS are using the education campaign to promote a global caring image whilst there are clearly additional commercial benefits for BS in terms of getting its brand name and soap products known. There is potentially an even wider benefit for BS in that it will increase awareness of personal hygiene as a concept which will have knock on benefits for the demand and sale of BS's other products such as shampoo.

The concept of responsible marketing suggests that companies should consider the wider social implications of their products and the needs of society at large. Thus BS's decisions to employ a team of direct sellers might be seen to help increase the wealth of local people and alleviate poverty; it will also help reach remote areas.

The BS campaign could be said to link the desire to improve education and welfare with the commercial reality of expanding the business's sales. To this end the interests of the company and the Brazilian government are aligned and soap could be seen as a product that will do social good by meeting people's functional needs.

Critics might argue that such marketing is actually just manipulative selling. The production of soap may involve chemicals which damage the environment, use of soap may pollute local water supplies, and access to clean water and street sanitation is more likely to have a significant influence on health and disease than the use of soap.

They would see BS as wasting the considerable resources needed to engage a Brazilian footballer in the campaign just to convince people to buy products they don't need, and using promotion to convince them that they will be dissatisfied or even unhealthy without them. The motivation might be seen to be to tap into a large potential market in the developing countries, when perhaps the domestic population would be better continuing to use more natural products or the traditional techniques available.

Also ethics could be considered in terms of whether BS is genuinely behind this as a concept – applying it to other countries etc – or whether it is simply a way of getting the Brazilian government to accept the company in the market.

Examiner note:

Candidates could choose to apply the legality/transparency/fairness/effect model here:

Legality – BS does not appear to be doing anything illegal

Transparency – BS appears to be being quite open in its plans

Fairness – there is nothing to stop other personal care companies doing the same thing (though Gomera for instance may not be able to pay the high fees of the footballer) and indeed there is nothing to stop consumers buying other soap products.

Effect – by raising awareness and creating education BS could be said to be having a positive effect on the local community.

Examiner's comments:

Finally part (d) asked candidates to assess the ethical implications of the proposed educational marketing campaign. This was poorly done by many candidates. There seems to be a tendency on the part of weaker candidates to approach the ethical requirements with great suspicion and to assume/conclude that what is being proposed is automatically unethical. A high number of candidates thought that the use of the Brazilian footballer was totally inappropriate and that in poorer countries it was unfair to try and influence people into buying anything at all (or indeed to wash their hands), with many focussing on the vulnerability of people in schools and hospitals. Some did apply the transparency, fairness and effect decision making approach, which tended to improve the quality of the answer by at least ensuring they were talking in ethical terms and applying a structured thought process. Only the best candidates provided an initial discussion of ethical marketing principles and concluded that linking marketing with corporate social responsibility is not necessarily unethical (manipulative selling). Some did question however whether the cost and high profile of using the footballer might undermine an otherwise reasonable attempt at CSR and ethical marketing. Answers to the ethics requirement, which is a consistent feature of the exam, continue to be variable and candidates wishing to score well are advised to adopt some form of framework for their answer and to produce a balanced argument rather than a one-sided discussion.

59 Maureen's Motors

Marking guide

		Knowledge	Skill	Marks
(a)	Generic strategy and market positioning	3	4	7
(b)	Service marketing mix	5	7	12
(c)	KIPs	2	4	6
		10	15	25

General comments:

Maureen's Motors is an eponymous insurance company that focuses its product on insurance for female drivers by offering benefits tailored to women that are not offered by most insurers: it provides additional cover for handbags and contents, pushchairs and car seats, and it has a network of female-friendly repairers and a helpline giving advice on all vehicle-related matters. Three famous actresses played the three Maureens in a long-running TV advertising campaign and MM then ran a competition to 'make me a Maureen' for ordinary women to star in their TV and billboard advertising campaign. Because of its brand image the current customer base for primary policy holders is 90% female. Since industry statistics show that women make significantly fewer claims than male counterparts and typically claim for lower amounts, this mix allows MM to make superior profits.

Like questions 1 and 2, this question was well attempted by most candidates.

(a) **Generic strategy and market positioning**

Competitive positioning can be viewed in a number of ways but essentially means giving a product or service a place relative to its competitors in terms of factors such as quality, price, image etc. A sustainable competitive advantage can be achieved where there is the ability to outperform competitors in the long run.

Porter identified two distinct generic strategies: cost leadership and differentiation.

A cost leadership strategy attempts to achieve the position of lowest cost producer which facilitates competition on price. Differentiation strategy assumes that competitive advantage can be gained by creating attributes of the product or service which customers value and are prepared to pay a premium for. Such a strategy can be pursued broadly across an industry eg Direct Line insurance which offers a range of cheap telephone/internet based insurance products, or by concentrating attention on one or more segments of the market (focus) eg SAGA who provide insurance and other products for the over 50s.

MM appears to have adopted a focus-based approach within Porter's model, targeting a particular segment of the insurance industry (motor) and within that a specific market niche (female drivers).

The concept of generic strategy has been developed further by considering a possible spectrum of price/quality combinations from low price, low quality/added value (a no frills strategy) through to a high priced, high added value strategy of focussed differentiation.

MM has created differentiation through its product features and also its marketing.

The additional benefits offered by its insurance product suggest that MM has attempted to differentiate its service (through female friendly repairers, helplines, additional cover for handbags and car seats etc). It has also attempted to create a strong lifestyle brand image via use of the 3

Maureens and competitions. Whilst the product attributes may be relatively easy for other insurers to copy, the strong brand image may be harder to replicate.

Another way of looking at the issue of market positioning for MM is through Kotler's 3 Cs: cost, customers, competition. This view sees the price/quality trade off in relation to competitors as the key issue. Competition for MM will come from other companies who decide to operate in the same market niche eg Sheila's Wheels and also from the generic motor insurance products offered by the wide range of general insurance companies. Parity pricing would see MM's price and quality as equivalent to competitors – at below parity price sales may be made at the expense of profitability; above parity MM's product will be uncompetitive if identical products are available from competitors at lower prices. This is where the importance of brand comes in to reinforce perceived value, since MM customers who are loyal to the brand may feel they are getting a superior product, even if the basics of the cover are the same, and therefore may be prepared to pay more for it.

Examiner's comments:

Requirement (a), which asked candidates to explain the strategy and positioning of MM, was very well attempted. The majority of candidates were well-prepared for a discussion of Porter's generic strategies and almost all identified MM as a differentiator, using appropriate information from the question, such as the provision of handbag cover and replacement car seats, to illustrate this. Some, but not all, recognised that instead of applying differentiation industry-wide, MM has focussed this strategy on a particular market niche resulting in a customer base that was 90% female. Whilst the weaker candidates restricted themselves to Porter, the better candidates also discussed positioning in relation to competitors and price/quality, pointing out that MM was likely to be at the higher end of the market when compared to the large motor insurers. A number also provided a discussion of Bowman's clock. Some weaker candidates spent too long on this requirement for the marks available, leaving themselves short of time for (b).

(b) **Marketing strategy**

Target market

MM appears to have taken the results of some preliminary market research and used it to identify potential customers that it wants to target: women drivers. It has then tried to address the fact that insurance is seen by many as a 'grudge' purchase and developed a concept of a certain lifestyle to appeal to this target market. Finally it has developed its car insurance service by considering the product benefits that are most likely to appeal to a female market eg handbag cover, female friendly repairers.

MM then needs to develop a marketing strategy to attract this target market, which can be considered using the marketing mix (the set of variables which a firm blends to produce the response it wants from its target market). In MM's case this includes the traditional 4 Ps (Product, Price, Place, Promotion) and the additional 3Ps for service industries (People, Processes and Physical evidence). Attracting customers in the first instance is key to market share since industry statistics suggest that women are then less likely to switch insurer.

Product

This refers to the qualities of the product as perceived by potential customers. MM's product offering is made up of three elements:

- The basic or core product which is motor insurance

- The actual product which in MM's case is motor insurance specifically tailored for women and finally this leads to:

- The augmented product consisting of the insurance services that MM believes women particularly value and are prepared to pay for eg female friendly repairers, additional cover for handbags, vehicle advice line etc.

Emphasising the fact that the service is particularly tailored to women will distinguish MM from the general motor insurers and is key to success.

Promotion

The MM brand is critical and promotion must be consistent with this and reinforce the image and alignment of the brand with the 3 Maureens. Advertising is likely to be the most important means of achieving this, hence the TV advertising campaign starring well known actresses has lead to coverage in women's magazines. Using the 'Make me a Maureen' competition strengthens the concept of MM being 'a reassuring brand for real women with real lives'. MM has created a strong brand image at relatively low cost but ongoing promotion will be required to maintain this, particularly if it continues to attract adverse publicity.

Brand recognition can be tested through market research.

Price

MM's pricing policy needs to be appropriate to the wider marketing strategy and consistent with its competitive positioning. The price that potential female customers are prepared to pay for additional benefits can be ascertained through market research. Given the differentiation strategy female customers may be more likely to be attracted to MM for its brand image and benefits its policy offers (perceived value pricing) rather than because it is necessarily the cheapest in price, although MM needs to consider the prices charged by competitors for similar products.

The EU directive means that MM cannot price discriminate between equivalent men and women but elements of the insurance package may be priced separately eg children's car seat cover may not be required by all women. This would also facilitate the product being offered to male drivers who otherwise may not be prepared to pay MM's higher prices for services which they do not value eg additional cover for handbag contents.

The pricing of insurance premiums is a largely risk-based actuarial calculation and so the cost of cover will vary depending on the nature and age of the vehicle, the age of the policy holder etc. The pricing strategy is also likely to include discounts for no claims and MM offers a loyalty bonus which will help retain customers and market share. It also offers discounts through a friend referral scheme.

MM should consider how people pay for their insurance eg it may charge a premium for people who wish to pay by instalments rather than annually. It may also decide to offer a discount for online purchase or for new customers.

Place

Place does not appear to be a key factor in the mix as it is not mentioned in the scenario. MM's products are likely to be sold through remote distribution channels (phone and internet), rather than face to face, and primarily online. MM could consider a possible agreement with certain car manufacturers to promote MM insurance along side new car purchases.

The people involved in this process will be key for MM and so the extension of the 4Ps to the 7Ps model for the marketing of services is relevant.

People

Recruitment of the right staff and training and development will be key to offering good female friendly customer service otherwise the attrition rate will be high.

Customer service staff taking calls and handling claims and those staffing the vehicle advice line will interact with customers and be key to providing a high quality service consistent with the MM brand and its association with the 3 Maureens.

The quality of the service offered by MM will also be heavily reliant on the female friendly repairers and MM will need to have a code of practice, training and monitoring to ensure this is adhered to.

Processes

As part of customer service, efficient administrative processes underpin a high quality provision. Processes need to be female friendly but also efficient. The speed of handling claims and making payments will be critical. If true, the adverse coverage in the newspapers suggests that MM has some work to do to improve in this area.

Technology can be used to ensure efficient processes for taking calls/selling policies/handling claims.

MM also need good processes to hire staff who are perceived by customers to be female friendly and who have the appropriate knowledge if they are manning the vehicle advice line. There will also need to be processes in place to manage the network of repairers and ensure the provision of replacement car seats.

Physical evidence

This is probably of minor importance but refers to items that give substance or evidence of the delivery surrounding MM's service eg. tangibles such as the MM logo, claim forms, cover letters and policy documents. MM could also brand the replacement car seats and send out free tax disc holders or key rings to those renewing policies.

Examiner's comments:

Requirement (b) asked candidates to discuss the marketing mix adopted by MM. Again the majority of candidates were well-prepared in respect of the knowledge for this question, with most recognising the fact that the service nature of the business meant considering the extra 3Ps (people, processes and physical evidence) in addition to the normal 4Ps of product, price, place and promotion. The aspect that was least well addressed was how to prioritise the 7Ps in relation to the facts in the question. The better answers identified the elements of the mix which were more important to MM and extracted salient information from the scenario to explain how these had been tailored to the target market. Some weaker candidates simply explained what each P represented rather than discussing how MM has chosen to use the various elements of the mix to market its insurance services. A significant minority limited their scores by discussing the 3Ps only, when it was very clear from the scenario that product, price and promotion were also relevant factors.

(c) **KPIs**

MM has been criticised for concentrating on new customers rather than existing ones. If this criticism is valid then MM needs to set targets for and measure the improvement in customer service and claims handling. Possible KPIs are as follows:

Note: candidates were expected to produce 3 KPIS in total, with at least one covering each area – more are however included here for marking purposes.

Customer service KPIs	Explanation
Average score from customer feedback surveys regarding claims handling/use of vehicle advice helpline/speed of response	An increase in this score over time would suggest that customers' satisfaction is increasing
Number of complaints – again split by the different elements of the service	If MM measures the % decrease in complaints received it can assess how effective the steps to improve service have been. By measuring the types of complaint MM can ascertain whether it is their staff or their associates (eg the car repairers) that are the cause of the problem
Number of referrals by customers to friends	An increase in the number of referrals would suggest that more customers are satisfied enough to recommend MM
Claims handling KPIs	
Speed of claim settlement	A reduction in the time taken to process and settle claims would indicate greater efficiency and a higher level of service for customers

Number of claims processed per employee / Case load per employee	Measuring the workload per employee and their productivity would help assess whether MM has allocated sufficient resources to this area
% of claim paid out	Customers will be keen to ensure that they receive the maximum possible amount of their claim and that they do not lose out due to any small print on the policy

Examiner's comments:

Requirement (c) asked candidates to explain and justify three KPIs that could be used to assess MM's claims handling and customer service. This was in the light of recent criticisms of both and the suggestion that MM cares more about attracting new customers than retaining existing ones. This part was quite poorly done by some candidates, who were clearly unsure about the distinction between KPIs and goals. For the weaker candidates, KPIs described could have been those for any business and it was not obvious that the candidate was discussing MM or specifically its need to improve claims handling and service to existing customers. Whilst customer satisfaction is relevant to all businesses and therefore customer feedback is vitally important, there was much information in the question, regarding the nature of MMs service and the recent criticisms, which could have been used to produce some high quality answers. The better candidates produced a reasoned justification of their choice of measure and demonstrated clearly how this could be used to track improvement in the relevant areas. Some candidates provided a long list of KPIs, despite the specific request for only three – these additional measures wasted time and did not attract marks.

60   Grassgrind Garden Mowers

Marking guide

			Knowledge	Skill	Marks
(a)	(i)	Analysis of performance	–	15	15
	(ii)	UK market share	2	3	5
	(iii)	Competitive positioning	2	5	7
	(iv)	Growth strategy	3	9	12
(b)		Ethical issues	2	4	6
			9	36	45

General comments

This is the mini case and also the data analysis question. The scenario relates to a company manufacturing lawnmowers (GGM). The company manufactures two types of upmarket, petrol-powered mower for use by UK households: tractor mowers and conventional mowers. The company is subject to a take-over bid by BB, which the GGM board is defending. A key issue is the proposed future strategy of BB, in comparison to the defensive strategy of the existing GGM board. The candidate is in the role of a business adviser for the accountants (PP) representing the existing GGM board. PP has been asked to prepare a report evaluating GGM and aspects of the bid strategies. More specifically, candidates are required to:

(i) Analyse the performance of GGM, and of each of its two products, in the financial years 2011 and 2012;

(ii) Determine the current UK market share of GGM, highlighting any problems that arise in defining market share in order to produce a useful figure;

(iii) Explain the competitive positioning of GGM in the UK mower market, and assess how this has changed between 2011 and 2012;

(iv) Compare the growth strategy of the GGM board with that of BB. Make relevant calculations and refer to appropriate strategic models.

In addition, candidates are required to explain the ethical issues that arise for GGM from a request by a potential new overseas customer to modify its mowers, but which may call into question health and safety aspects of the mowers.

(a) (i)

From: Business Adviser
To: GGM independent report to shareholders
Date: XX December 2012
Subject: Assessment of strategic plans

| | 2011 | | 2012 | | 2011 | 2012 |
	Conventional mowers	Tractor mowers	Conventional mowers	Tractor mowers	Total	Total
INCOME STATEMENT	£	£	£	£	£	£
Revenue	3240000	5400000	2952000	5076000	8640000	8028000
Variable cost	1944000	2700000	1771200	2820000	4644000	4591200
Contribution	1296000	2700000	1180800	2256000	3996000	3436800
Fixed cost	911250	303750	885600	338400	1215000	1224000
Profit	384750	2396250	295200	1917600	2781000	2212800
Profit/revenue %	11.9	44.4	10.0	37.8	32.2	27.6
% change in revenue			−8.9	−6.0		−7.1
% change in vc			−8.9	4.4		−1.1
% change in contribution			−8.9	−16.4		−14.0
% change in FC			−2.8	11.4		0.7
% change in profit			−23.3	−20.0		−20.4
% change in volume			−8.9	4.4		

2011
Conventional mowers

In 2011 conventional mowers made a contribution per unit of £160, giving a contribution margin ratio of 40%.

The profit per unit after allocating fixed costs was £47.50, giving an operating profit margin (using the method of allocation of fixed costs adopted by GGM) of only 11.9%. This reflects a high proportion of fixed operating costs in the cost structure and therefore a high degree of operating gearing.

In drawing any conclusions about the performance of each product, however, the validity of the operating profit figures depends largely on the validity of the method of fixed cost allocation. While all such allocations are arbitrary (to a greater or lesser extent) the allocation by unit of output seems to be inappropriate in determining a cause and effect relationship between fixed operating costs and production activity. This is particularly the case as the tractor mowers are significantly larger, and probably more time consuming to produce, meaning it is likely they will require more fixed costs.

Based on the information available, it is not possible to produce an accurate allocation (eg using activity based costing) but a better measure might be sales value (as suggested by the CEO), rather than sales volume, as this gives some recognition to the relative scale of productive activity per unit.

On this basis, the following revised data would be produced:

| | 2011 | | 2012 | | 2011 | 2012 |
	Conventional mowers	Tractor mowers	Conventional mowers	Tractor mowers	Total	Total
	£	£	£	£	£	£
Contribution	1296000	2700000	1180800	2256000	3996000	3436800
FC by value	455625	759375	450081	773919	1215000	1224000
Profit	840375	1940625	730719	1482081	2781000	2212800
Operating profit/revenue	25.9%	35.9%	24.8%	29.2%	32.2%	27.6%

Compared to the volume based method of allocation, the operating profit of conventional mowers in 2011 has more than doubled from £384,750 to £840,375.

In terms of viability, contribution is the most valid measure in the short term, as the issue of allocation of fixed costs is avoided. On this basis, the conventional mower creates a healthy £1,296,000 contribution in 2011, making it viable. This generates a reasonable operating profit margin of 25.9%.

Tractor mowers

In 2011 tractor mowers made a contribution per unit of £1,000 giving a contribution margin ratio of 50%.

The profit per unit after allocating fixed costs was £887.50 giving an operating profit margin (using the method of allocation of fixed costs adopted by GGM) of 44.4%. As already noted, this reflects the rather favourable treatment of tractor mowers using the original fixed cost per unit allocation method.

Using sales value, rather than sales volume, to allocate fixed costs, this gives a rather less favourable, though still profitable, picture for tractor mowers. Operating profit margin is now somewhat lower at 35.9% than it was under the original allocation method, although it is still higher than the operating profit margin of the conventional mowers.

Other costs

The operating cost and profit figures are only part of the picture in measuring performance. After taking account of finance costs the business may not be profitable at all. More information is needed in this respect.

Overall company profit

While the allocation of fixed operating costs is arbitrary at unit level, the overall cost and profit at company level is the same irrespective of the allocation method. While such costs may not be avoidable in the short term, in the longer term it is essential that they are covered in order to sustain the business.

Nevertheless, overall operating profit of £2,781,000 has been generated on revenue of £8,640,000. This generates a healthy operating profit margin of 32.2% in 2011.

2012

Conventional mowers

There has been no change in the selling price or in variable cost per unit of conventional mowers between 2011 and 2012. The key change affecting performance has therefore been a fall in sales volume of 8.9%. As selling prices have not changed, then sales revenue has also fallen by 8.9%.

The impact of fixed operating costs on conventional tractor profitability in 2012 is twofold. First, total operating fixed costs have risen by 0.7%, so the pool of costs to be allocated has increased. Second, the volume of conventional mowers sold has decreased, while the number of tractor mowers sold has increased. As a result, the proportion of the fixed overhead pool allocated to conventional mowers has fallen. The net effect of this for conventional mowers (under the existing allocation method) is that while fixed operating cost per unit has increased from £112.50 to £120 (+6.7%), the total fixed operating cost allocated to conventional mowers has decreased from £911,250 to £885,600 (a fall of 2.8%).

As already noted, the method of fixed cost allocation used by the company based on volumes is questionable. The revised sales value based allocation method shows that the overall fixed costs allocated to the conventional product fell from £455,625 in 2011 to £450,081 in 2012, a reduction of 1.2%.

Using these revised fixed cost allocations the operating profit margin has fallen from 25.9% in 2011 to 24.8% in 2012. The primary causal factor explaining why this has occurred is the fall in sales volume.

Tractor mowers

In 2012 the key factors affecting the change in profitability of tractor mowers were: (i) a 10% reduction in selling price from £2,000 to £1,800; and (ii) an increase of 4.4% in sales volume from 2,700 to 2,820. Variable costs per unit were unchanged.

The reduction in selling price may be causally linked to the increase in demand (downward sloping demand curve) but other factors may also have been relevant in that we do not know what would have happened to demand if the price had remained unchanged (see below).

Overall, in consequence of the price decrease and sales volume increase, revenues have fallen by 6% from £5.4m in 2011 to £5.076m in 2012. To the extent that the volume change was due to the price change, this would imply that demand is inelastic. As a consequence, the price reduction strategy could have significantly contributed to the fall in revenue of the tractor product in 2012 compared to 2011. The increase in fixed costs of 11.4% has also contributed to the reduction in profit of the tractor range.

Profitability of the tractor mowers has fallen as a result of the reduction in revenues. Using the sales volume basis for fixed cost allocation, operating profit has decreased by 20% from £2,396,250 to £1,917,600. Using the sales value basis for fixed cost allocation, operating profit has decreased by 23.6% from £1,940,625 to £1,482,081.

Comparison of the conventional and tractor range performance

Both conventional and tractor ranges have suffered a significant reduction in profit in 2012 compared to 2011 under both allocation bases.

In absolute terms, tractor mowers are more profitable than conventional mowers measured by both profit and contribution – although a more detailed review of overhead cost drivers may alter the data significantly.

The cause of the fall in profit for the tractor range may be largely endogenous ie choosing internally a price reduction strategy. It may therefore be within the company's control to reverse this price increase and restore future profitability to 2011 levels.

Overall profit

Overall operating profit has fallen by 20.4% from £2,781,000 in 2011 to £2,212,800 in 2012 (irrespective of the cost allocation method used). While the fall is substantial, the company remains reasonably profitable with an overall operating profit margin on revenue of 27.6%. If the price reduction is reversed, then some of the fall may be recovered in 2013.

Examiner's comments

Requirement (a)(i) requests candidates to analyse the performance of GGM, and each of its two products, in the financial years 2011 and 2012.

The majority of candidates answered this question in the report format that was required. The overall analysis of performance varied significantly from candidate to candidate. The higher scoring candidates used a variety of ratios such as change in revenues, profit margins and contribution. These data were used, in part, to explain the impact of the decrease in sales of conventional mowers. Also, the sales price of tractor mowers had reduced and, as a consequence, they had experienced an increase in sales volume. Some extremely good answers were produced in this respect, with candidates using price elasticity of demand to demonstrate the relationship between volume and price and thereby identify causal factors to explain the changes occurring in the data.

Only a minority of candidates developed their answers further and calculated the reallocation of fixed costs on a sales value basis. Most candidates calculated ratios for each of the two types of product separately and for the company as a whole for each year. This gave a structure for them to undertake further analysis.

The key issue which most candidates identified was the fact that tractor mowers were more profitable, but were aimed at a niche market. At the other end of the spectrum, the weaker candidates merely copied out the sales and cost figures from the question and made a vague attempt at analysing profitability. For these candidates there was normally no consideration of the relationship between price and volume, nor of the impact of changing the current method of allocation of fixed costs.

The lowest scoring candidates merely made assertions describing the changes in ratios, with little, if any, attempt at an analysis of causality. Some candidates spent too much time discussing market share in this section, rather than in (a)(ii).

(a) (ii)

Market share can be determined in terms of volume of sales or by sales value. Which is selected would depend on the purpose for which the analysis is being used.

A further issue is in defining the market. The broadest useful definition is likely to be the UK mower market. As GGM does not currently produce other powered garden tools and equipment then taking this wider definition does not seem appropriate. Within the mower sector there are various sub-sectors eg type of cutting blade; tractor and conventional; or method of power (petrol, electric, battery and hand-propelled).

The level of sub-analysis which would be appropriate could depend on a number of factors but one key issue would be whether consumers would readily substitute one good for another (eg it carries out the same function and is in the same price range). On this basis one could argue that the tractor mower is different from conventional mowers on the grounds of price and function in its suitability only for large gardens.

Taking the market split of tractor and then conventional mowers, a **sales volume** analysis of market share is as follows:

	2011		Forecast 2012	
	Conventional mower	*Tractor mower*	*Conventional mower*	*Tractor mower*
GGM (units)	8,100	2,700	7,380	2,820
Market (units)	1.5m	30,000	1.5m	30,600
Market share	0.54%	9%	0.49%	9.2%

In terms of **sales value**, market share is as follows:

	2011		Forecast 2012	
	Conventional mower	*Tractor mower*	*Conventional mower*	*Tractor mower*
GGM Revenue (£)	3,240,000	5,400,000	2,952,000	5,076,000
UK market at retail prices (£s) <W1>	360,360,000	35,640,000	367,640,000	36,360,000
UK market at wholesale prices (£s) <W2>	288,288,000	28,512,000	294,112,000	29,088,000
Market share at wholesale prices	1.1%	18.9%	1.0%	17.5%
Total market share at wholesale prices	2.7%		2.5%	

<W1> The UK market for mowers, by value, amounted to £396m in 2011 and £404m in 2012. Tractor mowers make up 9% of this market. However these are retail prices.

<W2> Retail prices are reduced to 80% (ie 1/1.25) to obtain wholesale prices.

Thus GGM has a very small share of the conventional mowers market at around 1%, but a reasonably significant share of the tractor mower market.

A further analysis could be of petrol-powered mowers alone but this might not add much to the usefulness of the information if petrol and electric mowers are close substitutes.

Note: the UK mower market share relates to the goods sold in the UK; as opposed to the UK mower industry, which is the goods manufactured in the UK.

Examiner's comments

Requirement (a)(ii) asks candidates to determine the current UK market share of GGM, highlighting any problems that arise in defining market share in order to produce a useful figure.

Most candidates attempted to determine market share for both products in terms of sales volume and sales value. Only a minority correctly adjusted for differences between wholesale and retail prices, and many ignored this issue altogether. Similarly, only a minority of candidates made a decent attempt at explaining the key problems in defining the market.

(a) (iii)

	2011		Forecast 2012	
	Conventional mowers	Tractor mowers	Conventional mowers	Tractor mowers
GGM				
Average price (per Question)	£400	£2,000	£400	£1,800
Retailer price x 1.25	£500	£2,500	£500	£2,250
UK MARKET				
UK market at retail prices (£s)	360,360,000	35,640,000	367,640,000	36,360,000
Market (units)	1.5m	30,000	1.5m	30,600
Average price	£240	£1,188	£245	£1,188

Conventional mower market

GGM is a minor participant in the UK conventional mower market with a market share of around 1% in both value terms and volume terms. This places it in a weak competitive position in this market.

The fall in conventional mower sales revenue in 2012 and the reduction in market share indicates a worsening of GGM's competitive positioning in this market. In volume terms, a decrease from 0.54% to 0.49% implies a worsening in competitiveness.

The fall in conventional mower sales revenue in 2012 and the reduction in value-based market share may indicate a worsening of GGM's competitive positioning in this market. Indeed, reduced conventional mower sales volume occurred despite no change in selling price by GGM and with competitors increasing selling price from an average of £240 in 2011 to £245 in 2012 (2%).

Within the conventional mower market, GGM is placed very much towards the quality end as its price of £400 becomes a retail price of £500 with a 25% mark up, which is more than double the market average of £245 in 2012. Its competitive position therefore needs to be considered against rival companies who also operate in the niche up-market sector of the conventional mower product market.

GGM may have suffered with consumers downgrading their purchases to cheaper products in the recession.

Tractor mower market

GGM is a significant player in the UK tractor mower market with a market share of 17.5% in value terms in 2012. This places it in a strong competitive position.

The fall in tractor mower sales revenue in 2012 and the reduction in value-based market share may indicate a worsening of GGM's competitive positioning in this market. However, in volume terms, an increase from 9% to 9.2% implies an increase in competitiveness on this basis at least.

Within the tractor mower market, GGM is placed very much towards the quality end as its price of £2,000 in 2011 is higher than the market average of £1,188 even allowing for differences between retail and wholesale prices. Even in 2012 with the price reduction to £1,800 it is still significantly higher than the market average. Its competitive position therefore needs to be considered against rival companies who also operate in the same niche up-market sector of the tractor mower product market.

The tractor mower range has increased sales volume by 4.4% in 2012. As already noted, part of this may be due to a price reduction. However there has also been market expansion of 2% in volume terms. So while GGM has increased sales this is partly due to market expansion and partly due to lower prices. Note that the average market price has been constant so GGM has lowered price and has captured more market share but reduced profit in the process.

Note also that as GGM has reduced price and is part of the market, then if the overall average market price has remained constant, on average competitors must have increased prices.

Overall competitive positioning:

In the UK market revenues amounted to £404m in 2012.

GGM's revenue is £8.028m, but when adjusted to retail prices it represents £10.035m.

GGM does not export outside the UK, so this is their total revenue. In terms of global sales therefore, GGM may overall be a small participant in the global industry and suffer competitive disadvantage in the UK market against international competitors from relative diseconomies of scale.

Examiner's comments

In requirement (a)(iii), candidates were asked to explain the competitive positioning of GGM in the UK mower market and to assess how this has changed between 2011 and 2012.

Most candidates answered this question by starting with Porter's generic strategies then making an attempt to link this with the scenario. Most did this by considering the two products separately.

A significant number of candidates said that the positioning was 'stuck in the middle' with regards to the tractor mower as they were reducing the price, but still trying to promote a quality product. Candidates also used other models such the BCG matrix and Bowman's Clock.

Very few candidates presented decent numerical analysis to this requirement. Most commented on the change in price of the tractor mower, but only stronger candidates commented on the fact that the average market price had also fallen.

(a) (iv)

GGM board's strategic plan

The Ansoff matrix is a useful model for identifying growth opportunities. There are four routes to growth in the model's two-by-two matrix of Products (new and existing) and Markets (new and existing).

The expansion strategy proposed by the GGM Board is one of product development in the Ansoff model. This means developing and launching new products into current markets.

The strength of this proposal is that GGM has experience and understanding of buyer and consumer behaviour in this market sector. Customers for the new products (petrol-powered garden tools and equipment including hedge trimmers, strimmers, chainsaws) are likely to be the same garden centres and DIY centres that already purchase the GGM mowers. GGM may therefore have knowledge of the customers, and trust from the customers.

Economies of scope may also occur in distributing goods to common locations, which may reduce common costs.

In terms of manufacturing capability there appear to be common elements and therefore core competencies in production that can be exploited to gain competitive advantage. This is likely to include using a smaller scale version of the petrol engines used on the mowers, but also other aspects such as cutting blades for hedge trimmers and chainsaws.

In terms of the size of market, the UK garden tools and equipment market is larger than the mower market as mower sales make up only 'about 45% of the overall gardening equipment industry.'

Data analysis

	Low demand	Estimated demand	High demand
Volume (units)	20,000	25,000	30,000
Price	£150	£150	£150
	£'000s	£'000s	£'000s
Revenue	3,000	3,750	4,500
Variable cost	(1,800)	(2,250)	(2,700)
Contribution	1,200	1,500	1,800
Fixed cost	(1,400)	(1,400)	(1,400)
Profit	(200)	100	400

Profitability

At the expected level of demand, the GGM board proposal makes a profit. However at only £100,000 this is extremely modest and will only relatively marginally add to the company's current profit for 2012 of £2,212,800. Even at the top end of the estimation range it will only add £400,000 a year to profit, and there may be a low probability to this level of demand occurring.

Unless there are synergies with existing production, the new strategy would not add significantly to profit and growth. Indeed, as a measure of the scale of new activity, profit in 2011 was £2,781,000 and so profit fell by £568,200 in 2012. This fall would not be made good by the new project even at the top end of the range of estimates.

Risk

A key feature of the new project is that it carries risk. In particular, while the contribution margin is high at 40%, there are also high fixed costs, making the operating gearing high. This is illustrated in the above table which shows that, in the worse case scenario, if sales volumes fall by 20% an operating loss of £200,000 will be made.

The break even revenue is:

£1.4m/0.4   =   £3.5m

Thus, the margin of safety from the 'most realistic estimate' is only £250,000 of sales. Therefore if sales fall by just 6.7% below the most realistic estimate, no profit will be made. A key issue in assessing risk therefore is how probable it is that sales will fall to this level.

While the market researchers indicate some uncertainty with respect to sales volumes this is only one variable. Other estimates are also likely to be surrounded by some uncertainty (eg price, variable cost, fixed costs).

Conclusion

This project does not look to be sufficiently profitable to improve growth significantly and contains risks which may reduce future profits. While most competitor mower manufacturers also produce petrol-powered garden tools and equipment, and qualitatively it seems a reasonable proposition for GGM, quantitatively, based on the data provided, it does not seem a way forward for GGM. Indeed, had it been so, perhaps the company would have entered this market some time ago.

BB's strategic plan

The expansion strategy proposed by BB is also one of product development in the Ansoff model in respect of UK sales.

However, there is also an element of diversification in the Ansoff model in respect of US sales. This involves moving away from core activities and developing new products for new markets, which involves the greatest risk of all strategies. It requires new skills, new techniques and different ways of operating. This is reinforced as not only has GGM not used battery technology before, but BB has not made mowers before.

A further way of viewing the potential acquisition is from BB's perspective. It is continuing a policy of downstream vertical integration.

In terms of UK sales there are similar advantages as the GGM board proposal (albeit with a different type of new product). There are economies of scope in distribution to the same customers, and there may be some common core competencies (eg the blades) with existing production methods and, although the battery element is new to GGM, it is core to BB.

At a marketing level however there are differences. In the BB case the new products are being separately branded so there is little reputational impact from the existing GGM brand. However BB may not be known in the UK, and consumer recognition in this market needs to be established.

The key advantage is that this proposal gives access to the US market through BB. However while BB operates in the US, it does not sell mowers in the US so the advantage of having BB to exploit its home market may be limited.

Data analysis

	High cost	Est cost	Low cost
Volume	20,000	20,000	20,000
Price	£500	£500	£500
	£'000s	£'000s	£'000s
Revenue	10,000	10,000	10,000
Variable cost	(7,000)	(7,000)	(7,000)
Contribution	3,000	3,000	3,000
Fixed cost	(3,000)	(2,000)	(1,000)
Profit	nil	1,000	2,000

Taking the data provided at face value, the BB proposal is far more profitable than the GGM board proposal and even at the lower end of the estimation range it does not make a loss, managing to break even. However this data has been provided by BB as part of its take-over bid hence a degree of professional scepticism needs to be applied to these estimates. Due diligence procedures will be needed to ascertain their validity.

The range of variation of fixed costs is considerable and yet only point estimates are given for all the other variables. Additional work is needed to ascertain why the variation is so high for fixed costs and no range of estimates is provided for other variables.

A further note of caution is that, unlike the GGM board's proposal, the BB plan is to produce more mowers. It may therefore be that consumers will buy the battery-powered mowers instead of buying a GGM petrol-powered mower. Due to this substitution, the sales noted above therefore may not be entirely incremental to the company.

Conclusion

Leaving aside these reservations, if the figures are valid, then the BB proposal looks to be a more substantial contribution to growth.

Tutorial note: Candidates may instead/also use other models such as the Lynch Expansion method matrix. The Lynch model is another two-by-two matrix of company growth (organic growth and external development) and geographical location (home (domestic) and international).

Examiner's comments

In requirement (a)(iv) candidates were asked to compare the growth strategy of the GGM board with that of BB, make relevant calculations and refer to appropriate strategic models.

Again, the standard of answers here varied significantly between the stronger and weaker candidates. There was data in the question in terms of best case, worst case and estimated demand which could have been used to analyse each strategy. Only the better candidates used the information to compute the profit under the different scenarios and then went on to compute break even and sensitivity analysis.

The majority of candidates tended to use the Ansoff model. The Lynch model was also used in the stronger answers to analyse the difference between the two strategies in terms of discussion of expanding internationally. In terms of the BB strategy, the use of the highest and lowest cost estimates was often ignored in favour of using the expected cost. For the most part, candidates concluded that the BB strategy was the most attractive because of the exposure to overseas markets.

Hardly any candidates expressed any sort of professional scepticism about the data presented by BB.

(b) Ethics pertains to whether a particular behaviour is deemed acceptable in the context under consideration. Here the issue is that Hetty's government has different laws for health and safety than the UK, but the underlying reasons for having the safety guard remain the same.

In making a decision as to how to proceed, GGM may find it helpful to apply the Institute of Business Ethics three tests:

- Transparency
- Effect
- Fairness

Transparency – would GGM mind people (existing customers, suppliers, employees) knowing that it has manufactured potentially dangerous equipment, even if it were legal . This test is partly about whether GGM's corporate ethics are open and transparent in its actions, rather than just what they claim in ethical statements.

Effect – whom does the decision affect/hurt? GGM stand to gain a major order if they are willing to control costs (by omitting the safety guard) and lower price. In the short term GGM would be making more profit as a consequence of the order.

However GGM risk reputational damage if it came to light it had manufactured unsafe goods and there may be repercussions in terms of lost customers in future.

Other losers would be any customers of Hetty (or other users of mowers) who got hurt in the event of a safety incident.

The ethical issue here is that GGM needs to recognise that, as a business, it has an obligation to the public interest and its wider stakeholders to behave responsibly. The requirement and expectation to make profits need to be constrained by these obligations, but such issues may themselves impact on long term profit.

There may also be certain industry codes of conduct that apply, and consequences from a breach of these, irrespective of where the items are sold.

Fairness – would the decision be considered fair by those affected? The issue for GGM is that they are being asked to manufacture mowers in the knowledge that they might cause harm. Should someone be badly hurt as a result of its actions, it is unlikely that they would perceive GGM's actions as fair, particularly if GGM was seen to have gained financially by winning more business.

Honesty

A final issue is one of honesty and professional scepticism. GGM should take legal advice regarding the legality of the modification being considered in order to substantiate the assertion that any such modification would be legal in Hetty's home country.

Response

GGM may believe that, even if the deal would be in its short term commercial interests, the additional profit is not worthwhile given the breach of corporate ethics that would be involved, even if no safety incident ever transpired from the modification.

One possible course of action would be to insist on fitting the safety guard but to offer a lower price anyway and thereby take a reduced profit per unit. However, GGM may feel that it is not in its interests to do business with a client of this nature even under these conditions.

Examiner's comments

Requirement (b) asked candidates to explain the ethical issues arising from a request to modify its mowers for a potential export contract.

Answers to this requirement varied but were, on the whole, disappointing. Candidates tended to approach this requirement in terms of a transparency, fairness and effect framework. What candidates did not then develop, however, were the next steps or draw any sort of conclusion.

A significant number of candidates mentioned the ICAEW code of ethics, self-interest and integrity. This question did not focus on the code of ethics as the client (from whose perspective the ethical issues are being considered) may not have any ICAEW members. Rather, the question required candidates, in a commercial scenario, to assess the legality and ethics of the proposal and the corporate social responsibility of GGM as a company.

The weakest candidates failed to see the issues at the corporate level and instead presented an answer as though it was an individual's ethical issue. Only some candidates gave sensible business advice, such as providing the mowers with the safety guard but not charging for this feature in the price, in order to break into that market. Instead they just stated that the contract should be refused. Whilst the approach to ethics has improved significantly over the years, there is still an inability of candidates to apply ethical principles to business situations.

61 Care 4U Ltd

Marking guide

		Marks		
		Knowledge	Skill	
(a)	SWOT analysis	3	9	12
(b)	Two strategies	4	15	19
		7	24	31

General comments

The scenario in this question relates to a private company which owns a large chain of retail pharmacies. It has a good reputation but it has had problems retaining and motivating individual salaried pharmacists.

There are also issues regarding the manner in which the outlets should be controlled and managed. The board has proposed two alternative strategies to expand the chain, to attract pharmacists and increase motivation. These proposed strategies have been identified as: (i) franchising; and (ii) shared ownership.

(a) **Strengths**

- C4U sells essential products for both prescription items and over-the-counter (OTC) medicines so market demand is likely to be robust to changes in the economy and (for the market as a whole) price inelastic.

- C4U has a significant number of outlets providing scale economies for purchasing (enabling discounts from pharmaceutical suppliers), IT (the centralised system is likely to be mainly a fixed cost enabling additional outlets to benefit at near zero marginal cost) and other central operational services (such as central administration which is likely to have a significant fixed cost element).

- There is a history of sustaining growth through good management which has a track record of competence.

- Funding available for expansion means the company has significant liquidity which lowers financial risk and provides opportunities for growth.

- Good reputation as community pharmacies with free tests, screening and advice increases goodwill and enables a loyal customer base to be established of regular customers/patients.

- Good control through the IT system means the performance of the business is monitored and controlled at the level of each individual pharmacy.

Weaknesses

- There is a shortage of well motivated pharmacists who are good managers which means that, whilst the technical functions may be competently carried out, the same people may not have the key business skills to build revenue and control costs at the pharmacy level of the organisation which is the key interface with customers.

- There are problems retaining pharmacists. This leads to retraining costs and the continued losses of a key human resource. The temporary nature of the employment may mean pharmacists have a low level of long term commitment to C4U.

- Generous salaries need to be paid to pharmacists which increases the cost base significantly and reduces profit.

Opportunities

- Increases in new drugs becoming available will mean that demand will increase both in terms of volume and, to the extent that new drugs are more expensive, may increase price.

- Pharmacy retailers have exited the industry thereby reducing competition from that source as there are fewer competitors remaining in the industry. There is therefore the opportunity to capture the markets of those leaving the industry.

- Capacity to charge in future for provision of advice, which is currently given free.

- Sell whole business to a large national chain.

- Expand through acquisition.

Threats

- Deregulation has made C4U susceptible to price competition for OTC drugs from supermarkets and other large companies in the industry who have scale economies and common costs with other functions in the store.

- Supermarkets are opening more in-store outlets offering increased non-price competition for all drugs. This competition comes in the form of 24 hour opening, convenience (shopping anyway for other goods), car parking out-of-town, scale of facility (and therefore range of items held in inventory giving choice).

- The prescription drugs market is susceptible to government regulation in terms of contractual conditions. Changes in such regulations are a risk to C4U.

- Government funding cuts will put pressure on prices paid to pharmacies in terms of the products that they will fund and the prices they are willing to pay for drugs and pharmacy services.

- Other goods sold by pharmacies are non-essential and are more susceptible to a sustained economic downturn and to competitive forces from a wider range of competitors outside the pharmacy sector.

- Alternative distribution channels for OTC are likely to be an increasing threat to high street pharmacy retailers (eg on-line sales, drug stores (OTC drug only shops)).

Conclusion

Key factors are:

- Reductions in government expenditure are key as this puts pressure on pharmacies for their main source of income which makes up 80% of revenue and if recoveries from government are reduced, with constant costs, then severe pressure is put on profits. Any cuts are also likely to be sustained as governments continually look to reduce public sector expenditure.

- Competition from supermarkets which: are pervasive in most regions; are instantly recognisable by consumers; have the ability to be low cost providers and tend to be trusted as providers of services (including healthcare).

Examiner's comments

Requirement (a) asks candidates to prepare a SWOT analysis.

Attempts at this requirement were generally good, with candidates demonstrating a strong understanding of the SWOT model and using the information in the question to produce high scoring answers. The key strengths and weaknesses identified centred around the brand name, the established reputation and the good IT control system, together with the problems in staff retention and the lack of management experience from the pharmacists.

The opportunities and threats were not as well identified, although the majority of candidates did manage to identify that the main opportunity was the increase in new drugs, whilst the main threat was government spending cuts. Some candidates attempted to use the PESTEL model, despite the question specifically asking for a SWOT analysis.

It was quite surprising that a number of candidates failed to summarise the key issues from the SWOT analysis despite the requirement specifically requiring a conclusion.

(b) (i) Profitability

Profit shares for average size pharmacy (first 5 years)

	Total	C4U's profit under franchising	C4U's profit under shared ownership
Revenue	600,000	30,000 (ie 5%)	
Operating costs (80%)	(480,000)		
Operating profit (20%)	120,000		
Management fee (under shared ownership option only)	(20,000)		20,000
Net profit	100,000		50,000
Up-front payment (amortised over 5 years)		5,000	–
Annual profit to C4U		35,000	70,000
Total profit for C4U (over 5 years)		175,000	350,000

Franchising

The up-front cash payment for the franchisee, averaging £25,000, is small by comparison to the shared ownership scheme which averages £40,000. However, with franchising, this payment would be recognised as revenue for C4U (amortised over 5 years) whereas the initial cash payment under the shared ownership scheme is a capital payment and would never be recognised in C4U's profit.

The up-front payment is small by comparison to the initial cost of opening a pharmacy so there is a small initial stake by the franchisee. This means that C4U has a high capital stake with franchising and may therefore expect a higher absolute level of profit to earn the same % return on investment.

Over the five year period the net cash investment by C4U for an average pharmacy under the franchise arrangement is £175,000 (£200,000 purchase price – £25,000 upfront fee). This is fully recovered according to the above table in terms of C4U's share of profits over the 5 year term (although this is not the case after tax and interest).

After 5 years C4U has all rights to the pharmacy business and the full profit stream. Meanwhile however there is an annual interest cost to C4U from providing the funds.

Shared ownership

C4U would receive the management fee in addition to the 50% share in profit, but the profit share is determined after the deduction of the management charge so in effect C4U is incurring half the cost of its own management charge.

As noted above, the additional capital stake is not recognised in C4U's profit.

The profit of the shared ownership scheme is overstated compared to the franchise arrangement as the revenue from intensive support is included but the incremental central costs in providing that support is not included.

The net cash investment by C4U for an average pharmacy under the shared ownership scheme is £160,000 (£200,000 opening cost – £40,000 pharmacist contribution). This is more than fully recovered according to the above table in terms of the C4U's share of profits over the 5 year term which amounts to £350,000. In this case profit will continue after the 5 years under the same arrangement unless one party decides to buy out the other.

As with the franchise arrangement, there is an interest cost to C4U in providing the initial funds to set up the pharmacy company. However to the extent that the interest is also a cost to pharmacy companies, it is an income to C4U, half of which is in effect paid by the co-owner.

Comparison

The above table shows that the profit per annum with the shared ownership scheme is double that of the franchise arrangement. At first sight this may suggest that the shared ownership route is better but:

- The start-up period may be a period of low profits as a new pharmacy business tries to become established against incumbents. If some costs are fixed this might mean low (or even zero) profitability in the short term, hence there may be little (or no) profit share for C4U at first with shared ownership. In contrast, under a franchise agreement at least some profit will be earned by C4U from a 5% share of revenue plus the amortised upfront franchise fee.

- The above table assumes that total revenue would be the same under either ownership choice. However if the incentives for the franchisee or the share ownership partner differ between the two options (see section below) then different levels of revenue may be generated from the same pharmacy and thus different levels of profit earned for C4U.

- The franchise profits are only for a period of 5 years after which full ownership can revert to C4U if it so choses. After the 5 years the profit stream to C4U would therefore be £120,000 per annum. Thus a lower short term profit will be compensated by higher long term profit with the franchise scheme compared to the shared ownership scheme.

- For both schemes, profits are likely to be overstated as there are likely to be additional central costs, interest and tax which are not reflected in operating profit.

- There may be some depreciation on the pharmacy outlet property.

(ii) Control and management

Franchising

- Control is exercised loosely by C4U through the franchise agreement contract. This is more on a negative basis in preventing certain courses of action (eg complying with contract terms to avoid damaging the brand) rather than on a positive basis in promoting positive actions.

- Autonomous management. Franchisees appear to be largely autonomous in being able to decide whether to accept or reject advice and support.

- Each pharmacy is separately managed so diversity of approach and management styles may develop between pharmacies.

- Some degree of auditing will be required by C4U in order to gain assurance regarding disclosed revenue figures to verify that the correct 5% franchise payment is being made. This will require direct access, or third party access, to accounting records and accounting systems.

- After 5 years, ultimate control reverts to C4U at which time it can choose to change or adapt the management style selected by the franchisee.

Shared ownership

- While the day to day management of pharmacies rests with the co-owner (the pharmacist), C4U manages and monitors the performances of individual pharmacies by providing 'intensive support advice, administration and IT facilities' to the company which would be 'a compulsory part of the agreement so C4U can manage the performance of its investment.'

- Thus, while the co-owner takes the day to day decisions, they have a high degree of monitoring by, and accountability to, C4U.

- If performance is poor and interest cannot be paid, ultimate control also rests with C4U, as the holder of the loan can force the company into insolvency.

(iii) **Incentives**

Franchising

- The contract is only 5 years, so franchisees will not have an incentive to build long term reputation.

- Even if a pharmacy performs badly and makes an operating loss, C4U still receives 5% of revenue so there are strong incentives for the franchisee to perform well and increase profit.

- Franchisees have incentives to reduce costs as this will increase profit but C4U will not take any share of this as they only have a share of revenues. This may incentivise franchisees to be efficient, but may also incentivise them to reduce quality.

Shared ownership

- The co-owner earns a salary and retains a half share of profits after management charges and interest. They are therefore incentivised to increase profit.

- The initial contribution by the co-owner pharmacist (£40,000 on average) is at risk if the venture fails and thus this provides an incentive to succeed.

- If the business succeeds then the co-owner pharmacist has an opportunity to buy out the other 50% at a fair value. There is thus the chance of owning his/her own business. However the more successful the pharmacy becomes the greater the cost of the buy-out. This may give a disincentive to over-performing while the pharmacy remains in joint ownership.

Examiner's comments

Requirement (b) requests candidates to compare the two strategies for expansion by considering: operating profit: control and management; and incentives.

Candidates produced few calculations in answering the operating profit part of this requirement, opting to spend more time on the discussion aspects of the question in respect of control and management and incentives. Where calculations were performed, many candidates treated the upfront payment of £25,000 as a cost in the first year and did not amortise it over five years as expected. This led to a computed profit of £5,000 according to the franchising agreement in the first year. Other errors included: not recognising 5% of the revenue; under the shared ownership arrangement attributing C4U 80% of the profit, rather than 50%; and not thinking about 'profit' by recognising the full cost of the PPE as an expense. It was clear from the answers produced, that candidates were familiar with how a franchising agreement operated, but often the comments were general and not applied to the scenario. Also, there was a lack of understanding of the nature and implications of the shared ownership arrangement, with candidates failing to grasp the fact that it gave a significant amount of control and accountability to C4U.

Answers to the incentives part of the question were often relatively brief, with candidates identifying that under the franchising agreement, the pharmacists still received 5% of revenues whereas under the shared ownership, the co-owners would be entitled to a half share of profit.

Overall, the information in the question could have been better used. Many answers to this part were very brief and did not compare the two strategies in sufficient detail or with sufficient insight.

62   The Mealfest Corporation

		Knowledge	Skill	Marks
(a)	Organisational structure, performance measurement and pricing	3	11	14
(b)	Benchmarking	3	7	10
		6	18	24

General comments

The listed company in question owns a chain of mid-market restaurants controlled from Germany, but also located in France, Switzerland and the UK. The company was originally centrally controlled and had homogeneous prices for all restaurants across Europe. At the beginning of 2012 it restructured, forming a separate division for each country. After the restructuring the prices were homogeneous within countries, but not between countries. The Mealfest board now wishes to monitor the success of the new structure and strategy.

(a)   (i)   Organisational structure

Pre-2012

MC is a multinational corporation. As such, its structure needs to consider not only operational size and diversity, but international variations in culture, taste, economic conditions, currencies, laws and regulations. The centralised nature of the organisational structure prior to January 2012 is in danger of ignoring, or minimising the significance of, these cross border variations.

Arising from this, there are a number of detailed issues with this structure and method of performance measurement (aside from the matters relating to foreign exchange rates highlighted by the finance director which are dealt with later below):

- Pre-2012 there was a very flat structure with each of 100 restaurants reporting performance directly to head office. This gives a wide span of control where head office staff in Berlin can have little knowledge of all local conditions and the causes behind the changes in the three performance metrics.

- The structure is also highly centralised with the key decisions relating to pricing, food sourcing and staff being taken centrally in Berlin. This may give economies of scale and discounts but narrows variety (eg different national cultures and food type preferences).

- There are differences in laws and regulations with regard to employment and social security law. Apart from Switzerland, the other four countries are in the EU which reduces, but does not remove, employment law differences. Specifically, national regulation issues include the following: the minimum wage differs between countries; social security payments vary; rights of employees from outside the EU to work in the EU differ; employees rights on redundancy or dismissal differ.

- It is unclear whether the performance of (i) the restaurants or (ii) the restaurant managers is being evaluated, or both.

- To the extent that it is the restaurant managers that are being evaluated, then they have little control over profit other than the volume of sales/customers. Menu prices, staff allocation, staff pay and sourcing of food are all fixed centrally. Restaurant managers are therefore being held responsible for matters beyond their control if they are being monitored as a profit centre.

- Centralised decisions fail to take account of local conditions. If, in a particular country, there is high unemployment, then staff may be recruited at lower pay than if labour market conditions are competitive.

Post-2012

The two key changes post-2012 are:

- A change in the degree of centralisation of decision making which is now at national level rather than corporate level (international).

- Additionally measuring performance at divisional level rather than only at restaurant level.

The decentralisation of decision making to national level reduces the issues arising from cultural, economic and legal differences. However, there may still be many of the above differences in cultural taste and prosperity within countries, as well as between countries.

In terms of measuring performance at divisional level, this seems more appropriate as most of the key decisions are now being taken at this level eg pricing (see below) and staffing, so the division is a profit centre (and also a revenue centre) and has control over most of the elements contributing to profit. The exception is food sourcing which remains at corporate level and is therefore an element of performance outside the control of divisional heads.

Other than revenue and profit, a third performance metric is return on assets. To make this a more valid element of performance evaluation, the divisional manager would need control over new investment and divestment (ie an investment centre). This is not the case, even under the post-2012 regime.

Exchange rate issues

MC's primary currency appears to be the euro. Germany and France have the euro as their currency so sales in these countries are not directly affected by currency translation. Food purchases from France and local labour in these countries are also payable in euro.

In the UK and Switzerland fluctuations over the year in exchange rates mean that the euro value of sales revenue is likely to change subject to macroeconomic influences, rather than just decisions at restaurant or divisional levels. Wage costs are in the same currency as revenues and so provide some natural hedging.

Given that food costs are in euro, this makes the euro denominated profit in UK and Swiss restaurants even more volatile than their revenues.

Given that performance comparisons are in euro as a common currency, the profit of a division or a restaurant is heavily dependent on the strength of the national currency, as well as the underlying performance of the business.

In measuring the return on assets in the UK and Switzerland, consideration also needs to be given to the exchange rate at which assets are translated.

(ii) **Pricing**

Pre-2012

Pre-2012 pricing exhibits three characteristics:

- The pricing decision is centralised
- Prices are uniform across all four countries
- Prices are only reset once a year

Centralisation

Centralisation means that pricing decisions fail to take account of local information which may be available to restaurant managers, but local conditions are unlikely to be known centrally on an up to date basis for all 100 locations in Europe. As a consequence, pricing decisions are unlikely to take account of local tastes and needs that customers may report back to individual managers.

Uniformity of pricing

Uniform pricing means that MC does not take account of local competitive conditions. This means that the company does not practise price discrimination by taking advantage of variations in price elasticity between either national markets or local restaurant markets.

Reset once a year

Prices are uniform within the year which means they lack inter-temporal flexibility. As an example, if there is seasonality, then prices would not reflect this. This might be particularly relevant where there is large tourist market in summer, but many fewer tourists in winter, generating different demand dynamics.

Post-2012

Of the three characteristics noted above, the third point remains the same (ie set only once a year) hence the problems (eg seasonality) are unchanged.

The first two issues (centralisation and uniformity) have changed and the underlying issues may have been moderated, but they have not been removed.

Centralisation

The degree of centralisation has been reduced from being company-wide to each national division. This is an improvement in terms of devolved decision making, but divisional managers might still not be aware of the local competitive conditions facing each restaurant manager.

Uniformity of pricing

There is still uniformity within countries, even though variations are permitted between countries. The issues here relating to a lack of price flexibility are reduced, but variations within a country in terms of competition, prosperity and taste can still be significant, leading to geographical variations in demand and price elasticity and a continued absence of exploiting price discrimination.

Exchange rate issues

Under the pre-2012 system of pricing, exchange rate variations have caused volatility in menu prices in the UK and Switzerland. Such exchange rate movements are likely to reflect macroeconomic conditions rather than the conditions in the restaurant market and may thus be distortionary, leading to arbitrary and suboptimal pricing.

Under the post-2012 system, there is discretion at national level to set prices and so the impact of exchange rates can be considered by divisional managers. A factor in this would be the relative rates of inflation in the UK and Switzerland compared to eurozone countries.

Examiner's comments

Requirement (a) asks candidates to compare pre and post 2012: (i) organisational structure and performance measurement; and (ii) pricing strategies.

Answers tended to be brief and concentrated on the fact that pre 2012, the structure was highly centralised and flat, whereas post 2012, the decentralisation of decision making eliminated some of the cultural differences previously experienced. There was normally little or no reference to the impact of exchange rate fluctuations and resulting issues in terms of revenue differences between countries and the impact on performance assessment. Although candidates acknowledged that within the different structures the performance would be assessed in terms of revenue and profits, very few considered return on assets.

In terms of pricing, candidates did not really seem to know how to approach the question and this often led to brief, unstructured answers which did not focus on the differences between the pre and post 2012 position, but instead merely repeated from the question that there had been a move from a centrally fixed pricing system to one now fixed at national level by divisional heads. There was very little analysis of how this would affect the behaviour of managers and customers or of exchange rate risk.

(b) Benchmarking compares the use of assets across the firm or across the industry and indicates best practice to show where assets might be better used to achieve sustainable competitive advantage (SCA).

One definition of benchmarking is 'The establishment, through data gathering, of targets and comparators, through whose use relative levels of performance (and particularly areas of underperformance) can be identified. By the adoption of identified best practices it is hoped that performance will improve.'

By comparing procedures and performance, internally and externally, MC can understand how to move towards best practice by learning how to reduce costs, improve service delivery in restaurants and thereby improve market positioning to align with market leaders in the sector.

There are four different types of benchmark that can be used: internal; competitive (industry wide); activity (best in class); and generic.

Internal (or historic) – internal benchmarking could be at the level of comparing individual restaurants or divisions with each other to determine those that are under- or over-performing. Comparisons of restaurants could be intra-country or company-wide. It may be however that certain restaurants are best at one function (eg food quality) while other restaurants are better at a different function (eg quality of service or ambience).

Historical comparison also looks at performance over time to ascertain trends/significant changes, etc.

Internal benchmarking is however restrictive as it could be that MC is generally under-performing and the true benchmark of best practice is to be found within external competitors who are out-performing MC.

Competitive (industry-wide) – this benchmark compares the performance of the restaurant or the division with equivalent units in other firms in the same industry or sector. This may assist MC in ascertaining ways to improve performance.

Comparing the performance of a division with a rival restaurant company in the same market sector may be possible if the rival is a company that is restricted to one country. In this case the published financial statements are likely to provide relevant data to compare key financial performance indicators. They may also provide some narrative information to evaluate non-financial performance indicators. Obtaining information about the performance and functions of rivals at the individual restaurant level is more challenging, as there is less information in the public domain. Industry publications and associations could be possible sources alongside informal contacts in the industry and personal visits to rivals.

If the whole national industry is under-performing, international comparisons may be more useful so comparisons could also be made with restaurants in other national markets (eg the US).

Activity (best in class) – compares with best practice in whatever industry can be found eg could compare MC table booking systems with online booking system for hotels or airline seats to ascertain whether there is scope for improved efficiency. Similarly, the levels of service could be benchmarked against other industry service practice (eg first class airline travel; hotel reception); food preparation could be compared to cookery competitions or the best home cooking.

Generic – against a conceptually similar process eg compare food preparation to the treatment of VIPs at visits and events. Food hygiene could be compared to a hospital operating theatre.

Examiner's comments

Requirement (b) asked candidates to explain how benchmarking may be used to evaluate performance of divisions and of individual restaurants.

A good knowledge was shown of the nature of internal, competitive, activity and generic benchmarking, with the majority of candidates displaying an understanding of each. However, answers' application to each type to the scenario tended to be very general with insufficient consideration of the circumstances of the scenario. Some candidates went on to use a balanced scorecard approach, identifying CSF's and KPI's. Whilst this identified some reasonable points, this approach was neither necessary nor entirely suitable for this requirement.

March 2013 exam answers

63 Mayhews Ltd

Marking guide

		Knowledge	Skill	Marks
(a)	Porter's five forces analysis	3	6	9
(b)	Performance evaluation	2	15	17
(c)	Advantages/disadvantages	2	4	6
(d)	Critical success factors (CSFs)	3	6	9
		10	31	41

(a) 5 Forces analysis – Filling stations

Threat of new entrants – low

Barriers to entry for fuel retailing are high. As well as needing sites in prime locations, there is the capital required to set up the filling station (underground storage tanks, fuel lines etc) and to comply with ongoing regulatory requirements. In addition the market is dominated by major brands (oil companies and supermarkets) and these larger players have significant cost advantages as a result of scale economies. Entry to the industry is also likely to be unattractive in the current environment given low margins and high levels of competition. As a result of these factors, the threat of new entrants is low although supermarkets may continue to open more filling stations at existing supermarket locations or new out-of-town sites.

Competitive rivalry – high

Because the industry is low margin, high volume, the level of competition is intense.

The supermarkets are keen to compete with each other on the price of fuel since if they can attract customers to the filling station they are also likely to buy other goods. The effect of competition is evidenced by the reduction in the number of filling stations and the failure of a significant number of the smaller independent filling stations.

Power of suppliers – high

Fuel supply is dominated by a few large petrol wholesalers who therefore wield significant power. This is increased by the fact that most are vertically integrated and also control some retail outlets. Suppliers are likely to exert more power in relation to the smaller independent filling stations than the supermarket-owned sites.

Power of customers – varied

Customers are fragmented so in that sense they have relatively low bargaining power in relation to the industry as a whole and the market price will largely be dictated by the petrol wholesaler and government taxes. However switching costs are low and petrol is a homogeneous commodity product so there is little brand loyalty. As a result customers are easily able to transfer business and in this respect they become more important to an individual operator within the industry as they are likely to choose the lowest price filling station in their area. Corporate buyers may have slightly more power because of the higher volume of business they represent.

Threat of substitutes – low

The threat of substitutes is limited although there is some scope for the manufacture and use of bio-fuels from vegetable oils and animal fats. The greater threat for the fuel retailing industry is that as the price of fuel increases people reduce their consumption by driving less, switching to electric cars and/or using alternative means of transport.

Conclusion

This is a highly competitive industry, which is particularly challenging for the smaller independent operators who struggle to compete with the economies of scale and brand loyalty of the supermarkets. With only 3 sites, Mayhews may lack sufficient throughput to sustain profitability in the fuel retailing industry in the longer term.

Examiner's comments:

Requirement (a) requested candidates to prepare a Porter's Five forces analysis of the UK fuel retailing industry which might help inform Mayhew's discussions regarding the viability of its filling station operations. This requirement was extremely well attempted by the majority of candidates. Whilst many were able to extract salient information from the question and use it to assess the strength of each force, only the better candidates concluded that the industry is extremely competitive, with high supplier power and that the future is relatively bleak for smaller independents such as Mayhews. A minority of candidates discussed only four of the five forces, omitting the need to consider competitive rivalry, which in the context of the scenario was one of the most important issues. A common error by weaker candidates was to discuss supermarket-owned filling stations under the heading substitutes instead of discussing substitutes for the purchase of fuel eg the use of electric cars or public transport.

(b)   Analysis of Mayhews' performance and closure plans

Note: The data to support the following commentary can be found in the Appendix

Mayhews' overall business performance

Between 2011 and 2012, despite the total revenue for the business remaining almost static at £4.29 million, there has been a 10.4% increase in gross profit and a 27.1% increase in net profit, resulting in an absolute increase in profit of £125,000. On the face of it therefore the business has done well in a difficult economic climate.

Although the revenue in overall terms has remained static, this masks the fact that the 11% reduction in fuel revenues has been almost exactly compensated for by an 18% increase in repairs revenue.

The movement in fuel revenue is explained by a 5.4% increase in price but a 15.5% reduction in volume. Within the industry fuel volumes are under pressure due to the economic climate and increased engine efficiency but the drop in volume of fuel sold by Mayhews may suggest that they are losing market share to competitors. This is not surprising since their average retail price is 136p/litre, over 2p/litre higher than the 2012 UK average and 5p per litre higher than the average supermarket price.

On average Mayhews is selling 1.47 million litres per site which is not only considerably lower than the branded petrol stations but also less than the 1.68 million litres sold by the average independent. The lack of volume will probably result in Mayhews having to pay higher prices to the wholesaler and will also result in higher overhead costs per litre, which may explain the higher prices being charged. This is also reflected in Mayhews' gross margin, which is only 11.3% whereas on average retailers keep 5% of the retail price, equating to a gross margin of 5/40 = 12.5% of the net of tax price.

The repairs revenue has grown by 18%. Given the economic climate it is unlikely that Mayhews will have put its prices up significantly and this is probably due to volume increases as a result of people needing more repairs and servicing as they hold on to their cars longer. It is also likely to reflect a move away from the dealers to local garages as customers attempt to keep their costs down.

Repairs and servicing now accounts for 44% of the total sales (compared to 37% in 2011). Since the gross margin on the repairs business is much higher at 52.1% than the margin on fuel (11.3%), this change in sales mix towards repairs has had a positive effect on the company's overall profit.

Operating costs have also remained relatively static at just under 16% of revenue. A breakdown of these would be helpful – since the premises are owned, in addition to the wages and salaries of the owner, filling station staff and garage mechanics, these costs are likely to consist of utilities, marketing and other administrative expenses. More information is required although on the face of it the business appears to have kept these under control.

Individual garages

If we consider the performance of the individual locations, it is clear that some garages are doing better than others. Garage C is performing best of all and contributing 40% of Mayhews' gross profit, which directly reflects its reduced reliance on fuel sales and a greater proportion of high margin servicing.

Garage B is the least successful. It is charging the highest price per litre (£1.38), selling the lowest volume of fuel (1.34m litres) and has lower margins on both fuel and repairs than the other two garages. It is also the most reliant on fuel revenues (over 62% of total revenue).

More information is required about the location of garage B but this may be in one of the less well populated rural areas or alternatively it may face strong competition in the vicinity eg it could be close to a filling station operated by a major supermarket.

Garage A appears to be performing reasonably and accounts for 36% of Mayhews' revenue and gross profit. Comparing the net margins is not particularly useful as the operating costs of garage A include the £45,000 salary cost of Barry which, once removed, shows garage A making a net margin of 14.9%.

If Mayhews is to focus more on repairs it should try and establish what garage C is doing to achieve margins of 55% and replicate that elsewhere (eg considering the procurement policy it has adopted for parts).

Interdependence of revenues and costs

A key issue for Mayhews is the extent to which the fuel and repairs revenue are interdependent. Should Mayhews decide to close one or more of the filling stations then they may lose some customers for repairs and servicing also.

Depending on how closely located the three garages are to each other, the Mayhews brand may be strong enough to close one garage completely but transfer its repair customers to one of the other locations.

Another consideration is the extent to which operating costs at a particular location will be reduced by closing the filling station part of the business.

Preliminary Conclusions and Recommendations

Mayhews has several choices available:

(i)   Continue as it is.

(ii) Close some/all of the filling stations but retain all three repairs and servicing businesses.

(iii) Close one or more garages in their entirety and sell off the sites to help fund investment in the new computer system and the repairs business at the remaining garage(s).

There is intense competition in fuel retailing and the Porters Five forces analysis in (a) suggests that this is a difficult industry for a business the size of Mayhews to make sustainable profits. Thus continuing as it is, Option (i), is unlikely to guarantee long-term future success.

Currently the filling station at each garage is making a positive contribution towards fixed operating costs. However the evidence between 2011 and 2012 indicates that it would be possible to improve profitability by increasing the proportion of the servicing and repairs business. Barry's comments about reputation indicate that there may be an opportunity to capitalise on the Mayhews brand and their reputation for honesty and reliability.

A preliminary assessment suggests that garage B is underperforming compared to the others and might be considered for closure. However more information is needed about the detailed performance of the individual garages, the likely savings in operating costs and the exit/compliance costs before deciding whether to close individual sites. An important consideration is the extent to which revenue and costs for the filling stations and repairs business are interdependent.

In the event that Mayhews decided to retain some/all filling stations, it could follow competitors and attempt to service local community needs through product diversification (forecourt shops).

In deciding on the future strategic direction of the business, another issue is succession planning, since Barry is 60. It is important to establish his personal aims and objectives for the business, including any exit plans. He may be keen to realise some of the capital tied up within the business, which the sale of one or more sites to a developer would allow him to do.

Further information required

- Details of the locations, markets and customer profiles of each garage
- Previous year's accounts for each garage
- Repairs revenue/margins split between individual and corporate customers
- Breakdown of operating costs between fuel/repairs/other to ascertain the likely savings in operating costs if one or more filling station is closed
- Exit costs associated with closure of one/more filling stations
- Break-even analysis of fuel sales
- Pricing policy for fuel sales
- Likely value of sites to developer
- Industry/sector information re gross margins/average labour costs/overheads

Appendix: Data analysis

Sales volumes and prices:

	Garage A	Garage B	Garage C	Mayhews 2012	Mayhews 2011
Litres sold (millions)	1.63	1.34	1.43	4.4	5.21
Ave price net of tax/litre	53.9pence	55.1pence	54.3pence	54.4pence	51.6pence
Ave retail price/litre (net of tax price/0.40)	£1.35	£1.38	£1.36	£1.36	£1.29

2012	Branded	Independent	Supermarkets	Mayhews
Litres sold per site (millions)	4.04	1.68	10.2	1.47
Ave retail price/litre	UK ave (whole market) = 133.8p		130.9p	136p
Ave price net of tax/litre	53.5p		52.4p	54.4p

Analysis by product/market:

Sales mix (%)

	Garage A	Garage B	Garage C	2012	2011
Fuel	56	62	51	56	63
Repairs	44	38	49	44	37

Gross margin (%)

	Garage A	Garage B	Garage C	2012	2011
Fuel	11.7	10.3	11.7	11.3	11.3
Repairs	51.6	48.0	55.0	52.1	52.1
Total	29.2	24.7	33.1	29.3	26.6

Breakdown of 2012 revenue by location (%):

	Fuel	Repairs	Total
Garage A	37	36	36
Garage B	31	24	28
Garage C	32	40	36

Breakdown of 2012 gross profit by location (%):

	Fuel	Repairs	Total
Garage A	38	36	36
Garage B	28	22	23
Garage C	34	42	41

Gross profit mix (%)

	Garage A	Garage B	Garage C	2012	2011
Fuel	22	26	18	21	27
Repairs	78	74	82	79	73

Operating costs and net profit

	Garage A	Garage B	Garage C	2012	2011
Operating costs as % of revenue	17.2 14.3%*	15.4	14.3	15.7	15.8
Net profit margin (%)	12.1 14.9%*	9.2	18.7	13.7	10.7
	(*) = adjusted for Barry's salary				

Mayhews: Overall change in performance 2011:2012

Decrease in fuel revenue	−10.9%
Increase in repairs revenue	+18.3%
Decrease in total revenue	negligible
Decrease in fuel gross profit	−11.2%
Increase in repairs gross profit	+18.2%
Increase in total gross profit	+10.4%
Reduction in operating costs	−1.0%
Increase in net profit	+27.1%
Decrease in litres sold	−15.5%
Increase in average retail price/litre	+5.4%

Examiner note:

A complete range of calculations has been provided here for marking purposes. Candidates were not expected to produce all of these given the marks and time available.

Examiner's comments:

Requirement (b) asked candidates to evaluate the performance of Mayhew's overall business and the individual garages and to justify a preliminary conclusion as to whether the company should close one or more filling stations to focus on maintenance and repairs. There were some excellent attempts at this requirement with even the weaker candidates typically scoring over half the marks available.

Most candidates produced a range of calculations for Mayhews business as a whole and for each of its garages, typically including margins, sales mix and revenue/profit growth. Better candidates also used the data to assess Mayhews' fuel prices and volumes in relation to the competition/market. At the other end of the spectrum, some weaker candidates produced hardly any numerical analysis and simply copied out absolute figures from the question or only made a vague attempt at analysing increases/decreases.

Most candidates identified the fact that despite falling fuel volumes, Mayhews has performed well, generating a 27% increase in profit from relatively static sales revenue. The key reason for this is that the mix of sales has changed in favour of maintenance and repairs, which has a significantly higher gross margin than fuel.

In relation to the individual garages, most candidates commented that Garage C is performing best of all and that garage B is the least successful. Better answers explained that this reflects C's reduced reliance on fuel sales, whereas B – the most reliant on fuel sales – is charging the highest price per litre and selling the lowest volume of fuel. A pleasing number of candidates identified that comparing the net margins of the three garages is not particularly useful since the operating costs of garage A include the £45,000 salary cost of the owner, which needs to be removed for a more accurate assessment. Better candidates did this calculation and commented on its results.

The strongest candidates identified that more information is required about the location of the garages and that B may be in one of the less well populated rural areas or alternatively face strong local competition. The lowest scoring candidates merely made assertions describing the changes in ratios, with little, if any, attempt at an analysis of causality.

Candidates were requested to make a preliminary conclusion about the closure of one or more filling stations and most did this, recommending that the filling station at either B or C be closed. Only the better candidates went on to qualify their conclusion, pointing out that more information would be required before making a final decision. The very strongest candidates raised the issue of the possible interdependence of costs and revenues, identifying that the filling station business was making a positive contribution at all garage locations and that failure to supply fuel may lead to the loss of customers for repairs.

(c)   Benefits of new information system

There are two aspects to the investment in IT: a new engine diagnostic system which will allow Mayhews to service more modern vehicles and a new computer system which will improve parts management and have marketing benefits.

Advantages

*   Mayhews will be able to handle all types of car and therefore attract greater volumes of business. It will also be able to undertake business that has previously had to be referred to the main dealer.

*   A customer database will increase marketing opportunities.

*   There will be increased revenue opportunities eg online booking of services and repairs, which might attract a different customer profile.

- The system will give Mayhews a competitive advantage. Contacting customers in advance of MOTs and anticipating service needs will improve the quality of the customer experience and enhance service levels. This may increase customer retention and lead to a greater share of their spend.

- The system should provide Barry with better management information and improve decision making – forecasting, customer profitability analysis, assessment of performance by location/product stream.

- A new system may help reduce costs through more efficient work scheduling, parts control etc.

- The system may help with knowledge management and reduce the business' reliance on Barry.

Disadvantage

- The costs of acquiring and installing the system may be prohibitive for a small business like Mayhews.

- Existing staff may lack the skills to use the system and/or to do work on modern cars. Mayhews will need to train staff to use the new systems and may encounter resistance.

- If Mayhews is currently receiving commission on referrals to main dealers it will lose this income.

- Implementation issues with the new system and the risk of system failures/downtime may cause delays/affect customer service levels. Data protection issues will need to be addressed.

- As the technology is likely to change in the future, particularly in relation to engine diagnostics, the system may need replacing or upgrading regularly.

- There is a risk that competitors will do this too – is it competitive advantage or catch up?

Conclusion

As Mayhews currently does not have the facility to carry out repairs to cars with more modern engine management systems, it appears that investing in a new system will be critical to the success of the strategy to increase the focus on the servicing and repairs business.

A detailed cost benefit analysis should be carried out to ensure the new system is commercially viable.

Examiner's comments:

Requirement (c) asked candidates to discuss the advantages and disadvantages of the proposed investment in information technology. The key to a good answer here was to identify that there were two aspects to the investment in IT: an engine diagnostic system that would allow Mayhews to service modern cars that they currently had to refer to the main dealers, and a new computer system which would provide a customer database and assist with parts management. Candidates who identified the two aspects tended to score well. Weaker candidates often listed the generic pros and cons of information systems, without applying this to Mayhews. Only the best candidates came to any form of conclusion – pointing out that the investment would be critical to Mayhews proposal to focus on repairs and maintenance and identifying the need for some form of cost/benefit analysis before such investment was undertaken.

(d) CSFs for Repairs and servicing

CSFs

Johnson, Scholes and Woodward define critical success factors as 'those product features that are particularly valued by a group of customers and therefore, where the organisation must excel to outperform the competition.' Mayhews has both individual and corporate clients and they may value different things eg corporate clients may be more concerned about speed of service whereas individual customers may focus on trust and reliability.

Alternatively a wider definition of CSFs is 'a small number of key goals vital to the success of an organisation – things that must go right.' Thus CSFs can consider not just the actual product/service but other factors vital to commercial success eg availability, competitive knowledge, cost or performance control.

Using CSFs for strategic control

The process of identifying CSFs will help Mayhews' management focus attention on what is important and the things that need controlling/improving. It will also identify areas of little value-added where for example costs could be eliminated.

Mayhews can measure achievement of the CSFs by calculating KPIs for periodic reporting (see below). These KPIs will assist in benchmarking the garages against each other and also against rivals. They can also help to guide the development of the new information system to ensure that Barry and the garage managers receive information about the factors that are critical to the performance of each location.

Possible CSFs for Mayhews repairs and servicing business

> **Examiner note:**
>
> a number of CSFs have been identified below for marking purposes. Only 3 were required.

(i)   Ability to attract and retain customers – Barry has identified that in this service-based market Mayhews has a reputation for being honest and reliable. Attracting and retaining customers will provide a stable source of income from annual MOTs and servicing and lead to word-of-mouth referrals which should generate growth. Maintaining and winning new corporate contracts will also be important.

(ii) Providing top quality service levels – Mayhews wants to differentiate itself by providing dealer quality service. Customers will expect that repairs carried out are of the highest quality and comply with safety regulations and that they are undertaken as quickly as possible.

(iii) Offering a competitively priced service – Mayhews has lower overheads and labour costs than the main dealers and its strategy is to capitalise on this by offering the same quality service but at affordable local garage prices. In the difficult economic climate, price may be a key factor for many customers.

(iv) Ability to recruit and retain mechanics with appropriate expertise – Mayhews' ability to offer a fast and reliable service will depend on this, particularly if it starts to undertake more complicated engine diagnostics.

(v)   Appropriate technology and information systems strategy to support business needs – Without investing in the new engine diagnostic system, Mayhews will struggle to compete with the main dealers. The reliability of the new computer system will also affect online bookings and will enhance the customer experience by predicting service needs.

Performance measures linked to CSFs:

> **Examiner note:**
>
> a wide range of KPIs has been identified below for marking purposes. Only one relevant KPI was required for each of the 3 CSFs identified.

(i)   **Attraction/Retention of customers:**

Number of cars referred to main dealer (measures Mayhews' ability to carry out work)
Number of contracts for corporate servicing
Average Customer satisfaction scores on post work feedback survey
Level of repeat business for MOTs and annual servicing
Geographical area of customer base
% of enquiries converted to booking for MOT/service

(ii) **Quality service levels**

Quality of work undertaken:
% of defects rectified
Warranty costs as a % of revenue
Level of complaints
% of vehicles maintained/repaired which have to be subsequently rechecked

Speed of service

Lead time between customer call and date job scheduled
Availability of parts
Hours taken per repair/service
% of jobs finished on time

(iii) **Competitively priced service**

Final price as a % of original Quotation
Hourly labour charge compared to main dealers' labour charges
Price of various work (MOT/routine service etc) compared to competitors
Recovery rates: Hours recharged to customers/Hours worked

(iv) **Staffing**

Qualifications undertaken/mechanic
Number of sick/absent days
Staff turnover compared to total number of staff

(v) **Technology and information**

Number of vehicles that Mayhews is unable to diagnose/need referring to main dealer
Number of mechanics trained in the new engine diagnostic system
Number of computer system breakdowns

Examiner's comments:

In requirement (d), candidates were asked to explain how the use of critical success factors might assist Mayhews in establishing a strategic control system. Candidates were required to justify three CSFs for the maintenance and repairs business and suggest one appropriate key performance indicator for each. This part was surprisingly quite poorly done. Many candidates restricted their marks by completely ignoring the element of the requirement relating to establishing a strategic control system and simply provided a list of CSFs and KPIs. The weakest candidates were clearly unsure about the distinction between KPIs and targets or goals. For some, the CSFs and KPIs described could have been those for any business and it was not obvious that the candidate was discussing Mayhews' repairs and maintenance business. Whilst customer satisfaction is relevant to all businesses and therefore customer feedback is vitally important, the information in the question could have been used to produce some higher quality answers. The better candidates produced a reasoned justification of their choice of each CSF and then demonstrated clearly how this could be measured. Some candidates provided a long list of KPIs, despite the specific request for only one for each CSF identified – these additional measures wasted time and did not attract marks.

---

64 Cabezada Ltd

Marking guide

		Knowledge	Skill	Marks
(a)	Business plan	4	12	6
(b)	Additional information	2	6	8
(c)	Market segmentation	3	5	8
		9	23	32

The scenario in this question relates to a relatively new company which uses steel shipping containers to create short-term living accommodation for events and contract clients. The directors are keen to expand globally and have begun to prepare a business plan to help attract appropriate local partners. Candidates were asked to take the role of a senior in the firm of business advisers which has been appointed to help develop the business plan.

The overall scores on this question were again very good.

(a) **Sections of Business Plan**

  (i) **Strengths and realistic market opportunities (section 2.2.1)**

  Our key strengths:

  Innovation – Cabezada are seen as a pioneer within the container accommodation industry and we have built up an extensive database, contact network and team of experienced designers and engineers.

  The Cabezada product range is extremely flexible and can be adapted to meet the needs of a wide variety of customers and target markets.

  There is a cheap and readily available supply of standardised containers, and with access to worldwide low-cost distribution systems we can quickly, easily and cheaply respond to customer needs.

  We have a strong leadership team as a result of the skills and experience acquired in our previous roles as chief executive of a hotel group and operations director of a large construction company.

  Realistic market opportunities:

  We believe that there are significant opportunities for rapid expansion into global markets via our local partnership model.

  Our proven success to date indicates that the container accommodation concept is likely to be successful in a range of other markets eg student accommodation, pop-up retail stores, mobile offices.

  The world's population is growing. Land shortages and cost implications mean there is likely to be an increasing need for this type of accommodation.

  Similarly the global demand for sustainability and a desire to conserve resources will lead to a growing demand for container accommodation over conventional structures.

  Cabezada may be able to further enhance its brand reputation and achieve recognition for corporate social responsibility by working with local governments and charities as potential partners in disaster areas/trouble zones. This and our sustainability ethos may widen market appeal and help attract future customers/investors.

  (ii) **Weaknesses and threats (section 2.2.2)**

  There is limited scope for Cabezada to expand alone due to current size and resources, which is why we have developed a partnership model.

  Some of the benefits of container accommodation are a result of the standardisation of containers, the ease of transportation and the readily available supply. These are also downsides as potentially this seems to be an easily replicated idea. Protection of IP in relation to our competitors will therefore be important. However Cabezada also benefits from experience and reputation gained as a result of first mover advantage and establishing a global network should help create barriers to entry.

  We recognise that as the business expands the two of us are unlikely to have sufficient time and expertise to manage the wider business. Neither of us has a financial background and we are well aware that many businesses fail because they lack sufficient financial expertise. We currently rely on our accountants to provide this expertise but we plan to appoint a finance director in due course and as the business expands we intend to appoint other directors to the Board.

Projects are heavily reliant on local infrastructure in relation to heat, light, sewerage etc. and delays may occur due to the political nature of certain projects. Cabezada's previous experience can be brought to bear here to ensure such risks are managed and to make sure that appropriate contingency plans are in place.

Legal and regulatory requirements differ between countries but this is mitigated by our use of the local partnership model.

Health and safety issues or accidents could be very damaging to our reputation. We pride ourselves on our unblemished health and safety record. We take this issue very seriously and we expect our partners to do the same.

A successful model will rely on the integrity of a wide range of local partners and we need to ensure goal congruence. Our partnership agreement will be carefully drafted to make clear the obligations on both sides to ensure the Cabezada brand is not diluted by variable standards. Our terms and conditions will also set out restrictive clauses and confidentiality agreements to protect our partners in the event that a local partner chooses to leave the business.

(iii) **Benefits of partnership approach for Cabezada and its local partners (section 3)**

Global business using a local model

Working with the right local partners will allow us to capitalise on our brand image as a pioneer in container accommodation, expand rapidly and generate competitive advantage for Cabezada.

It is easier for local customers and governments to do business with local offices, from a language and timing point of view, as well as culturally.

Local teams are better able to identify opportunities in a market and define appropriate price/quality combination.

Since building standards vary from country to country and requirements also change frequently it is better for the local office to work with architects, governments and planning experts.

Support for our local partner

In addition to exclusive rights to operate under the Cabezada brand in your defined area, we will provide you with a range of benefits that result from being part of a global business, and which are unachievable by setting up business alone:

1. A popular and tested product range suitable for many different uses in many markets and a reference list of successful projects in different countries

2. Access to an experienced team of designers and engineers dedicated to container accommodation

3. Marketing support including website, brochures and press articles

4. Our supplier and customer contact network and our extensive database of technical, financial and marketing information

5. Assistance with budgets and financial projections for projects

6. Ongoing support from a committed partner as evidenced by the fact that we are prepared to take a 20% stake in each partner business

Requirement (a) asked candidates to prepare three sections of the business plan:

(i) Strengths and realistic market opportunities
(ii) Weaknesses and threats
(iii)Benefits of partnership for Cabezada and its local partners

This was one of the higher skills elements of the paper and answers were quite polarised. Although candidates were clearly familiar with the knowledge required, which was based on SWOT analysis and methods of business development, weaker candidates struggled to apply this in the context of a business plan to attract potential partners. Candidates who appreciated the need to focus their content on the end user of the document and wrote in an appropriate style, scored very highly. The key here was to (i) emphasise why the company's strengths put it in an ideal position to capitalise on the global opportunities (ii) explain any potential weaknesses and threats and how they might be mitigated and (iii) highlight how the partnership proposition would be a win-win for both parties. Surprisingly, too many candidates did not produce an answer using the numbered section headings given in the requirement, missing out on an easy format mark. Weaker candidates often provided a bullet point list for each requirement which would not have been suitable for a firm to send to a client. Weak answers were often written as if the focus was on assessing the situation from Cabezada's point of view rather than considering how the information would be received by the partner (ie with a complete failure to consider the marketing/persuasive nature of the document). Another error was for candidates to write in a(i) and a(ii) about the strengths and weaknesses of the partnership arrangement, rather than of Cabezada, leaving themselves with little new to say in a(iii).

(b) **Additional information requirements**

A prospective partner will want sufficient information to be able to undertake appropriate due diligence and decide if the Cabezada business model makes sense given the current and future environment. They will use a range of criteria to assess the proposal and it is important to anticipate what these are likely to be and to cover them in the plan. The assessment criteria are likely to include:

- Viability of business model
- Costs
- Potential returns
- Risks (weaknesses and threats) and how these might be addressed
- Obligations of both parties
- Possible exit route

It would be useful for the plan to start with an executive summary setting out the highlights of the detail contained in the plan. In addition to the current content of the plan, a prospective partner is also likely to want the plan to include the following additional information about:

Owners of Cabezada

Background/track record/qualifications/expertise of owners;

Any other key stakeholders besides the two directors

Details of senior management

Financial security of the company

Recent accounts to indicate the long-term sustainability of the business and its ability to provide partners with on-going support.

Competition

Analysis of existing players in the market place, their USPs and how Cabezada differentiates itself in relation to their products/markets.

Detailed terms and conditions of joint venture

Terms and conditions of Cabezada's stake
Obligations of both JV parties
Details of amount and level of support and training to be provided by Cabezada
Restrictions on partners eg Regional protection; minimum performance requirements
Reporting structure for local partners
Control mechanisms to guarantee quality and performance of other partners
Restrictions on use of suppliers
Exit arrangements

Detailed financial information

The required investment level – the amount partners will have to pay for the franchise fee, monthly management charge and % royalty fee on sales.

Annual projections for a typical partner, showing likely profitability and cash flow.

Cabezada's attitude to any continuing financial obligations and the arrangements for financing in the event of expansion.

Evidence of key strategic relationships

Details of existing projects undertaken

Supplier contracts
Quotes/recommendations from existing satisfied customers
Details of any existing partners/references from them

Other information

Supporting technical detail on the different types of accommodation offered, including photos, plans, diagrams etc.

Examiner's comments:

Requirement (b) requested candidates to recommend any further information that should be included in the plan to help potential partners to adequately assess Cabezada's partnership proposition. Candidates who were familiar with the pro-forma contents of a business plan and who then applied this to the scenario tended to score well. Some weaker candidates merely provided a list of information without explaining how this might be useful to a potential partner. Better candidates provided a prioritised discussion, focussing on the fact that the current plan was completely lacking in any financial information – historic results, forecasts and details of the costs of the partnership arrangement – and that this would be vital if partners were to assess the likely returns from their investment. It is likely that partners would also want more information on the key directors with whom they were establishing a relationship.

(c) **Purpose and benefits of market segmentation**

Market segmentation is the division of the market into homogeneous groups of potential customers who may be treated similarly for marketing purposes.

The purpose of segmentation is to vary the marketing mix according to the needs of each chosen segment. This is likely to increase the effectiveness of marketing.

For example by dividing the market into events and contract clients Cabezada can tailor its product. Events clients may be more concerned with the appearance of the accommodation and want a range of designs; contract clients may focus on cost and functionality.

Benefits of market segmentation include:

- Identification of new marketing opportunities because it provides Cabezada with an opportunity to spot additional sub-groups or to dominate certain segments of the market (niche).

- Competitive advantage from having a better understanding of customer's needs and attitudes to price in each segment.

- It allows Cabezada to assess returns from each segment and thus assist in performance measurement/provide information for decision making.

Segmentation options for Cabezada:

Cabezada has currently chosen to segment the market by type of buyer: one-off short term events vs contract clients requiring longer term accommodation.

It could also consider segmentation by:

- Geographical location – this may help Cabezada organise its logistical operations and adjust elements of the price/product to local needs

- Type of accommodation: hotel & leisure; key worker; housing; media; temporary disaster recovery

- Quality of accommodation: basic, luxury, environmentally friendly

Examiner's comments:

In requirement (c), candidates were required to explain the purpose and benefits of market segmentation and discuss other approaches to segmentation that the company could adopt, besides the current split between contract and events clients.

The majority of candidates were able to define market segmentation and explain how it could be used to focus the marketing mix to specific customer needs. Again better candidates differentiated themselves by illustrating this with examples relating to Cabezada, rather than talking about segmentation in generic terms. Most candidates were able to make alternative suggestions for segmentation according to geography or quality, although a significant minority of suggestions were more appropriate for segmenting consumers than business customers. A small number of candidates discussed divisionalisation, generic strategy or product/market mix rather than segmentation; these answers were not relevant.

65 Chiba

Marking guide

		Knowledge	Skill	Marks
(a)	Ethical issues	2	3	5
(b)	Divestment/growth by acquisition	3	5	8
(c) (i)	Human resource management	2	3	5
(ii)	Change management	3	6	9
		10	17	27

General comments

Chiba is a Japanese company which manufactures a range of liquid foods including rice vinegar. Chiba wants to increase its market share in the UK by acquiring Malegar – a division of a large listed UK food business which makes the UK's leading brand of malt vinegar. Chiba's marketing director is however concerned that Malegar would not be for sale if it were a profitable business. Another potential integration issue is the fact that the two companies have very different cultures and attitudes to human resources management. There is also an ethical issue: the directors of Malegar are aware of a recent complaint from a major wholesaler concerning a contaminated batch of vinegar. As Malegar takes health and safety and quality control seriously, the directors believe the fault must lie with the supplier

(a) **Ethical issues**

The issue here is whether it is legal and ethical for the directors to keep the contamination confidential. As well as possibly damaging Malegar's reputation, the contamination will potentially have an effect on the wholesaler(s), the supplier of the bottles, the consumers of the vinegar and the potential purchaser, Chiba.

The directors need to investigate the cause of the problem and consider whether there has been any breach of the law or other regulations that may apply to the industry eg health and safety or food standards. It could be argued that since Malegar takes health and safety and quality control very seriously, there should have been procedures in place to avoid/detect the contamination before the product reached the wholesaler, irrespective of whoever caused the problem.

In the context of the potential acquisition by Chiba, the directors of Malegar have a duty to act in the best interests of the company and to obtain the best value for shareholders. However, since Malegar's parent, VM plc, is a UK listed company it is likely to have certain obligations regarding the disclosure of any information that could materially affect the purchase price. To this effect there may be a conflict of interest between the directors' duty to obtain the best price for their shareholders and their duty to treat Chiba fairly. The directors should therefore seek legal advice as to how much information they are required to disclose to a prospective purchaser and to what extent it is a case of 'buyer beware'. Chiba is likely to undertake due diligence to help understand the risks before taking on ownership and this will almost certainly involve an investigation into potential liabilities and warranties.

Knowingly making statements that are misleading or inaccurate is likely to be considered dishonest and unethical. The omission of information, which is a matter of transparency, is perhaps less clear cut, particularly where it might be argued that this is an acceptable treatment eg if the directors believe that the contamination issue has arisen with the supplier and is likely to be fully compensated.

Malegar's directors need to establish the facts and ascertain the cause of the contamination and then seek legal advice before deciding on the most appropriate course of action which fulfils their ethical obligations but minimises the risk of reputational damage for the company.

Examiner's comments:

Requirement (a) asked candidates to explain the ethical issues that arise for Malegar's directors in relation to revealing the possible contamination.

The quality of answers to this requirement varied considerably. The question required candidates to assess the ethical issues arising from the directors' intention to keep the contamination confidential and the responsibility of Malegar to its customers and the potential acquirer, Chiba. Many candidates approached this requirement in terms of a transparency, fairness and effect framework. However only the better candidates went on to develop the next steps or draw any sort of conclusion. The weaker candidates only considered the issue in relation to Chiba, ignoring the other stakeholders in the scenario (namely the wholesaler, glass supplier and end consumers). They often failed to see any grey area and simply stated that Malegar's directors must reveal the potential contamination or risk being sued by Chiba after it had acquired the business. Stronger candidates discussed the fact that the cause of the contamination was uncertain, and that the directors needed first to establish the facts and then decide whether to disclose. The best candidates also discussed whether Malegar would have any legal duty to disclose the issue to its customers or Chiba, which might be expected to undertake its own due diligence, or whether in the context of the acquisition it would be a case of 'buyer beware'.

ICAEW

(b) Strategy evaluation

As Chiba's marketing director notes, the UK parent may want to sell Malegar because the market is challenging and it is struggling to maintain margins etc. Even so, Malegar may still be worth buying as Chiba may be better placed to exploit benefits due to synergy with its existing brands and the ability to target other markets based on health benefits and alternative uses (eg cleaning).

However it could also be that the Malegar business is viable and that other reasons can be put forward for the divestment by the UK parent:

Reason for sale by UK parent

- Rationalisation of the business as a result of portfolio analysis – here we are told that VM plc wants to focus on a few key food brands (a reversal of diversification strategy). VM plc may have decided that there is a lack of strategic fit between vinegar and its other more profitable brands.

- VM may wish to generate funds for investment in other markets that will generate better growth opportunities. Malegar may be generating insufficient returns for the amount of management time/investment required.

- We are also told that the parent company has incurred significant borrowings. These may be incurring high interest costs and putting a strain on liquidity. A sale would raise funds to reduce this debt burden.

- If exit barriers are high (eg redundancy costs, termination penalties on leases etc) then it is better for VM to sell the business as a going concern rather than just withdraw the product.

- Finally the company may be trying to sell Malegar before the contamination becomes widely known and damages its brand/reputation

Chiba's growth by acquisition

The Ansoff model is a two-by-two matrix of 'Products' and 'Markets'. In the context of this matrix the acquisition of Malegar would involve market development and, to the extent that malt vinegar is deemed to be different from rice vinegar, product development. The Lynch expansion model is another two-by-two matrix of company growth and geographical location. Under this model, Chiba's proposed acquisition is international external development.

Arguments for growth by acquisition

- Chiba's management has identified a desire to increase its presence in the UK. Chiba has no track record in the UK market and the strong market presence of brand names such as Malegar creates barriers to entry that would make organic growth hard to achieve. Acquisition is likely to be faster than organic growth and potentially less risky.

- Acquisition of the market leader creates instant market dominance for Chiba and at the same time removes a significant player from the market.

- It will provide access to a strong brand name/reputation in the UK market and facilitate a better understanding of the UK market for a Japanese company. This reduces cultural risk and having a 'local image' may also reduce xenophobic tendencies.

- Acquisition gives Chiba instant access to the existing factory location and resources, including employees.

- The acquisition of a business in the UK may give rise to other future opportunities, eg expansion into Europe.

The price of the acquisition will be a major factor in assessing the overall merits of sale or purchase.

(c)   **HR strategy and change management**

(i)   **HR management by Malegar**

Malegar does not seem to have adopted a strategic approach to HRM. Its approach, which is very authoritarian, treats the staff merely as another resource, rather than as a valued asset. It may have resulted in a high degree of job-related tension, poor working relationships and some manipulation of data by functional managers accountable for their performance. There are likely to be limited prospects for career development.

The disadvantages of such an approach include:

- There is evidence that staff motivation may be a problem as there is a high staff turnover. The loss of staff loses experience and skills for the company with the costs of retraining and learning for new staff.

- There may be dysfunctional behaviour by staff in response to short-term targets instead of focussing on longer-term value-enhancing activities eg this may mean that short-term sales are made at the cost of long-term customer relationships.

- The hierarchical nature of the business and centralised approach to decision making may also have impeded team-working and stifled innovation.

HR management by Chiba

Chiba on the other hand appears to take a more strategic approach with emphasis on the human element. This recognises that collectively the staff are a valued asset and can contribute to competitive advantage.

Chiba is likely to do more to focus on personal and career development, gaining employees' commitment to the organisation's values and goals and creating a more participative environment.

As a result tension and manipulation are reduced and relationships are likely to be better.

The shared approach to decision making is likely to increase goal congruence, although a potential downside of Chiba's approach to HRM is that decision-making may be slower than in Malegar.

(i)   **Managing the change of culture**

It is clear that the two businesses are very different and that acquisition by Chiba will transform the existing structure, culture and values. As a result of the acquisition, Chiba's management will need to develop a strategy for creating and maintaining the necessary culture change, although the fact that the transition will take up to 12 months may help as the changes can be made gradually.

The changes may cause resistance from those wishing to preserve the existing state of affairs and the way that the changes are put forward and implemented will be crucial to Chiba's success. However given Chiba's approach to HRM, the change may be welcomed by many Malegar employees as better than they are used to.

Barrier to change

Barriers to change may be cultural or arise as a result of things which affect individuals and cause them to see the change as a threat (personnel barriers).

Cultural resistance arises as a result of structural inertia, group inertia and power structures.

- Structural inertia – Malegar has operated with a rigid hierarchy and short term targets which will take time to change. Its recruitment and promotion processes are likely to have resulted in certain types of employee who may not fit with Chiba's collective approach and participative decision making.

- Group inertia – this may be less relevant as Malegar's existing structure is unlikely to have led to cohesive teams. However the functional managers may act as a group in resisting change implementation and if employees are in one geographical location this may be a factor in increasing group resistance.

Power structures are threatened by the redistribution of authority or changing communication lines. This will in particular affect higher management in Malegar whose roles may change significantly after the new structure is implemented, as participation and collective responsibility is encouraged. Such management may be reluctant to implement changes which will be against their own interests. For example, managers may have viewed Malegar as having been very successful in the UK, therefore resenting the need to integrate and adopt the new values of a Japanese company.

Other Malegar employees who have been discontented under the existing system may however be supportive at the outset.

Personal barriers

There are also barriers which affect individuals and result in them seeing the change as a threat.

Malegar employees may feel threatened by the changes to their habitual way of working and the lack of familiarity (fear of the unknown). Junior employees may lack the confidence or skills to take on a new challenge and may take time to get used to the participative approach with its emphasis on shared responsibility. It is important that Chiba offers support and training to assist them.

Employees may have concerns over potential income levels and job security, although given the high staff turnover this does not seem to have been a feature of employment with Malegar. Chiba could provide statistics on staff turnover to help reassure employees about employment prospects and their earning capacity.

Selective information processing may cause employees to misinterpret or ignore the arguments for change put forward by Chiba's management.

Change management

Resistance to cultural change can be managed or reduced with genuine and visible support for the change by top management and good communication/participation systems associated with the change.

Chiba's management should identify the key stakeholders and influencers among the Malegar employees and provide communication and appropriate training.

Communication should focus on the benefits of the change to employees. Management needs to communicate Chiba's vision of the future and show how the Malegar employees can contribute to this. Given the gradual nature of the transfer of contracts, a negotiation strategy may be implemented where the process of bargaining leads to a situation of compromise and agreement. The advantage of a negotiation strategy is that Chiba can note possible conflict and deal with it in an orderly fashion, which prevents such problems as industrial action. Also ex-Malegar employees are more likely to support changes made and give positive commitment if they 'own' the change or have a stake in the future of the company.

Lewin suggests that managers should recognise the current state of equilibrium with forces pushing for change on the one hand and, equally, forces resisting change aiming to maintain the present situation. As a result Chiba's management would need to adopt the following process:

- **Unfreezing** – where management convince staff of the undesirability of the present situation, creating the initial motivation to change by emphasising the benefits of Chiba's longer term, participative approach.

- **The change process itself** – which will often involve new information, new attitudes and new concepts. This would involve the communication, negotiation and training outlined above.

- **Refreezing** – which reinforces the new pattern of work or behaviour by rewards, developing the belief that the changed situation satisfies organisational and personal values. Under Chiba's management employees are likely to have more opportunities for career development, staff turnover should reduce and Chiba can also implement non-financial motivators rather than focussing on the achievement of short term targets.

Examiner note:

This answer includes a wide variety of points for marking purposes and is far more comprehensive than would be expected for the marks available. As an alternative to Lewin, the Gemini's 4Rs framework for planned change could also be applied: Reframe, Restructure, Revitalise, Renew.

Examiner's comments:

In requirement (c), candidates were required to (i) contrast Chiba and Malegar's differing approaches to human resource management and (ii) explain the change management issues that Chiba is likely to face when integrating the Malegar employees.

Some candidates seemed less well prepared for (c)(i), with many weaker candidates restricting their answers to a comparison of structure and decision-making, which often was in fact little more than a repetition of points made in the scenario. Better candidates contrasted Malegar's 'hard' approach to HRM which treats employees as a short-term commodity, with Chiba's 'softer', more collective approach where employees are seen as a valued asset, and discussed the impact that this is likely to have on motivation, quality of decision-making and commitment to the organisation.

As usual candidates demonstrated good knowledge of change management in (c)(ii), with most discussing barriers to change and Lewin/Schein's iceberg model (although the Gemini's 4Rs framework could also have been used). It was disappointing that more candidates did not focus on the change in the context of the very different HRM strategy and culture/values of the Japanese company – a point that (c)(i) had been intended to highlight; weaker candidates instead discussed at length the general change management issues associated with acquisitions. The best candidates recognised that the change will transform the existing culture but is to take place over a gradual period of 12 months and, given some explanation, may be welcomed by most employees as better than their current position. Candidates who went on at length about structural inertia, group norms and job security failed to recognise that these might not be particularly relevant given Malegar's existing high staff turnover.

66 Hire Value Ltd

Marking guide

		Knowledge	Skill	Marks
(a)	Performance and competitive position	2	8	10
(b)	Shortfall in performance	–	16	16
(c)	Risk register	3	6	9
(d)	Ethical issues	3	7	10
		8	37	45

General comments

This is the mini case and also the data analysis question. The scenario relates to a small company (HV) operating in the self-drive, car hire industry. HV decided to expand the business just over a year ago by raising venture capital finance based on a business plan which forecast growth in sales and profits. Whilst there has been some growth, it has not matched the business plan projections and a one-year review has taken place to discover the reasons for this. The review also highlighted some transactions with directors which raised ethical issues. The question also provides information about the market leader, KK.

Data for (a) and (b)

	HV plan	HV Actual	Variance	%	KK
Revenue					
Business £000s	13,000	7,000	–6,000	–46.15	620,000
Leisure £000s	17,000	20,000	+3,000	+17.65	580,000
TOTAL REV £000s	30,000	27,000	–3,000	–10%	1,200,000
Profit £000s	1,200	1,000	–200	–16.67%	56,000
Vehicles	3,000	2,800	–200	–6.67%	68,000
Days hiring					
('000 days)	870	820	–50	–5.74%	21,100
Asset values					
Cars £000s	20,250	16,800	–3,450	–17.04%	816,000
Other £000s	10,000	10,000	0	0	664,000
Total assets £000s	30,250	26,800	–3,450	–11.40%	1,480,000

	HV plan	HV Actual	Variance	%	KK
Analysis					
% REVENUE					
– business	43.3%	25.9%			51.7%
– leisure	56.7%	74.1%			48.3%
PROFIT/REV	4%	3.7%			4.7%
REV per car pa	£10,000	£9,642.85			£17,647
REV per day hiring	£34.48	£32.93			£56.87
Days hire per car	290	293			310
Profit/assets	3.97	3.73			3.78
Profit/value of cars	5.93	5.95			6.86
Value of cars/cars	£6,750	£6,000			£12,000
Rev/value of cars	1.48	1.61			1.47

(a) Key differences between KK and HV which make performance comparisons more difficult are: the larger size of KK; and a different business sector, with KK being upmarket compared to HV's business model. However, both companies operate in a similar product and geographical market, being in the UK.

Competitive position

In assessing market share of KK and HV they are both operating in the short term rental sector which has revenues of £5,000 million. Any assessment of competitive position appears valid in relation to this market sub-sector.

With revenue of £1,200 million this gives KK a substantial 24% share of the short term car hire sector. In contrast, HV has a market share of about 0.5%. With a total industry revenue of about £5,000 million and 100 companies, the average company has a revenue of about £50 million giving it a 1% market share – almost twice that of HV.

As a consequence, HV is very much a niche player in the industry. It appears to adopt a slightly confused business model of a mid-market position in all respects except the key asset of the quality of the vehicles, which is downmarket. Perhaps, as a consequence, it is particularly weak in the business customer sector with only 26% of revenue from business customers.

In contrast, KK generates 52% of its revenue from the business customer sector. It also competes at the upper end of the market with a wide range of large company business customers and a series of partners offering exclusive access to some airlines making it impossible, in the short term at least, for smaller car hire companies, including HV, to compete.

KK's size enables it to have economies of scale and economies of scope for cost advantages and these also provide barriers to entry into this sector of the market making it hard for smaller companies, like HV, to compete.

Performance

In absolute terms, it is clear that KK earns a greater profit than HV. However this is to be expected from a larger company and it does not follow that it has performed better on this basis.

In terms of margins, the data table shows that KK has significantly better operating profit margins at 4.7% compared to 3.7% for HV. This may be due to: better cost control; economies of scale; or premium pricing.

Similarly, revenue per car is much greater for KK at £17,647 per year compared to only £9,643 for HV (83% higher). It would be misleading to conclude however that KK has better revenue generation from its assets on this basis. The table shows that the average value of a KK car is £12,000 while the average value of a HV car is only half that at £6,000. Thus, while KK's car value is 100% greater than that of HV, the revenue per car is only 83% higher. As a consequence, the data table shows that HV's annual revenue per £1 of car value is £1.61, compared to only £1.41 for KK. This may give some support for the HV business model of sourcing two year old used cars.

A key piece of data that indicates market positioning is the price per day of hire. For HV it is only £32.93, whereas KK is able to charge an average of £56.87, although this average may reflect some very high quality vehicles.

In terms of operating efficiency, KK also appears to outperform HV. KK cars are hired out 310 days per year giving a utilisation of 85% (on a 365 day year) compared to that of 80% already noted for HV.

It is clear therefore that in financial and operating terms KK has overall outperformed HV, but nevertheless the strategy of HV may have some favourable aspects and HV may have more potential to grow if it is able to win some large business customer accounts.

Examiner's comments:

Requirement (a) requested candidates to compare the performance and competitive position of HV with that of the market leader, KK. Attempts at this part were reasonable with most candidates producing some calculations including operating profit margin, average price per vehicle hired and average number of days hired. However, the interpretation of the data was, in many cases, limited. Candidates struggled with the comparison of a large business with a smaller business with many concluding little more than that KK had greater revenue and profit through its relatively greater size. Some of the reasons for the differences were very general, such as 'KK has economies of scale'. The comparison of competitive position was omitted altogether by a significant minority of candidates.

(b) **Revenue**

The above data analysis shows that overall revenues are lower than the business plan by £3m, which is a 10% shortfall on planned sales revenues.

The analysis by sector shows that there is a shortfall of £6m in the business customer sector, but that sales revenue in the leisure sector has exceeded the business plan by £3m. The reason for the shortfall in leisure needs to be investigated further in terms of the assumptions that were expected to lead to growth (eg number of new business customers, new lines of business, pricing policy, one or a few larger business customers expected to be won). It may be that negotiations are continuing on some accounts that are expected to be won in 2012/13 and that will come to fruition in 2013/14.

The excess over plan of leisure customer revenues should also be investigated further to continue to exploit any successes in the next period.

The impact of the revenue variances has made the company much more dependent on the leisure sector compared to the business sector (74% v 26%) than was envisaged in the business plan where the relative shares were reasonably equal (57% v 43%).

There is limited additional data on each customer sector but, looking at revenue overall, it can be seen from the above data table that the number of days hiring has fallen short of the plan by 50,000 hire days. In terms of volumes this is a 5.7% shortfall. The fact that sales revenues have fallen by 10% and volumes by only 5.7% implies that the rental charge has been lower than expected. This notion is substantiated by the revenue per vehicle hire day which was £34.48 per hire day in the business plan, but only £32.93 was actually achieved.

This result could be explained by: additional discounting, proportionately more hires of cheaper vehicles or failure to implement intended price increases. The result is, however, inconsistent with the shift in the proportion of business customers to leisure customers as business customers have 'preferential rates' and so one would expect the revenue per hire day to increase with a greater proportion of leisure customers. This matter requires further investigation and analysis by sector.

Profitability

The above data table shows that overall profit before tax is lower than the business plan by £200,000, which is a 16.7% shortfall on profit in the business plan.

The fall of 16.7% in profit based on a 10% fall in revenue may, in part, be due to operating gearing whereby fixed costs still need to be covered and therefore profit falls by a greater amount than revenue.

Profit margins are also lower than planned at 3.7%, compared to the forecast 4%. This also may be due to high operating gearing and lower sales than expected.

Return on assets

Having considered profitability in absolute terms, it is necessary to consider profitability in relation to the asset base generating that profit.

The revenue earning asset base (cars) is smaller than planned, with an actual average count of 2,800 vehicles rather than the 3,000 planned. The reasons for this need to be established. It may have been that with lower demand it was decided to reduce the number of cars held in order not to have surplus underutilised assets. It is possible however that the direction of causation is the other way around ie that it has proved difficult to source the right type of cars at the right price and the shortfall in vehicle capacity has meant that revenues have been affected. This latter explanation seems less likely, but further investigation is needed.

The return on total assets from the data table is 3.7% compared to the level in the business plan of 4%. This has occurred as, even though the asset base is £3.45m (11.4%) lower than expected, the profit is down 16.7% on the planned level.

Further analysis of assets shows that general non-revenue earning assets are constant at £10m. As a result the entire £3.45m fall in the asset base relates to hire cars. This is a 17% reduction. As a consequence, the return on the revenue generating asset base of cars is 5.95% which is slightly higher than the planned rate of 5.93%.

Further analysis shows that the reason for the lower hire car asset base is partly volume with 2,800 cars compared to the planned level of 3,000 (6.7% lower). However the value per car is also lower than planned at £6,000 compared to the planned value of £6,750. This may be due to: a higher proportion of purchases of smaller and cheaper cars than planned; the acquisition of older cars in the period; or a greater than expected fall in the value of the entire vehicle holding due to market conditions. Further investigations would be needed to ascertain the reasons.

Efficiency and utilisation

The number of days per year that cars are out on hire reflects utilisation and is a key factor in determining profitability. The data table shows that cars were out on hire 293 days per year compared to the planned level of 290 days (ie on a 365 day year this is 80% utilization). The most obvious reason for the higher level of utilization is that despite lower sales volumes than expected (ie hire days are 5.7% lower) the number of cars available is 6.7% lower.

The high utilization rates are good in one respect as they reflect high usage of revenue earning assets. In another respect however the high utilization could be seen as excessive. In particular as the business is seasonal then it may be significantly higher than 80% in peak season.

On the basis of the information provided, 30% of annual sales come in each of spring or summer. If there is on average 80% utilization then in summer/spring there is $80\% \times 30/25 = 96\%$. At a peak time of the week in peak season there may be 100% utilization for at least some types of vehicle. This may mean lost sales or lack of consumer choice in vehicle selection.

The utilisation and sales loss arguments need to be balanced. Further investigations are therefore needed regarding the number of lost sales from the inability to supply suitable vehicles to customers.

The Business Plan and Professional Scepticism

The shortfall from the business plan may have been due to over-optimistic forecasts in setting the plan rather than poor performance in delivering the plan. In particular, in order to raise finance from the venture capitalists, the HV board may have been incentivised to present the forecasts expected by the venture capitalists.

Examiner's comments:

Requirement (b) asked candidates to analyse and explain the shortfall between actual performance and the business plan forecast, then to highlight three matters for further investigation. The weakest candidates produced few or no calculations for this part, thereby providing purely qualitative answers. These types of data analysis and interpretation questions require numerical analysis of data but also explanations of underlying cause and effect relationships indicating why variances may have occurred in order to 'make the numbers speak'.

Many better candidates produced calculations which normally considered days hired, operating profit margins, return on assets and efficiency/utilisation ratios. Better answers also considered the validity of the projections in the business plan itself, questioning whether they were too optimistic in an attempt to obtain venture capital finance. The correct observation was often made that the necessary investment in new vehicles had not taken place hence somewhat diluting the firm's ability to expand the business sector.

Most candidates provided reasonable suggestions for further investigation. For example, some candidates indicated that prior year performance data would be useful in order to assess the reasons for the shortfall.

(c)

Risk	Impact and likelihood	Risk management
Legal liability from the operation of cars by customers and employees.	• High significance if there is personal injury. • Lower impact as damage will be to only one car. • With many vehicles being operated a reasonably high probability that accidents will occur.	• Insure risk. • Put in place procedures to ensure terms of insurance agreement are complied with. • Implement procedures to minimise the probability of accidents (eg restrict hires to 'clean' licence holders).
Regulation risk which may change the terms of business or the need for compliance costs to be incurred, including tax.	• Increased environment and tax legislation to reduce pollution seems likely. • With so many vehicles owned the impact could be significant.	• Consider acquiring more environmentally friendly vehicles. • Join industry pressure group to influence government.
Strong dependence on airline industry.	• Any problems with airline industry (recession, taxation, strike) are likely to affect the car rental industry.	• Form partnerships and work together with airline industry • Diversify with partners in other industries (eg insurance).
Competition risk. The internet has made capture of new bookings much easier for smaller companies to compete at the lower end of the market.	Competition may significantly affect price and have a major impact on profits of small companies such as HV. This is likely to occur and at the smaller end of the market there is already significant competition with over 100 UK operators.	• Develop reputation and identity. • Holding slots at airports is one way to restrict competition.
Seasonality means a risk of redundant assets in low season and insufficient capacity in peak season.	If seasonality is pronounced then the effects at the margin may be moderately significant. Highly likely as an established demand pattern.	• Price discrimination according to season. • Rent assets to acquire vehicles to meet short term peak rather than owning 100% of car pool. • Model seasonality so timings are predictable.

Risk	Impact and likelihood	Risk management
Car prices could change If cars increase in cost then this is the major capital asset and will affect profitability and liquidity.	The car industry is competitive which makes major price changes unlikely. However should it occur it may have significant impact.	• Have portfolio of different types of car of different ages. • Hold cars for longer if car prices temporarily increase.
Second hand values weaken meaning lower residuals at end of car life and greater depreciation and costs of ownership.	Second hand market is competitive but new legislation could mean older cars which are less environmentally friendly may become more costly to run and this reduces their value. Effect possibly significant.	• Lease some cars. • Monitor second hand market and new legislation affecting cars. • Hold cars for longer.
Operating cost increases – eg repairs, petrol, insurance, road tax.	Very likely given past evidence. Cumulative effect likely to be significant, although customers pay for own petrol.	• Review maintenance operations. • Industry wide effect so would not materially impact upon competitive position in the industry which may enable industry wide price increase to offset cost increases.
On-line communication or other computer failure would prevent all bookings for period of problem.	Likely to be short term and isolated but loss of customers to rivals and reputation risk.	IT back up facilities and contingency provisions for disaster recovery.

Note: only *four* risks were required from candidates.

Examiner's comments:

Requirement (c) asked candidates to prepare a risk register. There were some very general answers. For example some candidates merely cited operational or financial risk without being specific as to what these could be. That said, there were some really good answers at the other end of the spectrum which clearly identified very specific risks, their classification (eg financial or strategic), their impact and likelihood and what could be done to mitigate them. The higher scoring answers included the risks of the airline industry and their implications, issues with the online systems, as well as increase in fuel prices, values of vehicles and the ageing and depreciation of cars. Weaker answers typically displayed some or all of the following: covering only three risks; little detail or explanation of each point: highlighting insignificant risks; or identifying unlikely circumstances which were not suggested by the scenario. Most, but far from all, candidates used the columnar format suggested in the question.

(d) **Introduction**

In assessing the ethical issues and implications of the three matters raised it is important to assess both whether they are unethical, and the degree of ethical/unethical behaviour. This is particularly the case for the implications of the actions.

In the first instance, it is necessary to establish the full facts in each of the cases highlighted by Gatter LLP. At the moment they are merely accusations which need to be substantiated. An appropriate degree of professional scepticism must be applied to all concerned.

Issue 1 – Private use of company vehicles by executive directors

The company is a separate legal entity from the directors and shareholders, and no-one has rights to use or take the company's assets without due authority. Potentially, the use of company assets by directors, even where there is no loss of revenue, is an illegal act in breach of their statutory duties. In addition, it appears there is a corporate governance problem in that the directors, who are the company's agents, are pursuing their own ends rather than those of the company. It may be necessary to take legal advice. Initially it will be necessary to speak to each director to gather evidence of actions. It will also be necessary to examine director employment contracts with the company to investigate whether they confer rights to use company assets under any conditions. Additionally, it should be established whether there was any direct benefit to the company in directors using the assets in this manner.

The key potential ethical issue is honesty/integrity.

In addition however there is the issue of transparency to shareholders, even if only retrospectively, of the nature and extent of any actions of this kind.

In terms of effect, it needs to be established whether there has been any direct loss to the company (eg lost revenue) or additional cost (eg petrol used) which needs to be made good by the directors concerned.

The fairness of the transaction is in question, in that it may be contrary to the interests of the shareholders. Even where the directors are shareholders it is contrary to the interests of the other shareholders, in particular TopFin.

If any of the directors belong to a professional body, then there may be a code of conduct and guidelines to ensure members behave in an ethical and professional manner, with disciplinary action if they do not. Any director who is a member of the ICAEW for instance would face disciplinary proceedings unless the actions were legitimately within the terms of their employment contract.

There may also be an issue in directors not declaring a taxable benefit.

Issue 2 – The lending of a company vehicle by a director to a third party

The issues are similar to issue 1 except as follows:

- With issue 1, the practice appeared to be at least well known to the other directors. It is not clear whether there was any internal transparency over this incident, other than the one director who was informed.

- It seems implausible that this type of action is part of an employment contract with the director.

- There is potential for the director receiving some benefit from the friend in return for the loan of the car. This would be a key effect and would amount to a personal gain.

- Are there any further undisclosed transactions of this type?

In order to gain transparency internally amongst the directors, as well as externally to shareholders, these facts need to be established in addition to those in issue 1.

Issue 3 – The hiring of a private company vehicle by a director to a third party for personal gain

This is potentially the most serious ethical issue as there is an increased risk of fraud against the company. The distinguishing features from the first two issues are:

- There is a probability of a direct financial gain by a director from deliberate misuse of company property, in breach of her statutory duties as a director

- There is a potential direct effect on the company from loss of revenue on this contract

- Assuming the other directors were unaware of the incident, then there is an issue of internal control and transparency

The facts to be established are:

- Why and how this transaction occurred

- What happened to the proceeds gained? Why were they returned to the company after such a delay?

- Are there any further undisclosed transactions of this type?

Examiner's comments:

In requirement (d), candidates were asked to explain the ethical issues and implications arising from a series of transactions by directors.

Candidates' answers to this requirement were the weakest on the paper. Whilst most candidates were familiar with ethical language in terms of transparency, fairness and effect, only a small number of candidates considered honesty/integrity, legality and steps which should be taken to deal with each issue. Moreover, few candidates indicated that the full facts would need to be established prior to forming a firm conclusion. It was apparent in this question that candidates do not adopt a logical, methodical approach, which considers any additional information needed. Instead, many candidates merely concluded that the behaviour is illegal without questioning why or whether they have the legal knowledge or sufficient information to come to this firm conclusion. A significant number believed that Sandra Bevan's conduct amounted to money laundering. More balanced and questioning answers were required that do not assert conclusions without supporting reasoning and evidence. Few candidates questioned the powers and responsibilities of directors in the context of corporate governance or their legal duties.

67 Up 'n' Over Plc

Marking guide

		Knowledge	Skill	Marks
(a)	Expected variable cost/breakeven level	2	7	9
(b)	Report	5	16	21
		7	23	30

General comments

The scenario in this question relates to a manufacturer of low cost garage doors.

Although attempts had always been made to keep costs low to provide 'best value', losses had been made. As a consequence, a new chief executive was appointed a couple of years ago and pushed costs down further by reducing the quality of the raw materials and freezing all capital expenditure. Initially this had the effect of reducing costs and quality, increasing margins and turning the losses into a profit. More recently, however, there have been increasing customer complaints and falling sales, although profits remain higher than they were before the cost reduction exercise. The board is split between returning to the original strategy or retaining the new low cost strategy. The chairman has suggested a third choice, of ceasing to be a manufacturer and becoming an importer and wholesaler of garage doors from Thailand.

(a) (i) **2013**

Sales volume	=	£30m/£400	=	75,000 doors
Variable cost	=	£30m – £14m – £2m	=	£14m

| | VC per door | = | £14m/75,000 | = | **£186.67** |

(ii) Sales volume = £32m/£400 = 80,000 doors

2011

Variable cost	=	£32m – £15m + £1m	=	£18m
VC per door	=	£18m/80,000	=	£225
Contribution per door	=	£400 – £225	=	£175
Break even	=	£15m/£175	=	**85,714.28, ie 85,715 doors**

2012

Variable cost	=	£32m – £14m – £3m	=	£15m
VC per door	=	£15m/80,000	=	£187.50
Contribution per door	=	£400 – £187.5	=	£212.50
Break even	=	£14m/£212.50	=	**65,882.35 ie 65,883 doors**

Implications for operating risk

The high level of fixed costs of £15m and £14m in 2011 and 2012 respectively indicate high operating gearing. This is the seen more clearly when comparing fixed costs with the relative levels of variable costs of £18m and £15m in 2011 and 2012 respectively, which are only a little higher than fixed costs. The high operating gearing means that profits are volatile when changes in sales occur.

While there was a margin of safety of 14,117 units in 2012 (ie 17.6%) the probability of the margin being 'used up' in 2013 needs to be considered in the context of increasing customer dissatisfaction and possible cancellation of large orders. The fall in expected sales in 2013 from £32m to £30m (6.3%) is indicative of the operating gearing consequences.

Examiner's comments:

Requirement (a) asked candidates to compute variable costs and to calculate break even from data provided. For the majority of candidates, the computation of variable cost and the subsequent break even calculations did not pose any problems. There were however some mistakes in calculations, where candidates mixed up the revenue and cost figures or made calculations for the wrong years. The operating risk explanation was not dealt with very well, if at all, by many candidates.

(b)

From:	Business Adviser
To:	Up 'n' Over Board
Subject:	Future Strategy
Date:	12 June 2013

(i) **Return to policy of 2011 and prior years**

Benefits

Good reputation with customers for best value. The additional costs therefore enhance reputation as a strategic base on which to build, despite recent operating losses.

There is an existing customer base which is partially secured by some long term contracts with larger customers. This ties some major customers into UnO giving the opportunity to restore reputation before the next contract renewal if the cost reductions are reversed.

Problems

An operating loss of £1 million was made in 2011, which was the last year of the previous 'best value' policy. The breakeven calculation shows that there is a negative margin of safety of 5,715 units. This means UnO would need to sell another 5,715 doors in order to break even which would be a 7.1% increase in sales volume.

UnO's strategic positioning is unclear. It is neither a differentiator nor a cost leader in accordance with Porter's generic strategies. It therefore runs the risk of pursuing a strategy based on a subjective concept of 'best value' and may be 'stuck in the middle'. At the very least, it needs to be aware of its positioning in terms of price-quality within the industry.

There are 'competitive market conditions' which would make a price increase difficult as a means to increase sales revenues.

Sustainability

A sustainable enterprise is one that generates continuously increasing stakeholder value through the application of sustainable practices through the entire base activity (products and services, workforce, workplace, functions/processes, and management/governance).

The continued operating losses are not sustainable in the longer term as, without profit, the wider stakeholder need cannot be met as the company will not survive. The key question of sustainability is whether the loss in 2011 would be typical, or whether it could be reversed by efficiency gains or improvements in sales.

(ii) Cost reduction

Benefits

A profit is now being achieved of £3m in 2012 and there is an expected profit of £2m for 2013.

The breakeven calculation shows that there is a margin of safety of 14,117 units for 2012. This means UnO would need to sell 14,117 fewer doors at current prices and costs before profit fell to break even, which would be a 17.6% decrease in sales volume.

There has also been a share price increase in 2012. It is unclear whether this was entirely due to the cost reduction strategy or whether other factors also had an impact. However, assuming that the strategy was the major factor, this was a 114% increase in share price. While share price then fell to June 2013 by 29%, the share price remains above the 2011 level. The stock market does not therefore appear to expect UnO to return to losses.

Problems

While there was an initial favourable impact to cost reduction in achieving profit, there appears to be a lagged reputational effect as information gradually becomes available to show that the doors are becoming lower quality and less durable.

There is some evidence, from at least one customer, that they may cease to purchase doors from UnO if this continues.

There is some initial protection from large customers withdrawing arising from the long term contracts but, if they fail to be renewed, the impact may be sudden and substantial from reputational loss.

Moreover, as the large companies hold inventories, they may cease to purchase additional doors near the end of the contract and instead run down inventories.

Sustainability

The benefits of the cost reduction policy appear to be short term and unsustainable. While there is some margin of safety a major and systemic loss of reputation and customer demand from a poor quality product seems likely to push the company into losses fairly quickly.

(iii) Import from Thailand

Benefits

- Funds generated from closure of manufacturing may enable a return of funds to shareholders or investment and diversification into other distribution activities in the new wholesaler/importer role.

- If a contractual agreement can assure quality control procedures then UnO's reputation may recover.

- Most costs will be variable so the operating gearing will decrease so there is some protection from losses if sales fall.

- The existing distribution competencies of economies of scope and customer relationships can still be exploited.

Problems

- UnO needs to ensure continuity of supply. Given a new supplier and significant geographical distance, some measure of control over failure to supply is required.

- The timing of the supply chain may be more unreliable given the geographical distance, so the lead time may be longer and more variable causing disappointed customers and lack of agility in satisfying their needs unless UnO holds inventory.

- Transport costs may be substantial but appear, even when added to purchase costs, to be less than the current operating costs.

- Exchange rate risk may cause uncertainty over price and profit.

- If the new contract fails then the manufacturing base will be lost so UnO cannot return to the old strategy.

- Are there alternative suppliers at a similar price to diversify risk and maintain security of supply?

- Is there an exclusivity clause to prevent other UK companies importing the same goods from the same supplier?

- Is the contract price fixed for any period?

Sustainability

Continuity of supply in the longer term at a competitive price is key. This may not be from the same suppliers but by changing suppliers over time there may be continuity of supply.

Aside from business sustainability, environmental sustainability may be damaged by transport over such a long distance (eg climate change, pollution, emissions levels, waste, use of natural resources, impacts of product use, compliance with environmental legislation, air quality).

Conclusion

The cost reduction policy and the 2011 policy both appear to be unsustainable for different reasons.

The import policy has risks but if a suitable supplier can be found which is reliable then it may be a feasible and desirable strategy to follow.

Examiner's comments:

Requirement (b) requested candidates to evaluate the benefits and problems of the three strategies and assess the sustainability of each. Answers to this part varied in standard quite significantly. The better answers addressed all three strategies and all three key areas of each strategy being: benefits, problems and sustainability. Some very good points were made overall, in particularly a return to the old strategy would continue to generate losses and it would leave UnO 'stuck in the middle'. Therefore, in the longer term, the strategy was unsustainable. Discussion of the cost reduction strategy identified the reputational effect and the potential loss of customers. Most candidates opted for the third strategy but recognised that there were significant risks associated with importing from Thailand such as quality control, exchange risks and management of supplier relations. Poorer candidates showed some or all of the following weaknesses: failing to demonstrate an understanding of the differing strategies; failing to comment on sustainability; not providing a conclusion; failure to refer to the numerical analysis calculated in requirement (a).

68 Moogle plc

		Knowledge	Skill	Marks
(a)	PESTLE analysis	4	7	11
(b)	Internal/external information	4	10	14
		8	17	25

General comments

The scenario relates to the pet products section of a large supermarket chain. A new executive manager has been appointed to be responsible for UK pet products' profit, pricing and procurement. A key issue is the type of information the manager requires from the IT department to take decisions and control this section of the business.

(a) **Political**

Taxation effects of pet food – eg VAT may impact profitability significantly.

Social welfare policy – allowing people to keep pets in government housing, care homes and other regulated environments affects the number of possible pet owners.

Health and safety policies over pet foods may increase costs for suppliers.

Economic

Recession is likely to impact on the number of people who own pets and the amount they are likely to spend on pet products (eg premium foods) if they own an animal.

Exchange rates can affect the price of imported products.

Inflation may cause cost increases for pet food manufactures and increases in prices.

Social

Demographic changes are likely to lead to changes in pet ownership where ownership is concentrated in age groups, social classes or gender.

The total size of the population is likely to lead to changes in total pet ownership.

Trends in housing may affect the number and types of pets owned. For example, a trend towards inner city apartment dwellings is likely to mitigate against owning large dogs, compared to out of town houses with large gardens.

Use of social networking sites for pet owners can alter attitudes and demand by consumers making more informed purchase choices.

Social acceptability of owning some animals may influence market demand.

Social trends in animal accessories may also influence pet owners to purchase more (or fewer) pet products.

Technology

New technological developments may lead to new pet products (such as electronic tags) not previously available.

Information technology, including pet websites enabling purchasing on the Internet, can be a major rival to shopping in supermarkets and other pet stores. This may be particularly the case for bulk purchases of pet food which may not be easily achievable by some people (eg who do not own a car) when visiting a store in person.

Ecological

Animals can have an impact on the environment. Restrictions on behaviour to limit this (eg 'poop scoops') may be positive in providing an additional market for new products or negative in discouraging pet ownership.

Legal

Laws requiring minimum standards of care for animals may be the source of additional markets as owners purchase additional accessories in order to comply (eg kennels).

New onerous laws may however discourage pet ownership and thereby reduce demand.

Health and safety laws with respect to the quality of pet food may increase costs of manufacturers which could be passed on to consumers.

Some elements of the pet market such as pet insurance are heavily regulated, in common with other types of insurance product. This may present a barrier to entry into this sector, which may impact on sales and profits.

Conclusion

The key issues in the industry appear to be:

* Economic factors, and particularly the recession and customers' willingness to purchase premium foods and other luxury pet items

* Social trends determining pet ownership, which define the number and type of pets owned and therefore the scale of the pet market

Examiner's comments:

Requirement (a) asked candidates to prepare a PESTEL analysis for the UK pet products industry. Most candidates prepared the PESTEL analysis quite well, although they did struggle for ideas in relation to the political and ecological impacts of the industry. Some weaker candidates did an analysis for Moogle, instead of the pet industry overall, others just gave a list of points from the scenario without explaining the effects on the industry. Few candidates made an attempt to prioritise the points in any way. An overwhelming majority of candidates failed to present any conclusions to their analysis. Often, political and legal issues were addressed together, with candidates identifying that the pet insurance sector was stringently regulated and that government is recently far more conscious of animal welfare and may adopt policies in the future to continue to address this. Better candidates were good at thinking about the wider industry rather than only the points mentioned in the question.

(b)

NB MORE THAN 3 PIECES OF INFO ARE GIVEN TO GUIDE MARKERS FOR A RANGE OF POSSIBLE CANDIDATE ANSWERS

Information	Justification
INTERNAL	
1. UK sales from each product line compared to (i) the same period last year (ii) the previous month	This is important in order to observe overall trends at an early stage but particularly to assess the success or otherwise of new product lines.
	If we change prices of our products generally it will also be necessary to view demand effects. (If prices of individual products change only in some regions, this can be monitored by store managers.)
	The comparison with last year would control for seasonality to make valid comparisons but also predict intra period variations in order to inform purchasing patterns.
	While I would not have time to scrutinise every product, I do need to look at the risk areas where major changes have occurred so I can manage by exception. Please therefore order the data by product according to the size of the variation with the highest variances first and the lowest variances at the bottom of the list.
2. Shelf space (or floor space) for pet products in total	It is important to see whether allocations of shelf space impact on sales. If shelf space is being reduced then this could be a key factor affecting both sales and the number of items of inventory that can be procured.
	Dividing 1. UK sales by 2. shelf space would give me data to argue for efficient allocation of shelf space across the company if these data are also maintained for other product groupings.
	While I would not have time to scrutinise every store, I do need to look at the risk areas where the ratio of UK sales divided by shelf space is particularly high or low. Could you therefore extract data on a store by store basis but only report to me the top 10% and bottom 10% of stores?
3. Price changes by suppliers and notifications of price changes	In order to control costs and monitor the impact of cost changes on profit it is important that I am aware of any proposed or actual change in price by suppliers.
	This information will inform the procurement decision by triggering an investigation of the reasons for the price change, negotiations with the supplier and the possibility of ceasing to purchase from that supplier.
	This is essential in controlling costs.
	Where supplier price increases are accepted then the impact on profit needs to be monitored and the possibility of changing the prices we charge to our customers needs to be considered as a consequence.
4. New product information	If I introduce new products (eg pet insurance or on-line sales) this may require different types of information and closer monitoring than existing products.
	This is partly because of increased uncertainty and partly because of the different nature of products like insurance where aggregation with general sales would be unhelpful.

Information	Justification
5. Comparisons with our overseas stores	I would like to see key trends from our overseas stores to see if there are lessons to learn in the UK from pet product sales in the rest of the world.
	Key data may include: fastest growing product lines; successfully introduced new products; comparisons of product prices and costs (exchange rate adjusted) where there are large variations (eg same product selling at significantly different prices).
	There may be good reasons for variations but I may need to investigate.

EXTERNAL

1. Market trends	I need to know changes in the UK pet market from both market research and market trends.
	This may include our own data gathering (primary data) but also market intelligence (secondary data).
	Examples would be trends for buying:
	• Moist food or dried food • Premium or basic product lines • New product innovations
2. Competitor pricing	Our prices relative to competitors are a key factor in maintaining competitive advantage and impact on the reputation of the company generally for being good value.
	For branded products these are identical and we need price comparison shopping within the month so we can adjust our prices regularly.
	However I need to know at the month end where our prices have been higher or lower than key competitors. Please report all exceptions beyond a 2% threshold.
	Own brand products are not identical and therefore price comparisons are more difficult. Nevertheless I need to know price differences with our competitors beyond a 5% threshold.
3. Innovations and product launches	I need to know in advance any plans by suppliers about new products or changes in products (eg new recipes). We can then plan to purchase them or not at the earliest moment. We can also plan for price changes.

Examiner's comments:

Requirement (b) asked candidates to identify three pieces of internal information and three pieces of external information that the pet products manager would need and to explain why this information was needed. Candidates struggled to identify the correct level and type of information required. Often, sales per product from each store were given as relevant information, despite the question flagging that 'the bigger picture' was needed. Candidates did not appear to focus on cost information and discussed revenue, breakdown of sales by store, breakdown of inventory by store and overall store performance. Some candidates did not offer specific information and instead just described the difference between strategic, tactical and operational information and then contrasted information with raw data. In terms of the external information, again, the level of detail requested was too great for someone wanting a strategic picture. Revenue from competitor stores, number of pet owners in the UK and a breakdown of ownership between dogs and cats, were among the types of information discussed. Again, some of these were not relevant for the scenario or suggestion being discussed, and provision of some of the information was not realistic as it would be nearly impossible to get.

69 Funzie Ltd

Marking guide

		Knowledge	Skill	Marks
(a)	Performance evaluation	–	14	14
(b)	Profitability and stakeholder implications	4	9	13
(c)	Financial and strategic considerations	3	7	10
(d)	Ethical issues	3	3	6
		10	33	43

General comments

This is the mini case and also the data analysis question. It was the best attempted on the paper.

The scenario relates to a small independent TV production company which has been set up to produce educational and informative factual programmes. Funzie's margin depends on the difference between the fixed price agreed with the broadcaster when the programme is commissioned and the actual costs of making each programme. A significant amount of the production of the programme is outsourced, although Funzie is increasingly making use of computer graphics and wondering whether to bring this in-house. Although revenues are increasing, profits are falling. To ensure sustainability, Funzie needs to improve its budgeting and cost control or review its current range of programmes, although becoming a low-budget reality TV producer does not sit easily with all stakeholders. There is also an ethical issue in relation to the use of a programme idea which has been brought to Funzie by a newly employed programme director, but which may belong to a rival production company.

(a) Data analysis

Overall

Funzie is a reasonably successful, small independent TV production company which in 2011 made an operating margin of 13.2% on sales of £17.19m. Despite managing to increase its sales revenue by over 25% in 2012, operating profit has remained at £2.3m, the same level as 2011. The majority of Funzie's activities relate to the commissioning of TV programmes by UK broadcasters.

Budget

The budget for UK programming activities in 2012 appears to have been prepared on the assumption that the average commissioning revenue per hour would remain at 2011 levels (£230,000) and that both sales mix (95% UK, 5% International) and operating margins (11% UK and 55% International) would stay broadly the same.

Thus the budgeted increase in operating profit of £431,000 (19%) was due to come from volume increases in both areas of business – 16.3% in international sales leading to a £77,000 increase in profit, and a 19.7% increase in the number of UK programming hours sold, generating additional profit of £354,000.

Actual performance

Revenue

Between 2011 and 2012, Funzie's overall revenue actually increased by 25.9%, exceeding expectations. International sales increased by almost 40% but remain a small proportion of the overall business at just over 5.5% of total sales. The increase in UK sales revenue was 25.1 % – this was due to programming hours increasing by 28.2%, with an extra 20 hours of programmes being sold, however although volume increased, the average commissioning revenue achieved dropped from £230k to £224.6k per hour.

The increase in sales volume could be due to Funzie's growing reputation for high quality computer graphics helping it attract more programme commissions or re-commissions of earlier programme series. The drop in commissioning revenue per hour could be due to pressure from broadcasters for reduced prices, a reduction in the number of peak hour shows that were sold or an increase in the proportion of programme hours that relate to re-commissioned programmes (since these are typically at a discount of around 20% on the original programme price). Despite the fall in revenue per hour, Funzie is still earning above the industry average for factual programmes of £200,000.

Margins

Whilst on the face of it Funzie's ability to sell programmes appears to have improved, this has not led to an overall increase in operating profit, which is £8,000 less in 2012 than in 2011 (a drop of 0.35%). In fact profit on international sales increased by 52.2%, whilst the profit on UK sales fell by 14.2% compared to 2011 (and was 28.3% lower than budgeted). Thus whilst international sales attracted a margin of 60%, the margin on UK programmes fell from 11% to 7.5% and is now below the industry average margin of 10% for factual programmes. The operating profit per programme hour fell from £25,300 to £16,900. This is partly explained by the £5,400 reduction in average commissioning revenue per hour discussed above. The remaining £3,000 is due to increases in costs.

Costs

In-house variable costs have increased by 13.1% compared to 2011 but this is due to extra programme hours. In fact the in-house cost per programme hour has fallen by £5,400 which offsets the reduction in average revenue per hour. However the outsourced costs have increased significantly and, compared to 2011, Funzie are paying total costs of an extra £4,600 per programme hour. This could be due to the cost of unscheduled studio time and/or the late presenters.

It would be useful to ascertain whether the cost increases relate to the nature of the programmes being produced, eg more expensive computer graphics or celebrity presenters, or whether these are a function of poor planning and cost control (see (b)).

We also need to consider the extent to which in-house and outsourced costs are substitutes for one another. If Funzie has finite in-house resources then the increased volume of programme hours in 2012 will inevitably have led to an increased need for outsourcing.

Further information

It would be useful to know the breakdown of revenue between original commissions and re-commissions, and also the split of international revenue by programme or country.

It would be useful to know the profitability of each of the individual factual programmes or series that Funzie made during 2012 – it may be that some programmes have ended up making losses due to cost over-runs whilst others have returned large profits.

It would also be useful to know how much time and money is incurred developing programme ideas which Funzie are not able to sell to broadcasters.

Access to non-financial information or non-financial performance indicators would also be useful, eg programme ratings, other industry awards received.

Conclusion

Funzie's 2012 performance has been strong in terms of revenue but this has been at the expense of margins. This partly reflects broadcaster pressure on revenues but is also a reflection of increasing costs, especially outsourced costs, and so Vivian is right to suggest that Funzie should consider its approach to budgeting and cost control.

Appendix of key performance indicators:

	Budget	2012	2011
% Operating margin			
UK	11.0	7.5	11.0
International	55	60	55
Overall Funzie	13.1	10.5	13.2
KPIS per programme hour £000			
Commissioned revenue	230	224.6	230
In-house costs	45.5	40.2	45.6
Outsourced costs	151.0	159.9	150
Total prog costs	196.5	200.1	195.6
Revenue net of programming costs	33.5	24.5	34.4
UK operating profit	25.3	16.9	25.3

Change in 2012 results compared to Budget/2011:

% increase/(decrease)	2012 v Budget	2012 v 2011	Budget v 2011
UK programme hours	7.1	28.2	19.7
UK revenue	4.5	25.1	19.7
International revenue	20	39.5	16.3
Total revenue	5.3	25.9	19.5
UK operating profit	(28.3)	(14.2)	19.7
International op profit	30.9	52.2	16.3
Total operating profit	(16.3)	(0.4)	19.0
UK in-house v.costs	(5.4)	13.1	19.6
UK outsourced v.costs	13.4	36.6	20.5
Fixed costs	(1.3)	5.4	6.8

Mix of UK programming costs:

%	Budget	2012	2011
UK in-house v. costs	22.2	19.4	22.3
UK outsourced v. costs	73.8	77	73.3
Fixed costs	4.0	3.6	4.5

Sales mix:

%	Budget	2012	2011
UK	95.1	94.5	95.0
International	4.9	5.5	5.0

Examiner's comments:

Requirement (a) requested candidates to evaluate Funzie's 2012 performance in relation to both the 2012 budget and the 2011 actual results. Attempts at this part were very good, with most candidates producing a range of calculations including sales mix, margins and data per programme hour. As usual, the weakest candidates produced limited calculations, focussing on percentage increases/decreases or simply using absolute numbers in their discussion. Interpretation of the data was also on the whole quite reasonable, with most candidates identifying that revenue had increased (in relation to both budget and last year) but that the budgeted increase in profit between 2011 and 2012 had not materialised. The more insightful candidates went on to analyse the reasons for this, explaining that whilst the volume of programme hours has increased, revenue per hour is about £5,000 lower, reflecting the pressure on prices from broadcasters. Also whilst Funzie has controlled in-house costs, its reliance on outsourcing appears to have led to cost over-runs which are the primary cause of its failure to achieve the budgeted profit. Better candidates used the information in the scenario about the cost of last-minute studio time and the behaviour of presenters to suggest possible causes, including querying the accuracy of the original budget (hinted at in requirement (b)). The request to explain any further information required was overlooked by a significant minority of candidates and those who produced generic lists of standard information (cash flow, budgets, competitor results) severely limited their marks.

(b) Improving future profitability

Given the difficult industry climate, broadcasters are under pressure to reduce the cost of commissioned programmes. They may also change the nature of the programmes that they are prepared to buy, focussing on those that are likely to attract the widest audiences. Hence the requirement for peak-time documentaries to be entertaining as well as informative.

Budgeting and cost control

Budgeting and cost control needs to be done on an individual programme basis rather than say monthly. A budget needs to be prepared for each programme showing the costs for all aspects of making the programme. This should include the costs associated with using Funzie's in-house staff and equipment, together with details of outsourced people and facilities required and the estimated daily rate payable. When preparing the original budget it would be sensible to add an element of contingency for cost over-runs.

Funzie needs to carefully control the costs actually incurred in making the programme against the original programme budget since it is not able to claim more revenue from the broadcasters to cover over-runs. Regular monitoring of costs incurred to date, together with remaining costs required for completion of a programme, would allow Funzie to take action. Funzie may need to improve its management information system to provide such information.

Programme directors who are dissatisfied with the output can significantly increase the costs of studio time and so an authorisation process should be implemented for all anticipated cost over-runs. Bonuses could also be paid to those directors who manage the programme within budget.

Costs incurred presumably depend on the nature of the programme, the location in which it is made, the fees required by presenters and celebrities, costumes required and the extent to which expensive filming, editing or computer graphics techniques are required.

The need to reduce costs may cause conflict between financial and creative staff, since economies or efficiency savings may be considered to affect the quality of the final output. Funzie needs to ascertain to what extent any cost reductions would impact on the broadcasters'/viewers' perception of quality. Funzie may be able to reduce costs without affecting quality eg by negotiating discounts with regular freelancers/outsourced suppliers/studios in return for a guaranteed level of bookings. It should also amend contracts to give it the right to fine presenters who turn up late.

Increasing sales revenue

Currently all Funzie's programmes fall into the factual category. The range of commissioning revenue for this genre currently varies between £100,000 through to £300,000 for peak viewing. At average revenue of £225k per hour Funzie occupies an above average position in the industry – possibly because it has more peak time programmes or attracts higher revenues due to the use of computer graphics. However were Funzie's revenue to drop to £200k per hour, either due to price pressure or the fact that informative programmes are not attractive to peak-time audiences, then in 2012 Funzie would have made £2,236,000 less revenue and have fallen below break-even on UK programmes, with a £695,000 operating loss.

Funzie faces a conflict between shareholders' need/desire to maximise profit and the founders wish to stay true to their creative principles.

Due to the creative nature of the business, the individual interests and objectives of the employees and original founders are likely to have a strong influence on how Funzie is run and the types of programmes it produces. The founders' original aim was to produce innovative, high quality, non-fiction TV programmes that were informative to viewing audiences. Since Funzie's reputation "relies on its people and ideas', keeping them happy is going to be critical. It would be difficult for directors and producers to produce quality ideas and programmes if they were not interested in and therefore motivated by the concept.

However 60% of the shares are held by private investors – whilst Vivian and Sanaya probably control more than any one individual, they need to keep the other investors happy collectively.

These investors are more likely to be concerned with potential returns than the intellectual quality of the TV programmes being produced. It is clear from the industry statistics (see appendix) that factual programmes are not always the most profitable and there is pressure from the other shareholders to diversify into the drama documentary format to increase profitability. Funzie's survival may depend on addressing this. Industry statistics show that average revenue for such programmes is £250,000 per hour and that it is possible to make a 12% operating margin (or £30k per programme hour).

If changes are made to the nature of programmes then Funzie would be competing against others who specialise in these areas – there is no guarantee that would come up with successful ideas. Thus changing the nature of the programme mix may necessitate a change in the staff and/or different outsourcers.

Funzie is likely to have developed a clientele of broadcasters who will include those specialising in non-fiction, eg Discovery Channel, and those who show a much wider range of programmes of which non-fiction is only one element. Broadcasters' requirements are likely to be driven by cost and also by a desire to attract the highest possible audiences from which to generate advertising revenue. Generalist broadcasters will face a conflict between commissioning high quality informative programmes that are only of interest to niche audiences and those with much more wide-ranging appeal.

An alternative strategy for Funzie is to consider expanding its international sales which currently only form a small proportion of what it does (a form of market development under Ansoff's matrix) or to concentrate on sales to broadcasters who specialise in its market niche (market penetration).

International sales clearly contribute a high margin but are a relatively small proportion of Funzie's business. Since the hard work in generating the programme concept and then the programme has already been done this would appear to be an obvious source of additional revenue. Funzie should consider appointing a director to be in charge of International sales development to capitalise on its reputation as a high quality UK TV producer.

Seeking re-commissions for existing programmes may help, although as these are generally at a 20% discount on the original price. Funzie may find it hard to complete the programme on a tighter budget, particularly if estimates of the learning curve benefits are over-optimistic.

Conclusion

There is definitely scope for Funzie to attempt to improve profitability by improving its budgeting and cost control process. In terms of increasing revenue, it may find it easier to consider increasing international sales and re-commissions, rather than changing the nature of the programmes it makes. Performance related bonuses for staff based on meeting programme budgets, nominations for awards and successful programme ratings may incentivise them to come up with more revenue-earning ideas.

Appendix: Comparison with Industry average statistics

Programme type	Average revenue/hour £	Operating margin %	Operating profit/hour £
Funzie (UK only)	224.6	7.5%	16.9
Factual	200	10%	20
Period drama	425	8%	34
General Entertainment	150	13%	19.5
Comedy	225	11%	24.75
Drama documentary	250	12%	30

Examiner's comments:

Requirement (b) asked candidates to discuss Funzie's options for improving profitability and the implications for its key stakeholders. Candidates were asked to structure their answer using two headings: Budgeting and cost control; and Options for increasing sales revenue. Candidates who drew implications from the analysis they had performed in (a) to pick up on the key issues facing Funzie scored well here. Since the company has to agree a fixed price for the programme at the time it is commissioned, accurate budgeting of costs is key to understanding programme profitability. Also as cost over-runs cannot subsequently be passed on to the broadcasters, cost control during programme making is critical to realising anticipated profit. The best candidates discussed this in light of the fact that, despite a 5.3% increase in revenue, Funzie's actual profit is 16.3% down on budget and that, although in-house costs have reduced, outsourced costs appear to be out of control. Good answers highlighted the possible conflict between the programme directors' desire for creativity and quality and being held responsible for meeting the programme budget. They then went on to suggest relevant improvements to the budgeting process for individual programmes and specific approaches to controlling sub-contractor costs. Many weaker candidates made some generic references to cost control but ignored the budgeting aspect altogether.

Candidates seemed more comfortable discussing options to increase sales revenue, although few used the industry data in Exhibit 1 to support their arguments. Weaker candidates focussed on a shareholder's suggestion to expand into drama documentaries, whereas better candidates thought more widely and also considered options to increase sales of international and re-commissioned programmes, both of which might incur lower costs. A significant number of answers completely ignored the requirement to discuss the impact of the various options on the key stakeholders, despite the fact that the scenario highlighted the conflict between cost and quality for the programme directors and the founders' concerns about abandoning the original mission to create educational and informative programmes. Few candidates pulled their analyses of costs and revenue together to arrive at any sort of conclusion about improving profitability.

(c) **Computer graphics**

Outsourcing is where a business chooses to use an external supplier instead of providing the services in-house.

A key downside of outsourcing however is that the price paid will include a margin for the provider of the resources or service. Thus it is only cost effective if the supplier, due to its economies of scale, can provide the service more economically than the organisation can arrange internally. As part of its desire to control costs, Funzie is considering whether to bring its graphic design function entirely in-house.

Financial considerations

Do the fixed costs of any additional equipment, necessary software and staff outweigh the saving in variable costs charged by the supplier?

Equipment cost = £1.2m

Savings in outsourced time = 250 days x £2,250 = £562,500

So if the equipment lasts for three years then the savings will more than outweigh the cost.

Payback for investment in CG package = 2.13 years (1.2m/562,500)

However there may be additional costs in terms of the need for more in-house computer graphics technicians which would reduce the savings generated.

If the package only has a 2-3 year life, the decision would appear to be marginal. This calculation assumes the current amount of time outsourced will continue, however if CG is increasingly becoming Funzie's area of expertise then the number of days outsourced might increase in future, similarly if resources are limited then the CG company may put their prices up. Both these factors would increase the cost of outsourcing and hence make the move to in-house more attractive. Finally if the software can be upgraded for a relatively small amount to generate another 2-3 year life then the benefits will accrue over a much longer period of time.

Strategic considerations

However in addition to the financial perspective, there are also strategic considerations:

Outsourcing of activities that are common to the production of all TV programmes may make sense for small businesses such as Funzie, since one service provider can then benefit from the economies of scale available and pass this on to its customers (thus a production studio used by a number of independent producers is likely to be able to operate at near capacity). From Funzie's point of view the outsourcing of basic production activities is unlikely to lead to a loss in competitive advantage.

However if Funzie's competitive advantage increasingly relies on its use of computer graphics then it may make more sense to provide this service in-house provided that Funzie have the necessary expertise and competence to do so. This would avoid transferring organisational learning and IP to other firms. Presumably Funzie has the required competence, given that it already fulfils 50% of its need, although Funzie would need to consider whether bringing the additional graphic design in-house requires extra staff and equipment.

A potential downside is lack of flexibility. If Funzie acquires the relevant software packages etc these will quickly become out-of-date and it will face the need to update regularly rather than leaving this as the problem of its supplier. Funzie will also be less able to shop around or access other software packages or techniques.

Like many small TV producers Funzie makes use of outsourcing to reduce its need for its own expensive studios, equipment and full-time production staff. This is a good way of reducing fixed costs and transferring risk since Funzie only needs to pay for the relevant resources as and when it requires them. Bringing all CG in-house will increase Funzie's operating gearing.

However a downside of outsourcing is that Funzie may have to compete for time and resources at the supplier and may run the risk of non-availability which could impact on programme deadlines.

Conclusion:

It often strengthens a firm's value chain to outsource activities that are deemed to be weak links for an organisation. Here computer graphics is a critical success factor for Funzie, so retaining it internally may actually strengthen Funzie's value chain by protecting its competitive advantage. A more detailed cost-benefit analysis is required before a final decision is taken.

Examiner's comments:

Requirement (c) asked candidates to discuss the financial implications and strategic considerations of bringing all computer graphics in-house. Candidates were provided with clear numbers to help them do a 'back-of-the-envelope' calculation to assess the viability of the strategy. The weakest candidates either ignored the requirement to show supporting calculations despite the fact that these were very straightforward or focussed entirely on the financial aspects and failed to consider the strategic issues. Most candidates identified that, based on the figures provided, the software would pay for itself between 2 and 3 years but that more information was required on the costs of maintenance, staff training and the likely upgrade cycle. Since Funzie's use of computer graphics is growing and this is an area where costs have been difficult to control, other non-financial factors are also relevant. Better candidates applied their knowledge of outsourcing or vertical integration to the scenario to generate some relevant points here in relation to operating gearing, core competences and flexibility of choice. Few candidates pulled their discussions of the financial and strategic implications together to arrive at any sort of conclusion about whether to bring the operation in-house.

(d) **Ethics**

In general terms, ethics are 'the moral principles governing or influencing conduct'. Ethics pertains to whether a particular behaviour is deemed acceptable in the context under consideration. Ethics can also be viewed at the individual level (Conrad) and the corporate level (Funzie).

A key question here is legality in relation to the confidentiality of data/information.

There are two issues:

(1) Whether the IP for the programme concept belongs to Conrad or Dayze. If the former then there is unlikely to be a legal or indeed ethical issue.

   If the latter, then Conrad may be acting illegally in using information that belongs to his previous employer. Conrad's contract of employment with Dayze may provide the answer to this.

(2) Whether Funzie is acting legally in taking advantage of Conrad's actions. It is not clear here whether Funzie has been made aware of the source of Conrad's idea for the new programme, and therefore whether they are acting knowingly. However Funzie has an ethical obligation to make itself aware of the legality of the actions of its employee.

In making a decision as to how to proceed, it may be helpful to apply the Institute of Business Ethics three tests:

- Transparency
- Effect
- Fairness

Transparency – This test is partly about whether the action required contravenes business ethics principles and whether Funzie is 'doing the right thing' – it is not about whether Funzie can get away with the behaviour, provided they are not found out. Funzie needs to be open and transparent in its actions and comply with its own ethical code/any applicable industry codes. In an industry where IP is critical to competitive advantage, using a programme idea that belongs to someone else is unlikely to be considered ethical. Transparency also applies here in respect of whether Conrad has been open with Funzie about the fact that he had previously worked on this idea at Dayze.

Effect – who does the decision affect/hurt?

A clear loser here is Dayze. Even if it did not intend to go ahead with the production itself, if the IP belongs to the company rather than Conrad, then Dayze could still earn revenue by selling the programme concept to others. Funzie and the Australian broadcaster may make more profit as a consequence of the new programme. However Funzie's requirement and expectation to make profits needs to be constrained by its obligations to behave responsibly. Funzie (and potentially the Australian broadcaster) both risk reputational damage if it came to light that they had used someone else's IP for the programme.

Fairness - would the decision be considered fair by those affected?

The issue for Funzie is that they may benefit from Conrad's use of confidential information. In the context of business ethics, Funzie's behaviour, if it knowingly accepts the information, is to gain an unfair advantage over its rivals. The general principle within the industry appears to be that the IP for the programme concept remains with the production company and can be sold by them to broadcasters outside the UK. Thus the fact that Funzie would be selling the idea to Australian rather than UK producers is unlikely to make it 'fair'. The fact that Dayze were working on the idea before Conrad left them means they are unlikely to find his behaviour acceptable.

Honesty and integrity

Final issues are of honesty and integrity. Funzie needs to consider whether Conrad's actions are those of an honest employee and whether such behaviour may cause them to reconsider their employment decision.

Next steps

Conrad's use of general industry knowledge and experience obtained whilst working for his previous employer Dayze is not an issue, since it is common practice to employ staff with relevant experience.

However the use of the IP for the specific programme idea is a different matter. Assuming Conrad has been open in acknowledging the situation, the terms and conditions of Conrad's contract with Dayze and any duty of confidentiality to his previous employer need to be considered, and legal advice should be taken. Potentially discussions may also need to be had with Dayze.

Were the IP to belong to Conrad then commercially Funzie may be well within its rights to use the programme concept. If it wants to be seen to act ethically however, Funzie might consider approaching Dayze with a proposal that Funzie will use the programme concept outside the UK – leaving Dayze free to develop it in the UK.

If Conrad has acted illegally, Funzie should not benefit from those actions and may consider dismissing him. Were the legal case not to be clear-cut then Funzie would need to consider its ethical position and should probably decline to use the idea for the programme without discussing it with Dayze.

Examiner's comments:

In requirement (d), candidates were asked to explain the ethical issues presented by Conrad Jack's suggestion to develop a programme idea that he had been working on at his previous employer and to advise Funzie on appropriate next steps. Candidates' answers to this requirement were quite mixed. Those candidates who adopted a methodical approach and discussed the issue in terms of transparency, fairness and effect tended to fare better than those who simply concluded that copying the programme idea would be illegal or unethical without questioning why or whether they have the legal knowledge or sufficient information regarding the facts to come to this firm conclusion. Better candidates began by considering the legality of the suggestion in relation to the ownership of the programme IP and also the duty of confidentiality that Conrad is likely to owe to his former employer. They also discussed the fact that, even if the IP has not been protected, and commercially Funzie is free to pursue the idea, it may decide not to on ethical grounds. Only a few candidates went beyond the next step of suggesting Funzie take legal advice. The strongest answers explained that Funzie's response is likely to depend on the legal advice regarding who the IP belongs to, and it may include re-considering Conrad's employment or agreeing contract terms to protect Funzie from such behaviour in the future. As has been stated before, weaker candidates need to take note that more balanced and questioning answers are required that do not assert conclusions without supporting reasoning and evidence.

70   RESQ Ltd

Marking guide

		Knowledge	Skill	Marks
(a)	Organisational structures	5	4	9
(b)	Advantages/disadvantages	2	5	7
(c)	Profitability discussion	2	6	8
		9	15	24

General comments

At 24 marks, this was the shortest question on the paper. The scenario concerns a relatively new company RESQ which is a London-based key holding company. Customers pay a monthly subscription to RESQ which stores their spare house and car keys at a secure depot and provides a 24-hour emergency service in the event that the customer needs a set of keys urgently. RESQ has now been approached by a large insurance company, Genysis plc, which wants to offer the key holding service to its premium home insurance customers. This new contract will massively increase the customer base and require RESQ to have national coverage so the company, which currently has an entrepreneurial structure, needs the ability to cope with the new scale.

Candidates were asked to write a report to Gemma Devereux, the business owner, advising her on the implications of accepting the new contract. A surprising number of candidates failed to earn the mark available for setting their answer out in the appropriate format.

(a) **Structure**

From: Business Adviser
To: RESQ
Date: September 2013
Subject: Assessment of growth plans

Organisational structure defines how the various functions in an organisation are arranged. A successful strategy requires effective organisation of people and decision making.

RESQ currently has an entrepreneurial structure where all the key decisions are centralised on one person – Gemma.

In terms of Mintzberg's organisational forms, Gemma is at the strategic apex as a single owner-manager exercising direct control over the operational core below her. Other functions are reduced to a minimum and are fulfilled by a small number of administrators together with external professional assistance. The organisational structure is very flat.

The small size of the business and its localised geography (concentration in the London area) has meant that it is feasible for Gemma to manage the business and people personally. This is helped by the limited number of supplier relationships (there is a single courier contract).

However this is unlikely to be the case moving forward as the business would grow from handling 15,000 customers in one area to a database of 115,000 nationwide.

RESQ needs to move from dealing with individual customers with small buying power to dealing with a sophisticated buyer in the form of the insurance company. Genysis may also have a greater need for compliance and service level agreements that need to be monitored

Expansion nationally will involve finding a large number of depots and sourcing more courier companies, all of which will need to be subjected to appropriate security checks.

The entrepreneurial structure is likely to limit RESQ's expansion capability. As a company grows its organisational structure needs to evolve. Often a business will move to a functional structure and then to a divisionalised one. The latter is more applicable here. Divisions could be geographic or by type of customer (individual/corporate), with day-to-day decisions being decentralised to the division manager.

This would free Gemma up to concentrate on more strategic matters but a flow of management information will be important to success. Gemma may need to retain a degree of centralisation over pricing.

Such a structure would also lend itself to further growth in the future. It also has the advantage of succession planning as RESQ trains up people within the business with management capabilities

Another way of considering RESQ's structure would be as a network organisation, since its business is dependent on a number of partners, buying in services as and when needed: the courier activity is undertaken by external suppliers; depot facilities are leased.

Handy's Shamrock structure would see RESQ develop a flexible structure: a professional core of employed staff, a contractual fringe of couriers, depot owners and professional experts, and a flexible labour force who can be deployed when required (eg to cope with the initial data capture for all the new customers). Customers are a fourth cluster to whom RESQ may sub-contract certain tasks eg the responsibility for returning keys after a call-out.

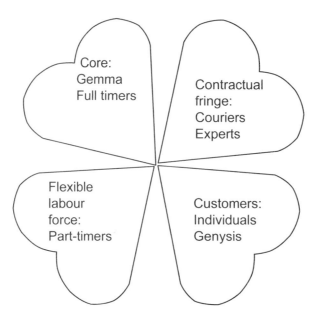

It would not be economical for RESQ to employ its own couriers as demand will vary considerably. As a result outsourcing the activity to local businesses will allow RESQ to meet its promises to customers in terms of delivery times more economically than it could do internally

Examiner's comments:

Requirement (a) asked candidates to explain RESQ's current organisational structure and advise on how this might need to adapt if the new contract is undertaken. Candidates were clearly very well-prepared for this requirement, which was the best attempted on the paper. However in some cases this meant that they wrote too much, at the expense of later parts. The majority of candidates identified the existing entrepreneurial structure and explained why this might no longer be suitable for an organisation that wanted to expand from London to a national scale. Many went on to suggest that a divisional structure on geographic lines would be more appropriate, often explaining this with the aid of a diagram. Candidates were asked to refer to relevant models and those who discussed RESQ's use of outside contractors and professional experts with reference to Mintzberg's organisational forms and/or Handy's shamrock structure produced answers that had more depth.

(b) **Developing business with Corporate customers**

Advantages:

- Corporate clients such as banks and insurance companies will have access to a wide customer base.

- The Genysis contract will provide rapid revenue growth without any significant marketing requirement.

- RESQ will have fewer individual customers to deal with.

- The company will gain an enhanced reputation from having a blue chip client.

- Economies of scale may arise from significantly increased numbers of customers (more buying power with couriers, depots etc).

- RESQ's product is a good fit with insurance product/company profile.

Disadvantages:

- RESQ will become very dependent on a single key customer, which increases concentration and therefore risk.

- Bargaining power of RESQ will be limited in relation to Genysis which is likely to be able to dictate service levels and prices. There may be pressure on margins and payment terms.

- RESQ is inexperienced in dealing with corporate clients.

- Compliance issues – the nature of the client means the need for monitoring and reporting is likely to increase. RESQ may also need to carry out more security checks

- Corporate customers may want exclusivity – eg Genysis may not want RESQ offering a similar service to competitors

- Larger customers may have greater requirements in terms of service levels which will increase costs.

- Will individual customers suffer?

  Rapid rather than gradual growth will necessitate instant rather than incremental change and additional resources/capital.

Conclusion

The new contract offers a potentially lucrative opportunity for growth and, depending on the financial assessment (see below), should probably be accepted if it is Gemma's objective and intention to expand the business. However it will require additional resources, the organisational structure will need to change radically and Gemma will need to take steps to manage the additional demands it is likely to place on the business eg recruit experienced managers to assist with this.

Examiner's comments:

Requirement (b) requested candidates to summarise the advantages and disadvantages of developing the business by working with a large corporate customer such as Genysis. This was also well done with many candidates pointing out that although there were obvious benefits to the expansion, RESQ would face the increased risk of being very dependent on one key customer and that Genysis was likely to have significant bargaining power regarding both price and service levels.

(c) **Factors affecting profitability**

Calculation of contract price:

Number of call-outs per annum	0	1	2	3	4
Probability	40%	30%	20%	5%	5%
Prob x call-out	0	0.3	0.4	0.15	0.2

EV call-outs per customer = 1.05

Incremental costs:	£
Key storage:100,000 × £8	800,000
Courier costs:100,000 × 1.05 × 15	1,575,000
Call handling costs:100,000 × 1.05 × 2	210,000
Additional fixed costs	150,000
Total costs	2,735,000

So RESQ needs revenue of £2,735,000 to break-even on the contract.

The breakeven contract price = £2,735,000. This equates to breakeven prices of £27.35 per customer per year or £2.28 per customer per month (£27.35/ 12)

RESQ's normal standard price for individual customers is £4 per month or £48 per year.

If it charged the standard price of £4 per customer per month, RESQ would receive £4.8million per year from Genysis and would make £2,065,000 profit on the contract (£4,800k - £2,735k).

Thus the maximum discount RESQ could offer on the standard price is 2,065/4,800 = 43%, but it would then only break-even.

Factors affecting profitability:

The contract costs are quite sensitive to the expected number of call-outs. Thus RESQ should build some slack into the price in case these increase. For example if the expected call-outs increased from 1.05 to 1.5 per customer then the contract costs would be £950,000 + (100,000 × 1.5 × £17) = £3.5m.

Genysis has asked for a discount, which will reduce RESQ's profitability. A discount of 25% ie a charge of £3 per month per customer would generate revenue of £3.6m and profit of £865k based on the original estimates, a margin of 24%.

Gemma could attempt to share the risk with Genysis by agreeing that she will offer a retrospective discount (bonus) if the level of call-outs is below a certain target.

RESQ may find it makes more profit if not all of Genysis customers decide to take up the offer of key-holding.

Clearly the profitability of the contract will also depend on the costs incurred.

The following assumptions have been made in respect of costs:

- Costs of key storage will be £8 per customer per annum irrespective of the number of Genysis customers who choose to store keys or the number of keys they store.

- Average courier cost for collection and delivery is £15 per request; in reality this will vary depending on customer location in relation to the key depot.

- Depot access charges are £2 per request.

- Fixed costs will increase by £150,000 to cope with the contract.

We have assumed that RESQ's existing costs will apply to the new contract. Costs may change considerably as a result of the expansion and may vary by location. It also ignores potential economies of scale and any volume discounts that RESQ may be able to negotiate with suppliers.

Note: RESQ's existing fixed costs have been ignored on the basis that they would be incurred despite the contract. However if there is spare capacity that will be used to service the Genysis contract then in the long run it could be argued that some element of these should be included in the costings.

Conclusion: The profitability of the contract is likely to be highly sensitive to the number of customers who take up the offer, the number of call-outs and the estimates of costs. RESQ needs to build in some contingency to the price to cover this.

Examiner's comments:

Requirement (c) asked for a discussion of the factors that would affect the profitability of the contract. Candidates were requested to show supporting calculations, including a break-even price, and to state any assumptions.

Candidates' ability to tackle the numbers in this question was extremely varied, reflected in the poor average score. A significant number quoted the break-even formula and used it to try and calculate a break-even number of customers rather than a break-even contract price, showing an inability to apply their knowledge. In fact the simplest approach here was to ascertain the break-even price by identifying the incremental costs of the contract, based on the assumptions provided. This required an expected value calculation to identify the likely number of customer call-outs during a year. Those that had not mis-managed their time then went on to identify a range of factors that would affect the final profit on the contract, although this often took the form of a list rather than a discussion. A significant number limited their marks by failing to state any assumptions despite the specific requirement to do so.

71 Inkpen Ltd

		Knowledge	Skill	Marks
(a)	Scenario planning	2	4	6
(b)	Current strategic position	2	6	8
(c)	Evaluation of alliance option	3	9	12
(d)	Pricing strategies	4	3	7
		11	22	33

General comments

The scenario concerns a family-owned chain of book stores specialising in the sale of textbooks to students and teachers. Historically profitable, the business has been finding the market more difficult due to severe competition from online retailers. Although e-readers are also having an impact, the majority of educational texts are still bought as physical books. Inkpen is proposing a link-up with an American textbook retailer, Livro, which has produced its own low-cost e-reader that has been very successful in the USA. Inkpen will earn commission by selling the e-reader in its shops and providing areas for customers to download e-books so that it can then earn revenue from every e-book sold in store. This will require the installation of wi-fi technology in Inkpen's stores. The hope is that the sale of e-readers will bring more people into the store who will then buy physical books as well as e-books once they are there, thus recapturing some market share from the online retailers. In order to create appeal for mixed text formats the company intends to offer bundle pricing deals for a combination of physical and e-books.

(a) Scenario planning

Scenario planning is useful in providing a long-term view of strategy, where a few key factors may influence success. In the face of a changing environment organisations can choose to do nothing, continue to make short-term forecasts or use scenario planning to consider potentially substantial shifts in the industry and its environment.

Technology has already radically changed the environment in which book retailers operate: firstly through the internet providing an alternative place to buy printed books; secondly through the advent of e-readers and e–books providing a different medium and perhaps also altering the nature of material that people read. A key question for Inkpen is: where will the industry be in 10 years' time?

Using scenario planning Inkpen would attempt to consider possible future situations (favourable or unfavourable) that may occur – 'what if?'– and how these might impact on its business – 'what is the effect of?' Consideration of these changes will help Inkpen determine how it can achieve a sustainable business model for the future.

The success of Inkpen's business depends on the demand for books. Possible scenarios for Inkpen to consider could be:

- A reduced demand for all forms of books

- Reduced demand for paper books but an increased demand for electronic books

- An increased demand for both electronic and paper books as readers move to multimedia

It will also need to consider the impact that this will have on the ways in which people purchase their reading material.

Finally, in assessing the impact of these different scenarios Inkpen needs to consider the whole supply chain of which it is a part. This will include asking what will publishers do faced with this future, how will universities and other academic institutions react, and what might competitors do?

Inkpen's management are right to consider that they need to find a new way of operating for the digital age. This type of scenario planning would give general rather than precise answers because of the uncertainties involved, but may allow Inkpen to anticipate changes, develop contingency plans and perhaps respond earlier than competitors.

Options might include:

- Abandoning stores and moving business completely to internet

- Becoming even more of a niche business

- Collaborating with publishers to try and increase demand for certain types of books

- Offering a range of complementary services, eg digital printing

- Working with faculties to respond to desire for course material from a range of content providers in a number of different forms

Examiner's comments:

Requirement (a) asked candidates to explain how Inkpen might benefit from scenario planning when developing strategic responses to the uncertainty facing its industry. This was very poorly done and the worst attempted requirement on the paper. Many candidates failed to appreciate or demonstrate that they understand the difference between scenario planning for an industry and the normal strategic planning process undertaken by an individual company. In this scenario, experts have identified that technology is causing major uncertainty regarding the future shape of the industry. As a result there will be substantial shifts, which will affect publishers, retailers and their customers. So a key consideration for Inkpen is where the industry will be in 10 years' time. A minority of candidates understood this and explained that if Inkpen wishes to have a sustainable business it needs to ask 'what if?' questions and come up with contingency plans, using information from the scenario to illustrate their answer. Many weaker candidates simply discussed a positioning based approach to strategic planning which failed to convey the fundamental nature of the uncertainties affecting the whole book industry supply chain.

(b) **SWOT analysis**

Inkpen is a niche differentiator, offering a high-quality service in the specialist textbook market. Analysing its current strategic position is effectively done by conducting a SWOT analysis of internal issues (S&W) and external issues (O&T):

Internal issues

Key strengths

- Inkpen is recognised as a premier academic book retailer in the UK and its prime location in many university towns and on-campus makes it convenient and accessible for a wide range of users and acts as a barrier to entry for physical bookstores.

- Inkpen is independent so can tailor its own stock and choose which books to recommend according to local customer profile. The reputation of its staff leads to good customer service and their specialist knowledge and expertise, together with the coffee shop ambience, give Inkpen a competitive advantage and may be beneficial in convincing customers to buy in-store (even if they are purchasing e-books) and to remain loyal.

- Inkpen has chosen to operate in a niche market which may be more profitable and to an extent offers some protection since demand for academic texts is less likely to be eradicated by e-books.

- Inkpen has tried to integrate its online business and offers online ordering in-store so is able to satisfy readers' demand to purchase online (11% sales currently made online). It was the first academic bookstore to offer an online service and management appear to be aware of the need to move with the times, as evidenced by the Livro proposal.

Key weaknesses

- Inkpen has a strong dependence on the academic market (70% sales) and on the sale of physical books (89%). It is therefore exposed given the fundamental uncertainty about the future of the industry. The limited amount of online business means it will find it hard to compete with the economies of scale of the major e-retailers such as Sahara plc.

- Financially Inkpen is likely to have suffered declining profit margins from greater competition and online book retailers and the need to carry physical stock places strain on its cash flow. Cashflow may also be affected by seasonality of demand based on the academic calendar, eg sales are likely to be higher at the start of the year/term when reading lists are issued for new courses (although as this has always been the case Inkpen is likely to be well-versed in managing its seasonal cash flows).

- Inkpen is likely to have low bargaining power with the large publishers.

External issues

Key threats

- Technology has significantly increased competition for Inkpen. This has led to a new generation of customers increasingly buying online rather than in the high street and the growing dominance of e-books which diminish the prospects for traditional printed books. There is a small risk that educational publishers may move to e–texts exclusively, although currently research suggests printed textbooks do still appeal to students.

- Another risk of the technology is that electronic material is easier to copy/pirate, reducing the need to pay for reading material.

- In addition to competition from the likes of Sahara, Inkpen faces competition from other book retailers which are increasingly fighting for survival, and from libraries and second hand sales, which are substitutes for buying the original text.

- Inkpen charges a higher price than competitors. In a recession demand is more price elastic and, with the rise in tuition fees, students in particular may become more price sensitive and choose to buy elsewhere. This would be particularly damaging given 70% of Inkpen's sales are textbooks.

Key opportunities

- Inkpen has a relatively strong competitive position within its niche market, so could continue to focus on market niches where strong demand for printed books will continue to exist. Ideas could include linking up with academic publishers to get exclusivity agreements for certain materials, or linking up with colleges and academics to ensure that Inkpen is stocking the books which are being recommended, and that students are given a web-link to Inkpen's online page for ordering.

- Inkpen needs to respond to the technological changes in its market place which are affecting both the method of reading and the method of book sales, so the sale of e-readers would allow Inkpen to target a wider range of customers. It could also consider the use of social media for marketing.

- Other ideas include having pop-up shops at the start of term on all university campuses and using its UK reputation to develop international sales.

- Inkpen could address the problem of substitutes by implementing a 'Rent a book' scheme or engaging in the sale of used books.

Conclusion

Inkpen operates in a mature industry where margins are increasingly under pressure as a result of online retailers. This has caused the closure of many small independent bookstores. Whilst the academic market may not yet have fully embraced e-readers, the growing dominance of e-books is a bleak prospect for a bookstore which only sells printed texts. Inkpen has built its reputation on a differentiation strategy and it needs to stay ahead of other bookstores by embracing the new technology. Its university location gives it access to a wide and captive market. It must use its key strengths – reputation, staff and customer loyalty – to become a multi-channel book seller, focussing on customers who want to buy books in both electronic and printed format.

Examiner's comments:

Requirement (b) requested candidates to analyse Inkpen's current strategic position, identifying the key internal and external issues and explaining why they are significant. Answers to this requirement were quite disappointing given that it was essentially asking for a SWOT analysis. Candidates would do well to note that when relatively basic techniques like PESTEL/SWOT or 5 Forces are asked for, the examiner expects more than a superficial or scatter-gun regurgitation of points mentioned in the scenario: key issues are required. Weaker answers typically displayed some or all of the following faults: highlighting minor points; little detail or explanation of the significance of each point; or listing only weaknesses and threats. Candidates who identified that what was required was a well-argued analysis, linking the most important factors affecting Inkpen, tended to do well. An overwhelming majority of candidates failed to present any sort of conclusion to their analysis, which is disappointing and also means they missed the opportunity to link Inkpen's current position to its possible reasons for exploring the alliance in (c).

(c) Strategy evaluation

Strategic fit

Inkpen currently operates a niche differentiation strategy. As a result of the knowledge and expertise of its staff it offers a premium service to customers. It has developed a reputation for focussing on a particular market niche – academic texts – and this is borne out by the location of its bookstores in university towns and campuses. However Inkpen is also aware of the need to move with technology as evidenced by the fact that it was the first bookstore to offer an online shop. Livro is an academic book retailer and the Cartilla has been designed with academic users in mind so on the face of it, it would appear to be good fit.

Inkpen's core market of students is likely to value features such as text annotation and low battery usage and are also likely to be price conscious, so will be attracted to a low-cost e-reader. The strategy also responds to the threat from online retailers and the fact that e-books are likely to reduce the sale of printed texts.

However Inkpen also needs to recognise that one form of product might be a substitute for another, so it may be in a position of cannibalising sales – it will make less money if a customer who would have purchased a printed book in-store now downloads it in e-form.

Resources and competences required

Inkpen already has an online business so may already have some of the information systems requirements in place to sell e-books.

All stores will need reliable Wi-Fi access and a sufficiently large e-reader area for customers.

Staff will need training to be able to demonstrate the Cartilla and help customers download e-books. Staff will also need to develop knowledge and expertise in relation to the range of e-books available – the service needs to be as good as the traditional area of business or Inkpen's reputation will be damaged.

Inkpen will need to have sample e-readers available although presumably these will be provided by Livro. There will need to be some security system in place to reduce the chance of theft.

Risks

The choice of partner in Livro Inc may not be appropriate – the success of the strategy depends on the Cartilla being seen as the e-reader of choice by Inkpen's customers.

The fact that it is successful in the USA may not mean automatic success in the UK, particularly given the dominance of Sahara.

It may also depend on Livro having strong links with publishers of academic e-texts.

This strategy does not address the issue of substitutes in the form of second hand book sales/libraries, neither does it prevent students viewing the Cartilla/e-books in store and purchasing elsewhere.

Whilst US publishers of academic texts may have begun to bring out e-books, UK publishers may be slower to follow suit. Alternatively publishers may decide to offer the facility to download e-books direct from their website and cut out Inkpen.

Some exchange rate risk may arise depending on how the agreement with Livro is structured.

Conclusion

Whilst the strategy is not without risk, Inkpen cannot afford to ignore the technological changes in the market place and a hybrid approach is likely to protect its future revenue stream. Since Livro will provide the technological know-how in respect of the product, this may be a relatively low risk, low cost method, and Livro's strong brand name in the USA may help Inkpen attract some market share from Sahara.

Examiner's comments:

Requirement (c) asked candidates to evaluate the proposed alliance with Livro, using three specific headings: strategic fit, resources and competences required, and risks.

Most candidates made a good attempt at this requirement and were able to discuss the benefits and disadvantages of the alliance under each of the given headings. Once again many poorer candidates failed to provide any sort of conclusion. The better answers concluded that in light of the potential impact of technology on the industry as a whole (requirement (a)) and given Inkpen's market niche and strategic position (requirement (b)), the alliance may offer a relatively low cost opportunity to respond to external factors, although whether Livro's brand name is sufficient to compete with market leader Sahara remains to be seen.

(d) **Pricing strategy**

Factors to consider when deciding on appropriate pricing strategies:

Competition – Inkpen is unlikely to be able to compete with economies of scale and hence match the discounted prices of Sahara and the other major e-retailers. However this may not be a problem as price is only one element of Inkpen's product offering. It also competes by offering customers a particular experience in terms of browsing environment, advice and service.

Costs – Inkpen may not be free to unilaterally decide on its own prices because of agreements with wholesalers which dictate the typical margins available or how products may be sold. Livro Inc will presumably influence the price for the Cartilla and possibly the e–books.

Customers – Inkpen needs to establish what premium its customers are prepared to pay for superior service. This is likely to differ for different groups of customers (the premium may not be very high if they are cash-strapped students).

The issue here is not that students may not buy the required reading text if the price is too high but that they might not buy it from Inkpen – instead going to a cheaper e-retailer or buying the text second-hand. To prevent this Inkpen could consider offering a buy-back scheme for texts (eg at 50% of original price) provided a new text is purchased at the same time.

Corporate strategy – Inkpen needs to be careful to align its pricing strategy with its niche differentiator status, so should avoid being a 'bargain basement' in terms of price.

Pricing strategies

Inkpen may be able to price discriminate for different types of books or customers. This will partly depend on customers' sensitivity to price (price elasticity of demand). We see this already in the industry for hardbacks and paperbacks.

Inkpen may be able to make different versions of product available, eg an introduction and summary of the text in e-text and the full text in printed form.

Bundle pricing, where Inkpen sells the e-text and printed version as a single package, may act as a barrier to entry to protect market share from sellers of second-hand texts.

Alternatively Inkpen could offer a special bundle price if all texts on a particular course reading list are bought from Inkpen in printed or electronic form.

There may be some scope for captive product pricing – so Inkpen could inflate the price of complementary e-material having sold the original text at a lower price.

Most bookstores use a range of promotional pricing: 3 for 2, book of the month, loyalty cards etc.

Inkpen could also incentivise local academics to refer students to Inkpen in return for discount on their own purchases or loyalty points.

Examiner's comments:

Requirement (d) requested candidates to discuss the factors that Inkpen needs to consider in developing suitable pricing strategies for both printed books and e-books. As usual candidates demonstrated good knowledge of pricing factors (the 4Cs) and pricing strategies. Only the better candidates scored highly by applying this knowledge to the specific circumstances in the question, in the context of Inkpen's stated desire to create appeal for mixed text formats.